PREFACE

Managers today face an unprecedented number of both challenges and opportunities. Among them are the warp-speed pace of innovations in technology and telecommunications, the spreading globalization of business organizations and their operations, a hypercompetitive business environment in many arenas, increasingly diverse and more vocal work forces, rapidly emerging new forms of employment relationships, intensifying pressures for service and products of exceedingly high quality, and evolving views of managerial leadership. All of these and other related developments make the field of management extremely stimulating and exciting but also, of course, highly challenging. It is exactly those challenges, and the opportunities they provide, that we hope to convey to the students who read this book.

At the outset of the text, in the very first chapter, in fact, we identify for students several perspectives that we think are especially important when analyzing these challenges and opportunities. Although the overall subject of this book—management—is typically segmented into familiar categories such as decision making, leadership, and control, we want students to place these topics in a context that reflects the true realities facing managers.

Managers do not operate in a world whose issues arrange themselves neatly into clearly defined, easily interpreted, and nicely compartmentalized situations. That is why, in Chapter 1, we point out immediately that managers operate within *organizational* contexts. Today, organizations come in every shape and size and with internal cultures that span the entire spectrum of values. Some organizations revolve around flawless execution, while others focus on speed and simplicity. The implication for managers, and therefore for students of management, is that the successful application of any concept or theory presented in the text requires thoughtful consideration of the organizational context within which the manager works.

We also emphasize to students in Chapter 1, and throughout the book, that people working in organizations today represent a greater spectrum of ethnic, religious, cultural, and educational backgrounds than ever before. This diversity includes superiors, peers, subordinates, customers, and suppliers—indeed, virtually any group with whom a manager comes in contact. Yet, despite this complex reality, managers must, as they always have, work effectively with and through people to accomplish goals.

The other three perspectives or themes that we stress for students in Chapter 1, as a basis for reading the material in the following chapters, include those of mastering dualities, willingness to become committed, and relishing the kaleidoscopic nature of management. Managers face dual pressures at almost every turn. They face competing pressures for speed and perfect quality, for flexibility and unbending integrity, for analysis and intuition. These dualities create tensions and demands for balancing skills never before experienced to this degree. To climb the Mount Everests of managerial challenges requires that successful managers be exceptionally committed to acquiring new knowledge and learning new skills and to investing their time and energies in adding value to other people's efforts, to organizations, and to society. It is important for students to understand that in meeting these challenges the activity of managing is multifaceted and cannot be dissected into discrete parcels. The emphasis is on management as an activity that takes place in a context of continually shifting and highly related parts that often appear to be exceedingly messy. Students need to understand that reality of management at the very beginning of their study.

All of this makes the education of future managers both difficult and exciting. It was this challenge that motivated us to embark on the journey of creating this text—and that also made us wonder at times whether we would be able to surmount the hurdles that the journey required. In our minds, the fundamental challenge was to present frameworks of management that are robust and, at the same time, to be able to relate them to the authentic environment that practicing managers face. That challenge was heightened by the fact that the terrain of management is constantly changing and therefore a moving target. Nevertheless, all of us who are management educators must strive to demonstrate the relevance of our theories, concepts, and approaches and provide students something of enduring value.

OVERVIEW

With these general issues as backdrop, we set off on our daunting journey. Writing a textbook is enjoyable but no easy feat, as anyone who has undertaken this task will tell you. We were guided in our journey by two major influences: our research and study of the field and our personal teaching, management, and consulting experiences. These influences led us to emphasize several specific objectives:

- A text that is solidly grounded in the scholarly literature, yet closely tied to the world of practicing managers.
- A text that is not only rich with examples but also replete with rich examples—examples that have enough detail to convey the complexity and interrelationships of real managerial situations.
- A text written in a style that speaks directly to the student reader and engages that reader.
- A text in which global dimensions of management are integrated throughout the book rather than set off in a separate chapter.
- A text with an accompanying *Instructor's Manual* and support materials that provide significant value and guidance to the instructor.

In contemplating our writing task, we were well aware of the large number of management textbooks already on the market. Many of them, frankly, are quite good. However, we thought that if we accomplished the objectives just outlined we could produce a text that makes teaching management more fun and successful for

MANAGEMENT
Meeting New Challenges

J. Stewart Black
Managing Director, Center for Global Assignment

Lyman W. Porter
University of California, Irvine

Prentice Hall
Upper Saddle River, New Jersey 07458

Executive Editor: Michael Roche
Assistant Editor: Ruth Berry
Editorial Assistant: Adam Hamel
Senior Marketing Manager: Julie Downs
Senior Marketing Coordinator: Joyce Cosentino
Production Supervisor: Louis C. Bruno, Jr.
Design Director: Regina Hagen
Cover Design: Leslie Haines
Cover/Photo: Images®copyright 1999 PhotoDisc, Inc.
Development, Design, Composition, and Project Coordination: Elm Street Publishing Services, Inc.

For permission to use copyrighted material, grateful acknowledgment is made to the following copyright holders:
p. 6   AP/Wide World Photos
p. 7   CORBIS/Ted Spiegel
p. 8   AP/Wide World Photos
p. 11   Images®copyright 1999 PhotoDisc, Inc.
p. 14   Images®copyright 1999 PhotoDisc, Inc.
p. 15   Images®copyright 1999 PhotoDisc, Inc.
p. 16   Images®copyright 1999 PhotoDisc, Inc.
p. 18   Images®copyright 1999 PhotoDisc, Inc.
p. 34   North Wind Picture Archives
p. 42   Images®copyright 1999 PhotoDisc, Inc.
p. 72   AT&T Archives. Reprinted with permission.
p. 77   Images®copyright 1999 PhotoDisc, Inc.
(credits continued on p. 629, which is hereby made part of this copyright page)

Copyright © 2000 by Prentice-Hall, Inc.
Upper Saddle River, New Jersey 07458

Library of Congress Cataloging-in-Publication Data
Black, J. Stewart.
  Management : meeting new challenges / Stewart Black, Lyman W. Porter. — 1st ed.
      p.   cm.
  Includes bibliographical references and index.
  ISBN 0-321-0147-3
  1. Management.   I. Porter, Lyman W.   II. Title.
HD31.B517   2000
658—dc21

                                         99-26073
                                              CIP

Prentice-Hall International (UK) Limited, London
Prentice-Hall of Australia Pty. Limited, Sydney
Prentice-Hall Canada, Inc., Toronto
Prentice-Hall Hispanoamericana, S.A., Mexico
Prentice-Hall of India Private Limited, New Delhi
Prentice-Hall of Japan, Inc., Tokyo
Pearson Education Asia Pte. Ltd., Singapore
Editora Prentice-Hall do Brasil, Ltda., Rio de Janeiro

Printed in the United States of America

10 9 8 7 6 5 4 3 2 1

instructors and that makes learning about management more stimulating and meaningful for students.

To pursue these objectives, we highlighted the following:

First, in grounding the book in the scholarly and research literature and linking that literature to the world of practicing managers, we present the concepts and theories that seem to us to make the most difference in actual managerial situations. In short, while we give considerable attention to people and their behavior in organizations, this is a book on management. Our focus, and our intended focus for students, is on the *managerial* implications of the material we present in the book.

Second, we felt that to write a text that included numerous real-world examples would require the use of a variety of formats. As a result, we have provided four different categories of examples:

- We start each chapter with an opening vignette, often a longer opening example than is typical of other texts. We did this because we wanted to preview a number of issues covered in the chapter and to provide a context of managerial realism.
- Each chapter is closed with a case, again longer than many such cases in competing texts. If students are to be skillful managers, they need to begin thinking about what they would do in actual managerial situations that have a degree of complexity. The closing cases provide the opportunity to do this.
- A third type of example is the "Managerial Challenges," which are set off within each chapter in box form. These examples are designed to illustrate and bring to life specific points in the text and to show how practicing managers have dealt with particular problems and issues. Some of these Managerial Challenge boxes are short, while others are somewhat longer. Their length was governed by what we thought was required to give the student useful elaboration of the points to maximize learning other than by an arbitrary standard.
- Finally, we also include many shorter in-text examples that help students apply the ideas and approaches they are studying.

Third, we wanted to speak directly to students. Students learn best when they are engaged. Consequently, we chose to write in a style that consistently positions student readers to think about what they are studying as though they were managers. Throughout the text, we pose questions and try to steer students away from just memorizing points or searching for easy, pat answers. That is one reason why, at the end of each chapter, we decided not to include a traditional chapter summary and instead to close with "Concluding Comments." These concluding comments speak directly to students about what we think about the issues covered in the chapter they have just read. We hope this reinforces our intention to motivate them to form their own conclusions about that same material.

Fourth, in attempting to integrate international dimensions of management into all of the chapters, we started with the fundamental assumption that globalization is not some glitzy, passing fad but rather a powerful force now and far into the future. While in one sense the world is getting smaller, for most managers the world is actually getting larger. Today, managers have to think about events in countries that were not even on their radar (or computer) screens a decade ago. Likewise, organizations often need to expand into countries that their managers could not even find on a map a few years ago—in some cases because the countries did not exist. We only need to look at recent, major events, such as the end of the Cold War, the ousting of dictators in certain developing countries, or debt and monetary crises erupting in major areas of the globe, to see how interconnected our world has become.

Our own experiences, as well as the conclusions from the Porter-McKibbin study of management education, suggest that given the pervasiveness of globalization, its implications for managers should be integrated into business subjects rather than simply relegated to a separate compartment. Consequently, there is no "International Management" chapter in this text. Rather, we have blended international considerations into each chapter. However, because some topics have had greater study and research from an international perspective, more is known about them. Also, some topics are intrinsically more amenable to international implications than are others. Therefore, we talk more about the interface of globalization and management in some chapters than in others.

Fifth, we have tried to create an *Instructor's Manual (IM)* that an instructor would actually use—because it is helpful. Most *IM*s have lecture notes and a few exercises. The lecture notes sometimes are nothing more than outlines of the chapter headings with a few elaborations. Because this typical format in many cases does not satisfy instructors' needs, we have taken a different approach. Our *IM* consists of fifty 45-minute teaching modules or sessions. Most chapters have between three and five such teaching sessions. This selection allows instructors teaching on either semester or quarter schedules to have a variety of session choices in constructing their courses. There are five basic categories of sessions: (1) lecture discussions, (2) exercises, (3) case-based discussions, (4) video-based discussions, and (5) hybrids (i.e., a 45-minute session that has two or more of the basic categories as part of the overall teaching plan for a given session). Each of the teaching sessions was developed to meet two key criteria: (1) be basically self-contained and (2) be written well enough that the instructor would say to him- or herself: "I could teach this, and I believe the class session would go well."

ORGANIZATION OF THE BOOK

The organization of this book does not differ greatly from other basic management texts. It starts off with an "Introduction and Historical Overview" (Chapters 1 and 2), provides a consideration of the "Environmental Context of Managing" (Chapters 3 through 6), and then considers five major functions of managing: "Planning and Decision Making" (Chapters 7 through 9), "Organizing and Staffing" (Chapters 10 through 12), "Leading" (Chapters 13 through 15), "Monitoring and Evaluating" (Chapters 16 through 18), and "Transforming" (Chapter 19). Two points about this organization deserve mention: (1) As already discussed, there is no separate chapter on the international dimensions of management; those issues are interwoven throughout all of the chapters, more in some chapters as befitting the chapter topic; and (2) in contrast with most other management texts, we place a consideration of innovation and entrepreneurship relatively early (Chapter 6) rather than toward the end of the book because we believe that way of thinking should influence students *before* they consider the various functions of management.

PEDAGOGY

Following are the key features of the pedagogy of this book:

- **Learning Objectives:** At the beginning of each chapter, the learning objectives provide a roadmap for students as they read the chapter. They also help students, after reading the chapter, to determine whether they have actually absorbed the major concepts and approaches to issues.
- **Opening Vignettes:** Each chapter starts with a relatively detailed description of real-life situations and the managerial issues involved. These vignettes are designed to stimulate students' thinking and awareness about various aspects of the topic to be covered in the chapter.
- **"Managerial Challenge" Boxes:** Each chapter contains two or so boxes that describe actual challenges faced by managers and the ways those managers dealt with them. These boxes are intended to provide extended and concrete examples of decisions that have confronted managers and the actions they have taken in their day-to-day efforts to solve organizational problems.
- **Review Questions:** The review questions at the end of each chapter are designed as a sort of summary. Each chapter has roughly 20 questions that provide a fairly comprehensive coverage of the major points and topics contained in the chapter material.
- **Discussion Questions:** The chapter discussion questions are different in purpose from the review questions. Each chapter has three to five discussion questions that are designed to be evocative and to get the student to think about the material. Some of the questions ask the student to speculate about the relevance or application of different concepts and approaches to situations they know from their own experience. In general, the aim of the discussion questions is to generate thinking versus merely memorizing the chapter contents. Many of the questions come directly from those we have used to generate discussion in our own classes.
- **Closing Cases:** At the end of each chapter, a fairly detailed closing case is provided. These cases, from various sources, are intended to elicit students' thinking about the issues and approaches covered in the chapter they have just read and then to apply those ideas to the dilemmas and decisions posed by the case descriptions. The cases are meant to be meaty enough to engage students in some serious consideration of the issues. At the conclusion of each closing case, a set of case discussion questions address key aspects of the case.
- **Marginal Definitions of Key Terms:** Throughout the book, concise definitions of key words and terms are provided in the margin to assist students in acquiring a ready understanding of the vocabulary of management.

TEACHING PACKAGE

Instructor's Manual

In addition to the fifty teaching modules mentioned previously, the *Instructor's Manual* also includes a *Test Bank* and a *PowerPoint Exhibit Gallery*. The *Test Bank* provides instructors with two midterm exams—each covering half the textbook—and a set of comprehensive short-answer and essay questions for a cumulative final exam. The exams provide more questions than would be necessary in a regular examination period, allowing the instructor flexibility in choosing questions pertinent to the chapters covered by his or her syllabus. The midterm exams include multiple-choice, true/false, short-answer, and essay questions. Grading suggestions and sample answers accompany the essay questions. The *PowerPoint Exhibit Gallery* provides thumbnails of all lecture and art slides included on the *Instructor's Resource Disk*. With these thumbnails, an instructor can reference slides mentioned in the teaching modules quickly. Also, PowerPoint thumbnails help the instructor to prepare and organize a lecture independent of the teaching modules. These supplements have been prepared by Jody and Holly Tompson of the University of Waikato, New Zealand.

Instructor's Resource Disk

This Windows-based CD-ROM provides Microsoft Word files for all teaching modules and *Test Bank* questions. An extensive set of Microsoft PowerPoint slides featuring lecture slides and textbook art has also been prepared by Jody and Holly Tompson.

Web Site

A Web site has been developed for this book. Here you can find links to other Web sites, as well as resources helpful to management students.

Videos

A collection of videos is available. In their teaching modules, Holly and Jody Tompson have provided a number of sessions where instructors can focus on these videos or integrate them into a lecture or discussion.

ACKNOWLEDGMENTS

Writing and producing a book of this size and complexity is without question a team—not just a group—effort. Over the several years since this text was first conceived, a large number of people have been involved. We are especially indebted to Melissa Rosati, the sponsoring editor who first signed the project, and to Mike Roche, the sponsoring editor who worked with us to the completion. Mike was always there with helpful advice and encouragement along the way, and without his many efforts on our behalf, there would be no book. Mary Clare McEwing was superb in her role as the supervising developmental editor, and Karen Hill at Elm Street Publishing Services was equally impressive in her accomplishments as the project developmental editor. Together, they provided numerous suggestions for improving the contents and organization of the text, and they also helped turn our occasional infelicitous phrasing into more readable prose. More than that, though, they did all this with both considerable warmth and sympathetic understanding of the authors' needs and a very high degree of absolute professionalism. Also, we want to extend a special thank-you for the developmental editorial work of Susan Messer on the early drafts of the chapters. Others who helped out along the way in the editing and production process of the book included Joan Cannon,

Arlene Bessenoff, Susan Peterson, Etta Worthington, Martha Beyerlein, and Andrea Coens.

Particular acknowledgment should be given to four scholars in the management field who wrote the basic drafts of the following chapters: Jerome Katz, Chapter 6 ("Managing Innovation and Entrepreneurship"); Helene Caudill, Chapter 17 ("Operations Management"); and Eli Cohen and Elizabeth Boyd, Chapter 18 ("Information Technology Management"). Each of these chapter authors demonstrated a high level of knowledge and insight in their respective areas of expertise, and together they have made a major contribution to the finished project.

We also want to express our great appreciation to all of the reviewers of various chapters of the manuscript, who are listed below. They provided us with extremely constructive and useful comments, criticism, and suggestions, and the final product is much improved as a result of their collective input.

Abel Adekola, *University of Wisconsin at Stout*
Clancey Allen, *Charles Sturt University (Australia)*
Debra Arvanites, *Villanova University*
Michael Buckley, *University of Oklahoma*
Gerald Calvasina, *University of North Carolina at Charlotte*
Tom Campbell, *University of Texas at Austin*
Gary Carini, *Baylor University*
George Carnahan, *Northern Michigan University*
Norma Carr-Ruffino, *San Francisco State University*
Jay Christensen-Szalanski, *University of Iowa*
James Crowley, *University College Dublin*
James Cunningham, *University College Galway*
Shirley Daniel, *University of Utah*
Tammy Davis, *Indiana State University*
Helen Deresky, *State University of New York at Plattsburgh*
Lora Dollar, *Sam Houston State University*
David Grigsby, *Clemson University*
Roulla Hagen, *Durham University (United Kingdom)*
Roy Hayhurst, *University of Limerick*
Dave Hunt, *University of Southern Mississippi*
George Jacobs, *Middle Tennessee State University*
Sel Kukalis, *California State University at Long Beach*
Wonsick Lee, *Central Connecticut State University*
Kathy Lovelace, *University of Massachusetts at Amherst*
Joseph Michlitsch, *Southern Illinois University at Edwardsville*
Thomas Miller, *University of Memphis*
Doug Peterson, *Western Illinois University*
Jose Proenca, *Widener University*
Clyde Scott, *University of Alabama*
John Shogren, *University of Denver*
Gregory Stephens, *Texas Christian University*
Ken Thompson, *DePaul University*
Siobhan Tiernan, *University of Limerick*
John Washbush, *University of Wisconsin at Whitewater*
James Wolff, *Wichita State University*
Joseph Yaney, *Northern Illinois University*

As authors of the text, we have worked with the publisher to produce an *Instructor's Manual* that we believe to be of high quality and one that we hope will be particularly useful and helpful to those who teach the basic management course. In this regard, we are very pleased to acknowledge with thanks the skill and scholarship of Jody and Holly Tompson, who have authored the *IM*. Jason Miranda, as the *IM* editor, was particularly helpful in the formative stages of developing the manual.

There is one person who deserves a very special place in our list of thank-yous. Without the tremendous dedication, perseverance, and expert reference sleuthing of Grace McLaughlin, this book would never have seen the light of day. Her efforts as our graduate research assistant on this project were simply outstanding. Grace: We salute you! You were, in a word, terrific!

Finally, but not least, we are deeply grateful to our wives, Tanya and Meredith, for their superlative and unhesitating support throughout this project. They deserve more than a few kudos—in fact, more than a few hundred.

J. Stewart Black
Lyman W. Porter

Brief Contents

CONTENTS

PART 2

ENVIRONMENTAL CONTEXT OF MANAGING

Chapter 3   Assessing External Environments 67

Strul-

Chapter 6   Managing Innovation and Entrepreneurship 144

PART 3

PLANNING AND DECISION MAKING

Chapter 17 Operations Management 508

Chapter 18 Information Technology Management 540

PART 7

TRANSFORMING

Chapter 19 Organizational Change and Renewal 571

PART 1

INTRODUCTION AND HISTORICAL OVERVIEW

CHAPTER 1

INTRODUCTION

After studying this chapter, you should be able to:

- Explain why management must be understood within the context of organizations and how organizations affect the practice of management.
- Describe the role of working with and through people in effective management.
- Explain duality in management and how working with paradoxes is at the core of management in today's environment.
- Specify the nature and extent of commitment required for managerial excellence.
- Explain why engaging in management can be considered like looking into a kaleidoscope.
- Describe and compare the different elements of managerial work and the different managerial roles.

Managing: Putting It All Together

Saturn, the division of General Motors that likes to boast that it is "a different kind of car company," often lives up to its slogan. At the end of 1998, the organization named Cynthia M. Trudell as president and chairman—the first woman to head a car division for an American or foreign auto manufacturer. Who is this new top manager for one of America's largest corporations? One writer calls her a "true car guy" who worked her way up through the ranks. She has spent nearly two decades learning the business from the inside, with stints managing engine and transmission factories, as well as a foundry.

Trudell spent her early years overseeing 150 workers who machined transmission gears. She thought that experience would help her learn manufacturing from the ground up. Trudell then worked for nine years in two GM transmission factories mastering the complexities of engines and transmissions because of the challenge and because, she said, "they're the heart and soul of the car." From there, she headed up IBC Vehicles in

England, a GM subsidiary that makes the Frontera sport utility vehicle for the European market. Other colleagues wonder at the determination involved in spending nine years in a transmission factory, but Trudell calls them "great years" in her career.

But the story of Cynthia Trudell isn't just about the woman executive who has shattered the glass ceiling in a traditionally male-dominated industry. It is also about the organizational context in which she has carried out her managerial activities. In contrast to GM's "yell and tell" approach to management, Trudell learned to work through people. She worked with factory workers and union leaders, forging strong relationships with both. "They bring a perspective that a lot of times I would never have thought about, and it makes a difference in execution," she explains. As head of IBC in England, Trudell managed to balance good relations with five separate unions. Thus, her appointment to Saturn, which is known for its partnership between labor and management, was, as she put it, "a dream come true."

Saturn has had its organizational problems, so Trudell will face multiple challenges for the new millennium. "She has not come into an easy place to be," says Eric Noble, an analyst with AutoPacific Inc. "Between the stagnant segment sales and GM's current bend toward centralization, she's got her work cut out for her." Trudell will also have to find new ways to reach women customers—who buy most of the Saturns—as well as balance the tensions between independence and coordination that satisfies employees, unions, and managers. As president, Trudell will oversee the manufacture, launch, and marketing of two important new products—a midsize car and a sport utility vehicle. All of this adds up to a juggling act that she welcomes. After all, she has years of hands-on experience to draw from—in fact, few could be better prepared.

Sources: Keith Bradsher, "From Factory to the Top of Saturn," *The New York Times*, December 20, 1998, p. 32; *The Detroit News*, December 15, 1998; Karin Miller, "GM Taps Woman to Run Saturn," *Yahoo! News, AP Headlines*, December 14, 1998; Micheline Maynard, "Female Exec to Run Saturn," *USA Today*, December 15, 1998.

We (the authors of this book) do not personally know Cynthia M. Trudell. We only know of her through accounts in the press, and those articles probably omit additional interesting information about her that would be worth knowing. Then why do we feature her in this opening chapter? It is not because she is a woman (which she is), or because she is married (which she is), or because she has two children (which she has). We would have been just as willing to feature a man (single or married) with no (or six) children. The reason we talk about her here is because we believe her career to date, and especially how she has approached managerial challenges during that career, comes very close to illustrating precisely some of the most important themes we will be emphasizing in this chapter and throughout this entire book:

- *Management occurs in organizations,* and by working for General Motors, she has certainly carried out her managerial activities in a large and complex organization.
- *Management requires getting things done through people,* and the opening story makes it clear that she has had an exceptionally strong focus on the people part of managing, once working simultaneously with five different unions.
- *Management is all about mastering duality,* and she has coped effectively with such dualities as keeping her eye on the big picture while attending to some of the most basic details of her job (such as machining transmission gears); and having a global perspective (managing in three different countries), yet also gaining a very local understanding of employees and customers.
- *Managerial excellence requires commitment,* and a knowledgeable observer of Ms. Trudell says, "she's obviously got a true love for the [automobile] industry, which is rare to find in anybody."
- *Management is like a kaleidoscope,* a fact which Ms. Trudell has encountered repeatedly in her managerial career experiences to date.

As you read through the remainder of this chapter, and the remaining chapters in this book, keep Cynthia M. Trudell in mind. Few people could surpass her as a role model for how to become an effective manager.

AN UNCONVENTIONAL INTRODUCTION TO MANAGEMENT

Here in Chapter 1 we're going to take a somewhat unconventional approach to introducing the topic of this book: management. In the first chapter, most textbooks start with definitions of basic terms such as "management" and "managers" and then describe various levels and types of managers, the essential managerial functions and roles, and categories of managerial skills. We'll do some of that, too, but later. Instead, we first want to map out some fundamental perspectives that cut across the entire managerial process. Our rationale for this approach is simple: We contend that when starting any journey, you must have a broad overview of the terrain you are about to travel *before* getting caught up in the details of the different parts of the trip. Otherwise, you risk moving from one checkpoint to the next without really understanding where you are heading and how to tie the different segments of the trip together into a meaningful and powerful adventure. And learning about the complexities of management is, we strongly believe, a journey that adds up to a definite adventure.

The broad perspectives that we want to share here early in the book are based on information and ideas from a wide variety of sources: our personal experiences and observations as educators, managers, and consultants; research findings from the scholarly literature; extensive study of the subject; and, particularly, hundreds of conversations and interviews with practicing managers over the years. In the next few pages, we will first state each perspective and some specific elaborations of it, followed by typical questions that might be asked about the perspective and our responses to those questions. In other words, for the next part of this chapter we will adopt a Q & A approach. We hope this approach will encourage you to be more involved with the material than is typically the case with a first chapter and that it will increase your curiosity about the subject and stimulate your interest in learning more about it.

PERSPECTIVE 1

MANAGEMENT OCCURS *IN* ORGANIZATIONS

The first thing to keep in mind as you begin your formal study of management is that there is an ever-present context for management and managers, much like the stage is the constant background for actors in a play. That managerial context is *organizations*.

Management Occurs in Organizational Contexts; It Does Not Happen in Isolation

Just as water is the necessary environment for fish, or air is for a plane, organizations are a necessary context for managers to manage. In fact, stated strongly, we could say that management does not exist without organizations.

But wait a minute. Can't there be management in nonorganizational settings like families, political groups, or ad hoc groups?

Good question. Managerial activities, such as decision making or communication, can happen in non-organizational settings such as a family. You can even engage in managerial activities, such as planning and goal setting, completely on your own without anyone else around. However, these activities in isolation do not constitute management. Management requires integration of all these activities and other people. This integration can only happen if there is an organizational context, just as dialogue can only happen if there's another person participating in the conversation—otherwise, it's a monologue.

Shaquille O'Neal is managed by his coach during the game; his finances and his contracts are managed by his agent. Should O'Neal be considered a manager since he takes an active role in evaluating his endorsements, movie roles, and other business propositions?

The worldwide organization of the Catholic church requires many managerial activities. Unique to this organization is the college of cardinals who are empowered to elect their leader, the pope.

OK, fine, but doesn't the type of organization matter? Doesn't it make a difference if the organization is small or large, whether it's for profit or nonprofit?

There is no question that the nuances of effective management change depending on the situation and type of organization. Managing in a small company, where you know every employee, is not identical to managing in a large organization, such as IBM with over 200,000 employees. In fact, in a tiny organization of less than a dozen people, you would hardly be talking much about management at all. So, in this book we focus on organizations with at least a moderate degree of complexity and size because that is where the premium for good management comes into play.

Regardless of the fact that some of the specifics of effective management will be affected by the size and type of organization, the fundamental substance of management does not change. If the basic essence and nature of management changed dramatically from one organizational type to another, we would need separate textbooks for small organization management, large organization management, private company management, public agency management, and so on. In our view, that is not only not required but instead would distract from a focus on the essentials of management as a critical and universal activity in all organizations.

Each Organization Has Its Own Set of Characteristics That Affect Both Managers and Those with Whom They Interact

While it is critical to understand that management occurs in the context of organizations, we do not want to create the impression that all organizations, even those of the same size or complexity, are the same. Each organization has its own "personality," if you will, and its own strengths, weaknesses, problems, and opportunities. These various personality characteristics affect the organization and all who work within it.

But what is it about organizations that create their particular characteristics, and do they influence effective management?

Organizations bring together people from different backgrounds, families, skills, and so on, who must then work together to serve common purposes, which ultimately will benefit each individual involved. In other words, in an organization, very different people must cooperate in working toward shared objectives. They can only do this by accepting existing ways of working together or by forming and agreeing to new ways. These ways of doing things come to constitute the personality, or culture, of the organization. Whatever one may think or assume about the personality or culture of, say, a typical unit of General Motors, it would probably be safe to presume it is different from that of Patagonia, the apparel manufacturer, where, at headquarters in Ventura, California, an office message board posts the local surfing conditions and both the CEO and employees have been known to head to the beach when the surf is up![1] Thus, although basic principles of effective management are relevant in any organization, the specific characteristics of an organization will almost certainly affect how those principles are applied.

Does this mean that if I am an effective manager in "Organization A" that I will automatically be an effective manager in "Organization B"? Or does this mean that because organizations have different personalities, effective management practices can't be transferred from one organization to another?

Sound approaches to management do transfer from one organization to another. This does not mean, however, that your behaviors can be identical and still be equally effective. For example, if you learn how to read music, you can apply that knowledge from one piece of music to another, but it does not mean that you can play each piece the same way. Furthermore, even if the musical score were the same, it does not mean that you would play the piece exactly the same way for different conductors or with different musical groups. But making adjustments in your playing does not change your fundamental understanding of how to read music

Victor Kiam, the venerable face that brought us "I liked it so much I bought the company ..." was a success as the owner/manager of Remington, yet failed in his subsequent ownership of the New England Patriots football team.

and your ability to adapt that knowledge to different circumstances.

Managing effectively is quite similar. You will need to change how you put management ideas into practice based on the nature of the organization in which you are working, but this fine-tuning does not lessen the importance of acquiring a basic understanding of management. In fact, having that understanding allows you to move from one organization to another and still be effective. This does not mean, however—and we want to emphasize this—that you can ignore the differences from one organization to another and manage precisely in one as you did in another. In fact, one of the quickest ways to be *in*effective as a manager is to remain rigid in how you carry out your managerial functions.

Managers Must Understand Something about Organizations

Because organizations are the context of management, managers must understand something about them. As we stated earlier, organizations are to management as air is to a plane. Yet, for a plane to fly effectively, a pilot must possess some essential knowledge about the characteristics and composition of air, such as how atmospheric density relates to temperature, in order to calculate how much lift it can provide. In the heat of the summer, planes taking off in Phoenix sometimes have to bump passengers when seats are still available on the plane. As the temperature rises (sometimes reaching 125 degrees Fahrenheit), the air becomes less dense, lift is more difficult, and the weight with which a plane can safely take off declines.

But in a practical sense, what does it mean to "understand organizations"? I can't possibly know everything there is to know about them, so how do I figure out what is more and less important to understand?

Just as a pilot does not have to be an astrophysicist or an aeronautical engineer to skillfully fly a plane, you do not need a Ph.D. in organizational science to be an effective manager. However, you do need a solid understanding of some basic features of organizations. Much of what follows in this textbook is designed to provide you with the fundamental knowledge you need in relation to the challenge of managing with skill. Of course, one textbook and one course in management will not by any means give you all the knowledge you will need in this regard.

Thus, while it is not practical to try to understand everything about organizations, you need to know something about how they can affect management practice. The key point is that just as a pilot cannot simply focus on the plane and ignore the conditions of the air, effective managers cannot simply focus on management and ignore the organizational context within which it gets practiced. Clearly, Cynthia Trudell knows the difference between what is required in the organizational context of a transmission parts factory and that of executive boardrooms.

MANAGEMENT REQUIRES GETTING THINGS DONE *THROUGH PEOPLE*

The act of managing involves an attempt to achieve an objective through the efforts of two, three, ten, a hundred, or even thousands of other people. Somebody acting entirely alone, whether he or she is writing a poem or making a critical investment decision, may be trying to achieve a particular goal, but that person is not managing. Management is, by its very nature, a people-based activity. Managers, no matter how talented, cannot do everything themselves. They need to be able to tap the skills and energies of other people, in addition to their own, if they are to be effective. The message is clear: If you don't want to work with and through other people, then don't become a manager. You won't like the activity, and you are unlikely to be successful.

Managers Must Be Adept at Assessing Other People's Capabilities

A critical managerial skill, and one that can be developed, is that of assessing other people's capabilities. Knowing what someone or a group of people currently can do, as well as judging what level of performance they might be able to reach with additional instruction, training, and motivation, is essential for building an effectively performing unit.

That sounds like something that is pretty difficult—to be able to size up other people with some degree of accuracy. How do you do it?

It's not easy and it takes time, effort, and, especially, experience to develop that kind of managerial skill. However, the important point

is that anyone who is going to be a manager has to *want* to do well on this task. In other words, a manager's own motivation and determination to enhance his or her competency in this area is critical to doing a good job at it.

Effective Managers Must Be Adept at Matching People's Capabilities with Appropriate Responsibilities

Knowing what a particular individual or particular group is capable of doing is only part of the equation for successfully getting things done through people. Another equally important part of the equation is being able to link people and tasks together in winning combinations. That doesn't just mean finding the right jobs for the person, though that is important. It also means making sure that they have the resources necessary to do the job. Therefore, the manager must be someone who is a resource provider (a resource finder and enhancer) as well as a resource coordinator.

That sounds good, but aren't resources always scarce in organizations?

Certainly, resources are finite in all organizations. A manager is never handed unlimited time, equipment, money, and, especially, people. That is why it is vital to be able to use human resources as skillfully as possible—to be able to connect people and tasks together effectively. Often, that process involves forming teams, where the whole is greater than the sum of the parts. Knowing who the people are and what their capabilities are is vital, but it also is essential to know a

Shift work at a restaurant is often the first job for a high school student. Franchise managers utilize this labor source as a way of achieving organizational goals through intensive training and numerous incentive programs.

lot about the tasks and the jobs to be done. Matching resources and tasks also demands considerable effort to explore whether additional resources are needed and not just assume that the existing resource base is all that is available. Management is an activity that requires initiative and not just passive acceptance of the status quo.

Effective Managers Must Be Adept at Motivating People

The third part of the equation for successfully getting tasks done through people is motivating them to accomplish those goals. In today's world, formal authority is declining almost everywhere as a useful means for influencing people. Thus, managers must have a good understanding of what people value—what they care about—if they are to be superior motivators.

Not every manager can be a psychologist, right? How can I know all the details about each person and what the individual values and wants out of work?

You are not expected to become a psychologist. What is important is that you know some basic approaches to motivation. In addition, you have to be able to have some sensitivity about how to apply those approaches to specific individuals. And that includes not only those who work for you but also your peers and your superiors.

But isn't management more than just motivating people or getting things done through people?

Absolutely. Management is a complex process that requires integration of many different types of tasks, from planning and organizing what is to be done to putting together budgets and evaluating outcomes. Motivating and leading people are just two components of this overall process. Nevertheless, unless managers can get things done through people, not much significant work will be accomplished. Managers need to be able to multiply the effects of their own efforts by influencing the efforts of other people.

PERSPECTIVE 3

MANAGEMENT IS ALL ABOUT *MASTERING DUALITY*

Like most things, if management were easy, everyone would be good at it. One of the important factors that separates great managers form mediocre managers is the recognition, acceptance, and mastery of "duality"—two sets of coping with forces that pull managers in opposite directions. Great managers do not avoid these tensions but embrace them, harness them, and utilize them.

Aren't you really just talking about trade-offs? Aren't you just saying that managers sometimes have to trade off one opposing force for another?

Yes, making trade-offs is one type of decision that managers have to make. Sometimes managers do, in fact, have to go with one plan to get certain results and in the process forgo another plan and its potential results. However, great managers do not automatically view competing forces in terms of trade-offs; they recognize that often the challenge is to respond to both forces simultaneously.

Management Is a Complex Process Requiring *Integration*, Yet Managerial Activities Are Often *Fragmented* and Do Not Occur in a Logical, Sequential Fashion

Management requires the integration of a variety of activities, such as planning, decision making, communicating, motivating, appraising, and organizing, yet a manager's day is typically fragmented with interruptions, breaks in sequence, and other distractions. In a sense, a manager is like a "plate spinner." The manager may need to keep several plates spinning at once and shuttle back and forth, giving each plate a boost to keep it rotating and stop it from crashing to the floor. Most

of the time the manager does not have the luxury of looking at the competing plates and deciding to keep one plate up and spinning while the others slow down until they fall off their sticks and crash to the floor.

Likewise, while the reality is that activities and information often confront the manager in discrete bits, it is the responsibility and challenge of the manager to pull those bits together and integrate them in a meaningful way. In a sense, the manager must be capable of seeing patterns and then coordinating information, people, and activities to achieve organizational goals.

Although I can see your point, when I go into the bookstore, management seems much more simple than you're describing. Isn't the key to simplify management and not make it more complex?

Management by "best-seller" may seem to simplify management, and certainly the authors of many of these books would like you to believe that if you just did "X" you would be a roaring success. But the reality is that management *is* complex and requires integration in a fragmented environment. Easy solutions may be appealing, but they often don't work. The truth of the matter is that if the simple tips in the best-sellers really worked as well as they claimed, there wouldn't be a new best-seller each month. No one would need the tip of the month.

This does not mean that there is not truth or value in best-selling management books. However, although simple solutions may work in a very specific situation, they are unlikely to work in most situations. Solutions that work across a variety of situations are likely to be more complicated. Effective managers understand that paradoxes—seeming contradictions—lie at the center of their roles and responsibilities and that one of their key challenges is to deal with those paradoxes effectively.

PERSPECTIVE 3

Business best-sellers, such as *Reengineering the Corporation* or *The Wisdom of Teams* provide very broad solutions to management problems. However, such sweeping solutions often fail to capture the complexities of situations, and overreliance on them by managers can sometimes make problems worse rather than solve them.

remain fairly constant, and others can be more open to change. For example, your fundamental values and ethics need to be fairly stable. People may not agree with your values or ethical standards, but they need to know what they are and need to know that you consistently hold to them. Otherwise, you will appear to others to be unpredictable and untrustworthy. You also need some consistency, without being overly rigid, in your basic approach to dealing with people and problems. People need to see that you are open to alternative ideas, but they will have difficulty if you are so changeable that you seem to be a chameleon.

Management Requires *Consistency* and *Flexibility*

Perhaps one of the most important paradoxes—or dualities—is that of consistency and flexibility. Without question, people need some consistency in their organizational life. Workers could not be expected to perform their jobs well if what they were to do or how they were expected to accomplish it changed each day. Without some consistency, chaos would reign, and no purposeful organizational objectives could be accomplished. Yet, in today's environment—with rapidly changing technology, government policies, customer preferences, and competitor capabilities—flexibility, change, and adaptation are essential for survival.

As a manager, how can I be consistent and yet remain flexible?

It is important to understand that everything about you as a manager does not need to be one way or the other—totally constant or completely flexible. Some of your characteristics as a manager should

Managers Must *Reflect* and *Act*

Talk to any manager today, and he or she will tell you that situations, decisions, problems, and opportunities fly at them with almost overwhelming speed. Quick action is often the difference between first and second place in the competitive marketplace, as Starbucks and Amazon.com have demonstrated in coffee houses and on-line book ordering. To some extent, capabilities such as quick thinking and decisiveness have become admired qualities of good managers. But there is an inherent problem with just focusing on the onslaught of daily activities. This problem is similar to running and focusing on the ground only a few feet in front of you. You may notice the stone in the path in time to avoid it, or you may notice a declining or inclining slope in the path and change your pace appropriately. Each individual step you take may be successful, but by focusing on only a few feet in front of you, you may not notice that you are running straight toward a wall or cliff.

Working long hours is often a requirement for today's managers. To be effective, and to be of long-term value to the organization, managers need to set time aside to reflect on what they are doing. This can take the form of personal time set aside for reflection—exercising or reading for instance—or in confidential discussions with colleagues.

But how can I get to all the things I need to each day and still have time to reflect? Managers can't be philosophers and just sit back in their offices thinking all day, can they?

Management is about activity; it is not about philosophy. But managers cannot know if they are headed in the right direction, if the current pace is appropriate, or if their current "running style" is effective, unless they *take* the time to reflect on things. Because management is about activity, you are unlikely to *find* time to reflect; you will have to make and take time out. In fact, many of the insights presented in this chapter have come from managers as we asked them to take time to reflect on management through our interviews. So, while managers must act and often must act quickly, they must also take time to reflect on what they are doing, how they are doing it, and, perhaps most important, why they are doing it.

Increasingly, Managers Need *Global Perspective* and *Local Understanding* of Specific Customers, Governments, Competitors, and Suppliers

International management consultants are fond of saying that in the future there will be two types of CEOs: those who have a global perspective and those who are out of a job. This overstatement captures one aspect of this future duality for managers, but it misses the other. The evidence for the increasing globalization of business is nearly overwhelming. It is virtually impossible to pick up a major magazine or newspaper and not find several stories related to global business in some form—companies going after international markets (e.g., the Daimler Benz–Chrysler merger), competing with foreign competitors (e.g., Boeing vs. Airbus), responding to a foreign government's policy change (e.g., companies adapting to 11 nations' adoption of the euro for currency exchange transactions),

PERSPECTIVE 3

The North American Free Trade Agreement (NAFTA) has created a free North American market for goods and services. Managers in Los Angeles, Mexico City, or Miami cannot assume that their products will be as appealing in Vancouver as they are in their home market. Very often this means modifying their products or finding a different way of positioning their product in other markets.

and so on. So, managers clearly need a global perspective. Yet, all business happens at a local level. Newspapers may talk about international business, but the business transactions and the management activities all happen in specific countries with specific employees, government officials, competitors, and suppliers.

But in a practical sense, how do I "think global and act local"?

A key is to be able to recognize the drivers behind these competing forces.

For many products, it is much cheaper to build one version for the entire world than to have variations for every country. Yet, for many of these products, customers in different countries do not have the same preferences. A compromise approach would try to find the middle ground and design the product so it had the widest appeal, recognizing that, as a consequence, the product would be unappealing to some potential customers. However, more sophisticated managers do not simply trade off global standardization for local appeal or vice versa. Instead, sophisticated managers recognize the inherent challenge of this duality and seek to standardize aspects of the product that have common appeal and customize those features that need adaptation to fit with local preferences.

For example, McDonald's has a worldwide identity, built on standardization of both product and service. The Quarter Pounder and Egg McMuffin are the same whether eaten in San Francisco, Singapore, or Moscow. The company also attempts to standardize managerial styles by requiring managers to learn the company's specific approaches to human resource practices, marketing, inventory management, and quality control. However, McDonald's corporate managers must also learn to deal with adjusting financial and marketing approaches to local conditions, just as their store managers in certain locations around the world must also know when to add specialized menu items to suit local tastes—black currant milkshakes in Poland, veggie burgers in the Netherlands, and salads with shrimp in Germany.[2]

You might think of it in terms of riding in a helicopter. Managers often have to "helicopter up" to a level in order to get a broad perspective of a situation, but then they need to come down to earth and make decisions or make things happen in a specific location. Managers who can only see what is directly in front of them risk being ineffective because they can't see "the forest for the trees." At the same time, managers who only fly at 20,000 feet also risk being ineffective because they miss the details and nuances that can influence the success or failure of specific decisions or tasks. Thus, effective management is not a matter of having only a broad global perspective or only a knowledge of the specific local situation; it is a matter of being able to have both.

PERSPECTIVE 4

MANAGERIAL EXCELLENCE *REQUIRES* COMMITMENT

As we have emphasized repeatedly, management is not a passive endeavor. To do it well requires deep commitment.

Commitment to what? To an organization or to a particular point of view?

No, although such commitments can be very important in particular situations and circumstances. Rather, we are talking about two fundamental types of commitment: one is to learning new skills and acquiring new knowledge; the other is to the goal of investing time, effort, and skills in creating something that didn't exist before and adding value to other people and to society.

Management Requires Commitment to Constantly Learning New Skills and Acquiring New Knowledge

Management is a complex process. It is not just about strategy, or organizing, or decision making, or leadership. It is about all of these activities and more, but espe-

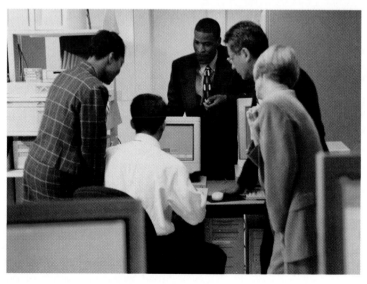

Regardless of the amount of their experience, managers must keep learning and improving their skills in order to meet new challenges and situations.

cially, it is about putting them all together. To integrate activities, managers require multiple skills: technical, conceptual, and interpersonal. These skills can be learned, or at least greatly improved by learning. They can, that is, *if* there is a commitment by a manager to such learning. No amount of experience by itself provides learning, but desire and effort to acquire new knowledge from those experiences can.

But do I really have to keep on learning about how to manage throughout my career? Isn't there a point where I've learned nearly everything there is to know about management?

That's a pretty dangerous assumption. As we said, the more experience the better, and the more effort to learn from that experience, the better. However, there will always be new situations and new challenges that you haven't encountered before, and a commitment to keep learning and keep improving as a manager is vital. There is a term called "hubris," which means overbearing pride or self-confidence, and it is the danger of developing hubris that should motivate you to keep pushing the frontiers of learning and skill acquisition as a manager, regardless of the amount of your previous experience and the knowledge you have gained from it.

Management Also Requires a Commitment to Adding Value to Other People and to Society

At its best, management is not a selfish activity. It should serve others, both in one's own organization and in society at large. This kind of commitment represents a challenge—a challenge to contribute something new and something that benefits more than yourself. Meeting this challenge requires not only a sense of obligation and of responsibility but also vision and a burning passion. Otherwise, why be a manager?

PERSPECTIVE 5

MANAGEMENT IS *KALEIDOSCOPIC*

Now that you've read this brief introduction to management, check the descriptors that you think apply to a manager's job:

_____ challenging
_____ sometimes frustrating
_____ often exciting
_____ occasionally boring
_____ frequently difficult
_____ seldom easy
_____ complex
_____ involves considerable variety
_____ full of ambiguities, paradoxes, and dualities
_____ time consuming
_____ usually personally rewarding
_____ often fun
_____ a means of making contributions to the larger society
_____ all of the above

Clearly, we believe the best answer is "all of the above," because management is kaleidoscopic: it deals with continually shifting, rapidly changing, and, often, extremely complex events. If any other answer were correct, management wouldn't be such a fascinating subject, and we would not have written this book.

Effective managers need to constantly heighten and polish their skills as the pace of change accelerates in the new millennium. Just imagine a sales manager in 1968: His sales representatives were probably all males; expected direction; may have heard about computers, yet never have seen one; managed a product line that consisted of stable, well-known brands; and had not yet witnessed the first moon landing. Today's sales manager oversees a diverse sales force; uses a personal computer, the Internet, and cell phones daily; manages people who weren't alive when Neil Armstrong first walked on the moon; and is constantly anticipating new products or competitors.

DEFINITIONS AND TERMINOLOGY

Before we go any further, it is essential that we take time to talk briefly about definitions and terms that will be used throughout this book. We recognize that definitions are, by themselves, dry and boring, but unless we have some common agreement on what key words mean, it is difficult to communicate. So, here is how we will be using the following terms as they relate to the overall focus of this book:

Management: This term has several different uses. The primary meaning for the purposes of this book is as an activity or process. More specifically, we define management as the process of assembling and using resources—human, financial, material, and information—in a goal-directed manner to accomplish tasks in an organization. This definition can in turn be subdivided into its key parts:

1. Management is a *process:* It involves a series of activities and operations, such as planning, deciding, and evaluating.
2. Management involves *assembling resources:* It is a process that brings together the means and assets to accomplish tasks.
3. Management involves *using resources:* It is a process that not only assembles resources but also puts them into use—to employ and deploy them.
4. Management involves assembling and using a *variety of types of resources:* It is a process that makes use not only of people but also of other types of resources, the most important of which are financial, material, and information.
5. Management involves acting in a *goal-directed* manner: It thus does not represent random activity but rather activity with a purpose and direction. The purpose or direction may be that of the individual, the organization, or, usually, a combination of the two.
6. Management involves the attempt to *accomplish tasks:* It includes efforts to complete activities successfully and to achieve particular levels of desired results.
7. Management, as we have already stressed earlier, involves activities carried out in an *organizational setting:* As we use the term, management is a process that is undertaken in organizations—that is, defined collections of people with differentiated functions put together for the long term to accomplish a variety of tasks. "Organizational settings," therefore, can refer to any type of work organization that employs people: companies, universities, law firms, hospitals, government agencies, and the like.

Management, as a term, also has several other meanings in addition to "a process" or set of activities. It is sometimes used to designate a particular *part* of the organization: the set of individuals who carry out management activities. Thus, you may hear the phrase "the management of IBM decided ..." or "the management of the University Hospital developed a new personnel policy...." Often, when the term is used this way, it does not necessarily refer to all members of management but rather to those who occupy the most powerful positions within this set (i.e., top management).

Another somewhat similar use of the term is to distinguish a category of people (i.e., "management") from those who are members of collective bargaining units ("union" members or, more informally, "labor") or those who are not involved in specific managerial activities whether or not they are union members (i.e., "non-management employees" or "rank-and-file employees"). We frequently use the term "member" to refer to any person (any employee) in an organization without regard to that individual's place in the organization. We will use the term *manager* to refer to anyone who has designated responsibilities for carrying out managerial activities, and *managing* to refer to the process itself.

So much for definitions. Let's now briefly talk about different categories of managerial work.

CATEGORIES OF MANAGERIAL WORK

Over the years, various systems have been developed to classify the types of work, functions, and roles managers carry out. These typologies can provide you with useful ways to look at the extremely varied nature of managerial jobs and responsibilities. In effect, they provide a form of road map for thinking about what management is.

Managerial Job Dimensions

An extremely useful way to try to gain an understanding of managerial work is to analyze the dimensions of managerial jobs. One particular approach was developed by a British researcher, Rosemary Stewart.[3] She proposed that any managerial job (and, in fact, any job anywhere in an organization) can be characterized along three dimensions:

- the demands made on it;
- the constraints placed on it; and
- the choices permitted in it.

Looking at managerial jobs in this way not only provides further understanding of what managers do but also permits direct comparisons of different jobs; for example, how the position of "manager of information systems" might compare with that of "financial analyst" or "marketing vice president" versus "plant manager."

Demands   This dimension of management jobs refers to what the holder of a particular position *must* do. "Demands" are of two types: activities or duties that must be carried out and the standards or levels of minimum performance that must be met. Demands can come from several sources, such as the organization at large, the immediate boss, or the way in which work activities are organized. Typical types of demands would include such behavior as attending required meetings, adhering to schedule deadlines, following certain procedures, and the like. No doubt, Cynthia Trudell has production and sales targets to meet in her CEO position at Saturn.

Constraints   "Constraints" are factors that limit the response of the manager to various demands. One obvious constraint for any manager is the amount of time available for an activity. Other typical constraints include budgets, technology, attitudes of subordinates, and legal regulations. The important point is that any managerial job has a set of constraints, and therefore a key to performing that job effectively is to recognize them and develop a good understanding of how they operate and how they can be minimized, overcome, or effectively confronted. Cynthia Trudell needs to work within the constraints of union contracts, supplier schedules, customer preferences, and even forces in the larger economy that she cannot control.

Choices   This dimension underscores the fact that despite demands and despite constraints, there is always room for some amount of discretionary behavior in any managerial job. Thus, there are a number of activities that a manager *may* carry out but does not have to. "Choices" can involve how work is to be done, what work beyond that absolutely required is to be done, who will do particular tasks, and what initiative not otherwise prohibited will be undertaken from almost infinite possibilities. In her past managerial positions, Cynthia Trudell has faced many choices and decisions, and in her new position she confronts a multitude of options in how to relate to hourly employees, how to demonstrate leadership, how to respond to changing conditions in automobile markets, and the like.

Managerial Functions

The system of analyzing the work of managers according to the different functions or processes they carry out dates back at least 80 years and has sometimes been criticized for not sufficiently representing what managers "really do." However, this system is still, after more than eight decades, widely utilized by management scholars and writers.[4] In fact, as we explain at the end of this chapter, a variation of this typology forms the basis for the organization of the chapters in this book (as well as most other textbooks on the subject of management). The four principal managerial functions that seem most applicable to modern organizations are planning, organizing, leading, and monitoring and evaluating.

Planning   Planning involves estimating future conditions and circumstances and, based on these estimations, making decisions about what work is to be done by the manager and all of those for whom she or he is responsible. This function can be thought of as involving two distinct levels or types: *strategic planning,* which addresses long-range goals and the broad approaches for achieving them, and *operational planning,* which focuses on short-range objectives and the specific means used to obtain them and on the related managerial activity of decision making.

Organizing   To carry out managerial work, resources must be put together systematically, and this function is labeled "organizing." Managers must deal with this function on two levels: the structure of relationships among people and positions—commonly called *organizational structure*—in the entire organization or major parts of it, and the structure of smaller units such as groups and teams. Since the world with which we deal is basically "messy" and thus full of uncertainties and ambiguities, the function of organizing is a critical challenge facing managers. At its most basic level, the purpose of this managerial function can be thought of as the attempt "to bring order out of chaos."

Leading   This function has typically had a number of different labels over the years such as "directing" or "leading." We prefer the latter term because it does not have the autocratic connotations associated with the world *directing*.

Monitoring and Evaluating   Often this function is labeled "controlling," but this label is not entirely satisfactory because it implies, as does the word *directing*, that the activity must be carried out in a dictatorial, autocratic fashion. This is, of course, not the case, although in a particular circumstance a manager might act in this manner. To avoid this possible misinterpretation, we prefer to call this overall

Managerial Functions

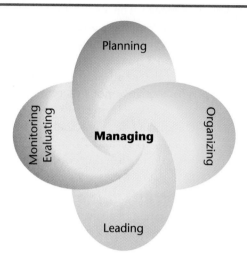

function "monitoring and evaluating." The essence of this function is to regulate the work of those for whom a manager is responsible. Regulation can be done in several different ways, including setting standards of performance in advance, monitoring ongoing (real-time) performance, and, especially, assessing a completed performance. The results of such evaluation are fed back into the planning process. Therefore, it is important to consider these four managerial functions as parts of a reciprocal and recurring process, as illustrated in Exhibit 1.1.

Managerial Roles

An alternative approach to describing managerial work was proposed some years ago by a Canadian scholar, Henry Mintzberg.[5] He based his classification system on research studies on how managers spend their time at work and focused on "roles," or what he called "organized sets of behaviors." Although this way of viewing managers' work activities has not replaced the functional approach, it has received a great deal of attention because it provides additional understanding and insights not readily apparent in that more traditional set of categories.

Mintzberg organized his typology of managerial roles into three major categories—interpersonal, informational, and decisional—each of which contains specific roles. There are 10 such roles in this system, as shown in Exhibit 1.2 and described in the following sections.

Interpersonal Roles   Interpersonal roles involve three types of behavior and, according to Mintzberg, derive directly from the manager's formal authority granted by the organization. They are

1. *The Figurehead Role:* This set of behaviors involves an emphasis on ceremonial activities, such as attending a social function, welcoming a visiting dignitary, or presiding at a farewell reception for a departing employee. A familiar term for this role of representing the organization, borrowed from the military, is "showing the flag." Although one particular occasion where this behavior

EXHIBIT 1.2

Managerial Roles

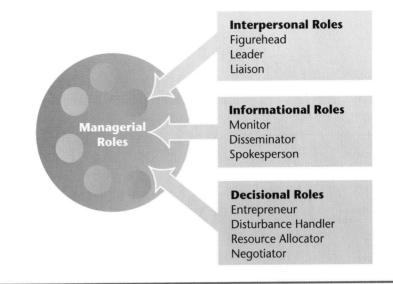

occurs may not be important in and of itself, the activity across a period of time is a necessary component of a manager's job.

2. *The Leader Role:* This role, in Mintzberg's system, is essentially one of influencing or directing others. It is the set of responsibilities people typically associate with a manager's job, since the organization gives the manager formal authority over the work of other people. To the extent that managers are able to translate this authority into actual influence, they are exercising what would be called leadership behavior.

3. *The Liaison Role:* This role emphasizes the contacts that a manager has with those outside the formal authority chain of command. These contacts include not only other managers within the organization but also many individuals outside it—for example, customers, suppliers, government officials, and managers from other organizations. This role also emphasizes lateral interactions, as contrasted with vertical interpersonal interactions, of a manager, and it highlights the fact that an important part of a manager's job is to serve as a go-between between his or her own unit and other units or groups.

Informational Roles   This set of roles builds on the interpersonal relationships that a manager establishes, and it underlines the importance of the network of contacts built up and maintained by the manager. The three specific informational roles identified by Mintzberg are the following:

1. *The Monitor Role:* This type of behavior involves extensive information seeking that managers engage in to keep aware of crucial developments that may affect their unit and their own work. Such monitoring, as previously noted, typically deals with spoken and written information and "soft" as well as "hard" facts.

2. *The Disseminator Role:* A manager not only receives information but also sends it. This often includes information that the receiver—such as a subordinate—wants but otherwise has no easy access to without the help of the manager.

3. *The Spokesperson Role:* A manager is frequently called upon to represent the views of the unit for which he or she is responsible. At lower management levels, this typically involves representing the unit to other individuals or groups within the organization; at higher management levels, this internal spokesperson role would be supplemented by an external component in which the organization and its activities and concerns often must be represented to the outside world, for example, making a presentation to financial securities analysts.

Decisional Roles   The final category of roles in this classification system relates to the decision-making requirements of a manager's job. Thus, this set builds on the two previous sets of roles, since interpersonal contacts generate information, which in turn is used to make decisions. Four such decisional roles are designated by Mintzberg:

1. *The Entrepreneurial Role:* Managers not only make routine decisions in their jobs but also frequently make decisions that explore new opportunities or start new projects. Such entrepreneurial behavior within an organization often involves a series of small decisions that permit ongoing assessment about whether to continue or abandon new ventures. Thus, this type of role behavior involves some degree of risk, but that risk is often limited or minimized by the sequence of decisions.
2. *The Disturbance Handler Role:* Managers initiate actions of their own, but they must also be able to respond to problems or "disturbances." In this role, a manager often acts as a judge or problem solver. The goal of such actions, of course, is to keep small problems or issues from developing into larger ones.
3. *The Resource Allocator Role:* Since resources of all types are always limited in organizations, one of the chief responsibilities of managers is to decide how the resources under their authority will be distributed. Such allocation decisions have a direct effect on the performance of a unit and an indirect effect of communicating certain types of information to members of the unit—for example, who is most important in the unit or what activity is regarded as highest priority.
4. *The Negotiator Role:* This type of managerial behavior refers to the fact that a manager is often called upon to make accommodations with other units or other organizations (depending on the level of the management position). Frequently, a given manager is, in effect, the "court of last resort" on whether a particular arrangement—that may have been negotiated by subordinates—is approved or not. The manager, in this decisional situation, is responsible for knowing what resources can or cannot be committed to particular negotiated solutions.

   In considering the 10 roles described in Mintzberg's analysis of managerial work, it is essential to keep in mind that the extent to which any particular role is important will vary considerably from one managerial job to another. Obviously, where a job fits in the organization will have a great deal to do with which particular role or roles will be emphasized. Nevertheless, Mintzberg maintains that the 10 roles form a "gestalt," or whole, and that to understand the total nature of any managerial job, *all* of them must be considered.

PLAN OF THE BOOK

Here at the end of Chapter 1, we want to share with you the overall structure and plan of the book. Most books on management, after starting with a set of introductory chapters, group the remaining chapters in clusters around the generally accepted four major functions of management: planning, organizing, leading, and monitoring/evaluating. This book is no exception. Although the chapter sequence is not original, the book's distinctiveness centers on how we present various topics and what we have to say about them.

The two chapters, including this one, in Part 1 are intended to provide an introduction and historical overview to the book's topic: management. Although the subject of Chapter 2, the history of management thought and practice, might not seem intrinsically appealing to some readers, it in fact helps to provide a useful grounding for understanding many contemporary management issues. A number of insights concerning modern management are gained by knowing how management developed in the past.

Part 2 provides a basic background for the four major managerial functions. Chapters 3 and 4 focus on the context for managing in organizations: the outside, or external, environment of management and the cultural environment. Particularly emphasized in these chapters are the various forces outside and inside the organization that affect how, and how well, a person can carry out managerial responsibilities. Chapter 5 presents the ethical issues that face every manager at the start of the new century. Although some books place this chapter toward the end of the book, we purposely place it near the beginning because of the prime importance we attach to this topic. Part 2 concludes with a discussion of innovation and entrepreneurship in Chapter 6. Understanding these two strong contemporary forces serves as an essential way to view the key functions involved in the process of managing in an organization.

The first of the four managerial functions, planning, is covered in the next set of chapters, 7 through 9, in Part 3. Chapter 7 provides an overview of basic planning principles and approaches, while Chapter 8 focuses on issues of broad strategy. Chapter 9 highlights the essential elements of decision making that are involved in bringing plans and strategies to concrete reality.

Chapters 10, 11, and 12, which form Part 4, deal with managerial issues involved with the function of organizing. Chapter 10 provides an overview of key elements of organization design and structure. Chapter 11 concentrates on organizational factors in the effective functioning of groups and teams. Chapter 12 discusses human resource factors involved in the staffing part of the organizing function.

The function of leading is the subject of Chapters 13, 14, and 15 in Part 5. First, an analysis of motivational principles relating to leading is provided in Chapter 13, followed by a focus on leadership itself in Chapter 14. In that chapter, special consideration is given to the similarities and differences between the concept of management and that of leadership. In Chapter 15, the topic of communication is explored for its implications for providing effective leadership in organizations.

In Part 6, Chapters 16 through 18, the fourth critical managerial function, monitoring and evaluating, is addressed from several different perspectives. Chapter 16 reviews some of the basic control challenges facing managers, while the following two chapters, 17 and 18, cover specific control issues involved in managing operations and managing information technology.

For the final part of the book, Part 7, Chapter 19 focuses on a central orientation that we think is imperative for anyone aspiring to work in a managerial job, namely, managing change. That theme, change, seems an especially appropriate one on which to conclude the book.

CONCLUDING COMMENTS

As we conclude this chapter, we want again to emphasize the five perspectives with which we started the chapter: Management takes place in an organizational context, management means getting things done through people, management involves mastering seeming contradictions and dualities, managerial excellence calls for significant commitments, and management is kaleidoscopic in nature. The challenge for you as a student is to learn more about the implications of these perspectives; that is, to learn more about the subtleties and complexities of the managerial process. This of course requires thought and analysis, but that, really, is only the beginning. To understand management also requires an ability to synthesize and integrate a diverse array of facts, theories, viewpoints, and examples—in a phrase, to be able to "put it all together" so that the whole is indeed more than the sum of its parts.

Above all else, however, beyond analysis and synthesis, management requires skill in implementation. This is, perhaps, one of the most difficult skills to develop—how to put into practice the results of analysis, synthesis, and decisions. If there is one skill that senior managers seem most concerned about among college graduates, it is in the area of implementation.[6] They believe that the typical graduate coming out of college is much better at analysis than at implementation. Obviously, acquiring experience in managing helps considerably in developing the skill to be able to implement effectively, as Cynthia Trudell has done. But experience by itself will not guarantee results. What is also needed is a heightened sensitivity to the importance of developing this skill. The lack of implementation skill is analogous to an athletic team formulating a good game plan but then fumbling the ball and dropping passes in the game itself. As you read through the remainder of this book, keep to the forefront the message that management is not just about knowing; it is also, and emphatically so, about doing.

And, as a final word to end this chapter, we want to reiterate another point made earlier: In today's world, if you aspire to manage at high levels in organizations, you will need to have a global *as well as* a local, or "own country," focus. Without both perspectives, your understanding and vision of how to implement effective management will be unnecessarily restricted. For that reason, we have made the international aspects of managerial issues and topics a major theme running throughout this book.

CHAPTER 2

HISTORY OF MANAGEMENT THOUGHT AND PRACTICE

After studying this chapter, you should be able to:

- Explain how conditions existing at the time influenced the development of management thought at the beginning of the 20th century.
- Describe the contributions of the scientific management approach and explain why it was so controversial.
- Discuss the differences and similarities of the ideas of the major contributors to the "classical" and "neoclassical" approaches to management.
- Compare the contributions to management thought of the behavioral, decision-making, and integrative approaches of more recent decades.

General Motors: How Pioneering Managers Struggled to Organize a New Industry

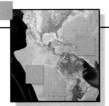

When the American auto industry came into being just after the beginning of the 20th century, new car manufacturers soon faced emerging problems, among them how to organize the work and lines of communication. For each of these companies to survive the tumultuous changes of the new century, including rapid growth, changes in technology, and market shifts, executives had to find a rational way to manage the workforce as well as the structure of the organization. One such top manager was Alfred P. Sloan, Jr., who served as CEO of General Motors from 1923 to 1946.

General Motors was founded in 1908. It is important to keep in mind that management theories, as they related to the new industrial era, were in their infancy then. By the early 1920s, when Sloan took over at General Motors, many manufacturers had adopted an approach called "scientific management" (discussed later in this chapter), which was designed to organize factory floor tasks. But usable and systematic approaches to management that dealt with the total organization had yet to evolve to any extent. Thus, Sloan and his colleagues struggled to find a solution.

Sloan recalled that, at General Motors, "It was ... management by crony, with the divisions operating on a horse-trading basis." In the first few years immediately following the end of World War I, divisions were competing against each other for available funds, which were often allocated based on top managers' preferences rather than unbiased evaluation. "The important thing was that no one knew how much was being contributed—plus or minus—by each division to the common good of the corporation. And since, therefore, no one knew, or could prove, where the efficiencies and inefficiencies lay, there was no objective basis for the allocation of new investment," observed Sloan.

Sloan recognized that the organization had to change. "I became convinced that the corporation could not continue to grow and survive unless it was better organized, and it was apparent that no one was giving that subject the attention it needed." With Sloan's support, late in 1920, General Motors' new President Pierre du Pont and new executive committee began to implement "a highly rational and objective mode of operation." Using the findings from an "Organizational Study" conducted by Sloan, they developed a new policy, which Sloan ultimately called a "trend toward a happy medium to industrial organization." General Motors' new policy was designed so that the organization could evolve in a strong yet flexible manner. The policy included decisions about the amount of responsibility that individual divisions would retain—and "thus initiated for the modern General Motors," Sloan wrote in 1964, "the trend toward a happy medium in industrial organization between the extremes of pure centralization and pure decentralization." Finding that "happy medium" is still a managerial problem that faces many organizations, including General Motors, even today some 80 years later!

Source: Alfred P. Sloan, Jr., *My Years with General Motors* (New York: Doubleday & Company, Inc., 1964), pp. 27, 42, 48, 52, 55; "General Motors History" at the GM Web site, accessed at http://www.gm.com, November 3, 1998.

As this opening story about the trials and tribulations of General Motors at the beginning of the 1920s demonstrates, industrial and other leaders throughout the 20th century struggled with how to approach the challenge of managing their organizations. In this task, they were assisted by various writers and scholars who contributed ideas and theories about this complex topic. Some of those more important thinkers and their ideas are covered in the remaining pages of this chapter.

In the pages that follow it is important to keep in mind a basic proposition: To understand the present, you must know something about the past. A review of the history of management thought, especially during the 20th century, can help us to gain a better understanding of different approaches to management—how those approaches have changed over the years and why they are the way they are now.

Although, as we will see, there have been ideas about management since antiquity, so-called "modern" management is only roughly 100 years old.

We begin with a brief look at the earlier origins of organized and systematic thinking about management, especially those that arose from the Industrial Revolution in England and later in the United States. Then we trace the development of the scientific management approach, classical management theory, and neoclassical theory. Later in the chapter, three more contemporary approaches are discussed: behavioral, decision-making, and integrative approaches. To give you some perspective, Exhibit 2.1 provides a timeline of the developments in management thought that places them in the historical context of other events that were occurring at the same approximate period of time. The exhibit is thus meant to emphasize the point that conditions and events in society and industry existing in a given time period strongly influenced the type of management theories and approaches being proposed.

EXHIBIT 2.1

History of Events and Management Thought and Practice

Date	General Events	Industrial Events	Management Thought/Practice
700–0 B.C.	First written laws of Athens Mayan civilization Greek civilization Rise of Rome	Canal between Nile and Red Sea Sundials, water clocks Mediterranean trade Great Wall of China (215 B.C.)	Sun Tzu, *The Art of War* (4th century B.C.)
A.D. 1–1450	London founded (A.D. 43) Fall of the Roman Empire (455—Vandals sack Rome) Dark Ages in Europe Mohammed (570–632) Oxford University founded (1167) Black Death decimates European population (1347–1349)	Applicants for public office in China required to take examinations (606) Postal and news services in the Caliph's empire (945) Trade between Asia and Western Europe via Venice (983) Coal mining begins in Newcastle, England (1233) Guild system Standardization of measurements in England Bankruptcy of Florentine banking houses (1345)	
1450–1700	Renaissance in Europe The Spanish Inquisition (1478–1834) Columbus lands in the Americas (1492) Age of Exploration Slave trade begins in Europe and Americas Plague in Europe (1563) New York City founded (1626) Harvard College founded (1636) Great Fire of London (1666) Newton's theories (1687)	Printing press (1455) Regular postal service in Europe (Vienna to Brussels to Madrid) (1500) Beginning of textile industry in England (1641) Hudson Bay Company founded (1670) Mitsui family trading and banking house in Japan founded (1673)	Machiavelli, *The Prince* (1513)

continued

EXHIBIT 2.1

Continued

Date	General Events	Industrial Events	Management Thought/Practice
1700–1800	Yale University founded (1701) American Revolution (1776) French Revolution (1789)	Bernoulli's work on hydrodynamics (1738) Benjamin Franklin invents the lightning conductor (1752) First iron mill in England (1754) The Industrial Revolution begins London Stock Exchange founded (1773) Steam engine (1775) New York Stock Exchange founded (1790) Whitney invents the cotton gin (1793) First telegraph, Paris–Lille (1794)	Smith, *An Inquiry into the Nature and Causes of the Wealth of Nations* (1776) Malthus, *Essay on the Principle of Evolution* (1798)
1800–1900	Century of Steam Luddite riots in England (1811) Trade union movement Darwin, *On the Origin of the Species by Natural Selection* (1859) American Civil War (1861–1865) Transcontinental railroad (1869) First U.S. business school: Wharton at the University of Pennsylvania (1881) Nobel Prizes established (1896)	First battery (1800) Robert Owen institutes social reforms at the Lanarck Mills (1800) Steam locomotive (1814) First typewriter patented (1830) Faraday works with electromagnetism (1831) British Factory Act provides system for factory inspection (1833) Morse demonstrates electric telegraph (1837) Standard Oil Company founded by John D. Rockefeller (1870) Telephone invented (1876) Phonograph invented (1877) Introduction of electric lights (1880) AT&T formed (1885) Eastman produces box camera (1888)	Babbage, *On the Economy of Machinery and Manufacturers* (1832) Cournot, *Researches into the Mathematical Principles of the Theory of Wealth* (1838) Engels, *The Condition of the Working Class in England* (1845) Marx and Engels, *The Communist Manifesto* (1848) Towne, *Engineer as Economist* (1886)
1900–1920	Century of electricity First MBA program established at the Tuck School, Dartmouth College (1900) Wright brothers flight (1903) Einstein's special theory of relativity (1905) World War I (1914–1918) Russian Revolution (1917)	U.S. Steel organized (1901) Ford Motor Company founded (1903) General Motors formed (1908) Weekends become popular (1910) Woolworth Co. founded (1912) Ford introduces assembly line (1913) Airmail service established from New York to Washington, D.C. (1918)	Taylor, *The Principles of Scientific Management* (1911) Fayol, *Administration Industrielle et Générale* (1916) The Gilbreths, *Applied Motion Study* (1917)

EXHIBIT 2.1

Continued

Date	General Events	Industrial Events	Management Thought/Practice
1920s	Lindbergh flies across Atlantic (1927) Stock market crash (1929)	Sloan reorganizes General Motors into multidivisional structure Beginning of chain stores	Mary Parker Follett, *Creative Experience* (1924) Hawthorne studies (1924–1932)
1930s	The Great Depression Social Security Act (1935)	First supermarkets Sit-down strikes Industrial Unionism as a challenge to managerial control	Mooney and Reiley, *Onward Industry* (1931) Mayo, *The Human Problems of Industrial Civilization* (1933) Barnard, *The Functions of the Executive* (1938) Roethlisberger and Dickson, *Management & the Worker* (1939)
1940s	World War II (1939–1945) The atomic age begins (1945) First session of the United Nations (1946) Partition of Palestine, creation of State of Israel (1947)	Commercialization of television ENIAC—Birth of general purpose computing (1946) Xerography process invented (1946) First supersonic flight (1947) Transistor invented at Bell Labs (1947) Creation of the World Bank and IMF	Weber, *Theory of Social and Economic Organization* (trans. 1947) Simon, *Administrative Behavior: A Study of Decision-Making Processes in Administrative Organization* (1947) Lewin, *Resolving Social Conflicts* (1948)
1950s	The Korean War Colonial independence movements Suburbanization U.S. Interstate Highway System USSR launches Sputnik (1957) European Common Market (1958)	Color television introduced in U.S. (1951) Electric power produced from atomic energy (1951) Transatlantic cable telephone service (1956) AFL merges with CIO (1955)	Maslow, *Motivation and Personality* (1954) Drucker, *The Practice of Management* (1954) Argyris, *Personality and Organization* (1957) March and Simon, *Organizations* (1958) Herzberg et al., *The Motivation to Work* (1959)
1960s	Civil Rights Movement Women's Movement Vietnam War Campus protests Assassinations of John Kennedy, Robert Kennedy, Martin Luther King, Jr. Berlin Wall constructed (1961) Cuban missile crisis (1962) Rachel Carson, *Silent Spring* (1962) Nobel prize for discovery of structure of DNA to Watson, Crick, and Wilkins (1962) Six Day War in Middle East (1967) First moon landing (July 24, 1969)	Conglomerates emerge as organizational form "Military-Industrial Complex" Jet travel Franchising Environmental Protection Agency Equal opportunity legislation	McGregor, *The Human Side of Enterprise* (1960) Likert, *New Patterns of Management* (1961) Chandler, *Strategy and Structure* (1962) Cyert and March, *A Behavioral Theory of the Firm* (1963) Sun Tzu, *The Art of War* (trans. 1963) Lawrence and Lorsch, *Organizations and the Environment* (1967)

continued

EXHIBIT 2.1
Continued

Date	General Events	Industrial Events	Management Thought/Practice
1970s	U.S. withdraws from Vietnam Western trade opened with China Oil embargo Airline deregulation	Dow Jones Index at 631 (1970) Birth of Apple Computer Hand-held calculators Fiber optics	Major growth in number of MBA graduates Quality circles Mintzberg, *The Nature of Managerial Work* (1973)
1980s	Deregulation Berlin Wall falls (1989)	Breakup of AT&T Major growth in personal computing Wal-Mart	M. Porter, *Competitive Strategy* (1980) Ouchi, *Theory Z: How American Business Can Meet the Japanese Challenge* (1981) Peters and Waterman, *In Search of Excellence* (1982) M. Porter, *Competitive Advantage* (1985) Just-in-time inventory systems
1990s	Soviet Union dissolves NAFTA European Union near reality	Internet Electronic commerce Microsoft Corporation dominance in software	Corporate downsizing Rightsizing Empowerment Reengineering Corporate governance issues Total quality management (TQM) Outsourcing Learning organizations Increasing emphasis on teams

The chapter concludes with a look at the status of management thought as we enter the 21st century. As you read the chapter, keep in mind two key questions to enhance your understanding: (1) What preceded the development of a particular way of thinking about management? (2) What was the world—in particular, the world of work—like at the time the theory or approach emerged?

THE ORIGINS OF MANAGEMENT THOUGHT

The topic of how to manage organizations did not receive systematic and wide-scale attention until virtually the start of the 20th century. However, writers have been commenting on, and even analyzing, managerial issues throughout the past 3,000 years. As we will see in the next few pages, a scattering of writers and record-ed examples from a small number of organizations in different places in the civilized world did leave their mark on management thought and practice before the beginning of the 20th century.

Pre-Industrial Revolution Influences

As the Managerial Challenge box, "Even Ancient Civilizations Faced Managerial Challenges," shows, as far back as roughly 1,000 B.C., perceptive officials in China were writing about how to manage and control organized human activity. Five hundred or so years later (approximately the 4th century B.C.), an illustrious

MANAGERIAL CHALLENGE

EVEN ANCIENT CIVILIZATIONS FACED MANAGERIAL CHALLENGES

Although this chapter primarily focuses on the history of management thought and practice dating from the 18th century, we can turn even further back in time to gain an understanding of how organizations function. Four thousand years ago, Chinese rulers faced the same challenge that today's managers face: how to organize people (including different levels of officials) in order to complete tasks and achieve goals. Until 250 B.C., China was made up of many states of differing sizes, populations, and natural resources. In fact, China resembled a modern, large, multidivisional corporation. Then, between 250 B.C. and 206 B.C., China became a centralized empire with tight control from the top, a structure that is not totally unfamiliar in some of today's large companies.

What methods did Chinese rulers develop over centuries to meet the challenge of governing such a large country, and how do they relate to today's methods? *The Officials of Chou,* developed either by King Ching of Chou or the Duke of Chou sometime around 1100 B.C., outlines in great detail many of the features that management experts now think of as tenets of a true bureaucracy, including clear, specific job descriptions for officials at every level; explicitly stated rights, powers, and obligations of senior officials; division of labor based on specialization (and, ultimately, technical competence in those areas); clear hierarchy of authority; clearly defined work procedures; and promotion or advancement based on merit (technical competence). King Ching also outlined several important "rules of good management," including personal qualities such as carefulness and economy, the quest for self-improvement, the necessity of making bold decisions as well as conforming to rules, and the importance of promoting subordinates. All of these char-

acteristics probably sound quite familiar, as if they might be found in an employee's or manager's handbook for a large, contemporary corporation.

Leadership style also played an important part in the governing of ancient China. In addition to the rules of good management, high-level officials were encouraged to be benevolent in their methods of governing because this behavior would, in the end, engender support from the people. E Yin, who was prime minister around 1750 B.C., wrote, "Do not slight the concerns of the people: Think of their difficulties.... Be careful to think about the end at the beginning. When you hear words against which your mind sets itself, you must inquire whether these words are not right. When you hear words that agree with your own thinking, you must ask whether these words are not wrong." Being able to communicate effectively with subordinates and citizens and win their support was crucial to the survival of a leader's power—and perhaps his life. China's social system was clan based, and many of the clans had their own armies. Apparently, a number of rulers were overthrown simply because their behavior and style of governing were unacceptable to the clans.

With their global reach and capacity for instantaneous communication, today's corporations may not appear to resemble ancient China's agrarian civilization. But it is clear that even four thousand years ago, rulers searched for efficient, effective ways to manage people. In some respects, they came up with answers that sound very familiar today.

Source: Violina P. Rindova and William H. Starbuck, "Ancient Chinese Theories of Civilization," *Journal of Management Inquiry,* 6, no. 2 (June 1997), pp. 144–59; copyright 1997 Sage Publications, Inc.

Chinese military leader of the time, Sun Tzu, wrote about his views of principles of leadership (e.g., the need for the leader to promote unity within an organization), ideas that many consider are still relevant to today's organizations.[1]

Other civilizations, such as those of ancient Egypt and, later, Rome, were able to organize large numbers of people to carry out coordinated activities that required a form of what today we would call "management." The Egyptians built pyramids as far back as 2700 B.C., and the Romans in the early centuries A.D., and even before, were able to develop highly organized and well-led armies that exercised control over wide areas of territory. Thus, although relatively little was written systematically at the time about how these feats of organization and leadership were carried out, the results demonstrated that management was being successfully practiced in terms of achieving goals and objectives.

In the late Middle Ages (15th and 16th centuries), city-states in Europe such as Venice and Florence were managing certain activities with procedures that today we

Similar to a modern public works project, the pyramids of ancient Egypt were constructed with thousands of workers under the leadership of pharoahs. These sophisticated structures are proof that ancient civilizations practiced management to coordinate the work of thousands.

would consider "modern." For example, Venice had a large shipyard at that time that, in effect, adopted such managerial control procedures as the standardization of parts, inventory control, and analysis of costs of materials.[2] Also in this era, Machiavelli (in 1513) published his famous treatise—*The Prince*—on opportunistic and, some would say, crafty techniques for leaders of state to rule their subjects.

Although all of these and other developments relevant to management thought and practice took place before the 18th century, it was not until the middle of that century that the issue of how to manage organizations started to become a more prominent concern. Until that time, most organizations (with a few exceptions such as those noted, the Catholic Church, and military organizations), were still relatively small and simple in structure. For this reason, it had been unnecessary to give serious thought to the way jobs were carried out, work divided among people, and their efforts coordinated. All this was about to change around 1750 when the Industrial Revolution began in England. (This period of societal transformation was not called by that name at the time but was given that label by historians many decades later.) It would take some years, however, before that "revolution" would spread to other places, including the Western hemisphere and Asia.

The Industrial Revolution in England

The fundamental changes that took place in human work performance in the latter half of the 1700s received their impetus from one key source: advances in technology, especially those related to mechanized power. Up to that time, work was accomplished almost solely through human or animal effort, sometimes supplemented by wind or water power. Consequently, work was organized around the family and was located typically within each family's dwelling. The nature of this system—subsequently labeled the "domestic system" by historians[3]—made it difficult to perform more complex work, to produce more complex products, and especially to turn out goods in high volumes.

The beginning of the end of the domestic production system was signaled by the introduction of power-driven machinery, especially the steam engine. Although the now-famous inventor, James Watt, produced the first functional steam engine in 1765, it was another 20 years before it was put into general use.[4] From then on the steam engine, and what it could do, rapidly altered the ways many types of goods were produced. In fact, its development was perhaps the single most important step in the rise of the factory system. The steam engine made it possible to increase vastly the volume of production; however, increased production also required more materials and hence more capital. To put those resources to more efficient use in turn required more people working together in one location. This meant, in effect, bringing people to the work rather than bringing work to the people. Hence, the factory seemed to answer the emerging question of how to take the greatest advantage of the potential of steam power for increased productivity.

Once factories were established at the end of the 1700s in England, it became clear that although they solved one problem, they created another: how best to coordinate workers' efforts for maximum efficiency. One approach was to divide up the work so that each person performed a limited number of tasks; in other words, specialized tasks. This idea, which came to be called **division of labor**, was especially championed by one of the founders of modern economics, Adam Smith. In 1776, about the time the Revolutionary War was beginning in America, Smith published his seminal work, *The Wealth of Nations*. That book (consisting of several volumes) contained a very clear description of the advantages of the division of labor:

division of labor
the division of work so that each person performs a limited number of tasks (specialized tasks); first used early in the Industrial Revolution

> *This great increase of the quantity of work which, in consequence of the division of labour, the same number of people are capable of performing, is owing to three different circumstances: first, to the increase of dexterity in every particular workman; secondly, to the saving of the time which is commonly lost in passing from one species of work to another; and lastly, to the invention of a great number of machines which facilitate and abridge labour, and enable one man to do the work of many.[5]*

Interestingly, some people today forget that Smith also had great insight in anticipating the potential *dis*advantages of the implementation of the division of labor idea, especially as it related to the workers who would be involved:

> *The man whose whole life is spent in performing a few simple operations... naturally loses, therefore, the habit of [mental] exertion, and generally becomes stupid and ignorant as it is possible for a human creature to become.... His dexterity at his own particular trade seems ... to be acquired at the expense of his intellectual, social, and martial virtues.[6]*

In addition to the issues of how to divide up the work efficiently, the other problem relating to factories was how to coordinate the efforts of all of the workers—in other words, how to manage them. There were a number of aspects to the management problem. The owners of early factories and their immediate family were also the managers. As factories grew in size, however, it became impossible for family members to supervise all the workers. This meant that other people had to be hired for supervision. But who was to do this?

At the beginning of the Industrial Revolution, there were no trained supervisors or managers, because this task had never existed before. The early nonfamily supervisors were usually "illiterate workers promoted from the ranks because they evidenced a greater degree of technical skills or had the ability to keep discipline."[7] As management historian Daniel Wren has summed up the situation: "The transformation of England from an agrarian to an industrial society meant that there was no managerial class or, in modern terms, no professional managers. First, there was no common body of knowledge about how to manage.... Second, there was no common code of management behavior, no universal set of expectations about how a manager should act."[8]

The need for attention to the process that would come to be known as "management" became more acute as England entered the 19th century and the Industrial Revolution became more widespread and affected more and more people. Several prominent individuals, typically entrepreneurs or factory owners themselves, in the early 1800s in England and Scotland did consider how best to organize the activities of factories and direct the work of the people employed in them. Some of these earliest management thinkers, such as Robert Owen and Charles Babbage, even published their ideas in books. Consequently, they can be thought of as the first "management writers" of modern times, but their impact was relatively limited. Book reading in that era was not widespread, and the typical factory manager was busy coping with his own day-to-day problems, not worrying about other people's thoughts on how to run factories more efficiently. Also, much of this early writing focused on techniques applicable to specific firms rather than on general principles or theories about management. Formal writing about principles of management was still more than half a century away.[9]

The Industrial Revolution in America

The Industrial Revolution started in England, but it was in the New World in America that it flourished. One contributing factor to its success was the abundance of raw materials and natural resources, such as water, timber, and minerals. Another factor was the general absence of old traditions to slow the adoption of new methods. Also, American manufacturers gained an advantage from early trial and error of their English counterparts, some of whom migrated to the United States and brought their most successful methods with them.

Three types of industrial enterprises in the first half of the 19th century accounted for most of the improvements in managing enterprises in the United States: textile manufacturing, arms manufacturing, and railroads.[10] As one historian has noted, "The American Industrial Revolution began in textiles."[11] Textile manufacturing was the principal industrial activity that benefited most from a large number of people working together in one location. Manufacturers of arms and weapons, on the other hand, were the key developers of interchangeable parts. In doing so, they advanced the practice of using division of labor and high degrees of employee specialization and significantly increased the ability of a manufacturer to turn out products requiring precision work.

In the railroads, however, the first systematic thinking emerged about how to *manage* a company more effectively. The critical challenge to railroads, from a management standpoint, was quite different from that faced by manufacturers. Railroads had to organize, coordinate, and supervise multiple operations in widely dispersed geographical locations. Although armies and the Catholic Church had been coping with such problems for many years, those organizations had unique sources of discipline and control unavailable to private-sector industrial organizations. In the decades just before and after the Civil War, several far-sighted individuals connected with railroads began to propose specific methods to deal with organizational problems. One such person was David McCallum, general superintendent of the Erie Railroad in the 1850s. McCallum instituted a number of procedures and policies that we now take for granted, but for the time they were quite innovative. He developed organizational charts, regular reports from lower and middle managers, formal job descriptions, and promotions based on merit.[12] The issue of how best to run railroads efficiently and safely set the stage for more formal, systematic approaches to managerial activities. We turn next to a review of the insights and ideas of those who contributed such systematic approaches, the pioneers of modern management theory.

PIONEERS: THE SCIENTIFIC MANAGEMENT APPROACH

The rapid growth in the number and size of factories following the end of the American Civil War in 1865 resulted in increased attention to the issue of how to improve industrial efficiency. By the 1880s, professional engineers were beginning to address this problem directly. In fact, a paper delivered in 1886 in Chicago at a meeting of the American Society of Mechanical Engineers is regarded as the beginning of "modern" management in the United States.[13] This paper, titled "The Engineer as Economist," was presented by engineer Henry R. Towne, who was the co-founder of the Yale Lock Company. The significance of Towne's paper is that it represented one of the first formal calls for serious attention to the business aspects of engineering activities. Specifically, Towne urged engineers to consider that "the matter of shop management is of equal importance with that of engineering as affecting the successful conduct of most, if not all, of our great industrial establishments, and ... the *management of works* [Towne's italics] has become a matter of such great and far-reaching importance as perhaps to justify its classification ... as one of the modern arts."[14]

Frederick W. Taylor (1856–1915)

Towne's call was not immediately heeded by most of his engineering colleagues. However, at roughly the same time period (i.e., the 1880s), an engineer working at the Midvale Steel Company in Philadelphia was thinking along somewhat the same lines. His name was Frederick Winslow Taylor, and he was to become one of the most famous people in the Western world in the early years of the 20th century.

To put Taylor's ideas into perspective, it is necessary to take a brief look at what the United States was like around the turn of the century. At that time, the typical education level of an industrial worker was less than the sixth grade, and there were only about 15,000 college graduates per year in a population of over 58 million. (Compared with education levels over 100 years later in the mid-1990s when the respective numbers were 1.7 million degrees conferred and a population of 260 million, the ratio of college graduates per year to the total population has thus changed from .03 percent to .7 percent.) Also in the 1880s, approximately 85 percent of all firms were manufacturing enterprises, while today they comprise only 15

FREDERICK WINSLOW TAYLOR, 1856–1915

Frederick Winslow Taylor was born in 1856 in Germantown, Pennsylvania. His father was a prosperous lawyer, and Taylor grew up in an affluent family. Taylor's family was of Puritan decent, arriving in the United States in 1629 at Plymouth, Massachusetts. This ancestry instilled in Taylor many Puritan values, including the need to search for the truth, to avoid waste of any type, and to judge by observation of the facts. These values in part drove Taylor's search for the "one best way" even in his youth. For example, while just a boy, Taylor searched for the one best way to play croquet and the best way to make a cross-country walk covering the greatest distance with the least fatigue.

Although he enrolled in Harvard Law School to follow his father's footsteps, he had to withdraw because of poor health and eyesight. After leaving Harvard, Taylor started as an apprentice at Enterprise Hydraulic Works of Philadelphia and finished his apprenticeship in 1878 at the age of 22. During this time he developed an appreciation for workers' points of view and saw problems with worker "soldiering," (i.e., loafing), poor quality of management, and poor relations between workers and management.

In 1878, Taylor moved to Midvale Steel (Pennsylvania) and worked as a common laborer. Within six years he moved from laborer to clerk, to machinist, to gang boss of machinists, to foreman of the machine shop, to master mechanic, to chief engineer. While working full-time at Midvale, Taylor also enrolled in a home study course from Stevens Institute of Technology in New Jersey. He attended classes only to take examinations. Two-and-a-half years after enrolling, Taylor graduated in 1883 with a degree in mechanical engineering.

Source: Frank B. Copley, *Frederick W. Taylor: Father of Scientific Management*, 2 vols. (New York: Harper & Row, 1923).

percent. It is crucial to keep such facts in mind when considering what Taylor proposed and why he advocated the ideas and procedures he did.

Taylor began his life's work as a common laborer and as an apprentice tool and die maker. Thus, hard-earned, on-the-job experience in blue-collar jobs provided his initial ideas and motivation about how to improve the efficiency of industrial plants. Taylor developed a strong belief that only through rigorous scientific experimentation could better methods be developed. He was particularly keen on time study and analysis of workers' individual tasks—a truly innovative concept for its day. In fact, as noted management author Peter Drucker has written, "Taylor was the first man in history who actually studied work seriously."[15] In some respects, the emphasis on gathering factual data about tasks and jobs might be regarded as Taylor's greatest contribution to the advancement of the practice of management.

Taylor's Principles of Scientific Management   Even though most of Taylor's fact-finding studies concentrated on the hourly employee and the first level of supervision, his total approach as it evolved and expanded over the years came to be called **scientific management**. The essence of Taylor's scientific management approach focused on a few key principles that gradually evolved over years of extensive study of task and supervisory practices and how they could be combined for

scientific management
approach developed by Frederick Winslow Taylor focusing on basic principles for improving performance, such as studying jobs by using objective measurements in order to determine the one best way, selecting the best persons for the job, training them in the most efficient methods, and providing sufficient monetary incentive to those performing the work

EXHIBIT 2.2

Basic Elements of Scientific Management

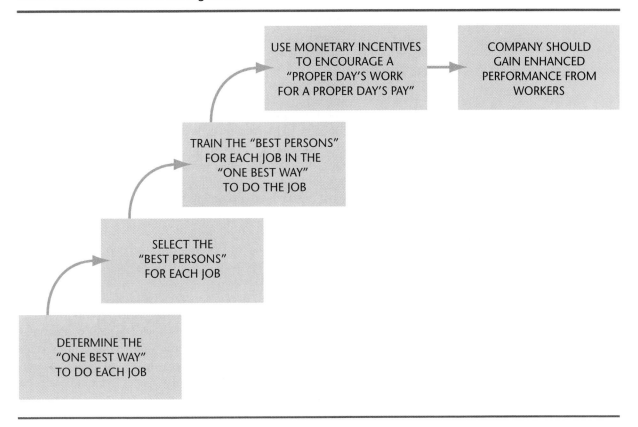

improved performance. The basic elements of scientific management (shown in Exhibit 2.2) were the following:

- **Determine the one best way to do each job through precise, objective measurement:** Taylor's entire approach was fundamentally based on meticulously studying and measuring the efforts involved in performing each task and movement that constituted a job, and then determining from the data the single best way to carry out the total set of procedures.
- **Select the "best persons" for the job:** For many of the blue-collar jobs Taylor investigated, such as loading pig iron, the best person meant the strongest person with the strongest desire to do a good job. For other jobs not involving sheer strength, this meant the person with the most aptitude for a particular set of tasks.
- **Train the "best person" in the most efficient methods of performing the task(s), i.e., the one best way:** Taylor stressed that it was management's—not the worker's—responsibility to study the task and determine scientifically the optimal way to perform it. This might mean retraining workers who had already been performing the task.
- **Provide sufficient monetary incentive to the workers to perform the task correctly and meet a defined hourly or daily target rate of output**

(a "proper day's work"): Taylor believed that it was only fair for workers to share directly in the rewards of higher levels of output that would result when correct methods were used and when the prescribed rate of performance was achieved. These rewards were to be in the form of sharply higher take-home wages for individuals who met or exceeded the standards, compared with the wages of workers who produced at slower rates and did not meet assigned targets.

Taylor's Impact   By the time Taylor's major work, *The Principles of Scientific Management,* was published in 1911, he already had attained considerable notoriety, both within the business world as well as in the wider society. Companies were beginning to explore ways to implement versions of Taylor's approach in order to increase the performance level of their operations. At the same time, however, some of the labor unions of the day were becoming more and more concerned and vocal about the possible exploitation of workers if Taylor's methods were used widely. Indeed, even the U.S. Congress took note of Taylor, when hearings were held in 1911 and 1912 by the House Labor Committee. The committee examined Taylor's views on how scientific management was affecting the ordinary worker, among other matters.

The major criticism of Taylor and his overall approach (see Exhibit 2.3) was that his methods not only placed undue pressure on workers but also disproportionately rewarded management compared with employees. Taylor himself maintained that companies and their workers should have a joint and mutual interest in improving output through scientific management principles and that increased levels of efficiency and production would benefit both parties.[16] He also argued

EXHIBIT 2.3

Contributions and Criticisms of Scientific Management

CONTRIBUTIONS	• Emphasized the Gathering of Factual Data Concerning Jobs and Tasks • Persuaded Managers to Abandon Haphazard Approaches to Planning and Organizing Work • Stressed the Role of Management in Organizing Work, Training Workers, and Instituting Incentives	
	FROM ORGANIZED LABOR	FROM BEHAVIORAL SCIENTISTS
CRITICISMS	• Too Much Pressure to Perform Placed on the Workers • Unfair Division of Rewards Between Management and Labor	• Presents an Oversimplified Approach to Worker Motivation • Pays Insufficient Attention to Social Factors in the Workplace that Affect Worker Behavior • Too Authoritarian in Approach • Demands Excessive Specialization of Jobs and Tasks

that he was not anti-union, but that unions would become unnecessary if management fairly shared productivity gains with workers. Of course, what constitutes an equitable sharing of gains (including protection against layoffs caused by increased rates of production) has never been resolved, and thus organized labor has always remained extremely wary of many features of scientific management.

In later years, some behavioral scientists criticized Taylor and the scientific management approach on several grounds (as shown in Exhibit 2.3), including the following: (1) scientific management was an oversimplified approach to motivation that emphasized the importance of wage incentives; (2) it payed insufficient attention to other, especially social, factors that affect employee behavior in work settings; (3) it was an authoritarian, management-dominated approach; (4) it placed too much emphasis on specialization of tasks and jobs; and (5) Taylor failed to give credit to those who helped develop the ideas and procedures commonly identified with "scientific management."[17] Some of these criticisms have been challenged by other management scholars, and thus the validity of the criticisms is still disputed.

Nevertheless, several facts ought to be kept in mind about Taylor and the impact of his contributions:

1. **The influence of his times:** Just as we all are products of our own times, so was Taylor. He was strongly influenced by many factors at the turn of the century (e.g., the average education level of the work force) that have changed considerably in the intervening 90-plus years. Were today's conditions present then, he undoubtedly would have modified some of his views.

2. **Order out of chaos:** Taylor spent a great amount of effort, as we have noted earlier, on systematically studying jobs and work. As a result of his research and demonstrations, he helped persuade managers to abandon a haphazard approach to planning and organizing work and instead to base it on facts, especially at the hourly worker's level and the first level of supervision.

3. **Managerial responsibilities:** Taylor continually stressed that it was management's responsibility to organize the work, train the workers, and institute an effective incentive system. In his own words, he wanted to bring about "a complete mental revolution," not only on the part of the workers but also, and particularly, "on the part of those on the management's side—the foreman, the superintendent, the owner of the business, the board of directors—a complete mental revolution as to their duties toward their fellow workers in the management, toward their workmen, and toward all of their daily problems."[18] This, perhaps, was Taylor's most enduring legacy to the development of management thought.

Other Leaders of Scientific Management

Although Frederick Taylor was the acknowledged founder and central figure in the scientific management movement, several others played important roles in advancing and extending the general approach to fact-based and orderly processes for managing industrial organizations. Three of those, whom we briefly mention here, were Henry L. Gantt and Frank and Lillian Gilbreth.

H. L. Gantt (1861–1919)
Gantt was a young engineering colleague of Taylor's at the Midvale Steel Company at the end of the 1880s, but by the early 1900s he was

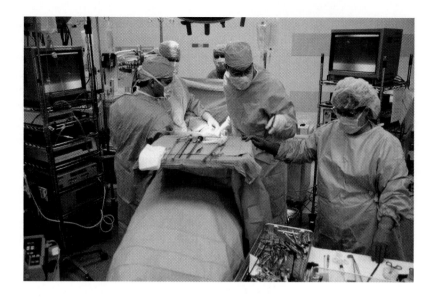

One of today's operating room procedures was developed by Frank Gilbreth (along with Frederick Taylor) in an efficiency study of medical operations. The next time you see a surgeon extend an opened hand and a nurse place an instrument into it, think of time and motion studies. Prior to this change in method, doctors wasted much time searching for the right tool.

well launched in his own career as one of the first bona fide management consultants. He was heavily influenced in his early career by Taylor's views, but he subsequently became known chiefly for developing graphic methods to aid in organizing and coordinating multiple tasks in complex production jobs. While serving as a volunteer consultant to the U.S. government during World War I, he perfected a type of bar chart that showed the order in which tasks had to be initiated and the time allotted for each. Versions of this graphic display, now called Gantt charts, have been widely used and were the direct forerunner of modern-day PERT (Program Evaluation and Review Techniques) methods. The importance of Gantt's graphic approach was that it reinforced the need for systematic planning in order to sequence tasks efficiently and for more direct control over the time allotted to them, which in turn directly lowered costs and increased performance.

Frank and Lillian Gilbreth (1868–1924 and 1878–1972)   This husband-and-wife team were strong advocates of Taylor's general approach, but they were able to add their own unique contributions. Frank Gilbreth was a contractor who became intensely interested in studying how various construction tasks could be performed more efficiently and with reduced fatigue for the worker. Using the recently invented motion picture camera, he developed techniques to analyze each motion that went into performing a task, such as bricklaying. Eventually, Gilbreth was able to categorize any motion into one of 17 basic types (which he called "Therbligs," a reversal—with t and h transposed—of the spelling of "Gilbreth"). In theory, this categorization of motions made it possible to develop the most effective combination for performing any physical task. Lillian Gilbreth was one of the first doctoral-level industrial psychologists in the United States. In her early career, she worked closely with her husband on his analytical studies of motions. She concentrated on the "mental" tasks facing management and on how psychological principles could further the application of a scientific management approach that would benefit both worker and manager. Lillian Gilbreth (who died in 1972 at the age of 93) achieved many "firsts"—e.g., she was the first woman member of both the Society of Industrial Engineers and the Society of Mechanical Engineers—and in later years her peers called her "the first lady of management."[19] Not the least of the two Gilbreths' many joint accomplishments was their success in raising 12 children, the story of which was immortalized in a book, *Cheaper by the Dozen,* and a movie of the same name. The Gilbreths thus applied scientific management principles in the home as well as in their extensive investigations of industrial jobs. It was in the latter area, however, where their individual and combined efforts had worldwide impact.

PIONEERS: CLASSICAL MANAGEMENT THEORY

classical management theory
ideas concerning the management of organizations arising from pioneers such as Taylor, Fayol, Weber, and Mooney and Reiley, together with emerging concepts identified with the scientific management approach

While Taylor and various associates were spreading the gospel of scientific management in the United States and Europe in the first two decades of the 20th century, others also were beginning to think seriously and insightfully about how to manage organizations. Four of those who had the greatest impact on subsequent management thought and practice will be discussed here. Two of them essentially worked and wrote individually, and the other two jointly authored a book. One was French, one was German, and the other two were Americans (see Exhibit 2.4). Their ideas, together with some of the emerging concepts identified with the scientific management approach, have come to be called "classical management theory."

Classical management theory focuses on the study of the principles and functions of management and the authority structures of organizations. In some cases, the term "administrative theory" could be used interchangeably with "management theory." Of course, the term "classical management theory" was never attached to

EXHIBIT 2.4
Contributors to Classical Management Theory

	HENRI FAYOL (French)	MAX WEBER (German)	J. D. MOONEY & A. C. REILEY (American)
WROTE	*General and Industrial Management*	*The Theory of Social and Economic Organization*	*Onward Industry!*
STATED/ DEFINED	• Five Functions of Management • 14 Principles of Management	• Three Basic Types of Authority Relationships • Bureaucracy	• Four Basic Principles of Management
(COMMENT)	Focused on middle and upper management activities in multi-unit organizations	Writings aimed more for scholars than practicing managers, but ultimately influenced society as a whole	Fayol and Weber had not yet been published in America, so the similarity of Mooney and Reiley's descriptions of management was used to argue the universality of management principles

this broad set of ideas during the era in which they appeared (from roughly 1900 to the early 1930s). It has only been more recently applied. The ideas and thoughts are considered classical because they had some relatively enduring qualities and served as a springboard for others' thinking and action. As we will see later in this chapter, they even served as a model against which newer and quite different theories and approaches were contrasted.

Henri Fayol (1841–1925)

Henri Fayol was a French mining engineer who rose rapidly in his company to become president at age 37. Under his leadership, his company became a large, integrated mining, iron, and steel organization, which took raw materials and transformed them into finished product. Fayol's relatively early and extended exposure to the top management position of a sizable firm gave him an opportunity to reflect on what was required to manage the total enterprise. Using his experience to good advantage, Fayol put some of his ideas on management into written form, culminating with the publication of his most famous work in 1916, a monograph entitled *Administration Industrielle et Générale* ("General and Industrial Management").

Fayol's publication had lasting impact for two reasons. First, his attempt to define management as consisting of five key elements was a major advance.[20] His approach was analytical and focused attention on management as a legitimate, specialized set of activities, and it identified what those activities were: planning (in French, "prévoyance"), organizing, command, coordination, and control. These "elements," as Fayol termed them, have subsequently been called (in English) **functions of management**, and in slightly modified form, they have prevailed to the present day. The alert reader, in fact, will recognize that Fayol's list of elements is quite similar to the major sections of this text and nearly all other contemporary management texts. The most common current version of the list collapses the functions to four (allocating coordination activities across the other four functions) and changing the term "command" to "influencing" or "leading." In short, even with the passage of more than 80 years since the publication of *Administration Industrielle et Générale*, few improvements have been made on Fayol's "classic" list of management functions.

functions of management
basic elements of management as originally identified by Henri Fayol, consisting of planning, organizing, command, coordination, and control

The other reason Fayol's work received a great deal of attention in later years was that it also presented a list of 14 management "principles," or, more accurately, guidelines that he found effective and thought could be used to improve the performance of a wide variety of organizations. Some of the more important of these (paraphrased) were: division of labor (specialization of work); unity of command (each person in the organization should receive orders from only one other person); unity of direction (all persons in a part of the organization must govern their actions by the same, single plan); and "scalar chain" (there must be a clear line of authority from the bottom to the top of the organization). (See Exhibit 2.5 for the complete list of Fayol's principles). These principles have been challenged in recent years, but they appeared at a time when business and industrial activity was quite different from that of today and the context (government, society, technology, etc.) in which such activity took place was profoundly different.

The importance of Fayol's contributions was not fully recognized in the English-speaking world until later translations appeared (e.g., in 1949), but the

EXHIBIT 2.5

Fayol's 14 Principles of Management

1. *DIVISION OF WORK*	Divide work into specialized tasks and functions, each assigned to specific individuals.	
2. *AUTHORITY*	Authority must be accompanied by responsibility.	
3. *DISCIPLINE*	Sanctions are necessary to minimize or prevent the recurrence of behavior that violates agreed-upon expectations.	
4. *UNITY OF COMMAND*	"For any action whatsoever, an employee should receive orders from one superior only."	
5. *UNITY OF DIRECTION*	There should be "one head and one plan for a group of activities having the same objective."	
6. *SUBORDINATION*	"The interest of one employee or group of employees should not prevail over that of the [organization]."	
7. *REMUNERATION*	"… should be fair and, as far as is possible, afford satisfaction both to personnel and firm (employee and employer)."	
8. *CENTRALIZATION*	The amount of centralization or decentralization necessary to a firm is a function both of the size of the firm and the ability of the manager(s). Organizational effectiveness is increased by determining the optimal level of centralization.	
9. *SCALAR CHAIN*	"The scalar chain is the chain of supervisors ranging from the ultimate authority to the lowest ranks. The line of authority is the route followed—via every link in the chain—by all communications which start from or go to the ultimate authority."	
10. *ORDER*	There must be order in both material and personnel. For material: "things [must] be in their place suitably arranged … so as to facilitate all activities." For personnel: "Perfect order requires … that the place be suitable for the employee and the employee for the place … the right man in the right place."	
11. *EQUITY*	To encourage employee loyalty and performance, employers must treat employees fairly, combining kindness and justice, but not excluding forcefulness or sternness.	
12. *STABILITY OF TENURE OF PERSONNEL*	It requires time for an employee to develop the skills necessary to perform his or her work well. Therefore, successful companies are those with low turnover (high stability of tenure) of personnel. "Instability of tenure is at one and the same time cause and effect of bad [management]."	
13. *INITIATIVE*	"At all levels of the organizational ladder zeal and energy on the part of employees are augmented by initiative [the thinking out and implementation of plans]. The initiative of all, added to that of the manager, and supplementing it if need be, represents a great source of strength for businesses."	
14. *ESPRIT DE CORPS*	"Union is strength. Harmony, union among the personnel of a concern is great strength in that concern. Effort, then, should be made to establish it."	

Source: Adapted from H. Fayol, *General and Industrial Management* (London: Pitman, 1949), chapter 4. (Translation by C. Storrs from 1916 French edition, *Administration Industrielle et Générale.*)

originality of his ideas and the clarity and systematized way in which they were presented endure. Also, it should be noted that Fayol's focus, in contrast to much of Taylor's work, was directed toward the middle and upper levels of managerial activities of multi-unit enterprises rather than toward shop floor supervision and the management of individual factories. In that sense, Fayol's ideas were consistent with Taylor's, but they covered new ground—ground that would be especially relevant to the types of firms and corporations prominent in the last half of the 20th century.

Max Weber (1864–1920)

Although Max Weber lived at approximately the same time as did Taylor and Fayol, he neither influenced them nor was influenced by them. Weber was a German academic and scholar who never managed an organization, or even part of one, but who was one of history's most perceptive organizational observers. As one of the early forerunners of modern sociology, Weber was an organization theorist and not a management theorist per se. We mention him here, however, because by the mid-20th century he had become extremely influential in how leading thinkers viewed the management process in organizations—industrial or otherwise.

Weber's most significant work dealing with organizations, *The Theory of Social and Economic Organization,* although originally published in 1922 after his death, was not translated into English until 1947. He was a product of the German culture and society of his era, and this background no doubt had a strong bearing on the kinds of intellectual issues he chose to analyze. With respect to organizations, those issues centered on the concept of authority, especially the questions of "Why do individuals obey commands?" and "Why do people do as they are told?"[21] He theorized that three basic types of authority relationships or structures could be used to classify organizations:

1. **Traditional authority:** authority exercised on the basis of custom or past practice. According to Weber, its weakness as a source of authority in organizations was that it emphasizes precedent for its own sake rather than making the best possible decisions.

2. **Charismatic authority:** authority based on "devotion to the specific and exceptional sanctity, heroism, or exemplary character of an individual person."[22] The weakness of charismatic authority, as stressed by Weber, is that it does not provide a basis for succession of authority relationships when the charismatic leader leaves the scene, and hence this threatens the continuity of the organization.

3. **Rational-legal authority:** authority exercised to achieve specifically designated goals and based on the legal right of the person in a particular office (*buro* in German) to issue commands. In Weber's analysis, this type of authority is best suited for larger, complex organizations because it emphasizes obedience to orders issued by someone—*whoever that person is*—fulfilling an official position and acting on the basis of powers conferred on that position (and not to a particular person). This basis for authority overcomes, in Weber's view, the disadvantages of the other two forms of authority.

Weber went on to describe the type of organization that would result if the use of rational-legal authority were maximized: namely, a "bureaucracy." In describing bureaucracies, Weber was not necessarily advocating that every organization should become one, only that if this type of authority were put into place throughout an organization, it would have certain features; for example:

- An explicit set of rules to govern official actions
- Clearly defined duties for each office (i.e., position)
- Competence and technical qualifications as the basis for selection of office-holders
- Comprehensive training for people occupying particular positions

In assessing the impact of Weber and his writings on the history of management thought, several points should be made. To begin with, it should be reiterated that Weber has affected society's views about the management of organizations by influencing scholars rather than by directly addressing managers. Nevertheless, although Weber wrote independently of others who concentrated specifically on ways to improve the performance of managerial activities, his analysis of the advantages of bureaucratic organization was consistent with the prescriptions for managers provided by Taylor and Fayol. It is also necessary to keep in mind that Weber's concept of a bureaucracy was that of a form of organization based on a specified type of authority and not the caricature of a sluggish, rule-strangled organization that the term has come to mean in recent years. In fact, if Weber were alive today, he would probably think of that type of organization as a sort of bureaucracy run amok and not at all what he envisioned.

J. D. Mooney (1884–1957) and A. C. Reiley (1869–1947)

The final set of classical management theorists to be discussed here are two American executives, James D. Mooney and Allan C. Reiley. Both were upper-level managers within the General Motors Corporation, with a particular interest in the historical evolution of organizational principles. In the depths of the Great Depression (in 1931), they published a book that had the bold title of *Onward Industry!* This book, which gained considerable visibility for its authors, attempted to demonstrate how all great organizations of the past and present tended to follow several fundamental principles, principles we now refer to as the center of the classical approach to management:

1. The *coordinative principle:* the need to obtain a high degree of coordination of actions toward a common purpose.
2. The *scalar principle:* the need to designate the precise delegation of authority from the top to the bottom of the organization.
3. The *functional principle:* the need to achieve a tight grouping of specialized functions or duties.
4. The *staff principle:* the need to provide managers in the direct chain of command (the line) with ideas and information from specialized experts (the staff), and the related need to distinguish clearly between the two types of positions.

Although Mooney and Reiley apparently had never read the works of either Henri Fayol or Max Weber (since they had not yet been translated into English), their managerial and organizational principles were remarkably similar to those that these two theorists had developed in other countries and cultures some two decades earlier. Some management writers later took this to be evidence for the universality of management principles.

The Impact of Classical Management Theory

As we said at the beginning of this section, the term "classical management theory" is a label that has been applied in recent years to the collection of ideas put forth by people such as Fayol, Weber, Mooney and Reiley, and others in the first 35 years of the twentieth century. Those ideas do not constitute "theory" in the strict scientific use of that word. Rather, they are a loose set of concepts and principles that have provided a coherent and, above all, rational way to think about how organizations

EXHIBIT 2.6

Assumptions Underlying
Classical Management
Theory

1. "Efficiency of an undertaking is measured solely in terms of productivity."
2. "Human beings can be assumed to act rationally."
3. "[Employees] are unable to work out the relationships of their positions without detailed guidance from their supervisors."
4. "Unless clear limits to jobs are defined and enforced, [employees] will tend to be confused …"
5. "Human beings prefer the security of a definite task and do not value the freedom of determining their own approaches to problems …"
6. "It is possible to predict and establish clear-cut patterns of future activities and the relationships among activities."
7. "Management involves primarily the formal and official activities of individuals."
8. "The activities of [employees] should be viewed on an objective and impersonal basis …"
9. "Workers are motivated by economic needs …"
10. "People do not like to work, and therefore, close-supervision and accountability should be emphasized."
11. "Coordination will not be achieved unless it is planned and directed from above."
12. "Authority has its source at the top of a hierarchy and is delegated downward."
13. "Simple tasks are easier to master and thus lead toward higher productivity by concentrating on a narrow scope of activity."
14. "Managerial functions … have universal characteristics and can be performed in a given manner regardless of the environment and qualities of the personnel involved."

Source: J. L. Massie, "Management Theory," in *Handbook of Organizations,* ed. J. G. March (Chicago: Rand McNally, 1965). Reprinted with permission of J. G. March.

should be structured and managed. Because this cluster of ideas—along with those of Taylor and the scientific management approach—amounted to such an advance in thinking, they were indeed influential. They provided guidance for those who wanted to develop and operate more effective and efficient organizations. Furthermore, and this should not be overlooked, many of these notions have persisted to this day in one form or another. Anyone who has ever worked in a company, a government office, indeed in almost any organization cannot help but notice how often and how widespread is the attempted application of many of the so-called principles of classical management theory over 80 years after they were first proposed.

Despite the progress in management thinking that classical management theorists represent, there were (and are) major problems with their basic approach. To obtain a sense of some of those problems, we need only to consider the underlying assumptions, which are summarized in Exhibit 2.6. First and foremost, as summarized in Exhibit 2.7, the underlying assumptions implied an extremely limited view of the role of people in organizations. Second, and also quite important, the classical management approach was essentially a static view of how organizations should be managed and did not deal sufficiently with the effects of changing conditions. Classical theory implicitly assumed that all organizations should be managed in

EXHIBIT 2.7
EXHIBIT 2.7

Contributions and Criticisms of Classical Management Theory

CONTRIBUTIONS	• Provided a Coherent and Rational Way to Think about the Structure and Management of Organizations • Provided Directions for Managers Attempting to Increase Effectiveness and Efficiency in Their Organizations • Many of the Principles Have Persisted in One Form or Another to the Present
CRITICISMS	• Assumed an Extremely Narrow View of the Role of People in Organizations • Assumed There is "One Best Way" to Manage Businesses • Assumed (Implicitly) a Static Role for the Business Environment

"the one best way." As with its close cousin, scientific management (often classified as a classical theory), it was clearly a product of its times, even though this fact was not apparent to those who proposed its principles nor especially to those who to this day still believe that what worked in 1925 will still work just as well in 2005!

NEOCLASSICAL ADMINISTRATIVE THEORY

By the beginning of the 1920s, the world of work was changing. The size and complexity of organizations were increasing, as shown in the General Motors example that opened this chapter, and the skills, abilities, and expectations of employees were also becoming more complex. These changes made it obvious that the traditional approach to managing was not adequate nor always appropriate. Revisions in the ways of thinking about how to manage organized work activity began in the 1920s and continued to the 1940s. As might be expected, the new thinking drew from the accepted wisdom of basic management principles, even though it went beyond those principles in interesting new directions. Because these ideas had at least some links to past thinking, this approach is now often called neoclassical management theory. **Neoclassical management theory** continued to emphasize the study and analysis of managerial functions and organizational structures but expanded to include situational and social considerations such as communication and cooperation. Two individuals closely associated with this label were Mary Parker Follett and Chester Barnard, as shown in Exhibit 2.8.

neoclassical management theory
thinking about organized work activity and how to manage that drew from classical theory in its emphasis on study and analysis of the workplace but expanded to include situational and social considerations (i.e., communication and cooperation)

Mary Parker Follett (1868–1933)

Lillian Gilbreth was not the only prominent woman who contributed to management thought in the early part of the 20th century. Mary Parker Follett was a writer, lecturer, and independent consultant who early in life became interested in political philosophy but who later turned her attention to the management of organizations. She was especially influential in the 1920s.

EXHIBIT 2.8		
Contributors to Neoclassical Management Theory		

	MARY PARKER FOLLETT	**CHESTER BARNARD**
WROTE	*Creative Experience*	*The Functions of the Executive*
AGREED WITH CLASSICAL THEORISTS ON	• Importance of Detailed Analysis of Work Settings • Coordination of Work Activities	• Importance of Detailed Analysis of Work Settings
EMPHASIZED	• Cooperation between Managers and Subordinates • Integration of Interests of Organization and Employees • The Use of the Type of Authority Appropriate to the Situation	• A View of Organizations as Cooperative Social Systems • The Need for Managers to Obtain Voluntary Cooperation from Their Workers • The "Zone of Indifference" • The Need for Efficient Organizational Communication
(COMMENT)	Forerunner of many modern ideas of management, particularly the contingency approach	Views on authority were innovative and anticipated later behavioralist thinking

---

MARY PARKER FOLLETT, 1868–1933

Mary Parker Follett was born in Boston, Massachusetts. Although a contemporary of Taylor, Follett was much more a philosopher than manager. She was educated at what is today called Radcliffe College. Her early interests in John Fichte (1762–1814), a German philosopher who espoused a nationalism in which freedom of the individual had to be subordinated to the group, led her to write the book *The New State*. In this book, Follett argued that an individual could only find his or her true self through group orientation.

She began to be more of a business philosopher in 1924 after she published *Creative Experience*. This book was widely read by businessmen of the day. In 1924 and 1925, Follett gave a series of lectures in New York that were sponsored by the Bureau of Personnel Administration. The lectures were well received and led Follett to focus most of her later writings and lectures on principles of business organization and administration.

Source: Henry C. Metcalf and Lyndall Urwick, *Dynamic Administration: The Collected Papers of Mary Parker Follett* (New York: Harper & Row, 1940).

In many respects, Follett's thinking was consistent with Taylor's and the scientific management movement in that she placed great importance on detailed study and analysis of the work setting and on the necessity for careful coordination of activities. However, she also emphasized the need to generate a spirit of cooperation between managers and their subordinates and to integrate the interests of the organization and its employees. In this regard, her ideas differed from the typical views of many contemporary advocates of scientific management. Also, in contrast to Weber's analysis, Follett focused not on the formal powers conferred on an office but rather on the dictates of the **law of the situation**, that is, the authority—based on a person's knowledge and experience—that seems appropriate to the circumstances. This type of thinking anticipated by some 40 years a prominent modern approach to management, the contingency approach, which is discussed later in this chapter. In summary, although Mary Parker Follett and her ideas are often classified as being associated with classical management theory, she was in fact someone who was a clear forerunner of much of modern management thought that has dominated the last half of the 20th century. Thus, we have placed her here in the neoclassical category of management thinkers.

law of the situation
Mary Parker Follett's emphasis on the need to generate a spirit of cooperation between managers and their subordinates with a focus on the authority (based on a person's knowledge and experience) that seems appropriate to the circumstances

Chester Barnard (1886–1961)

A long-time executive at AT&T and ultimately president of then New Jersey Bell Telephone company, Chester Barnard spent a considerable amount of time and thought in formulating his unique and detailed ideas regarding the nature of organizations and the role of its managers and leaders. This effort resulted in a highly regarded book published in 1938, *The Functions of the Executive*, that has had considerable influence on the field of management ever since.

CHESTER BARNARD, 1886–1961

Chester Barnard was born to a farming family in Malden, Massachusetts. Through his talent and hard work, he earned a scholarship to Harvard University, where he studied economics. While a student, Barnard supplemented his income by tuning pianos and running a small dance band. He completed his studies in three years but was not granted a degree because even though he had passed a certain course with distinction, he had been too busy to take the laboratory section.

Barnard left Harvard in 1909 and joined the Statistics Department of American Telephone and Telegraph. He worked hard and applied both the formal learning he had received at Harvard and the knowledge he gained from his own studies. Despite being a "Harvard drop-out," Barnard was a scholar who read Vilfredo Pareto in French and Kurt Lewis and Max Weber in German. In 1927 he was named president of New Jersey Bell.

Barnard also spent considerable time and energy working in voluntary organizations. He helped David Lilienthal establish the policies of the U.S. Atomic Energy Commission. He worked with the United States Service Organization and served as its president for three years. He also served as the president of the Rockefeller Foundation for four years.

After 10 years as president of New Jersey Bell, Barnard gave a series of lectures at the Lowell Institute in Boston. An expansion of the lectures was published in Barnard's famous book, *Functions of the Executive*, published by Harvard University Press in 1938.

Source: William B. Wolf, *How to Understand Management: An Introduction to Chester I. Barnard* (Los Angeles: Lucas Bro. Publishers, 1968).

Barnard, as did most classical management theorists, provided a very systematic but nonempirical (nondata) analysis of the tasks of management. In this sense, the starting point for his analysis could be considered somewhat similar to classical theorists. However, Barnard differed sharply from the standard classical approach by viewing organizations as cooperative social systems. In fact, as it was for Mary Parker Follett, cooperation was at the center of Barnard's thinking about the nature of organizations. He believed that all organizations, no matter what type, required (1) willingness to cooperate, (2) common purpose, and (3) communication. In particular, he stressed the need for managers in organizations to obtain the voluntary cooperation of those they lead. Additionally, his strong focus on the need for communication as an essential ingredient in any organization was also a ground-breaking notion for its day.

In his discussion of the concept of authority, however, Barnard probably achieved his greatest influence on others. He argued that the source of a manager's authority depends on the acceptance of his or her orders by the subordinate. This was a truly radical idea for its time, because until then traditional management theory had always insisted that the source of authority was solely determined by the position of the manager and that the higher the position, the greater the authority possessed by the person occupying it. Barnard elaborated on his perspective by defining what he called the "zone of indifference" (which others later labeled the "zone of acceptance"). This zone consisted of orders that would be accepted by the subordinate without question. Barnard did believe (in line with classical theory) that this zone was wider the higher the position of the order giver, but he also contended that the leadership skills and abilities of the manager were critical to broaden the scope of orders that a subordinate would accept without dispute or resistance. His thinking thus foreshadowed later behavioral approaches to the process of management.

BEHAVIORAL APPROACHES

Early management theorists, especially Frederick Taylor and the proponents of a scientific management approach, did not entirely ignore the human component of organizations. Rather, they viewed the human dimension of organizations in very specific and limited ways. Scientific management and classical management approaches placed great emphasis on initial selection of workers for jobs and thus, in effect, on individual capabilities, such as differences in physical agility or strength. They also believed that worker motivation stemmed almost solely from the financial incentives offered by hourly and piecework wages linked directly to the amount of output. What was not given much, if any, attention in these approaches were the following:

- Capacities of employees for further development after they are hired for particular jobs
- Other sources of employee motivation in addition to financial rewards
- The impact of relationships among employees and with their supervisors

While it is easy to say with the benefit of hindsight that even the earliest management theorists ought to have paid more attention to these factors, remember that the level of education of the average person was much lower then than now and that the social and cultural conditions that existed in those times resulted in different employee and management expectations compared with those of today. Put another way, traditional ways of operating were much different then, and those traditions exerted a powerful influence on management theories of that era.

The neoclassical theorists, such as Mary Parker Follett and Chester Barnard, with their strong focus on the need for cooperation in organizations, did begin to bring the human element more to the forefront in discussions of how enterprises should be managed. Nevertheless, it took the dramatic findings of a years-long set of research studies, the Hawthorne studies, to focus a spotlight on how the human factor impacted work performance at the shop floor level. These findings led to a whole new approach called the human relations approach.

The Human Relations Approach

human relations approach
approach springing from the findings of the Hawthorne studies that focused on the importance of relationships among people in the workplace

Hawthorne studies
a series of research studies at the Hawthorne plant of the Western Electric Company that focused a spotlight on the importance of the human factor in productivity

The **human relations approach** to management did not suddenly emerge full blown. Instead, it evolved as the findings from the **Hawthorne studies** began to achieve prominence toward the end of the 1930s, with the publication of the famous book, *Management and the Worker,* by Roethlisberger and Dickson in 1939. This series of investigations started in the mid-1920s at the Hawthorne plant of the Western Electric Company (a manufacturing subsidiary of the American Telephone and Telegraph Company [AT&T] at the time) outside Chicago. They were directed initially by researchers from the Massachusetts Institute of Technology.[23] However, as time went by, the research program became more associated with two well-known Harvard professors, the Australian social scientist Elton Mayo and a management professor by the name of Fritz Roethlisberger.

The first studies at the Hawthorne plant, as befitting the times, were designed to determine the effects of changes in the physical working environment, namely lighting, on productivity. However, when the early findings were analyzed by the researchers, it became apparent that what seemed to be causing the largest effects on worker performance was not the amount of light in the workplace, but rather the relations among the workers and between them and their supervisors. (Analyses of the data carried out some years later suggested that changes in the wage incentive system at the time also may have played a role in determining changes in worker output in some of the test conditions.)[24]

These initial results led to other studies over the next half-dozen years at Hawthorne (in the late 1920s and early 1930s) that were designed to gather more detailed data on the nature of these relationships among workers and supervisors and on how they affected employee output. The additional studies included observations under researcher-controlled conditions about how a group of workers could act together to exert considerable influence on the performance of individual members of the group. The researchers also carried out extensive interviewing of employees regarding their attitudes toward their work. The overall findings from the series of studies that spanned some eight years were then summarized in the 1939 Roethlisberger and Dickson book. Among other prominent outcomes of the Hawthorne studies, incidentally, was the demonstration of the apparent effect on worker behavior of having that behavior observed and given special attention. That phenomenon became known as the *Hawthorne effect.*

Although the Hawthorne studies have received criticism for inadequacies in research design and in the way in which some of the data were analyzed, the highly publicized findings did in fact strongly impact many managers.[25] In effect, as management historians have put it, "the Hawthorne studies ... introduced a new way of thinking about the people factor."[26] It became evident that if those who ran factories or companies were interested in improving productivity, more attention—than had been the case in most organizations up to that time—would have to be paid to the way in which the people relationships were handled, thus leading to the origin of the term "human relations approach." Simply instructing employees on how to operate machines or equipment and providing them with a wage incentive for doing so was not sufficient.

Those advocating more attention to human relations concentrated particularly on the role of the first-line supervisor and his (since in those days it usually was a "he") interactions with subordinates. The advice was to treat subordinates not as impersonal cogs in a machine but as individual human beings with feelings and emotions and needs other than just financial. This approach also stressed that it was the task of upper management to provide the necessary support and backing for the first-level supervisors, or foremen, in the time and effort they devoted to improving relations. The logic involved was that if workers felt better about their relationships with their supervisor and their working conditions, they would have a greater desire to produce more—or, at least, have less of a desire to try to restrict output.

The Human Resources Approach

The human relations movement flourished in the 1940s and 1950s, as many organizations attempted to implement a more human and humane approach to their treatment of employees. Again, it must be emphasized that the assumption—sometimes explicit but often implicit—was that improved worker satisfaction would result in better performance. By the 1960s, as a result of continuing research carried out in a variety of work circumstances, the human relations approach was shown to be incomplete at best and highly misleading at worst. In effect, the findings from these studies demonstrated that there was seldom a direct connection between satisfaction and performance and that, furthermore, from a psychological perspective, it should not be presumed that more satisfied workers necessarily will be more productive workers. Such results, coupled with additional analyses, led to new behavioral formulations relevant to the management process. One of these, called the human resources approach, provides a distinct contrast to the human relations approach and puts particular emphasis on starting from a different set of managerial assumptions concerning people. Exhibit 2.9 shows the basic differences between these two approaches.

human resources approach

approach involving a basic belief that people possess and want to make greater use of their talents and capabilities and that if allowed to do so, performance and satisfaction will increase

In essence, the core of the **human resources approach** to management thinking—led by such scholars as Douglas McGregor, Rensis Likert, and Chris Argyris—stresses a fundamental belief that most people possess and want to use more talent and capabilities in their work than may be readily apparent from their past or present job assignments. If so, it becomes management's primary role to develop these untapped human resources through increased opportunities for self-direction and self-control. The logic is that if human resources are better utilized, performance will be enhanced. Increased satisfaction, if it occurs, becomes the by-product rather than the cause of this improved performance. Direct evidence for the effectiveness of the human resources approach is not easy to obtain, but this

EXHIBIT 2.9
EXHIBIT 2.9
Differences between Human Relations and Human Resources Approaches to Management

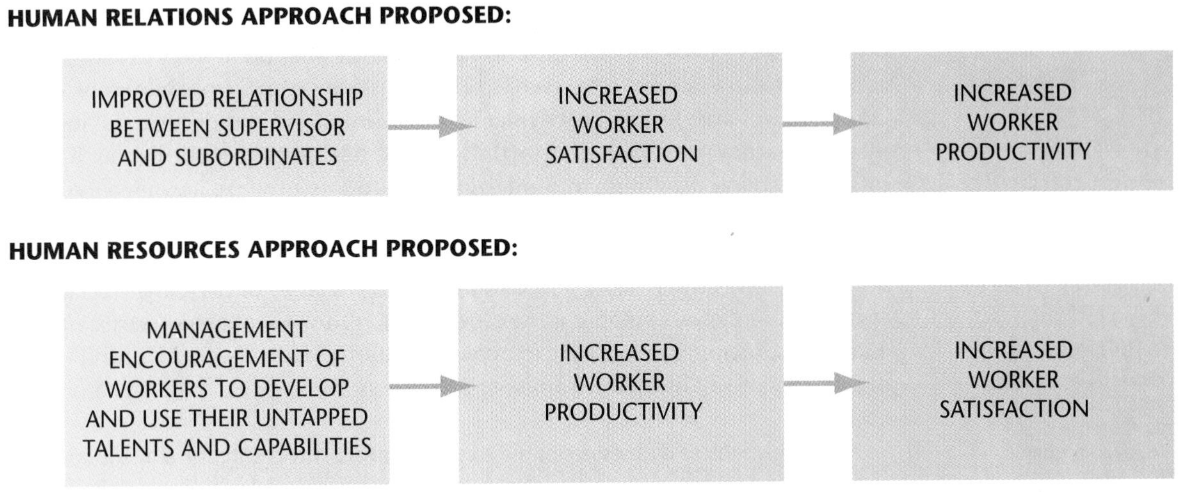

HUMAN RELATIONS APPROACH PROPOSED:

IMPROVED RELATIONSHIP BETWEEN SUPERVISOR AND SUBORDINATES	→	INCREASED WORKER SATISFACTION	→	INCREASED WORKER PRODUCTIVITY

HUMAN RESOURCES APPROACH PROPOSED:

MANAGEMENT ENCOURAGEMENT OF WORKERS TO DEVELOP AND USE THEIR UNTAPPED TALENTS AND CAPABILITIES	→	INCREASED WORKER PRODUCTIVITY	→	INCREASED WORKER SATISFACTION

general orientation toward the human component of organizations underlies the basic behavioral approach to management in a large number of organizations as we enter the new century.

DECISION-MAKING APPROACHES

The behavioral approaches just described emphasize the motivation of individuals to excel at their jobs. Although it is hard to deny the importance of such perspectives, other processes taking place in organizations also have considerable consequences for their overall effectiveness. One of the most crucial is decision making. Good decisions can mobilize many people, and bad decisions can undercut and even jeopardize the continued existence of the organization. Despite the importance of decision making for the fate of organizations, it was not until after World War II that this process received concerted attention from management theorists. When this did happen, two lines of inquiry developed, one more behavioral and one more mathematical. We will look at both briefly here but only in terms of their historical significance.

Behavioral Decision-Making Approach

The emphasis on decision making as a critical element in the management process is generally credited to Herbert Simon, a Nobel Laureate in economics, who originally received his doctoral training in political science. Early in his academic career, Simon turned his attention to the concept of "economic man," the notion that individuals are totally rational and that in their decisions they can evaluate all alternative courses of action and their consequences and then select that one that has the best chance of maximizing goal attainment (e.g., profit). Simon was particularly interested in how this concept worked in practice in real organizational settings. His analyses led him to develop an alternative model, "administrative man." In contrast to economic man, administrative man—managers in real-life organizations—does not have information on all possible alternative courses of action and also does not have complete information on the probabilities of various consequences arising from particular actions. Simon did not dispute the idea that managers attempt to make rational decisions, but he proposed that such thinking is constrained by human limitations and results in what he called **bounded rationality**. Because of their "bounded," or constrained, rationality, according to Simon, managers do not search indefinitely for the best alternative (i.e., goal maximization) but rather make a decision that "satisfices." **Satisficing** is a decision that results in an acceptable course of action, although not necessarily the best course. Satisficing is necessary, in actual situations, according to Simon, because managers almost always must operate under conditions of uncertainty rather than certainty.

bounded rationality

Herbert Simon's concept that managers attempt to make rational decisions, but their thinking is constrained by human limitations

satisficing

decisions that result in an acceptable course of action rather than the best alternative, or goal maximization

Although Simon's ideas probably have had more direct effect on academics who study management than on managers themselves, they nevertheless have been extremely influential, as attested to by the Nobel award. His 1940s writing on decision making led to additional important work on this topic in the 1950s and 1960s by himself and his colleagues at Carnegie Mellon University, James March and Richard Cyert. The latter two scholars authored an important book in the early 1960s, *A Behavioral Theory of the Firm,* which provided an all-encompassing view of organizations from a decision-making perspective.

Quantitative Decision-Making Approaches

Quantitative, or mathematical, approaches to managerial problems, especially problems requiring specific decisions, did not emerge until after World War II. Utilizing techniques that had been developed during wartime, a new field of study was developed called **management science**, or **operations research**. Each of these terms caused some confusion, the former because of its similarity to the term scientific management and the latter because it did not convey precise meaning. Nevertheless, the field (which we will refer to as "management science") grew rapidly in popularity for its ability to provide precise solutions to decision problems involving many variables and complicated connections among those variables. In effect, management science techniques such as linear programming (a mathematical procedure for determining the optimal combination of resources under specific constraining conditions) and various mathematical modeling procedures provided valuable tools to managers to assist in planning and forecasting activities. Along with **simulation** techniques, where various potential combinations of variables can be mathematically manipulated in advance of actual decisions to determine the possible effects of changes in one or more variables, such mathematical modeling approaches have greatly improved the quality of managerial analyses of complicated decisions. However, such techniques do not in themselves provide comprehensive theories of management and hence have not had the same impact as some of the other major conceptual approaches to management covered earlier in this chapter. Nevertheless, their introduction did bring a much stronger analytical approach to some management tasks.

management science (operations research)

quantitative or mathematical approaches to managerial problems, especially those requiring specific decisions

simulation

a set of techniques in which various potential combinations of variables can be mathematically manipulated in advance of actual decisions to determine the possible effects of changes in one or more variables

INTEGRATIVE APPROACHES

integrative approaches
recent approaches to management that include systems theory and contingency approaches and emphasize a consideration of a wide range of factors

The final set of approaches to management that we consider in this chapter are more recent and can loosely be labeled **integrative approaches**, that is, approaches that attempt to combine a number of different variables or elements into a more wholistic approach to the broad process of management. Since they are so relatively recent, it is questionable whether they should be included in a chapter on the *history* of management thought. But we include them to provide background on current management thinking and to show how historical approaches have been modified to the present. Also, you will encounter them, in one form or another, throughout this book, and therefore we only introduce them briefly here. The two that are most encompassing and that most widely affect contemporary management thinking are systems theory and contingency approaches.

Systems Theory

system
an interconnected set of elements that have orderly interactions that form a unitary whole

systems theory
the processes involved in how "inputs" get transformed by the organization into "outputs"

What has been called General Systems Theory (GST) was developed as early as the 1920s and was especially utilized in biology ("living systems") and engineering ("mechanical systems"), among other scientific areas of endeavor.[27] This approach was not applied to organizations until the 1960s, but since then it has been a prominent form of organizational analysis with considerable implications for understanding the process of management. A **system** refers to an interconnected set of elements that have orderly interactions that form a unitary whole. Thus, **systems theory** in the organizational context refers to the process involved in how "inputs" get transformed by the organization into "outputs," as illustrated in Exhibit 2.10. Organizational inputs are generally considered to be of three major types: financial, material, and human resources. These inputs are combined and modified by technological and managerial actions into the two major types of organizational outputs, goods and services. Thus, from this perspective, management can be viewed as a type of transformation process, with the manager's role being one of converting a collection of resources into useful output. Understanding how all of these elements relate to each other and effectively integrating units and processes provide two major challenges for managers.

EXHIBIT 2.10
Systems Theory Applied to Organizations: An Example

INPUTS	TRANSFORMATION PROCESSES	OUTPUTS
FINANCIAL, MATERIAL, AND HUMAN RESOURCES	ACTIONS OF EMPLOYEES, MANAGERS, AND TECHNOLOGY — Through Use of Latest Computer Technology, Combined with Employee Motivation and Managerial Leadership	GOODS AND SERVICES
Ideas of Artists, Writers, and Directors		New Animated Motion Picture

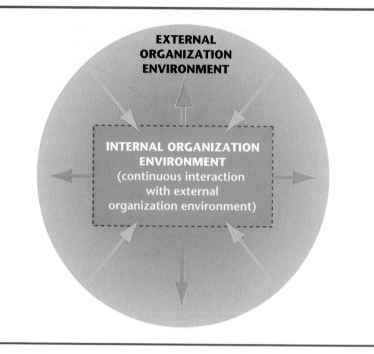

EXHIBIT 2.11

Open System

EXTERNAL
ORGANIZATION
ENVIRONMENT

INTERNAL ORGANIZATION
ENVIRONMENT
(continuous interaction
with external
organization environment)

closed system

a system in which there is no
interaction of the elements
with the outside environment

open system

a system in which there is
interaction of the elements
with the outside environment

Systems theory also distinguishes between **closed systems** and **open systems** as shown in Exhibit 2.11. In the former, there is no interaction of the elements of the system with the outside environment, and in the latter there is. Therefore, organizations can be considered open systems that constantly interact with their environment, importing resources from it into the organization and exporting goods and services back out into the outside world. Since traditional management theory often seemed to treat organizations as if they were more or less closed systems, it tended to overlook many of the important impacts that relations with the outside environment could have on functions inside the company or plant. Viewing organizations as open systems, on the other hand, provides an appropriate, and necessary, perspective for any manager operating in the rapidly changing world of the 21st century.

Contingency Approaches

A cornerstone of scientific management and classical management theories was that there was *one best way* of doing a job, including the various functions of management. If an employee or manager performed tasks in any other way, the outcome, according to those theories, would be a reduction in effectiveness. Furthermore, these approaches specified what should characterize this one best way as it related to managerial jobs and roles: namely, unity of command, clear hierarchy of authority, precise specification of job duties, and so forth. The central theme of the "one best way" persisted for decades after the idea was first proposed by Taylor and others.

What was challenged over the years, particularly in the 1940s and 1950s, was the nature of what the one best way should be. That is, in some organizations a version of a human relations approach replaced the traditional way of operating. Thus, for such firms and agencies there was an effort to substitute a more responsive and employee-centered approach that stressed increasing employee satisfaction and morale and providing more flexible rules and regulations. It was almost as if some organizations had made 180-degree turns in their attempts to do things differently. Sometimes this change met with success, but often companies and other organizations found that they had simply exchanged one type of problem (employee dissatisfaction) for another type (casual or sloppy performance).

By the end of the 1960s, interesting research findings were emerging that suggested that perhaps what was being overlooked was how well different approaches to management (e.g., the highly structured traditional approach versus the flexible, employee-centered approach) worked in different sets of organizational circumstances.[28] In effect, the findings tended to indicate that the highly structured approach (sometimes called the **mechanistic approach**) was better suited to stable external environments, highly repetitive tasks, and employees with limited technical or professional expertise. On the other hand, the flexible approach (often labeled the **organic approach**) seemed better suited for rapidly changing and complex environments, nonrepetitive tasks, and employees with considerable training and competence. The Managerial Challenge box, "Success at Semco," tells the story of one manager's radical shift toward such an approach. Collectively, the research findings led many management scholars to the view that the most effective type of management would be a **contingency approach** that took into account the circumstances that existed, especially the nature of the organization's environment, its technology, the tasks to be performed within the organization, and the types of individual members—with their particular capabilities—the organization could attract and retain.

In its narrower sense, then, the term "contingency approach" refers to a choice between more traditional forms of organizational structure and methods of management and more flexible and less specified structure and methods. This choice, as it relates to the process of management, is well summed up in the often-quoted statement of the former manager of the Los Angeles Dodgers, Tommy Lasorda: "Management is like holding a dove: squeeze it too hard and it dies; hold it too loose and it flies away."

In its broader sense, the contingency approach simply means that there are no general principles of management that can be applicable to *all* situations. What is best will depend on a whole host of variables, many of them beyond the manager's direct control, but most of which should be considered in deciding how to proceed. Interestingly, in management theory, we have gone from one extreme—"one best way"—to another extreme—"it all depends." Although this latter stance does not appear on the surface to provide much obvious guidance, it is clearly more suited to the current era of exceedingly rapid and often discontinuous change. It also puts the burden squarely where it belongs: on managers themselves to develop their diagnostic and analytical skills to provide effective approaches for changing circumstances.

mechanistic approach

highly structured traditional management approach, which may be better suited to stable external environments, highly repetitive tasks, and employees with limited technical or professional expertise

organic approach

a flexible, employee-centered management approach that seems better suited for rapidly changing and complex environments, nonrepetitive tasks, and employees with considerable training and competence

contingency approach

a management theory that emphasizes matching a structured or flexible management style to the organization's environment, its technology, the tasks to be performed, and the types of employees

ENTERING THE 21ST CENTURY

As a new century, indeed a new millennium, begins, it is useful to take an overview of where management thought is currently. One conclusion that can be stated unequivocally: There is no single, grand theory or all-encompassing approach that dominates the thinking about management. Rather, as we have seen in the preceding sections, there are a variety of perspectives that have been developed in recent

MANAGERIAL CHALLENGE

SUCCESS AT SEMCO

As experts continue to debate the efficacy of different managerial approaches, Ricardo Semler, the young CEO of Semco, backed up his words with action. Semco is a family-owned business in Sao Paulo, Brazil, that manufactures everything from high-speed commercial dishwashers to rocket-fuel propellant mixers for satellites. While still in his early 20s, Semler took over management of the company, which had been run in a dictatorial style by his father. Factory work was organized in a mechanistic manner; dress codes and time clocks were strictly enforced; and watchmen eyed every move that workers made. Then Semler collapsed on the factory floor from stress. He realized that, if both he and his company were to survive, things must change.

Semler decided that flexibility in the workplace was vital, both to the health of employees and to the health of the company, so he set about democratizing his company. First, he abolished dress codes and time clocks. Then he threw away the rule books. "Thousands of rules work fine for an army or a prison system," he explains, "but not, I believe, for a business." Next, he flattened the organization's hierarchy, which also changed the way work itself was organized. Now employees engage in a more organic approach to their jobs; they typically work in clusters or teams, and all have mastered more than one job. According to Semler, most employees know how to drive a forklift and will do so to get a job done faster. The purchasing and engineering departments are scrambled so that everyone sits together, near the factory floor. Even the machines themselves have been moved; instead of being aligned in rows, they are set at odd angles so that teams can work around them more easily. Semler has taken this democratization a step farther by making sure that every employee knows how to read a balance sheet and a cash-flow statement, and workers share in nearly 25 percent of the company's profits.

All this shifting of tasks and roles gave Semler some unexpected ways to cut costs as well. Semco no longer has a receptionist or secretaries. "We don't believe in cluttering the payroll with ungratifying, dead-end jobs. Everyone at Semco, even top managers, fetches guests, stands over photocopiers, sends faxes, types letters, and dials the phone.... At Semco we have stripped away the unnecessary perks and privileges that feed the ego but hurt the balance sheet and distract everyone from the crucial corporate tasks of making, selling, billing, and collecting," Semler explains.

Semler believes that he has found the true way to run a business, and many other corporations are beginning to agree. For instance, companies such as IBM, General Motors, Ford, Kodak, Bayer, Nestlé, Goodyear, Chase Manhattan, and Dow Chemical have all sent executives to Semco to attend special seminars conducted by Semler on his managerial approach. And Semler claims that productivity at Semco has increased over the two decades since the change, from $11,000 in annual sales per employee to $135,000 in annual sales per employee. It should not be concluded, however, that Semler's highly organic approach—what he calls "natural business"—is right for every company. Rather, it is an approach that seems to work in this particular set of circumstances and with this particular leader, which may be applicable with appropriate adaptations to at least some other companies.

Sources: Jill Muehrcke, "Let Tribal Customs Thrive," *Nonprofit World* 16, no. 1 (January/February 1998), pp. 2–3; Donald J. McNerny, "Maverick: The Success Story Behind the World's Most Unusual Workplace," *Organizational Dynamics* 24, no. 2 (Autumn 1995), pp. 92–93; "People Power: Enlisting Agents of Change," *Chief Executive*, Brief Supplement, May 1995, pp. 15–16; "From Fear to Freedom," *Fortune*, February 6, 1995, pp. 70, 74, 78; Ricardo Semler, "Who Needs Bosses?" *Across the Board* 31, no. 2 (February 1994), pp. 23–25.

years that have shaped how both academic scholars and practicing managers view the challenge of managing organizations effectively. Many of these more recently developed frameworks discussed in the past few pages have been based on rigorous research and related analysis; that is, they have been based on attempts to develop a science of management (not to be confused with "scientific management" or "management science"). Such research and analysis are continuing at a brisk pace at the turn of the century and could lead to new insights and major innovations within the next decade or so.

Management thought at the end of the 20th century, however, has also been influenced by more practitioner-oriented writers and observers. They have helped introduce a number of approaches and ideas—such as total quality management, re-engineering, and learning organizations—that will be discussed later in this book. While not comprehensive management theories in themselves, these concepts and techniques have had a fair amount of influence on the day-to-day practice of management, such as raising the priority for all employees—managers and non-managers alike—of producing products and services of exceptional quality and reliability. Indeed, some of these writers have used the competition among countries, as well as among companies, as a way of focusing attention on improving management.

For example, not so many years ago, a pair of former management consultants, Tom Peters and Robert Waterman, in the early 1980s published a book called *In Search of Excellence* that sold over one million copies within its first three years. It sold so well and was read by so many managers, especially in the United States, because it claimed to show that a number of American companies were being managed as competently as the leading Japanese companies of the time. In effect, this kind of popular writing emphasized the idea of benchmarks or examples of "best" management practices as a way of motivating other managers and companies to improve.

Nevertheless, to reiterate, the reality at the beginning of the 21st century is that the competitive world of organizations, especially business organizations, is so complex and so fast-changing that no single, overall theory or approach to management can be expected to provide *the* way of thinking about this topic. Managers, and those who expect to be managers in the future, need to draw their ideas from many different sources and be able to take into account—but critically evaluate—multiple approaches to managing. That would seem to be the clear message and challenge as we enter the 21st century.

CONCLUDING COMMENTS

The history of management thought and practice up to this point in time can be compared to a flowing river. In the centuries before 1900, there was only a relatively tiny stream of ideas about how to manage organizations of any size and complexity. Like small brooks forming the source of a river, the ideas of ancient writers made their individual contributions to the development of management thought, but it was not until other events occurred, in this case the Industrial Revolution, that a major river was formed.

The needs of expanding industrial societies provided the setting and the impetus for concentrated attention on the subject of management. Even within that fertile context, however, it took the exceptional efforts and dedication of a relatively small number of people, such as Taylor, Follett, the Gilbreths, and Barnard, to increase the flow of ideas. They not only increased the size of the river, but they also changed its course, while always being strongly affected by events and circumstances of the times in which they lived. They brought greater rationality to a former haphazard process and, over time, a broader and more complex view of what the process of management was all about. It took the Hawthorne studies and the publication of their findings in the late 1930s, however, to bring additional clarity to the river of management ideas by emphasizing the centrality of the people component of organizations and the importance of the human relations that existed within them.

In the years following World War II, the management river broadened out considerably with the input of such major tributaries as the behavioral, decision-making, systems, and contingency theory approaches to management. Each of these sets of ideas added to those that preceded them and often opened up whole new ways of thinking about managerial issues. Now, here at the start of the new century, the river of management history has, in effect, arrived at a sort of delta, with a very large spread of ideas and practices. With all of the influences of significant forces for change in the external environment—such as leapfrog advances in information technology, the increasing diversity of workforces, the expanding globalization of business, and the intensifying use of "voice" (i.e., speaking up) by employees and society at large—it makes it extremely difficult to chart the future of management. That task, though, forms the basis of the case for you to tackle at the end of this chapter!

KEY TERMS

bounded rationality 56
classical management theory 43
closed system 58
contingency approach 59
division of labor 35
functions of management 44
Hawthorne studies 53
human relations approach 53

human resources approach 54
integrative approaches 57
law of the situation 51
management science (operations research) 56
mechanistic approach 59
neoclassical management theory 49

open system 58
organic approach 59
satisficing 56
scientific management 38
simulation 56
system 57
systems theory 57

REVIEW QUESTIONS

1. Why was management, as a topic, not widely addressed before the beginning of the Industrial Revolution?
2. Why did the factory system replace the domestic production system?
3. What was the single most important technological advancement that led to the Industrial Revolution, and why was it so important?
4. What developments caused the need for industrial enterprises to start to change to a system of using more professional managers (i.e., individuals who would make management a career)?
5. What were F. W. Taylor's greatest contributions to management thought and practice, and for what could he be most strongly criticized?
6. What did H. L. Gantt contribute to the development of scientific management?
7. How were Fayol's contributions to management thought similar to, and different from, those of Taylor?
8. What are the three basic types of authority as described by Weber?
9. Describe the similarities and differences between classical and neoclassical management thinking.
10. What is the basic distinction between the human relations and the human resources approaches to management?
11. Why is it important to consider organizations as *open* systems?
12. What is the basic assumption behind the contingency approach to management?

DISCUSSION QUESTIONS

1. Provide an example of how conditions and events of a particular time period shaped the managerial approaches that emerged during or around that period.

2. To what extent do you see the ideas of scientific management reflected in organizations today? In what type of organizations, if any, are these ideas still relatively prominent? Provide at least three examples.

3. The human relations school of thought argued that happy workers would be productive workers. Why do you think that subsequent research generally has failed to provide evidence for a strong relationship of this type?

4. The so-called "classical approaches" provided managers with specific steps to take in improving organizational performance, while the contingency approach maintains that "it all depends." Does the contingency approach offer useful help to managers, and if so, in what ways?

CLOSING CASE

Management Trends for the New Millennium

Imagine that you are a manager in the new millennium. You have studied the history of management thought and understand where business has been, especially during the past century of the 1900s. Now you must determine where business is headed to help your company develop a competitive edge. As a manager, you need to be a good forecaster of human capital and other resources in the future. Experts agree that some important trends that will influence organizations in the coming decades are already emerging.

Globalization has begun, and it will continue as companies search for new markets and cheaper places to manufacture goods. Globalization has been possible, in part, because of technological advances such as advanced telecommunications, which in turn has allowed rapid transfer of information from one place to another throughout the world. Globalization means that workforces are becoming increasingly diverse; in fact, an international or multinational organization may have employees in many countries, immersed in different cultures, speaking different languages. Managers will be looking for the best way to manage these diverse workforces, who may be working collectively around the clock, around the world (as one shift ends a workday in Europe, another may be beginning in Asia).

Technology will continue to have an immense influence on the way organizations are run. Thus, employees must be educated to utilize new technology, and companies must be able to adapt production facilities and other systems quickly to keep up with technological changes and consumer demands. Speed is now a major factor in many organizations' chances for success. Should managers then work toward a decentralized organizational structure to keep their companies as flexible as possible? If organizations become more decentralized, then employees' roles and responsibilities are likely to change. One change in the way companies use their personnel has already begun—it is the outsourcing of work, or the hiring of contract workers instead of full-time employees. This may reduce costs, but it also means a reduction in the number of key, educated workers who contribute their efforts exclusively to the company.

Demographers predict that people will continue to move away from urban centers, which means businesses must follow (or businesses may move away, and their workers will follow). More people will work from home, either as full-time employees or as contract workers, as mentioned previously. Employees are also demanding improved working environments, with less stress. In addition, workforces in the United States and elsewhere continue to become more diverse. As demographic shifts take place in the workforce, so are other shifts taking place in the marketplace. Baby boomers have entered middle age, and many are already becoming empty nesters. Before the end of the next century, ethnic groups will make up the majority of the U.S. population, and the increase in population of those who are age 85 and over will be dramatic. Each of these trends will influence the strategies that organizations develop to serve new markets and manage their workforces.

Finally, there is the issue of the economy—both at home and abroad. In the United States, experts predict that the economy probably will continue to grow, at least until early in the 21st century. This means that consumers will keep buying homes, furnishings, automobiles, and electronics, as well as travel and recreation products, despite occasional economic slowdowns. While managers are not expected to be trained economists, they will need to pay attention to general economic trends to determine where and how their companies should concentrate their best efforts.

QUESTIONS

1. Given the trends that seem probable over at least the next decade or so, to what extent is it likely that some new, comprehensive theory of management will emerge that will be widely applicable to almost all types of companies and organizations in almost any country around the world?
2. Nearly everybody acknowledges that ever-increasing globalization is a force that will affect most companies of any size in the future. How can students of management best take into account that trend in order to become effective managers?
3. How should managers adjust their approaches to managing people in view of the fact that the U.S. population (as in many other countries) is both aging and growing more diverse?
4. Provide arguments for and against the following proposition: Organizations of the 21st century will become so decentralized, so flat (i.e., very few levels from the top to the bottom of the organization), and so information-intensive that virtually no management will be needed.

Sources: Graham T. Molitor, "Anticipating Change: Socio-political Global Trends and Issues," *Executive Speeches* 12, no. 4 (February/March 1998), pp. 24–29; Michael A. Hitt, "1997 Presidential Address: Twenty-First-Century Organizations: Business Firms, Business Schools, and the Academy," *Academy of Management Review* 23, no. 2 (April 1998), pp. 218–19; John Howard, "The Forces of Change," *Presidents and Prime Ministers* 7, no. 2 (March/April 1998), pp. 6–9; David Hummels et al., "Vertical Specialization and the Changing Nature of World Trade," *Economic Policy Review* 4, no. 2 (June 1998), pp. 79–99; Susan Bady, "Six Emerging Markets," *Professional Builder* 61, no. 18 (November 1996), pp. 76–82.

PART 2

ENVIRONMENTAL CONTEXT OF MANAGING

CHAPTER 3

ASSESSING EXTERNAL ENVIRONMENTS

LEARNING OBJECTIVES

After studying this chapter, you should be able to:

- Explain the five forces of a firm's industry environment.
- Describe the critical forces in the domestic environment.
- Describe the key elements of an organization's international environment.
- Describe the key considerations in conducting an effective country analysis.
- Differentiate between environmental instability and risk.

Russia's Black Gold or Black Hole?

The former Soviet Union has 141 giant oil and gas fields—fields that hold more than 500 million barrels of oil or three trillion cubic feet of gas. Russia alone has more natural gas than any other nation in the world, including Saudi Arabia. The western Siberian basin, which is only a fraction of Russia, has 16 percent of the world's discovered oil reserves. However, 20,000 wells in Russia still have vast amounts of untapped oil because the natural pressure that pushes the oil to the surface is gone, and Russians lack the technology to force the remaining oil out of the ground. Because of the political pressures to divert human and financial resources into a military that could compete with the West, the old Soviet government neglected maintenance and new technology for the oil industry, leaving much of the equipment in near useless condition. Current financial troubles in Russia have only worsened the situation. Consequently, production has fallen from its peak in 1988, when the Soviet Union was the largest producer of oil in the world, by an estimated 20 to 30 percent. In fact, what Russia stopped producing was equal to all the oil produced in the North Sea each year. Oil production and transportation in Russia were so poor that an estimated one million barrels a day spilled on the ground. Depending on the price of oil, this represented between $10 and $20 million a day, or $3 to $6 billion a year! Unlike in most other countries, finding oil in Russia is not a problem.

So what is the problem? The problem is chaos in the wake of the breakup of the Soviet Union. Prior to the collapse, the Ministry of Energy in Moscow held an iron-fisted grip on the vast reserves and projects throughout the land. Like the military, the ministry issued orders from Moscow that were carried down through the chain of command. Given the vastness of the country, the chain was long and complicated. With the collapse came breaks in the chain, and many of the local oil-producing associations grabbed as much power and authority as they could. Recently, there have been cases of "spontaneous privatization;" that is, local oil companies simply refuse to take orders and produce, ship, and sell oil at their pleasure.

The vast reserves of oil and gas and growing global demand mean that the potential profits are extraordinary, which greatly raises the stakes. However, much of this black gold lies beneath land that is subject to some of the longest and coldest winters in the world. Workers in places such as Tyumen live in log cabins and huts without indoor plumbing. The high stakes, long winters, poor living and working conditions, and free-flowing vodka provide an explosive combination. Travelers to the region describe it as similar to the Wild West in the United States back in the 1800s. In Tyumen, things got so wild that many of the elite Black Beret military units that were pulled out of Latvia and Estonia were sent to Tyumen to try to keep order.

How does a foreign firm successfully conduct business in such an environment? Should it even try? Most of the Western oil companies such as British Petroleum, Exxon, and Chevron see the discovered oil and gas reserves of this region as nearly irresistible. Finding oil is such a difficult process in the rest of the world now that most firms still risk the turmoil and venture into the oil fields in the former Soviet Union. In 1996, there were 164 oil and gas joint ventures between foreign oil companies and former Soviet states.

Permission to explore, drill, extract, transport, or sell oil and gas used to be tightly controlled by the central oil ministry. Now, if you want to drill in Kazakhstan and ship crude oil to Italy for refining, you would have to negotiate separate agreements with Kazakhstan, Russia, and Georgia, depending on the chosen transportation route. With the political turmoil in Georgia and Russia, there is no guarantee that the government that signed the agreement today would be the same one in power tomorrow.

In addition, with Russia's economic crisis in 1998, the political financial stability remains uncertain. Add to that a tumble in oil prices worldwide, and you have a volatile situation that could explode.

Clearly, if you are a manager in a large multinational oil firm, you cannot ignore the potential opportunities or the chaos of the surrounding environment. But even a manager in a small oil-drilling parts supply firm can be affected by global unrest.

Source: Adapted from Ahmed Rasid, "The Next Frontier," *Far Eastern Economic Review*, February 4 1993, pp. 48–50; Erik Kreil, "Oil and Gas Joint Ventures in the Former Soviet Union," U.S. Energy Information Agency, accessed at http://www.eia.doe.gov, August 1996; Sebastian Alison, "Russia Sees Second Devaluation as Oil Price Slumps," Reuters Limited, November 23, 1998.

Consider this lesson from nature: A cactus will drown in the tropics but flourish in the desert; an orchid will wither in the desert but blossom in the tropical rainforest. Just as in the natural world, organizations live and die as a function of their fit with their external environment. This is why, as a manager, you must have a solid understanding of your organization's external environment. For example, if you don't understand the political environment in the various countries of the former Soviet Union, you may invest money to drill for black gold only to find that it turns into a black hole into which you can forever pour money but from which you never get a return.

external environment
a wide variety of forces and institutions outside the organization that can influence its performance

The **external environment** consists of a wide variety of forces outside the organization that can influence its performance (see Exhibit 3.1 for an overview). In this chapter, we examine the major aspects of the external environment. We first explore the most immediate environment—the industry environment—and then the more general environments—the domestic and international environments—in which an organization exists.

EXHIBIT 3.1

External Environment Forces

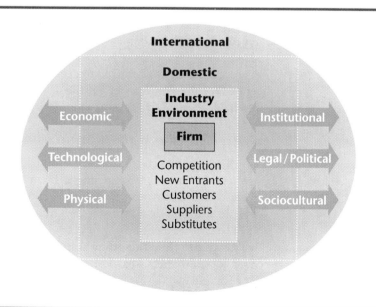

But what if you do not plan to work in an organization with any national or international orientation or activities? Why should you need to extend your understanding to encompass global issues? You need to understand the international environment because increasingly even domestic organizations and managers are feeling the influences of international forces. For example, as a manager, you may be completely focused on your customer within a small region of your domestic market. You may not be focused on, care about, or even be aware of competitors in Thailand. However, this does not mean that competitors in Thailand are not focused on you. Furthermore, it does not mean that your customer doesn't care about the competitors in Thailand if they can offer a better value, such as equal or better quality at lower cost.

As we examine the domestic and then international environments, you will notice that many of the forces are the same, though they behave slightly differently. Just as wind, humidity, temperature, and rainfall exist in the general environment and the more extended environment, the economic, sociocultural, legal-political, and technological environmental forces exist in both the domestic and international environments. However, there are two additional forces in the international environment that you should know and understand. We examine why each force is important for managers to understand and explain why two additional forces should be considered in analyzing the international environment.

INDUSTRY ENVIRONMENT

industry environment
the industry in which the firm competes and the factors that have the greatest impact on the nature of competition in that industry

The **industry environment** is the most immediate environment within which an organization survives and flourishes. Consequently, it typically has the largest influence on the organization, and the fit between the organization and the industry environment is critical for a manager to understand. Forces in the industry environment exert a significant influence on the organization. Because the industry environment plays a significant role in the competitive and strategic position of an organization, we will examine certain aspects of these forces in more detail later in Chapter 8 when we explore the topic of strategic management.

Perhaps the most well-known analysis of industry for us is Michael Porter's Five Forces model.[1] This framework contains five industry environment forces that can significantly influence the performance of the organization (see Exhibit 3.2). The original research was designed to explain why some industries were more profitable as a whole than others and why some organizations within industries were more profitable than other organizations in the same industry.

Competitors and the Nature of Competition

The first aspect of the industry environment to consider is who your competitors are and the nature of competition. In any form of competition, one of the first things you need to know is your competitor. For example, you need to know how big and strong your competitors are relative to you. If you are small and weak relative to your competition, you may choose to stay out of their way and go after business that is less interesting to them. In your analysis of competitors, you also need to know their weaknesses. Those weaknesses may represent opportunities that you can exploit.

Just For Feet took this view. Just For Feet was a latecomer to the athletic footwear retail business. Competitors such as Foot Locker already had hundreds of

EXHIBIT 3.2

EXHIBIT 3.2

Five Forces

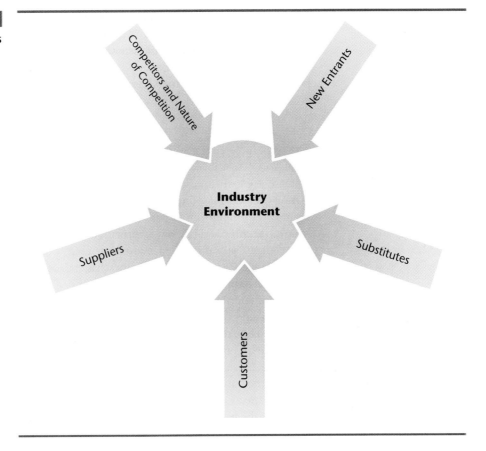

retail outlets across the nation when Just For Feet was established. But despite the overall size of Foot Locker, their individual stores were relatively small. To Just For Feet, this weakness represented a great opportunity. Just For Feet established stores that were three to five times the size of Foot Locker's stores. Just For Feet wanted these stores to be entertainment centers and not just sneaker stores, so they included basketball practice courts, loud music, pro athletes signing autographs, and an endless selection of sneakers in their stores. Just For Feet soon became the fastest growing athletic footwear retailer in the country and one of the 100 fastest growing companies listed in *Fortune* magazine.[2]

In addition to understanding your competitors, you also need to consider the nature of competition, or rivalry, in your industry. In general, competition can be based on price or on quality. Simplified, competitors can try to outdo each other by offering the lowest price to customers or by offering the best product. The more competition is based on price, the lower the profits. This is primarily because it is easier to lower prices than costs. As prices decline faster than costs, profit margins shrink. For example, competition in the airline business has been based on airfare prices since deregulation in 1977. With the stroke of a pen or computer key, airlines can slash prices to try to attract customers. They cannot so easily lower the price of new planes, fuel, or the wages of pilots or flight attendants. Consequently, most U.S. airlines lost billions during the 1980s and early 1990s. The notable exception has been Southwest Airlines. This is primarily because Southwest has had the lowest cost structure of any major airline. Only as fuel prices declined in the late 1990s did airlines in general start making money again.[3]

In contrast to the airline industry, competition in the luxury automobile industry is primarily based on quality. Issues of safety, engineering, and handling, not price, dominate the ads for Mercedes, Lexus, BMW, and Infinity.

New Entrants

The second element of the five forces is the extent to which it is easy or difficult for firms to enter the industry. All other elements being equal, new entrants will increase competition. Unless the size of the entire industry pie is expanding, the greater the number of new entrants, the thinner the slice of pie for each participant. Increased competition usually leads to lower profit margins because customers have more choices. Unless it is difficult and expensive to switch from one company to another (typically called **switching costs**), companies are forced to pass on greater value to customers when they have more choices. This greater value usually comes from lowering profits. For example, if there are five grocery stores within a block of your house, and its costs you very little to go to one store over another, you are likely to go to the store that offers the best deal. As the stores compete for your business, they typically have to lower their profits to offer you a better deal.

The factors that keep new entrants out are termed barriers. **Entry barriers** are the obstacles that make it difficult for firms to get into a business. The bigger the barriers, the harder it is to get into the business. The harder it is to get in, the fewer new entrants. Generally, the fewer the new entrants, the fewer the total number of players in the industry. This typically means that each player gets a larger slice of the

switching costs
expenses in time, effort, and money to change from one supplier to another

entry barriers
factors that make it more difficult for new firms to enter markets

For some years after the breakup of AT&T, there were only two other national long-distance telephone carriers in the United States: MCI and Sprint. The enormous cost of setting up the infrastructure (fiber-optic networks) made it difficult for other competitors to quickly jump in.

industry pie. It also means that customers likely have fewer choices, and that usually translates into higher profits for the firms already in the industry.

Substitutes

Substitutes as an industry force focus on the extent to which alternative products or services can substitute for the existing product or service. Substitution does not involve a choice of one grocery store over another. Rather, it involves opting for another alternative, for example, going to a restaurant instead of the grocery store when you are hungry. One of the factors that severely hurt the passenger bus industry is the substitution effect of flying. When it costs $59 for an hour flight from Irvine, California, to Phoenix, Arizona, and it costs $42 for an eight-hour bus ride, most people fly rather than take the bus. Generally, the fewer the available substitutes, the greater the profits. For example, if you have no choice to satisfy your hunger except by going to the grocery store for food (i.e., no substitute), grocery stores would make more money.

Customers

All managers in organizations have customers to serve. To the extent that there are relatively few customers and these customers are united, they have more power to demand lower prices, customized products or services, or attractive financing terms from producers. The greater the power of customers, the more value they can extract. Unless you can quickly and significantly lower your costs, the more value customers extract, the lower your profits will be. For example, suppose you worked for a diamond mine. To make money, you would need to sell the diamonds you extracted. One company, DeBeers, purchases an estimated 80 percent of the world's diamonds.[4] As a diamond mining company, you are unlikely to make big profits because DeBeers basically determines the price they will pay for the diamonds they buy from you. Because of their significant power as a customer, they will pay you a low price.

Suppliers

Every organization also has a set of suppliers. To the extent that there are relatively few suppliers and they are united, they have more power to place demands on producers. In general, the greater the power of suppliers, the lower the industry profits. For example, suppose you work for one of the major airlines and you need to purchase a commercial airliner that will hold 350 passengers and travel nonstop from New York to Tokyo.[5] Boeing is in a fairly powerful supplier position. Its 747 is one of the few planes that can fulfill these requirements. Because you have few alternatives, Boeing can extract a high price for its 747s. This higher price raises your costs. Unless you can raise your prices to the same degree or lower other costs to offset the high price paid to Boeing, your profits will decline.

Industry environment forces have a powerful influence on organizations and their performance. Exhibit 3.3 summarizes the general industry forces and their subcomponents that lead to higher or lower profits.

Industry environments are important, but they do not predetermine success or failure. That is, you can position your organization within an industry so that your organization performs better than your competitors. We mention this because we

- Few Competitors
- Quality-Based Competition
- High Entry Barriers
- Few New Entrants
- Few Substitutes
- Many Customers
- Fragmented Customers
- Many Suppliers

Higher Profits

- Many Competitors
- Price-Based Competition
- Low Entry Barriers
- Many New Entrants
- Many Substitutes
- Few Customers
- United Customers
- Few Suppliers

Lower Profits

do not want to create the impression that if you are in an "unattractive" industry (i.e., one in which the industry forces are generally aligned to result in lower profits), you are doomed to lower profits. Most airlines have lost money because of the nature of the five forces in that industry; however, as we mentioned, Southwest has made money. In fact, it has made so much money that if you had bought $1,000 of Southwest stock when it was issued about 20 years ago, your stock would now be worth $26 million! So clearly, organizations can survive and flourish even in hostile environments. How you can accomplish that is the subject of Chapter 8 on strategic management.

DOMESTIC EXTERNAL ENVIRONMENT

macro environment
the broader environment in which a firm finds itself that affects not just the industrial firm but the industry it is in

Now that we have examined the most immediate environment to an organization, we turn to the more extended environment—the domestic **macro environment**. For a quick appreciation of the link between the industry and domestic environments, just think about the school or university you are now attending. It competes with other schools for bright, capable students in its industry. However, the nature of competition or other competing schools, the availability of substitutes, and power of suppliers or of customers such as yourself are not the only environmental forces that influence the school. A variety of forces in the general domestic environment can also have an influence. These forces are typically divided into four major categories: economic, sociocultural, legal-political, and technological. We examine each of these forces and how they affect organizations.

Economic Forces

A wide variety of economic forces in the external environment can significantly influence organizations. Not all economic forces affect all organizations equally. The exact nature of the business and industry determines the specific factors that influence an organization. Economic forces can be grouped into three general categories: current conditions, economic cycles, and structural changes.

EXHIBIT 3.4

Overall Economic Cycles and Industry Cycles

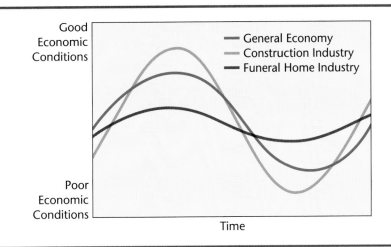

Current economic conditions are important for obvious reasons. The current level of inflation can directly affect how quickly costs rise. The current level of unemployment can directly affect how easy or difficult it is to find the type of labor you need. The current interest rates can determine how easy it is to borrow money or even how much money a firm can borrow to finance activities and expansions.

But economic activity is not static, and current conditions do not necessarily predict what the economic conditions will be in the future. Economic activity tends to move in cycles. Although it is difficult to predict exactly when an upturn or downturn in economic conditions will occur, understanding that cycles exist and the key factors that move them is critical for managerial activities such as planning. It is also important to understand that specific industry cycles can be more or less pronounced than the general economic cycle of the country (see Exhibit 3.4). So in addition to the general economic cycle, you need to understand the economic cycles of a particular industry to make good planning decisions. For example, the construction industry tends to have higher peaks and lower valleys than the overall national economy, and the funeral home business tends to have lower peaks and higher valleys than the overall economy. If you were unaware of the nature of your particular industry, you might make poor management decisions. For example, if you were unaware of the exaggerated cycles of the construction industry relative to the peaks and valleys of the general economy, you might not plan for enough labor or materials for the upturn in the cycle and might order more materials or hire more people than necessary during downturns in the cycle.

Perhaps the hardest yet most critical thing to understand about economic conditions is knowing whether structural changes are taking place. **Structural changes** are changes that significantly affect the dynamics of economic activity now and into the future. The shift from an agrarian (agricultural) to industrial economy and then from an industrial to service economy were all structural changes that took place in the U.S. economy. They affected where people worked, what work they did, the education level they needed to do the work, and so on. If structural changes are taking place and you are unaware of them, you can easily make poor managerial decisions. For example, a structural shift to a more knowledge-based

structural changes

shifts in economic dynamics that result in new economic activities becoming important forces while other, older activities decline in power work environment may change not only the nature of workers but what motivates them. Without understanding this, you may try to motivate them in ways that worked in the past but won't in the future because the type of people you employ change and they bring with them new values.

Sociocultural Forces

Though business managers may have a natural tendency to pay attention to economic forces, sociocultural forces are also important. They can be divided into two categories: demographics and values.

demographics
descriptive elements of people in a society

Demographics are essentially the descriptive elements of people in the society, such as average age, birth rate, level of education, literacy rate, and so on. For example, everyone has heard about the baby boomers born between 1946 and 1964. They constitute nearly a third of the population of the United States. They are the major force behind a variety of shifting demographics, including the rising average age in the United States. Increased life expectancy also contributes to this rising average age. In 1920 the average life expectancy was 53.6 years, and by 2010 it is estimated to be 77 years.[6]

But why should you as a manager care about baby boomers or other demographics? Simplified, demographics can significantly affect both organizational inputs and outcomes. For example, the average level of education and the birth rate in the United States combined can have a significant impact on the supply of workers with a given level of education and training. Specifically, a low birth rate and a stagnant level of education could have a significant impact on your ability as a manager in a high-tech firm to find the technicians you need to run your business. Or consider that people are living longer and that the largest demographic group in U.S. history is about 15 years away from the age at which health problems begin to increase. This could present the health care industry with significant opportunities as well as challenges.

societal values
the endstates that a major portion of the society deem important and right at a given point in time

Although demographics can tell us important statistics about our population, societal values largely translate those numbers into business implications. **Societal values** determine the extent to which the products or services your firm provides have a market. For example, a switch in values from status to functionality moved firms such as Calvin Klein out of the spotlight and L.L. Bean into consumer demand in the early 1990s. In the mid- and late-1990s, it seems that the values about status and clothes have again reversed themselves and so have the fortunes of these two companies.

Astute managers need the ability to combine demographics and societal values.[7] For example, during the eighties the majority of the baby boomers were in their thirties. Like most "thirty-something" individuals, baby boomers were beginning to establish themselves in their careers and reap the early economic benefits. This meant that there was a large group in the population with significant spending power. Add values to these demographics that stressed status, especially in visible possessions like cars, and you get some interesting results. One result was the biggest selling spurt that BMW has ever experienced. BMW became the symbol of success and status for these "Yuppies" (Young Urban Professionals).[8] Astute managers can combine demographics and values to see sociocultural forces that might present either challenges or opportunities. Accurately reading these forces can greatly facilitate advance planning.

The trend toward a healthy lifestyle has benefitted health clubs, athletic apparel manufacturers and retailers, and health-food producers. Conversely, it has had a negative effect on tobacco farmers and cigarette producers.

Legal and Political Forces

Legal and political forces can also have dramatic impacts on organizations. Laws frame what organizations can and cannot do. As a consequence, they can create both challenges and opportunities. For example, new pollution laws significantly increased the operating costs of coal-burning power plants. At the same time, other laws created new business opportunities for firms such as Corning that developed and sold new filter systems for these plants.[9] Tax laws can also have a profound effect on businesses. In the 1970s, tax breaks for oil and gas exploration led to massive activity in states such as Texas. The repeal of those laws pushed many firms, and nearly the state, into bankruptcy.[10]

Perhaps one of the most important political aspects of the external domestic environment is federal government spending. On the one hand, increases or decreases in government spending can have a significant impact on the overall economy. Total government spending at the local, state, and national levels can account for 20 percent of **gross domestic product**. At this level, increases or decreases in total government spending can have a significant impact on overall business activity. However, even if total spending remains unchanged, if significant spending moves from one area to another, then government spending can still dramatically affect businesses. Consider the nearly threefold increase in military spending during the Reagan presidency. Firms such as General Dynamics profited considerably from this spending. Interestingly, the decrease in military spending that then followed put many businesses, including General Dynamics, out of business or into the arms of another firm.[11]

More complicated, but perhaps even more important, is whether U.S. government spending pushes the deficit up or down. For example, generally when federal spending pushes the federal deficit up, interest rates also go up. As interest rates go up, money becomes more expensive for firms to borrow, and as a consequence, they borrow less. As firms borrow less, they expand their business activities at a

gross domestic product
the total economic value produced within the national borders of a given country

slower rate or even contract their overall activity. This can push unemployment up, which in turn pushes consumer spending down, creating full-fledged economic downturn. So while the political process governing federal spending and the deficit can be quite complicated, managers cannot afford to ignore its effects.

Technology Forces

Technological forces can have brilliant or devastating effects on organizations. A specific technological innovation can spell the birth and growth of one firm and the decline and death of another. For example, the invention of the transistor created firms like Texas Instruments and spelled the death of vacuum tube manufacturers that did not adapt to this technological environment change. While the techno-logical environment can be quite complicated, managers need to keep in touch with both product and process technological changes.

product technological changes

changes that lead to new products, features, or capabilities

Product technological changes are those that lead to new product features, capabilities, or completely new products. As a manager, you need to know what product technology changes are occurring, especially in your industry. For example, managers at Xerox were caught flat-footed when new, small personal copiers from Canon were able to produce the volume and quality of copies at half the price of larger Xerox machines.

process technological changes

changes that alter how products are made or how firms are managed

Process technological changes typically relate to alternations in how products are made or how enterprises are managed. For example, a new computer coloring technology brought back animated feature films because it substantially lowered production costs compared with the old individual frame-by-frame, hand-painted technology.[12] Management information system technology (MIS) such as that used by Wal-Mart (the largest retailer in the world with over $100 billion in annual sales) allows managers to track merchandise on a daily or hourly basis and thereby know which products are selling and which ones are not. This in turn allows them to effectively order merchandise so that they do not run out of hot-selling items (and miss out on the sales revenue) and avoid overstocking poor-selling items (and tie up valuable cash in inventory).[13]

To summarize the major forces in the macro domestic environment, let's return to the example of your school to see their impact. How does the general health of the economy influence your school? In good economic times, companies might have more money to donate to research, scholarships, or other important aspects of the school that almost always need money. How does having money for research or scholarships affect the school's ability to compete with other schools in the indus-try? The answer to the question is obvious and shows how the economic environ-ment can affect the industry environment in attracting good students and faculty.

What about sociocultural forces? How have they affected universities? As one example, consider that following the baby boomers (80 million strong) were the "baby busters" (only 40 million). Although the percentage of students going to college increased between these two generations, it did not increase enough to offset the overall decline in the number of people of college age. Many schools had expanded to accommodate the large increase in college students of the baby boomer generation, so when the smaller number of baby busters led to declines in enrollment and tuition dollars collected, these schools were severely hurt.

How have legal-political forces affected universities? At about the same time schools were trying to cope with declining enrollments, government loans to stu-dents also started to dry up. This meant that schools fortunate enough to have independent scholarship money in the bank were able to compete better for students. These healthier schools saw their enrollments decline less, while the weaker schools saw their enrollments decline more than the average.

Finally, consider the influence of technological forces. One of the current technological issues is live broadcasting of classes and remote location learning. What if technology allows the classroom to be taken to the students rather than bringing the students to the classroom? How will this affect universities? How is your school addressing this technological force in the external macro domestic environment?

If you were a manager in your school, you would need not only an understanding of your industry environment but the macro domestic environment as well. How could you make effective plans without understanding these forces? How would you know what direction to lead the organization without understanding these forces? Though these external environmental forces may seem somewhat removed from day-to-day managerial activities, they are quite relevant.

THE INTERNATIONAL ENVIRONMENT

As in the domestic environment, economic, sociocultural, legal-political, and technological forces exist and are important to analyze in the international environment. In addition, two other forces play an important role: institutional and physical forces. The reason they deserve special attention when examining the international environment is that they are much easier to understand in the domestic environment, but in the international environment, institutional and physical forces are not as readily apparent.

The Increasing Importance of the International Environment

Although all managers should pay attention to the international environment, its importance varies depending on the organization's size and scope of business. For small organizations, the domestic environment may generally be more important because their operations tend to be concentrated at a more local level and so the domestic environment has a much stronger impact. However, for medium-size and large firms, the international environment can be as important or even more important than the domestic environment. This is especially true as the percentage of international sales increases part of total sales. For example, 70 percent of Coca-Cola's revenues come from international sales; consequently, the international environment is critical to the company's performance. For firms that do not just operate in multiple countries but integrate operations into an almost borderless enterprise, the line between the domestic and international environments can blur to the point that for all practical purposes, the two are indistinguishable.

But even for small firms, the relevance of the international environment is growing almost day by day. Previously, if you were a manager in a small, local business, the key external forces were the competitor across the road, customers in the surrounding country, a supplier in the next town, the economic conditions of the state, the city council up the street, and general opinions of key townspeople. With the spread of technology and instantaneous global communications, for most managers those days are gone—never to return. Consider the following Managerial Challenge.

MANAGERIAL CHALLENGE

STORMY SEAS AT KNIGHT-CARVER, INC.

In the late 1980s, Dan Carver, the president of a medium-size yacht-building company, Knight-Carver (K-C), located in peaceful and sunny San Diego, California, was content and happy. His company was doing about $10 million a year in custom yacht building and repair. Carver was about as worried about the international external environment as he was about an iceberg floating into San Diego bay from Alaska.

At its peak, the company had 90 employees making and repairing small to medium-sized yachts. Nearly all of its customers were from the West Coast, and all the work was done in a small complex at the San Diego harbor. K-C did most things as well as the next competitor, but when it came to custom interiors, they had superior craftsmanship.

Despite the peaceful atmosphere at K-C, a storm was brewing that would blow the company into the middle of the global waters of international business. In 1990, the U.S. government put a 10 percent luxury tax on boats. This instantly added $120,000 to a typical $1.2 million custom boat. At about the same time, the U.S. economy took a nosedive. The tight economy and the new tax laws caused customers to look for lower-cost boat builders. Suddenly, K-C found that its customers were having their boats built by Taiwanese, Korean, Indonesian, and Brazilian competitors

that it never knew existed. To survive these stormy seas, K-C reduced the number of employees from 90 to about 30. It also reached out to customers in Japan and Saudi Arabia and started gathering information on suppliers in other countries such as Korea. The company also tried to assess the quality of its new foreign competitors' products.

Ironically, one of the key life preservers for this previously domestic company came from the largest *international* boat race in the world, the America's Cup. Thanks to San Diego resident and captain of America3, Dennis Conner, the America's Cup and international sailing teams from Japan, France, New Zealand, and Australia descended on San Diego in the summer of 1994. Racing spectators from around the world came to watch. International racing teams needed space for their boats and leased space from K-C. Leveraging these lease payments, making international connections, and taking advantage of an improving U.S. economy, K-C was able to keep the bank from taking over the business.

But the business was never the same. Never again could K-C afford to take its eye off foreign competitors or ignore suppliers from throughout the world. Now, it tracks foreign exchange rates daily, monitors supplier costs around the world, and calls on an international base of customers. All this, and K-C is still only a $10 million a year yacht builder.

The Special Nature of the International Environment

When we think of the international environment, we often think of more general issues such as general economic trends or regional trade agreements. For example, we might think about the managerial implications of regional trade agreements such as NAFTA (the North American Free Trade Agreement) or the European Union. Will they dismantle economic walls within regions but erect greater trade barriers between trading blocs? Clearly, these general international issues are important to consider, but we need to remember that there is actually no such thing as truly global business.

When considering the international environment, countries and their laws affect how organizations and their managers can conduct business. All legal economic activities take place, are recorded, and accounted for in at least one nation state. Consequently, that country is at the center of international environmental analysis.

If foreign countries are at the heart of international environmental analysis, then we must understand the characteristics that form a country. The central issue for all nations is sovereignty.[14] **State sovereignty** is the right for a group of people and its government to influence the rules and policies within the borders of their country and be relatively immune from outside influences. This right has two critical implications for managers. First, countries can establish laws, rules, practices, languages, currencies, standards, and cultural norms different from each other. These differ-

state sovereignty
the right for a group of people and its government to influence the rules and policies within the borders of their country and be relatively immune from outside influences

ences make monitoring the international environment significantly more complex and challenging than the domestic environment. Second, when these differences conflict, as they invariably do, there are no international institutions with enforcement power to resolve the conflicts between differing national laws. For example, what if British Petroleum strikes a deal with Kazakhstan's government and the government later decides to change the rules? British law states that the firm has a right to expect Kazakhstan to comply with the original agreement or compensate the firm for breach of contract. However, no institution has the power to enforce the terms of the previous contract—not the World Court, the United Nations, or any other institution. In practical terms, state sovereignty makes environmental analysis much more costly than in a domestic setting, where institutions within a country have power to review disputes, make judgments, and, most importantly, enforce them.

So managers need to look broadly at the international environment, but for business decisions, managers need analyses of specific countries. Day-to-day decisions involve selecting countries in which to do business, assessing the risk, and continuing or discontinuing business when changes occur.

Country and Political Risk Analysis

risk
the extent to which an event can have an impact on an organization

country risk analysis
the process of examining a country and its characteristics relative to a firm's proposed or existing business activities and determining the extent to which the environment is favorable or unfavorable

political risk analysis
the process of examining the political aspects of a country relative to a firm's proposed or existing business activities and determining the extent to which the political environment is favorable or unfavorable for the business

In the context of business, **risk** exists if a destabilizing event will significantly affect your organization.[15] Managers have several ways of assessing risk, among them analysis of the country's general business environment and its political system.

The process of analyzing a country in the international environment is typically called country risk analysis. **Country risk analysis** is the process of examining a country and its characteristics relative to a firm's proposed or existing business activities and determining the extent to which the environment is favorable or unfavorable. **Political risk analysis** is essentially a subcategory of country risk analysis and can be defined as the process of examining the political aspects of a country relative to a firm's proposed or existing business activities and determining the extent to which the political environment will have a favorable or unfavorable impact on the other environmental forces.

Essentially, country and political risk analyses help managers decide whether they should enter a nation or not, and if they are already in, whether they should stay in or get out. Exhibit 3.5 lists some sources that are useful for assessing a country's risk. In both analyses, managers examine six major environmental forces: economic forces, sociocultural forces, legal and political forces, technological forces, institutional forces, and physical forces. But before we examine these six environmental forces, we first need to understand two special aspects: instability and risk.

Economic Development and Instability

Whether it is the war in Bosnia, Hong Kong's return to China, the breakup of the Soviet Union, a coup attempt in Indonesia, abolishment of apartheid in South Africa, or the Asian financial crisis, destabilizing events rarely escape our notice. The Internet and global 24-hour media coverage bring events to our doorstep as they happen. Unfortunately, managers often make poor decisions when considering these events because they fail to place them in a larger context.[16]

One of the most important things to understand is that instability varies with economic development. On a continuum from low levels of economic development

EXHIBIT 3.5		
Some Useful Sources for Assessing International Risk	*Culturgrams*	International newsletter from the David M. Kennedy Center for International Studies at Brigham Young University, 800/528-6279 or http://ucs.byu.edu/kenncent
	Craighead, Inc.	Country profiles available to businesses considering relocation, 203/655-1007 or http://www.craighead.com
	Economist Intelligence Unit	Source of global business intelligence, including briefings and a comprehensive database, http://www.eiu.com
	U.S. Department of Commerce	Information on trade policy, http://www.doc.gov, including the International Trade Administration, http://www.ita.doc.gov
	Central Intelligence Agency (CIA)	Information on foreign or international economic and political information, available from the U.S. Government Printing Office, Superintendent of Documents, Washington, DC 20402; press releases available at the CIA Web site, http://www.odci.gov/cia/public_affairs
	U.S. State Department	Information on regions of the world, http://www.state.gov

to high levels of economic development, the pattern of political instability resembles an inverted "U," with instability peaking in the middle stages of economic development (see Exhibit 3.6).

In the early stages of economic development, the expectations of a country's citizens are focused primarily on survival; economic expectations are low. On average, basic economic expectations are realized. However, as a country becomes more economically developed, its citizens' economic expectations often rise quickly. As economic conditions and standards of living improve, people expect even better conditions. These expectations can be enhanced through technologies such as TV and radio, because they provide people with information about better standards of living in other countries. Generally, economic expectations rise more rapidly than

EXHIBIT 3.6	
Pattern of Instability	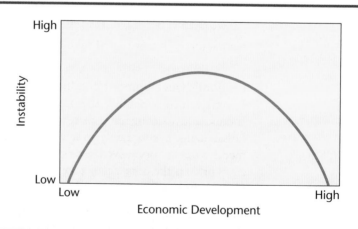

actual economic conditions. Consequently, ,
tion—increases as the country moves from lc
the middle stages. As the gap widens, political
a country moves toward the high end of econoɪ
narrow again. Expectations continue to rise but a
have a house, two cars, an automatic garage door
microwave, a dishwasher, an electric can opener, a
computer, how dissatisfied can you be?

Instability and Risk   In addition to understandin
between economic development and instability, as a mᵢ   ᵤ differentiate between instability and risk. Instability in a coun   ᵢcal system does
not necessarily put business at risk. Consequently, instabiliɪ, *aoes not* equal risk. For
example, even though the Tiananmen Square incident in 1989 was a significant
event in China, foreign toy manufacturers in China were largely unaffected by it.
This was primarily because the event was limited to Beijing in the north of China
and most of the toy manufacturers were located in the south of China.

Not only can firms be unaffected by instability, but they may also benefit. For
example, the overthrow of the Peronist regime in Argentina, the demise of Suharto
in Indonesia, or the ousting of the communists in Hungary all had positive effects
for most foreign firms in those countries. Some of the reasons that foreign firms
benefited were that tariffs came down, import restrictions were reduced, and capital was allowed to flow more freely.

Analyzing International Environmental Forces

As a manager, how do you determine which countries are "good" to do business in
and which ones are not? Let's take Brazil for example. Is it a good country in which
to do business? During the late 1970s and early 1980s, Brazil looked like a great
place for foreign firms to do business. Brazil was borrowing billions of dollars to
build up its economy and was a nation rich in natural and human resources. Then
Brazil ran into difficulty repaying these billions in loans. This severely hurt the
economy and business climate. Recently, foreign firms have begun to return to
Brazil (see the Managerial Challenge box). Given Brazil's up-and-down economic
and political history, would you advise doing business in the country? How would
you assess the opportunities or risks of doing business there?

As the situation in Brazil helps illustrate, most countries have both positive and
negative aspects. In the abstract, these aspects mean very little, but the key to an
effective analysis of the country is relating them to a specific industry or organization, and its circumstances. Because industries and businesses operate differently
and have different needs, specific policies or government actions pose unequal
threats. For example, because Pizza Hut can source nearly all of its needed raw
materials within Brazil, changes in import duties do not matter. However,
Volkswagen must import many components for the cars it builds in Brazil and
therefore cares very much about changes in tariffs. To thoroughly analyze a country, you should examine the following environmental forces.

Economic Forces   Economic data on most countries are readily available from
sources such as the World Bank. Statistics on inflation, gross domestic product

MANAGERIAL CHALLENGE

BOOM OR BUST FOR BRAZIL?

Firms such as Goldman Sachs & Company; J. C. Penney; Saatchi & Saatchi; McDonald's; Pepsi; and Pizza Hut have all recently announced or begun new operations in Brazil. Foreign investment in Brazil will have catapulted from $25 billion in 1993 to over $100 billion in 2000. Pizza Hut is typical of this new boom of foreign investment. The company plans to expand from 38 restaurants to over 400 in the São Paulo metropolitan area alone. Their logic? Pizza Hut has 438 restaurants in Australia, which has roughly the same population as that of São Paulo. The company plans to double the number of restaurants in Brazil each year for the next several years. Pepsi plans to invest $90 million in Brazil over the next several years. In addition to selling pizzas, it also wants a share of the 1.4 billion gallon soft drink market in the country; the third largest in the world behind the United States and Mexico. Are these firms rushing prematurely into Brazil?

Those that argue that it is time to move back into Brazil point to several key positive changes in the country:

- Rescheduling of the country's $49 billion in commercial debt
- Lowering of tariffs from an average of 78 percent to 12 percent

- Dropping of the list of banned imports
- Lowering of the inflation rate to under 10 percent
- Expansion of foreign investment to nearly $18 billion, offsetting a trade deficit of $10 billion

Those that argue against bold moves into Brazil also point to specific negative factors, including:

- Large and persistent government budget deficits
- Continued high unemployment and crime rates
- High social security and government pension payments
- Lack of training in the labor force

Should foreign firms try to get into Brazil to take advantage of the impending boom, or should they avoid the country and its possible bust? Clearly, Pepsi has made a big bet on the positive future of the country, and time will tell whether that bet pays off.

Sources: Adapted from James Booke, "U.S. Businesses Flocking to Brazilian Ventures," *New York Times*, May 9, 1994, pp. C1 and C4; Caspar W. Weinberger, "Brazil in 1997," *Forbes*, July 28, 1997, p. 37; Caspar W. Weinburger, "Brazil: Weathering the Asian Storm," *Forbes*, May 4, 1998, p. 37.

(GDP is the total economic value produced within the borders of the country), interest rates, unemployment, economic growth rates, and so on are now widely available and should be examined. For example, GM expects 90 percent of its revenue growth over the next 10 years to come from outside the United States. Furthermore, it expects a majority of that international growth to come in Asia. GM has particularly focused on China and is investing $2 to $3 billion over the next several years in the country. Interest in China is driven largely by the high expected economic growth rate in China (8 to 10 percent through 2005 compared to 2 to 3.5 percent in the United States), current low car ownership rates, and rising income levels. Even though the Asian debt crisis of the late 1990s caused some retrenchment on GM's part, the expected population and economic growth of the region still made it the key strategic region for GM.[17]

Sociocultural Forces   In addition to economic data, social forces are also important to an in-depth analysis. Sociocultural forces include demographics such as literacy rates, average age, birth rate, average education level, and average life expectancy. It can also include cultural issues such as role of the family in elder care or the extent to which consumption of goods is encouraged or discouraged. For example, a software firm proposing to establish operations in India would want to know the literacy rates and other measures of education levels for the country.

Otherwise, it might find that the pool of qualified programmers is not large enough to support the firm's growth plans.

Legal and Political Forces   Government policies are important to examine because in most countries, different groups have differing policy preferences. Consumers may want stricter laws covering biodegradable products, while industry groups want less restrictions. Because governments have limited financial resources, different policy areas compete with each other for funding. Education spending may compete with law enforcement for government dollars, or defense spending may compete with environmental spending. Consequently, it is important to examine decisions across areas, as well as within one category, to receive critical insights into the priorities of the government.

The following represent policy areas common to most governments:

- *Foreign/defense policy,* especially any orientation toward military buildup or downsizing
- *Fiscal policy,* especially changes in spending, taxes, or surpluses or deficits
- *Monetary policy,* especially changes in money supply, interest rates, and exchange rates
- *Income policies,* especially those concerning the poor
- *Foreign trade and investment policies,* especially concerning tariff and nontariff barriers, foreign investment and ownership, and capital flows
- *Industrial policy,* especially those concerning growth in specific industries
- *Social policies,* especially concerning labor, education, population control, and religion

Technological Forces   An environmental analysis would be incomplete without an assessment of the technological context. Firms increasingly win or lose as a function of their technological advantages and disadvantages, and it is important to keep in touch with technological advances in other countries. For example, in the multibillion dollar global disposable diaper industry, absorbency technology shifted from "fluff pulp" (a paper-based product) to absorbent chemicals. Procter & Gamble, maker of Pampers, almost lost its dominant position in the U.S. marketplace because it didn't keep up with the new absorbency technology that emerged in Japan.[18]

For many firms, technological advances in telecommunications and data transmission are and will have significant influences on their fortunes. For example, in 1995, virtually none of Cisco's revenue came from purchase orders over the Internet. By 1998 over 50 percent of their nearly $10 billion in revenue came over the Internet. Interestingly, a majority of the products Cisco sells are high-speed switches used in transmitting data over the Internet.

Institutional Forces   The institutional context involves the key organizations in the country. Although the strength and power of institutions can vary from one country to another, they constitute an important consideration in any environmental analysis. Institutions to assess include the government, labor unions, religious institutions, and business institutions. These organizations are also important in analyzing the domestic environment, although they usually function differently in other countries. It takes special effort to adequately understand how they function in the international environment.

Physical Forces   Physical features such as infrastructure (e.g., roads, telecommunications, air links, etc.), arable land, deepwater harbors, mineral resources, forests, and climate can have a dramatic impact on existing and potential operations in a country. For example, China has vast coal resources deep in its interior, but they are not an attractive business opportunity because of the poor rail and road infrastructure in those regions. Clearly, physical conditions in the domestic environment are also important, but most managers have a good understanding of domestic conditions. However, physical conditions in foreign countries can vary widely, can substantially affect business, and, as a consequence, deserve special attention in any analysis of the international environment.

ENVIRONMENTAL SCANNING

Given all the elements of the environment that we have covered, it should be clear that effective managers need to scan the environment constantly to monitor changes. Part of the design of this chapter is to help that process by pointing out the different critical areas to monitor. The external environment is a big place, and trying to monitor everything would simply be overwhelming. Consequently, the first principle of effective environmental scanning is knowing what to scan.

However, even if you know what to scan, you will still need a plan of how to scan. What do you look to to provide you with information on economic, sociocultural, legal and political, and technological forces? Where do you look for information on competitors, new entrants, substitutes, customers, and suppliers? Business publications such as *Fortune, Business Week, The Economist, Financial Times,* and *The Wall Street Journal* are probably good starting points. However, for industry-specific information, you likely will need to turn to more specialized trade journals.

The key to keep in mind concerning public sources of information is that everyone has equal access to them. Consequently, as a manager you have two basic means of gaining advantage. First, you can work at being superior to others in analyzing publicly available information and anticipating how it relates to your job, company, and industry. Second, you can seek advantage by gaining information from nonpublic sources. For example, this may be as simple as asking people you meet in your business (or even personal) travels about developments in any of the areas mentioned in this chapter. For example, an acquaintance may inform you of rising worker unrest in China that could affect your joint venture there long before word shows up in local or, especially, international newspapers. This advance information may help you anticipate and prepare for events rather than just react.

But whether you focus on public or private sources of information, effective scanning has few basic components (see Exhibit 3.7).

- *Define:* The first step involves determining what type of information you should scan for and where and how you plan to acquire the information.
- *Recognize:* Next you must recognize information as relevant.
- *Analyze:* Once you have recognized information, you need to analyze it and determine its implications.
- *Apply:* Finally, the full force of the information lies in its application to your job, company, or industry. Essentially, in this stage you are answering two key questions: What impact will this information have and how can I respond effectively?

EXHIBIT 3.7
Environmental Scanning

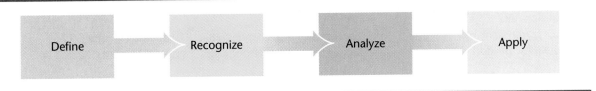

CONCLUDING COMMENTS

Managers sometimes think that the task of external environment analysis is the job of specialized analysts. In large organizations, entire departments may be dedicated to analyzing the economic or political forces in the environment. Although reports from others inside or outside the company can be valuable, managers need to be personally aware of and understand these forces. Without such personal awareness and understanding of critical environmental forces, you might not recognize valuable information even if you had it in your hands. As manager, you must accurately and systematically identify critical factors in the external environment and understand cause-and-effect relationships. Only then will you be able to anticipate, rather than simply react to, management challenges.

Certainly effective analysis of all the various forces within the industry, domestic, and international environments is a big challenge. However, two even larger challenges remain. The first is to begin to see links among the various forces within an environment. For example, it is one thing to do a good analysis of the substitution and customer forces within the industry environment. It is quite another to see that the lack of substitutes and the fragmented nature of customers combine to offer an unprecedented opportunity for growth. Only in drawing the connections can you plan effectively and exploit opportunities for growth.

The second major challenge is seeing the connections between a particular business and its industry, domestic, and international environments. Seeing relationships among them is a quality of a truly gifted manager. If we return to our natural environment analogy, seeing relationships among these environments is like being able to see causes and effects between a plant and its environment. Finding the right conditions to favor growth and survival is as important to business as it is in nature. Organizations thrive or perish according to their fit with their environment.

Meeting the basic challenge of understanding and analyzing individual environmental forces is a significant accomplishment for a manager. Meeting the challenge of seeing relationships among different forces within an environment is exciting. Meeting the challenge of seeing relationships among different environments is a never-ending challenge—one that makes management such an exciting and invigorating profession.

KEY TERMS

country risk analysis 81

demographics 76

entry barriers 72

external environment 69

gross domestic product 77

industry environment 70

macro environment 74

political risk analysis 81

process technological changes 78

product technological changes 78

risk 81

societal values 76

state sovereignty 80

structural changes 75

switching costs 72

REVIEW QUESTIONS

1. Define the external environment and explain why it is important for managers to be able to analyze it.
2. Define country risk analysis. How is it similar to and different from political risk analysis?
3. What are the key features of a country's physical environment?
4. Name three key institutions that should be included in an environmental analysis.
5. What are the key elements of a country's political context?
6. Explain the inverted "U" relationships between political instability and economic development.
7. Why does political instability not equal business risk?
8. Why does a manager need to be aware of societal demographics?
9. What role do society's values play in business?
10. How are structural economic changes different from economic cycles?
11. Why is government spending important to consider when analyzing the legal and political environment?
12. What are the key differences between product and process technological changes and why is an awareness of both critical to an assessment of the technological environment?

DISCUSSION QUESTIONS

1. What factors do you think will increasingly force managers to be proficient at assessing international variables when conducting environmental analyses?
2. Are there industries in which the domestic aspects of the external environment are and will remain the most dominant? Name at least four and explain why you think they apply.
3. What are the most difficult environmental analysis skills to develop? What are some possible means of ensuring that you have these valuable skills?
4. Debate the following statement: Computers and news media have made international environment analysis simpler.
5. Pick a country and go to the library or the Internet to find some information about its resources, government, political and legal systems, and physical infrastructure. What type of business would do well in that country? Why?

CLOSING CASE

Kaufman & Broad Home Corp.: Their Business Is Building

You might not think of home building as big business; after all, the stereotypical house builder is a small, owner-contractor operation. But that stereotype is changing. Consider Los Angeles–based Kaufman & Broad Home Corp., which is the largest home builder in California and the third largest in the United States (the company also has projects in Europe). Kaufman & Broad builds nearly 15,000 homes per year.

How does a company like this manage to survive and grow in an industry whose external environment is subject—quite literally—to the winds of change? For instance, weather conditions, from average rainfall to outright disasters such as hurricanes and tornadoes, affect the rate at which homes can be built in a given region. General economic conditions, such as interest rates, affect whether people can afford new homes. Even demographics affect the demand for new homes. For example, people tend to purchase their largest and most expensive home while they are in their 40s near the peak of their earnings and when they typically have children still at home. The majority of the 80-million-strong baby boom generation were in their 40s during the 1990s and into the early part of the twenty-first century and the housing industry set new records for homes built.

Competitors are another important factor that affects construction firms. Although Kaufman & Broad may be one of the largest builders in the country, the company still faces stiff competition not only from other large builders but also from local builders who are successful because they know their suppliers and their customers personally. Bruce Karatz, CEO of Kaufman & Broad, takes this competition seriously. When the company land-purchase committee reviews a proposed land purchase, one of the important considerations in the purchase is who the local competitors are. "You have to keep score," notes Karatz.

Kaufman & Broad also has to keep an eye on substitutes for single-family homes. Suppose a potential customer expresses the desire to purchase a condominium instead of a Kaufman & Broad single-family home. In a case like this, Kaufman & Broad could direct a potential buyer to one of its lower-priced housing developments, where houses are located on smaller lots, thus providing the customer with two of the advantages of condominium living (lower price and less maintenance), while avoiding the major downside of condominiums (shared walls).

Are there enough customers to support a company like Kaufman & Broad, and if so, who are they? Currently, Kaufman & Broad's home base of California is experiencing a housing boom; in fact, the company keeps running out of homes to sell. This is largely because of low mortgage rates and high consumer confidence in the economy. Low mortgage rates make home buying accessible to more people; high consumer confidence makes people willing to take the chance on buying a home. In addition, California is experiencing another population spurt due to both internal growth and migration. So there are more customers who are available and able to buy homes.

Even if there are enough customers who want to purchase homes, builders like Kaufman & Broad face a unique barrier to entry: Desirable communities are becoming "more and more restrictive in the amount of development that they will permit," explains Bruce Karatz. "As restrictions pile on top of each other, the end result is less new development in the areas where the demand is greatest, and therefore prices tend to go up and out of reach of first-time buyers or even first-time move-up buyers."

Finally, when the domestic economy is booming, so is the building industry. But when recession arrives, many builders do not survive. Kaufman & Broad has already survived the recession of a decade ago; it did so by focusing on building inexpensive housing financed on easy terms through its own mortgage company. How does Karatz view the future macroeconomic environment? "No one knows what is happening on a macroeconomic level. No one really knows what is going to happen six months from now. We cannot be overly consumed with that kind of discussion because it is beyond our control. The issue is to operate our business in the here and now, executing as best we can, day in and day out.... Of course, we're not just a Southern California home builder, so the conditions here may vary from those in other areas of the country or even in France, so that's another factor enabling us to withstand a downturn."

QUESTIONS

1. What are the key environment factors that could dramatically affect the success of Kaufman & Broad?
2. What steps might Kaufman & Broad take to be prepared for another economic downturn?
3. What steps might Kaufman & Broad take to be ready to supply desirable homes for the aging baby boomer population?

Sources: "Kaufman's Shares Soar 16% on Earnings News," *Los Angeles Times,* Wednesday, June 24, 1998, p. D2; "Homeward Bound," *Los Angeles Times,* June 16, 1998, p. D10; Meghan Drueding, "Daring in Denver," *Builder* 21, no. 3 (March 1998), p. 114.

CHAPTER 4

MANAGING WITHIN CULTURAL CONTEXTS*

GE Medical's Sick Patient in France

General Electric (GE), in an effort to increase its global strategic position in medical technology, bought Companie Générale de Radiologie (CGR), a French company. The company was owned by the state and manufactured medical equipment, with a specific emphasis on X-ray machines and CAT scanners. When GE acquired CGR, GE received $800 million in cash from state-controlled Thomson S.A. in return for GE's RCA consumer electronic business. The acquisition of CGR was viewed as a brilliant strategic move, at the time. Combined with GE's strong position in medical imaging technology in the United States, the acquisition of CGR gave GE an immediate and significant position in Europe. GE projected a $25 million profit for the first full year of operations. However, things did not turn out as the strategic planners projected.

---

*Parts of this chapter have been adapted with permission from a chapter written by J. Stewart Black, appearing in *Globalizing People Through International Assignments* (Reading, Mass.: Addison-Wesley, 1999).

One of the first things GE did was to organize a training seminar for the French managers. GE left T-shirts with the slogan "Go for Number One" for each of the participants. Although the French managers wore them, many were not happy about it. One manager stated, "It was like Hitler was back forcing us to wear uniforms. It was humiliating."

Soon after the takeover, GE also sent American specialists to France to fix CGR's financial-control system. Unfortunately, these specialists knew very little about French accounting or financial-reporting requirements. Consequently, they tried to impose a system that was inappropriate for French financial reporting and for the way CGR had traditionally kept records. For example, the two systems differed in what was defined as a cost versus an expense. This cultural conflict (and the working out of an agreeable compromise) took several months and resulted in substantial direct and indirect costs.

GE then tried to coordinate and integrate CGR into its Milwaukee-based medical-equipment unit in several other ways. For example, because CGR racked up a $25 million loss instead of the projected $25 million profit, an American executive from Milwaukee was sent to France to turn the operations around. Several cost-cutting measures, including massive layoffs and the closing of roughly half of the 12 CGR plants, shocked the French workforce. Additionally, the profit-hungry culture of GE continued to clash with the state-run, noncompetitive history and culture of CGR. As a consequence, many valuable managers and engineers left the company.

GE's efforts to integrate CGR into the GE culture through English-language motivational posters, flying GE flags, and other morale boosters were met with considerable resistance by the French employees. One union leader commented, "They came in here bragging, 'We are GE, we're the best and we've got the methods.'" Although GE officials estimated that GE-CGR would produce a profit in the second year, it lost another $25 million.

Despite these initial cultural blunders, today GE Medical Systems is one of the strongest competitors in the United States and globally. In fact, some managers believe that the culture clashes experienced in France made everyone aware of the important role national and organizational cultures play in how people see and react to different events. As a consequence, senior GE Medical Systems managers changed their mental maps to recognize that people do not view the world or management the same everywhere. To facilitate this awareness in others, general cross-cultural training, as well as training specifically in French culture and the business environment, was provided for all Americans transferred to France. With this greater awareness of culture and efforts to understand specific elements of the organizational and national cultures, GE was able to leverage the knowledge and alternative perspectives of managers in the French acquisition into a powerful and globally competitive enterprise.

Source: J. Stewart Black, *Globalizing People Through International Assignments,* (Reading, Mass.: Addison-Wesley, 1999).

As the GE Medical Systems example illustrates, even companies that have strong reputations and many years of experience can run aground on unseen cultural reefs as they navigate in culturally diverse business waters. Yet, awareness and understanding of culture at both the organizational and national levels can foster creativity and innovations—and ultimately enhance team and organizational performance.

As a manager, you need a thorough understanding of culture because it affects people's beliefs and actions. For that reason, we devote an entire chapter to it. You will encounter increasing cultural diversity as a manager, and its strong influence can affect performance in the workplace and ultimately an organization's competitiveness.

MANAGERIAL RELEVANCE OF CULTURE

Culture affects both people and their organizations, so it is important to understand why it is relevant to you as a manager. There are at least three major reasons why you should have a deep understanding of culture:

1. Culture can significantly influence behavior.
2. As a manager, you will increasingly encounter greater cultural diversity in the workplace.
3. Culture can be used to accomplish a variety of managerial objectives.

We briefly examine each of these reasons.

Impact of Culture on Behavior

As a manager you need to understand culture because it can dramatically influence important behaviors. For example, culture can influence how people observe and interpret the business world around them.[1] Even when viewing identical situations, culture can influence whether individuals see those situations as opportunities or threats.[2] Culture can contribute to preexisting ways of interpreting events, evaluating them, and determining a course of action.[3] Identification with the culture can cause individuals to exert extra effort and make sacrifices to support the culture and the people in it.[4] If culture can significantly influence these and other behaviors, which in turn can influence individual, group, or organizational performance, then it is critical for you to understand what culture is, how it is formed, and how it can be changed or leveraged.

Cultural Diversity in the Workplace

Given culture's influence on behavior, the fact that you will face greater cultural diversity in your career than perhaps has ever been encountered before in history justifies time spent understanding it. To get an idea of the greater cultural diversity you will face, simply consider the following statistics:

- More than half the American workforce is currently composed of women, minorities, and immigrants.
- By the year 2000, white males will represent only 15 percent of people entering the workforce.
- Approximately 84 percent of all immigrants to the United States now come from Asian or Latin American countries, not from Europe.
- At current rates of internationalization, by the year 2015, the volume of international business will equal that of domestic business on a worldwide basis.[5]

These and other statistics point out that as a manager you will encounter an increasingly culturally diverse U.S. workforce and a growing likelihood of interacting with individuals from foreign countries and cultures. These cultural differences present both managerial challenges and opportunities—challenges that if ignored can have negative consequences for individuals and their organizations and opportunities that if captured can lead to superior outcomes and organizational competitiveness.

Culture as a Management Tool

Finally, as a manager, you need to thoroughly understand culture because it can help accomplish managerial responsibilities. Once established, culture serves as a constant guide to and influence on behavior. An organization's culture can thus guide what people do and how they do it without managers needing to monitor and direct them constantly. This is particularly important now and with the increasingly complex and geographically dispersed organizations we see today. In many cases, managers may not be present to watch over and direct people. To the extent that culture can guide behavior, it can be a powerful management tool.

THE ESSENCE OF CULTURE

We have already used the word "culture" several times in this chapter. What do you think of when someone uses the term? Many people think culture is something an organization, region, or country has—something you can see, hear, touch, smell, or taste. People who take this view often point to clothing, customs, ceremonies, music, historical landmarks, art, and food as examples of culture. However, these markers are only the most visible, and in many ways the least powerful, aspects of culture.

culture
a learned set of assumptions, values, and behaviors in response to common challenges that has been accepted as successful enough to be passed on to new generations through symbolic means

Definition of Culture

To appreciate the full importance and impact of culture, we need to take a somewhat complex and broad view of it.[6] Although a team of anthropologists identified over 160 different definitions of culture,[7] we define it as follows: **Culture** is a learned set of assumptions, values, and behaviors that has been accepted as successful enough to be passed on to new generations. This definition gives us a thorough picture of what culture is and how it forms. As the definition suggests, a culture begins when a group of people face a set of challenges. In an organization, the culture might begin to form when the early members face the initial challenges of starting the organization—securing funding, creating products, distributing products to customers, and so on. The assumptions, values, and behaviors that are successful get taught to newcomers. In an organization, these newcomers are new hires. In a national culture, newcomers are essentially children born to the group. So for the newcomers, the culture is learned, not inherited. Culture is taught to newcomers primarily through symbols and communication, such as stories, speeches, discussions, manuals, novels, poems, art, and so on. Over time, specific assumptions, values, and behaviors come to be shared among the members of the group. However, because circumstances change, what are considered successful responses can also evolve and change. As a consequence, culture is adaptive. Although we will address specific differences of organizational culture as opposed to national culture at the end of this chapter, the essence of culture is the same. So, organizational culture simply means the assumptions, values, and behaviors that have worked well enough in the organization to be taught to newcomers.

LEVELS OF CULTURE

artifacts

physical discoveries that represent a culture and its values, such as buildings, pottery, clothing, tools, food, and art

values

enduring beliefs that specific conduct or end states of existence are personally and socially preferred to others

assumptions

the beliefs about fundamental aspects of life

Although we typically think of culture as one entity, it consists of three distinct but related levels.[8] The structure of these elements is like a tree (see Exhibit 4.1). Some elements are visible. These are often termed **artifacts**, or visible manifestations of a culture such as its art, clothing, food, architecture, and customs. The base of the culture, like the trunk of a tree, is its values. **Values** are essentially the enduring beliefs that specific conduct or end states are personally or socially preferred to others. However, what holds the tree up is invisible. Most of the components of culture lie below the surface and are hard to see unless you make an effort to uncover them. These are the **assumptions** of the culture, or the beliefs about fundamental aspects of life.

Cultural Assumptions

Assumptions are like the soil in which a tree grows. The nature of the soil determines many characteristics of the tree. Still, like the natural world, different varieties of trees can grow in the same soil. For example, pine trees can grow in the same soil as an aspen. Groups with similar underlying cultural assumptions can also share somewhat different values and exhibit different behaviors. But this does not mean a given tree can grow anywhere. An aspen won't grow in the sand of a beach, and a palm tree won't grow in the soil of a high mountain. Certain cultural values and behaviors are only possible with certain underlying cultural assumptions. One of the key implications for you as a manager is that if you understand the fundamental cultural assumptions of a group, you can then begin to understand the values and behaviors of the group.

Consequently, although assumptions may seem the most abstract dimension of culture, they are in fact one of the most practical. Remember that values and behaviors grow out of assumptions. If you can understand the underlying assumptions, you can begin to understand the types of values and behaviors they support.

EXHIBIT 4.1

Levels of Culture

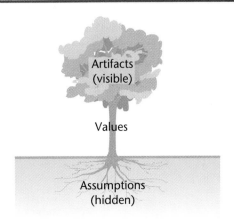

Without an understanding of assumptions, you might make a number of mistakes in trying to understand, change, or even create a new culture. For example, your might mistakenly try to change the existing culture in ways that are not possible because they conflict with the underlying assumptions. For example, your attempt to reward individual performance in Vietnam might yield poor results because of the underlying assumptions concerning groups and fitting in. Without understanding cultural assumptions, you might not recognize that "to change the fruits, you need to change the roots." But changing the fundamental assumptions of a culture is not easy. Generally, they are taken for granted and have been reinforced over many years.

Most scholars agree that there is a universal category of assumptions represented in all groups. Although different groups can hold some different assumptions, they share six basic assumptions.[9] Exhibit 4.2 summarizes these assumptions and provides examples of the specific forms they might take, as well as their management implications.

Humanity's Relationship to the Environment   The first set of assumptions concerns those made about the relationship of humanity to nature. For example, in some cultures (the United States is one example), the assumption is that humans should dominate nature and use it for the wealth and benefit of mankind. In other cultures, the assumption is that humans and nature should coexist harmoniously. The implications of these differing assumptions can be quite significant. In the United States the dominance of men over nature can be see in structures and industry: damming rivers for electricity, mining iron to make steel for automobiles, or logging trees to make homes. However, the implications of this belief may reach beyond these basic activities to strategic planning or management practices in business as well. Consider how most U.S. firms view their business environment and how they strategically approach it. Is the business environment viewed as something that people must accept and with which they must try to harmonize? Or is it viewed as something that must be mastered and dominated if possible? Americans' assumption that the business environment is something to dominate is evident in antitrust laws. Antitrust laws and regulations in the United States are not in place because Americans think they must be submissive to the environment but simply to

EXHIBIT 4.2

Basic Assumptions and Their Management Implications

Managerial Implications	Specific Assumptions		Specific Assumptions	Managerial Implications
Firms should seek positions that allow them to coexist with others.	People must coexist harmoniously with the environment.	Humans and the Environment	People are meant to dominate the environment.	Strategic plans should be developed to enable the firm to dominate its industry.
Provide people with opportunities and responsibilities and encourage their development.	Work is as natural as play for people.	Human Nature	People are generally lazy.	Implement systems for monitoring behavior and establish clear punishment for undesired behavior.
Cooperation with and contributions to the group should be evaluated and rewarded.	People exist because of others and owe an obligation to them.	Human Relationships	Individuals have certain rights and freedoms.	Individual performance should be measured and rewarded.
Planning the future only gets in the way of enjoying the present.	People should react to and enjoy whatever the present provides.	Human Activity	People create their own destinies and must plan for the future.	People who fail to plan should plan to fail.
Opinion leaders are how you influence people and decisions.	Truth is what is socially accepted.	Truth and Reality	Truth objectively exists.	Facts and statistics are how you convince and influence people.
Taking advantage of the moment is valued. Arriving late for appointments is not a character flaw.	Time is like a lake, what you don't use today will be there tomorrow.	Time	Time is like a river, what you don't use wisely today is gone forever.	Time management is a critical skill. Appointments are made well in advance and punctuality is valued.

counteract marketplace domination by a single firm. For example, the recent difficulties Microsoft has had with the U.S. Justice Department grew out of Microsoft's determination to dominate its environment. Groups that assume humans must subjugate themselves to nature often are characterized by strong notions of fate. As a consequence, the idea of having a strategic planning department is ridiculous because it is not possible for humans to dominate something as powerful as the environment or God's will.

Human Nature   Different groups also make different assumptions about the nature of people. Some cultures assume people are fundamentally good, while others assume they are inherently evil. You can see the direct influence of this category of assumptions in different organizations. Douglas McGregor captured this

Theory X managers
managers who assume that the average human being has an inherent dislike for work and will avoid it if he or she can

Theory Y managers
managers who assume that work is as natural as play or rest

notion well in his classic book, *The Human Side of Enterprise*.[10] McGregor argued that every manager acted on a theory, or set of assumptions, about people. **Theory X managers** assume that the average human being has an inherent dislike for work and will avoid it if he or she can. Managers accepting this view of people believe that they must be coerced, controlled, directed, and threatened with punishment to get them to strive toward the achievement of organizational objectives. If enough managers in an organization collectively share these assumptions, the organization will have monitoring systems and detailed manuals on exactly what workers' jobs are and exactly how they are to do them. On the other hand, **Theory Y managers** assume that work is as natural as play or rest. Consequently, managers accepting this view of people believe that employees exercise self-direction and self-control to accomplish objectives to which they are committed. Commitment to objectives is a function of the rewards associated with their achievement. Organizations in which Theory Y is the dominant assumption would be more likely to involve workers in decision making or even allow them some autonomy and self-direction in their jobs. For example, Hewlett-Packard (H-P) is known as an organization with a culture based on more Theory Y assumptions about human nature.

Human Relationships   Assumptions about human relationships really deal with a variety of questions:

* What is the right way for people to deal with each other?
* How much power and authority should one person have over another?
* How much should someone be concerned with him- or herself versus others?

power distance
the extent to which people accept power and authority differences among people

In addressing these and other related questions, Geert Hofstede studied over 100,000 employees within a single firm across 40 different countries.[11] He found four dimensions along which individuals in these countries differed. One of those four dimensions was the construct of power distance. **Power distance** is the extent to which people accept power and authority differences among people. Power distance is *not* a measure of the extent to which there are power and status differences in a group. Most organizations and most societies have richer and poorer, more and less powerful members. Power distance is *not* the existence or nonexistence of status and power differentials in a society but the extent to which any differences are *accepted*. In his study, people from the Philippines, Venezuela, and Mexico had the highest levels of acceptance of power differences. In contrast, Austria, Israel, and Denmark had the lowest levels of acceptance.

Even though Americans tend to be at the low end of the power distance continuum, the extent to which this assumption exists can vary across organizations. For example, Southwest Airlines would be at the lower end of the power distance continuum while American Airlines would be at the higher end. The egalitarian attitude in Southwest Airlines seems to stem from its founder and CEO, Herb Kelleher (or "Uncle Herb," as he is known to all Southwest employees). At Southwest, status differentials such as big private offices for upper management, reserved parking places for senior managers, and so on do not exist. These and other symbols of status are much more common and accepted within American Airlines.

individualism
the extent to which people base their identities on themselves and are expected to take care of only themselves and their immediate families

A second dimension in Hofstede's study was the extent to which cultures valued individualism or collectivism. **Individualism** can be thought of as the extent to which people base their identity on themselves and are expected to take care of themselves and their immediate family. Hofstede's study found that people from the United States, Australia, and Great Britain had the highest individual orientations. Individuals from these countries tended to have "I" consciousness and exhibited higher emotional independence from organizations or institutions. They tended to emphasize and reward individual achievement and value individual decisions. **Collectivism** can be thought of as the extent to which identity is a function of the groups to which individuals belong (e.g., families, firm members, community members, etc.) and the extent to which group members are expected to look after each other. People from Venezuela, Colombia, and Pakistan had the highest collective orientations. People from these countries tended the have "We" consciousness and exhibited emotional dependence on organizations or institutions to which they belonged. They tended to emphasize group membership and value collective, group decisions.

collectivism
the extent to which identity is a function of the groups to which individuals belong and to which members are expected to look after each other

Once again, even within a society, the extent to which people within organizations share the assumption that individuals matter more than the group or that the group matters more than the individual can vary. For example, Goldman Sachs has stronger individualistic assumptions than Motorola. In Goldman Sachs, rewards are based primarily on individual performance, while in Motorola rewards are based on individual, group, and overall organization performance.

Human Activity Assumptions about human activity concern issues of what is right for people to do and whether they should be active, passive, or fatalistic in these activities. In the United States people brag about working 80 hours a week, about having no time for vacations or to watch TV, and about doing several things at the same time on their computers. They believe in phrases such as "people who fail to plan should plan to fail" and "plan the work and work the plan." In other cultures, such emphasis on work is not valued and may even be seen as a waste of time and energy. Other cultures believe that such preoccupation with planning only gets in the way of enjoying the present.

In sharp contrast to the United States, most Europeans receive a minimum of four weeks vacation time for their jobs. The American culture places such a strong emphasis on the importance of work that many Americans do not even use all of their allocated time off.

masculine societies

those in which the activities of society are directed toward success, money, and possessions

feminine societies

those that emphasize caring for others and enhancing the quality of life

Hofstede's work also addressed this issue. He argued that there were masculine and feminine societies. **Masculine societies** value activities focused on success, money, and possessions. **Feminine societies** value activities focused on caring for others and enhancing the quality of life.

Truth and Reality   Different groups also form differing assumptions about the nature of reality and truth and how they are verified or established. The famous CEO of ITT, Harold Geneen, always talked about "the unshakable facts," those that would hold up even after intense scrutiny. Truth was assumed to exist and could be discovered through rigorous examination. In other groups, reality is much more subjective and dependent on what people believe it to be. Consequently, opinion leaders or persuasive stories rather than unshakable facts are used to influence people and business decisions.

The famous analogy of the three baseball umpires may serve to illustrate the basic assumptions that people can make relative to reality and truth. The first umpire stated, "There are balls and there are strikes, and I call them as they are." The second umpire stated, "There are balls and there are strikes, and I call them as I see them." The third umpire stated, "There ain't nothing till I call it." Clearly, the nature of the game can change dramatically depending on which umpire is calling the pitch. Have you been in an organization in which the assumption of the first umpire dominated the group? Even if you haven't, you can probably imagine such an organization. In fact, ITT under Mr. Geneen had a "first umpire" type of culture.

uncertainty avoidance

the extent to which people feel threatened by ambiguous situations and create beliefs and institutions to try to avoid uncertainty

Hofstede found that cultures differed in the extent to which they need things to be clear or ambiguous. He labeled this **uncertainty avoidance**. Societies high in uncertainty avoidance can be thought of as most comfortable with a first umpire type of culture and least comfortable with a third umpire type of culture. They create structures and institutions to reduce uncertainty. Societies low in uncertainty avoidance can be thought of as most comfortable with a second or third umpire type of culture and somewhat disliking of a first umpire type culture.

Time   Different groups also form differing assumptions about the nature of time. Is time viewed as a river or a lake? Those that view time as a river generally hold linear assumptions about time. Like a river, time moves on in a linear fashion. What you do not take advantage of today will be gone tomorrow. This assumption creates a great emphasis on time management, being punctual for appointments, keeping appointment books, and so on. The phenomenal success of Franklin Quest (now Franklin Covey), a producer of relatively expensive day planners, is testimony to this orientation in the United States. Franklin has grown at a rate several times that of the general economy for the last decade. Recently, it has moved with great success into Japan, another culture with linear assumptions about time. Those that view time as a lake generally hold nonlinear assumptions about time. Like a lake, what you do not dip from the lake today will still be there for you to use tomorrow. This has nearly the opposite effect on management behaviors: being late for an appointment is not seen as a character flaw and setting specific day, hour, and minute schedules is seen as unnecessary.

short-term or long-term orientation

extent to which societies view time as something that, once passed, can never be recouped or as something that is endless

Hofstede's work also addressed this fundamental assumption. Hofstede found that societies could be segmented based on whether they had a **short-term or long-term orientation**. Short-term oriented societies tend to view time as a river and focus on immediate results and maximizing time management. Long-term

EXHIBIT 4.3

Questions to Get at Cultural Assumptions

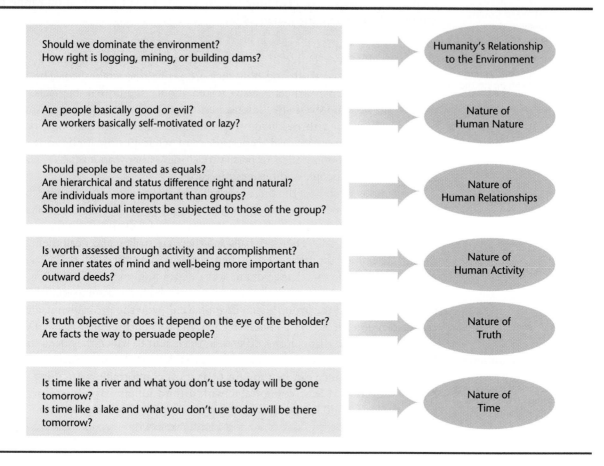

oriented societies tend to view time as a lake and focus on developing relationships, not expecting immediate results or returns on current efforts.

All groups confront issues represented by these six categories of cultural assumptions. Different organizations can hold differing assumptions. Different societies can hold different assumptions. Whether you are trying to understand an organization or a country, you must look at the fundamental assumptions first. In general, this involves asking a general set of questions. Exhibit 4.3 provides illustrative questions for each of the six categories of cultural assumptions. Given that all groups have formed assumptions relative to these six categories, you could use the questions to begin to understand an organization or national culture new to you.

Cultural Values

Values are typically defined as enduring beliefs that specific conduct or end states of existence are personally and socially preferred to others.[12] Values are like the trunk of a tree, harder to see from far away but critical to the nourishment and stature of the tree. Fundamentally, values guide behavior because they define what is good or ought to be and what is bad and ought not to be.

EXHIBIT 4.4 Classification of Values	*Theoretical people* value the discovery of truth. They are empirical, critical, and rational, aiming to order and systematize their knowledge.
	Economic people value what is useful. They are interested in practical affairs, especially those of business, judging things by their usefulness.
	Aesthetic people value beauty and harmony. They are concerned with grade and symmetry, finding fulfillment in artistic experiences.
	Social people value altruistic and philanthropic love. They are kind, sympathetic, and unselfish, valuing other people as ends in themselves.
	Religious people value unity. They seek communication with the cosmos, mystically relating to its wholeness.

Source: G. W. Allport, P. E. Vernon, and Q. Lindzey, *A Study of Values* (Boston: Houghton Mifflin, 1966).

We can view managerial values as enduring beliefs about specific ways of managing and conducting business that have been deemed successful enough to be passed on. Although some comprehensive frameworks have been proposed for values in general (see Exhibit 4.4 for an early classic), no widely accepted framework for organizing managerial beliefs and values exist.

Because values address what ought or ought not to be, differences in values often lead to clashes and negative judgments about others. For example, American programmers at Microsoft often play "nerf basketball" while trying to solve difficult problems, believing that these types of activities contribute to creative problem solving. In contrast, nerf basketball is not a common sight in the halls of General Motors' programming offices in Detroit. Because of their differing values, Microsoft's programmers in Washington might look on GM's programmers in Michigan as being boring, dull, and uncreative. GM programmers might look on Microsoft's programmers as childish or unprofessional.

This tendency to judge different values negatively can be problematic for an organization with operations in multiple countries. For example, programmers in Germany generally do not play nerf basketball to help solve problems. What happens when programmers from Microsoft's German operations have to work on a project with Microsoft's Redmond, Washington, programmers? It could be a serious barrier to productivity if the two sets of Microsoft programmers do not understand each other.

Because values define what is good or bad, right or wrong, they not only guide behavior but are the source of actions that you can see. In part, this is why archeologists and anthropologists seek out artifacts; they hope to find ones that will help them deduce the values of people who are no longer around to observe. In organizations, this is also why artifacts, such as stories, can provide valuable insights into the organization's culture. For example, what insights into the UPS culture can you glean from the following well-known story?

Just before Christmas, a railroad official called a regional UPS manager to inform them that a flatcar carrying two UPS trailers had unfortunately been left on a siding in the middle of Illinois. Most of the packages in these two cars were Christmas presents. Without permission or authorization, the regional manager paid for a high-speed diesel locomotive to fetch the stranded flatcar and

EXHIBIT 4.5

Culture and Managerial Behaviors

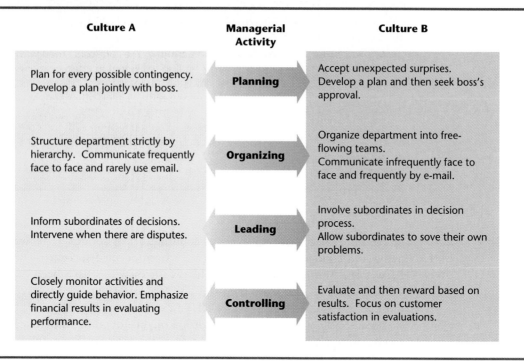

Culture A	Managerial Activity	Culture B
Plan for every possible contingency. Develop a plan jointly with boss.	Planning	Accept unexpected surprises. Develop a plan and then seek boss's approval.
Structure department strictly by hierarchy. Communicate frequently face to face and rarely use email.	Organizing	Organize department into free-flowing teams. Communicate infrequently face to face and frequently by e-mail.
Inform subordinates of decisions. Intervene when there are disputes.	Leading	Involve subordinates in decision process. Allow subordinates to sove their own problems.
Closely monitor activities and directly guide behavior. Emphasize financial results in evaluating performance.	Controlling	Evaluate and then reward based on results. Focus on customer satisfaction in evaluations.

haul it to Chicago. The manager then diverted two of UPS's Boeing 727 jets to Chicago to pick up the packages and fly them to their destinations in Florida and Louisiana in time for Christmas. Headquarters wasn't even informed of these extraordinary expenses until weeks after the incident. Once informed, top management applauded the regional manager's decision.[13]

What does this story tell you about UPS's values concerning customer service? Managerial autonomy? Decision making? Because values guide behavior, they are critical for any manager to understand. Not recognizing that values could be different even among employees in the same organization can often lead to unproductive clashes among employees. Later in the chapter, we will talk about sources of cultural diversity within the United States and ways in which you can not only manage employees with diverse values but can use their strengths for greater productivity.

Cultural Artifacts and Behaviors

The visible portions of culture are referred to as artifacts and behaviors. In general, the term *artifact* is most often associated with physical discoveries that represent a culture and its values, such as buildings, pottery, clothing, tools, food, and art. Archeologists find artifacts when they dig in the jungles and deserts of the world looking for lost civilizations. In modern organizations, important artifacts include such things as office arrangements (individual offices for all versus open offices with no walls), parking arrangements (reserved spaces for some versus open spaces for all), or clothing. Consider the "uniforms" that managers wear at IBM in New York and Silicon Graphics in California. When you walk in the door at Silicon

Graphics, you are more likely to see a manager in Levi's and a polo shirt than one in a suit and tie. Although no official dress code policy existed that required all male managers at IBM to wear a white shirt and tie, until recently, if you walked into an IBM office, all the men would be wearing a white shirt and tie. A senior IBM executive once commented that several years ago, he decided that since there was no policy, he would go to work with a different color shirt (not white) and tie. Less than an hour after arriving, he went home to change because he "felt naked without a white shirt on, even though no one said anything."[14]

Artifacts and behaviors are closely linked. For example, while the clothing worn in an organization or even in a country might be a cultural artifact, wearing a certain style of clothing is a behavior. But culture can influence behaviors well beyond what to wear. Culture can influence key managerial behaviors, as Exhibit 4.5 illustrates.

ORGANIZATIONAL DIVERSITY

As a manager, you will encounter greater organizational diversity in the future. As we mentioned in the beginning of the chapter, diversity comes from two primary sources: (1) greater diversity in the cultures of employees and (2) increased international activity of organizations.

Even if you manage in an organization whose primary focus is domestic, supervisors, peers, and subordinates will not be exactly like you. Differences in age, race, ethnicity, gender, physical abilities, and sexual orientation, as well as work background, income, marital status, military experience, religious beliefs, geographic location, parental status, and education, can all influence the assumptions, values, and behaviors of people.[15] Within an organization, such diversity can enhance competitiveness or, if ignored or unmanaged, can lower productivity (see Exhibit 4.6). As illustrated in Exhibit 4.6, culturally homogeneous groups in general produce a normal distribution; that is, most groups with culturally similar members produce average results, with a few groups doing quite well and a small minority doing quite poorly. In contrast, most culturally diverse groups either produce significantly worse or superior results with very few culturally diverse groups

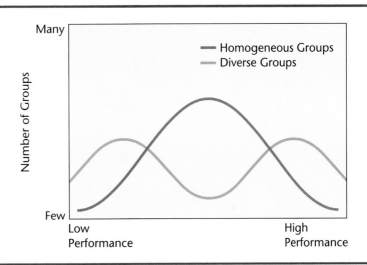

EXHIBIT 4.6

Effects of Cultural Diversity on Productivity

EXHIBIT 4.7	
Managing Cultural Diversity for Competitive Advantage	
1. Cost	As organizations become more diverse, the cost of a poor job in integrating workers will increase.
2. Resource Acquisition	Companies with the best reputations for managing diversity will win the competition for the best personnel. As the labor pool shrinks and becomes more diverse, this edge will become increasingly important.
3. Marketing	For multinational organizations, the insight and cultural sensitivity that members with roots in other cultures bring should improve marketing efforts.
4. Creativity	Diversity of perspectives and less emphasis on conformity to norms of the past should improve creativity.
5. Problem Solving	Cultural diversity in decision and problem solving groups potentially produces better decisions through consideration of a wider range of and more thorough critical analysis of issues.
6. System Flexibility	Cultural diversity enables the system to be less determinant, less standardized, and therefore more fluid, which will create more flexibility to react to environmental changes.

Source: T. H. Cox and S. Blake, "Managing Cultural Diversity: Implications for Organizational Competitiveness," *Academy of Management Executive* 5 no. 3 (1991), p. 23.

producing results in the middle.[16] The culturally diverse teams that did better than culturally similar teams leveraged diverse perspectives, ideas, and innovations into superior performance. The culturally diverse teams that did worse than culturally similar teams were unable to manage the differences among members effectively. This was in part because members of these groups viewed the differences as liabilities rather than as assets. Exhibit 4.7 provides a summary of the general arguments for viewing cultural diversity as an asset rather than a liability.

STRONG AND WEAK CULTURES

Culture is not simply the total collection of a group of people's assumptions, values, or artifacts. This is because not all of the assumptions, values, or behaviors are equally influential nor are they equally shared among members of a group. In other words, their strength varies.

To help in understanding this aspect of culture, think of it in terms of mental road maps and traffic signals. The road map, or culture, tells you what the important and valued goals are and what highways or backroads can get you there. However, just as the severity of consequences for assorted traffic violations vary, so too do the consequences for breaching accepted cultural beliefs. A helpful way of thinking about **strong versus weak cultural values** is to conceptualize the cultural rules along two dimensions: (1) the extent to which they are widely shared among group members and (2) the extent to which they are deeply held. This conceptualization is illustrated in Exhibit 4.8.

The assumptions, values, or rules of the culture that are widely shared and deeply held are generally those that are accompanied by substantial rewards or punishments. For example, in UPS the value of customer service appears to be

strong versus weak cultural values
the conceptualization of cultural rules along two dimensions: (1) the extent to which they are widely shared among group members and (2) the extent to which they are deeply held

Matrix of Cultural Strength

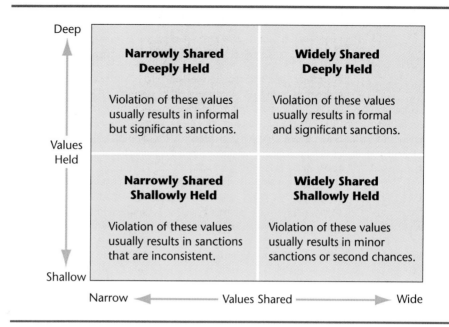

widely shared and deeply held. Employees who take steps to satisfy customers even though their actions are not specifically prescribed in a company manual, such as the UPS regional manager who ordered services of two Boeing 727s, are rewarded and recognized. These rewards and recognition both demonstrate the strength of customer satisfaction as a value in the organization's culture and further strengthen that value. Consider how the strong customer service culture at Nordstrom has affected employee behavior (see the Managerial Challenge box on p. 106).

What about the case in which the value is deeply held but not widely shared? This is perhaps the best definition of a **subculture**. Organizationwide cultures may not develop because the needed conditions, such as consistent reinforcement or time, are not present. Consequently, subcultures may be as common, or in some cases more common, than an overall corporate culture. Because the subculture by definition does not have overall organization legitimacy, violations of the subculture's norms usually carry informal rewards and punishments. For example, in the United States, burping after a meal is considered by some to be a serious violation of proper behavior, but this view is not held strongly by all. Consequently, you are unlikely to be put in jail for burping. However, you might be cut out of particular social circles if you violate that rule. In other cultures, you may offend a host by *not* burping after a meal because it indicates that you were not satisfied with the meal.

In the case of widely shared but not deeply held rules, violations of the rules often carry uniform but rather mild punishments. In many cases, infrequent violation of these rules may carry no punishment at all. For example, not interrupting people when they are talking to you is a generally accepted rule of conduct in the United States. However, if one occasionally interrupts, it is unlikely that this behavior will be accompanied by any serious punishment.

The importance of conceptualizing cultural values in terms of their strengths is that you then recognize that not all aspects of a culture are created equal. As we

subculture

a subgroup within a larger group that cohesively holds values some of which are noticeably different from the larger group

MANAGERIAL CHALLENGE

CULTURE AND MOTIVATION AT NORDSTROM

Few retailers have a stronger customer-service reputation than Nordstrom. Its sales employees (or "Nordies," as they call themselves) are famous for extraordinary efforts to satisfy customers. The most famous story of customer service involves an elderly widow who came to Nordstrom to return tires her husband had bought not long before he died. Nordstrom does not sell tires. Still, the clerk took the tires and gave the woman a full refund. The clerk then had to take the tires to the right store across town to obtain a refund. It is not uncommon for Nordies to drive to another Nordstrom store to retrieve an out-of-stock item for a customer, to drive to a customer's home to make a delivery, to take back merchandise bought at a competitor's store, to call customers to inform them of new merchandise or sales, to write personal thank-you notes for purchases, or to gather items from different parts of the store to assemble a complete outfit. This customer-service culture pays dividends not only to the customer, but to the sales clerks as well. The average Nordstrom sales clerk earns approximately $30,000 a year, or about twice the industry average. Top clerks earn over $90,000 a year!

This organization culture of customer service is reinforced through an incentive system. Nordies are paid a commission of between 6.75 percent and 10 percent on net sales if they exceed the "sales per hour" quota. The sales per hour ratio is simply the net sales an employee makes divided by the number of hours for which the employee is clocked in.

This places a premium on repeat customers. First-time customers require significant time to discover what they like and don't like, what their price ranges are, and what types of clothes and accessories they need. Sales clerks already know this about repeat customers. Consequently, Nordies can serve repeat customers much more efficiently. It is not uncommon for regular customers to insist on working with only a certain sales clerk.

This organization culture contributed to sales per square foot that were twice the industry average, and to net sales that have gone from $400 million to $4.5 billion over the last 15 years!

Source: Robert Specter, "The Nordstrom Way," accessed at www.training-university.com/magazine/may_june97/nordstrom.html, November 18, 1998.

---

will explore shortly, even when we boil culture down to its most fundamental elements, the number of specific assumptions, values, beliefs, rules, behaviors, and customs is nearly infinite. Consequently, trying to learn about all aspects of a new corporate or country culture can be overwhelming. The simplified matrix presented in Exhibit 4.8 provides some mental economy in trying to understand a new culture. This is likely to be of particular relevance to you as you enter a new organization after graduation.

First and foremost, because rewards and punishments are greatest for those aspects of culture that are widely shared and deeply held, these values and rules are worth learning early. While true mastery of a culture may require understanding all aspects of the culture, focusing first on the widely shared and deeply held values can facilitate early learning and adjustment.

To the extent a specific behavior is widely shared, deeply held, and directly related to one or more of the six fundamental assumptions, the behavior will be difficult to change. It might be called a **core value**. Newcomers to an organization should place a premium on making sure that the organization's core values match theirs. You are unlikely to be very happy in an organization with core values that clash with yours. In an international context, a business may have to modify its home office operations, management systems, products, and policies that conflict with those of a foreign country if it is to be successful. For example, in the United States, most people strongly believe that rewards should be tied to individual behavior and that they should not be distributed equally among members of a

core value

a value that is widely shared and deeply held, and difficult to change within a group

group regardless of individual performance. This belief is supported by deep-rooted assumptions concerning individualism. Firms based in other countries that set up operations in the United States and attempt to implement egalitarian reward systems are likely to find limited success.

CREATING AND CHANGING ORGANIZATION CULTURE

Since organization culture can be a mechanism for guiding employee behavior, it is as important as the company's compensation or performance evaluation systems. In fact, to create and reinforce a particular set of values or corporate culture, alignment between the desired values and other systems in the organization should exist.

Today's organizations face business environments that are more complicated and more dynamic than perhaps at any other point in history. If an organization tried to create specific policies for all possible situations in such a dynamic environment, the resulting manual would be several phone books thick, and consequently of little practical use. Furthermore, by the time it was printed and distributed, the environment probably would have changed enough to make it obsolete. If, on the other hand, employees could be given a set of assumptions and values to use in assessing situations and determining appropriate actions, then the organization could distribute a simple and short booklet on the company's values and let that guide behavior. Because of this, organizational culture, which many managers originally thought was a "fluffy" topic, is increasingly being seen as a strategic issue that can have a significant impact on the firm's bottom line.

But what can managers do to create effective cultures or to change cultures that are ineffective to match the environment? There are at least five critical strategies to effectively manage organizational culture (see Exhibit 4.9). In fact, you can think of them as spokes on a wheel. When all five are in place, the wheel of organization culture is much easier to push where you want it to go.

Selection

One way to create or change a culture is to select individuals whose assumptions, values, and behaviors already match those that you desire. Disney uses this mechanism with great success in creating a culture of "guest" service in its theme parks. In fact, former president of EuroDisney, Steve Burke, attributes some of that park's problems (now called Disneyland Paris) to poor selection practices and hiring individuals whose attitudes toward friendly customer service were not compatible with Disney's culture. This was also one of the first things Mr. Burke changed upon his arrival in France.[17]

Socialization

Even if selection is perfect, congruent cultural values can be introduced and reinforced in new hires through socialization. These efforts might include early orientation, training, and arranged interactions with experienced organizational members on a group or individual level. But managers should keep in mind that individuals are not just blank sheets upon which the organization can write whatever cultural scripts it desires. Individuals actively seek out information and try to learn the organization's culture.[18] Consequently, managers should try to facilitate

EXHIBIT 4.9

Strategies to Manage
Organizational Culture

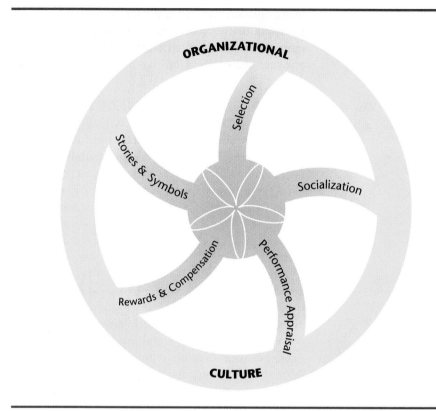

these efforts and monitor them to ensure individuals are truly coming to a correct understanding of the organization's culture.

Performance Appraisal

Few things signal more clearly to newcomers in an organization what the organization values than what it measures and evaluates. For example, it would do Nordstrom little good to claim that the organization values customer service but then evaluate employees primarily on punctuality. Nordstrom uses "customer praise letters" as well as customer complaints as part of employee evaluation to reinforce its customer service culture.

Rewards and Compensation

Rewards and compensation may be among the most powerful means of signaling what the organization values and reinforcing desired behaviors in newcomers. If we return to the Nordstrom example, it would do the company little good talk about customer service as a cultural value and then base bonuses on stockroom inventory control. To reinforce the customer-service value, Nordstrom bases rewards on sales per hour. The best way to achieve high sales per hour is to work with repeat customers who purchase most of their clothes from you rather than from competing stores. The best way to get repeat customers and have them make most of their clothing purchases with you is to serve them better than anyone else. As a manager, it is important to remember that although you may not be able to change the formal reward and compensation system of the organization, you directly control many informal rewards that can significantly affect subordinates (which will be discussed in more detail in Chapter 13 on motivation). For example, what you praise and recognize people for can significantly influence their values and behaviors.

Stories and Symbols

Organizational culture is also created and reinforced through a variety of symbols. For example, stories can be a powerful means of communicating company values. Earlier, we cited the famous UPS story. Basically, organizational stories tell employees what to do or not to do. Symbols such as physical layout can also communicate and reinforce specific values of the corporate culture. For example, suppose you were hired by company X and on your first day at work, as you pulled into the parking lot, you noticed that the first two rows of parking spaces were all reserved and that the spaces closest to the front door were reserved for the most senior executives in the company. What values would you begin to suspect the company held relative to hierarchy or participative decision making? You obviously would want more information before drawing final conclusions, but seemingly small symbols can communicate and reinforce an organization's culture. **Rituals** play a key role in the symbolic communication of an organization's culture. For example, in Japan most major corporations hold a common ritual when their newly hired college graduates join the company. Along with their parents, these new hires gather at a large assembly hall. A representative of the new hires gives a speech in which he pledges loyalty to the company on behalf of the new hires. A representative of all the parents then gives a speech in which he or she commends their children into the company's hands. A senior executive of the company then gives a speech in which he vows on behalf of the company to take care of and continue to nurture these new hires. More effectively than any memo or policy statement, this ritual reinforces the core value of belonging and loyalty.

rituals
ceremonial acts associated with particular events that are consistently repeated when those events occur

INTERNATIONAL CONTEXTS AND CULTURES

All of the basics of culture that we have covered thus far apply to cultures at a national or local level. However, just as it is sometimes difficult to generalize about an organizationwide corporate culture, so too it is difficult to generalize about national cultures. Often, important subcultures exist within the boundaries of a nation. Interestingly, Hofstede's study, which has been criticized because it consisted of subjects from within one company, adds important insights precisely because all the subjects are members of the same organization. The organization was IBM, which in general is thought to have a rather strong corporate culture. This strong corporate culture might have dampened the differences across national cultures. Yet, in general, Hofstede found greater differences in cultural values between nationalities than within nationalities.

Perhaps one of the most useful concepts for examining and understanding different countries' cultures is cultural context.[19] **Cultural context** is the degree to which a situation influences behavior or perception of appropriateness. In high-context cultures, people pay close attention to the situation and its various elements. Key contextual variables are used to determine appropriate and inappropriate behavior. In low-context cultures, contextual variables have much less

cultural context
the degree to which a situation influences behavior or perception of appropriateness

Doing business abroad requires an understanding of cultural differences such as gestures and public manners, proper business attire, and even business card etiquette. In Japan, for instance, there is an appropriate way to accept business cards: the card must be taken in both hands and studied.

impact on the determination of appropriate behaviors. In other words, in low-context cultures, the situation may or may not make a difference in what is considered appropriate behavior, but in high-context cultures, the context makes all the difference. For example, in Japan there are five different words for the pronoun "you." The context determines what form of the pronoun "you" would be appropriate in addressing different people. If you are talking to a customer holding a significantly higher title than yours, who works in a large company such as Matsushita, and is several years older, you would be expected to use the term *"otaku"* when addressing the customer. If you were talking to a subordinate, several years younger, *"kimi"* would be the appropriate pronoun. Exhibit 4.10 provides a list of some low- and high-context cultures.

Context can influence a number of important managerial behaviors, including communication, negotiation, decision making, and leadership. While we will examine many of these implications in greater detail in subsequent chapters, the Managerial Challenge box helps illustrate the concept and some of its implications.

EXHIBIT 4.10

Low- and High-Context Cultures

Low-Context Cultures	High-Context Cultures
American	Vietnamese
Canadian	Chinese
German	Japanese
Swiss	Korean
Scandinavian	Arab
English	Greek

Source: Adapted from E. Hall, *Beyond Culture* (Garden City, N.Y.: Doubleday, 1976); S. Rosen and O. Shenkar, "Clustering Countries on Attitudinal Dimensions: A Review and Synthesis," *Academy of Management Review* 10, no. 3 (1985), p. 449.

MANAGERIAL CHALLENGE

MANAGING SALES IN A DIFFERENT CULTURE

To Richard DeVos Jr., president of Amway, Japan represented an eye-popping opportunity and head-pounding challenges. With 120 million of the world's most affluent consumers, Japan represented one of the two or three top international opportunities for Amway. However, its high-context culture posed a significant barrier to success, especially given the strong American and low-context roots of Amway. In fact, the name Amway stands for American Way.

Founded in 1959 by DeVos's father and a co-founder, Amway has been an American icon for over three decades. DeVos Sr. began the company by selling household products door to door in Ada, Michigan. From its humble beginnings, the company grew to over $5 billion in sales, with most of the recent growth in international markets. In 1984, 15 percent of Amway's revenues came from international sales; 10 years later, 65 percent of revenues came from international sales in over 60 countries.

Amway's entry into Japan was not easy or simple. For the first five years, its operation in Japan produced nothing but red ink. The key to success in Japan was for Amway to find a way to adapt its basic concept to the culture of Japan.

In Japan, the complex distribution system for retail goods reflects its high-context culture: loyalty is king. When an individual joins a group, that person gains an identity and a strong sense of belonging. In high-context cultures, greater distinctions are made between insiders and outsiders than in low-context cultures. Consequently, the Japanese distribution system is not easily opened to newcomers. Retailers depend on wholesalers to deliver desired products, provide credit, and maintain inventory. Wholesalers, in turn, depend on manufacturers for their goods. A retailer or wholesaler that adds products from a new manufacturer is often considered disloyal to the group. A new product may represent new sales and growth to a retailer, but its overall sales still largely depend on existing products, which are supplied by the existing network of wholesalers and manufacturers. Thus, both wholesalers and manufacturers have leverage over retailers by delaying shipments or reducing credit.

How could Amway meet the challenge of introducing its products to consumers in a culture in which the distribution system is so close-knit? The company was able to circumvent the established distribution system and sell its products through 1.2 million individual distributors who sell directly to consumers. Most of these distributors do not work for Amway full-time but earn some supplemental cash. The distributors put up $70 in cash for a kit that includes Amway literature and sample products. If a distributor wants to quit, he or she can get a refund for the kit.

Amway tried to capitalize on Japan's high-context culture by encouraging new distributors to sell to people with whom they already had relationships. Incentives were established for distributors to encourage other people—usually people they knew—to become distributors. In this way, key distributors emerge by developing their own network of related distributors. Using this strategy, Amway Japan has become the third largest direct-selling company in the country. In fact, Amway sales in Japan are close to surpassing those in the United States.

DeVos believes that 75 percent of the company's revenues should come from outside the United States over the next several years. Many of the potential markets are other high-context cultures such as China, Vietnam, and India. It will be interesting to see whether the lessons learned in Japan can apply to these new countries.

Sources: "Challenging Japan's Sales Culture." *Institutional Investor,* May 1994, p 23; "Global Expansion, the Unstoppable Crusade," *Success,* September 1994, p. 18; John Hayes, "Global Way," *Forbes,* July 18, 1994, p. 318; Neil Weinberg, "Garlic and Licorice, Anyone?" *Forbes,* November 18, 1996.

CONCLUDING COMMENTS

What we wear, how we talk, and when we speak are all heavily influenced by cultural assumptions, values, and beliefs. Groups, whether they be a department, a company, or a country, typically develop a shared set of mental road maps and traffic signals to effectively interact with each other. The managerial challenge relating to culture is threefold: understanding, changing, and leveraging culture.

In understanding cultures, you should keep in mind that culture consists of assumptions, values, and behaviors that exist because they have been successful in the past. The six basic areas of assumptions presented can facilitate your ability to understand a new culture. This is not to say that every behavior, custom, or tradition you observe can be traced to one of these six categories of assumptions; but many of the fundamental aspects of a culture can be linked to beliefs about humans' relationship to the environment, human nature, human relationships, human activity, truth and morality, or time. The more widely and deeply the assumptions and values are shared, the stronger the cultural value. The stronger a particular cultural value, the greater the rewards or punishments associated with compliance or noncompliance and the more difficult it is to change.

Changing a culture is always a challenge. Behavioral change and compliance can be achieved with enough monitoring and reinforcement of desired behavior and punishment of undesired behavior. But doing so will extract a heavy cost of time, energy, and money if the new behaviors are not consistent or compatible with widely shared and strongly held values and assumptions. For example, Japanese executives discontinued wearing traditional kimonos and instead changed to wearing Western clothes. However, Japanese executives did not adopt Western individualistic values and start wearing all sorts of different styles of business attire. You only need spend a few moments in any business district in Japan to see the modern business attire (dark suit, white shirt, modest tie) is as pervasive as traditional kimonos were. Why? Because, in Japan, people value the group and conforming to it more than individuality. This is a core value, and it has not changed. With this in mind, the challenge in effecting change is to link new desired behaviors to existing values and assumptions. Where this is not possible, old cultural trees—soil, roots, trunk, leaves, and all—must be extracted and replaced with new ones. For most people, this is traumatic, and they usually resist the effort. So to be successful, you must correctly determine not only the behavior, values, and assumptions that fit with the environmental conditions but also the change strategy and the amount of effort needed to implement it effectively.

The third challenge lies in using cultural diversity effectively. In today's environment, you will encounter individuals—whether customers, competitors, suppliers, subordinates, bosses, or peers—who have a different cultural background from your own. They will have assumptions, values, beliefs, communication styles, management philosophies, and decision-making processes different from yours. Research suggests that if you simply label those differences as good or bad based on your own assumptions and values, you are not likely to be effective in culturally diverse management situations.[20] If, however, you stop and say, "That's interesting; I wonder why it's that way?" you are more likely to be effective in a diverse environment.

KEY TERMS

artifacts 94	masculine societies 99	Theory X managers 97
assumptions 94	power distance 97	Theory Y managers 97
collectivism 98	rituals 109	uncertainty avoidance 99
core value 106	short-term or long-term orientation 99	values 94
cultural context 109		
culture 93	strong versus weak cultural values 104	
feminine societies 99		
individualism 97	subculture 104	

REVIEW QUESTIONS

1. Define *culture*.
2. Describe the three levels of culture.
3. What are the key differences between artifacts and assumptions?
4. Describe the six basic assumptions and provide contrasting examples for each.
5. What are the key differences between Theory X and Theory Y managers?
6. Define *power distance* and provide an example of how it affects managerial behavior.
7. Define *individualism-collectivism* and provide an example of how it affects managerial behavior.
8. How does the extent to which cultural values are widely shared and/or deeply held affect the strength or weakness of a culture?
9. What is a subculture?
10. What strategies can managers use to create or change culture?
11. What are the key differences between high- and low-context cultures? How do they affect managerial behavior?

DISCUSSION QUESTIONS

1. All organizations have cultures. What are the key cultural aspects of your school? What links are there between key assumptions and values and visible artifacts such as clothing, behaviors, or rituals? Compare your school's culture with that of other schools: How do they differ? How are they the same?
2. The stronger an organizational culture, the greater the impact it can have on behavior; however, the stronger the culture, the more difficult it is to change. Unfortunately, the environment changes, and values that fit the environment today may be inappropriate tomorrow. What can an organization do to keep the positive aspects of a strong culture and still reduce the risk of becoming extinct by not changing its culture fast enough to accommodate environmental shifts?
3. If you look forward to working with individuals from a variety of cultural backgrounds, or perhaps even working in foreign countries, what can you do to better prepare yourself for those future opportunities?
4. What are the key work values you want in an organization you work for? List at least 10. How can you assess the extent to which potential employers have these desired values?

CLOSING CASE

Cultural Change at the Savings Bank of Utica

We often think of banks as having conservative cultures—from the formal dress of their employees to a rigid hierarchy to which all workers adhere. The Savings Bank of Utica (SBU) used to have a buttoned-down organizational culture like this. In fact, it seemed to many of its employees and customers that the bank's most deeply held, widely shared value was that rules were made to be obeyed, never questioned or changed. Gary Gildersleeve, senior vice president for retail banking, discovered that rules did not necessarily enhance the bank's relationships with its customers; in fact, they could cause the bank to lose its competitive edge. Once, Gildersleeve observed a customer telling a branch manager that a certain rule was ridiculous. Instead of listening to the customer and trying to solve the problem, the manager handed the customer a copy of the bank's policy manual and said, "Here. You read it; it's the law."

It's true that banking is highly regulated business, but with a rapidly changing environment, increased competition, and new financial products, banks must now reach out to their customers in much the same way that other service industries do. To accomplish this, a bank's organizational culture must be flexible enough to serve individual customers needs. "We needed to change," reflects Gildersleeve, "and change our people."

Gildersleeve and Gary Gemmill, a professor or organization and management at Syracuse University (not far from Utica), collaborated on ways to change the culture at SBU. First, they instituted a reward system intended to reinforce the bank's new value of sales and service efforts. Some managers balked at the idea. "You mean, you are going to pay [employees] for selling a checking account? It's [already] their job." Branch managers had been so entrenched in rules that they had lost track of the goal of attracting and serving customers. But Gildersleeve and Gemmill pressed forward.

Next, they tried a new strategy—a series of management retreats called WAVE (Working to Achieve Visions of Excellence) aimed at developing a team style of management. Prior to this, collectivism was a foreign concept to bank managers; individualism as managers was a deeply held value. The idea of WAVE was to "get people to think they are a critical part of the process" and to encourage "people to take initiative, be creative, experiment with possibilities, take a systemwide approach, and talk openly about things that ordinarily are not discussible."

WAVE amounted to retaining employees at different levels, including managers, and some senior managers resisted this. Their assumption was that their senior position placed them beyond the need for training. (If they needed to be trained, they reasoned, something must be wrong with their own performance.) Some decided to

leave the bank, but those who stayed, as well as their successors, support the program.

Sandra Wilczynski, vice president of human resources, supports the way that WAVE has changed the bank's organizational culture. She believes that the program has helped establish team spirit, improved working relationship, and led to improved customer service. "What's important is the sense of community and the line of sight of how employees' jobs fit into the big picture. It's important that they understand how their work affects another worker … and … helps the organization achieve its goals."

Ultimately, WAVE actually decreased the power distance in the bank. Instead of waiting for higher-ranking managers to handle problems, SBU employees now actively search for solutions themselves. Executive secretary Dorothy Bailey comments, "I used to just give Gary Gildersleeve messages; now I can find a solution." She recalls a recent incident in which an elderly customer had trouble having a check cashed at a bank branch. Bailey received the complaint, but instead of waiting for Gildersleeve or someone else to handle it, she contacted a manager and arranged for the customer to use a special courtesy card.

There is still room for improvement at SBU. Gildersleeve believes that more employees need to take the message of WAVE seriously, not just view it as a good training exercise or as a pat on the back. He also wants more managers and employees to take their own initiative toward changing the culture, rather than simply looking to him for answers and ideas. And WAVE is not necessarily a panacea for all banks, but it does provide some insights into avenues for cultural change.

QUESTIONS
1. How might SBU managers respond to the assumption, "Rules are rules?"
2. In addition to those stated in the case, what do you think might be some of the new values that SBU would like to instill in its managers and employees?
3. What additional steps might SBU take to reinforce its new values?

Sources: Clifford C. Hebard, "A Story of Real Change," *Training and Development* 52, no. 7 (1998), pp. 47–50; www.aba.com; and www.acbankers.org.

ETHICS AND SOCIAL RESPONSIBILITY

After studying this chapter, you should be able to:

- Describe the rationale for why an understanding of basic approaches to ethical decision making and corporate social responsibility is important.
- Explain the basic approaches to ethical decision making.
- Point out the different implications of each approach in real-life situations.
- Explain the basic approaches to corporate social responsibility.
- Draw different implications for each approach to corporate social responsibility.

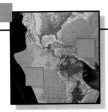

Nicolo Pignatelli and Gulf Italia

Nicolo Pignatelli, president of Gulf Italia (a subsidiary of Gulf Oil), stared at the notice from the Italian government. "How could this be possible?" he thought. The notice informed Pignatelli that although he had just completed construction of an oil refinery with a capacity of almost 6 million tons, he had authorization to produce only 3.9 million tons. On top of that, the notice made it clear that not only did Pignatelli have to obtain government permission to operate at full capacity, but he would also have to get a separate authorization to implement the permission. Pignatelli didn't know whether to be intimidated or infuriated. The cost of the project was already well past $100 million, and the refinery would lose millions if it did not operate at or near capacity.

Pignatelli was understandably upset—he had spent seven long years implementing a strategy to take Gulf Italia from one of the small fries in the Italian oil and gasoline industry to one of the major players. He had bought Fiat's oil-related businesses and the gasoline stations of Marathon Oil (700 service stations in central and southern Italy). Gulf now had crude oil and gas stations. It needed its own refinery to complete the chain from the wellhead to the gas pump.

Building a refinery in Italy proved to be a long and expensive task. Even after receiving permission to build the refinery in northern Italy, local opposition resulted in five location changes. These changes cost Gulf an additional $16 million. To ensure that the smoke and fumes would not get trapped close to the ground, Pignatelli spent extra money on a 450-foot smokestack (twice as tall as normal). Pignatelli also installed a special combustion chamber so that flare towers (used to burn off waste gas) and their common loud noise and noxious fumes were not necessary. He also added a state-of-the-art water purification system. In fact, Pignatelli demonstrated the quality of the system by drinking the waste water. These environmental additions added over $1 million to the project.

To ensure that the refinery was profitable, Pignatelli arranged a joint venture with Mobil Oil. Mobil had many service stations in northern Italy (where Gulf's refinery was located), whereas Gulf's service stations were concentrated in central and southern Italy. The money Mobil put up for its equity share would reduce Gulf's financial burden in building the refinery. However, Mobil would pull out of the deal if Gulf's refinery could not operate at capacity.

It had taken seven years to get the refinery approved and built. Millions of dollars were on the line. Trying to get approval to operate at capacity and then to get authorization to implement that approval might take many more months, if not years. Pignatelli wondered if he was being purposely set up by government officials.

Three options occurred to Pignatelli: (1) play it straight and try to get government authorization, (2) pay a large sum of money ($1 million deposited to a Swiss bank account) to a "consultant" who had "debottle-necked" problems like this before and who promised Pignatelli that he could fix the situation within six months, or (3) try to get his more influential partners to put pressure on government officials.

Pignatelli considered each option. Playing it straight would likely take several months and possibly years before government authorization could be obtained. In the meantime, the refinery would not operate or would operate at such a low capacity that it would lose millions. Given the cost of the project already, the thousands of jobs that depended on an operating refinery, and time pressures, $1 million seemed like a small price to pay to get government approval. Pignatelli was not sure that pressure from his other partners would influence government officials. He wondered about the effect of going to the media.

Source: A. K. Surdaram and J. S. Black, "Nicole Pignatelli and Gulf Italia," *The International Business Environment,* 1995, pp. 166–74.

As the story of Pignatelli illustrates, managers face perplexing ethical issues. Pignatelli seems to be leaning in the direction of hiring a consultant, who might use part of the money for bribes. If Pignatelli does not pay the bribes directly, does this absolve him of responsibility? If bribes are common practice, does this justify paying them even if they are illegal? Does Gulf have a responsibility to Italian citizens to build an environmentally friendly refinery if not required by law? Is it right for Gulf to spend this extra money and essentially take it away from shareholders? What if you were a lower-level employee in the company and learned that Pignatelli were going to pay bribes to get things "debottlenecked." What would your ethical obligations be? Should you ignore the situation? Confront Pignatelli? Inform your direct boss?

Individuals at all levels of an organization face a variety of ethical dilemmas. Just consider the following real but disguised case.

After working 11 months in her position with Dresden Inc. since graduation, Martha received an attractive job offer from a competing firm. Her current employer, Dresden, paid bonuses to employees based on performance after a year of employment. Martha was expecting a $10,000 bonus from Dresden. In discussions with the competing firm, Martha had negotiated for them to pay her the $10,000 if Dresden Inc. failed to do so. Part of the reason they were willing to do this was because Martha had been exposed to a number of strategic operations and plans in her first year of employment at Dresden. Given her somewhat junior position in the company, she had not been asked to sign, nor had she signed, a "noncompete" clause that would have prevented her from taking a job with a competitor for a specific time period. Legally, she was free to take the job with the competitor.

This case raises several ethical questions. Does Martha's current firm have an ethical obligation to pay her the $10,000 bonus even though she plans to leave only a few days short of completing 12 months of employment? If you were Martha, in trying to negotiate payment of the bonus, would you feel an ethical obligation to tell Dresden that the competitor had promised to pay the bonus if it didn't? Would you have any ethical misgivings about taking the new job and then relating all you knew about your previous employer's strategic plans?

managerial ethics
the study of morality and standards of business conduct

corporate social responsibility
the obligations that corporations owe to their constituencies

Both of these cases focus on the two key issues of this chapter: managerial ethics and corporate social responsibility. **Managerial ethics** is essentially the study of morality and standards of business conduct. **Corporate social responsibility** is concerned with the obligations that corporations owe to their constituencies, such as shareholders, employees, customers, and citizens at large.

MANAGERIAL CHALLENGES

You may be wondering, "Why should managers care about ethics and social responsibility? Aren't these the types of issues that philosophers worry about?" To answer this question, you need only pick up recent newspapers or business magazines. Everything from Wall Street trading scandals to environmental pollution cover-ups seem to be in the press daily. For example, Cendant lost $20 billion in market value when it was established that managers in a firm it had recently acquired had falsified revenue figures. The former president of the acquired firm,

EXHIBIT 5.1

Excellence in Ethics Award Winners

Award Criteria
1. Be a leader in their field, out ahead of the pack, showing the way ethically.
2. Have programs or initiatives in responsibility that demonstrate sincerity and ongoing vibrancy, and reach deep into the company.
3. Have a significant presence on the national scene, so their ethical behavior sends a loud signal.
4. Be a standout in at least one area, though recipients need not be perfect, nor even exemplary, in all areas.
5. Have faced a challenging situation in recent years and shown they can overcome it with integrity.

Winners
Xerox Corporation
Honored in 1995 for commitment to diversity in the workplace. (Also awarded the first-ever Sear's Award for World Class Employee Relations.)
Home Depot
Honored in 1995 for commitment to community involvement at all levels of the organization.
Odwalla, Inc.
Honored in 1995 for minimizing the impact of business operations on the environment.
General Motors
Honored in 1996 for excellence in environmental performance.
Reebok
Honored in 1996 for support of human rights initiatives around the world, both inside and outside of the company.
BankAmerica
Honored in 1996 for judging the ethical, as well as financial, merits of loan funding.
Herman Miller Inc.
Honored in 1997 for commitment to eco-efficiency in business operations. (The company reduced waste to landfills from 21 million pounds in 1994 to 6 million pounds in 1996!)
Life USA (Insurance Co.)
Honored in 1997 for its place as the first and only employee-owned insurance agency in the country.
Medtronic
Award for General Excellence in Ethics. Honored in 1997 for its continued commitment to the highest legal, moral, and ethical standards by all of its employees in all 120 countries where it operates.

Sources: Data from D. Kurschner, S. Gaines, and M. Scott, *Business Ethics* 9, no. 6 (1995), pp. 30–36; S. Gaines, "The 8th Annual Business Ethics Awards," *Business Ethics* 10, no. 6 (1996), pp. 14–18; J. Makower, "The 9th Annual Business Ethics Awards," *Business Ethics* 11, no. 6 (1997), pp. 7–9.

Walter Forbes, claimed he knew nothing of the illegal accounting practices. This, however, did not keep him from being forced to resign. This story generated over 300 articles in newspapers and magazines over the space of less than 30 days. Clearly, poorly managed managerial ethics and corporate social responsibility can generate negative publicity, hurt a company's stock price, or make it difficult for the firm to recruit high-quality employees. In contrast, well-managed ethical behavior and corporate social responsibility can have significant, positive consequences for employees, customers, shareholders, and communities. Exhibit 5.1 provides a listing of companies honored for "Excellence in Ethics" by *Business Ethics* magazine. As you read these examples, you might consider whether you would be more or less likely to work for one of these firms, or if it might be easier for you as a manager in one of these firms to recruit or motivate employees.

In addition to recognizing both the negative and positive impact that managerial ethics and social responsibility can have, managers need to understand the various approaches for making ethical and social responsibility decisions in order to make better decisions themselves and understand decisions made by others.

The Development of Individual Ethics

By this point in your life you no doubt already have a fairly well-established set of ethical beliefs and values. How did you come by them? What role did family, friends, peers, teachers, religion, job experiences, and life experiences have on the development of your ethical beliefs? To explore this issue, you might think of someone who has made quite different ethical judgments from your own. What if you had been born in a different country, raised by a different family, attended a different school system, experienced different religious influences, had different friends, and held different jobs? Would you hold the same ethical values you do now? Would you reach identical ethical judgments to those you reach now?

There is little debate that family, friends, peers, teachers, religion, job experiences, and life experiences play a significant role in the development of individual ethical values and judgments. What is debated is which factors play the strongest role because their influence varies from person to person.

Managers need to understand that a variety of factors play a role in the development of individual ethical values and judgments. First, managers must recognize that others may differ in their judgments of what is right or wrong. Second, differences in conclusions usually have more to do with differences in family background, friends, peers, teachers, religion, job experiences, and life experiences than anything else. Third, managers typically cannot allow employees to reach their own conclusions about what is ethical employee conduct and what is not. Consequently, if managers want to shape employees' ethical behaviors, they must understand their employees' backgrounds and how their employees evaluate ethical situations.

Understanding Basic Approaches to Ethics

Although most managers already have well-established values and beliefs, many have not clearly formulated a means of thinking through ethical dilemmas. This can sometimes lead managers to make decisions that they later regret. The pressures of the moment can overwhelm them, especially if they lack a systematized and explicit framework for thinking through dilemmas. For example, you may believe that paying bribes is wrong, but if you were in Pignatelli's situation, it is possible that the stress of the moment—your $100 million refinery, your nearly 1,000 service stations, your employees' jobs, your own job—might push you into making a decision and taking action contrary to your stated beliefs.

Understanding the basic approaches to ethical decision making can also help you recognize when others are using an ethical decision-making approach different from your own. Different approaches can lead to opposite judgments of ethical actions. Failure to recognize this can lead to endless arguments, damaged relationships, and no clear course of action. Understanding various approaches may enable you to avoid these negative results and more effectively deal with other people.

In an increasingly diverse workforce and global business environment, encountering people who use widely different approaches and reach different conclusions about ethical conduct is quite likely. This is illustrated in a recent study that examined the extent to which salespeople from the United States, Japan, and Korea viewed a set of actions as posing an ethical issue or not. The study found significant difference among these three nationalities.[1] For example, Korean salespeople did

EXHIBIT 5.2

Ethical Perspectives from Three Countries

Do the following situations present an ethical situation? (1= No; 5 = Yes)

Situation	United States	Japan	Korea
Seeking information from customers on competitors' quotation for the purpose of submitting another quotation.	3.07	3.12	2.83
Giving free gifts to a purchaser.	2.81	2.97	2.40
Making statements that exaggerate the seriousness of a problem in order to get a bigger order from a purchaser.	3.45	3.24	3.46
Allowing personal feelings toward a purchaser to affect price, delivery, and other terms of the sale.	3.14	3.11	3.43
Gaining information about competitors by asking purchasers for information.	2.48	3.11	2.71

not think that seeking information from a customer on the price quotation offered by a competitor in order to resubmit a more competitive bid was much of an ethical issue, unlike American and Japanese salespeople. Also, Korean salespeople did not think that giving free gifts was as much of an ethical issue as did American or Japanese salespeople. How do you view these issues? To what extent do you see each of these items in Exhibit 5.2 as an ethical issue?

Without understanding how or why people from other cultures come to different conclusions about ethical behavior, it is easy to judge their beliefs and decisions as wrong and to label people holding "wrong" beliefs as inferior. Ethnocentric evaluations have been demonstrated in research to be harmful for managers, especially in culturally diverse or international contexts.[2] So, it is important for new managers to be able to examine the basic approaches to ethical decision making to broaden their understanding.

BASIC APPROACHES TO ETHICAL DECISION MAKING

Several frameworks, or approaches, to ethical decision making exist. We examine four of the most common: the utilitarian, moral rights, universalism, and justice approaches. An understanding of basic approaches to ethical decision making can help you as a manager examine personal ethics and help you understand and work more effectively with others who have different ethical perspectives.

Utilitarian Approach

utilitarian approach
an approach to ethics in which the ethical or right course of action is based on what results in the greatest good

The first basic approach, the utilitarian approach, focuses on consequences of an action. Simplified, using a **utilitarian approach**, you judge the most ethical course of action to be the one that results "in the greatest good." For example, assume you are trying to sell grain to a developing nation and a key customs agent demands an extra fee before he will clear your shipment. From a utilitarian perspective, you would try to determine the consequences of the options available to you, for example, (1) pay the bribe, (2) do not pay the bribe, or (3) seek intervention from a third party. Once you have considered the alternatives, you then deter-

In an effort to win the 2002 Winter Olympics for Salt Lake City, members of the Salt Lake Olympic Committee made unauthorized payments to International Olympic Committee members and their relatives. Two top officials in the city's Olympic bid were accused of ethical, but not criminal, wrongdoing in a corruption scandal. Winning the Olympics brings tremendous benefits and prestige to a city.

mine which action would result in the greatest good. If there are starving people waiting for the grain, you might argue that because the grain would make the difference between life and death, paying the customs agent to release the grain results in the greatest good and is, therefore, the most ethical course of action. However, it is important to point out that most of the time, the determination of the greatest good is subjective. Factors such as culture, economic circumstances, and religion can all affect the value you might place on particular outcomes compared with the value that others place on the same outcomes. For example, you might highly value the preservation of jobs, while someone else might think unemployment is just a natural consequence.

In addition to the difficulty of trying to assess the value that others place on the consequences of your actions, there is a much bigger challenge with a utilitarian approach. In addition to positive outcomes, you must also consider negative ones. For example, in addition to the benefits received by the starving people as a result of bribing the customs official, you also need to examine the loss to shareholders and the value they attach to the loss. If a significant sum, say $1 million, is paid to the customs official, that money cannot be returned to the shareholders—money that should be theirs. Suppose the firm has 1,000 shareholders. The bribe results in a direct loss to each shareholder of $1,000. You may decide that the loss of $1,000 for each of 1,000 shareholders is less than the benefit to all those that received the grain.

If you were Pignatelli and were using a utilitarian approach, would the benefits of 2,000 people keeping their jobs outweigh the losses to shareholders and justify the extra payments to secure the needed authorizations? If this rationale may justify the actions of an individual manager in one case, can it justify a whole category of similar actions such as bribery in general? If all managers could justify paying bribes, then couldn't it become the basis of how contracts were won? Wouldn't this result in less emphasis on product cost, quality, and safety? The negative consequences from higher costs and lower quality and safety for consumers might easily outweigh the initial benefits. Therefore, a key challenge for those using the utilitarian approach is considering more distant as well as immediate consequences of a particular course of action.

Moral Rights Approach

moral rights approach
an approach to ethics that focuses on examining the moral standing of a given action independent of its positive or negative consequences

The **moral rights approach** to ethical decisions focuses on an examination of the moral standing of actions independent of their consequences. It holds that some principles are simply right or moral, independent of consequences. When two courses of action both have moral standing, then the positive and negative consequences of each should determine which course is more ethical. From this approach, your intention to act in conformance with moral principles, as well as the consequences of that action, must be considered in determining whether an action is ethical or unethical. From a moral rights approach, if paying bribes is simply wrong and doesn't have moral standing, then saving 2,000 jobs does not justify the action.

Universal Approach

universal approach
an approach to ethics in which ethical action is determined by the moral imperative "do unto others as you would have them do unto everyone, including yourself"

Immanuel Kant, perhaps one of the most famous moral philosophers, articulated the best-known ethical imperative, or **universal approach**. Simplified, Kant's moral imperative was "do unto others as you would have them do unto everyone, including yourself." This imperative contends that to determine whether a course of action is ethical, you must first determine whether it can apply to all people under all situations. Second, you must ask yourself if you would want the rule applied to yourself. At the heart of universalism is the issue of rights. For Kant, the basis of all rights stem from freedom and autonomy. Actions that limit the freedom and autonomy of individuals generally lack moral standing and, therefore, rarely can be justified. If you were in Pignatelli's situation and took a universal approach to the decision of what to do, it might be difficult to justify paying bribes. To meet the "do unto others as you would have them do unto everyone" criterion, you would have to be willing to let everyone use bribes as a means of getting the ends they desired.

Justice Approach

justice approach
an approach to ethics that focuses on how equitably the costs and benefits are distributed among people

The **justice approach** focuses on how equitably the costs and benefits of actions are distributed as the principal means of judging ethical behavior.[3] In general, costs and benefits should be equitably distributed, rules should be impartially applied, and those damaged because of inequity or discrimination should be compensated.

distributive justice
a particular justice approach that focuses on distributing rewards and punishments based on performance

Distributive Justice Managers ascribing to **distributive justice** distribute rewards and punishments equitably based on performance. This does not mean that everyone gets the same or equal rewards or punishments; rather, they receive equitable rewards and punishments as a function of how much they contribute or detract from the organization's goals. A manager cannot distribute bonuses, promotions, or benefits based on arbitrary characteristics such as age, gender, religion, or race. This is the basic rationale behind the U.S. Civil Rights Act of 1964. Under this law, even if a manager has no intention of discriminating against a particular minority group, if a minority group can demonstrate inequitable results (called *disparate impact*), legal action can be brought against the firm. For example, if 50 percent of a firm's applicants for promotion were women, but 75 percent of those receiving promotions were men, these data could be used to file a claim of discrimination based on the underlying notion of distributive justice.

procedural justice
a particular justice approach that focuses on ensuring that people affected by decisions conform to the decision-making process and that the process is administered impartially

Procedural Justice Managers ascribing to **procedural justice** make sure that people affected by managerial decisions consent to the decision-making process and that the process is administered impartially.[4] Consent means that people are informed about the process and have the freedom to exit the system if they choose. As with distributive justice, the decision-making process cannot systematically discriminate against people because of arbitrary characteristics such as age, gender, religion, or race.

compensatory justice
a particular justice approach that focuses on compensating people injured when distributive and procedural justice approaches break down

Compensatory Justice   The main thesis of **compensatory justice** is that if distributive justice and procedural justice fail or are not followed as they should be, then those damaged by the inequitable distribution of rewards should be compensated. This compensation often takes the form of money, but it can take other forms. For example, compensatory justice is at the heart of affirmative action plans. Typically, affirmative action plans ensure that groups that may have been systematically disadvantaged in the past, such as women or minorities, are given every opportunity in the future. For example, special training programs could be instituted for women who were passed over for promotions in the past because they were denied access to certain experiences required for promotion.

MORAL INTENSITY IN ETHICAL DECISION MAKING

moral intensity
degree to which we see an issue as an ethical one

In addition to different approaches to ethical decisions, managers should also be aware of the power an ethical issue can have.[5] The degree to which we see an issue as an ethical one, termed **moral intensity**, is largely a function of the content of the issue. Moral intensity has six components, as illustrated in Exhibit 5.3: (1) magnitude

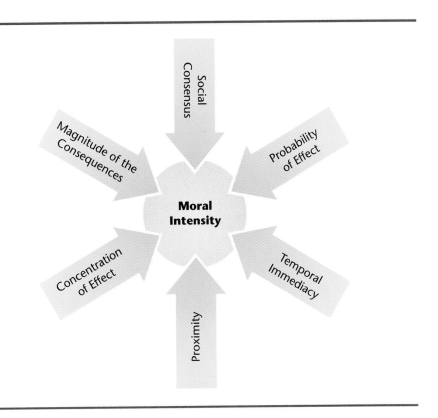

of the consequences, (2) social consensus, (3) probability of effect, (4) temporal immediacy, (5) proximity, and (6) concentration of effect.[6]

magnitude of the consequences
the level of impact anticipated with the outcome of a given action

The **magnitude of the consequences** associated with the outcome of a given action is the level of impact anticipated. This impact is independent of whether the consequences are positive or negative. For example, laying off 100 employees because of a downturn in the economy has less of an impact than if 1,000 employees join the ranks of the unemployed.

social consensus
the extent to which members of a society agree that a particular act is either good or bad

Social consensus involves the extent to which members of a society agree that an act is either good or bad. For example, in the United States, there is greater social consensus concerning the wrongness of driving drunk than speeding on the highway.

probability of effect
how likely people think the consequences of an action are

The third component of moral intensity is **probability of effect**. Even if a particular action could have severe consequences and people agree about the positive or negative nature of that impact, the intensity of the issue rises and falls depending on how likely people think the consequences are. Nearly all people agree that a baby food that causes permanent brain damage should be banned and company officials punished; however, because of safeguards, the possibility of this occurring is quite remote and therefore generates little ethical debate. In contrast, the probability that people will be injured in car accidents is quite high. This concern constantly raises discussions and debates about the moral obligation of auto manufacturers to make safer cars.

temporal immediacy
the time interval between the time the action occurs and the onset of its consequences

Temporal immediacy is the fourth component of moral intensity and is a function of the interval between the time the action occurs and the onset of its consequences. The greater the time interval between the action and its consequences, the less intensity people typically feel toward the issue. For example, even if industrial pollution were certain to lead to global warming and result in catastrophic changes to weather patterns, because the consequences are likely to happen 50 years from now, the moral intensity of industrial pollution would be much less than if the effects happened next year.

proximity
the closeness of the decision maker to those affected by a decision

The fifth component is **proximity**. All other factors being equal, the closer the decision maker feels to those affected by the decision, the more the decision maker will consider the consequences of the action and feel it has ethical implications. It is important to keep in mind that an affinity between the decision maker and those affected could be a function of many factors, including nationality, cultural background, ethnic similarity, organizational identification, or socioeconomic similarity.

concentration of effect
the extent to which consequences are concentrated on a few individuals or dispersed across many

The last component is the **concentration of effect**, or the extent to which consequences are focused on a few individuals or dispersed across many. For example, even though laying off 100 people has a lower magnitude of effect than laying off 1,000 people, laying off 100 people in a town of 5,000 has a greater concentration of effect than laying off 1,000 people in city of 12 million such as New York.

The importance of these six facets of moral intensity is twofold. First, as a manager, you can use these facets to anticipate issues that are likely to be seen as significant ethical dilemmas in the workplace. If you can better anticipate issues that are likely to become ethical debates, you have more time to prepare for and may be more effective at handling ethical dilemmas. Second, if you are working with a group that is using the same basic ethical approach and still can't agree on the ethical course of action, you can use these facets to determine the source of the disagreement. The disagreement may stem from different perceptions of the situation on one or more of the moral intensity components. For example, your group may be arguing over the ethics of terminating a relationship with a long-time supplier. In examining the source of the disagreement, you may discover a difference in perception as to the concentration of effect and magnitude of impact that the termination might have on the supplier. Once the source of the disagreement is uncovered, it is then possible to examine more carefully the reasons for the different perceptions and explore the possibility of resolving those differences.

MAKING ETHICAL DECISIONS

Increasingly it seems that individuals and organizations are embracing a philosophy of business ethics perhaps first and best articulated in 1776 by Adam Smith in his classic book, *The Moral Sentiments of Reason*. Smith's basic thesis was that it is in individuals' and organizations' self-interest to make ethical decisions. Still, a significant challenge remains to you as a manager: How can ethical decisions be fostered and encouraged?

The Manager

As we mentioned at the outset, part of the reason for exploring various approaches to ethical decision making is to help you refine your own approach so that when pressures arise, you can make decisions consistent with your ethical framework. To this end, there is perhaps no substitute for taking personal responsibility for ethical decisions. To illustrate this, put yourself in Caren Wheeler's position (see Managerial Challenge box). What approach would you use and what decision would you make?

How much moral intensity does this situation have? What is the magnitude of consequences if Creative Applications is dropped as a supplier? How many jobs might be lost? How likely is this? How soon would it happen? If there is some degree of moral intensity to the situation, what approach would you use to come to a decision? Is it right to drop Creative Applications? Caren is expected not only to provide a recommendation but also a rationale for it. Although it is probably impossible to argue that one of the approaches presented in this chapter is best, applied consistently, each approach does allow a consistent pattern of ethical decision making. This consistency may matter more to those with whom you interact than whether your decisions are always in agreement with theirs.[7]

The Organization

Just as managers try to foster ethical decisions, organizations try to encourage them among their managers. Although there are a variety of ways organizations might accomplish this objective, codes of ethics and whistle-blowing systems are perhaps two of the more visible efforts.

code of ethical conduct
a formal statement typically one to three pages in length outlining types of behavior that are and are not acceptable

Codes of Ethics   Given the ethical dilemmas that managers face and the different approaches for evaluating ethical behavior, many firms have adopted codes of ethics to guide their managers' decision making. A **code of ethical conduct** is typically a formal statement of one to three pages that primarily outlines types of behavior that are and are not acceptable. Exhibit 5.4 reprints the Johnson & Johnson credo, one of the oldest among U.S. corporations. The credo was first adopted in 1945 and has been revised four times to its current version.

MANAGERIAL CHALLENGE

CHANGING HORSES

Caren Wheeler was a young purchasing manager at Johannson Wood Products, a 12-year-old company in the Midwest. Like many innovative midsized firms, Johannson Wood Products had formed strong partnerships with a limited number of suppliers to receive supplies on a just-in-time basis and then ship its finished goods in a timely fashion to retail stores. One of those partner suppliers was Creative Applications.

Creative Applications was a small, family-run company that would store and mill Johannson Wood Products' lumber into finished parts. The partnership, negotiated three years ago, had worked well for Creative Applications. Over 60 percent of its revenues were obtained from Johannson Wood Products. In fact, the agreement had come just when Creative Applications was in financial trouble. Though they were not out of the woods yet, the agreement with Johannson Wood Products was critical to Creative Applications' survival.

Recently, however, the partnership had not worked well for Johannson Wood Products. As its sales increased, Creative Applications was having difficulty meeting deadlines. Caren had mentioned this problem to Steve Jackson, Creative Applications' plant manager (and the son of the owner), but no real improvement occurred.

When Caren met with Tom Masters, the president of Johannson Wood Products, and several other managers to discuss the situation, a variety of opinions emerged. Some saw this as an ethical issue and others did not. First the group focused on Steve Jackson's abrasive personality and management style. Many in the meeting felt that he was "a control freak" and could not delegate authority. Consequently, as demand increased, Steve became a bottleneck in Creative Applications' ability to meet delivery deadlines.

One of Johannson Wood Products' managers who disliked Steve Jackson stated, "I don't think that continuing a relationship with Creative Applications is going to work for us. It's one of those cases where the management capabilities of a small-time operation can't make the transition to a

---

EXHIBIT 5.4

Johnson & Johnson
Credo

We believe our first responsibility is to the doctors, nurses, and patients, to mothers and all others who use our products and services. In meeting their needs everything we do must be of high quality. We must constantly strive to reduce our costs in order to maintain reasonable prices. Customers' orders must be serviced promptly and accurately. Our suppliers and distributors must have an opportunity to make a fair profit.

We are responsible to our employees: the men and women who work with us throughout the world. Everyone must be considered as an individual. We must respect their dignity and recognize their merit. They must have a sense of security in their jobs. Compensation must be fair and adequate, and working conditions clean, orderly, and safe. Employees must feel free to make suggestions and complaints. There must be equal opportunity for employment, development, and advancement for those qualified. We must provide competent management, and their actions must be just and ethical.

We are responsible to the communities in which we live and work and to the world community as well.

We must be good citizens—support good works and charities and bear our fair share of taxes. We must encourage civic improvements and better health and education.

We must maintain in good order the property we are privileged to use, protecting the environment and natural resources.

Our final responsibility is to our stockholders. Business must make a sound profit. We must experiment with new ideas. Research must be carried on, innovative programs developed, and mistakes paid for. New equipment must be purchased, new facilities provided, and new products launched. Reserves must be created to provide for adverse times.

When we operate according to these principles, the stockholders should realize a fair return.

larger producer. We can't afford to keep nursing along a relationship that's not working."

Another manager thought it was unfair to bring personal feelings for or against Steve into the discussion and replied, "We've always told our vendors that if they were there for us, we'd be there for them. For over two years, Creative Applications really put out to perform for us. Are we going to pull out now that they are facing tough times? Remember 18 months ago, when we pressured them to lease an expensive piece of milling equipment because of our increased volume? The equipment dealer would only do it on a three-year lease. Creative did it even though it elevated their costs. If we pull the rug out from under them now, that's not fair, and it will hurt their chances of survival—we're still 60 percent of their business. Is it ethical to just pull the plug now?"

A third individual interjected, "I propose that we make an offer to either purchase Creative Applications or start our in-house capability for milling the products. Here is a proposal that details the capital that would be required for either option and the potential savings that could be generated over a three-year period."

"Caren, what do you recommend?" asked Tom Masters. Several different issues raced through her mind. Johannson Wood Products was always stressing loyal partnership relationships. Was it ethical to sever the relationship with Creative Applications? On the other hand, the delays being caused by Creative Applications were beginning to hurt Johannson Wood Products' ability to meet store orders faster than its competition. Caren did not really like Steve's personality, but she wondered if it was right to factor personal feelings about Steve Jackson into the decision. Were there ethical issues in this decision or not? What was the right thing to do?

Source: Adapted from Doug Wallace, "Changing Horses," *Business Ethics*, November–December 1994, p. 34.

An examination of 84 codes of ethics in U.S. firms found three specific clusters of issues addressed in these statements.[8] The first cluster included items that focused on being a good "organization citizen" and was divided into nine subcategories. The second cluster included items that guided employee behavior away from unlawful or improper acts that would harm the organization and was divided into 12 subcategories. The third cluster included items that addressed directives to be good to customers and was divided into three subcategories. Exhibit 5.5 provides a list and description of the clusters and specific categories of issues addressed in these written codes. Most firms did have items in each of the three clusters, though not in all 30 subcategories.

A study of codes of ethics for firms in the United Kingdom, France, and Germany found that a higher percentage of German firms had codes of ethics than British or French firms (see Exhibit 5.6).[9] The greater cultural emphasis on explicit communication in Germany may partially explain this finding. Although only about one-third of the European firms in this study had codes of ethics, approximately 85 percent of U.S. firms have formal codes.

Exhibit 5.7 provides information about the content of the codes of ethics for the firms that in fact had formal codes. Interestingly, while 100 percent of the European firms covered issues of acceptable and unacceptable employee behavior in their codes, only 55 percent of U.S. firms covered these issues. By contrast, only 15 percent of the European firms covered issues of political interests (i.e., business/government relations) and 96 percent of U.S. firms covered these issues in their codes.

Research on codes of ethics indicates that organizations believe codes of ethics to be the most effective means of encouraging ethical behavior in their employees.[10] Indeed, if a given firm had a code that covered all 30 categories listed in Exhibit 5.5, employees would have a comprehensive guide for behavior. Unfortunately, the

EXHIBIT 5.5

Categories Found in Corporate Codes of Ethics

Cluster 1

"Be a dependable organization citizen."

1. Demonstrate courtesy, respect, honesty, and fairness in relationships with customers, suppliers, competitors, and other employees.
2. Comply with safety, health, and security regulations.
3. Do not use abusive language or actions.
4. Dress in businesslike attire.
5. Possession of firearms on company premises is prohibited.
6. Follow directives from supervisors.
7. Be reliable in attendance and punctuality.
9. Manage personal finances in a manner consistent with employment by a fiduciary institution.

Unclustered Items

1. Exhibit standards of personal integrity and professional conduct.
2. Racial, ethnic, religious, or sexual harassment is prohibited.
3. Report questionable, unethical, or illegal activities to your manager.
4. Seek opportunities to participate in community services and political activities.
5. Conserve resources and protect the quality of the environment in areas where the company operates.
6. Members of the corporation are not to recommend attorneys, accountants, insurance agents, stockbrokers, real estate agents, or similar individuals to customers.

Cluster 2

"Don't do anything unlawful or improper that will harm the organization."

1. Maintain confidentiality of customer, employee, and corporate records and information.
2. Avoid outside activities that conflict with or impair the performance of duties.
3. Make decisions objectively without regard to friendship or personal gain.
4. The acceptance of any form of bribe is prohibited.
5. Payment to any person, business, political organization, or public official for unlawful or unauthorized purposes is prohibited.
6. Conduct personal and business dealings in compliance with all relevant laws, regulations, and policies.
7. Comply fully with antitrust laws and trade regulations.
8. Comply fully with accepted accounting rules and controls.
9. Do not provide false or misleading information to the corporation, its auditors, or a government agency.
10. Do not use company property or resources for personal benefit or any other improper purpose.
11. Each employee is personally accountable for company funds over which he or she has control.
12. Staff members should not have any interest in any competitor or supplier of the company unless such interest has been fully disclosed to the company.

Cluster 3

"Be good to our customers."

1. Strive to provide products and services of the highest quality.
2. Perform assigned duties to the best of your ability and in the best interest of the corporation, its shareholders, and its customers.
3. Convey true claims for products.

Source: Donald Robin, Michael Giallourakis, Fred R. David, and Thomas E. Moritz, "A Different Look at Codes of Ethics." Reprinted from *Business Horizons* (January–February 1989), Table 1, p. 68. Copyright 1989 by Indiana University Kelley School of Business. Used with permission.

research does not support a strong link between codes of ethics and actual employee behavior. Firms without formal codes seem to have no higher or lower incidents of unethical behavior than those with formal codes.[11] This may be because simply having a formal statement written down is not sufficient. For example, although nearly all of the Fortune 500 U.S. firms have codes of ethics, only about one-third have training programs, about 33 percent have ethics officers, and roughly 50 percent have distributed formal codes to all their employees.[12]

Successfully Implementing Codes of Ethics   Establishing a formal, written code of ethical conduct is an important first step. However, actions speak much

EXHIBIT 5.6

**Adoption of
Codes of Ethics**

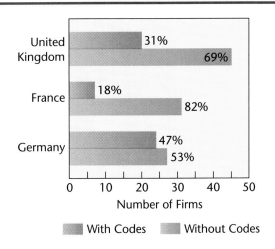

louder than words, and employees are unlikely to conform to the formal code unless other actions taken by the organization reinforce the code and communicate that the company is serious about compliance.

Communication.   The first step in effectively implementing a code of ethics is communicating it to all employees. For maximum impact, this communication needs to take a variety of forms and be repeated. It is not enough to simply send out a one-time memo. Rather, the code will need to be communicated in memos, company newsletters, videos, and speeches by senior executives.

Training.   For the code of ethical conduct to be effective, people will likely need training. For maximum impact, the training needs to be engaging. For example, at Motorola, they have developed approximately 80 different short cases. Each case presents a situation requiring a manager to make a decision. Participants in the training program individually and then collectively decide what they would do and discuss the ethical aspects of the decision. Participants then hear what senior executives, including the CEO, think about the situation and what decisions and behaviors they believe would be in keeping with the firm's code of ethics. Lockheed Martin also takes an engaging approach to ethics training with an interesting innovative twist (see the Managerial Challenge box).

Although officials at organizations often think that ethics training programs are effective, current research does not yet support that conclusion. And research provides even less guidance about the length or structure of training programs and their effectiveness.

Reward and Recognition.   In addition to communicating the code to employees and training them, it is critical to make sure that those who comply are recognized and rewarded. Otherwise, employees will simply view the written code as the "formal rhetoric but not the real deal." Exxon is a company that recognizes the importance of this principle. It regularly celebrates the story of an individual who has honored the company's code of conduct even when doing so might have cost the company money. For example, recently one of its drilling teams was setting up to drill for oil in the jungles of a developing country. A government official came by and stated that before they started the drill they needed to pay an operating permit. However, the official wanted the payment (approximately $10,000) paid to him

EXHIBIT 5.7

Subjects Addressed in Corporate Codes of Ethics

Subjects	UNITED KINGDOM n = 33 Number of Firms	%	FRANCE n = 15 Number of Firms	%	GERMANY n = 30 Number of Firms	%	TOTAL EUROPEAN COUNTRIES Number of Firms	%	UNITED STATES n = 118 Number of Firms	%	SIGNIFICANCE Europe vs. U.S.
Employee conduct	33	100	15	100	30	100	78	100	47	55	SIG
Community and environment	21	64	11	73	19	63	51	85	50	42	NS
Customers	18	39	14	93	20	67	52	87	96	81	SIG
Shareholders	13	39	11	73	18	60	42	64	NA	NA	NA
Suppliers and contractors	7	21	2	13	6	20	15	19	101	86	SIG
Political interests	4	12	3	20	5	17	12	15	113	96	SIG
Innovation and technology	2	6	3	20	18	60	26	33	18	15	SIG

NS = Not significant
NA = No comparable data available
SIG = Significantly different

personally in cash. This was against Exxon's code, so the team manager refused to pay. The drilling team and their expensive equipment sat idle for more than a week at a cost to Exxon of over $1 million. Finally, the government official admitted that all the paperwork and permits were in order and the team was allowed to proceed. Exxon celebrated this incident in its newsletter to reinforce to its employees that the company took its code of ethical conduct seriously and rewarded people who honored it even if it cost the company money.

whistle blower

an employee who discloses illegal or unethical conduct on the part of others in the organization

Whistle Blowing A **whistle blower** is an employee who discloses illegal or unethical conduct on the part of others in the organization. While some firms have implemented programs to encourage whistle blowing, most have not.[13] As a group, whistle blowers tend *not* to be disgruntled employees but instead are conscientious, high-performing employees who report illegal or unethical incidents. In general, they report these incidents not for notoriety but because they believe the wrongdoings are so grave that they must be exposed.[14] Research suggests that the

In response to the space shuttle *Challenger* disaster, NASA has implemented a whistle-blowing system so that anyone working on a shuttle project can alert NASA to a safety problem and maintain his or her anonymity. Engineers at Morton Thiokol had alerted NASA to the ill effects of cold conditions on the O-rings in the solid rocket boosters, but managers at Morton Thiokol and NASA did not heed the warnings because they did not want to delay the program.

more employees know about the channels through which they can blow the whistle and the stronger the protection of past whistle blowers, the more likely employees are to initially use internal rather than external channels such as the media.[15] Battelle Memorial Institute developed a whistle-blowing system for NASA (the National Aeronautic and Space Administration) with a central individual, an ombudsman, following the explosion of the space shuttle *Challenger*. According to Michael Hanley, the project manager, "the system enables anyone working on the shuttle project to alert NASA to any potential safety problem while maintaining their anonymity."[16] IBM receives up to 18,000 letters a year from employees making confidential complaints through IBM's "Speak Up" program. Firms such as Hughes Tool Co., General Motors, and Bloomingdale's offer financial rewards to employees who report valid claims.[17] In general, research suggests the following steps can be effective in encouraging valid whistle blowing:

- Clearly communicate whistle-blowing procedures to all employees.
- Allow for reporting channels in addition to the chain of command or reporting incidents to one's boss.
- Thoroughly investigate all claims based on a consistent procedure.
- Protect whistle blowers who make valid claims.
- Provide moderate financial incentives or rewards for valid claims.
- Publicly celebrate employees who make valid claims. [18]

By following these steps, managers can catch problems before they become national media events and seriously damage the firm's reputation. In addition to these steps, there are now laws in the United States that both protect and reward whistle blowers. Employers cannot discharge, threaten, or otherwise discriminate against employees because they report a suspected violation of the law. Employees who blow the whistle on companies with federal government contracts can actually receive a small portion of the judgment if the company is found guilty.

The Government

The governments of the United States and many other countries have also tried to foster ethical behavior. The U.S. government has enacted a number of laws and regulations designed to achieve this objective. Perhaps the most discussed, given today's global environment, is the Foreign Corrupt Practices Act.

Foreign Corrupt Practices Act

a law passed in the United States in 1977 that makes it illegal for U.S. citizens to pay bribes or to have reason to know that bribes will be paid to foreign government officials

U.S. Foreign Corrupt Practices Act   Few issues of ethical behavior have received more attention than questionable payments or bribes. For American managers, this issue is at the heart of the **Foreign Corrupt Practices Act** (FCPA). This act was passed in 1977 primarily in response to the disclosure that U.S. firms were making payments to foreign government officials to win government contracts and receive preferential treatment.

One of the key incidents that sparked the FCPA was the revelation that Lockheed Corporation had made over $12 million in payments to Japanese business executives and government officials to sell commercial aircraft in that country. Subsequent discoveries showed that nearly 500 U.S. companies had made similar payments around the world, totaling over $300 million.

Lockheed Chairman Carl Kotchian argued that the payments represented less than 3 percent of the revenue gained from the sale of aircraft to Japan. Further, these sales had a positive effect on the salaries and job security of Lockheed workers, with positive spillover benefits for their dependents, the communities, and the shareholders. Mr. Kotchian said that he was "between a rock and a hard spot;" if he made the payments, people might criticize his actions as unethical, and if he did not make the payments, a competitor would. Consequently, the competition would get the contracts, and some Lockheed workers might lose their jobs. Whether you agree with Mr. Kotchian or not, it is instructive to assess which ethical approach he seems to be using. Is it a moral right approach, justice approach, or utilitarian approach?

Until the passage of the FCPA, these dilemmas were purely ethical ones. Upon its passage, many of these decisions became legal ones because the FCPA made it illegal for employees of U.S. firms to corrupt the actions of foreign officials, politicians, or candidates for office. The act also outlaws employees from making payments to *any* person when they have "reason to know" that the payments might be used to corrupt the behavior of officials. The act also required that firms take steps to provide "reasonable assurance" that transactions are in compliance with the law and to keep detailed records of transactions.

The FCPA does not cover payments made to business executives. For American managers, payments made to executives are ethical decisions, not legal ones. The FCPA also does not prohibit payments to low-level government employees to perform in a more timely manner the duties they normally would have performed. These types of payments are typically called *facilitating payments*. For example, payment of $100 to a customs inspector not to delay the inspection of an imported product would not violate the FCPA because the payment simply facilitates something that the customs inspector would do anyway. However, the payment of $100 to pass a product without inspecting it would be a violation of the FCPA because the payment would entice the customs agent to do something he or she is not supposed to do.

Penalties for violation of the FCPA range up to $1 million in fines for the company and $10,000 in fines and up to *five years'* imprisonment for the responsible individuals. Clearly, a $1 million fine is not a deterrent when deals can be worth $100 million. Rather, the prison terms for individuals are the real teeth in the law.

Clearly, making ethical decisions is not easy. It takes an understanding of various frameworks at the individual level and intervention at the organization and government level if compliance with particular points of view is to be achieved. While this section has focused on making ethical decisions from the individual point of view, the next section examines the general issues of ethics focusing on the organization. Typically, the issues we cover next are discussed under the general banner of corporate social responsibility.

BEING SOCIALLY RESPONSIBLE

Corporate social responsibility is concerned with the constituencies to which corporations have obligations and the nature and extent of those obligations. Organizations have been coming to terms with the amount of resources they should devote to being socially responsible. Consider the following questions that confront managers daily:

- Should a firm implement environmental standards greater than those required by law?
- Should a firm insist on the same high level of safety standards in all its worldwide operations even if the laws of other countries accept lower standards?
- Do all employees, regardless of nationality or employment location, have the same rights?
- Should managerial actions that are illegal or morally unacceptable in one country be allowed in another country in which they are legal or morally acceptable?
- Should managers consider the interests of employees, customers, or general citizens over those of shareholders?

Questions such as these form the substance of social responsibility debates. Both social responsibility and managerial ethics focus on the "oughts" of conducting business. Although several approaches to corporate social responsibility exist, an examination of two fundamental perspectives will help you reflect on how you personally view the issue and how you might effectively interact with others holding differing perspectives.

The Efficiency Perspective

efficiency perspective
a particular perspective of corporate social responsibility that argues that the obligation of managers is to maximize profits for shareholders and leave social causes to governments and other organizations

Perhaps no contemporary person presents the **efficiency perspective** of social responsibility more clearly than Milton Friedman.[19] Quite simply, according to Friedman, the business of business is business. In other words, a manager's responsibility is to maximize profits for the owners of the business. Adam Smith is perhaps the earliest advocate of this approach. Smith concluded that the best way to advance the well-being of society is to place resources in the hands of individuals and allow market forces to allocate scarce resources to satisfy society's demands.[20]

Managers as Owners   When a manager of a business is also the owner, the self-interests of the owner are best achieved by serving the needs of society. If society demands that a product be made within certain environmental and safety standards, then it is in the best interests of the owner to produce the product accordingly. Otherwise, customers will likely purchase the product from competitors. Customers are more likely to purchase from firms that comply with widely shared and deeply held social values, so it makes sense for businesses to incorporate those values into their operations and products. To the extent that the cost of incorporating society's values is less than the price customers are willing to pay, the firm makes a profit.

Managers as Agents   In most large organizations today, the manager is not the owner. The corporate form of organization is characterized by the separation of ownership (shareholders) and control (managers). Managers serve as the agents of the organization's owners. Within this context, Friedman argues that managers should "conduct business in accordance with [owners'] desires, which will generally be to make as much money as possible while conforming to the basic rules of society, both those embodied in law and those embodied in ethical custom."[21] From Friedman's perspective, managers have no obligation to act on behalf of society if it does not maximize value for the shareholders. For example, packaging products in recycled paper should be undertaken only if doing so maximizes shareholder wealth. Whether such an action satisfies or benefits a small group of activists is irrelevant. Managers have no responsibility to carry out such programs; in fact, they have a responsibility *not* to undertake such action because it does not maximize shareholder wealth. Similarly, charitable donations are not the responsibility of corporations. Instead, managers should maximize the return to shareholders. Shareholders can then decide whether and to whom they want to make charitable donations.

From the efficiency perspective, it is impossible for managers to maximize shareholders' wealth and simultaneously attempt to fulfill all of society's needs. It is the responsibility of government to impose taxes and determine expenditures to meet society's needs. If managers pursue actions that benefit society but do not benefit shareholders, then they are exercising political power, not managerial authority.

Concerns with the Efficiency Perspective   The efficiency perspective assumes that markets are competitive and that competitive forces move firms toward fulfilling societal needs as expressed by consumer demand. Firms that do not respond to consumer demands in terms of products, price, delivery, safety, environmental impact, or any other dimension important to consumers will, through competition, be forced out of business. Unfortunately, however, corrective action often occurs after people are injured.

Arnold Dworkin, the owner of Kaufman's Bagel and Delicatessen in Skokie, Illinois, learned to pay attention to public safety the hard way. On a Wednesday, calls trickled in to the restaurant from customers complaining of vomiting, nausea, and stomach pains and by Friday the restaurant had to be closed. Customers were suffering from salmonella bacteria, which was traced to corned beef being cooked at only 90 degrees rather than the 140 degrees required by local health regulations. Although corrective measures were taken, three weeks later another customer was hospitalized with salmonella poisoning. This time the cause was traced to a leaky floorboard above a basement meat-drying table. Kaufman's lost approximately $250,000 in sales and $10,000 in food, and its insurance company paid out more than $750,000 for individual and class-action suits and hospital claims. Interestingly, because Dworkin dealt with the situation in a straightforward manner by disclosing all the information he had with customers and the media, quickly making every repair, and following all the recommended actions suggested by the safety and health board regardless of cost, his business returned to 90 to 95 percent of its original level within two years.[22]

The other major concern with the efficiency perspective is that corporations can impose indirect consequences (externalities) that may not be completely understood or anticipated. For example, the government of the United Kingdom enticed

Nissan with tax and other incentives to build a new automobile plant there. However, the trucks going in and out of the plant created traffic congestion and wear on public roads that were not completely accounted for in the government's proposal. These conditions slowed deliveries to the factory and also created inconveniences for the citizens. To some extent, the Nissan managers took actions that hurt Nissan shareholders and U.K. citizens as a function of externalities. Consider another example. Because of imperfect information, it may be difficult for you to correctly assess the costs of a chemical disaster at a grass fertilizer plant. Consequently, as a consumer you are unlikely to be willing to pay the appropriate price for the fertilizer that would cover the costs of adequate safety practices surrounding its production. As the plant manager, this may cause you to skip necessary safety practices in order to keep costs low and make a profit. It is not until inadequate safety policies and practices result in a chemical disaster and people are killed or injured that the impact of the externality (i.e., the chemical disaster) is fully appreciated by consumers and therefore appropriately priced in the market.

Social Responsibility Perspective

The social responsibility perspective contends that society grants existence to firms; therefore, firms have responsibilities and obligations to society as a whole, not just shareholders. Thus, while the efficiency perspective states that it is *socially responsible* to maximize the return to the shareholder, the social responsibility perspective states that it is *socially irresponsible* to maximize only shareholder wealth because shareholders are not the only ones responsible for the firm's existence. For instance, creditors of a corporation cannot go beyond the assets of the corporation and seek repayment from the assets of the owners. This protection is termed *limited liability*. This privilege to the corporation is granted by society, not by owners.[23] Thus, the existence of the firm is not solely a function of shareholders, and, therefore, the responsibilities of the firm cannot be restricted just to shareholders.

stakeholders
individuals or groups that have an interest in and are affected by the actions of an organization

Stakeholders   In the social responsibility perspective, managers must consider the legitimate concerns of other stakeholders beyond the shareholders. **Stakeholders** are individuals or groups that have an interest in and are affected by the actions of an organization. They include customers, employees, financiers, suppliers, communities, society at large, and shareholders. Customers have special standing within this set of constituencies because they provide the company with revenue.[24] Shareholders are also given special status, but in the stakeholder approach, shareholders are viewed as providers of risk capital rather than as sole owners. Consequently, shareholders are entitled to a *reasonable* return on the capital they put at risk, but they are not entitled to a *maximum* return because they are not solely responsible for the existence of the firm. To maximize the return to shareholders would take away returns owed to the other stakeholders. Thus, managers must make decisions and take actions that provide a reasonable return to shareholders, balanced against the legitimate concerns of customers, employees, financiers, communities, and society at large.

Concerns with the Social Responsibility Perspective   One of the key concerns with the social responsibility perspective is that important terms such as "reasonable returns" or "legitimate concerns" cannot be defined adequately. Given that reasonable returns to shareholders and legitimate concerns of other stakeholders could come into conflict, not knowing exactly what is reasonable or legiti-

EXHIBIT 5.8

Comparing Efficiency and Social Responsibility Perspectives

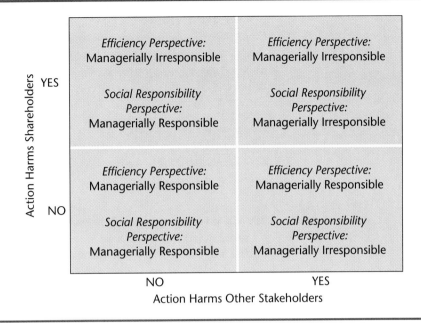

EXHIBIT 5.8

Comparing Efficiency and Social Responsibility Perspectives

mate reduces managers' ability to find the appropriate balance and act in socially responsible ways. It is possible that customers, employees, financiers, communities, and society at large will have conflicting and competing concerns. In such cases, how are managers to determine the most socially responsible action? Customers may be one of the most important stakeholders, but how much more important are they than the others? If customers want plastic bags for groceries but communities want paper bags, how can a manager decide which action is socially responsible?

Comparing the Efficiency and Stakeholder Perspectives

The efficiency and social responsibility perspectives differ mainly in terms of the constituencies to which organizations have responsibilities. The two perspectives differ little in their evaluations of actions that either harm or benefit both shareholders and society (see Exhibit 5.8). Their evaluations differ most markedly when actions help one group and harm the other. Actions that benefit shareholders but harm the other legitimate stakeholders would be viewed as managerially responsible from the efficiency perspective, but from the social responsibility perspective they would be viewed as socially irresponsible. Actions that harm shareholders but benefit the other legitimate stakeholders would be viewed as managerially irresponsible from the efficiency perspective, but from the social responsibility perspective would be viewed as socially responsible.

The following quotes illustrate how differently CEOs can view the issue of corporate social responsibility.[25]

Profits are like breathing. If you can't breathe, you can forget everything else that you're doing because you're not going to be around much longer.
—Robert E. Mercer, Goodyear Tire & Rubber

To talk about business altruistically going out and solving the world's problems is nonsense. The role of business is primarily to be successful and profitable, a good employer, and effective in its relationships with all its constituencies, not the least of which are its owners. There are problems that are in the best interest of the health of our economic system and the business that are part of it if they are solved. And there are some social problems that should not be our responsibility other than to support government action by the tax we pay. I do not think that you should look at business as having a primary role in life to solve social problems.

—Robert H. Malott, FMC

I work for the shareholders. I work for the employees. I work for the customers. If I don't make a good profit, I'm not doing a very good job for the owners and for the employees. If I make too much profit, my customers worry. And it's a constant balancing act.

—Richard E. Heckert, Du Pont

The only way for a corporation to exist and capitalism to survive is to be part of the whole society. Companies have to be concerned with the owners—the share-holders, the employees, and the customers.

—David T. Kerns, Xerox

Corporations can be short-sighted and worry only about our mission, products, and competitive standing. But we do it at our peril. We may need the goodwill of a neighborhood to enlarge a corner store. We may need well-funded institutions of higher learning to turn out the skilled technical employees we require. We may need adequate community health care to curb absenteeism in our plants. Or we may need fair tax treatment for an industry to be able to compete in the world economy. However small or large our enterprise, we cannot isolate our business from society around us.

—Robert D. Haas, Levi Strauss

Corporate Responses

As the previous quotes illustrate, how corporations react to the various pressures and constituencies connected to the topic of social responsibility varies widely. These reactions can be simplified and laid out on a continuum that ranges from defensive to proactive, as illustrated in Exhibit 5.9.

EXHIBIT 5.9

Corporate Responses

	Defenders	**Accommodaters**	**Reactors**	**Anticipators**
Belief:	We must fight against efforts to restrict or regulate our activities and profit-making potential.	We will change when legally compelled to do so.	We should respond to significant pressure even if we are not legally required to.	We owe it to society to anticipate and avoid actions with potentially harmful consequences, even if we are not pressured or legally required to do so.
Focus:	Maximize profits. Find legal loopholes. Fight new restrictions and regulations.	Maximize profits. Abide by the letter of the law. Change when legally compelled to do so.	Protect profits. Abide by the law. React to pressure that could affect business results.	Obtain profits. Abide by the law. Anticipate harmful consequences independent of pressures and laws.

Defenders   Companies that might be classified as defenders tend to fight efforts that they see as resulting in greater restriction and regulation of their ability to maximize profits. These firms often operate at the edge of the law and actively seek legal loopholes in conducting their business. Typically they change only when legally compelled to do so.

Accommodaters   These companies are less aggressive in fighting restrictions and regulations but they change only when legally compelled to do so. This type of firm tends to obey the letter of the law but does not make changes that might restrict profits if they are not required to.

Reactors   Reactor firms make changes when they feel that pressure from constituencies is sufficient such that nonresponsiveness could have a negative economic impact on the firm. For example, the firm might change to recycled paper for packaging only when the pressure from customers becomes strong enough that nonresponsiveness would lead customers to boycott their products or to simply choose a competitor's products that use recycled paper for packaging.

Anticipators   Firms in this category tend to believe that they owe an obligation to a variety of stakeholders—customers, employees, shareholders, general citizens, and so on—not to harm them independent of laws or pressures that restrict or regulate their actions. Firms in this category not only abide by the law, but they might take action to avoid harming constituencies, even when the constituencies might not be aware of the potential danger. For example, a firm might take steps to protect employees from harmful chemicals within the workplace even before employees suffered negative side effects sufficient for them to demand work environment changes.

Thinking about the two general approaches to corporate social responsibility and the four general categories of responses, how would you evaluate the case of Nike discussed in the Managerial Challenge box?

CONCLUDING COMMENTS

There is no universal opinion concerning managerial ethics or the social responsibility of corporations. Gray areas remain, and important questions go unanswered regardless of which fundamental perspective you adopt concerning ethical behavior or corporate social responsibility. For example, the efficiency approach argues that managers should seek to maximize shareholders' returns but must do so within the laws and ethical norms of the society. In today's increasingly global environment, a given firm may operate in a variety of societies. What if the norms of one society clash with those of another? Which societal norms should be honored?

A social responsibility approach also operates within equally large gray areas. For example, how can you calculate, let alone incorporate, conflicting needs of constituencies across countries? How can a Korean consumer's needs for low price for paper be balanced against the environmental concerns of Indonesian or Brazilian societies where large forests are being cut to produce paper? How can all of these concerns be balanced against the potential worldwide concern for the depletion of critical oxygen-providing trees?

MANAGERIAL CHALLENGE

IS NIKE'S CORPORATE RESPONSE TO CRITICISM SOCIALLY RESPONSIBLE?

Nike is facing a new challenge of Olympic proportions: a lawsuit filed in San Francisco Superior Court accusing the company of violating California's consumer laws by deliberately misleading consumers about the working conditions of thousands of its offshore laborers in countries like Vietnam, China, and Indonesia.

Nike employs about 22,000 people but has an additional 450,000 workers in Asian factories that are run by subcontractors who manufacture most of the company's active sportswear. According to the lawsuit, these factory workers are subjected to substandard working conditions, such as exposure to dangerous toxins and carcinogens; poor ventilation and/or air quality, forced overtime, and corporal punishment and abuse. For instance, the suit alleges that several female workers in Vietnam were forced to run laps around the perimeter of three warehouses as punishment from a supervisor. In addition, there is the issue of pay and whether or not these workers receive a fair wage. At the Yueyuan Factory No. 3 in Dongguan, China, the average monthly wage is 600 renimbi, which equals $73. Meals and living quarters are also provided. But in Vietnam, the monthly wage is about $40 per month, and workers must pay for their own accommodations. Finally, there is the problem of child labor law infractions, which is complicated by the differing age requirements found in different countries. For instance, the national minimum age requirement for workers in Indonesia is 14, whereas in the United States it is 16.

Nike has responded to the suit and its allegations (as well as other critics) in a variety of ways. The company claims that it will increase the outside monitoring of its overseas plants and raise the minimum age of its shoe factory workers to 18 and its apparel workers to 16. "At 18, the worker is generally more mature, has more work experience, is easier to train in health and safety issues, and therefore better suited to work in a footwear factory," claims Phil Knight, CEO of Nike. "Nike has zero tolerance for underage labor." The company has also agreed to apply U.S. safety standards for air quality to its foreign operations and says it has converted its use of toxic chemical solvents to water-based

products in the assembly of its footwear. And Nike employs a staff of 1,000 labor-practices managers to institute a program called SHAPE—Safety, Health, Attitude of Management, People, Environment. "We are the only company that has people dedicated exclusively to labor-practice enforcement," notes Brad Figel, Nike's lobbyist in Washington.

But Nike refuses to budge on the issue of wages; nor will it move its manufacturing back to the United States. "Americans pay $100 for a pair of shoes that a worker gets $3 a day to make," observes Kimberly Myoshi of San Francisco's Global Exchange. "They pay Michael Jordan $40 million to endorse them. Can't they find more money to pay the workers?" No, answers Nike, who maintains that the wages they pay foreign workers are good, based on the standards of the workers' countries. The recent 69 percent drop in earnings experienced by the company probably means that Nike will not be raising its wages anytime soon.

Nike is in a difficult position. The lawsuit and other vocal critics, including various human rights groups, have tarnished the company's corporate image, yet the company staunchly resists criticism. "The action as filed appears to be more of a press release dressed up like a lawsuit," says Nike in a prepared statement released from its Oregon headquarters. The company consistently claims that the suit is relying on anecdotes, not facts. "This is something we take seriously because of our respect for California courts, our shareholders, and consumers," says Nike spokeswoman Vizhier Mooney. "But perhaps one positive aspect is that a court of law is a forum where facts triumph over anecdotes." In turn, attorneys for the plaintiffs in the California lawsuit say that they will travel to Asia to see firsthand exactly what is going on in Nike's foreign factories.

Sources: "Nike CEO: I Can Change," CNN Web site, May 12, 1998; Aurelio Rojas, "Nike Faces Suit over Factory Conditions," *San Francisco Chronicle*, April 21, 1998; "Unsafe Conditions at Nike Factory in Vietnam Revealed in '96 Audit," HoustonChronicle.com, November 9, 1997; Bill Saporito, "Taking a Look Inside Nike's Factories," *Time* 151, no. 12 (March 30, 1998) [no page numbers; online articles].

In addition to the difficulty of determining the relative weight of different constituencies, managers face the challenge of trying to determine the weights of different groups within one category of constituencies across national borders. How are such determinations made? For example, firms may have employees in many countries, and the concerns of these employees will most likely differ. Employees in Japan may want the firm to maximize job security, while employees in England may want the firm to maximize wages. Similarly, German consumers may want firms to have high global environmental standards, and Indonesian consumers may have no such concerns. Which standards should be adopted?

The general debates concerning ethics and social responsibility have raged for generations. The purpose of this chapter has not been to resolve the debate but rather to examine the assumptions and rationales of fundamental perspectives. We hope this examination enables you to evaluate your own views, so that you will be prepared when situations arise concerning ethics or social responsibility. Perhaps then the pressure of the moment will be less likely to cause you to take actions that you might later regret. Understanding the general frameworks also helps you to better appreciate others who have differing perspectives and, thereby, interact more effectively with them.

KEY TERMS

code of ethical conduct 125	magnitude of the	social consensus 124
compensatory justice 123	consequences 124	stakeholders 136
concentration of effect 124	managerial ethics 117	temporal immediacy 124
corporate social responsibility 117	moral intensity 123	universal approach 122
distributive justice 122	moral rights approach 122	utilitarian approach 120
efficiency perspective 134	probability of effect 124	whistle blower 131
Foreign Corrupt Practices Act 133	procedural justice 122	
justice approach 122	proximity 124	

REVIEW QUESTIONS

1. Define *managerial ethics*. What are the key differences between managerial ethics and corporate social responsibility?
2. The utilitarian approach to ethics is often called the "greatest good" approach. What are the key challenges in determining the greatest good?
3. What are the two key elements of the moral rights approach to business ethics?
4. How is the universal approach different from the "golden rule" of do unto others as you would have them do unto you?
5. What are the key elements of distributive, procedural, and compensatory justice, and how are the three related to each other?
6. What is moral intensity?
7. What are the six factors that influence moral intensity? Describe and give an example of each one.
8. According to Adam Smith, it is in the best interests of managers and organizations to make ethical decisions. What is the basis of his argument?
9. What is a company code of ethical conduct and what areas are typically addressed in such codes?
10. Why do companies without codes of ethics seem to be no worse off than companies with codes of ethics in terms of the number of incidents of ethical wrongdoing?
11. What is a whistler blower?

DISCUSSION QUESTIONS

1. Countries such as India and Mexico and states such as Georgia and Utah have "employment at will" laws or practices (i.e., the right of an employer to fire an employee for any reason or for no reason). Is this ethical from each of the basic ethical decision-making approaches? Why or why not?

2. Which of the basic approaches to ethical decision-making most closely matches your approach for dealing with ethical dilemmas?

3. Is it wise for a government to try to legislate ethics through laws such as the FCPA?

4. What is the ethical climate like in your school? What is your school's policy or honor code concerning cheating? What is your ethical responsibility if you see someone cheating?

5. Would you be willing to be a whistle blower? On what type of issue would you blow the whistle? Inflated overtime submitted on a government contract? Sexual harassment? What organizational and personal factors would you consider?

6. Consider the following scenario: A sales representative from a textbook publisher calls on your professor to try to get him or her to adopt a new textbook. Is it okay for the professor to accept a free lunch from a publisher's sales representative? If it is okay for a professor to accept a free lunch, what about a free game of golf? What about a free set of golf clubs after the game?

CLOSING CASE

Ben & Jerry's: Is Sainthood Impossible?

Can companies successfully pursue their profit objectives while honoring their commitment to social responsibility? Many cynics indicate that the term "business ethics" is a contradiction—and that the main motive for business is profit, which is contradictory to ethical behavior. Milton Friedman once asserted that a business's real social responsibility is "to make lots of money for its shareholders, create jobs for the community, and pay taxes to the government." This perspective has been the challenge of one business that has been held up as the epitome of an ethical company: Ben & Jerry's Homemade, Inc.

The story of how Ben & Jerry's got started is now legend. Two self-described ex-hippies, Ben Cohen and Jerry Greenfield, started their super-premium ice cream business in 1978 as renegade competitors to ice cream giant, Pillsbury (then owner of Häagen-Dazs). Part of the company's appeal was "the small guys versus the big, bad corporation," and Ben & Jerry's taunted its main competitor by taking out an ad in Rolling Stone magazine and asking readers to "help two Vermont hippies fight the giant Pillsbury Corporation." Jerry Greenfield even picketed

Pillsbury headquarters in Minneapolis and handed out pamphlets asking, "What's the Doughboy Afraid of?"

The other part of the company's appeal was the social responsibility upon which the company was built. As part of its promise to society, Ben & Jerry's regularly contributed 7.5 percent of its pretax corporate income to charities (compared with a national corporate average of 1.5 percent), maintained a strong commitment to recycling, and developed creative products to promote its many social causes. One such product was Rainforest Crunch ice cream, which contained Brazil nuts from the rainforests of South America, to help promote the growth of agriculture in the rainforests. Brownies used in other ice cream flavors came from a New York bakery that employed homeless people. The company advertised in its packaging that its products were "all natural," something that their competitors could not necessarily claim.

Ben & Jerry's growth exploded from the late 1970s to the early 1990s. By 1994, however, the company began to have financial difficulties in the face of strong competition from Häagen-Dazs and an overall downturn in the economy. The company's long-term mission of social responsibility did not help its short-term financial objectives, and stock prices plummeted. To survive, Ben & Jerry's had to hire a "real" CEO—giving the company a more corporate image than it had previously had—and make profit a priority. Unwillingly, the small, renegade company started to approach the corporate image that it had always fought while trying to maintain its image of ethical purity.

It was during this downturn that the media discovered some of the skeletons hidden behind Ben & Jerry's saintly façade. The "all natural" product claims were disputed, as the media found that many of Ben & Jerry's ice cream varieties contained artificial flavors and preservatives. One of its flavors, Cherry Garcia (named after the rock musician of the Grateful Dead, Jerry Garcia), was discovered to have sulfur dioxide as a preservative.

In addition, some of the social causes Ben & Jerry's helped to promote turned sour. A clergyman, James Carter, who ran a New Jersey bakery that employed recovering drug addicts to churn out apple pies, struck a deal with Ben & Jerry's. Carter delivered his bakery's pies to Ben Cohen at the company's Vermont headquarters, which Ben & Jerry's turned into a new apple pie frozen yogurt. After two years of business together, sales of the apple pie yogurt fell, and Ben & Jerry's was forced to eventually cut off the business. Carter had to lay off his employees and was left with a half million dollars of debt in the form of unused apple pie inventory. "It's pretty cute, this social mission," Carter said bitterly. "But the bottom line is, Ben & Jerry's buried my company."

There was even controversy over the Rainforest Crunch ice cream. Under the "Save the Rainforest" crusade, the label on Rainforest Crunch promised that "money from these nuts will help Brazilian forest peoples start a nut-shelling cooperative that they'll own and operate." North American consumers fell in love with the campaign, and the flavor was so successful that the Xapuri cooperative—the South American growers who supplied the nuts for Rainforest Crunch—collapsed under the demand. The cooperative sold whatever land they could after the collapse to purchase cars and houses. Their leaders complained that

the growers had been lured by the promise of dollars, not by the encouragement to cultivate the rainforests. To continue production of Rainforest Crunch, Ben & Jerry's ended up buying 95 percent of the nuts from commercial suppliers, including the Mutran family, a notorious business that had reportedly killed labor organizers.

Did Ben & Jerry's innocently step into situations from which they could not escape, or did they have the same profit motives as the rest of corporate America? Was it possible to turn the socially conscious attitude of the 1960s into a 1990s ad slogan without destroying its intent? In an ironic twist of fate, Ben & Jerry's sent a pint of its newly created Cherry Garcia (under the slogan "What a Long Strange Dip It's Been") to their inspiration, Jerry Garcia, himself a popular promoter of social causes. What they received in return was a letter from his lawyer demanding royalties for the use of his name and music. Years later, Ben & Jerry's finally got their revenge: As soon as Jerry Garcia's death was announced, sales of Cherry Garcia frozen yogurt shot through the roof. Still, the return to shareholders from this saintly strategy has not been heavenly. Since its high of $32 in 1992, the stock price for Ben & Jerry's has dropped essentially in half.

QUESTIONS

1. In your opinion, did Ben & Jerry's compromise its mission in the pursuit of profit? What other strategies might it have used?

2. If an ethically sound company such as Ben & Jerry's cannot maintain corporate sainthood, can other companies expect to do so?

3. How could Ben & Jerry's have managed expectations of its "do-good" image a little better?

4. Would you attribute these outcomes to inexperience, nature of the business, unethical behavior on Ben & Jerry's part, or something else? Support your answer.

Sources: Adapted from: Alex Taylor III, "Yo, Ben! Yo, Jerry! It's Just Ice Cream!" *Fortune,* April 28, 1997; and Hanna Rosin, "The Evil Empire: The Scoop on Ben & Jerry's Crunchy Capitalism," *The New Republic,* September 11, 1995, pp. 22–26.

CHAPTER 6

MANAGING INNOVATION AND ENTREPRENEURSHIP*

LEARNING OBJECTIVES

After studying this chapter, you should be able to:

- Differentiate know-how and know-who issues in preparing for self-employment.
- Compare and contrast the American, European, and Asian models of entrepreneurship.
- Explain the life cycles of new ventures, new industries, and the innovation process.
- Describe the three different models of entrepreneurship.
- Explain the concept of the innovation adoption curve and its implications for choosing customers for new products, services, or firms.
- Describe the types of learning that apply to organizational innovations.

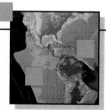

Marc Andreessen of Netscape Communications

At 21, University of Illinois undergraduate Mark Andreessen made $6.85 an hour as part of a six-person team at the National Center for Supercomputer Applications (NCSA) writing code for a graphics program to run on NCSA's supercomputer. But Andreessen divided his time between his official project and his personal pet project—a "hack," or program, called a "browser." This program would provide a graphical interface for the Internet, just as Windows provides a graphical interface for a personal computer. In particular, the browser would provide graphical access to a new type of 'Net service, called the World Wide Web, that combined text, graphics, and connections, or "hotlinks," to other Internet resources.

Andreessen's NCSA boss, Larry Smarr, didn't even know about the browser until he saw Andreessen demonstrating it to some visiting government researchers, but seeing the prospects, and the outsiders' reactions, Smarr made the project an official high priority. Andreessen,

*This chapter was written by Jerome Katz of Saint Louis University and edited by the authors of this book.

computer whiz Eric Bina, and four others created the graphical browser now called Mosaic, which the center made available for free to everyone.

Like Visicalc for the Apple II, or Lotus 1-2-3 for the IBM-PC, Mosaic was called a breakthrough product, one that created and legitimized a new computer program niche—the Internet browser—transforming the Internet from the playground of researchers, professors, and students into the Information Superhighway and the new market of the 1990s.

Andreessen believed that Mosaic could be improved. When contacted by Jim Clark, the founder of Silicon Graphics, he set out to develop a better browser. Their company, Netscape Communications, was launched in April 1994. By the end of the year Andreessen, who was now Netscape's Vice President of Technology, and his team produced a graphical browser that was at least 10 times faster than Mosaic. It also offered more options for displaying graphics, and it could deal directly with more of the Internet than Mosaic. The product was called Netscape Navigator, and like Mosaic, it was made available free to nearly everyone using the Internet. Within a year, Navigator controlled 75 percent or more of the market for browsers. More important, Navigator was a key factor in the 10,000-fold increase in World Wide Web usage in the intervening year.

When Netscape made its initial public offering of stock in 1995, it corralled over $2 *billion* for a firm with only a handful of products and a balance sheet still in the red. (In comparison, software giant Microsoft was worth around $56 billion.) Andreessen's 2.6 percent share of Netscape brought him over $50 million initially, and over $250 million within six months. He was now in charge of a team of programmers that was doubling in size every three months, trying to complete a new generation of browser every three months, and meanwhile competing head-to-head daily with the largest and best-financed personal computer software company in the world—Microsoft. All this and he was still only 23.

By 1998, Andreessen held the title of Executive Vice President of Products for Netscape, when America Online bid $4 billion for Netscape's stock. At the time, he owned or had options on 2,000,000 plus shares of Netscape, guaranteeing him around $90 million in AOL stock. By now he was 26, and with nearly six years racing at the pace of Internet time, he was one of the "old men" of an industry that didn't even exist a decade before.

Andreessen's ideas and hunches made millionaires, even billionaires, of others. For example, in 1995, he invited a couple of Stanford doctoral students in electrical engineering to move their list of Netscape bookmarks over to Netscape's servers. The students were twenty-somethings Jerry

Yang and David Filo. The bookmark list was the first version of the Web directory service we know as YAHOO!, and by late 1998, both Young and Filo passed the $1 billion mark in personal wealth.

Sources: John Markoff, "6 Tips on How to Earn $52 Million by Age 24," *New York Times,* August 14, 1995, Late Edition—Final, Section D, p. 5; "Spinning a Golden Web: Marc Andreessen's Internet Software Earned Him $50 Million in One Day," *People,* September 11, 1995, Money Section, p. 74; James Collins, "Business: High Stakes Winners," *Time* 147, no. 8 (February 19, 1996), pp. 42–47, J. Hodges, "Hello, My Name Is Croesus," *Fortune,* August 3, 1998; personal communication with Sue Walton, press relations, Netscape Communications, December 12, 1998 (swalton@netscape.com).

Just as all managers are likely to face ethics issues at some times, perhaps many, in their careers, so will they be likely to innovate. The need to approach managerial opportunities from a creative, innovative, and entrepreneurial perspective is becoming more and more critical in today's rapidly changing environment. Not only the perspective, but also the spirit, of innovation and entrepreneurship is essential for dealing with a wide variety of managerial issues and opportunities. Mark Andreessen, Jerry Yang, and David Filo are examples of a growing list of people who have seized those opportunities and transformed the way the world works. This chapter discusses how such people have revolutionized business, what obstacles they have overcome, and which ingredients are necessary for an individual or firm to instill a stronger entrepreneurial approach to the practice of management, whether in start-up or existing organizations.

Specifically, in this chapter we begin with a discussion of the importance of innovation and entrepreneurship for managers and organizations and indicate the relation between these two key terms. Next, we address the issue of "what is an entrepreneur?" and the implications of the answer for career choices. This is followed by a comparison of the predominant models of entrepreneurship that exist in three major regions of the world: the United States, Europe, and Asia. Cutting across all of those models, however, is the new-venture life cycle. The principal sources from which individuals and organizations obtain their innovative and entrepreneurial ideas that can initiate that life cycle—technology, the market, and the organization—is the subject of the next section. The chapter concludes with a consideration of issues of managing the pace and stages of innovation, and with a look at the role of learning in the overall innovation process.

THE IMPORTANCE OF INNOVATION AND ENTREPRENEURSHIP

innovation
the creation of new ideas, products, services, or processes through improvement, discovery, or invention

entrepreneurship
a special type of innovation applied to creating and exploiting new commercial opportunities

Innovation is the creation of new ideas, products, services, or processes through improvement, discovery, or invention. Innovation can occur anywhere—in business, education, sports, or families. **Entrepreneurship** is a special type of innovation applied to creating and exploiting new commercial opportunities, a new product or service, a new way of distributing goods, a new market, or a new organization. Economist Joseph Schumpeter called entrepreneurship the process of "creative destruction," because so often new commercial opportunities challenge old ways of doing business.[1] For example, as personal computers took over business desktops, the makers of "big iron"—mainframe computers—saw their sales plummet.

Entrepreneurship has three important impacts on business. The most obvious one is as a career choice: Almost half of all business school graduates are expected to be self-employed at some time in their career. Second, entrepreneurship lies at the core of how people organize a business. Entrepreneurial firms start out small, even when they are units of large companies, and these small firms follow predictable patterns in regard to their structure and operation. Third, entrepreneurship represents the major push behind innovation in capitalist societies, as people try to improve or create new products or services to capture markets and profits.

Entrepreneurship also has a special significance in political and economic spheres of life, because the entrepreneurial process is the foundation for free enterprise systems. The constant search for, creation of, and exploitation of opportunities require several forms of freedom, such as the freedom to associate with others, the freedom to travel, the freedom to enter into contracts, and the freedom to create and possess private property, such as land, or intellectual property, such as patents or copyrights.

WHAT IS AN ENTREPRENEUR?

Those who practice entrepreneurship are called entrepreneurs, and there are generally thought to be three types. Being able to recognize the different entrepreneurial types helps managers, and even other entrepreneurs, better understand the aspirations of the entrepreneur and predict the most likely business strategies and organizational goals of the entrepreneur's business.

High-growth entrepreneurs are business owners who are primarily interested in achieving a major impact in their business—through increasing the worth of their business when sold or increasing the size, market share, or technological leadership of the firm. Such entrepreneurs usually talk about their firms in terms of milestones they have met or that lie ahead, and their focus is on achievement rather than survival. Bill Gates of Microsoft is a clear example of the classic high-growth entrepreneur.

Corporate entrepreneurs, or intrapreneurs, share the outlook of the high-growth entrepreneur, but they are employees of a larger organization. Don Estridge was the IBM corporate entrepreneur who created the IBM personal computer, and Hyman Rickover was a corporate entrepreneur in the military who championed the creation of the nuclear submarine force.

Not everyone is suited to the high-risk, high-growth path, however. The third type of entrepreneur, **small business owners**, aims for survival for the business and a comfortable living. Small business owners talk more about day-to-day business issues than grand strategies and milestones. They can be found in most professions—for example, a doctor's office is a small business specializing in delivering medical services—and in the businesses we frequent every day, such as restaurants, shops, and service firms.

high-growth entrepreneurs
business owners who are primarily interested in achieving a major impact in their business—through increasing the worth of their business when sold or increasing the size, market share, or technological leadership of the firm

corporate entrepreneurs (or intrapreneurs)
innovative employee-managers within established firms

small business owner
an entrepreneur who owns a business that is not dominant in its field and employs a small number of people (generally fewer than 500)

ENTREPRENEURSHIP AS A CAREER CHOICE

Despite evidence of the innovative, often unpredictable, role entrepreneurs play in the economy, most social scientists tend to look at entrepreneurs and intrapreneurs as simply managers in a different setting. As a result, few theories of entrepreneurial behavior or entrepreneurial personality have been formulated to date.

Evidence in the real world indicates that there is not one "entrepreneurial type." Rather, a wide variety of people can be successful entrepreneurs. Consider two famous media entrepreneurs. Carl Sagan held a Ph.D. in astrophysics and was a paragon of organization. His dissertation was on cleaning up noise from the Venus probe satellite. He became a nationally recognized expert on space and science generally, one of the people on whom public broadcasting depended to interpret science for the masses. His production company created the PBS series *Cosmos* and best-selling books *Cosmos* and *The Dragons of Eden*. He was a leading advocate for politically liberal causes before his death in 1996.

Rush Limbaugh dropped out of college when he got exasperated with outlining a talk in his speech class. To this day, he organizes his work using dozens, sometimes hundreds, of little notes. He became a radio announcer and worked his way up through bigger and more powerful stations, finally creating a conservative radio talk show that became the standard for dozens of imitators, conservative and liberal alike. "The Rush Limbaugh Show" is America's highest-rated radio program. Limbaugh's newsletter is one of the top sellers in the United States, and each of his books has become a national best-seller. He is one of the most widely known supporters of U.S. politically conservative causes today.

These two men share little in terms of background, work habits, or world view. Yet they were both successful entrepreneurs in the same industry, in the same locale, at the same time. The lesson for potential entrepreneurs is that it is possible to be successful without fitting a particular mold. What would Limbaugh and Sagan have in common? Both were reported to be exceptionally hard workers, both had tremendous passion for their work, both could articulate a vision of what was special or unique about their work, both had a clear idea of what their products were and who their customers were, and both were good at inspiring others to join. Thus, with perseverance at work, vision regarding goals, and clear thinking about what is sold and who will buy it, it is possible to be a successful entrepreneur.

Entrepreneurship is also highly likely among specific groups, such as immigrants, family-owned businesses, or people who choose vocations (such as dentistry) where the majority of people are self-employed.[2] Also, people who choose to work in new industries tend to be self-employed. For example, when personal computers were introduced, they were sold by hundreds of small stores owned by entrepreneurs. All four of these sources of entrepreneurs depend on long-standing structural elements in an economy. They are fairly stable factors in the United States, for example. If one or more of these structural factors apply to you, your likelihood of becoming self-employed rises dramatically.

Personal circumstances also make some individuals more likely to become self-employed. One that we just mentioned is vocational choice. Choosing a profession such as surgeon, writer, or lawyer can lead some people to entrepreneurship. Another personal factor is location. You may live in a city where there are no firms that need your skills, learning, or knowledge.[3] To use your talents, you may need to start your own business.

What can be done to prepare for self-employment? The answer is to build up knowledge and professional contacts, or know-how and know-who. Know-how consists of five types of knowledge: product or service (what is being sold), industry (what competitors are doing and how they do it), market (who buys it, where, why, and for how much), management (planning, employee management, etc.), and self-employment (taking total responsibility, creating organizational goals, choosing and managing risks). Today, over 1,400 U.S. colleges offer courses in entrepreneurship and small business, providing much of the needed know-how as part of a business degree. A traditional way to gain know-how is to work for someone else in a similar firm before starting out on your own. Experience gained in this manner helps a new entrepreneur become recognized in an industry, market, and product or service. Taking on managerial responsibilities somewhere along the line makes sense, too. Even if not in your chosen industry, being the manager of any business or department helps prepare you for your own firm. Along the same lines, running even a small business of your own—lawn care, sales, or the like—helps you gain understanding and the basic credentials to show you can manage your own business.

sole proprietorship
a form of organizing a business in which one person owns the business in its entirety

partnership
a form of organizing a business where two or more people own the firm together

corporation
a form of business created through application to a state for a "corporate entity;" stock is issued representing ownership

Know-who is an often-overlooked element in entrepreneurship. Most entrepreneurs are **sole proprietorships**, a business form where the firm and the entrepreneur are the same. Other ways to organize are as **partnerships**, where two or more people share business ownership, and as a **corporation**, where the state legally recognizes a specially created "corporate entity" composed of stock held by one or more people. Sole proprietors usually are not solo. They tap the expertise of advisors such as bookkeepers, accountants, lawyers, and other entrepreneurs. They get advice from customers and salespeople who call on them. They seek out financial support from and have to impress bankers, investors, or companies that agree to sell to the proprietor on credit. So, personal contacts with other businesspeople are a vital part of an entrepreneurial venture.

The lesson of entrepreneurship as a career choice is that nearly any type of person and firm can be successful. This chapter is filled with examples of people who differ in age, gender, nationality, occupation, personality, and style who created businesses, both large and small, and made successes of them. They may have given us products as mundane as Halloween leafbags or as path-breaking as the personal computer, but their diverse stories and achievements mean there is room for nearly every person and idea in the segment of our workforce we call entrepreneurs.

MODELS OF ENTREPRENEURSHIP

Entrepreneurship as the creation and exploitation of opportunities has been around for a long time. In the Mediterranean 2,200 years ago, Phoenician trading vessels were floating small businesses. At the heart of all the great explorations like those of Marco Polo, Ferdinand Magellan, Christopher Columbus, and Meriwether Lewis and William Clark lay a hope of new ideas to exploit, new riches to be made, and new markets to tap. Small shop owners were the economic engine for much of China. But entrepreneurship is not uniform around the world. Today, there are three distinct societal models for entrepreneurship: American, European, and Asian.[4]

American Model

The American model of entrepreneurship emphasizes economic freedom and social freedom, what economists often call classic free enterprise. Economic freedom involves the ability to create, enter into, and execute contracts without prior government approval or involvement; the ability to make and use profits autonomously; and the ability to enter into economic activities such as selling or buying with minimal government control. In practice, government does get involved in the U.S. free enterprise process through activities such as registering corporations and company names; through inspection standards for the Occupational Safety and Health Administration (OSHA), the Equal Employment Opportunity Commission (EEOC), and other agencies; and through taxation. But the American model shows relatively low government involvement compared with other places in the world.

Social freedom refers to the autonomy individuals and firms possess within the society. It includes those ideas often called freedom of choice—the ability to choose with whom you work or play, what you buy, and what you read or watch. It also refers to the amount of power an individual holds in dealings with the government. In the U.S. system, the Bill of Rights protects individuals against government interference in the economic arena, the legal arena, and the media. Phrases such as "innocent until proven guilty," "freedom of speech," "freedom from unreasonable search and seizure," "freedom from cruel and unusual punishment," and the like mean that U.S. citizens are free to pursue their personal interests without government retribution, even when a person or firm is critical of the government. The American model tries to favor the rights of the individual over the rights of the government, and in U.S. law a business is viewed as an individual. Under the American model, the powers of individuals and firms generally balance each other, so individual rights such as consumer protection and business rights such as free markets balance each other most of the time.

European Model

The European model of entrepreneurship places social freedom ahead of economic freedom, viewing businesses as trades within a society and giving "the people" as a whole substantial rights. When businesses and government disagree on what should be done, the goals of the people—the larger society—are almost always placed ahead of the goals of business. Under this model, the role of government is to create a level playing field for businesses and consumers and to achieve the societal aims of equality and quality of life through regulation. Under the European model, government provides detailed instructions to firms about how to organize and treat employees, how to build products, and how and where they may be marketed. Private property exists, as does the power of contracts, but the legal power of the individual, as consumer or employee, is greater than that of the firm.

Asian Model

The Asian model of entrepreneurship places economic freedom ahead of social freedom, in effect making traders and governments closer to equal in power in the society, with individuals holding less power. Under the Asian model, a firm has the right to do business unhampered by government or may even have direct government support. Regulation, where it exists, serves to protect local industry from imports. Individuals under these models may have fewer rights than under the American or European models, and in return, a greater part of the individual's social and legal support comes from his or her firm than under the other two models.

What is important for a manager or entrepreneur to understand about these models is that the process of entrepreneurship and its business consequences differ around the world. The classic European and Asian models erect very specific standards for products, but they do so for different reasons. European models do so to protect the consumer, Asian models to protect existing industry. American, European, and Asian models protect the rights of workers in entrepreneurial firms, but they do so in different ways. Americans have numerous laws and precedents permitting individual legal suits, but under European models the state is more likely to intervene for wronged workers, and under Asian models workers often have to fend for themselves. Why should an entrepreneur or intrapreneur worry about these different models? For the firm that decides to conduct business world-wide, recognizing the different variations of entrepreneurship is essential to a successful strategy. Although the manufacturing technology for a firm might be the same around the world, the legal, social, and political environments of the firm will differ, sometimes dramatically, under the three models, and to be equally successful, the wise entrepreneur or intrapreneur adapts the business to fit the different models of entrepreneurship.

THE NEW VENTURE LIFE CYCLE

Although a society's model of entrepreneurship establishes the context or environment in which new products, services, and firms emerge, the process of how a business is formed represents the central idea of entrepreneurship and innovation. Newness is what makes innovation and entrepreneurship distinctive from the stable, ongoing processes of established firms. Regardless of the industry, entrepreneurial firms tend to follow patterns of birth, growth, and stabilization or death. These patterns are called the new venture life cycle.

new venture life cycle
a five-stage model of the development of organizations: existence, survival, success, takeoff, and resource maturity

The **new venture life cycle** is drawn from the development models of individuals. Like people, firms go through stages, in effect being born and experiencing changes similar to childhood, adolescence, adulthood, and maturity. Different issues surface at each stage, although there are remarkable consistencies in the types of issues that firms face at any one stage.

Research into the new venture life cycle identifies five stages: existence, survival, success, takeoff, and resource maturity (see Exhibit 6.1).[5]

Existence

Existence is the "birth" process for a new firm. The goal of an entrepreneur at this stage is simply to get a business started. Studies have shown that at any moment, 4 percent of American workers are thinking about or working on starting a business,

EXHIBIT 6.1

The New Venture Life Cycle

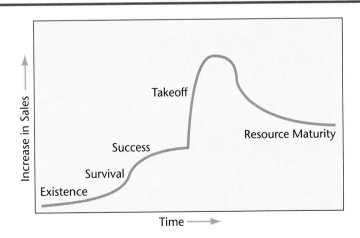

but only about 0.4 percent actually succeed in starting one.[6] Other research examined the conditions under which start-ups succeed, and four properties were found to be necessary to create a firm:

- Resources, such as capital, time, and raw materials that can be committed to the creation process
- A boundary, or a place for the firm to gather and protect its resources or simply in which it can exist—for example, a store or office in a physical space or a corporate charter in the legal arena
- Intention, the entrepreneur's decision to start or continue a business
- Exchange, making trades with customers—in effect "doing business"[7]

The four properties may occur in different orders. For example, Michael Dell of Dell Computers started by making a personal computer in his dorm room for himself. Friends and classmates were so impressed by the value that they asked him to make computers for them. Only after prospective customers made their exchange offers did Dell find he intended to start a business.

The four properties also identify what a prospective entrepreneur needs for her or his business to exist. The desire to have a business, called intention, alone is not enough. To be able to launch a viable business, the entrepreneur also needs resources such as a business idea and money; a physical or virtual business place, which is defined by a boundary; and, most of all, customers willing to buy the product or service. Lacking one of the four, the business is unlikely to start.

Survival

Survival is the "early childhood" of firms, and like young children, young firms face problems because of their lack of size, reserves, or experience. Many industries have rules of thumb about how long it takes before the survival of a firm is relatively certain. For a restaurant, for example, surviving two years after opening its doors usually marks the restaurant as a long-term survivor.

The problems faced by survival-stage firms are varied. They usually have little money in the bank, so they live from their cash flow and are dependent on the cash cycle. For example, retailers need products to sell when they open their doors, and obtaining those products will cost hard dollars until the firm can build a credit history. Although a good stock of merchandise is needed on opening day, it may take weeks to sell all the merchandise and replenish the funds paid for the merchandise, especially because some customers buy on credit and can stretch out payments. This time lag between full bank accounts describes the cash cycle. For a new firm, with its money tied up in the inventory and credit extended to customers, any unexpected problem that eats up the remaining money used for wages, utilities, taxes, and the like—the working capital—can force the firm into bankruptcy. From a managerial perspective, this problem is critical. The single greatest cause of business failure is financial inadequacy—in other words, not enough money when you need it.

The other two major problems are finding and refining a steady base of customers and gaining legitimacy as a professionally run business in the eyes of financiers and other businesses. Without customers, a business cannot grow, and even with customers and cash, if a business is not seen as legitimate, it always works at a disadvantage in the marketplace. Entrepreneurs, especially innovative ones, face this problem all the time. Consider Chris Whittle, the young magazine entrepreneur who developed a string of campus magazines and successfully turned around *Esquire*. His next project was Channel One, a commercially financed educational television channel distributed for free to schools. The benefits to participating schools were twofold: high-quality educational programming provided for students and bundled state-of-the-art television equipment provided free to every schoolroom hooked into Channel One. However, many educators, parents, and traditionalists in the media objected to the idea of companies paying Whittle to gain commercial access to young students. While fighting negative public opinion, Whittle struggled to sell advertising to commercial sponsors leery of boycotts or negative public reaction. He sold Channel One after two unprofitable years of operation.[8]

Ten years ago, the belief was that over one-half of all new firms close within two years, but almost a decade of research has shown that new firms do much better than previously thought. Statistics published by the U.S. Small Business Administration show that 80 percent of new firms survive two years, and nearly half are still in business five years after starting.[9] Still, starting a business is one of the riskiest actions an individual can undertake in business, since she or he must make a tremendous commitment of personal and financial resources, both time and money.

Success

Success occurs once the firm is established in its market. It is marked by consistent performance, either continuing growth or stabilization at some level of business. Its level of performance must be adequate to produce a profit and even to create slack resources the small business owner can use, such as time off from work, a slower pace at work, or hiring additional personnel to take on more of the tasks of the owner.

The goal of the success stage is to consolidate the gains made and systematize them, in effect to make the business more "businesslike." At this stage, employees begin to receive training, procedures become standardized, and sales turn into marketing. The small business owner becomes more businesslike to gain the benefits of repetition. For example, if there is an established, written procedure for opening the business each day, and employees are trained in how to do it, the owner can delegate that task. Many small business owners hope the success stage lasts a long, long time. However, for high-growth and corporate entrepreneurs, this is the period during which they can catch their breath and lay the groundwork for rapid growth.

Takeoff

Takeoff refers to a period of rapid growth in the lives of firms, but it especially characterizes the high-growth and corporate entrepreneurship approaches. Takeoff is seen when sales increase in multiples. In the example of Netscape's Navigator, usage went from none to approximately 4 million copies in less than one year. Although takeoff might seem to be a state of unbridled joy for the entrepreneur, it can be devastating. During takeoff, the firm tries to balance surging customer demand with the limitations it always faces in manufacturing the needed products or services. Consider, for example, the challenge posed by the success of the Halloween leaf bag in the Managerial Challenge box.

Netscape cleverly avoided an availability problem. By making the Navigator program available for immediate downloading through the Internet, customers could obtain copies without straining the finances or manufacturing capabilities of the fledgling Netscape Communications Corporation. Clearly, managing takeoff means

MANAGERIAL CHALLENGE

BALANCING BETWEEN TAKEOFF AND TAKEDOWN

In 1990, Ben Zinbarg's 17-year-old Sun-Hill Company introduced the Stuff-A-Pumpkin home Halloween decoration. It was an ordinary plastic leaf bag, but it was bright orange instead of the regular dark color. Once filled with leaves, it was designed to display a giant jack-o'-lantern face. The new product, marketed through discount stores, was an overnight success. Orders for millions of bags came flooding in, completely overwhelming Zinbarg's ability to provide the product. Seeing Sun-Hill stretched to its limit, Zinbarg's personal banker of 17 years stopped his credit line, and 23 other banks turned Sun-Hill down, despite millions of dollars of orders in hand.

Competitors quickly realized Sun-Hill's weakness and muscled into the market. Only by securing financing from a friend, investing all his own money, and convincing suppliers and employees to delay receiving money owed them was Zinbarg able to buy additional production capacity to fill his orders. Meanwhile, he aggressively pursued legal action against competitors who infringed on the patent and copyright he held for the Stuff-A-Pumpkin. Even for an experienced company, an unexpected takeoff can be a near-death experience.

Source: Joan Stableford, "For Sun-Hill Industries, Success Last Year Was in the Bag," *Fairfield County Business Journal* 22, no. 19 (May 27, 1991), Section 1, p. 10.

that the entrepreneur or manager needs to do careful planning to anticipate and then facilitate increased production or to develop clever distribution strategies.

Resource Maturity

Resource maturity occurs when a small business begins to look more and more like a large business. Managing maturity is a major problem facing many businesses today. The life span of the typical family firm (which describes over 90 percent of all businesses in the United States) is 24 years. Looked at another way, family business experts report that 70 percent of existing family businesses never survive into a second generation. To achieve the desired longevity, attention to management succession planning is required. In succession planning, the key resources become the knowledge of the outgoing generation, such as customer contacts and favors owed to the firm, and the skills and ideas of the incoming generation of managers along with their sensitivity to the existing culture of the organization. For survival, the firm will depend on its new leaders and the creative spark they provide. This, in turn, brings us to the questions: From what directions does that innovative spark arise? What sources set it off?

ENTREPRENEURIAL DIRECTIONS FOR INNOVATIONS

What do superstores and supersaver airfares have in common? Each was a major innovation, a process by which a new idea or practice is made useful. Understanding innovation is essential to modern business managers because it is one of the driving forces in business today, and one of the greatest challenges managers and entrepreneurs face.

Innovations can come from any of three directions (see Exhibit 6.2).[10] They can come from technology, which is focused on how something gets done; from the

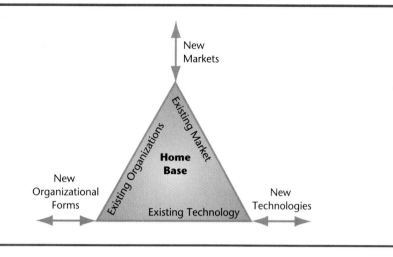

EXHIBIT 6.2

The Three Directions of Innovation

market, which focuses on who will use the innovation; or from the organization, which is where the innovation takes place. In practice, innovations require changes on all three dimensions. A new technology may require a new market to sustain it and a new organization to sell it. This was true for automobiles when they first came out in the late 19th century, and it remained true for personal computers in the 1970s. Both new technologies required specialized organizations such as car dealers and computer retailers such as Computerland. Both technologies looked for markets to legitimize themselves, although in both cases the first markets were hobbyists with an interest in technology and a willingness to tinker with their new "toys."

In the following sections, we consider each of the major factors in innovation—the technology, the market, and the firm—to understand the role innovation plays in managing the modern firm.

Technology Innovations for Products and Services

product innovation
innovations based on truly new product ideas or on superior functional performance

process innovations
improvements in an existing product or service, usually with the goal of reducing manufacturing costs

Innovations in goods tend to fall into one of two types. The classic new product idea, called a **product innovation**, is most often associated with small entrepreneurial businesses. Usually these innovations are based on truly new product ideas, such as the personal computer, or on superior functional performance, such as Compaq Computers were over IBM-PCs in the early 1980s. At the other end of the scale are large businesses and their **process innovations**, typically (but not always) small improvements in an existing product or service, usually with the goal of reducing manufacturing costs.

Consider the airline industry as a source of both product and process innovations.[11] Major product innovations have included replacing propeller-driven planes with jet aircraft and introducing computerized reservation systems. The most important change from a college student's perspective, however, came with the truly extreme process innovation of Freddy Laker, father of the "no frills" airline. He combined several opportunities, such as old jets available at extremely low lease rates and the availability of secondary airports like Newark instead of New York's JFK, with a low-service approach to create ultracheap fares. In the United States, People Express copied Laker Airways's formula, and the major airlines suddenly faced a tremendous loss of revenue. Laker, a solo entrepreneur, turned the

The concept of surfing on snow was started by Jake Burton Carpenter in 1977 with his introduction of the snowboard. He started his company, Burton Snowboards, which is the largest snowboarding company in the world. Snowboarding has gained acceptance and extreme popularity worldwide, even becoming an Olympic event.

airline industry on its head like no one had done before, and he did it with a radical innovation.[12]

Given the new low prices of the no-frills carriers, the established airlines sought a way to compete. Some matched prices, but at the cost of their profits. Some abandoned routes to the no-frills carriers. Some tried to increase their share of full-fare (primarily business) travelers. But in the end, the winning formula took the form of another process innovation, one based on operations research and computerized information systems at American Airlines (see the Managerial Challenge box).

Innovation never ends, and the next page in the story was written by Herb Kelleher, who made hundreds of incremental changes in staffing, organizing, and operating airlines to create the second generation of no-frills carrier, and the reigning champ in per-mile profitability, Southwest Airlines.[13]

Market Innovations

market

a general term in business for the population of customers, and can include people and/or firms that will use an innovation or buy a product or service

market innovation

a change in the way products or services are distributed, or offerings that are expanded into new areas

Innovations can focus on products and processes or on **markets**. A **market innovation** is one that either introduces a new way of distributing products or services or expands offerings into new areas. In both cases, the innovation is centered on the end user of the innovation (the person who will use the product or service), rather than on the product or service itself. While sometimes not as evident as product or process innovations, market innovations can have profound impacts.

Distribution Distribution refers to the process of getting goods or services from their creators to their purchasers or users. Although distribution is normally considered part of marketing rather than management, market innovations are important to managers. Consider superstores or "category killers," as they are called by retailers. Office Depot, Home Depot, HQ, Office Max, CompUSA, Computer City, Circuit City, Best Buy, PetsMart, and Baby Superstore are all category busters.[14] They offer customers a new way to purchase items, with a focus on a narrow range of products and tremendous selection of brands and levels within that range. They compete on price and tend to do without elaborate store displays. Their major competition is department stores such as Sears and J.C. Penney and discount stores such as Kmart and Wal-Mart.

Much of the growth in market innovations recently has come from the growth of media. Examples include selling via television (e.g., the Home Shopping

MANAGERIAL CHALLENGE

MAKING DATA PAY

Robert Crandall of American Airlines was losing money to no-frills airlines every day. But he saw that virtually every American Airlines flight had some empty seats, and American had better information than most competitors because of its extensive computerized reservation system, SABRE. Using the wealth of data accumulated flight by flight over the years, Crandall instructed American Airlines operations researchers to predict how many empty seats would occur on *every* American Airlines flight. Crandall assigned fares to that number of seats comparable to those of the no-frills airlines, and supersaver fares were born.

When you see the disclaimer "seats are limited" in airline ads, it is because the number of seats available is determined on the likely number of empty seats. With these pricing policies, the airline gets the maximum price possible from every seat on the plane. Travelers were able to get low fares on traditional airlines that had amenities such as reservations, free baggage checking, free in-flight meals, and bigger seats. They flocked to these new fares that American developed—and that virtually every other traditional airline copied. The process innovation of supersaver fares made it possible to offer reduced-cost air travel to millions, effectively combatting the first generation of no-frills carriers like Laker and People Express.

Source: "United Airlines versus American Airlines—Crying for Wolf," *The Economist,* August 6, 1988, Business, finance and science section, p. 55.

Network), by catalog (e.g., Lands' End), or most recently via the Internet (e.g., Amazon.com).[15] In each case the idea is the same: Get products or services to the same people through new methods, methods that will entice them to spend more money or buy more often.

A geographical approach to distribution comes as companies offer their products or services to people who have not seen them before. Part of the stock analysts' optimism about Wal-Mart comes from the fact that Wal-Mart does not have stores in all 50 states yet; it still has room to grow. In addition, many thought McDonald's had reached its limit in the fast-food market, but McDonald's innovative response came in two forms. First, it expanded overseas. The McDonald's in Moscow was a worldwide news item, but it was only one store in a massive international expansion. Second, McDonald's created new outlets for its burgers in their home market. By a process innovation that lowered the cost of equipment, McDonald's was able to create mini-McDonald's that could be placed in other stores such as Wal-Mart or gas stations. These mini-stores reflect both process and market innovations.[16]

innovation adoption curve

a model that categorizes people into five groups based on when they buy or use an innovation: innovators, early adopters, early majority, late majority, or laggards

The Innovation Adoption Curve   Perhaps the idea most critical to market-driven innovation is the **innovation adoption curve** (Exhibit 6.3), which categorizes people by when they adopt, that is, buy or use, an innovation. Five groups were identified based on how soon individuals adopt an innovation after it is introduced:

- *Innovators* represent around 2.5 percent of the market for a product or service. These people value being "state of the art" and perhaps even being perceived as risk takers. Innovators are willing to pay a premium to have the product first. They are also willing to accept the problems that come from using a new, and possibly untried, product.

- *Early adopters* represent around 13.5 percent of the market, but they are the opinion leaders of the market. They have the power to legitimize innovations because, unlike innovators, who are often viewed as eccentric, they can serve

EXHIBIT 6.3

The Innovation
Adoption Curve

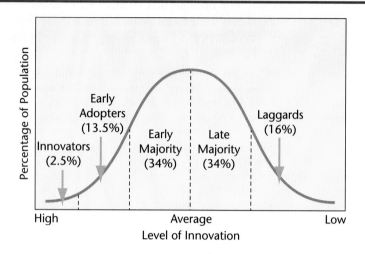

as role models. Early adopters are only a little more innovative than the average person, which makes them a key target market for assuring sales.

- *The early majority* constitutes 34 percent of the market. Such people are aware of innovations but approach them deliberately, checking them out thoroughly before adopting.
- *The late majority* also constitutes 34 percent of the market, and the term describes people who adopt after the average member of the market. These people wait until it is very clear that an innovation is safe and widely accepted. Even after adopting, they remain skeptical about innovations until they have been proven.
- *Laggards* describe the remaining 16 percent of the market. They are focused on the traditions of the past rather than the innovations of the present or future. They tend to adopt innovations when they no longer have a choice.[17]

The market for personal computers in the home demonstrates the implications of the innovation adoption curve. The people who bought PCs first were innovators. They were willing to pay exorbitant prices for the newest machines and willing to tinker with them to iron out problems. Often, they were hard-core computer lovers. They may have used the machines to develop their own programs. Those they convinced of the value of PCs were the early adopters, who bought brand-name machines and commercial programs, using them for word processing, spreadsheets, and other functions. These forward thinkers may have printed out the first computer holiday greeting cards and put the church finances on a spreadsheet as an exercise. Seeing this potential, the early majority began to buy PCs so their children would have the advantages of the early adopters. They may have read *Consumer Reports* or the upcoming computer magazines and comparison shopped for the best price. Today, the home PC market is working through the early majority stage. More and more people are coming to believe that they need a PC in their home. The late majority are beginning to take notice, since PCs are becoming more common. Home PCs are sold at most appliance, department, and discount stores. The late majority may not be buying yet, but they are beginning to look. The laggards still shake their heads and stubbornly cling to their pens, typewriters, and calculators.

For the manager or entrepreneur, the speed of adoption is a critical factor. It allows firms to get an early competitive foothold in new markets. As we noted previously, for Netscape, using the Internet to distribute free copies of Netscape Navigator gave the fledgling company a highly accelerated adoption rate. Other companies entering the market had to contend with Netscape's widespread use. By targeting their free downloads at Internet-savvy innovators and early adopters, who were already actively using the Internet, Netscape got the attention of most of the world's computer experts and computer consultants, further locking up the market. The major lesson for managers here is the so-called **first-mover advantage**, a strategy in which the first firm to move into a market is likely to establish market dominance.

first-mover advantage
a strategy that suggests that the first firm to move into a market is likely to establish market dominance

Managers also need to be concerned with planning the transition from introduction of an innovation to gaining profits. Generally, the slower the rate of adoption, the longer it takes for an innovation to break even. Innovations usually cost money, and these costs are recouped through sales. Managers, including those at Netscape, know that the key to subsequent sales is capturing the innovator and early adopter groups—the first for innovation visibility and the second for innovation legitimization. Mass introduction over the Internet may not be feasible for all products, but certain techniques permit managers to target innovators and early adopters. Matching demographic profiles or compiling lists of adopters of other innovations may yield gains since innovators tend to use many products in their early stages. Once entrepreneurs or managers target these prospects, they may offer them special deals to gain exposure. For example, to make money from its innovation, Netscape began selling technical support for its Navigator program. To obtain the technical support, users had to buy the program, which contained access numbers for support. Netscape managers had to plan for this change. They did so by setting up technical support staff, producing the for-sale packages, and getting the new products out into stores.

Firm Innovations

The link between innovation and entrepreneurship is clearest when we look at firms as innovations themselves. **Firm innovation** occurs when a new type of business is created. The act of creating a firm can itself spur other future innovation. Consider the situation of a divorced mother of three who became national training director of a direct-sales firm (also known as house-to-house sales). This woman eventually was laid off because she was earning too much money. When this happened to Mary Kay Ash, she started a business of her own, selling beauty products. But the real innovation came in the way she and her son designed their next firm, a direct-sales organization to compete with Avon Products. Using innovations such as in-home beauty shows, the highest commissions in the industry for salespeople, and extravagant incentives, such as the famous pink Cadillacs, Mary Kay Cosmetics became an organizational innovation and a model for other direct-sales firms.[18]

firm innovation
creation of a new type of business

The nature of an organizational innovation can, in turn, have a profound impact on the technological or market aspects of innovation. Consider Emmett Culligan. Culligan saw the potential profitability of mechanical water softeners, and he started a business to sell them. The business failed, however, because the cost of the machines was too high. He invented an organizational innovation on his second try by offering a water softening *service* in customers' houses, for $2 a month. The water softening equipment remained Culligan's property, and the company

In 1994 Jason and Matt Olim conceived the idea of using technology to build a better music store and started CDnow. CDnow is the world's leading online music store and has changed the music store business.

maintained it. With this change from a sales to a leasing organization, Culligan became hugely successful.[19] The lesson for managers is that often success for an innovative product requires an innovative approach to organizing the business.

When truly innovative products or services enter the market, they usually create a new, dominant organizational form. The new organization becomes a formal standard that redefines the expected practice in a particular industry. For example, restaurants have been a dominant organizational form for hundreds of years. The fast-food restaurant was a 20th century invention that was spun off from traditional sit-down restaurants, and the drive-through restaurant was a further organizational innovation. How did they become dominant? By fulfilling customer needs for faster and faster service and by being profitable.

Investors, government, customers, and suppliers continually look for new sources of useful cost-effective and efficient products. Culligan adopted the Bell Telephone System's approach of selling phone service but retaining ownership of the equipment. Using a familiar practice but adapting it to a new industry legitimized the approach among customers and business. The new alternative to a high-cost technology was readily accepted. Culligan's competitors had two choices: either adopt a service-selling plan like Culligan's or develop a new technology to cut the cost of water-softening equipment to levels where people would buy it. Culligan thus defined the industry's new organizational form. Persuading customers to adopt an innovation is not an easy matter, however. Entrepreneurs and managers must plan their efforts well for success to occur.

MANAGING ENTREPRENEURIAL INNOVATION

Just as college graduates in the job market do not always have expertise, so do new organizations in an industry face a set of conditions called the "liability of newness."[20] **Liability of newness** is the theory that new forms—organizations, innovations, recent graduates—face severe challenges from the environment because of

liability of newness
a theory that new forms, whether new organizations, new innovations, or individuals without experience, face severe challenges from the environment because of lack of resources or experience

a lack of resources or experience. New firms or forms are especially susceptible to threats from the environment. For a new organizational form, the threat could be that potential customers believe that the innovation is not likely to gain market acceptance in the future. CB radio restaurants, for example, a forerunner of the computer bar of today, survived only as long as the American gas crisis did. The firm may also lack the resources to meet its obligations. This classic problem parallels one that new college graduates seeking work face—they lack experience. There are two good ways around this problem.

The first way for an innovator to gain acceptance is to have expertise from which its customer or employer can immediately benefit. If the innovator has an answer to a problem they face, lack of experience may diminish in importance. The second approach is to go into a field so new that no "right" way to perform is yet established. World Wide Web consulting firms in the late 1990s, for example, faced almost no certification or standardization, so a wide variety of methods, skills, and organizational forms were tolerated. In a slightly older industry, such as Internet service providers, legitimization becomes more significant because customers and government regulators are now aware of what "good" Internet connectivity should be.

The lesson for future managers is that innovation and entrepreneurship can be managed. What makes managing innovation and entrepreneurship possible is knowing how they unfold in business, just as knowing the job-hunting process helps college students prepare for starting their careers. Two ideas about the process of innovation and entrepreneurship can give prospective managers good insight: understanding the pace of innovation and the stages of innovation.

The Pace of Innovation

The pace of innovation is increasing. Typing was fundamentally unchanged from the invention of the typewriter in the late 19th century until the introduction of the computer-based word processor in the early 1960s. These early programs ran on mainframe computers, and they offered new flexibility and ease of document revision. Next came stand-alone word processors by IBM and Wang in the mid-1960s, and then personal computer–based word processors on TRS-80 and Apple II computers in the 1970s. By the early 1980s, state-of-the-art word processors were on the Apple Macintosh and in the IBM environment. Knowing how to use a typewriter served typists for 70-plus years. Knowing how to use a mainframe computerized word processor served typists for a decade, then with desktop computers for less than a decade. Similar advances in technologies in other business functions and industries have also accelerated the pace of change.

The Stages of Innovation

The number of settings in which innovations occur is also increasing. For example, a manager might be juggling technological innovations such as network computing, social innovations such as diversity training, process innovations such as computerized inventory control, and market innovations such as expanding to new markets overseas all at the same time. Clearly, the modern manager must be able to manage innovation. Innovation *can* be managed, but that requires understanding innovation and how it is accepted in organizations. Researchers suggest a five-step process to describe the life cycle, or stages, of innovation in business: (1) invention,

EXHIBIT 6.4

The Five Stages of Innovation

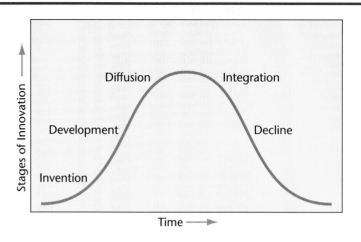

(2) development, (3) diffusion, (4) integration (a variant of consequences), and (5) decline (see Exhibit 6.4). Let's consider the stages using the story of 3M's Post-it Notes as a model.[21]

invention
the first stage of the five-step innovation process, which occurs with the creation of a new idea or process

Invention is the creation of a new idea or process, but invention is not the same as innovation. Spence Silver, a 3M engineer, was looking for promising new adhesives among industrial chemicals produced by another company. In the process, he stumbled on a formula for an adhesive that did *not* stick well. He prepared the details for producing this weak adhesive but could not think of a use for it. No one else at 3M could either, since they were focused on creating stronger adhesives.

development
the second stage of the five-step innovation process, which involves taking the invention and making it practical for some purpose or market

Development involves taking the invention and making it practical for some purpose or market. In the case at 3M, another scientist, Art Fry, was having trouble keeping bookmarks in place in his hymnal at church. He remembered Spence Silver's weak adhesive and put it on bookmarks. To do this, however, he built the equipment for applying the adhesive to paper in his basement. Eventually, to take the machine out for use at 3M, he had to blast out a wall of his basement!

diffusion
the third stage of the five-step innovation process, which occurs when the innovation is put into use by end users or customers

Diffusion is the process of getting the innovation into use. When 3M showed Post-it Notes to prospective customers in focus groups, none of them thought they were useful. Results from surveys were even more negative. Thus, diffusion strategies included handing out free samples and getting an executive secretary who worked for 3M's CEO to send samples to *other* Fortune 500 executive secretaries. Sales began to pour in—finally.[22]

integration
the fourth stage of the five-step innovation process, which occurs when the change is made permanent within an organization

Integration refers to the process of making the change permanent. For Post-it Notes, integration came in two forms. First, 3M dedicated part of the organization to selling and further developing the Post-it product line. For the market, 3M undertook a massive campaign to provide potential users with an initial supply of Post-it Notes in order to create demand for the new product. Today, it is hard to find a desk at home or in an office without Post-it Notes. When you cannot imagine what you would do without something, the product has been integrated into the market.

decline
the fifth stage of the five-step innovation process, which occurs when an innovation stops being used

Decline occurs when an innovation stops being used. Typewriters still exist, but in smaller numbers and in a somewhat changed form—electronic typewriters.

Typewriter producers such as SCM have gone out of business. Although the electronic office has not diminished the amount of paper, several computerized versions of Post-it Notes are vying to make 3M's paper-based product obsolete in the increasingly electronic age.

THE ROLE OF LEARNING IN INNOVATION

In the end, the processes of innovation and entrepreneurship depend on learning. Such changes do not come about in static environments, nor do they occur when people are uninterested in improving their own positions or that of their organizations. As we have already seen, these creative breakthroughs involve one or more of the following: (1) product innovations, which deal with the new technology for products and services; (2) market innovations and ideas such as adoption curves; and (3) firm innovations, or new ways to present innovations to the world. In effect, these are both the sources or directions from which innovations emerge and the destination areas for those innovations. As shown in Exhibit 6.5, a model has been developed to emphasize the link between each of these directions and a particular type of learning.[23] We discuss next the implications of that model.

One such type of learning is learning by doing. Consider, for example, that a new product or service in a business gets handled three times—by the inventors, by the producers who make it, and by the marketers who convince end users to buy and adopt it. In a small business, the entrepreneur may perform all three tasks, subcontract some or all of them, or delegate them to employees. In a large firm, separate units such as research and development, manufacturing, and marketing handle each of the tasks. To do this, learning by doing is often involved when the problems

EXHIBIT 6.5

Learning in Innovation

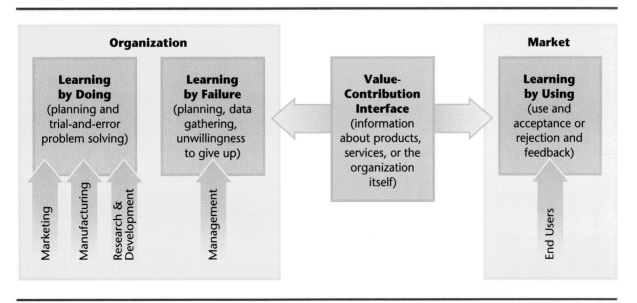

of the new firm, new product, or new service are worked out through a combination of planning and trial-and-error problem solving.

Another type of learning involves learning by failure. As Chris Whittle's experiences pointed out, being successful in one setting, such as turning around *Esquire* magazine, may not prepare a person to deal with other problems, such as public resistance to Channel One TV. Problem solving becomes a unique skill for innovators and entrepreneurs, and nothing improves problem-solving skills better than facing and overcoming failure. Handling failure, of course, can be done by improving planning and data gathering. The emotional element of failure, however, is a different matter. The classic entrepreneur or innovator may have a strong emotional reaction to failure, but what also characterizes this person is an unwillingness to give up. He or she will face what went wrong, deal with the loss of legitimacy or acceptance, and try again, the next time better prepared. Today we see Sears, Roebuck as a major national retailer, almost a sure survivor. But the entrepreneurs who started it came to their partnership from a rocky path. Richard Sears had owned and failed at several businesses before forming a fateful first partnership with Alvah Roebuck. But Roebuck sold the firm to others, only to seek out Sears three years later, at age 30, to found the Sears, Roebuck we know today. From their experiences, the two men learned the right way to set up a retailing operation and how to weather the problems that emerge.[24] Similarly, Mary Kay Ash was forced out of a company, a move typically viewed as a failure, but this experience taught her how to motivate and reward salespeople. Learning by failure focuses on dealing with both the emotions and the practicalities of bouncing back from a failure.

In the market, customers or users deal with innovation by a technique called learning by using. When alternate long-distance phone services (e.g., MCI and Sprint) were first introduced, customers had to punch in long strings of access codes. Only innovators and a few early adopters, or extremely budget-conscious individuals, used the services. But these people also became the core market supporting the companies, and they legitimized these fledgling long-distance services in the public's and government regulators' eyes. These competitors to AT&T realized the disadvantage posed by dialing the added numbers, and they petitioned for the right to easier access.[25] In personal computing, the first time a person learns how to use a word processor, it takes a long time to master all the new terms, commands, and methods. But regardless of the program a user learns first, the second is much easier and faster because many fundamentals remain the same. Savvy manufacturers facilitate this transfer. For example, Microsoft Word has a special set of help menus and other devices to ease the transition of former users of the WordPerfect word processor.

Between the market and the organization occurs another type of learning, called the value-contribution interface. In organizational activities and settings such as a store, sales call, or catalog, information about the product, service, or firm flows in two directions, back and forth between the organization and the customers. With this experience also comes the actions essential to business—customers' monies coming to the firm and the firm's products and services going out to customers. It is here at this interface that the essence of innovation, entrepreneurship, and even business in general occurs. Innovations are sent out to the market and are accepted or rejected. A business receives money and market feedback and transforms them to new ideas for the future. The interface is constantly changing and constantly in action, and it is where managerial innovators and entrepreneurs need to focus their attention in the learning process.

CONCLUDING COMMENTS

As much as anything, innovation and entrepreneurship involve a mind-set or a frame of mind that is oriented toward *being* innovative and entrepreneurial, whether inside or outside an established company or other organization. In other words, a desire to be innovative, along with developing a heightened alertness to possibilities, to opportunities, and to unmet needs of others, is critical. However, good intentions or good ideas by themselves are usually not enough to achieve successful innovation. What is needed in addition, in many cases, is a more sophisticated understanding of such concepts as the basic elements of new venture life cycles, innovation adoption curves, and the various stages of innovation. Having strong entrepreneurial motivation *coupled with* a thorough knowledge of the process and of the potential pitfalls and ways to overcome or deal with them is probably the best recipe for carrying out innovations and entrepreneurial ventures that thrive and accomplish or surpass their goals.

As this chapter—as well as this part of the book on the "Environmental Context of Managing"—concludes, it is important for you to retain a focus on innovation and entrepreneurship in the remaining chapters of the book. The following sections of the book deal with the various functions of management (planning, organizing, leading, and evaluating), and all of these functions require managers to think innovatively and to maintain an entrepreneurial mind-set of the type symbolized by the examples in the present chapter. To manage effectively involves considerable attention to the nature and complexities of the several major functions of the overall managerial process. But the *way* those functions are carried out is equally crucial. That is where innovation and entrepreneurship come in, regardless of the setting.

KEY TERMS

corporate entrepreneurs (intrapreneurs) 147
corporation 149
decline 162
development 162
diffusion 162
entrepreneurship 146
firm innovation 159

first-mover advantage 159
high-growth entrepreneurs 147
innovation 146
innovation adoption curve 157
integration 162
invention 162
liability of newness 161
market 156

market innovation 156
new venture life cycle 151
partnership 149
process innovations 155
product innovation 155
small business owner 147
sole proprietorship 149

REVIEW QUESTIONS

1. What is the difference between know-how and know-who? Why are they important to entrepreneurship?
2. Is there one entrepreneurial type? Explain.
3. What is the difference between success and takeoff in the new venture life cycle?
4. How does the liability of newness affect just-started firms?
5. The four properties of emerging organizations (boundary, resources, intention, exchange) can occur in different orders. Pick two orders and describe what a firm following that sequence would be doing.

6. What is the role "legitimization" plays in assuring the survival of new firms, products, or services?
7. What are the three sources for innovation?
8. Differentiate the three types of learning that occur in the innovation process.

DISCUSSION QUESTIONS

1. Think of two or more entrepreneurs whom you know personally (that is, not just ones you have read about). What are their similarities and what are their differences?
2. How could a person who is just beginning a managerial career be an innovator in her or his first few managerial positions (in the lower levels of an organization)? Would there be some ways of being an innovator in this circumstance that would likely be more successful than other ways?
3. What is the relationship between experience and the liability of newness, and how can a potential entrepreneur exploit it?
4. Think of a business organization (e.g., a bank, grocery store, airline, hotel) with which you have had personal contact as a customer. Could managers in that organization have used information from the value-contribution interface to do a better job of meeting your needs as a customer? Explain your answer.
5. Describe some examples in your own personal experiences where you learned by failure to come up with new, innovative ways of carrying out an important task.

CLOSING CASE

Walt Disney: From 18 to 40

Walt Disney was born in 1901. At the age of 36, he brought out his first full-length animated movie, *Snow White and the Seven Dwarfs*. Produced by a team of over 1,000 employees, it was the most ambitious animated undertaking of all time. Bringing such a massive project together required experience, and Disney had over 15 years of film animation experience, plus a real passion for control.

Walt Disney was not an overnight success. His first animation business was a partnership, the Iwerks-Disney Commercial Artists Company, started in 1919, when Disney was 18 and attending art school. Unlike his later businesses, this company had trouble generating enough business. Disney's partner, Ub Iwerks, took another job, and Disney, working alone in Kansas City, saw the

company flounder. In 1923, the renamed company, Laugh-O-Grams, closed its doors.

That same year, Disney moved to California, where his brother Roy lived, and the two brothers, with Iwerks a 20 percent partner, started the Disney Brothers Studios, renamed the Walt Disney Studios by 1925. The new studio served as an animation subcontractor, turning out cartoons for larger studios, such as the Oswald the Rabbit series for Universal Studios. Doing this kind of work helped the Disney Studios establish connections in the movie industry and paid the bills while the Disneys and Iwerks developed their business.

Few entrepreneurs are as controversial as Walt Disney. But his management style did bring the studio that bore his name remarkable success. Disney Studios introduced several innovations in animation, including the first cartoon with sound (*Steamboat Willie* in 1928), the first color cartoon (*Flowers and Trees* in 1932), and the first feature-length cartoon (*Snow White and the Seven Dwarfs* in 1937). Walt Disney also was able to make extraordinary use of the talents of others. For example, partner Ub Iwerks was a legendary animator, able to turn out 700 drawings a day, with quality that garnered the respect of junior animators everywhere.

The presence of those junior animators came from Disney's application of scientific management principles for animation published by John Randolph Bray, in which senior artisan animators (all men) created single drawings of key scenes and less-skilled, and much less highly paid, junior animators (also all men) completed the drawings connecting the key scenes. Color and ink were added by even less highly trained and less highly paid women. All were supervised closely and were clocked to assure efficient performance. With this highly organized, tightly controlled animation organization, the Walt Disney Studios was able to operate the 1,000-person animation team needed to produce *Snow White and the Seven Dwarfs*.

Walt Disney went to great lengths to control his organization; the use of scientific management principles was only one part. He was the sole judge of which projects would go forward and which would be terminated. He checked the quality of nearly all work, including that of his partner, Ub Iwerks—even though he did so after Iwerks went home for the night. He personally reviewed all budgets in the organization and was the sole public image and voice of the entire studio.

Although eminently lovable when describing his studio's work and characters, Walt Disney was not necessarily an easy man to work for, even when he was young. In the studio's early days, four animators from the Oswald the Rabbit team left to join a competitor, Charles Mintz. Ub Iwerks, Disney's top animator and partner, got so fed up with Disney's insistence on scientific management approaches over artistic approaches, and on reworking his animations, that Iwerks quit the partnership in 1930, only to return 10 years later as an employee. Disney's acceptance of Iwerks's return was at odds with his usual practice for animators who challenged the Disney way. Animators

who went on strike in an attempt to start a union at the Disney Studios were all eventually laid off or fired by Disney. He knew who they were because he kept photographs of the strikers on a wall in his office.

Disney not only sought to control his organization, he extended this control to his characters themselves. George Borgfeldt asked permission in 1932 to use Mickey and Minnie Mouse's names and likenesses to sell children's products. The result was a new revenue source for Disney. Building on the success of Mickey Mouse commercial products, the Disney company created its first Mickey Mouse book and had it published by a commercial publisher. In its first year, the book sold just under 100,000 copies, cementing Disney's place in the highly profitable business of licensing and spin-off products. He would carefully review potential licensing opportunities and spin-off products personally, as he did so much of the business, continuing to exercise control wherever possible.

In short, except for Disneyland (which would not open until 1955), almost all the modern elements of the Disney organization were in place by 1937, when *Snow White* was released. Even then, Walt was not even 40 years old.

QUESTIONS

1. How did Walt Disney obtain his know-how for the animation business?
2. What are examples of Disney's innovative moves from home base in terms of technology? Organization? Markets?
3. Growing from three partners in 1925 to the 1,000-plus team of *Snow White* in 1937, did the Disney Studios fit the new venture life cycle? Explain why or why not.
4. Walt Disney would contend that tight controls made his studio successful. Do you agree with that assessment?

Sources: David M. Boje, "Stories of the Storytelling Organization: A Postmodern Analysis of Disney as 'Tamara-Land,'" *Academy of Management Journal* 38, no. 4 (August 1995), pp. 997–1035; M. Eliot, *Walt Disney: Hollywood's Dark Prince* (New York: Birch Lane Press, Carol Publishing, 1993); R. Holliss and B. Sibley, *The Disney Story* (London: Octopus Books, 1998); R. Schickel, *The Disney Version: The Life, Times, Art and Commerce of Walt Disney,* rev. ed. (New York: Simon & Schuster, 1985); J. Van Maanen, "Displacing Disney: Some Notes on the Flow of Culture," *Qualitative Sociology* 15, no. 1 (1992), pp. 5–35.

PART 3

PLANNING AND DECISION MAKING

CHAPTER 7

PLANNING

Procter & Gamble in Eastern Europe

Procter & Gamble (P&G), the marketer of Tide detergent, Vidal Sassoon hair care products, and hundreds of other well-known consumer brands, relies heavily on its international markets to sustain long-term growth. About 55 percent of its business occurs outside the United States. The company serves more than 140 countries with 300 different brands, 140 manufacturing plants, and 54 operations around the world. Western Europe generates $8.5 billion in annual sales, a volume larger than the entire company earned just 15 years ago. Germany alone represents 10 percent of the entire company's annual sales.

Because of its presence in Western Europe, it was only natural that P&G took an interest in the opening of Eastern Europe. In 1989, as the Berlin Wall fell, the company entered Eastern European countries that had been deprived of quality Western material goods. However, rather than enter rapidly and make mistakes, the company formulated a methodical plan. The steps to this plan included (1) analyzing the environment, (2) setting objectives and strategies, (3) determining resources, and (4) monitoring outcomes.

171

Analyzing the Environment

Given the instability of the Eastern European countries, P&G took time to analyze the environment before expanding. In February 1990, company executives took a tour of major markets to assess strengths and weaknesses among the countries, including Hungary, the Czech Republic, and Russia. Executives returned to the United States with notes and impressions on both risks and benefits.

Risks

- Poor infrastructure
- Unstable governments and tense political atmosphere

Benefits

- 400 million consumers
- Highly educated workforce
- Movement to a free market system

Based on the environmental assessment, the company decided to focus first on Poland, the Czech Republic, and Hungary and to enter Russia very cautiously.

Setting Objectives and Strategies

P&G's next step was to set objectives for its expansion into Eastern Europe. In addition to long- and short-term financial objectives, the company had several strategic objectives. Two important objectives were (1) to achieve lowest cost and best quality sourcing and (2) to achieve superior distribution.

To provide low-cost, high-quality product, P&G determined that it would eventually need regional production capacity. However, the company also wanted to start up fast without too much risk, so the option of building plants was not feasible.

The next option was to acquire local manufacturers. Though the option carried some risk—how could an Eastern European plant manufacture as productively as a Western plant?—it was less risky than building from scratch. One such acquisition occurred in the Czech Republic, where P&G found a company called Rakona. P&G engineers worked with Czech employees at the Rakona plant to conduct test runs of Ariel detergent—the equivalent to Tide in Europe. After a few weeks, the detergent produced in the Czech plant was identical to that produced in Western Europe.

To achieve the highest market share, P&G needed to expand rapidly. But the company found that distribution channels in Eastern Europe were very poorly developed. In the United States, a case of detergent can be delivered to almost any location in 24 hours. However, even under favorable circumstances in Russia, it could take three weeks for a case of detergent to move from Moscow across Siberia to Vladivostok on the eastern shore.

Determining Resources

Once objectives and strategies were set, P&G determined what resources were needed. The company figured that the most critical resource was human—employees who would build the business in Eastern Europe. Both experienced P&G managers from other parts of the world and local men and women would be needed. And these employees would need both technical and managerial skills to succeed.

Monitoring Outcomes

During the implementation of its plan, P&G was careful to monitor the outcomes, both financial and strategic, in each of the countries it entered. The results have reflected an overall success story in Eastern Europe. After four years of operation, annual sales rose to $500 million, making the company the largest consumer goods firm in the entire region. Twenty-five brands served the markets, and most were among the top two or three in their product categories. The business also became profitable within the first four years, whereas in Western Europe it had taken eight years to turn a profit.

P&G remains optimistic about its long-term business in Eastern Europe. Because of its careful, methodical planning, the company expects to net high returns over the long term.

Source: John Pepper, "Leading the Change in Eastern Europe," *Business Quarterly*, Autumn 1995, pp. 26–33.

The opening case clearly illustrates the importance of a firm's ability to formulate and implement effective plans. Although planning has been an important managerial activity for some time, it is perhaps more important and perplexing now than ever before. The rise in competition means that if an organization, department, or individual manager fails to plan and loses momentum, competitors are likely to overtake it. Yet, the speed of change and rapid flow of information increasingly require flexibility and adaptability to a dynamic environment. In today's world, rigidity can be as fatal as no plan at all. As important as competition and the rate of change are, both must be viewed within the context of globalization for a manager to be successful today and in the future. Increasingly as a manager, you must not only be aware of competitors down the street but around the world. In addition, you must recognize that because information flows throughout the world nearly instantaneously, it can lead to dramatic changes in your plans.

AN OVERVIEW OF PLANNING

objectives
end states or targets for which organizational managers aim

plans
the means by which managers hope to hit desired targets

planning
a decision-making process that focuses on the future of the organization and how it will get where it wants to go

Few activities are more basic to management than deciding where the company is going and how it is going to get there. Organizational **objectives** are the end states or targets for which managers aim. **Plans** are the means by which managers hope to hit the desired targets. **Planning**, then, is essentially a decision-making process that focuses on the future of the organization and how it will get where it wants to go. Setting organizational objectives precedes the development of organizational plans. Without objectives or targets, plans make very little sense. Objectives help set direction, focus effort, guide behaviors, and evaluate progress.[1] Interestingly, managers sometimes spend so much time formulating objectives that they neglect to develop detailed plans that will enable them to achieve their goals. This is akin to making a commitment to graduate from college without any idea about what classes to take or when certain classes need to be taken. So both objectives and planning are crucial for an organization's success. We now explore the types of plans that exist, the basic planning process, and the methods for implementing plans effectively.

Types of Plans

Today, few organizations offer just one product or service. As a consequence, they cannot develop a single plan to cover all organizational activities. For example, TRW has businesses ranging from automotive parts to financial reporting services. Even within the real estate reporting business, TRW has a variety of functional areas such as finance, accounting, human resources, and customer service. To understand the planning process for complex organizations, we need to differentiate among three types of plans (see Exhibit 7.1).

strategic plans
plans that focus on the broad future of the organization and incorporate both external environment demands and internal resources into the actions managers need to take to achieve the long-term goals of the organization

Strategic Plans   **Strategic plans** focus on the broad future of the organization and incorporate both external environment demands and internal resources into the actions managers need to take to achieve the long-term goals of the organization. Typically, strategic plans cover the major aspects of the organization, including its products, services, finances, technology, and human resources. Although "long-term" has no precise definition, most strategic plans focus on how to achieve goals three to five years into the future. For example, after the passage of NAFTA (the North American Free Trade Agreement), the Mexican state of Sonora, which borders Arizona, had a strategic plan to revitalize its economy. In evaluating their strengths and weakness, government officials decided that the most effective way to revitalize their economy was to take advantage of their beautiful beaches and encourage tourists to come and visit.

tactical plans
plans that translate strategic plans into specific goals for specific parts of the organization; they have shorter time frames and are narrower in scope, typically affecting a single business unit within an organization

Tactical Plans   **Tactical plans** translate strategic plans into specific goals for specific parts of the organization. Consequently, they tend to have shorter time frames and to be narrower in scope. Instead of focusing on the entire corporation, tactical

EXHIBIT 7.1
Types of Plans: Key Differences

	Strategic Plans	**Tactical Plans**	**Operational Plans**
Time Horizon	Typically 3–5 years	Often focused on 1–2 years in the future	Usually focused on the next 12 months or less
Scope	Broadest; originating with a focus on the entire organization	Rarely broader than a strategic business unit	Narrowest; usually centered on departments or smaller units of the organization
Complexity	The most complex and general, because of the different industries and businesses potentially covered	Somewhat complex but more specific, because of the more limited domain of application	The least complex, because they usually focus on small, homogenous units
Impact	Have the potential to dramatically impact, both positively and negatively, the fortunes and survival of the organization	Can affect specific businesses but generally not the fortunes or survivability of the entire organization	Impact is usually restricted to specific department or organization unit
Interdependence	High interdependence; must take into account the resources and capabilities of the entire organization and its external environments	Moderate interdependence; must take into account the resources and capabilities of several units within a business	Low interdependence; the plan may be linked to higher-level tactical and strategic plans but is less interdependent with them

plans typically affect a single business unit within an organization (see the Managerial Challenge box). Although tactical plans should complement the overall strategic plan, they are often loosely coordinated. Returning to our example of the Mexican state of Sonora, part of Sonora borders the northeastern portion of the Gulf of Baja and has wonderful beaches and harbors. The tactical plans of the transportation department called for improving the roads leading from the border with Arizona to the beach resorts. The tactical plans of the commerce department called for making special low-interest loans available to companies that would build Western-styled quality hotels in the targeted region. While the tactical plans of the transportation and commerce departments were different, both served to support the overall strategic plan of Sonora.

operational plans
plans that translate tactical plans into specific goals for small units of the organization and focus on the near term (typically 12 months or less)

Operational Plans Operational plans translate tactical plans into specific goals and actions for small units of the organization and focus on the near term, typically 12 months or less. These plans are the least complex of the three and rarely have an impact beyond the department or unit for which the plan was developed. For example, in the case of the Mexican state of Sonora, the purchasing section within the department of transportation created an operational plan that called for the purchase of several new road graders and a new steamroller to expand the main highway from a two- to a four-lane highway.

MANAGERIAL CHALLENGE

THE BELLAGIO: TACTICAL PLANNING FOR A NEW HOTEL

When Mirage Resorts decided to build the Bellagio, a new luxury hotel in Las Vegas, it was no small feat. The blueprints called for 3,000 rooms, a large gallery to hold a fine-art collection, a glass-domed conservatory, a theater equipped to hold Cirque du Soleil's new water show, an eight-acre replica of Italy's Lake Como—along with the usual designer shops and gourmet restaurants. The cost of all of this, before the Bellagio's doors opened, would run about $1.6 billion. In addition, Mirage had to find a way to recruit nearly 10,000 workers to staff the hotel. Clearly, the company needed a tactical plan to accomplish these goals.

As construction got under way, Mirage began its hiring process. Because of the number of jobs that needed to be filled—by the right candidates—Mirage had to come up with a plan for receiving and sorting through applications, interviewing, and making employment offers. First, the company budgeted $1 million on a computer software system that would screen as many as 75,000 job candidates in three months to eliminate those who were not suitable and cull those who might be. Second, Mirage planned to run newspaper ads announcing that it was hiring employees for the new hotel, providing a toll-free number that applicants could call to make an appointment to fill out an application. Once the software system had screened candidates, Mirage planned to spend two and a half months interviewing the 26,000 finalists, at the rate of nearly 700 per day. (Mirage hired and specially trained 180 interviewers to handle the process.) Interview results would then be entered into a database for later reference.

The applicants would be narrowed further. If a candidate was unwise enough not to show up for a job interview without notifying someone at the company, he or she would be dropped from the process. "If people didn't show up for their appointments, we figured they'd be no-shows at work too," explains vice president Arte Nathan. Mirage also anticipated conducting background checks on about 18,000 finalists. Eventually, Mirage planned to offer positions to its final candidates, in many cases over five months after the initial application.

How successful was this hiring plan? Computer screening actually reduced the length of the process, which had previously taken nine months instead of five. Arte Nathan claims that his company saved $600,000 on items such as paper, temporary help, and file space. The Bellagio is now open for business, with employees in place.

Sources: Eileen P. Gunn, "How Mirage Resorts Sifted 75,000 Applicants to Hire 9,600 in 24 Weeks," *Fortune,* October 12, 1998, p. 195; John Gurzinksi, "A Raft of Preparations at Bellagio," *Las Vegas Review Journal,* September 30, 1998; "Bellagio," *Time,* October 26, 1998.

As summarized in Exhibit 7.1, strategic, tactical, and operational plans differ from each other on five important dimensions: time horizon, scope, complexity, impact, and interdependence.[2] While these differences are important, in many organizations today, a complete understanding of strategic, tactical, and operational plans requires us to examine one more issue: organizational levels.

Organizational Levels

Exhibit 7.2 depicts the three primary levels of a corporation. Managers at each level attempt to address somewhat different questions.

Corporate Level   Most corporations of even moderate size have a corporate headquarters. However, complex and large organizations, such as Brunswick with $3.9 billion in annual sales, often divide the various businesses of the company into large groups. For Brunswick, these groups are marine and recreation. The heads of these groups typically report to executives at the corporate headquarters. Executives at the corporate level in large firms include both those in the headquarters and those heading up the large corporate groups. These corporate-level executives primarily focus on questions such as the following:

EXHIBIT 7.2
Organizational Levels

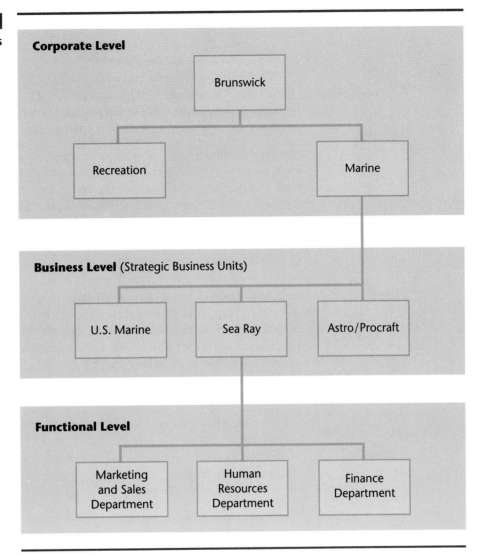

EXHIBIT 7.2
Organizational Levels

- What industries should we get into or out of?
- What markets should the firm be in?
- Is it time to move aggressively into China? If so, what businesses should move first?
- In which businesses should the corporation invest money?

In the case of Brunswick, if coordination across the recreation, marine, or businesses within the groups is needed or beneficial, corporate-level managers are responsible for recognizing and capturing those opportunities.

Business Level   The next level is sometimes referred to as the SBU, or strategic business unit, level. At this level, managers focus on determining how they will compete effectively in the market. For example, within Brunswick's recreation group are a variety of specific businesses, including LIFEcycle exercise equipment, bowling balls, billiards, and Brunswick recreation centers. Managers in these specific businesses attempt to address questions such as the following:

* Who are our direct competitors?
* What are their strengths and weaknesses?
* What are our strengths and weaknesses?
* What do customers value in the products or services we offer?
* What advantages do we have over competitors?

In the next chapter we will examine strategic management tools that business-level managers use to answer these questions, but you can tell from the planning questions listed that SBU-level managers are focused more on how to compete effectively in the business of today than on what businesses to be in tomorrow. If coordination across different departments (e.g., finance, marketing, product development) or units within the SBU is needed or beneficial, SBU-level managers are responsible for recognizing and capturing those opportunities.

Functional Level At the functional level, managers focus on how they can achieve the competitive plan of the business. These managers are often heads of departments such as finance, marketing, human resources, or product development. Depending on the SBU's structure, functional managers may include managers responsible for the business within a specific geographic region or managers who are responsible for a specific product or service. Generally, these functional managers attempt to address questions such as the following:

* What activities does my unit need to perform well to meet customer expectations?
* What information about competitors does my unit need to help the business compete effectively?
* What are our unit's strengths and weaknesses?

The main focus of functional managers' planning activities is on how they can support the SBU plan. If coordination between individuals within a unit is needed or beneficial, functional-level managers are responsible for recognizing and capturing those opportunities.

Interaction between Plan Types and Levels

Strategic plans typically are developed at the corporate level. In fact, strategic planning is arguably the key planning responsibility of corporate managers. Corporate managers, however, tend not to develop tactical or operational plans. Business unit managers may be involved in developing strategic plans for their business units and are usually involved in developing tactical plans for their business. However, business unit managers typically do not develop operational plans. In contrast, functional-level managers are not often involved in developing either strategic or tactical plans. Instead, their planning responsibilities tend to focus on the development of operational plans. Exhibit 7.3 illustrates the general pattern of planning responsibility by organizational level. Keep in mind, however, that specific patterns in organizations could be different. For example, the size of the organization could affect the pattern. In small organizations, corporate managers might be involved in developing strategic, tactical, *and* operational plans.

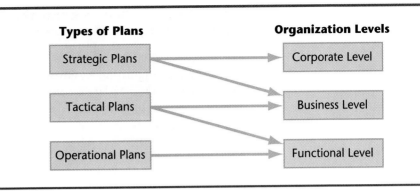

THE PLANNING PROCESS

The planning process has seven key elements: environmental analysis, objectives, requirements, resources, actions, implementation, and outcomes (see Exhibit 7.4). In this section we will examine each of these elements and their role in the overall planning process.

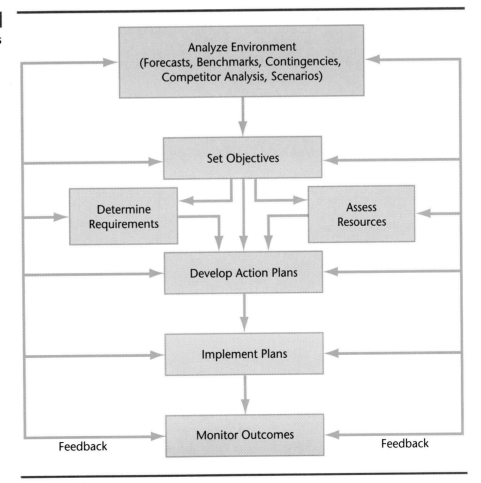

Greeting card companies develop new products that are relevant to contemporary lifestyle trends. American Greetings has introduced a new line of religious cards that reflect the growing influence of spirituality in our society and the increasing demand for religious and inspirational products.

Analyzing the Environment

The first element of the planning process is an assessment of the environment. Plans formulated or implemented in the absence of environmental assessment may very well fall short of the desired results.

Forecasts   One of the principal tools managers use in assessing the environment is a forecast. Forecasts can be made for virtually any critical element managers believe could affect the organization or their area of responsibility. For example, if you were in the residential construction business, forecasts of interest rates would be important to you. Generally, as interest rates go up and borrowing money becomes more expensive, fewer people purchase new homes. Those that still purchase new homes must purchase less expensive homes than they could if interest rates were lower. Planning for the number of houses to build in the coming year, as a consequence, would be influenced by the interest rate forecast.

Interestingly, there is a cascading effect of forecasts. For example, if you forecast that you will build only 1,000 homes instead of 1,500 homes over the next year because interest rates are expected to rise from 7.5 percent to 8.75 percent, then you might also forecast a decline in revenues. This may lead the purchasing manager to plan for smaller purchases of lumber and may lead the human resource manager to plan for a smaller number of construction workers.

Environmental Uncertainty   The extent of uncertainty in the environment affects the utility of forecasts and other assessments of the environment.[3] Environmental uncertainty can come from a variety of factors. For example, it might be that change in key factors affecting your business is unknown. Your export business might be significantly affected by changes in the exchange rate. As the dollar becomes stronger (i.e., appreciates) against the German mark, your products become more expensive to Germans. As a consequence, they may purchase less from you, and your revenues decline. However, no one may be able to forecast the dollar's movement relative to the German mark. Uncertainty could also come from unpredictable changes of significant magnitude. For example, your export business might be shipping a significant amount of product to the Russian government. However, if the president of Russia has a heart attack and dies, this could significantly affect your business as new leaders and government priorities or purchasing practices are brought in.

The key issue for managers and their planning activities is that the greater the environmental uncertainty, the more flexible their plans need to be. In some cases, managers may even develop **contingency plans**. Contingency plans typically identify key factors that could affect the desired results and specify what different actions will be taken if changes occur.[4] For example, if you are in the residential construction business and interest rates are a key factor that affects your business, you might form a contingency plan stating that if the interest rate rises more than one full point, you will offer customers reduced financing charges or include certain upgrades, like more expensive carpet, in their home purchase.

contingency plans
plans that identify key factors that could affect the desired results and specify what different actions will be taken if changes occur

Benchmarking A more recent and popular means of assessing the environment is benchmarking. **Benchmarking** is the investigation of the best results among competitors and noncompetitors and the practices that lead to those results.[5] In terms of results, managers might assess competitors that have the highest revenue-to-employee ratio as a means of assessing productivity. Managers could then compare their own revenue-to-employee ratio and get an idea of where they stand relative to competitors. In this assessment, they might also investigate practices that seem to contribute to high revenue-to-employee ratios. For example, they might find that firms with the highest ratio tend to have fewer levels of managers because they push decision-making authority down in the organization and have a strong focus on participative management and employee involvement.

benchmarking
investigation of the best results among competitors and noncompetitors and the practices that lead to those results

The same type of assessments might also be made of noncompetitors. Benchmarking noncompetitors has potential pitfalls and benefits. Noncompetitors can have underlying business factors that make comparisons difficult. For example, a telemarketing company that sells relatively inexpensive items over the phone will have a much lower revenue-to-employee ratio than a maker of supercomputers. The telemarketing firm has a relatively labor-intensive business, while the maker of supercomputers has a technology-intensive business.

However, organizations can gain fresh insights by looking beyond their competitors and industry. Consider Outback Steak House. Even though the steel industry was totally different from the franchise restaurant industry, Outback Steak House found a motivational practice used by several "mini-mills" in the steel industry to be successful in their business. Like any franchise restaurant, Outback makes money as its restaurants make money. The person who makes or breaks a restaurant is the local restaurant manager. In particular, the manager must hire the right people and motivate them effectively to ensure good food and service for the customers. The key for Outback is how to motivate the restaurant managers. The "best practice" that Outback adopted was giving the restaurant managers some ownership in the restaurant. That way if the restaurant made money, so did the manager. The manager then felt and acted more like an owner and less like a employee. The adoption of this best practice has had a positive effect on Outback

Steak House's success. Thus, even though benchmarking noncompetitors requires some judgment as to what is relevant or appropriate, it can also lead to ideas and practices that put you ahead of the competition.

Setting Objectives

The second element in the planning process is setting objectives, or desired outcomes, for the entire organization, a specific unit, or even an individual. As we mentioned at the beginning of this chapter, it is difficult to establish or implement specific actions without an idea of where those steps are intended to go or what they are expected to achieve.

Priorities and Multiple Objectives One of the first challenges for managers as they set objectives is to determine priorities.[6] Not all objectives are of equal importance or value. Furthermore, some objectives might be important now and less important later. Without a clear understanding of which objectives are most important and when, employees may be working at odds with each other or create unnecessary conflicts.[7]

Consider your own university. Most universities have multiple and sometimes conflicting objectives. For example, students pay tuition in order to learn current and useful concepts from the best professors the school has to offer. Universities cannot ignore the expectations of this important set of constituents. At the same time, to generate current and useful knowledge, universities must hire top researchers and fund their research. Without a clear idea of the priorities, managers, such as department heads, may find it difficult to determine how best to allocate the department budget. How much of the budget should go toward activities that help develop the teaching skills of the faculty? How much should go toward funding research?

Similar potential conflicts might exist for a company regarding objectives for market share and profitability. Though not necessarily the case, a greater share of a market can often be gained by lowering prices, which usually hurts profits. Managers would have a difficult time making and implementing plans without having a clear understanding of the firm's priorities

Timing of objectives is also important.[8] For example, a new firm in an already established market might determine that its current objective is to gain customers quickly and thereby establish a presence in the market. This objective would most likely have a strong impact on the pricing and product promotion plans of the firm. However, once it had 10 percent of the market, the firm might determine that profitability objectives take priority over broadening its customer base. Without a clear understanding of the shift in priorities, managers could easily work against the firm's objectives or against each other.

Measurement of Objectives Even if the priority of objectives is clear, the ways objectives are measured and therefore the ability to determine whether they have been met must be clear. For example, a firm might determine that financial performance is the number one objective. However, financial performance can be measured in a variety of ways, among them profits relative to sales or profits relative to assets.[9] The important point to understand is that the type of measurement can significantly affect people's planning activities and behavior in general. For example, if financial performance is measured in terms of the ratio of profits to sales, managers can improve that ratio by reducing costs and keeping sales steady or by keeping costs steady and increasing sales. In contrast, measuring financial performance in terms of profit to assets focuses on getting greater productivity from the assets. This may mean getting more product out of a given piece of machinery. Thus, the specific measurement of the objectives can have a significant impact on the plans managers make, as well as their general behavior.[10]

Determining Requirements

The third element in the planning process is the determination of requirements. Managers essentially address the question, "What will it take to get from here to there?" The "there" is the objectives discussed previously. The "here" requires an assessment or knowledge of where the organization is today.

To begin the process, you must first understand the key drivers. For example, let's suppose you are in the shoe manufacturing business, and your objective is to increase your market share from 10 to 15 percent. What is it that drives market share? You may need to expand your product line into other types of shoes. As a consequence, you determine that one of your requirements is a new line of shoes at the top end of the market, where you currently have none. To expand your market share in the middle-priced running shoe segment, you may determine that cushion technology is one of the key drivers. You may determine that customers purchase running shoes based on their shock absorption during running. As a consequence, you also determine to pursue a new cushion technology. The point is that the identification of critical requirements is likely to flow from determining key drivers of firm objectives.

Assessing Resources

The fourth element in the planning process is an assessment of the required resources and the resources available to the organization or manager. This element is closely tied to the identification of requirements, but the two are not the same. The easiest way to differentiate may be to think of requirements as what is needed to achieve the objectives and resources as how much is available.

Resources Required   Let's return to our athletic shoe example and the key requirement of a new line of shoes at the top end of the market. Relative to this key requirement, the first critical question is, "What resources are needed to produce a new high-end product?" Let's suppose you determine that it will take three top product-design engineers two months and a budget of $100,000 to produce a prototype. Further, you determine that it will take new equipment at a cost of $500,000 to manufacture the new high-end shoes. Finally, you determine that it will take an advertising and promotion budget of $2 million to effectively launch the new line. These, of course, do not address all the resources required to design, produce, and sell the new high-end product line, but they do illustrate the financial, human, equipment, and technology resources that might be required.

Resources Available   Knowing what resources are required leads naturally to the next assessment: What resources are available? Clearly, for a plan to be effective, it must not only be well formulated but feasible to implement.[11] If the resources required significantly exceed those available, either new resources need to be acquired or the plan must be changed. Changing the plan may require changing the objective. In assessing resources available, managers must ask themselves questions such as the following:

- Do we have the needed human talent to meet the requirements?
- Even if we have the needed talent, are they available? Can we take people off what they are currently working on in order to put them on this new project?
- If we don't have the necessary talent, can we develop or acquire it within the needed time frame?
- Do we have the financial resources available? Can we get additional funding from the debt or equity markets?
- Do we have the required technology or can we gain access to it at a cost-effective price?

While these questions are certainly not the only ones managers need to ask, they do provide a flavor of the questions that need to be addressed to determine whether there is a gap between the resources required and those available. If there is a gap, managers must determine whether it can be bridged or whether objectives and key requirements need to be changed to fit the available resources.

Developing Action Plans

The fifth element in the planning process is the development of specific action plans. The action plans are essentially the marching orders that everyone uses to accomplish the established objectives.

Sequence and Timing   One of the key elements of an effective action plan is the sequence and timing of the various specific steps in the plan.[12] One of the common tools used to graphically display the sequence and timing of the specific actions is a Gantt chart, first mentioned in Chapter 2 (see Exhibit 7.5). Time is typically on the horizontal axis and the tasks to be done are on the vertical axis. The chart shows when actions are to be started and how long they are expected to take. It shows which actions are first, second, or last in the process and whether a preceding action must be completed before a subsequent one can be started or whether there is overlap.

In addition to the planned sequence and timing, actual progress can be charted as well. This allows managers to track their progress against the plan and make adjustments.

Accountability   The second key aspect of effective action plans is a specification of who is accountable for which actions. Knowing who is responsible for what coordinates different people's actions in the overall plan.[13] Accountability also increases the likelihood that steps will be taken when they should be and done as well as they need to be.

Implementing Plans

Once an action plan has been created, it needs to be implemented. The quality of the implementation can affect the actual results as much as the quality of the plan itself. However, much of the success of implementation can be assured by following the previous steps in the planning process well. Plans often fail in the implementa-

EXHIBIT 7.5

Gantt Chart

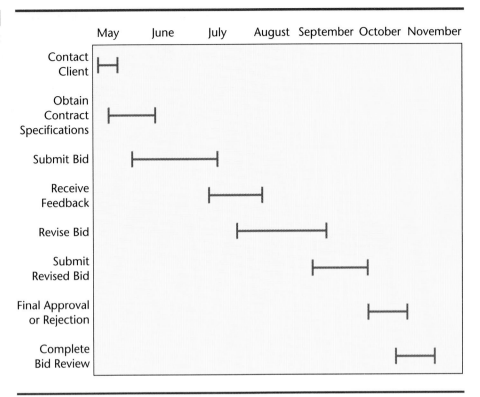

tion stage because of inadequate assessment of resources—both those required and available. Returning to our shoe example, suppose at a critical point the workers who will operate the new sewing machines must be trained. However, because of poor communication with the workers, they mistakenly think the new machines will require fewer workers. As a consequence, they resist the training. Their resistance delays the production of the new shoes, and a critical window of opportunity in the marketplace may be lost.

This example illustrates in a simple way why implementation can be as critical and sometimes more critical than the overall objectives. However, no matter how carefully you implement a plan, you will still need to monitor and adjust your efforts.

Monitoring Implementation   Even if all previous steps in the planning process are done well, there is no guarantee that the plan will be successfully implemented. So, it is essential for you to monitor the implementation and to consider in particular three critical factors.

First, you need to monitor the progress of the plan. Are those responsible for taking actions aware of their responsibilities and the timing of them? Are they adequately motivated and prepared to implement their portion of the plan? Are the necessary actions being taken at the right time? Are they being done at the desired level of quality? As a manager, you need to ask questions such as these to monitor the progress of the implementation.

Second, as a manager you need to monitor the level of support that the plan receives as it is being implemented. Are you as the manager providing the required support—encouragement, funds, coaching—for the implementation? Few plans of any complexity can be effectively implemented without continual support. Are the other key supporters providing the encouragement needed? One of your key responsibilities as a manager is to monitor and ensure that the required support is there.

Third, as a manager you need to monitor the level of resistance. We address managing change in a later chapter, but it is important to point out here that many plans and their implementation involve change. To the extent that they do, you should anticipate and monitor resistance.

Time Adjustment   Because we live in a dynamic environment, any plan whose formulation and implementation last more than a few days or weeks is likely to need adjustment. As the environment changes, what was originally an acceptable objective may become unrealistic or too easily achieved and therefore need to be changed. Likewise, what were perfectly reasonable timeframes and required resources at one point may become unreasonable because of economic, political, technological, or competitive changes.

This realization has at least two implications. First, it suggests that as a manager working in a changing environment, you need to plan the way a fire department does. A fire department cannot anticipate exactly where or even when fires will break out. Their plans are built upon certain principles and around general categories of fires. Second, living in dynamic environments may suggest in general that as a manager you need to foster in your people a recognition and acceptance of the need to adapt plans as they are being carried out. You may also need to foster skills such as adaptability in your subordinates. These skills might include good environmental scanning skills and quick requirement and resource assessment abilities. The key point to remember is that in today's dynamic environment, a fixed plan may be as dangerous as no plan at all.

Monitoring Outcomes

The final element in the planning process involves monitoring outcomes. If the objectives have been well defined from the outset of planning, there should be little question what outcomes are to be monitored or how they are to be measured. If the plan was expected to result in increased financial performance and it was to be measured in terms of increased sales, then the outcome to monitor is clear.

However, most plans also produce unanticipated consequences.[14] The plan and its implementation may produce negative or positive unanticipated consequences. Both can be valuable sources of learning. Let's return to our athletic shoe case. Let's suppose that through implementing the plan, you discover it takes more advertising money than anticipated to launch your new high-end line of shoes. You find that customers have an image of your firm as a middle-range shoe manufacturer and have difficulty believing you can produce a line of athletic shoes with the technology, quality, and "sizzle" of other makers that are already in the high end of the market. On the unexpected positive side, you also discover that a stitching machine that you bought for your high-end shoes produced a straighter and stronger stitch at a lower price than the machines you were using for your lower-end shoes. Using the new machines on both your lower-end and high-end shoes will lower your costs, yet allow you to promote higher quality. This may help you compete with other makers at the lower end of the market who have lower quality.

Thus, while it is critical to monitor the outcomes that match the objectives set at the outset of the planning process, managers should try to capture all results possible. They in turn should feed those results back into any and all relevant elements of the planning process.

PLANNING TOOLS

Managers use a variety of planning tools. For example, earlier in the chapter we referred to Gantt charts as one of the tools managers can use to time and sequence actions. In this section we discuss two tools that are widely used and that, if you have not encountered already, you are quite likely to early in your career: budgets and management by objectives.

Budgets

budgets
tools that help quantify and allocate resources to specific activities

capital expenditure budget
the amount of money to be spent on specific items that have long-term use and require significant amounts of money to acquire, such as equipment, land, or buildings

expense budget
a list of the amount of money a unit or organization allocates to each of its primary activities

Budgets are used to quantify and allocate resources to specific activities. In most organizations, budgets are proposed and set annually. A variety of resources can be quantified in budgets, but money is the most commonly used. There are several types of budgets. For example, a **capital expenditure budget** specifies the amount of money to be spent on specific items that have long-term use and require significant amounts of money to acquire. These items might include such things as equipment, land, or buildings.

Another common budget is an expense budget. An **expense budget** typically includes all the primary activities on which the unit or organization plans to spend money and the amount that is allocated for each item. Virtually all profit and nonprofit organizations have expense budgets, both for planning and for control purposes.

In the energy industry, exploration demands traveling to some of the most exotic places on earth in search of crude oil, natural gas, and other energy sources. Managers in Texaco's global exploration unit will budget hundreds of millions of dollars this year to explore for oil and gas.

proposed budget

a plan of how much money is needed that is submitted to a superior or budget review committee

approved budget

authorization to a manager to spend money on certain activities and the amount that may be spent

incremental budgeting approach

budgeting system in which managers begin with the approved budget of the previous year and then present arguments for why the upcoming budget should be more or less

Most organizations have a two-phased process for budgeting. The first consists of managers looking ahead and planning their needs. They then put together a budget specifying things such as expected capital expenditures or expenses. This **proposed budget** provides a plan of how much money is needed and is submitted to a superior or budget review committee. Once the proposed budget is submitted, it gets reviewed, often along with other proposed budgets. An **approved budget** specifies what the manager is actually authorized to spend money on and how much.

Two main approaches to the budgeting process can be taken. The first approach is typically called the **incremental budgeting approach**.[15] In this approach, managers typically use the approved budget of the previous year and then present arguments why the upcoming budget should be more or less. Incremental budgeting has the advantage of efficiency because managers do not need to spend significant time justifying the allocation of money toward items that remain the same from year to year. The principal negative consequence of incremental budgeting is that items can build "budget momentum." In other words, items that have been given money in the past may be given money in the future just because they were funded before. Consider the true case of a small town in North Carolina. Every year, sometime near Christmas, all of the parking meters on the main street are turned off. People park for free. Most of the city residents think that this is just the city's way of giving folks a nice Christmas gift. Actually, it is the City Council's way of maintaining their budget level given the incremental approach the mayor takes to budgeting. The council figures out any surplus still on hand toward the end of the year and computes how many days of free parking downtown will be needed to eat up the surplus. They allocate that many days of free parking and consequently maintain the same level of funding for the next year. As in this case, incremental budgeting can create a "use it or lose it" mindset, which in turn can lead to inefficient use of valuable resources.

zero-based budgeting approach

budgeting system in which all allocations of funds must be justified from zero each year

The **zero-based budgeting approach** assumes that all allocations of funds must be justified from zero each year.[16] In other words, just because your department was given $100,000 for computer equipment purchases last year, that does not justify the need for money for additional computers this year. You must start from a base of zero funds and justify the resources being requested for each activity. The benefit of this approach to budgeting is that items that cannot be justified on their own current merits (regardless of their past merits and allocated budgets) will not get money. So zero-based budgeting frees up money available for other items or activities. In general, this system can lead to a more effective allocation of the organization's financial resources. However, zero-based budgeting takes time because each item must be justified each year. Some items to which an organization should allocate money may cost more time and energy to justify than they are worth.

In either approach, budgets are typically used as planning tools by managers to determine priorities, required resources, and keys to implementation. See the Managerial Challenge box, "Budgeting Is Not Just Academic," to see how one manager budgets for his department. Because money is usually a scarce resource in most organizations—there is almost never as much available as there are requests for it—allocating money among various activities almost forces an organization to prioritize activities. This is true at all three organization levels. For example, department managers are likely to find they have more demand for money than they have money to allocate. Similarly, corporate officers are likely to find departments and

MANAGERIAL CHALLENGE

BUDGETING IS NOT JUST ACADEMIC

As head of the Management Department at Columbia College–Chicago, Dennis Rich must regularly juggle strategic planning for the college with tactical planning for his department. Columbia is an urban private college of more than 7,000 students, focusing on education in the arts, communications, and public information. "Good management skills are vital to everyone," he says. "We focus most on educating those committed to the arts, entertainment, media, and fashion industries."

Although his planning activities are part of the college's overall strategic planning initiative, Rich can see the most progress in his own department. Rich admits that when he came to Columbia several years ago, it was one of the better arts management programs around. Now there is no question in his mind that it's first rate. And he attributes the success largely to a smoothly running team—one that's productive and uses management skills for the benefit of the department.

Planning for his department is critical, because Rich must vie with the 13 other academic departments for college resources. The budget that Rich presents each year to the administration is one developed by the eight full-time faculty

members. To build a budget, he meets with his faculty and asks them quite simply what they need. Rich admits that on occasion he'll return budget requests to faculty members, believing the numbers to be out of line. Mostly, however, individual faculty members know how to plan for what they need and then ask for it. Basic to successful planning is building a realistic budget. "Don't come asking me for money in the middle of the year," Rich warns his faculty members. The result has been a department that has a balanced budget every year. This, of course, is something Rich expects—after all, it is a management department.

Admittedly, Rich can't always perform miracles, and it sometimes takes more than one year to influence administration to allocate resources for needed facilities or programs. Such was the case with the computer lab that now sits on the seventh floor of the building that houses his department. Rich says that it wasn't easy getting the lab, and it took repeated requests.

Columbia proudly promotes the fact that, in addition to full-time staff, much of its faculty is part time—people who do what they teach others to do. And so in the management department of this college, the faculty is attempting to show as well as teach good management practice.

business units requesting more money than the organization has. This leads to a determination of which units and activities are of highest priority and should receive budget approval.

In this sense, budgets can be an effective means of integrating and quantifying many aspects of the corporate, business, and function plans. Although the budgeting process per se does not guarantee that managers will make good decisions about integrating and coordinating activities about priorities, it does help ensure they will at least be discussed.

Management by Objectives

management by objectives (MBO)
system in which specific performance goals or objectives for individuals are jointly determined by the individual and his or her immediate boss; specific time frames are attached to these objectives, and feedback is provided

The second major planning tool is **management by objectives (MBO)**. MBO is a system in which specific performance goals or objectives for individuals are jointly determined by the individual and his or her immediate boss. Moreover, specific time frames are attached to these objectives, and feedback is provided. As this definition illustrates, MBO has four basic components: (1) specific goals, (2) participative decision making, (3) explicit time periods, and (4) feedback on performance.

Exhibit 7.6 provides a graphic illustration of how MBO works. First, specific goals are set. The achievement of these goals should translate into results that support the organization's strategic, tactical, and operational plans and objectives. The individual goals need to be jointly set because research suggests that goal

The Process of MBO

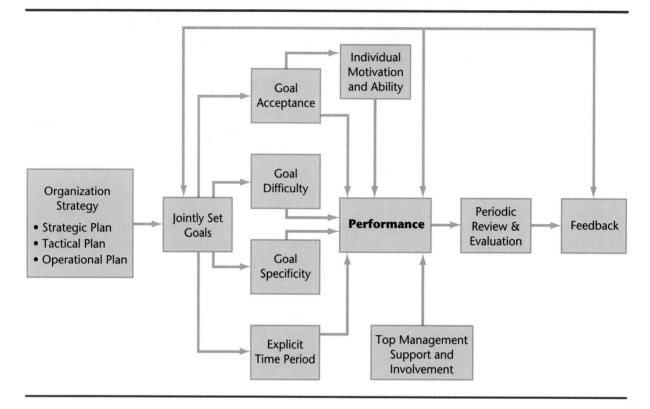

acceptance and goal difficulty (i.e., a challenging goal) are enhanced by participation.[17] Goal acceptance in turn has a positive impact on both motivation to perform and actual performance.[18] All other things being equal, goal difficulty also has a positive impact on performance.[19] As mentioned, goals need to be specific and have explicit time periods attached. For example, rather than setting a goal of "trying to improve customer satisfaction," you would "increase customer satisfaction from an average of 85 percent to 90 percent within the next six months." Research also suggests that MBO systems are most effective if top management demonstrates its clear support for and involvement in the system.[20] Although not directly part of the MBO system, individual capabilities must be kept in mind when setting objectives. Obviously, setting specific goals and time periods that an individual does not believe can be achieved hurts motivation and performance. Thus, goals need to be difficult but achievable. Clearly, if goals have specific time frames, then periodic review and evaluation are necessary. The final and perhaps most powerful element of MBO is performance feedback.[21] Individuals need to know if what they are doing is on or off target so that they can retain or adjust their behaviors. Also, feedback can affect the goal-setting process. Specific feedback may indicate that the original goals were too easy, too difficult, or just not directed at appropriate targets.

The general research results concerning MBO are positive.[22] Properly followed, MBO does seem to result in higher performance and can be effective in translating corporate strategy into individual actions and results that collectively lead to corporate objectives.

CONCLUDING COMMENTS

Planning requires a determination of where the organization wants to go and how it is going to get there. This process includes an assessment of the organization's external and internal environments. Early in their careers, managers typically are more involved in operational plans.

But it is important for them to understand the entire process. First, lower-level managers are more motivated to implement their specific responsibilities if they know the larger plan and can see how their actions can help carry it out. Second, lower-level managers face thousands of decisions daily. They cannot make wise decisions if they do not understand overall objectives. Doing so would be like deciding to turn left or right and slowing down or speeding up without knowing where you were trying to go.

In a global business environment, managers are simultaneously faced with three critical planning challenges. First, they must try to learn from the past. Many things that went right or wrong in the past may be helpful in guiding action and shaping plans for the future. Second, managers must keep their ears and eyes closely tuned to signals in the current environment—signals from competitors, customers, and governments. The rate of change in the current environment is so fast that lack of flexibility and adaptability in the present could forfeit the future. Finally, managers must think about and plan for the future. It is the incorporation of three different time perspectives (past, present, and future) that makes planning one of the most challenging managerial activities.

KEY TERMS

approved budget 188

benchmarking 181

budgets 187

capital expenditure budget 187

contingency plans 181

expense budget 187

incremental budgeting
   approach 188

management by objectives
   (MBO) 189

objectives 174

operational plans 175

planning 174

plans 174

proposed budget 188

strategic plans 174

tactical plans 174

zero-based budgeting
   approach 188

REVIEW QUESTIONS

1. What are the key functions of setting objectives?
2. What are the key differences between strategic, tactical, and operational plans?
3. What impact does organizational level have on managerial planning activities?
4. What are the key issues on which managers at the corporate, business, and functional level focus relative to planning?
5. What are the seven elements in the planning process?
6. Under what conditions are contingency plans most beneficial?
7. What is benchmarking and what role does it play in planning?
8. Why is determining the priority of objectives important?
9. How can budgeting be used as a planning tool?
10. Describe the two basic approaches to budgeting.

11. What are the strengths and weaknesses of incremental and zero-based budgeting?

12. What is the role of MBO in strategy formulation and implementation?

DISCUSSION QUESTIONS

1. Why is the articulation of objectives and priorities important to planning?

2. Think of an action plan in which you were recently involved either at work or in an organization. Which elements of the planning process were done well? Which ones were done poorly? What was the impact of these strengths and weaknesses on the outcome?

3. As you look at your own experience and capabilities, where are your strengths and weaknesses relative to the seven elements of the planning process? What is your plan of action for strengthening your planning capabilities?

CLOSING CASE

Whirlpool: Planning for the Next Century

The management of Whirlpool—one of the world's largest appliance manufacturers—faced a critical but not uncommon question: how to continue the company's growth into the 21st century. Several growth options were available to Whirlpool: to diversify into related product areas, to integrate vertically (by entering the retail industry), or to expand internationally. Whirlpool decided instead to "stick to its knitting" and rededicate itself to what it did best: sell large appliances. Its long-term goal was to become the global market leader of major appliances.

That quiet decision had an enormous impact on the entire corporation. Like any company engaged in planning its long-term course, Whirlpool used the goal of becoming the global market leader as its launch pad into planning efforts in all areas of the company. The goal drove strategies that involved the company's geographic presence, its management structure, and its marketing efforts.

On the way toward its goal, Whirlpool formed a joint venture with N. V. Philips of the Netherlands, and later took full ownership of Philips' major appliance business. Joint ventures in various countries also followed, including the fast-growing Asian markets. Closer to home, Whirlpool integrated its U.S., Canadian, and Mexican major appliance operations and created the North American Appliance Group (NAAG). It placed stronger emphasis on major appliances, as opposed to smaller ones, to remain consistent with the overall long-term global goal.

Another major change involved the company structure. For years, Whirlpool had been organized around strategic business units for each brand franchise, typical of the industry. This had allowed employees to manage their own brands separately from the rest of the brands. With the new global initiative, the company disbanded the brand management structure and adopted a cross-functional team structure called "Product Business Teams" (PBTs). Each PBT included professionals from marketing, engineering, procurement, logistics, and other functions. In turn, each PBT was assigned to a specific product—such as dishwashers—and was accountable for all the elements that determine the success of that product. The team approach allowed the company to push decision making down to the trenches, to the employees who knew the marketplace intimately.

Whirlpool also adopted the "Dominant Consumer Franchise" strategy, defined as "giving the consumer a compelling reason beyond price for buying Whirlpool's products over the competitors' products." The Dominant Consumer Franchise was the driver of all plans that related to the marketing of Whirlpool's products. Through marketing research, Whirlpool discovered six distinct appliance consumer segments, all women: (1) the Traditionalist (who has a very strong home focus), (2) the Housework Rebel (who juggles her responsibilities between a full-time job and housework well), (3) the Achiever (who is educated and sees an opportunity to display her good taste by acquiring the right appliances), (4) the Self-Assured (a younger, well-educated woman who takes a casual view of housework), (5) the Proven Conservative (similar to the Traditionalist, but younger), and (6) the Homebound Survivor (an older woman who has few outside interests). Using the Dominant Consumer Franchise strategy, a PBT would determine which market segment best fit its product, and planned all its activities around this segment.

In its planning efforts, Whirlpool clearly decided to narrow its product focus to large appliances but to broaden its geographic focus to global markets. Will this product focus allow Whirlpool to become the global market leader? Whirlpool's planning will undoubtedly have a major impact on its business in the 21st century, and the success of that planning remains to be seen. But Whirlpool now manufactures products in 13 countries and markets products in about 140 countries worldwide.

QUESTIONS

1. What steps did Whirlpool take in its planning to c its strategic direction?
2. Is Whirlpool's Product Business Team structure very different from its original brand management structure? Explain.
3. Though Whirlpool has clearly decided to narrow its product focus to large appliances, it has expanded its geographic focus to global markets. In your opinion, will this trade-off sustain long-term growth? Support your opinion.

Sources: Adapted form "Dedication to Majors," *Appliance Manufacturer,* May 1994, pp. W-4, W-35; Jennifer J. Laabs, "Whirlpool Managers Become Global Architects," *Workforce Magazine* online, accessed at http://www.workforceonline.com/archive/2310.html on October 7, 1998; and "How We Got Here," from the Whirlpool Corporation Web page timeline, accessed at http://www.whirlpoolcorp.com on October 7, 1998.

CHAPTER 8

STRATEGIC
MANAGEMENT

After studying this chapter, you should be able to:

- Define strategy.
- Explain the role of environmental analysis in strategy formulation.
- Explain the strategic planning process.
- Utilize strategic planning tools, such as the product life cycle model, portfolio matrix, and SWOT analysis.
- Describe strategy implementation tools such as the Seven S model.
- Describe the differences between intended and emergent strategies.

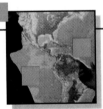

Planning the Strategic Future of Microsoft

Not only is he the richest man in the United States, but Bill Gates may be one of the best strategic visionaries and planners as well. When Bill Gates dropped out of Harvard University in 1975 to found Microsoft, along with his partner Paul Allen, few others saw the potential in computer software that they did.

Through the 1960s and 1970s, most computers were large, complicated machines used almost exclusively by large companies or research organizations, such as universities. In 1980, IBM was the uncontested leader of the computer world, with sales of nearly $30 billion. But as technologies advanced, computers became smaller and more accessible to individuals. In the beginning, these personal computers (PCs) had little computing power and were slow, with little memory, few applications, and built-in operating systems. When IBM decided to enter the personal computer segment, it decided the potential for making money would be in hardware not software. Its background in making large mainframe computers gave it little insight into the extent that PC hardware, such as disk drives, would later become commodities.

However, IBM's initial decision to stay out of the PC software business gave Microsoft the opportunity it needed. In 1980, Bill Gates and Microsoft signed a contract with IBM to provide the operating system for IBM PCs. Microsoft developed MS-DOS (Disk Operating System), which acted as the control system for the computer and the interface between the computer and specific application programs, such as word processing.

With better vision than perhaps anyone else at the time, Gates recognized that application software companies could save significant sums of money if they could write one version of their application program to work with a standard operating system, instead of writing several versions to run on multiple proprietary operating systems. Thus, they would have an incentive to direct their software-development activities toward the standard operating system. Gates needed DOS to become the industry standard.

With this in mind, he quickly convinced IBM to allow Microsoft to sell MS-DOS to other computer manufacturers. By 1983, Microsoft sales had grown to $63 million. The high cost of developing an alternative operating system to MS-DOS (about $500 million) and the popularity of MS-DOS on IBM and IBM-compatible PCs created a significant entry barrier to other software companies.

Although MS-DOS solved many problems, it still was not "user friendly." Consumers had to learn what terms like "config.sys" meant. Apple Computer was determined to solve this problem by designing an operating system that didn't require typed commands. The introduction of the Apple Macintosh in 1984 and its amazingly easy-to-use operating system posed a serious threat to Microsoft.

Microsoft found itself in a difficult competitive position. Although its operating system had captured nearly 80 percent of the market, executives believed their position was not sustainable because most consumers wanted user-friendly systems. A customer's initial decision about operating systems was critical, because once a system was chosen, switching to the other was quite costly. Consequently, few customers changed operating systems once they made their initial decision.

In a competitive countermove, Microsoft developed "Windows," a more user-friendly system that presented the user with an interface of icons and words that could be accessed through clicking. Microsoft narrowed the gap between itself and Apple significantly with the launch of its updated Windows 95 and 98. To ensure that the product was a success, Microsoft spent over $100 million in marketing the new products.

Computers and computer literacy are now virtually commonplace. Information is increasingly becoming the currency of exchange and power. In answer to the growing needs of consumers, Microsoft is planning for the next arenas of competition—the information superhighway and interactive television. Microsoft launched Microsoft Network, an on-line information network, to compete with companies such as America Online.

Whether this or other strategic moves and planning will enable Microsoft to continue its strong competitive position in the ever-changing software industry is yet to be seen. It faces several competitive threats, chief among them a U.S. Department of Justice antitrust case regarding its Internet browser and a breach of contract lawsuit brought by Sun Microsystems for changes to Sun's Java programming language. Time will tell whether Microsoft can face and meet these challenges.

Sources: Daniel Ichbiah and Susan L. Knepper, *The Making of Microsoft* (Rocklin, Calif.: Rima Publishing, 1991); Kathy Rebello, "Windows 95," *Business Week,* July 10, 1995; Brent Schlender, "Bill Gates and Paul Allen Talk," *Fortune,* October 2, 1995; John R. Wilke, "Microsoft Case: Tapes, E-Mails, and Meetings," *The Wall Street Journal,* October 5, 1998, pp. B1, B4; Steve Hamm, Amy Cortese, and Peter Burrows, "No Letup—and No Apologies: Antitrust Scrutiny Hasn't Eased Microsoft's Competitiveness," *Business Week,* October 26, 1998, pp. 58–64.

For Microsoft to successfully navigate the future threats and opportunities it faces, it must have a strategy for how to compete effectively. Although firms have always needed plans to compete, often referred to as competitive strategies, the dramatic rise of competition in recent years has raised the importance of strategy and the strategic management process. For an illustration of this increasing competition, we need only look as far as the parking lot. As recently as 25 years ago, the largest automobile market in the world, the United States, was dominated by only three major manufacturers: General Motors, Ford, and Chrysler. In contrast, today when a country such as Poland, with only one-sixth the population of the United States, opens its automobile market, a host of players including BMW, Daimler-Chrysler, Daewoo, Fiat, Ford, GM, Honda, Hyundai, Isuzu, Kia, Nissan, Renault, Subaru, Suzuki, Toyota, and others converge on the market opportunity at once. As the list of automobile competitors indicates, globalization is one of the most powerful forces behind increasing competition. Today competitors from every corner of the world can converge on markets. This means that just to survive, firms have to be world class. In this context, firms that fail to plan well might as well plan to fail.

STRATEGIC MANAGEMENT PROCESS

strategic management
type of planning in which (1) the organization's general direction and objectives are determined, (2) a plan is formulated and implemented to achieve the objectives, and (3) the results are monitored and necessary adjustments made

Strategic management is a type of planning process in which (1) the organization's general direction and objectives are determined (its strategic intent and mission), (2) a plan is formulated and implemented to achieve the objectives, and (3) the results are monitored and necessary adjustments made. To understand what this means, we need to examine each step in this overall process (see Exhibit 8.1).

Because a strategy is a plan for the future of the company, many of the key elements in the strategic management process are similar to those we covered in the previous chapter on planning. Consequently, we will highlight key similarities in the following sections. In advance, however, we should make clear that while one could think of strategic management as happening at the corporate, business unit,

EXHIBIT 8.1

**Strategic Management
Process**

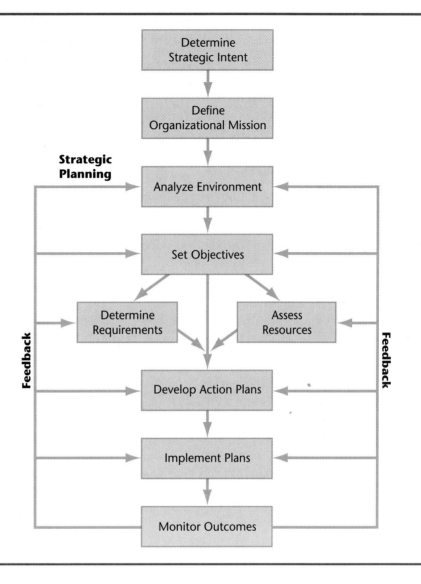

EXHIBIT 8.1

Strategic Management
Process

and operational levels, we typically think of it in terms of corporate and business levels. However, like planning in general, the scope of strategic management typically narrows as we move down organization levels.

Strategic Intent

strategic intent
what an organization ultimately wants to be and do; the first step in the strategic management process

The first step in the strategic management process is the determination of the firm's strategic intent. **Strategic intent** is not easy to define, but it can be thought of as what the organization ultimately wants to be and do.[1] For example, Ford Motor Company's strategic intent is to "be the number one automotive company in the world." British Airways intends to become "The World's Favourite Airline." Xerox Corporation states its strategic intent in equally simple terms: "The World's Document Company." Kellogg's strategic intent is to have "Kellogg's Products on Every Table in the World." As these four examples illustrate, strategic intent captures the general identity, direction, and level of aspirations of the organization. A key point to keep in mind is that while the other specific elements in the strategic planning process constitute the body of a strategic plan, strategic intent is the heart of the plan. As such, one of its key objectives is to inspire.[2] This is why most statements of strategic intent are also statements of "strategic stretch." That is, to live up to the strategic intent, the organization must stretch far beyond where it is today.

Mission

Although statements of strategic intent are typically only a sentence in length, mission statements are usually much longer. A **mission statement** articulates the fundamental purpose of the organization and often contains several components, among them

mission statement
articulation of the fundamental purpose of the organization, often containing several components such as company philosophy, company identity (self-concept), principal products or services, customers and markets, geographic focus, obligations to shareholders, and commitment to employees

- Company philosophy
- Company identity, or self-concept
- Principal products or services
- Customers and markets
- Geographic focus
- Obligations to shareholders
- Commitment to employees[3]

An example of a mission statement is provided in Exhibit 8.2. As the example illustrates, while mission statements provide more detail concerning the purpose of the organization, they should support and be consistent with its strategic intent.

Environmental Analysis

The external environment of a firm has many possible components as we discussed in Chapter 3. Each one of these components can significantly affect the strategy a firm might develop as well as whether the firm is likely to succeed or fail. In Chapter 3, we examined Porter's "five forces" framework for analyzing a firm's external environment.[4] In terms of the strategic management process, the key contribution of analyzing customer power, supplier power, new entrants, substitutes, and nature of competition is that it informs you of the relative difficulty (or ease) of your position in particular segments of your overall business. For example, suppose customers have power because they are few and coordinated and your suppliers

EXHIBIT 8.2

Mission Statement for the Internal Revenue Service

> **✦ IRS Mission Statement ✦**
>
> The IRS mission is to "provide America's taxpayers
> top quality service by helping them
> understand and meet their tax responsibilities
> and by applying the tax law with
> integrity and fairness to all."

have power because they are few and have high control over critical inputs. This would inhibit your ability to make money in this segment. Consequently, from a strategic perspective, you may be better off emphasizing and putting resources into other segments of your business. If the results of the analysis look bad enough, it may suggest that strategically you should get out of a particular segment of business because it is just too difficult to make money in that segment.

Competition   An assessment of competition is a part of virtually any strategic management process because a firm's position of strength or weakness relative to customers is always a function of how it stacks up against competitors. One increasingly popular means of assessing this is in terms of the value proposition a firm presents to customers. A **value proposition** is essentially the ratio of what customers get from a firm and how much it costs them. Clearly, customers can get many things that they value from a particular product or service. If the product is a car, the customers get a certain level of performance, reliability, styling, and so on. For that, they have to pay a price. The key question from a strategic management perspective is, "How much of what the customer really wants do I provide and at what price relative to my competitors?"

To illustrate, let's simplify things a little. Let's say that you are in the automobile business. Further, let's say that what customers really care about is reliability. Assuming we have objective measures of reliability, such as repair expenses per 10,000 miles driven, we can actually draw the value propositions by plotting differing reliability levels by the price of the car (see Exhibit 8.3). The diagonal line represents essentially equal value. That is, as you move up the line, you get greater reliability, but you pay for it. The customers who really value reliability are willing to pay a higher price for the car. Those who don't value reliability as highly prefer to pay less. But in terms of value, all points along the line are considered equal. From a strategic management perspective, what you care about is your relative position to competitors within a given customer segment. A **customer segment** is essentially a group of customers who share similar preferences or place similar value on product features. For the sake of illustration, we have divided customers into three segments: low, medium, and high value placed on reliability.

Let's say you produce cars of medium reliability. The attractiveness of the value proposition you present to customers is a function of where you are relative to competitors. In Exhibit 8.3, which company, A, B, or C, represents the best value for the customers? Clearly, it is company C. Company C has a lower price and higher reliability than either companies A or B. Now, of companies A and B, which represents the better value to customers? Actually, their value propositions are quite similar. Company B produces cars with higher reliability than company A, but customers have to pay a higher price for the increase in quality. If you were company B, competing with companies A and C, where would you have to move to offer a more competitive value to your customers? In general, you would have to move up and to the left. In other words, you would have to lower your price and increase your reliability. Specifically, if you matched company C's price and beat them on reliability, you would then offer a superior value proposition, which should enhance your competitive position.

The bottom line is that any assessment of the external environment from a strategic management perspective must include an analysis of your competitors and your relative position to them. Although other tools can be used in this

value proposition
ratio of what customers get from a business and how much it costs them

customer segment
a group of customers who share similar preferences or place similar value on product features

EXHIBIT 8.3

Value Proposition for
Three Car Companies

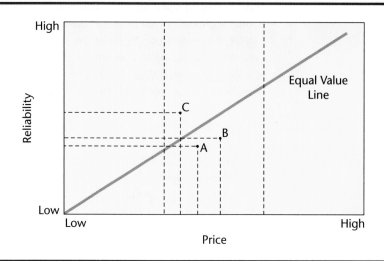

process, value proposition has become increasingly widespread because, in the final analysis, it is customers who pay companies' bills and provide profits.

Economic Conditions   Economic conditions also affect a firm's fortunes. Important economic factors include inflation, unemployment, interest rates, trade balance between countries, and currency exchange rates. For example, interest rates determine how expensive or cheap money is to borrow and, therefore, what rates of return firms need to achieve on their investments into plants, equipment, and technology to pay borrowed money back and still be profitable. Exchange rates and their fluctuations, especially in a global marketplace, can also have a significant impact on a firm's fortunes or even survival. Suppose you were an American manufacturing firm trying to sell your products in Japan. As you examined your Japanese competitors, you found that your costs were 10 percent higher than theirs. Clearly, this would constitute a cost disadvantage. However, what would happen if the yen-to-dollar exchange rate went from ¥120:$1 to roughly ¥80:$1? Without doing anything, you would have gone from a 10 percent cost disadvantage to a 20 percent cost advantage. In contrast, suppose you were manufacturing some of your products in Malaysia and importing them into the United States. What would happen if unemployment in Malaysia went from 10 percent to less than 2 percent? You would likely find that you had to pay more for quality labor. This might cause you to raise your prices in the United States to keep your profit margins the same. Furthermore, what would happen if your major competitor manufactured its product in China, where unemployment and inflation had remained stable? You could easily be put at a cost and price disadvantage. The key point here is that the increasing globalization of business means managers cannot afford to ignore global economic swings in the future.

Political Conditions   Political conditions, and the laws and regulations that result from the political process, can also have a significant impact on firms. For example, changes in minimum wages can significantly affect the profits or even survivability of firms that depend on unskilled labor and low wages in creating their products or services. Laws can keep you out of otherwise attractive markets or make what was once an attractive market unattractive. For example, when the Indian government insisted that Coca-Cola share its secret formula with a local partner, Coca-Cola decided to withdraw from the market. It withdrew mainly because it was worried that it would not be able to keep the firm's traditional high standards of quality and product consistency and that it would simply be creating a new competitor. In 1993, a new government reversed the policy, and Coca-Cola decided to reenter the market. This time, however, it was more careful to weave itself into the fabric of the country by forming alliances so that it would be harder and more costly for the Indian government to reverse its decision and try to boot Coca-Cola out of the country.[5]

Culture and Society   Cultural conditions and social values constitute an additional aspect of the environment you must analyze. As discussed in Chapter 4, culture consists of values that are passed from one generation to the next. The importance of culture is perhaps most obvious when a firm discovers that what was successful at home does not work abroad. A classic example of this issue is the Chevy Nova. While the car and the name were relatively successful in the United States, they failed in Mexico. Why? Essentially, *no va* in Spanish means "no go."

The importance of the external environment for firms is clear. To help illustrate this, imagine trying to compete and survive in the clothing industry under the following conditions:

- Many customers have money to spend, but they change their minds frequently about what they like.
- Competitors twice your size have significant resources to spend on advertising.
- Three suppliers control the fabric trade.
- Suppliers sell you lesser-quality fabrics several months after your larger competitors receive higher-quality fabrics.
- An economic recession is in full swing in the United States.
- New laws have been proposed regulating the number of hours employees under the age of 21 can work.
- Social values are placing less emphasis on outward appearance.

It only takes a little imagination to see why external environmental conditions are critical to a firm's success. You now can see why external environment analysis is a critical part of the strategic management process.

Strategic Objectives

Unless organizational dreams and purposes are translated into specific performance goals, they are likely to remain statements of good intentions and unrealized achievements. Furthermore, an analysis of the environment is an academic exercise unless the implications find their way into strategic objectives. **Strategic objectives** translate the strategic intent and mission of the firm into concrete and measurable goals. Setting strategic objectives is a critical step in the strategic management process because it facilitates a firm's ability to (1) allocate resources appropriately, (2) reach a shared understanding of priorities, (3) delegate responsibilities, and (4) hold people accountable for results.[6] Specifically, strategic objectives might address any of the following issues:

- Revenue growth
- Profitability

strategic objectives
translation of the strategic intent and mission of the firm into concrete and measurable goals

* Customer satisfaction
* Market share
* Financial returns (e.g., return on equity, return on assets)
* Technological leadership
* Cash flow
* Operating efficiency (e.g., costs per unit, expense per employee)

It is important to note that strategic objectives differ from other performance objectives in one fundamental use. Strategic objectives are longer term in nature. They are not yearly objectives or goals. They represent targets for which the company aims over the long term. Although setting strategic objectives is critical, much of the time managers actually spend on strategic management is taken up in the subsequent steps of the process. These principally involve analyzing the organization's internal environment, formulating a strategy, developing an implementation plan, and monitoring the results.

Organizational Analysis

An analysis of the organization's internal environment is equally important to an analysis of its external environment. As we discussed in the previous chapter, this assessment involves two related but separate processes. The first is an assessment of requirements, and the second is an assessment of resources.

The process of assessing requirements from a general planning process or from a strategic planning process is similar enough that we can be fairly brief in our review. As we discussed previously, once we know what our objectives are, we can begin to determine what is required to achieve them. Returning to our value proposition example, if you were to try to move company B up and to the left, while still maintaining previous profit levels, what would be required? First, to move up, you would need higher levels of reliability. Does this take investment in research and development? Better manufacturing processes? More highly skilled workers? Second, to move to the left (i.e., lower prices) and still maintain previous levels of profits is likely to require cutting costs to offset the lower revenue per car. However, if your objectives focus on total profits and not profits per car, you may not have to cut costs as much if, in lowering your price, you attract more customers and sell more cars. Your profit per car would be lower, but your overall total profits could be higher than before.

The process of assessing resources from a strategic planning process is somewhat more specialized than from a general planning perspective. Consequently, this aspect of the strategic planning process requires a more detailed discussion.

A firm can assess its internal resources and how it relates to the firm's competitive position from a variety of ways. However, the "value chain" approach proposed by Michael Porter is arguably one of the most cited and widely utilized.[7] The **value chain** is essentially a set of key activities that directly produce or support the production of what a firm ultimately offers to customers. Porter separates the internal components of a firm into five primary activities and four support activities (see Exhibit 8.4). The **primary activities** are those that are directly involved in the creation of a product or service and getting it into the hands of the customer and keeping it there. As the label suggests, **support activities** facilitate the creation of the product or service and its transfer to the customer. Porter stresses that rather than assessing the cost of these activities, managers must assess the value they add to the product or service to truly understand the firm's ability to compete. The

value chain
key activities that directly produce or support the production of what a firm ultimately offers to customers

primary activities
business activities that are directly involved in the creation of a product or service and getting it into the hands of the customer and keeping in it there

support activities
business activities that facilitate the creation of the product or service and its transfer to the customer

EXHIBIT 8.4

The Value Chain

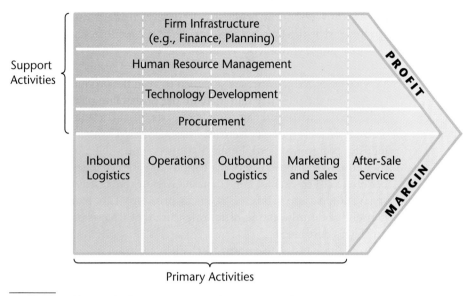

Source: Adapted from Michael Porter, *Competitive Advantage* (New York: Free Press, 1985).

absolute value of a product or service is a function of how much customers are will-ing to pay and how many customers are willing to purchase the product or service. A firm makes a profit if it can produce something whose value exceeds its costs. To determine where value is added in the firm's internal value chains, managers need to understand each of the nine activities in the chain.

Inbound Logistics   This component of the value chain consists of activities that are designed to receive, store, and then disseminate various inputs to the products or services. Raw materials, receiving, transportation, inventory, information, and so on are commonly a part of inbound logistics. In the beer industry, inbound logis-tics involve getting hops, barley, and malt to various brewing sites.

Operations   A wide variety of activities are included within the operations com-ponent of the value chain. Activities that transform inputs into the products and services of the firm are at the heart of operations. In addition, such activities as maintenance that keep machines in working order would also be included in the operations segment of the value chain. In our beer example, operational issues may involve beer recipes for different products and markets as well as the process of bottling and labeling the products.

Outbound Logistics   Simply stated, outbound logistics include activities that get the product or service from the firm to the customers. Our beer factory would need to warehouse the finished product, process the orders, schedule delivery trucks, and distribute its products (either directly or through distributors) to get the product delivered to stores, bars, ballparks, restaurants, and other places where it can be sold.

Marketing and Sales Marketing and sales activities are designed to let customers know about the products and services that are available and entice them to purchase what the firm has to offer. The beer manufacturer would need to advertise, promote its products, sell them, and price them.

Service Service activities are designed to keep the product in the hands of the customer after the purchase and increase the probability of a repeat purchase. Service activities may involve repair, supply of parts, installation, or product adjustment.

Each of these primary activities has associated costs. They enhance the firm's industry position and profitability if a customer is willing to pay more for them than they cost. The importance of the various activities changes depending on customer preferences. For example, in the fashion industry, customers often want the latest styles, colors, and fabrics as soon as possible. This places a premium on both inbound and outbound logistics to ensure that what is produced can be delivered quickly to customers.

In addition to the five primary activities, there are four support activities. As illustrated in Exhibit 8.4, these activities cut across all five of the primary activities; that is, elements of a given support activity facilitate each of the five primary activities.

Procurement The activity of procuring usable and consumable assets is found in each of the primary activities. For example, not only must raw materials used in products be purchased within inbound logistics, but also delivery trucks and scheduling software for the fleet must be purchased so that those materials can arrive for processing. The purchases of machinery and replacement parts are examples of specific procurement activities within operations. Firms often have purchasing departments, but procurement may be handled by various people—from purchasing agents to secretaries.

Technology Development Technology development revolves around expertise and the tools or equipment related to the exercise of that expertise. The technology may be as simple as a pencil for manually recording information or as complicated as a supercomputer and its software. Although technology development is concentrated on product development or process innovation, technology and the means by which it is applied to tasks also has an impact on all five primary activities.

Human Resource Management Given that no activity is completely removed from humans (even automatic processes and equipment are designed and implemented by someone), the process of acquiring, training, evaluating, compensating, and developing human resources is present in all five primary activities. Capable and motivated people can have a profound impact on all activities of a firm, so human resource management is a key support activity. In service firms such as law, consulting, or accounting firms, the quality of the people is what customers purchase. Therefore, this component of the value chain is critical to a service firm's fortune or failure.

Firm Infrastructure Although infrastructure usually brings plant, utilities, and equipment to mind, a firm's infrastructure has less to do with brick and mortar

than with functions that support all primary activities
planning, finance, accounting, legal, government relatic
the information supplied by these functions to the vari
example, legal information concerning worker safety st
operations, and legal information on truth in advertisir
keting and sales.

Just as each primary activity has associated costs, so
Support activities enhance the firm's position and profi
they assist primary activities and contribute to final proc
tomers value. Like primary activities, the importance of the support activities also
changes depending on customer preferences. Returning to our earlier example of
the fashion industry, customers' preference for the latest styles, colors, and fabrics as
soon as possible may increase the importance of planning information to businesses in that industry. Planning information that relates forecasting trends, buying sea-
sons, purchasing cycles, and ways they help satisfy customer preferences would be
valuable. Customer preferences might also increase the importance of technology
development support activity, especially those that support flexibility such as technology that allows clothes to be dyed *after* they have been knit into a sweater
rather than in the yarn stage, because this allows the latest color preferences to be
incorporated at the last minute.

Leveraging the Value Chain   Knowing your firm's value chain is one thing;
leveraging for an advantage in the marketplace is quite another. The first step in
managing the value chain for greater profits and performance is to determine
where in your value chain you have the potential to add the greatest value. If we
return to our beer example, let's say that our German customers value a rich-tasting
beer and that they are less sensitive to price. If the flavor of beer is largely determined by the quality of the ingredients and that quality varies widely, we know we
need to concentrate on procurement. We must be sure that we have the highest-
quality ingredients. Further, let's suppose that being able to identify high-quality
ingredients is primarily a function of experienced buyers who can see, smell, and
taste quality differences. Now we know that we must be sure that our human
resource management systems are superior in terms of recruiting, selecting, and
training these ingredients' buyers. The power of the value chain model lies in that
it helps us segment business activities and see the important linkages. However, the
model per se does not tell us which specific activities add the most value or which
linkages among activities are the most important. That all comes from our analysis.

Core Competencies   In addition to the activities involved in the value chain,
organizations and their managers need to consider one other element for effective
internal analysis—core competencies. **Core competencies** are activities on which a
firm focuses and has an **internal comparative advantage**.[8] While comparative
advantage means being able to do one thing better than another, core competency
is essentially what a firm does best out of the many things it does. Few firms are
equally good at all things they do. For example, a firm might be better at creating
new products than it is at designing effective marketing plans for the products. All
aspects of the value chain are potential sources of core competencies. The challenge
is to determine at which ones the firm is best and ensure that those handful of core
competencies add value in the eyes of the customer. For example, Honda believes
that one of its core competencies is the technology behind and the manufacturing

core competencies
activities on which a firm or
individual focuses and has an
internal comparative
advantage; that is, essentially
what a firm does best out of
the many things it does

**internal comparative
advantage**
doing some things better than
others

of combustion engines. This has led it from motorcycles (which it produced long before its first car) to cars to lawnmowers. Honda determined that one of its support activities (i.e., technology development) was one of the key things at which it was best and let that drive its strategy.

Resource-Based Approach   The resource-based approach to strategy argues that the most important determinant of corporate success is determining and then exploiting the internal strengths of the company.[9] A couple of simple analogies may help illustrate this. Suppose you had a group of gifted orchestra musicians. Even if a large group of customers loved jazz, the resource-based approach would argue against trying to turn orchestra musicians into jazz musicians. Likewise, it would be silly to design a passing offense as a strategy in American football if you had a great running back but a quarterback with a terrible throwing arm.

But the resource-based approach to strategy does not assume that you are forever stuck where you are. It does argue, however, that the resources you build or add should have some key characteristics. First, the resources should result in things customers value; for example, resources that enable a firm to produce low emission engines only help their competitive position if customers value this. Second, the resources should be rare. The logic here is quite straightforward. If all, or even most, competitors possess a given resource, such as a particular piece of manufacturing equipment, then there is little possibility for one competitor to produce a product significantly superior to another competitor using the same piece of equipment. Third, the resources should be hard for competitors to copy. This may include things such as patents and copyrights that legally are protected as well as things that aren't protected but are still hard to copy, such as the brilliance of a top researcher or the creativity of an advertising specialist.

Fit Approaches

While the resource-based approach to strategy examines the external environment, its focus is on internal capabilities. Fit approaches place much more emphasis on the environment and take the perspective that a successful strategy requires a good fit between the firm and its external environment.[10] This does not mean that for a given environment, there is only one appropriate strategy. The relationship between environment and strategy is much like the relationship in the natural world. Certain conditions of an environment, such as rainfall, temperature, amount of sunshine, humidity, and altitude, can determine which varieties of plants can grow, but they do not limit growth to only one type of plant. For example, the lack of rain and high temperatures in Australia's deserts preclude the natural occurrence of orchids. However, a wide variety of plants thrive there. The severity of some environments, such as Antarctica, can limit the range of viable plants, but such extremes tend to be the exception rather than the rule.

The same is true in the business environment. Most business environments are temperate enough that a variety of strategies are feasible. However, this does not mean that any strategy is feasible or that all feasible strategies will be equally successful. For example, suppose your firm existed in the following business environment:

- Suppliers of a critical raw material are in short supply.
- Your business requires large economies of scale (e.g., it takes a facility with a million square feet to produce enough product to be profitable).
- Three of your largest competitors control 60 percent of the market.

* Each of these three competitors is four times your size.
* Customers are quite price sensitive and can easily switch to lower-priced products.

Under these conditions, a strategy aimed at competing on price and purchasing all your raw materials from suppliers is unlikely to succeed. Why? The strategy does not fit the environment. Short supply of raw materials and three large competitors mean that suppliers have an incentive to supply these large firms first. The large economies of scale mean that larger firms are in a better position to spread costs over more sales. This gives competitors a cost and potential price advantage. If you try to achieve a profit margin similar to your competitors by pricing your product above theirs, price-sensitive customers will buy your competitors' cheaper product. Furthermore, your small size means you will have difficulty reducing the costs per product to the level of your competitors. Thus, if you price products at the same level as competitors, your cost *dis*advantage will result in lower profit margins and, in the worst case, may actually result in losses.

The fit approach requires a careful assessment of the external environment *and* of your organization's internal capabilities for success. Consider a simple example. Suppose there was a 100-yard dash, and the winner would receive $1 million. You are one of five people entered in the race. The $1 million means very little unless you can run fast—and run fast compared with the other entrants. Similarly, a fit analysis requires you to examine market opportunities and threats and your firm's ability to deal effectively with those conditions. Although a variety of tools and techniques can help you integrate your internal and external analyses, product life cycle, portfolio, and SWOT analyses are three widely used and effective techniques with which you should be familiar.

Product Life Cycle Analysis   Like people, products go through a life cycle that starts with birth and ends with decline (see Exhibit 8.5). When a product is first born, or developed, it is similar to a baby—it needs constant care and does not produce much. During the birth period, most products provide very little revenue and yet require significant investments of time and money. Revenues during this early stage are provided by "early adopters," or consumers that buy products before they

EXHIBIT 8.5
Product Life Cycle

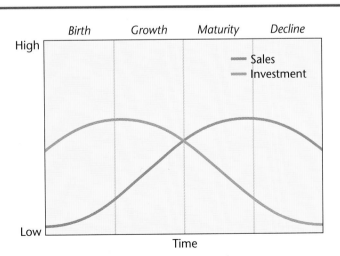

are widely accepted in the marketplace. Often these early adopters can provide valuable information on product or service characteristics that can help broaden product acceptance. This in turn enhances the next stage—growth.

The steepness and height of the life cycle line during the growth period are primarily a function of how quickly and how widely customers accept the product.[11] The degree to which a firm can exploit economies of scale is one of the most important factors that influences the extent of investment needed during the growth stage.[12] The greater the economies of scale, the relatively less investment that is required during the growth stage. For example, it takes between $500 million and $1 billion to develop a new operating system for a personal computer. However, once that initial investment is made, it takes hardly any money to make a thousand or a million copies of the operating system to sell during the growth stage.

The mature stage of the product life cycle occurs when the product or service produces its greatest profits.[13] During this stage, the highest levels of revenues and lowest costs per unit are achieved.

Unless a product is rejuvenated, it typically enters the decline stage because new products or services make it obsolete. The extent to which the new products are "better" (faster, cheaper, more powerful, longer lasting, etc.) is an important factor in how steep the decline curve will be. Switching cost is often another powerful factor. The lower the switching costs, the steeper the decline curve. Obviously, significant new product qualities and low switching costs could combine to produce a steep and dramatic decline.

One of the most attractive aspects about an international marketplace is that, for a given product, firms can seek out new markets to start the product life cycle all over again (see Exhibit 8.6). A firm can extend the life of a product by taking it international. The key to success for this strategy is managers' abilities to correctly identify countries whose economic, social, cultural, and political conditions match the product and to identify any modifications that could be accomplished economically and would enhance its acceptance in a particular country.[14] The Managerial Challenge box discusses a product that was kept alive by an international marketplace—the VW Beetle.

In summary, product life cycle analysis helps you examine the product and how it matches its environment to estimate the likely shape of its life cycle curve. Having

EXHIBIT 8.6
International Product Life Cycles

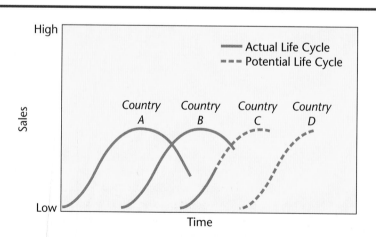

MANAGERIAL CHALLENGE

FLASHBACK, FLASH FORWARD: KEEPING THE VW BEETLE ALIVE

Peace, Flower Power, and Herbie the Love Bug were all components of the "groovy" 60s. None are buzzwords today. While the fading of popular words from the social scene may be of little consequence, the decline of consumer interest in the Beetle posed a significant threat to Volkswagen.

Instead of simply accepting the market loss, Volkswagen took some time to assess its options and selected Brazil as the next market for the Beetle. Brazil was chosen for several reasons. First, it was a developing country whose auto industry was starving for affordable but reliable cars. Second, Brazil's roads were not in great condition, and the four-wheel independent suspension of the Beetle was ideal for rough roads. This was one of the reasons the Beetle was a car of choice for off-road races.

Because the Beetle was well matched to the market conditions in Brazil, it achieved a popularity there nearly as strong as it had enjoyed in the United States 15 years earlier. Volkswagen produced the Beetle in Brazil into the mid-1980s.

When the car's popularity declined in Brazil and production was stopped, Volkswagen moved production to Mexico. Consumers in Mexico had been purchasing "bugs" since 1964, but moving production to Mexico allowed Volkswagen to capture more of the market by avoiding import duties and other restrictions.

Surprisingly, Volkswagen reopened production in Brazil in 1993, with hopes of again marketing the Beetles in the United States. However, here Volkswagen may have tried to squeeze too much from a product that was in the decline stages of its life cycle relative to these markets. The reintroduction of the Beetle into the United States did not approach the success of its original peak. Convinced that there was still interest in the United States and other countries in the original concept, VW totally redesigned the Beetle. It changed the styling, suspension, and engine and even moved the trunk from the front to the back. The reintroduction of this car in the late 1990s was a huge success, boosting VW sales nearly 63 percent in September 1998 to its best performance since 1985. Back orders were common, and discounts were nowhere to be found. In fact, demand was so strong that some dealers were able to sell Beetles above the suggested list price. How long the success will last is anyone's guess, but VW's ability to extend the life cycle of the product by taking it to less-developed markets and then redesigning it for developed markets has allowed the Beetle model and brand to outlive most other car models by decades.

Sources: Jerry Dubrowski, "VW Unveils New Beetle," Cable News Network online, January 5, 1998; Casey Wian, "Beetle Mania Spreads," Cable News Network online, May 5, 1998; Gregory L. White, "U.S. Car Sales Jumped by 6% in September," *The Wall Street Journal*, October 6, 1998, pp. A3, A8; "Volkswagen U.S. September Sales Best Since 1985," Reuters Limited, October 2, 1998.

an idea of a product's life cycle—the steepness of the curve and how long each stage will last—can significantly enhance your ability to plan properly for increases or decreases in equipment purchases, advertising, or distribution.

Portfolio Analysis   In many ways, portfolio analysis is an extension of product life cycle concepts. It starts with the assumption that a firm has multiple products and that those products are at different stages of their life cycles. Portfolio analysis is an attempt to determine where various products currently are in their life cycles. Based on this analysis, corporate plans of where the firm ought to place its strategic investments can be developed.

One of the earliest portfolio analysis techniques was the BCG matrix, developed by the Boston Consulting Group. This tool requires managers to assess the market attractiveness of a particular product or business and the attractiveness of the current position in the market, primarily in terms of market share (see Exhibit 8.7).

Products or strategic business units (SBUs are units that are considered strategically important and have profit and loss accountability) that have relatively low market share in unattractive markets are classified as **dogs**. These products are often in the decline stage of their life cycle. If a way cannot be found to teach the

dogs
products or strategic business units that have relatively low market share in unattractive markets; they are often products in the decline stage of their life cycles

EXHIBIT 8.7

BCG Matrix

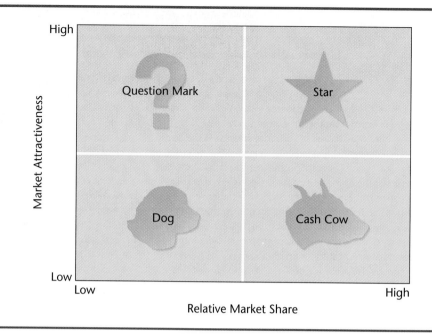

old dog a new trick, the product or business is often sold or shut down. For example, 5¼-inch diskettes and drives were made in the millions and made millions in profits during the 1980s, but they were dog products in the 1990s.

Products or SBUs that have relatively low market share in attractive markets are classified as **question marks**. Managers need to find a way to increase their share of the market, be satisfied with a relatively small share, or get out. You may wonder, "If we're in an attractive market, why would we exit?" The answer is typically found in the internal organizational analysis. For example, you would choose to exit an attractive market because you simply do not have the capabilities or resources to be successful, including such things as technology or capital to invest. For example, in the early 1990s, CDs and CD-ROM drives looked like hot markets, but they required different technology and manufacturing capabilities than 5¼-inch diskettes or disk drives. As a consequence, only a few leading companies, such as Sony, were able to make a successful transition to the new products.

Products or SBUs that have relatively high market share in markets with unattractive futures are classified as **cash cows**. In this case, managers need to feed the cow enough to keep it alive but milk it for all it is worth. Cash cow products or businesses are typically at the maturity stage of their life cycle. Often, the excess cash that is generated is used to fund investments in question marks or promising new products. For example, 3½-inch diskettes and disk drives might easily be considered cash cow products for the mid and late 1990s.

Stars are products that have relatively high market share in markets with attractive futures. Typically, stars are in the birth or growth stages of their life cycle. As we discussed in the section on product life cycles, the birth and growth stages usually require the highest investments of time and money. While CDs and CD-ROM drives might have been considered question marks for Sony in the early 1990s, they were considered star products in the late 1990s. Also, Internet technology is an area in which businesses are investing for the future.

question marks
products or SBUs that have relatively low market share in attractive markets

cash cows
products or SBUs that have relatively high market share in markets with unattractive futures; typically, cash cows are at the maturity stage of their life cycles

stars
products or SBUs that have relatively high market share in markets with attractive futures; typically, stars are in the birth or growth stages of their life cycles

Cell phones are star products for companies like Nokia and Motorola. There are roughly 38 million cellular phone subscribers in the United States and over 80 million worldwide, and the number of users is rising steadily.

The basic idea behind portfolio analysis is to make sure that the corporation is diversified and does not have too many dogs, does not spend too much time on question marks, and has enough cash cows to fund the stars. The exact products or businesses that constitute a balanced portfolio change over time. Some stars may mature and become cash cows or even decline and become dogs.

The same basic idea of analyzing market attractiveness and your firm's capabilities and strengths can also be used to construct an international portfolio analysis and plan (see Exhibit 8.8). In constructing a matrix such as in the exhibit, you

EXHIBIT 8.8

International Matrix

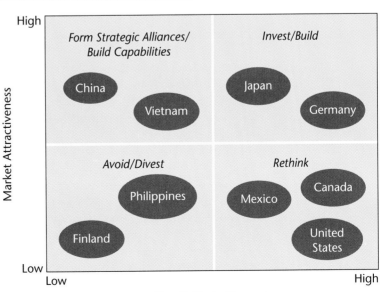

essentially assess the attractiveness of different countries and your ability to compete in those markets. In this context, dogs are markets that are unattractive and for which you have a low ability to compete successfully. For example, in Exhibit 8.8, Finland and the Philippines are dog markets for our hypothetical company. The strategic planning and management implication here is to avoid dog markets and, if you are in one of these markets, to get out.

Markets that are unattractive but in which you have strong competitive capabilities require some rethinking (United States, Mexico, and Canada in Exhibit 8.8). You need to ask questions such as, "Do those markets have segments that could be attractive? Can we introduce new products that leverage our current strengths?" If nothing can be done to make the market more attractive, the company should milk its current products while preparing to exit the market.

If particular markets are attractive (China and Vietnam in Exhibit 8.8), but you have low competitive capabilities, you have two basic options. First, you can form strategic alliances with partners who have capabilities you lack and who can benefit from those you have. Second, you can take the time and money to build the capabilities you need to compete in the market. For example, China might represent a very attractive market for your new beverage product, but you lack managers who understand the Chinese distribution system. You can take on a partner who has this understanding, or you can train or hire managers with this understanding.

Finally, you should invest and build in markets that are attractive and in which you can be competitive (Japan and Germany in Exhibit 8.8). These "star" markets can provide significant revenues in the future.

In summary, most portfolio analysis techniques are designed to assist you in assessing the attractiveness of a market (within a country or across countries) and your current or potential competitive position in that market. Thus, these techniques bring together many of the insights gained from the external and internal analyses discussed in the previous sections.

SWOT analysis
assessment of an organization's strengths, weaknesses, opportunities, and threats

SWOT Analysis   In assessing an organization's competitiveness, managers need to consider its strengths and weaknesses as well as any opportunities and threats for its continued operation. **SWOT analysis** stands for strengths, weaknesses, opportunities, and threats. SWOT analysis is more a basic framework than a specific strategic planning tool.[15] In conducting a SWOT analysis, you first evaluate your firm's strengths or core competencies. Next, you evaluate your firm's weaknesses. The value chain framework previously discussed can be used to work through the strengths and weaknesses during the internal analysis. For example, what parts of the value chain do you do well? Sourcing? Marketing? What do you perform poorly? Customer service? Public relations?

Once a firm has considered its internal environment, it then moves to the external environment. First, you ask, "What are the opportunities facing our firm?" Insights gained from a product life cycle analysis or portfolio analysis can help address this part of the SWOT analysis. For example, what products or businesses are about to enter the growth stage? What countries have conditions conducive to growth for particular products or businesses? Also, insights gained from using the five-forces framework can help identify not only potential opportunities but threats as well. For example, new products that could become substitutes for your products or new entrants into your markets could constitute serious threats.

The important insights of a SWOT analysis come only after you examine the matches and mismatches between the organization's strengths and weaknesses and the environment's opportunities and threats. For example, Wal-Mart (the largest retail organization in the world with over $100 billion in sales) currently has many international opportunities. Representatives from several countries, such as Chile, have approached Wal-Mart executives, inviting them to open stores in their countries. Wal-Mart's strengths include the ability to get large volumes of products to customers at low prices. However, as a result of its strong focus on the U.S. market, very few Wal-Mart managers have experience or knowledge of foreign markets. Fortunately for Wal-Mart, few competitors can capture immediately these international opportunities. This very simple SWOT analysis suggests that while Wal-Mart has some time to respond to international opportunities, it cannot wait forever. If an opportunity to make money exists in these foreign markets, a competitor *will* seek out the opportunity. To effectively respond, Wal-Mart must find a partner that has knowledge of global markets, develop managers within Wal-Mart, or hire people who can help them expand internationally.

STRATEGY FORMULATION

Once you understand the environment in which an organization competes, its internal capabilities and resources, and the extent to which the two do or do not fit, you can formulate a specific strategy to be competitive.

Competitive Advantage

competitive advantage
the ability of a firm to win consistently over the long term in a competitive situation

You rarely read a business newspaper or magazine without running into the term *competitive advantage*, but what is competitive advantage? At its essence, the concept of **competitive advantage** is the ability of a firm to win consistently over the long term in a competitive situation.[16] In the case of for-profit organizations, this means consistently gaining greater profits than competitors. If competitive advantage consists of factors that lead to a consistent winning record, what then are these factors?

Competitive advantage is created through the achievement of the following:

- Doing things better than others do them.
- Doing things that are difficult for others to replicate.
- Doing things that customers value.
- Doing things that are difficult to substitute.
- Doing things that have greater than average cost-value margins.[17]

Let's examine each aspect in further depth.

comparative advantage
the ability to do something better than most others

First and foremost, organizations must have comparative advantage. **Comparative advantage** is the ability to do something better than most others. As a student, you no doubt find that you have a comparative advantage at some subjects in school; maybe you are better than most of your classmates at writing or statistics. Sony has been able to miniaturize audio and video products (for example, radios, tape players, CD players, and video players) better than most other electronics firms. Thus, Sony has a comparative advantage at the miniaturization of audio and video products. For firms to have *competitive advantage*, they must first have *comparative advantage*.

Comparative advantage alone will not guarantee competitive advantage, however. In addition, organizations must create entry barriers concerning their comparative advantages.[18] For example, suppose you are better at statistics than most of

Sony has a comparative advantage in the miniaturization of electronics products. It is the first company to offer a laptop computer that is less than 1 inch thick and weighs 2.7 pounds, the Sony Vaio 505.

your classmates. Further, suppose that your comparative advantage is a function of having taken several math classes in high school and college. For others to become as good at statistics as you are, they would need to take a similar number of classes. The more classes they have to take, the greater the barrier. Disneyland is often cited as having a comparative advantage in friendly employees. While today Disney might be superior to other firms when it comes to friendly employees, *if* it is easy for other firms to replicate this, Disney's comparative advantage will soon disappear. But how easy is it to find and keep employees who can smile for hours on end even while someone asks them where the nearest restroom is for the ten thousandth time that day?

Value-adding activities constitute the third factor for competitive advantage. **Value** consists of activities to which customers attach economic worth. You may be better at statistics than your classmates and they may face high barriers to become as good as you. However, this will not necessarily translate into a competitive advantage in the job market, unless potential employers value the ability to use statistics. If you are interested in a market research position, then your comparative advantage in statistics could easily translate into a competitive advantage in the job market. Similarly, being able to miniaturize audio and video products better than others would lead to few profits for Sony unless the majority of customers wanted smaller radios, video recorders, and CD players. Although providing products that customers value may seem obvious, many well regarded firms and their employees have engaged in activities that added no value to their customers.

In addition, a firm's comparative advantage must be difficult to substitute. Substitution is concerned with whether or not an activity or its output can be replaced by something else, *not* whether it can be copied. For example, the Swiss firm Nestlé is famous for its chocolate products. Nestlé has a significant comparative advantage in the taste and smoothness of its chocolate. Nestlé's specialized knowledge makes it difficult for other firms to replicate. The millions of chocolate lovers in the world mean that Nestlé has a comparative advantage that is valued.

value
activities to which customers attach economic worth

However, none of this guarantees Nestlé a competitive advantage. If Nestlé is to have a sustainable competitive advantage, customers must find it difficult to substitute the sweet taste and smooth texture that they get from eating chocolate with something else. If chocolate lovers find they can satisfy their desire for sweet taste and smooth texture by eating Ben & Jerry's premium ice cream, Nestlé's comparative advantage would not sustain its competitive advantage.

The final element necessary for competitive advantage is the concept of supernormal returns. **Supernormal returns** are the profits that are above the average for a comparable set of firms. These greater-than-average profits are primarily a function of greater-than-average cost-value margins. For example, if the average cost in the industry for a 3½-inch high-density disk is $1 and the average value or price is $1.50, then the average margin is $.50. A supernormal return would be anything above $.50 in profit.

supernormal returns
profits that are above the average for a comparable set of firms

Strategies for Competitive Advantage

How can firms achieve supernormal returns? The two most-discussed generic strategies involve seeking competitive advantage through cost leadership or differentiation.[19] Let's return to our computer disk example. If the industry average profit is $.50, how can a firm make more than this?

Cost Leadership **Cost leadership** simply involves competing by striving to be the lowest-cost producer of a product or provider of a service. To the extent a firm has lower costs than its competitors (i.e., cost leadership) and can command prices similar to its competitors, it can achieve above-average profits. For a computer disk manufacturer to obtain supernormal returns through cost leadership, it would need to lower its costs below the industry average (from $1 to say $.75) and still be able to charge the industry average price (i.e., $1.50). In this case, the firm would make a profit of $.75 instead of the industry average of $.50. It is important to understand that the cost leadership strategy does not necessarily imply price leadership. For example, if the cost leader had costs of $.75 per disk but also charged the lowest price ($1.25), it would earn normal returns (i.e., the industry average of $.50).

cost leadership
competing by striving to be the lowest-cost producer of a product or provider of a service

Differentiation A firm using a **differentiation** strategy seeks to make its product or service different from those of competitors on dimensions highly and widely valued by customers. If it can do so, it can command a premium price. If the firm can also keep costs at approximately the industry average, the premium price it gets allows it to earn above-average profits. For a computer disk manufacturer to obtain supernormal returns through differentiation leadership, it would need to keep its costs at approximately the industry average, while adding features that would allow it to command a premium price (say $1.75 instead of $1.50). In this case, the firm would make a profit of $.75 instead of the industry average of $.50. Any number of characteristics might provide the basis for differentiation. These characteristics might be directly related to the product or service itself or might be indirectly related through any of the aspects of the firm's value chain. Eveready batteries, for example, might command a premium price because they provide longer-lasting power. In contrast, Caterpillar's tractors might command a premium price because Caterpillar can deliver service and spare parts anywhere in the world within 24 hours.

differentiation
making a product or service different from those of competitors on dimensions highly and widely valued by customers

When customers highly value a variety of product attributes, competing firms can successfully pursue different differentiation strategies. For example, Apple

Computer might try to differentiate its products based on how easy they are to use, while Compaq might try to differentiate its products based on how fast and powerful they are. If, on the other hand, customers highly and widely value only one attribute for a given product or service, then firms have fewer options for differentiation strategies. The most successful firm will be the one that is the best at the attribute customers value and that can keep costs low relative to competitors. For example, if customers only value computer speed, then the firm that produces the fastest computer will likely earn the highest profits. For a differentiation strategy to lead to sustainable above-average profits, products must achieve unique advantage on attributes highly valued by customers, and the source of the differentiation must not be easy for other firms to imitate or match. Otherwise, the extra profit potential of premium prices can be negated by high costs.

strategic scope

the extent to which a strategy is broad or narrow in its focus

Strategic Scope   A firm can limit the scope of its strategy (its **strategic scope**), or breadth of focus, by focusing on a specific segment of customers. Although the restriction reduces the total volume and revenue the firm can obtain from a product, it does not necessarily affect its ability to earn supernormal returns. For example, Ferrari differentiates its product based on style and performance and focuses on a very narrow segment of customers (not many people can afford a $250,000 car). A narrow scope strategy also applies to cost leadership. To the extent that the cost leader can provide products or services sufficiently valuable to command prices near the industry average for some targeted segment of customers, it can achieve above-average profits.

niche strategy

a strategy focused on a small segment of a market generally ignored by larger competitors

To succeed when pursuing a limited scope, or **niche strategy**, there must be significant differences among targeted customers or among geographical segments of customers. For example, in selling cars, clear segments exist. Some people value gas mileage, while others value performance. Thus, you can make a high-performance sports car and not really worry about small economy cars taking away your customers. Geographical segments may also exist. First, customers in different locations may prefer different features. If you design and sell suits costing $1,000 or more, you need to know that customers in hot and humid climates prefer cotton fabrics while those in drier and cooler climates prefer wool fabrics. If your firm is particularly strong in wool fabrics, you have a clear geographic segment of customers you can pursue with a differentiation, niche strategy. Second, geographical segments also occur when customers have similar preferences but do not have universal access. The most common reason for this is government intervention. For example, a firm might be able to gain access to customers in France but not in Egypt because of government restrictions, even though Egyptian customers have similar preferences.

sustainable competitive advantage

maintaining success over the long term by making old sources of competitive advantage obsolete before competitors do; thus, firms must continually build temporary competitive advantages, replacing old ones with new ones

Firms pursuing any one of the four generic strategies (see Exhibit 8.9) must remember that in our fast-changing world, today's competitive advantage may be obsolete tomorrow. Firms that succeed over the long term make their old sources of competitive advantage obsolete before their competitors do. Thus, to have **sustainable competitive advantage**, firms must continually build temporary competitive advantages, replacing old ones with new ones.

International Orientation

In today's global environment, a firm's international orientation can significantly affect its long-term success or failure. Research suggests that much of an organization's international strategy grows from the orientation of its senior executives.[20]

EXHIBIT 8.9

Generic Strategies
and Scope

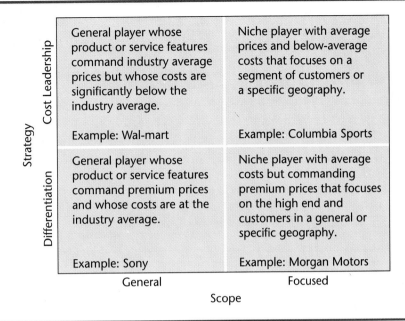

Organizations in which senior executives have an ethnocentric orientation tend to think that what has worked in their home country will work in other countries as well. They assume business is business and good management is good management and tend to launch products in other countries without making any modifications. For example, a U.S. golf ball manufacturer tried to sell its balls in Japan packaged in its normal set of four. However, in Japanese, the number four has the same pronunciation as the word for death. Consequently, in Japan very few things are sold in groups of four.

Organizations in which senior executives have a policentric orientation tend to develop separate strategies for each country. This approach can sometimes lead to inefficiencies. For example, GM spent over $2 billion on the design and development of separate compact cars for three geographic segments, for a total of $6 billion. In the end, although each car was designed and developed for separate markets, approximately 80 to 90 percent of the cars' parts and components could have been identical. GM's policentric orientation may have cost it an unnecessary $3.5 billion in duplicate design and development costs. However, a policentric orientation is not bad per se. For example, a policentric orientation is appropriate when a product is *not* universal and customer preferences are *not* common across countries. For example, funeral services are tied to local culture and customs, so a policentric orientation works well in this case.

Geocentric organizations tend to have senior executives who take the middle ground—they do not believe that what worked in their home country will work everywhere else, nor do they believe that products and services need to be designed and delivered uniquely for each country. They try to capture commonalties where they exist but at the same time be sensitive to cultural and country differences. Currently, GM is trying to move toward a much more geocentric orientation. It is trying to make major components such as chassis and engines common while adjusting components such as suspension to match regional differences.

MANAGERIAL CHALLENGE

TRANSLATING STRATEGY INTO ACTION AT ASHLAND CONSULTING

Kathy Freeman could hardly believe it had been only five years since she graduated from a state university in California with her B.S. in business and joined Ashland Consulting, a small firm specializing in strategic consulting. During those five years, she had advanced from research associate to associate consultant to consulting team leader. As team leader, Freeman was now responsible for a team of four people specializing in strategic market entry projects and reported directly to one of the five senior partners.

Recently, Freeman and all the other employees in the firm had participated in a two-day company retreat. During those two days, the senior partners had outlined the new strategic vision and plan for the company. In the past, the firm had focused on clients in the Bay Area near San Francisco and in the states of Oregon and Washington. Additionally, the firm had become somewhat specialized in consulting for firms interested in expanding into Asian markets and helping Asian firms, especially Japanese, set up subsidiaries in the western United States. The senior partners believed that the firm needed to broaden its geographical scope beyond the West Coast and Asia and to broaden its offerings beyond new market entry.

In the past, the firm's revenues came from doing many small projects for a variety of clients. The new vision called for doing more involved projects or just doing more projects with fewer clients. Essentially, the rationale was that Ashland could add more value, and therefore be harder for competitors to dislodge, if it focused on fewer clients and developed much deeper relationships with them. This involved a shift from short-term project focus to long-term relationship development and from specialized project service to general strategic consulting.

Freeman's job was to translate these general new strategic directions into the goals and activities for her team.

The first thing she did was to hold a one-hour team meeting in which she briefly restated the new strategic directions and then asked her team members what general implications they saw for themselves as a result of the new strategy. Quickly, several team members mentioned that they would need to broaden their base of competencies from new market entry to such areas as reengineering.

After the initial meeting, Freeman reviewed the team's past clients to look for repeat customers or other indications of potential for deeper client relationships. She identified three firms out of the 15 or so that her team had worked with over the last 14 months.

She next called another brief team meeting to review her assessment with the team and get their ideas about how they might develop deeper relationships with these repeat clients. One of the most promising ideas was to make some unsolicited bids on projects. Several team members had heard of projects the clients were undertaking in the near future on which Ashland could bid.

After this second team meeting, Freeman realized that one of her greatest opportunities for translating the new strategic vision into action would be in redoing individual performance plans (similar to an MBO system) that she had recently conducted with each team member. In particular, it was clear to Freeman that to have a team who could provide a variety of strategic consulting services to a few targeted clients, each of her team members would need to develop new areas of competency. Yet, it didn't seem possible for them all to be equally competent in all the new areas of consulting, at least initially. Her next big task would be to crystallize her thoughts about what each team member should add to his or her skills to capitalize on the interests and strengths of each person and create overall team balance.

STRATEGY IMPLEMENTATION

Once a strategy has been formulated, it must be effectively implemented for desired results to materialize. Some evidence indicates that an average strategy superbly implemented is better than a great strategy poorly implemented.[21] Consequently, strategy implementation is at least as important as strategy formulation. Consider the case of Kathy Freeman at Ashland Consulting in the Managerial Challenge box.

Seven S's

Perhaps the most widely used strategy implementation framework is that developed by one of the largest and best-known strategy consulting firms—McKinsey Consulting. About 20 years ago, McKinsey discovered that when many of its clients implemented strategic plans it recommended, things actually got worse for the clients. McKinsey realized that having clients do worse when they follow your advice is not the way to build a successful consulting firm. What emerged from McKinsey's efforts to unravel this mystery was the Seven S framework (see Exhibit 8.10).

Essentially, McKinsey discovered that the reason clients were doing worse when they implemented the new strategies was because they were being implemented within old structures, shared values, systems, skills, styles, and staff. These old aspects of the organization were inconsistent with the new strategy. The old framework worked against and overwhelmed the new, and the results were negative.

EXHIBIT 8.10

Seven S Model

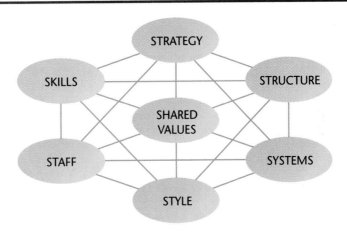

1. **Strategy** — Plan or course of action leading to the allocation of firm's resources to reach identified goals.

2. **Structure** — The ways people and tasks relate to each other. The basic grouping of reporting relationships and activities. The way separate entities of an organization are linked.

3. **Shared Values** — The significant meanings or guiding concepts that give purpose and meaning to the organization.

4. **Systems** — Formal processes and procedures, including management control systems, performance measurement and reward systems, and planning and budgeting systems, and the ways people relate to them.

5. **Skills** — Organizational competencies, including the abilities of individuals as well as management practices, technological abilities, and other capabilities that reside in the organization.

6. **Style** — The leadership style of management and the overall operating style of the organization. A reflection of the norms people act upon and how they work and interact with each other, vendors, and customers.

7. **Staff** — Recruitment, selection, development, socialization, and advancement of people in the organization.

Source: Richard Pascale, *Managing on the Edge* (New York: Simon & Schuster, 1990).

MANAGERIAL CHALLENGE

STRATEGY IMPLEMENTATION AT CONTINENTAL AIRLINES

In 1993, Continental Airlines emerged from Chapter 11 bankruptcy protection for the second time. Clearly, something had to change if the company wanted to stay in the air this time. New owners and new management decided that they would move away from direct battles with the big airlines, such as American, Northwest, Delta, and United, and would copy the battle plan of the most profitable airline in the industry—Southwest Airlines. To facilitate this, Continental's CEO, Robert Ferguson III, hired Donald Valentine, a former marketing executive with Southwest, to be the new Continental marketing chief.

A strategic plan was developed by a team of marketing, planning, and finance executives. The plan called for a new service, "CALite," involving short-haul (typically under two hours' flying time), direct route, business-oriented, no-frills, low-price service. To avoid a direct fight with Southwest, which concentrated most of its flights in the southwestern United States, managers at Continental decided they would focus on the southeastern United States.

Not heeding the advice of his managers may have insulated CEO Ferguson from information about needed revisions in the new strategy and implementation plan. Reportedly, a number of managers who questioned the implementation plan and pointed out potential problems were ridiculed, demoted, or even removed from their jobs. Consequently, soon everyone fell in line without question.

In nine months, Continental moved hundreds of flights from its hub in Denver to the Southeast, where it immediately tried to implement its new strategy by starting flights on 50 short routes. Southwest, on the other hand, had made its service changes over five years. In its effort to become immediately successful, CALite's routes were not well planned. Many of its initial routes did not need new service, and the demand was not equal to the frequency of flights CALite provided. Continental also added new planes to serve these routes. These new planes added significant expense to Continental's cost structure. Low prices, half-full planes, and higher operating costs made CALite's profit margins extremely thin.

CALite also ended special treatment for frequent fliers—one of its former advantages because of the generous schedules for redeeming miles for free trips and upgrades. Its business customers were upset that even though they were flying planes owned by Continental, they could not accumulate frequent-flier miles or use miles they had already earned.

Continental's employees were also not prepared for the dramatic change in work rules. For example, at Southwest, planes are turned around in approximately 20 minutes, because flight attendants help with cleaning the planes. In contrast, Continental had a long history of narrow job descriptions where flight attendant and cleanup crews had separate and nonoverlapping responsibilities.

Thus, while the plan of offering CALite as a new service may have had sound strategic logic, its poor implementation was its eventual undoing. Instead of being an important strategic thrust out of bankruptcy and toward profitability, CALite ended up losing millions of dollars. CALite executives had learned a painful lesson—poor strategy implementation can kill even the best strategy formulation.

Did CALite's nosedive sink Continental? Surprisingly, no. The company went back to the drawing board to draft a new strategy. Its Go Forward plan, begun in 1995, refocused the company's efforts away from competing with Southwest Airlines and toward international routes, especially to Europe. Continental reported a 19 percent traffic increase from September 1997 to September 1998, with international traffic up 15.5 percent during the same period. The company consummated a strategic global alliance with Northwest Airlines which should expand Continental's network and lower costs.

Sources: Adapted from Bridget O'Brian, "Heavy Going: Continental's CALite Hits Some Turbulence in Battling Southwest Airlines," *The Wall Street Journal*, January 10, 1995, p. A1; Carol Huang, "Continental, Northwest Consider Forming Global Pact," Reuters Limited, October 2, 1998; "Continental Airlines Reports the Highest September Load Factor in Company History," Continental Airlines press release, October 2, 1998, PR Newswire; "Company Profile: Go Forward Plan," accessed at the Continental Airlines Web site at http://flycontinental.com on October 7, 1998.

The Seven S McKinsey framework asserts that while each S is important, it is the congruence and fit among them that is critical. For example, IBM has a strategy of leveraging solutions developed for one client, such as Bank of Tokyo, for other clients in the same industry, such as Citibank. This strategy requires significant sharing of information across organizational units. First, to be successful, a structure must facilitate full and timely information exchange. Second, success also requires organizational members who trust each other and who value sharing information.

Third, compensation systems must reward people on more than their personal results because the positive effects of their information sharing could easily show up in another unit or even another country. Fourth, effective information sharing also requires data gathering, analysis, and dissemination skills. People are not necessarily gifted in all these activities. Fifth, there are key positions where information is generated and transferred. Staff with the highest information skills must be placed in these critical positions. Finally, the leadership style of senior managers must be consistent with the other aspects of the model. This simplified but true example helps illustrate that the key to successful strategy implementation is having an internal organization that is consistent with and supportive of the strategy. Continental Airlines provides an interesting illustration of what can happen when aspects of the organization are inconsistent with the strategy, as discussed in the Managerial Challenge box.

Strategy Evaluation

The final step in the strategic management process is evaluation. Just as evaluation and feedback can improve individual performance, so can they enhance organizational performance. When a small number of managers are responsible for the organization's strategic, tactical, or operational objectives, their individual performance evaluations can often provide a rough indication of how the organization is doing. If the individual's personal objectives are tied directly to operational objectives and they are all meeting or exceeding their goals, the organization as a whole is likely meeting its operational objectives. Most organizations carry out annual or even quarterly organizational performance evaluations. Typically, the strategic results are given to the more senior executives, and the operational results are disseminated principally to lower-level managers. Like individual feedback, organizational performance evaluation is used to reinforce efforts that have contributed to desired results and to correct those that have not.

STRATEGY AS PATTERN

The dominant view of strategy is that it is and should be a rational, conscious plan of action. This perspective is not universally shared, not even in Western firms. As pointed out earlier, many cultures believe that humans do not control their destiny and that strategic management is a vanity born of not knowing one's place in the universe. But even if we do accept the perspective of using planning and strategy as rational, conscious, and purposeful action, we often may not act on that belief. Scholars such as Henry Mintzberg have argued that strategies often emerge from patterned behavior rather than from planned and intended actions.[22]

According to Mintzberg, observers often assume that the actions an organization takes were planned. Also, journalists often impute a strategy to a corporation based on observed patterns of actions, whether the managers who took those actions had those purposes in mind or not. Mintzberg argues that often the pattern results from a string of actions rather than intentions and explicit plans. That is, certain actions were reinforced by positive consequences, and they were repeated and expanded only as long as positive consequences continued. In turn, these patterns were interpreted by observers as intended. Sometimes even organizational members later interpret these patterns as though they were intended from the outset. Thus, even in firms with managers who believe in planning and strategic management, strategy may form from actions that had positive consequences rather than intentions. Floris A. Maljers, co-chair and CEO of Unilever, echoes the view of strategy as pattern:

> *Unilever is often described as one of the foremost transnational companies. Yet our organization of diverse operations around the world is not the outcome of a conscious effort ... the company has evolved mainly through a Darwinian system of retaining what was useful and rejecting what no longer worked—in other words, through actual practice as a business responding to the marketplace.*[23]

Mintzberg points out that we need to recognize the existence of both *deliberate* strategies and *emergent* strategies. The importance of this distinction is that strategies focus our attention on analyzing key factors in the domestic and international environment and trying to plan for the future. In contrast, emergent strategies focus our attention on the consequences of past and present actions. An awareness of both types of strategies allows us to focus on the past, present, *and* future and incorporate our own judgments and the environment when we assess what works or doesn't work in the competitive marketplace.

CONCLUDING COMMENTS

Because strategic management is a process of determining where the organization wants to go and how it will successfully compete, it is a critical managerial function. The logic that senior managers must understand the strategic management process is self-evident. Yet it is equally important for entry-level managers to understand the process. Entry-level managers may not be involved in strategy formulation, but they must implement the strategy for it to succeed. Furthermore, entry-level managers need to know what the corporate-, business-, or functional-level strategies are to make decisions that support overall goals. Managers make many daily decisions, and those decisions can have a complementary or conflicting impact on the overall direction and performance of the organization. So, it is important that they make informed decisions; it is too costly to monitor all managers to determine whether they are consistent with the overall strategy. Rather, they can be more effective and efficient when they are guided by a clear understanding of strategic management process in general and the strategy of the company in particular.

KEY TERMS

cash cows 210
comparative advantage 213
competitive advantage 213
core competencies 205
cost leadership 215
customer segment 199
differentiation 215
dogs 209
internal comparative advantage 205

mission statement 198
niche strategy 216
primary activities 202
question marks 210
stars 210
strategic intent 197
strategic management 196
strategic objectives 201
strategic scope 216

supernormal returns 215
support activities 202
sustainable competitive advantage 216
SWOT analysis 212
value 214
value chain 202
value proposition 199

REVIEW QUESTIONS

1. What is the purpose of strategic intent?
2. What elements are typically included in a mission statement?
3. What are the key elements in an environmental analysis?
4. How can a firm's value chain be used to conduct an organizational analysis?
5. What is the difference between primary activities in the value chain and support activities?
6. What is the difference between comparative advantage and competitive advantage?
7. What are the five elements you need to have a competitive advantage?
8. What are the typical stages in a product's life cycle and how can this be used in strategic planning?
9. How can a portfolio analysis be used in developing global strategies?
10. What are the elements of the Seven S model?
11. What is the key principle behind the Seven S model?

DISCUSSION QUESTIONS

1. How does the articulation of strategic intent affect the strategic planning and management process? Could organizations be just as effective without clear statements of strategic intent? Give examples.
2. What would a SWOT analysis of your university look like? What are your school's key strengths and weaknesses? What are the major threats in the external environment? What are the opportunities? Make a list of all you can think of.
3. Looking at your life, to what degree do you have an intended versus emergent strategy? Are the classes you're now taking and planning to take in the future more a function of intended steps or of positive and negative consequences encountered as you took classes over time?
4. With this assessment in mind, what do you see as the positive and negative aspects of intended and emergent strategies for individuals or for organizations?

CLOSING CASE

Blockbuster Faces a New Era in Entertainment

After over a decade of successful growth, Blockbuster, the world's largest video-rental chain, began to see storm clouds on the horizon. Video-rental sales began to flatten as new VCR sales matured in the United States. Other video-rental store chains copied Blockbuster's concept and fragmented the market. Deep discount stores further dampened video-rental sales by selling their own retail videotapes for consumers to own. New technology—in the form of video on demand—threatened Blockbuster's future

existence. To ensure future growth, Blockbuster would need a new strategy.

A young entrepreneur, David P. Cook, created the first Blockbuster video-rental store. The Blockbuster concept was built on the premise that consumers were generally dissatisfied with mom-and-pop video rental outfits. Most rental stores offered a limited selection of titles, often focusing too much on current hit titles; had short hours of operation; and made no effort to create an ambiance. To capitalize on that dissatisfaction, Cook created the video superstore, where customers could delight in browsing through movies. Blockbuster's typical store was 6,000 square feet and brightly lit, with current videos playing overhead for previewing. Each store offered a minimum of 6,500 titles, not only ranging from a wide selection of current hits but also offering the most popular titles in different film genres: classics, foreign, musical, western, action, drama, animated, and even music videos. Videos were displayed forward so that the original jackets could be easily read. An important difference in the video selection was that Blockbuster consciously omitted X-rated videos, which were considered a necessity in most small video stores. To rent videos, customers would become club members for free.

The Blockbuster concept was an instant hit. By the end of its second year, there were 78 Blockbuster video-rental stores generating revenues of $20 million. The store's success was brought to the attention of Wayne Huizenga, an investor. After visiting his first Blockbuster store, Huizenga saw a great opportunity and invested $18 million into the business, giving him a 35 percent share of the company. When Blockbuster's management cashed out in 1987, Huizenga took over the business.

Under Huizenga's energetic leadership, Blockbuster's growth exploded. Over the next decade, the number of stores increased from 238 to 5,000. Revenues increased from $50 million to $4 billion. At its peak, Blockbuster captured a 25 percent share of the U.S. video-rental market. The blue-and-yellow Blockbuster card, carried by 40 million members, became more widely held than the American Express card.

Several strategies were employed to turn Blockbuster into the world's largest video-rental chain. First, both mom-and-pop shops and large chains, such as the 200-store Erol's chain, were bought and converted into blue-and-yellow Blockbuster centers. The rationale for the frantic buying was the belief that Blockbuster really did not have a proprietary business and that being the first and the biggest would make it more difficult for others to imitate the concept. The growth in store count also came from newly built stores.

In addition to massive acquisitions, Blockbuster pursued an aggressive franchising plan, signing up impressive franchisees such as George W. Baker, a former executive of Kentucky Fried Chicken, and the Zale family, who had made its fortune in the nation's largest jewelry business. By the time the company had 2,000 stores, half of them were franchised.

The concept of a video superstore was unique not only in the United States but in other regions of the world as well. Part of the expansion strategy was to capture promising international markets, particularly in industrialized nations, where VCR ownership was the highest. Thus, the first regions that Blockbuster entered were Canada, Western Europe, and Japan, where the VCR market was the most developed.

Stores were acquired or built in as many as 20 different countries extending beyond the Western developed nations, including Australia, Mexico, and Brazil. Especially successful was the entry into Brazil, where the first store in São Paulo amassed first-month sales of over $300,000, making it the best one-month performance of any Blockbuster store in history.

Though video-rental business always represented Blockbuster's core business, Huizenga found it necessary to diversify for further growth. Rather than defining the business as the "video-rental business," Huizenga envisioned Blockbuster as a future "entertainment conglomerate" that would operate alternate outlets, such as music stores, amphitheaters, indoor playgrounds, entertainment centers, and stadiums.

Blockbuster also entered TV and motion picture production by acquiring major stakes in Spelling Entertainment, the producer of such TV shows as *Melrose Place* and *Beverly Hills 90210* and in Republic Pictures Corporation.

Blockbuster's diversification strategy was considered by its executives to be well in place once video rentals represented about half its total revenues.

The diversification strategy was driven in part by the flattening of video rentals. By 1993, sales for the entire video rental business began to flatten as quickly as they had risen in the late 1980s. Several factors led to this trend. First, the market for VCRs in the United States began to mature as penetration of American homes hit its peak. Second, the retail market for videotape sales started to pick up, and deep discount stores such as Wal-Mart and Kmart could sell them more cheaply than Blockbuster, which was slow to enter this market. Third, competition from other video rental stores such as Hollywood Video further carved out market share.

Perhaps the largest threat to Blockbuster's existence was video-on-demand technology. Video on demand allows consumers to receive digitized videos over a high-speed network to a TV set. This, in essence, brings an entire video store into American households. Consumers can select any video or TV show from the comfort of their living rooms, avoiding the inevitable out-of-stocks of popular titles and the necessity of driving to the nearest Blockbuster. The new technology may take years to reach most U.S. homes. But the price of videos on demand is expected to be very competitive with retail video rentals.

QUESTIONS

1. How can Blockbuster avoid becoming a dinosaur as emerging technologies bring movies and other entertainment into the home?
2. Has the Blockbuster concept lost its novelty in the U.S. market?

3. Should Blockbuster push hard into other international markets, where the video-on-demand technology is still not available?
4. Should Blockbuster redefine its own business and continue to pursue other options in entertainment, as it did in the early 1990s? Or would this strategy fragment the business?

Sources: Richard Sandomir, "Wayne Huizenga's Growth Complex," *New York Times Magazine,* June 9, 1991, pp. S22–26. Sally Goll Beatty, "Viacom's Blockbuster Rethinks Strategy," *The Wall Street Journal,* November 20, 1995, p. A1; Johnnie L. Roberts, "Chips Off the Block," *Newsweek,* February 20, 1995, pp. 42–43; Jeffery D. Zbar, "Blockbuster Adjusts to New Era," *Advertising Age,* September 18, 1995, p. 40.

CHAPTER 9

INDIVIDUAL AND GROUP DECISION MAKING*

LEARNING OBJECTIVES

After studying this chapter, you should be able to:

- Explain the traditional model of decision making.
- Recognize and account for the limits of rationality in the decision process.
- Describe the role of risk and uncertainty in decision making.
- List the conditions when decisions are best made individually and when they are best made collectively.
- Name the steps to facilitate group participation in decision making.
- Describe the barriers to effective decision making and ways to overcome them.

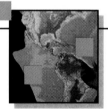

IBM's Decision to Buy Lotus

In a surprise move, IBM made a hostile bid to buy Lotus for approximately $3.5 billion and in the process shocked the employees of both companies and impressed industry watchers and analysts with both its decision and near flawless execution.

IBM decided to go after Lotus because of its strong position in personal computer (PC) software. Lotus basically pioneered spreadsheet software with its Lotus 1 2 3 product and more recently had developed the best-selling "groupware" software, Lotus Notes, which allowed individuals in different locations to work together and share information electronically as though they were working side by side. It was these products and especially the brainpower behind them that IBM wanted. But that was the dilemma of this decision for IBM—the only real asset Lotus had was its people, and they could leave if IBM did not implement its decision well.

IBM explored the possibility of forming an alliance by talking with Lotus and its CEO, Jim Manzi, about various forms of cooperation. However, several months after discussion began, key IBM executives,

---

*Portions of this chapter have been adopted from *Organizational Behavior*, 5th Edition, by Richard M. Steers and J. Stewart Black with permission from the authors and the publisher.

including CEO Lou Gerstner, were convinced that Lotus was nervous about the high level of cooperation IBM wanted. Gerstner began losing patience and considering a hostile bid. The decision whether to make a friendly offer or a hostile bid for Lotus was influenced by several factors.

According to one key insider in IBM, "Several times, we asked ourselves if and why we had to do it on a hostile basis. The answer was simple. If we bear-hugged Jim [offered Manzi a friendly deal] he could go to a third party and make a deal to sell the company or, worse, he could encumber Notes [the groupware product], giving certain rights to Notes to a third party. This was the risk."

Another key factor that influenced the decision to make a hostile bid was that the Lotus bylaws allowed IBM to appeal directly to Lotus share-holders. If the buyout price was high enough, shareholders would approve the sale and cash out because they could make a substantial profit.

But how much should IBM offer for Lotus? It wanted to offer enough to attract the interest of Lotus shareholders, but it did not want to overpay. At the time, Lotus shares were selling for about $30 per share. Based on past sales in the software industry, a premium of nearly 100 percent was standard, which translated into a $60-a-share offer. According to one IBM insider, "The question was whether to lob a low price and get coaxed up, or to lob a higher price to send a message to other potential suitors that we were interested in concluding the deal quickly because we wanted to minimize the chance that there would be a pirating of Lotus developers by rivals." As a consequence, IBM went with a "we're serious" bid of $60 a share. It thought this would be high enough that Lotus could not ignore it and that rivals, such as AT&T or Oracle Systems, could not top it.

In addition, IBM had to decide how to finance and structure the offer. It could offer to swap IBM shares, borrow money, or pay cash. It chose to make the offer simple and compelling by offering *all* cash. IBM's $10 billion in cash reserves made this possible. Moreover, this decision made it difficult for anyone to shoot down the deal because of questionable financing.

For the takeover decision to be implemented successfully, several things had to happen. The most important was to ensure that key software developers at Lotus did not jump ship, which was a real risk given the difference between the blue-suit culture of IBM and the Levi's-and-T-shirt culture of Lotus. The challenge was, "How to get information about IBM's intentions to Lotus employees as soon after the public announce-ment as possible in order to calm some of their fears." Legally, IBM could not make a direct appeal to Lotus employees. However, IBM solved this implementation problem creatively. It posted detailed information about the deal and IBM's intentions on IBM's Internet home page immediately after the public announcement. Anyone, including Lotus employees, could access the information. According to one IBM executive, "We thought that Ray Ozzie's [the key developer of Lotus Notes] principal interest would be the success of Notes, so our interests and his would be closely aligned. We thought that as long as we didn't do something stupid, he would stay."

Although the ultimate results of the decision to buy Lotus have been mixed, senior IBM executives believe that the decision was correct and that they were successful in achieving their objectives. Lotus was able to release products more quickly and to a wider market under IBM's umbrella. But changes in technology come swiftly. The increasing use of the Internet and its familiar features has cut into Lotus Notes' market share. Its share of the groupware market is down from a high of 64 percent in 1995 to 41 percent in 1997. Worse yet, those key employees have begun to desert Lotus, seeking greener pastures in start-ups. Time will tell whether the decision to buy Lotus was wise.

Sources: *New York Times,* June 22, 1995, pp. D1 and D28; Jeff Angus, Karen M. Carillo, Justin Hibbard, and Bruce Coldwell, "IBM and Lotus Get Closer," *Information Week* Online, July 28, 1997; David Lyons, "The Decline and Fall of Lotus," *Forbes,* August 10, 1998.

In the minds of many, decision making is the most important managerial activity. Management decisions may involve high-profile issues such as acquiring or selling assets, moving into or out of product segments, or launching national or international ad campaigns. But not all managerial decisions are as visible as IBM's buyout of Lotus. Many involve behind-the-scenes issues such as hiring a new employee or changing a production process. Regardless of the decisions, what makes them important is the impact they have. Managers usually make decisions with limited financial, technical, information, or human resources. These constraints and pressures create some of the most powerful challenges in managerial decision making. Consequently, managers need to understand the basic processes of decision making in organizations and the factors that influence them. Several frameworks are available to help explain managerial decision making. Each framework is based on different assumptions about the nature of people at work. So, as an informed manager, you need to understand the models and the assumptions underlying each.

In addition, in many situations you must determine the involvement of others (e.g., subordinates, peers) in decisions. When are group decisions superior (or inferior) to individual ones? How much participation is realistic in organizations in which managers still assume responsibility for group actions? How do these phenomena affect the quality of decisions? Finally, what strategies can managers use to improve decisions in organizations? A knowledge of effective decision making can help you as a manager make the most efficient use of your limited time and resources.

BASIC DECISION-MAKING CONCEPTS

decision making

a process of specifying the nature of a particular problem or opportunity and selecting among available alternatives to solve a problem or capture an opportunity

formulation

a process involving identifying a problem or opportunity, acquiring information, developing desired performance expectations, and diagnosing the causes and relationships among factors affecting the problem or opportunity

solution

a process involving generating alternatives, selecting the preferred solution, and implementing the decided course of action

A characteristic of effective leaders and effective work groups is their ability to make decisions that are appropriate, timely, and acceptable. If organizational effectiveness is defined as the ability to secure and use resources in the pursuit of organizational goals, then the decision-making processes that determine how these resources are acquired and used is a key building block. For our purposes here, we define **decision making** as a process of specifying the nature of a particular problem or opportunity and selecting among available alternatives to solve a problem or capture an opportunity. In this sense, decision making has two aspects: the act and the process. The act of decision making involves choosing between alternatives. The process of decision making involves several steps that can be divided into two distinct categories. The first, **formulation**, involves identifying a problem or opportunity, acquiring information, developing desired performance expectations, and diagnosing the causes and relationships among factors affecting the problem or opportunity. The **solution** phase involves generating alternatives, selecting the preferred solution, and implementing the decided course of action. Following the implementation of the solution, the manager monitors the situation to determine the extent to which the decision was successful. The Managerial Challenge box discusses a decision involving the spin-off of some AT&T businesses.

Competition from other blue-jeans manufacturers has led managers at Levi Strauss & Company to the decision to close 11 of their 22 plants in the United States and Canada and lay off 5,900 workers. Levi's is virtually the last major apparel manufacturer to move its operations offshore. These decisions reflect part of a strategy to move more operations overseas so that the company can improve earnings.

MANAGERIAL CHALLENGE

THE REINVENTION OF A GIANT

For a century, AT&T was *the* telephone company. But "Ma Bell," as it was known, lost its monopoly on telephone services in 1984 when the company finally settled the lawsuit brought against it by the Justice Department. As a result of that settlement, AT&T divested itself of seven regional telephone companies, known as "Baby Bells." AT&T executives thought the divestiture turned the remaining company into a strong marketing entity.

From that position of strength came a surprising announcement about a decade later. AT&T would break up into three smaller parts—this time of its own volition. AT&T announced the decision to a startled press, outlining plans for a slimmed-down AT&T focused on communication systems. A second, smaller business from the Network Systems group took the name of Lucent Technologies and handled phone and network equipment for systems and technology markets. A third company, Global Information Services, left the personal computer market and became a business computer service company operating under the name of NCR.

As surprising as the announcement was, the CEO at the time, Robert Allen, was under tremendous pressure to do something, because most of the business expansions and acquisitions of the past had not paid off for the company. The hostile takeover of NCR in 1991 resulted in a business that only limped along. Losing hundreds of millions of dollars in the computer industry, AT&T's attempt to enter that market had clearly not succeeded. This raised questions on Wall Street when AT&T did not sell the unit off in spite of the red numbers on its income statement.

Another problem facing AT&T came from Washington. Congress was debating a bill allowing the Baby Bells to enter the long-distance market, but it still prohibited AT&T from competing in the local phone service market. No amount of money AT&T spent on lobbying seemed to favorably influence this vote.

AT&T was also struggling with internal competition among business units, which often resulted in cannibalization of revenue from customers. Perhaps the company had become too big. Part of the problem was that the network services business unit was selling switches and equipment to a variety of AT&T competitors. "I was probably as frustrated as I'd ever been trying to coordinate across our various businesses," reported CEO Allen. Because of poor performance, AT&T stock seriously lagged behind the S&P average. To keep operations as stable as possible, Allen limited knowl-

edge of the impending split. The decision to unbundle the conglomerate into three separate companies was so well hidden, in fact, that as few as 40 persons in the top management of the company knew about it prior to the news conference announcing the change.

Allen announced his intentions to the AT&T board of directors and at that time took into his confidence only two AT&T executives, CFO Richard Miller and general counsel John Zeglis. The team was joined by Jeff Williams, a managing director at Morgan Stanley, the investment banker for the company, and Martin Lipton, from the law firm of Wachtell Lipton Rosen & Katz. These latter two added one colleague from each of their firms to form what Allen called the "Circle of Seven." This team hammered out a plan for the restructuring.

Change of this magnitude is hard to keep under wraps, yet secrecy was critical as the plan progressed. To avoid suspicion, the team met secretly in some unused AT&T space in Manhattan. Documents were destroyed at home by Allen, who professed to have done his own copying and distributing. After three months, the plan was well enough developed to alert a few other top executives of the process. Roughly six months after they first heard the plan, the board of directors was given full details, which they approved. Allen then took this news to Wall Street. The immediate response was positive, with the share price of AT&T stock zipping up over $11 per share in a matter of hours.

The move positioned the pared-down company that still bears the AT&T name to respond more quickly to market challenges. For example, recently, AT&T announced a joint venture with giant British Telecom to focus on international long-distance business opportunities, a market segment that has increased severalfold over the last few years. It also recently merged with Teleport Communications Group to enable it to capture business in local phone service. This merger has helped the company offset its losses in long-distance services. The new CEO, C. Michael Armstrong, was pleased with the company's progress but said, "There's no question in my mind or any minds of the leadership we still have further to go."

Sources: Peter Elstron, "AT&T: Dialing for Direction," *Business Week,* July 14, 1997; Manuel Schiffres, "Ma Bell's Brood Grows Up," *Kiplinger's Personal Finance Magazine,* February 1998; David E. Kalish, "AT&T Profits Rise 68 Percent," The Associated Press, October 26, 1998; "FCC Approves AT&T and TCG Merger," Communications Media Center at New York Law School, July 23, 1998.

INDIVIDUAL DECISION MAKING

It is no easy task to outline or diagram the details of the decision-making process. Research has been mixed about how individuals and groups make decisions.[1] Even so, at least three attempts to describe the decision-making process are worth noting. These three models are (1) the rational/classic model; (2) the administrative, or bounded rationality, model; and (3) the retrospective decision-making model. Each model is useful for understanding the nature of decision processes in organizations. While reading these models, pay special attention to the assumptions each makes about the nature of decision makers; also note the differences in focus.

The Rational/Classical Model

rational model (classical model)
a seven-step model of decision making that represents the earliest attempt to model decision processes

The **rational model** (also known as the **classical model**) represents the earliest attempt to model decision processes.[2] It is viewed by some as the classical approach to understanding decision processes. This approach involves seven basic steps (see Exhibit 9.1).

Step 1: Identifying Decision Situations   In the classic model, the decision maker begins by recognizing that a decision-making situation exists; that is, that problems or opportunities exist. A **problem** exists when a manager detects a gap between existing and desired performance. An **opportunity** exists when a manager detects a chance to achieve a more desirable state than the current one. For example, in IBM's case, the market was increasingly shifting toward personal computer networks and software that allowed individuals in different places to work together electronically. IBM was weak in this area of software. The company had to recognize this before it could consider the purchase of Lotus or some other alternative.

problem
a gap between existing and desired performance

opportunity
a chance to achieve a more desirable state than the current one

Step 2: Developing Objectives and Criteria   Once a manager has identified the decision-making situation, the next step is to determine the criteria for selecting alternatives. These criteria essentially represent what is important in the outcome. For example, before you can decide which job applicant to hire, you need to determine the important characteristics or outcomes needed. If you need the new hire to be effective at sales, then good interpersonal skills might be a criterion. However, it is rare that a single criterion will be sufficient to guide the decision-making process, in part because one factor rarely produces all the desired results. For example, good interpersonal skills *alone* will not likely lead to great sales results; also needed are superior motivation and knowledge of the selling process. When several criteria are involved, it is often necessary to weight the various criteria. For example, you might decide that a new hire's sales depend on four things: interpersonal skills, motivation, product knowledge, and understanding of the selling process. However, the impact of these factors may not be equal. As a manager, then, you might assign a weight to each criterion: for example, motivation, 30%; interpersonal skills, 25%; understanding of the selling process, 25%; product knowledge, 20%.

Step 3: Generating Alternatives   Once the objectives and criteria are established, the next step is to generate alternatives that achieve the desired result. How

EXHIBIT 9.1

Classical Decision-Making Model

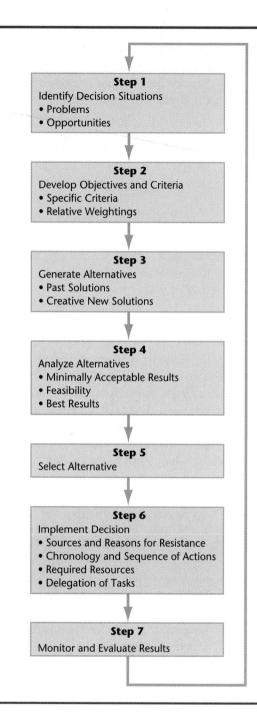

Step 1
Identify Decision Situations
• Problems
• Opportunities

Step 2
Develop Objectives and Criteria
• Specific Criteria
• Relative Weightings

Step 3
Generate Alternatives
• Past Solutions
• Creative New Solutions

Step 4
Analyze Alternatives
• Minimally Acceptable Results
• Feasibility
• Best Results

Step 5
Select Alternative

Step 6
Implement Decision
• Sources and Reasons for Resistance
• Chronology and Sequence of Actions
• Required Resources
• Delegation of Tasks

Step 7
Monitor and Evaluate Results

can a particular problem be solved or a given opportunity captured? Most of us consider first the alternatives that we have encountered or used in the past. If a current situation is similar to the past, past solutions can be effective. However, if the current situation is dissimilar to the past or if past solutions have not succeeded, we must generate new alternatives. However, creative alternatives may be needed even when the current situation is familiar and past solutions have worked. This is because even though a particular solution was effective in the past in what may seem to be a similar situation, no two situations are identical and subtle differences may reduce a past solution's effectiveness today. Second, even if the past solution could succeed today, alternative solutions might be even more successful.

Step 4: Analyzing Alternatives   The fourth step in the process involves analyzing the alternatives generated. To begin, you need to determine which alternatives would produce minimally acceptable results. Any alternatives that are unlikely to at least achieve the minimally acceptable outcome can be eliminated. Next, you need to examine the feasibility of the remaining alternatives. Returning to our hiring example, you may have found three candidates for your sales position who would likely produce the minimally acceptable sales results. But one candidate's salary needs exceed your budget; therefore, that person is not feasible. Once infeasible alternatives are eliminated, the next step is to determine which of the remaining alternatives would produce the most satisfactory outcome. Typically, the criteria and weights produced in Step 2 are applied at this point. For example, of the two remaining candidates for the sales position, John and Jane, you might rate both people on each of the four criteria (see Exhibit 9.2).

As you can see, even though Jane scored lower than John on both sales and product knowledge, Jane is the better candidate. Her higher overall score is a function of scoring higher on the most important criteria (i.e., motivation and interpersonal skills).

Step 5: Selecting Alternatives   Selecting an alternative flows naturally out of your analysis. The classical model argues that managers will choose the alternative that maximizes the desired outcome. This idea has often been expressed by the term **subjectively expected utility (SEU) model**. This model asserts that managers choose the alternative that they subjectively believe maximizes the desired outcome. The two key components of this model are the expected outcome produced by a given alternative and the probability that the alternative can be implemented. In our hiring example, Jane would seem to be the candidate who will

subjectively expected utility (SEU) model
a model of decision making that asserts that managers choose the alternative that they subjectively believe maximizes the desired outcome

EXHIBIT 9.2
Applying Criteria in Analyzing Alternatives

Candidate	Criteria	Rating*	x	Weight	=	Score
John	Motivation	8	x	.30	=	2.40
	Interpersonal	6	x	.25	=	1.50
	Sales knowledge	7	x	.25	=	1.75
	Product knowledge	6	x	.20	=	1.20
				Total Score	=	6.85

Candidate	Criteria	Rating	x	Weight	=	Score
Jane	Motivation	9	x	.30	=	2.70
	Interpersonal	8	x	.25	=	2.00
	Sales knowledge	6	x	.25	=	1.50
	Product knowledge	5	x	.20	=	1.00
				Total Score	=	7.20

*1 = Low; 10 = high

produce the greater sales because she received the higher total score on the criteria believed to lead to sales success. The SEU model suggests that before you select Jane, you will assess the probability that if Jane is offered the job, she will come to work for you. If Jane is the better candidate but won't work for you, then she really isn't the better candidate; John is.

Step 6: Implementing the Decision   In the classical model of decision making, effective decision implementation has four components. First, you assess sources and reasons for potential resistance to the decision. For example, Joe, a district sales manager in your company, might resist the decision to hire Jane because John is his personal friend, and Joe told John he could help get him the sales job. Second, you determine the chronology and sequence of actions designed to overcome resistance to the decision and ensure that the decision is effectively implemented. For example, you know that Joe believes sales process and product knowledge are the most important things in hiring a new salesperson. You also know that John was rated higher on these criteria than Jane.

Consequently, you might decide to first explain to Joe that in making your decision, you weighted motivation and interpersonal skills much higher than sales process or product knowledge and explain that company and independent studies support this weighting. Further, you might assign Jane to a district sales manager other than Joe to ensure that she gets a good start with the company. You might also decide to place her in a month-long training program to better familiarize her with your products and send her to a one-week course on "The Selling Process" when it is next offered. Setting the chronology and sequence of actions leads naturally into the third step: an assessment of the resources required to implement the decision effectively. For example, you know it will cost you $4,500 for the sales training course for Jane. Moreover, you need to determine whether you could delegate implementation steps to others and can ensure that those individuals understand and are held accountable for those steps and outcomes.

Step 7: Monitoring and Evaluating Results   The final step in the classical model involves monitoring and evaluating the results. To do this, you must gather information and compare results to the objectives and standards you set at the beginning. This is trickier than it may seem. First, you must gather the right information or the evaluation will be distorted at best and meaningless at worst. For example, in the case of hiring Jane, gathering information only on the number of sick days she has taken is unlikely to help you evaluate her early job performance. You might think it is silly that anyone would gather information on sick days taken when sales are what is important, but it is not uncommon for information that is easy to collect to obscure what is important. Often, the most important information is the hardest to gather. For example, gathering information on the number of sales calls Jane makes is much easier than gathering information on the attitude she presented to the customer during those sales calls. Yet, the latter may be more important than the former in closing the sale. In addition, the longer the lead time between actions and results, the more important appropriate performance indicators are, even if they are not easy to gather or evaluate. The key point here is the importance of monitoring and evaluating results in order to detect problems with the original decision and its implementation so that corrective actions can be taken. If the appropriate information is not gathered, the purpose of this final step is defeated.

To many, the classical model makes considerable sense. However, it is important to understand the assumptions upon which it is built:

- Problems are clear.
- Objectives are clear.
- People agree on criteria and weights.
- All alternatives are known.
- All consequences can be anticipated.
- Decision makers are rational:
  - They are not biased in recognizing problems.
  - They can process all relevant information.
  - They appropriately incorporate immediate and future consequences into decision making.
  - They search for the alternative that maximizes the desired result.

The potential weaknesses of the classical model are easily exposed if you just recall your own decision about what university to attend. How clear was the problem or your objectives? Did everyone agree on the criteria and weights for evaluating alternative schools? Did you know or even consider all the possible alternative universities? Could you fully anticipate the consequences associated with attending each school? Were you completely unbiased in your definition of the problem or the opportunity of which school to attend, and did you objectively review all the relevant information? Did you appropriately emphasize short-term and long-term consequences? Did you search for alternatives until you found the one that maximized your desired outcome? If you answered no to some of these questions, you're not alone. A large body of research has shown that people are not as rational as the classical model assumes.[3] In fact, we can identify a series of factors that inhibit people's ability to accurately identify and analyze problems, as shown in Exhibit 9.3.

EXHIBIT 9.3	*Informational bias*	A reluctance to communicate negative information.
Factors That Inhibit Accurate Problem Identification and Analysis	*Uncertainty absorption*	A tendency for information to lose its uncertainty as it is passed along, resulting in information that is seen as more precise than it really is.
	Selective perception	A tendency to ignore or avoid certain information, especially ambiguous information.
	Stereotyping	Deciding about an alternative on the basis of characteristics ascribed by others.
	Cognitive complexity	Limits on the amount of information people can process at one time.
	Stress	Reduction of people's ability to cope with informational demands.

Source: Adapted from R. N. Taylor, *Behavioral Decision Making* (Glenview, Ill.: Scott, Foresman, 1984), pp. 16–23.

Thus, while the rational, or classic, model shows how decisions *should* be made (that is, it works as a prescriptive model), it falls somewhat short concerning how decisions are *actually* made (that is, as a descriptive model).

The Bounded Rationality Model

bounded rationality model (administrative man model)

a model that assumes that people usually settle for acceptable rather than maximum options because the decisions they confront typically demand greater information-processing capabilities than they possess

An alternative model, one not bound by the above assumptions, has been presented by Herbert Simon.[4] This model is called the **bounded rationality model** (or the **administrative man model**). As the name implies, this model does not assume individual rationality in the decision process. Instead, it assumes that people, while they may seek the best solution, usually settle for much less, because the decisions they confront typically demand greater information-processing capabilities than they possess. They seek a kind of bounded (or limited) rationality in decisions.

The concept of bounded rationality attempts to describe decision processes in terms of three mechanisms. First, using **sequential attention to alternative solutions**, people examine possible solutions to a problem one at a time. Instead of identifying all possible solutions and selecting the best (as suggested in the rational model), people identify and evaluate various alternatives individually. If the first solution fails to work or is evaluated as unworkable, it is discarded and another solution is considered. When an acceptable (though not necessarily the best) solution is found, people stop searching for new alternatives. Thus, if the first alternative is workable, the search-and-analysis effort is likely to stop.

sequential attention to alternative solutions

the tendency for people to examine possible solutions one at a time instead of identifying all possible solutions and to stop searching once an acceptable (though not necessarily the best) solution is found

heuristic

a rule that guides the search for alternatives into areas that have a high probability for yielding success

The second mechanism is the use of heuristics. A **heuristic** is a rule that guides the search for alternatives into areas that have a high probability for yielding success. According to the bounded rationality model, decision makers use heuristics to reduce large problems to manageable propositions so decisions can be made rapidly. They look for obvious solutions or previous solutions that worked in similar situations. For instance, some companies continually hire MBAs from certain schools because in the past such graduates have performed well for the company.

satisficing

the tendency for decision makers to accept the first alternative that meets their minimally acceptable requirements rather than pushing them further for an alternative that produces the best results

The third mechanism is the concept of satisficing (not to be confused with "satisfying"). **Satisficing** is selection of a minimally acceptable solution rather than pushing farther for an alternative that produces the best results. Whereas the rational model focused on the decision maker as an optimizer, this model sees him or her as a satisficer. As explained by March and Simon:

> *An alternative is* optimal *if (1) there exists a set of criteria that permits all alternatives to be compared and (2) the alternative in question is preferred, by these criteria, to all other alternatives. An alternative is satisfactory if (1) there exists a set of criteria that describes minimally satisfactory alternatives, and (2) the alternative in question meets or exceeds all these criteria.... Finding that optimal alternative is a radically different problem from finding a satisfactory alternative.... To optimize requires processing several orders of magnitude more complex than those required to satisfice.*[5]

On the basis of these assumptions about decision makers, it is possible to outline the decision process from the standpoint of the bounded rationality model:

1. Set the goal to be pursued, or define the problem to be solved.
2. Establish an appropriate level of performance, or criterion level (that is, when do you know that a solution is acceptable, even if it is not perfect?).
3. Employ heuristics to narrow the solution to a *single* promising alternative.

4. If no feasible alternative is identified, lower the aspiration level, and begin the search for a new alternative solution (repeat steps 2 and 3).

5. After identifying a feasible alternative, evaluate it to determine its acceptability.

6. If the individual alternative is unacceptable, initiate a search for a new alternative solution (repeat steps 3–5).

7. If the identified alternative is acceptable, implement the solution.

8. Following implementation, evaluate the ease with which the goal was (or was not) attained, and raise or lower the level of performance accordingly on future decisions.

This decision process is quite different from the rational model. In it we do not seek the *best* solution; instead, we look for a solution that is *acceptable*. The search behavior is sequential, involving evaluation of one solution at a time. Finally, in contrast to the prescriptive rational model, the bounded rationality model is *descriptive;* that is, it describes how decision makers actually identify solutions to organizational problems.

The Retrospective Decision Model

A third model focuses on how decision makers attempt to rationalize their choices after they are made. It has been variously referred to as the **retrospective decision model**, or the **implicit favorite model**.[6]

retrospective decision model (implicit favorite model)

a decision-making model that focuses on how decision makers attempt to rationalize their choices after they are made

This model emerged when MIT professor Per Soelberg observed the job choice processes of graduating business students and noted that, in many cases, the students identified implicit favorites (that is, the alternative they wanted) very early in the recruiting and choice process. For example, one student might identify a manufacturer in Arizona as a favorite. However, students continued their search for additional alternatives and quickly selected the best alternate (or second) candidate, known as the "confirmation candidate." For example, the student might select a high-tech firm in California as his alternate firm. Next, the students would attempt to develop decision rules that demonstrated unequivocally that the implicit favorite was superior to the confirmation candidate. They did so by perceptual distortion of information—that is, highlighting the positive features of the implicit favorite over the alternative. For example, the student might leave out vacation time as a criterion because his favorite firm in Arizona has a very poor vacation policy compared with the alternate firm in California. However, the student might heavily weight a criterion of housing costs because they are cheaper in Arizona, the student's favored choice. Finally, after deriving a decision rule that clearly favored the implicit favorite, the student announced the decision and accepted the job in Arizona.

Ironically, Soelberg noted, the implicit favorite was typically superior to the confirmation candidate on only one or two dimensions. Even so, decision makers generally characterized their decision rules as being multidimensional. For example, in the case of the two firms in Arizona and California, the jobs offered were quite similar, and the salary, travel, benefits, and promotion prospects were also nearly identical. Yet the students would claim that the Arizona firm was superior on several counts.

The entire process is designed to justify, through the guise of scientific rigor, a decision that has already been made intuitively. By this means, the individual becomes convinced that he or she is acting rationally and making a logical, reasoned decision on an important topic. Consider how many times you have made a decision in a similar way when looking for clothes, cars, stereo systems, and so on. You start with an item that catches your eye and then spend considerable time convincing yourself and your friends that this is the "best" choice. If your implicit favorite is the cheapest among the competition, you emphasize price; if it is not, you emphasize quality or styling. Ultimately, you end up buying the item you favored, feeling comfortable that you made the right choice.

Types of Decisions

In addition to the basic models of decision making, the type of decision can affect the process. Most decisions can be divided into two basic types: programmed or nonprogrammed. A **programmed decision** is a standard response to a simple or routine problem. The nature of the problem is well defined and clearly understood by the decision maker, as is the array of possible solutions. Examples of programmed decisions can be seen in college admission decisions, reimbursement for managers' travel expenses, and promotion decisions with many unionized personnel. In all these decisions, specific criteria can be identified (e.g., grade-point average and test scores for college admission, per-diem allowances for expense account reimbursements, or seniority for union promotions). The programmed decision process is characterized by high levels of certainty for both the problem formulation and the problem solution phases, and rules and procedures typically spell out exactly how to respond.

On the other hand, **nonprogrammed decisions** occur in response to problems that are either poorly defined or novel. For example, should a university president with limited funds expand the size of the business school to meet growing student demand, or should she expand the university's science facilities to bring in more federal research contracts? No alternative is clearly correct, and past decisions are of little help; instead, you must weigh the alternatives and their consequences carefully to make a unique decision—a nonprogrammed decision.

In most organizations, a significant relationship exists between the programmed and nonprogrammed decisions and organizational hierarchy. As shown in Exhibit 9.4, for example, top managers usually face nonprogrammed decisions, as in the case of the university president. On the other hand, college deans or department heads—let alone faculty or students—seldom get to make such decisions. Furthermore, lower-level managers (such as first-line supervisors) typically encounter

programmed decision
a standard response to a simple or routine problem

nonprogrammed decision
a decision about a problem that is either poorly defined or novel

EXHIBIT 9.4

Decision-Maker Level and Type of Decision

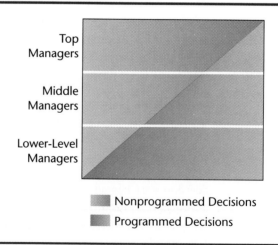

Top Managers

Middle Managers

Lower-Level Managers

■ Nonprogrammed Decisions
■ Programmed Decisions

Employees at Jiffy Lube follow standard operating procedures for automobile maintenance such as oil changes.

mostly programmed, or routine, decisions. Their options and resources, as well as risks, are usually far less than those of top managers. And, as we might expect, middle managers fall somewhere in between.

One final point should be made here concerning the relationship between programmed and nonprogrammed decisions. Programmed decisions are usually made through structured bureaucratic techniques. For example, **standard operating procedures (SOP)** are often used for programmed decisions. SOPs specify exactly what should be done—the sequence of steps and exactly how each step should be performed. In contrast, nonprogrammed decisions must be made by managers using available information and their own judgment, often under considerable time pressure. Managers tend to let programmed activities overshadow nonprogrammed activities. Thus, if a manager has a series of decisions to make, he or she will tend to make those that are routine and repetitive before focusing on those that are unique and require considerable thought. Presumably, this happens because managers wish to clear their desks so they can concentrate on the really serious problems. Unfortunately, however, because of time pressures, managers often don't actually get to the more difficult—and perhaps more important—decisions. This tendency is called **Gresham's law of planning**.[7]

The implications of Gresham's law for managerial decision making are clear. Decisions must be made in a timely fashion. Organizations accomplish this in many ways, including having special organizational units, such as a corporate planning unit, or, when a unit cannot be devoted to planning, having time management programs train managers to better allocate their limited time. However it is done, it is important that nonprogrammed decisions receive the time and attention they deserve.

Balancing Risk and Uncertainty with Environmental Scanning

Especially in nonprogrammed decisions, managers often face problems and challenges that are characterized by higher levels of risk and uncertainty. If the university president, for example, makes the wrong decision about the direction his

standard operating procedures (SOP)
established procedures for action used for programmed decisions that specify exactly what should be done

Gresham's law of planning
the tendency for managers to let programmed activities overshadow nonprogrammed activities

MANAGERIAL CHALLENGE

JOFFREY BALLET: TO BE OR NOT TO BE?

Dance companies come and go. Given the nature of some companies, it may be hard to think of them as businesses. But they are, and most operate as not-for-profit corporations. For the Joffrey Ballet, a world-class ballet company, the decision facing it was basic—how could it survive?

The 30-year-old ballet company had been beleaguered by problems since the death of founder Robert Joffrey in 1988. In his will, Joffrey stipulated that Gerald Arpino should take over as artistic director. For Arpino, who had started dancing as a teenager when he met Joffrey, leading this ballet company was an appropriate challenge. Arpino had been instrumental in the company's founding and had worked side by side with Joffrey, both as dancer and choreographer.

As new artistic director, Arpino waged a war with a board divided over his taking over. What should have been a smooth transference of power was marked by chaos. Infighting drove Arpino into contests that almost toppled him. Arpino dug in, restructuring the company and raising needed funds. Although Arpino's decisions helped keep the company afloat in the short term, ultimately they were not enough to keep the company from floundering. In fact, it had to cancel its 1992 season in New York because it would have put the company further in the red. The company did continue touring around the country and the world. But, according to Executive Director Arnold Breman, things came to a screeching halt three years later. "There was no money and lots of debts. We felt we just couldn't go on."

Arpino reexamined the situation. As he did, several things became clear. First, the company was in serious trouble and a decision of how to go forward was needed, and needed soon. Second, whatever decision he made, he was absolutely committed to making it work. As he considered his options, Arpino recognized that although its home was in New York, the Joffrey Ballet also had a big support base in Chicago. The company had performed in the city 50 times in 40 years and had a "huge following" there, Breman said. Another critical factor was that several key financial supporters of the Joffrey Ballet lived in Chicago. Arpino recognized that the Joffrey was one of several major dance companies in New York, but in Chicago there was room for a world-class ballet company to shine. It seemed a natural fit for a city with a major orchestra, a major opera company, and major museums but no major dance company.

After Arpino mulled the situation over, he pulled in Bruce Sagan, a Chicago supporter, to discuss the feasibility of relocating. The first step was to explore the financial support available, which Arpino did with Sagan's help. Supporters cautioned Arpino from flouncing into Chicago ready to take over the dance scene. So Arpino commenced discussions with the struggling Ballet Chicago about a merger. These negotiations continued for seven months, although the deal ultimately fell through. The two companies could not agree on crucial issues such as the budget, artistic direction, and administration. Breman admitted that the Joffrey then considered Los Angeles as a possible site,

organization should take, it could be costly, both financially and politically. In fact, the president's job may depend on making the right decision. If you expand the science facility, you still have no guarantee that the added faculty will bring in more contracts and grants; besides, by doing so, you may be denying admission to a large number of qualified business students. You may also alienate the business students and faculty. On the other hand, building the business programs will almost certainly alienate the science students and faculty, may allow a rival university to get ahead, and may prompt many of your best scientists to go elsewhere. Risks and uncertainty permeate nonprogrammed decisions.

As a result, decision makers usually do considerable environmental scanning prior to making the decision. That is, they seek as much useful information as they can from outside the organization. In this case, if, as the university president, you discover that a rival school is about to expand its own science complex and wants to hire away your best scientists, you may wish to defend what you have, especially if you view the business school as less important to your institution's goals. On the other hand, if your state's governor and legislature have made it clear that they want more business education, you may have to factor this into your decision as but Chicago still was favored, mostly because of the monetary support available.

The committee of financial supporters in Chicago posed a challenge to Arpino at this point. He could bring the company to Chicago with their full support if the company came debt free. This wasn't easy since the Joffrey was carrying over $1.7 million in debt. More than half this amount was back pay owed the dancers. An additional $750,000 was from loans made to the company by board members—loans that had as collateral costumes and other assets of the company.

Arpino, viewing Chicago as the last hope for the company, was able to negotiate with the dancers to accept partial payment of what was owed. This was possible, Breman said, because the dancers believed in the company and wanted to continue dancing. Board members waived outstanding debt and offered the costumes to a newly formed company. Although Arpino made the initial explorations into moving the company to Chicago by himself, Breman said it was very much a joint decision, shared by the ad hoc committee of Chicago Joffrey supporters.

A Chicago office was opened and reorganization launched. A new Illinois corporation was formed with a new board, primarily Chicagoans, and new bylaws. Administrative positions, other than Breman's, were filled by Chicago area residents. Fast work paved the way for the first rehearsal of the newly relocated dancers. How did the dancers react to the prospect of being transported?

"They're a special breed of dancer," Breman said. "They wanted to dance with the Joffrey."

The Joffrey Ballet of Chicago is a touring company including foreign destinations. Recent stops were in Israel, Istanbul, and Ephesus, Turkey. The company has a subscription series for its regular season in Chicago, as well as a four-week summer residency in Telluride, Colorado. Less than five months after the dancers took the floor in Chicago and little more than a year after the need for a drastic decision presented itself, the Joffrey Ballet of Chicago eliminated its old debt and continues on solid footing.

Breman admits the decision to move was scary, especially when the merger with Ballet Chicago fell through. "But it was the group of supporters that said we should go on." It is because of that support that Arpino packed his bags and his dancers packed their tights. As he put it, "The roots of this nationally and internationally acclaimed classical ballet company have grown strong and are flourishing in the fertile soil of the heartland...."

Sources: Adapted from articles in *Dance Magazine,* May 1992, October 1995, December 1995; and the Joffrey Ballet of Chicago Web site, accessed at www.joffrey.com on October 22, 1998.

well. In other words, through environmental scanning, managers attempt to gain useful information that can lead to a higher-quality decision.

Influences on Decision Making

At least three general factors influence decisions (see Exhibit 9.5).[8] First, there are the characteristics of the decision maker. Such factors as his or her knowledge of the problem, ability to analyze and solve the problem, and motivation to solve it affect the decision. Second are the characteristics of the problem itself, including the extent to which the problem is familiar to the managers, the ambiguity and complexity of the problem, and the extent to which the problem is stable or volatile. Third, the decision is influenced by the environment in which the decision is made. Included in the environment are the degree to which the decision is irreversible, its significance or importance, the person accountable for the decision and its consequences, and any time or money constraints involved in the decision process. Taken together, these factors represent the major ingredients involved in the decision. The Managerial Challenge box discusses the environmental and problem characteristics that influenced the Joffrey Ballet's move to Chicago.

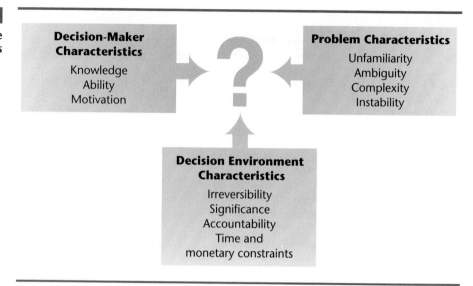

EXHIBIT 9.5
Influences on the
Decision Process

GROUP DECISION MAKING

The three models described at the beginning of the chapter attempt to explain certain aspects of individual decision making. However, those models can also illuminate aspects of group decision making. Many of the basic processes remain the same. For instance, using the rational model, we can observe that both individuals and groups identify objectives. Both individuals and groups may also attempt to identify all possible outcomes before selecting one and, more than likely, both will fail in that attempt. Both individuals and groups are often observed engaging in satisficing behavior or using heuristics in the decision process. And both individuals and groups develop implicit favorites and attempt to justify those favorites by procedures that appear to others to be rationalization.

Impact of Groups on Decision Making

What makes group decision making different from individual decision making is the social interaction in the process, which complicates the dynamics. In some situations, group decision making can be an asset, but other times it can be a liability. The trick for you as a manager is to discover when and how to invite group participation in decisions. Some assets and liabilities of group decision making are shown in Exhibit 9.6. Going one step further, let us look at what we know about the impact of groups in the decision process itself, especially relative to nonprogrammed decisions:

- In *establishing objectives,* groups are typically superior to individuals in that they bring greater cumulative knowledge to problems.
- In *identifying alternatives,* individual efforts ensure that different and perhaps unique solutions are identified from various functional areas that later can be considered by the group.
- In *evaluating alternatives,* group judgment is often superior to individual judgment, because it involves a wider range of viewpoints.

EXHIBIT 9.6

Assets and Liabilities of Group Decision Making

Assets +	Liabilities −
• Groups can accumulate more knowledge and facts. • Groups have a broader perspective and consider more alternatives. • Individuals who participate in group decisions are more satisfied with the decision and are more likely to support it. • Group decision processes serve an important communication function, as well as a useful political function.	• Groups often work more slowly than individuals. • Group decisions involve considerable compromise that may lead to less-than-optimal decisions. • Groups are often dominated by one individual or a small clique, thereby negating many of the virtues of group processes. • Overreliance on group decision making can inhibit management's ability to act quickly and decisively when necessary.

- In *choosing alternatives,* involving group members often leads to greater acceptance of the final outcome.
- In *implementing the choice,* individual responsibility is generally superior to group responsibility. Whether decisions are made individually or collectively, individuals perform better in carrying out the decision than groups do.[9]

From this list you can see that you cannot conclude that either individual or group decision making is superior. Rather, the situations and the individuals involved should guide the choice of decision technique.

One question about the effects of group participation remains to be asked: Why does it seem to work in many instances? A partial answer to this question has been offered by Ebert and Mitchell.[10] First, they suggest that participation clarifies more fully what is expected. Second, participation increases the likelihood that employees will work for rewards and outcomes they value. Third, it heightens the effects of social influence on behavior. That is, peers will monitor and exert pressure on each other to conform to expected performance levels. Finally, it enlarges the amount of control employees have over their work activities. In many cases, participation in decision making can be useful in both organizational goal attainment and personal need satisfaction.

Because participation helps involve employees and increases satisfaction and interaction, it has been an important part of quality improvement efforts. For example, team-based efforts to improve products and processes have always worked best when they included significant participation in decision making.

CONTINGENCY MODEL OF PARTICIPATIVE DECISION MAKING

A central issue facing managers is the extent to which they should allow employees in the work group to participate in decisions affecting their jobs. Participation decentralizes authority and influence throughout an organization, but in many cases it can lead to improved decision quality, increased commitment of members to decision outcomes, and increased satisfaction resulting from involvement. These results are often associated with effective organizations.

Participative decision making is not a panacea. Research suggests that it is not appropriate for every situation.[11] If participative decision making is not appropriate for all situations, how can you as a manager determine when it will and won't be effective?

Participative Decision Makers

To determine some of the variables that make up good participative decisions, researchers have explored the characteristics of the decision makers. Essentially, researchers have asked the question, "When participative decision making is effective, what do the people involved look like?" First and foremost, research suggests that those participating in the decision-making process must have sufficient knowledge about the content of the decision. Companies such as Ford, Federal Express, Procter & Gamble, and Boeing have put together **cross-functional teams** (consisting of members from marketing, finance, operations, human resources, etc.) for new product launches because each member has unique knowledge that adds value to the overall product launch decision. In contrast, asking people to become involved in decisions that are completely outside their area of expertise does not lead to either better-quality decisions or more commitment to the decisions and their implementation.

In addition to content knowledge, members also need to have a general desire to participate. Not everyone wants to become involved in decisions. The desire to participate results from the individuals' believing that (1) they have relevant content knowledge, (2) their participation will help bring about change, (3) the resulting change will produce outcomes they value or prefer, and (4) participation is valued by the organization and fits with its goals and objectives. When Chrysler first started encouraging more employee involvement in decisions, workers resisted the effort because they did not believe it was "for real." This belief was based on the fact involvement was not a part of the company's history; in the past, decisions were made by managers and implemented by employees. As a consequence, it took sustained support from top management before workers believed participation was legitimate.

Participative Decision-Making Process

Like individual decision making, participative decision making involves related, yet separate processes. Using the classical model of decision making, a participative group moves through the same seven steps, but involvement of group members can vary in each of those steps. Low involvement allows members to communicate their opinions about the problem, alternatives, and solution but not to influence the final determination. High involvement allows members not only to communicate their opinions but to make final determinations. Thus, degree of involvement could range from high to low on each of the seven elements of the classical decision model. Exhibit 9.7 provides a sample in which a particular group has high involvement in the front end of classical decision making but low involvement on the back end.

Since involvement can vary for each step of the classical decision-making model, a question naturally arises whether any configuration is better. One study directly examined this question.[12] This study found that high involvement in generating

---

cross-functional teams
employees from different departments, such as finance, marketing, operations, and human resources, who work together in problem solving

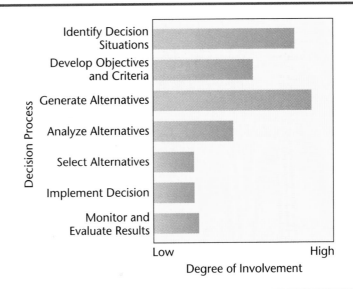

alternatives, planning implementation, and evaluating results was significantly related to higher levels of satisfaction and work group performance. The authors argued that involvement in generating alternatives was important because solutions almost always came from alternatives generated. They argued that involvement in planning the implementation was important because the outcome was affected more by the way a solution was implemented than by the solution itself. Finally, they argued that involvement in evaluating results was important because feedback is critical before beginning the cycle again.

One of the interesting implications from this line of study is that group members also need to understand group processes for participative decision making to be effective. That is, skill in analysis, communication, and handling conflicts can be as important as knowledge and the desire to participate. For example, one of the critical capabilities in identifying problems is environmental scanning. Not everyone is skilled at scanning the environment and recognizing problems or opportunities; yet, it is hard to begin participative decision making without members who can recognize problems and opportunities. For generating alternatives, a critical capability is creativity. For selecting a solution, a critical process capability is managing conflict—it is unlikely that a group can agree on a preferred solution without some conflict. As a consequence, managing that disagreement effectively is a critical process skill.

Exhibit 9.8 provides a summary of the questions a manager should ask in determining whether participative decision making is likely to be effective.

On the basis of a long-term research project, Victor Vroom and his colleagues Phillip Yetton and Arthur Jago also developed a theory of participation in decision making that has clear managerial implications.[13] It is possible to categorize this model as either a model of leadership or a model of decision making. The model considers how managers should behave in decision-making situations but also prescribes correct leader behavior regarding the degree of participation. Given its orientation toward leadership behavior, we cover this theory in depth in Chapter 14.

EXHIBIT 9.8	1. Do potential group members have sufficient content knowledge?

Contingency Factors for Effective Participative Decision Making

1. Do potential group members have sufficient content knowledge?
2. Do potential members have sufficient process knowledge?
3. Do members have a desire to participate?
4. Do members believe that their participation will result in changes?
5. Do members positively value the expected outcomes?
6. Do members see participation as legitimate and congruent with other aspects of the organization?
7. If the answer to any of the above questions is no, is it possible to change the conditions?

Source: N. Margulies and J. Stewart Black, "Perspectives on the Implementation of Participative Approaches." *Human Resource Management* 26, no. 3, (1987), pp. 385–412.

DECISION SPEED AND QUALITY

In the early 1980s, Gavilan Computer was at the forefront of computer technology and had a virtual monopoly on the developing—and lucrative—lap-top computer market. By 1984, however, Gavilan had filed for bankruptcy. Despite a $31 million stake from venture capitalists, the company experienced long delays and indecision that cost it its early technological and market advantage. Competitors entered the market niche, and Gavilan failed to exploit its advantage. As one executive observed, "We missed the window."[14] What happened to Gavilan has occurred with alarming frequency in corporations—especially those involved in high-technology industries—as the indecisive fall by the wayside.

In a series of studies of decision making in industries characterized by frequent change and turbulence—so-called high-velocity environments—researchers Kathleen Eisenhardt and L. J. Bourgeois attempted to determine what separates successful decision makers and managers from unsuccessful ones.[15] In high-velocity industries (e.g., microelectronics, medical technology, genetic engineering), high-quality, rapid decision making by executives and their companies is closely related to good corporate performance. In these industries, mistakes are costly; information is often ambiguous, obsolete, or simply incorrect; and recovery from missed opportunities is extremely difficult. In view of the importance of speed for organizational innovation, performance, and survival, how do successful decision makers make high quality, rapid decisions? And how are those decisions implemented rapidly?

Eisenhardt and Bourgeois found that five factors influenced a manager's ability to make fast decisions in high-velocity environments (see Exhibit 9.9). These five characteristics are moderated by three "mediating processes" that determine the manager's and group's ability to deal with the quantity and quality of information:

1. *Accelerated cognitive processing.* The decision maker must be able to process and analyze great amounts of information quickly and efficiently. Some people—and some groups—can simply process information faster and better than others. Obviously, the faster a manager can process what is presented, the quicker the decision.

2. *Smooth group processes.* To be effective, the manager must work with a group that has smooth, harmonious relations. This is not to say that everyone always

EXHIBIT 9.9

Factors of Fast Decision Making

1. *Real-time information.* Fast decision makers must have access to and be able to process real-time information—that is, information that describes what is happening right now, not yesterday.
2. *Multiple simultaneous alternatives.* Decision makers examine several possible alternative courses of action simultaneously, not sequentially (e.g., "Let's look at alternatives X, Y, and Z altogether and see how each looks."). This adds complexity and richness to the analysis and reduces the time involved in information processing.
3. *Two-tiered advice process.* Fast decision makers make use of a two-tiered advisory system, whereby all team members are allowed input but greater weight is given to the more experienced co-workers.
4. *Consensus with qualification.* Fast decision makers attempt to gain widespread consensus on the decision as it is being made, not after it is made.
5. *Decision integration.* Fast decision makers integrate tactical planning and issues of implementation within the decision process itself (e.g., "If we are going to do X, how might we do it?").

agrees. Quite the contrary—members of effective groups often disagree. However, it is the way they disagree and resolve their disagreements that counts. Fast decisions are aided by group members who share a common vision and who are mutually supportive and cohesive.

3. *Confidence to act.* Finally, fast decision makers must not be afraid to act. Some managers are reluctant to make decisions in the face of uncertainty, and they tend to wait until they can reduce the uncertainty. Unfortunately, in high-velocity environments, this uncertainty is never reduced. Thus, to be effective, fast decision makers must be willing to choose when the appropriate time comes.

Remember that this research is focused on high-velocity environments, not all organizational environments. That is, in businesses that are characterized by relative stability (e.g., the funeral home industry), rapid decisions may prove disastrous. Because stability allows time for more complete data collection and processing, managers in stable environments have less need for immediate action. Thus, as a manager, you need to assess the time factors that characterize your industry. Then you will be able to make decisions appropriate for your industry.

PROBLEMS IN GROUP DECISION MAKING

At least two problems can negatively affect decision effectiveness in group decision making: groupthink and escalating commitment to a course of action.

Groupthink

groupthink
a mode of thinking in which pursuit of agreement among members becomes so dominant that it overrides a realistic appraisal of alternative courses of action

Increased attention has been focused in recent years on a phenomenon known as **groupthink**. This phenomenon, first discussed by Irving Janis, refers to a mode of thinking in which pursuit of agreement among members becomes so dominant that it overrides a realistic appraisal of alternative courses of action.[16] The concept emerged from Janis's studies of high-level policy decisions by government leaders.

EXHIBIT 9.10

The Groupthink Process

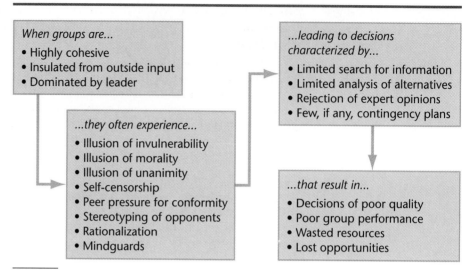

Source: Adapted from Gregory Moorhead, "Groupthink: Hypothesis in Need of Testing," *Group and Organization Studies* 7, no. 4 (December 1982), pp. 429–44. Copyright © 1982 by Sage Publications, Inc. Reprinted by permission of Sage Publications, Inc.

These included decisions by the U.S. government about Vietnam, the Bay of Pigs, and the Korean War. In analyzing the decision process leading up to each action, Janis found indications pointing to the development of group norms that improved morale at the expense of critical thinking. A model of this process is shown in Exhibit 9.10.

Symptoms of Groupthink   In studies of both government and business leaders, Janis identified eight primary symptoms of groupthink. The first is the *illusion of invulnerability.* Group members often reassure themselves about obvious dangers, becoming overly optimistic and, thus, willing to take extraordinary risks. Members fail to respond to clear warning signals. For instance, in the disastrous Bay of Pigs invasion of Cuba in the 1960s, the United States operated on the false assumption that it could keep its invasion of Cuba a secret. Even after news of the plan had leaked out, government leaders remained convinced of their ability to keep it a secret.

Victims of groupthink also tend to collectively *rationalize* and discount warning signs and other negative feedback that could lead to reconsideration of the course of action. For example, many American firms discounted the new economic potential of a united Europe in the 1990s by saying that because Europeans have never been able to cooperate in the past, they wouldn't in the future.

Next, group members often believe in the inherent morality of the group. Because of this *illusion of morality,* they ignore the ethical or moral consequences of their decisions. Leading tobacco companies continue to run advertisements about free choice about smoking, completely ignoring the medical evidence on the hazards involved.

Stereotyping the enemy is another symptom of groupthink. In-group members often stereotype leaders of opposition groups in harsh terms that rule out negotiation on differences of opinion. Often they also place tremendous pressure to conform on members who temporarily express doubts about the group's shared illusions or who raise questions about the validity of the arguments supporting the group decisions.

Moreover, group members often use *self-censorship* to avoid deviations from group consensus. They often minimize to themselves the seriousness of their doubts. Partly because of self-censorship, the *illusion of unanimity* forms. Members assume that individuals who remain silent agree with the spoken opinions of others and falsely conclude that everyone holds the same opinion.

Finally, victims of groupthink often appoint themselves as *mindguards* to protect the leader and other members of the group from adverse information that could cause conflict over the correctness of a course of action. The mindguard may tell the dissident that he or she is being disruptive or nonsupportive or may simply isolate the dissident from other group members. For many years, FBI agents in the Washington headquarters who expressed views contrary to the party line found themselves transferred to less desirable locations.

Consequences of Groupthink   Groupthink can have several adverse consequences for the quality of decision making. First, groups plagued by groupthink often limit their search for possible solutions to one or two alternatives rather than all possible alternatives. Second, such groups frequently fail to reexamine their chosen action after new information or events suggest a change in course. Third, group members spend little time considering nonobvious advantages to alternative courses of action. Fourth, such groups often make little or no attempt to seek experts' advice either inside or outside their own organization. Fifth, members show interest in facts that support their preferred alternative and either ignore or disregard facts that fail to support it. Finally, groups often ignore possible roadblocks to their choice and, as a result, fail to develop contingency plans. This last consequence is similar to retrospective decision making—the decision is made and then data are selected that support the decision. Because the decision is reinforced by peers, unwillingness to reexamine and change directions is even more powerful than in individuals.

Overcoming Groupthink   Because a groupthink mentality poses such serious consequences for organizations, we must consider how to minimize its effects. Janis suggests several strategies. To begin, group leaders can reduce groupthink by encouraging each member to evaluate proposals critically. Also, leaders can ensure that the group considers a range of alternatives by not stating their own positions and instead promoting open inquiry.

Other strategies for preventing groupthink involve getting more suggestions for viable solutions. This can be done by assigning the same problem to two independent groups. Or before the group reaches a decision, members can seek advice from other groups in the organization. Another technique is to invite experts outside the group to challenge members' views at group meetings.

Groupthink may also be prevented with strategies directed at the group members themselves. For example, for each group meeting, a member can be appointed to serve as a **devil's advocate**, a person whose role is to challenge the majority position. Also, after reaching preliminary consensus, the group can schedule a second-chance meeting. This allows group members an opportunity to express doubts and rethink the issue.

devil's advocate
a group member whose role is to challenge the majority position

EXHIBIT 9.11

Guidelines for
Overcoming Groupthink

For the company:
- Establish several independent groups to examine the same problem.
- Train managers in groupthink prevention techniques.

For the leader:
- Assign everyone the role of critical evaluator.
- Use outside experts to challenge the group.
- Assign a devil's advocate role to one member of the group.
- Try to be impartial and refrain from stating your own views.

For group members:
- Try to retain your objectivity and be a critical thinker.
- Discuss group deliberations with a trusted outsider, and report back to the group.

For the deliberation process:
- At times, break the group into subgroups to discuss the problem.
- Take time to study what other companies or groups have done in similar situations.
- Schedule second-chance meetings to provide an opportunity to rethink the issues before making a final decision.

If groups are aware of the problems of groupthink, they can use the steps discussed to minimize the likelihood of falling victim to this problem. These steps, summarized in Exhibit 9.11, offer advice for leaders, organizations, individuals, and the process itself.

Escalating Commitment to a Decision

escalating commitment
the tendency to exhibit greater levels of commitment to a decision as time passes and investments are made in the decision, even after significant evidence emerges indicating that the original decision was incorrect

Whereas groupthink helps to explain how policy-making groups put blinders on and stifle dissenting opinions when making major decisions, the concept of **escalating commitment** to decisions offers an explanation of why decision makers adhere to a course of action after they know it is incorrect (that is, why managers "throw good money after bad"). To understand the problem of escalating commitment, consider the following true examples:

- At an early stage of the United States's involvement in the Vietnam War, George Ball, then Undersecretary of State, wrote the following in a memo to President Johnson:

  The decision you face now is crucial. Once large numbers of U.S. troops are committed to direct combat, they will begin to take heavy casualties in a war they are ill equipped to fight in a noncooperative if not downright hostile countryside. Once we suffer large casualties, we will have started a well-nigh irreversible process. Our involvement will be so great that we cannot without national humiliation stop short of achieving our complete objectives. Of the two possibilities, I think humiliation would be more likely than the achievement of our objectives—even after we have paid terrible costs.

- A company overestimated its capability to build an airplane brake that met certain technical specifications at a given cost. Because it won the government contract, the company was forced to invest greater and greater effort meeting the contract terms. As a result of increasing pressure to meet specifications and deadlines, records and tests of the brake were misrepresented to government officials. Corporate careers and company credibility were increasingly staked on the airbrake contract, although many in the firm knew the brake would not work effectively. At the conclusion of the construction period, the government test pilot flew the plane; it skidded off the runway and narrowly missed injuring the pilot.
- An individual purchased a stock at $50 a share, but the price dropped to $20. Still convinced about the merit of the stock, he bought more shares at the lower price. Soon the price declined further, and the individual was again faced with the decision to buy more, hold what he already had, or sell out entirely.[17]

How do we account for such commitment by individuals and groups to obvious mistakes? At least three explanations are possible. First, we can point to individual limitations in information processing. People may be limited in both their desire and ability to handle all the information for complex decisions. As a result, errors in judgment may occur. For example, the company in which our stock investor purchased shares may have significant operations in countries in which negative changes in exchange rates are occurring or in which government regulations have changed. Our investor simply may not be able to completely comprehend these issues and how they are hurting the company's performance and subsequent stock price. A second approach is to explain decision errors as a breakdown in rationality because of group dynamics. For example, our stock investor may have received the tip from a trusted friend or he could be the friend of the company's CEO and therefore have a strong emotional commitment. Although both explanations may help us understand the error, Staw suggests that they do not go far enough. "A salient feature … is that a series of decisions is associated with a course of action rather than an isolated choice."[18]

To help explain such behavior, Professor Barry Staw turned to the social psychological literature on forced compliance. In studies of forced compliance, individuals are typically made to perform an unpleasant or dissatisfying act (e.g., eating grasshoppers) with no external rewards. In general, after they comply, individuals bias their own attitudes to justify their previous behavior (e.g., grasshoppers are high in protein). This biasing of attitudes is most likely to occur when the individuals feel personally responsible for the negative consequences and when the consequences are difficult to undo.

On the basis of these findings, Staw and his colleagues carried out a series of experiments to find out how willing people would be to continue to commit valued resources to a course of action after it was clear that the original decision had been wrong. They found that decision makers actually allocated more money to company divisions that were showing poor results than to those that were showing good results. Also, decision makers allocated more money to a division when they had been responsible for the original decision to back the division. In short, decision makers were most likely to spend money on projects that had negative consequences when they were responsible.

EXHIBIT 9.12

**Contributing Factors
to Escalation of
Commitment to
Decisions**

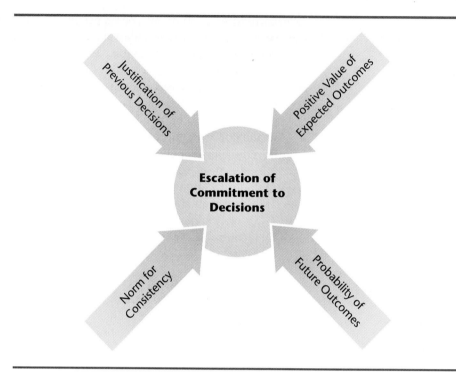

To find out why, Staw suggested a model of escalating commitment (Exhibit 9.12). This abbreviated model shows that four basic elements determine commitment to an action. First, people are likely to remain committed to a course of action (even when it is clearly incorrect) because of a need to justify previous decisions. When people feel responsible for negative consequences and a need to demonstrate their own competence, they will often stick to a decision to turn it around or "pull a victory out of defeat." This is referred to as *retrospective rationality;* that is, the individual seeks to appear competent in previous actions. For example, banks that loaned billions of dollars to Latin American countries in the late 1970s and early 1980s continued to loan more money even after it was clear that the governments would have great difficulty repaying the loans. They continued these loans in part to support their original decision. If they didn't continue the loans, they might be forced to recognize that their original decision was a mistake.

In addition, commitment to a previous decision is influenced by a *norm for consistency.* That is, managers who are consistent in their actions are often considered better leaders than those who flip-flop from one course of action to another. For instance, in a Gallup poll on President Clinton's popularity, respondents who were dissatisfied with his performance described him as "inconsistent."

Finally, two additional factors—the perceived probability and value of future outcomes—jointly influence what is called prospective rationality. *Prospective rationality* is simply a belief that future courses of action are rational and correct. When people think they can turn a situation around or that "prosperity is just around the corner," and when the goal is highly prized, they exhibit strong commitment to a continued course of action, influenced in part by the feeling that it is the proper thing to do.

Overcoming Escalation of Commitment Because escalation of commitment can lead to serious and negative consequences for organizations, we must consider how to minimize its effects. First, as a manager, you should stress in your own mind and to others (superiors, peers, and subordinates) that investments made in the past are sunk costs—that is, they cannot be recovered. All finance theory argues that sunk cost should be ignored in making future decisions, and only future costs and benefits should be considered. Second, you must create an atmosphere in which consistency does not dominate. This requires stressing the changing aspects of the competitive, social, cultural, and commercial environment surrounding a business and focusing on the importance of matching current decisions to current and expected future environments rather than to past decisions. Third, you can encourage each member to evaluate the prospects of future outcomes and their expected positive value critically. You can invite experts from outside the group to challenge members' future expectations. As with groupthink, a member can be appointed to serve as a devil's advocate to challenge the majority position.

In summary, when we consider effective decision-making processes in organizations, we must ward off the threats of groupthink and escalating commitments. Each can subvert even the most carefully considered decisions.

CULTURAL DIMENSIONS OF DECISION MAKING

To this point we have talked about decision making as though it applied the world over. Although we still have much to learn about decision making in different countries and cultures, we can identify several factors that affect decisions. Many stem from the cultural differences we examined in Chapter 4.

One of the factors affecting decision making is the extent to which a culture adopts an individualist or collectivist orientation. For example, in exploring a contingency framework for participative decision making, we cited research suggesting that participation was not effective in all situations and that it should be used when it matches specific elements of a situation. The fundamental factor is an individualistic orientation. Most researchers of participative decision making have come from individualistic cultures such as the United States, Canada, and the United Kingdom. In countries such as Japan, Indonesia, and Korea, managers and employees have a much stronger collectivist orientation. So involving others in decision making may not simply be a function of contingency factors but should be done because it is simply the "right" thing to do. In collectivist cultures, even when an individual decision maker believes he or she has all the relevant knowledge, a strong collectivist value often leads to the inclusion of others in the decision-making process.

These cultural clashes can often be seen when individuals from opposite orientations must work together. For example, when managers from more individualistic cultures are assigned to work in more collectivist cultures, they quite frequently experience difficulties because they tend to make too many individual decisions and not include others.[19]

Basic values concerning hierarchy can also influence decision making across countries. As discussed in Chapter 4, managers in countries such as Malaysia, India, and Thailand have a higher acceptance of hierarchical differences between people (high power distance, in Hofstede's terms), while managers in countries such as Israel, Australia, and Denmark do not. Power difference can significantly affect the problem-analysis stage of decision making, especially when it involves group decisions. In low-power-distance cultures, group members tend to openly and directly disagree with each other in discussing the merits or risks of a given alternative. In high-power-distance cultures, such open discussions are less acceptable when individuals of differing ranks are involved. For example, in Thailand, if a lower-ranked individual had a significant difference of opinion with his or her superior, directly raising this during a group meeting would not be acceptable. Rather, the individual would try to find a time, perhaps after work, in which his or her ideas could be presented privately to the superior.

On the surface, one might expect organizations in cultures that have high levels of power distance to suffer from problems of groupthink because employees are less willing to voice their concerns or make critical comments, especially when superiors are present. Interestingly, many of these cultures have developed business practices to counterbalance this potential problem. For example, in Japan, managers use a technique called *nemawashi*. This term is borrowed from gardening and refers to the process of gradually snipping the roots of a tree or bush that is to be transplanted to reduce the shock to the plant. In business, *nemawashi* translates into many private or semiprivate meetings in which true opinions are shared before a major decision-making meeting. This allows differences of opinion to be stated while protecting respected hierarchical status. In addition, meeting after work at a bar or restaurant also allows for more direct discussions and disagreements. Both of these practices serve to counteract groupthink fostered by high power distance.

In addition, the extent to which cultures differ in their tolerance of risk can affect decision making. In countries with a relatively low tolerance of uncertainty and risk, such as Japan and Germany, nonprogrammed decisions are avoided as much as possible by using standard operating procedures. For example, the operating manual at BMW for how to work through an engineering problem is thick and detailed. Even though the specific engineering problems may vary, BMW executives have tried to make the decisions as programmed as possible. In contrast, managers in countries with relatively high tolerance of uncertainty and risk, such as Hong Kong and the United States, tend to seek out nonprogrammed decisions and to give senior management more responsibility for nonprogrammed decisions.

In addition to cultural values and the way they can affect the decision-making process, social and even corporate cultural values can affect nearly every aspect of decision making. For example, what is seen as a problem, what is viewed as an acceptable or desirable outcome, what criteria are used in assessing various alternatives, how an alternative is chosen (e.g., by the highest-ranking member, majority votes, consensus, etc.), or who is involved in planning the implementation can all be influenced by the underlying organizational or national culture. However, knowing the basic building blocks of decision making helps you ask the right questions and discover important differences in decision making when you work with people from other cultures.

STRATEGIES FOR IMPROVING DECISIONS MAKING

Now that we have focused on the problems and processes involved in decision making and have examined several decision models, differences between individual and group decisions, participation in decision making, constraints on effective decision making, and cultural influences, we can consider additional ways of improving

EXHIBIT 9.13	Structured Debate (Problem Formulation)	Creativity Stimulants (Problem Solution)
Techniques for Improving Decision Making	Devil's advocate Multiple advocacy Dialectical inquiry	Brainstorming Nominal group technique Delphi technique

the decision-making process. At the beginning of the chapter, we mentioned that decisions can be divided into two phases: problem formulation and problem solution. Strategies to improve decision making can also be divided into the same two categories.[20]

Improving Problem Formulation

Problem formulation focuses on identifying the causes for unsatisfactory behavior and finding new opportunities and challenges. This process is often inhibited by the failure of group members to look beyond the familiar. Groupthink and escalating commitment often limit critical analysis or comprehensive searches for information and solutions. As a result, improvement in problem formulation may require the use of structured debate. **Structured debate** is a process to improve problem formulation through the use of a devil's advocate, multiple advocacy, and dialectical inquiry (see Exhibit 9.13).

structured debate
a process to improve problem formulation that includes the processes of devil's advocate, multiple advocacy, and dialectical inquiry

Devil's Advocate   As discussed earlier, a devil's advocate is a group member whose role is to disagree with the group. For example, if you asked a group of American automobile company executives why their sales are down, they might blame Japanese imports. In this case, a devil's advocate would argue that the problem lies not with the Japanese, but with the Americans themselves and their poor product quality. Through this process, the group is forced to justify its position and, as a consequence, develop a more precise and accurate picture of the problem and its underlying causes.

multiple advocacy
a process to improve decision making by assigning several group members to represent the opinions of various constituencies that might have an interest in the decision

Multiple Advocacy   **Multiple advocacy** is like the devil's advocate approach, except that more than one opposing view is presented. Each group involved in a decision is assigned the responsibility of representing the opinions of its constituents. Thus, if a university is concerned with accommodating racial and cultural diversity on campus, it might establish a commission including African Americans, Hispanics, Asians, women's groups, and so forth. The resulting dialogue should lead to the identification of a useful agenda for discussion.

dialectical inquiry
a process to improve decision making by assigning a group member (or members) the role of questioning the underlying assumptions associated with the formulation of the problem

Dialectical Inquiry   **Dialectical inquiry** occurs when a group or individual is assigned the role of questioning the underlying assumptions of problem formulation. It begins by identifying the prevailing view of the problem and its associated assumptions. Next, an individual is asked to develop an alternative problem that is credible but has different assumptions. By doing so, the accuracy of the original assumptions is examined and possibly altered. As a result, group members are forced to "think outside the box" and look at new ways to analyze a problem. These efforts are particularly helpful in overcoming groupthink and escalating commitment, because they question the underlying assumptions of group behavior.

Improving Problem Solution

Problem solution involves development and evaluation of alternative courses of action and selection and implementation of the preferred alternatives. To improve this process, group members must be as thorough and creative as possible. Stimulation of creativity expands the search for and analysis of possible alternatives. Three such mechanisms are useful.

brainstorming
a process of generating many creative solutions without evaluating their merit

Brainstorming   **Brainstorming** is a process of generating many creative solutions without evaluating their merit. It is a frequently used mechanism to provide the maximum number of ideas in a short period of time. A group comes together, is given a specific problem, and is told to propose any ideas that come to mind to solve the problem. In such sessions—at least at the early stages—criticism is minimized so as not to inhibit expression. Once all the ideas are on the table, the group considers the positive and negative aspects of each proposal. Through a process of continual refinement, the best possible solution under the circumstances should emerge.

nominal group technique
a process of having group members record their proposed solutions, summarize all proposed solutions, and independently rank solutions until a clearly favored solution emerges

Nominal Group Technique   The **nominal group technique**, typically referred to as NGT, consists of four phases in group decision making.[21] First, individual members meet as a group, but they begin by sitting silently and independently generating their ideas on a problem in writing. This silent period is followed by a round-robin procedure in which each group member presents an idea to the group. No discussion of the idea is allowed at this time. The ideas are summarized and recorded (perhaps on a blackboard). After all individuals have presented their ideas, each idea is discussed to clarify and evaluate it. Finally, group members conclude the meeting by silently and independently ranking the various ideas or solutions to the problem. The final decision is determined by the pooled outcome of the members' votes on the issue.

The NGT allows the group to meet formally, but it does not allow members much discussion; hence, the term *nominal* group technique. A chief advantage of this procedure is that everyone independently considers the problem without influence from other group members. As we found, this influence represents one of the chief obstacles to open-minded discussion and decision making.

delphi technique
process in which group members do not meet face to face but provide written input on potential solutions through an interactive process until a clearly favored solution emerges

Delphi Technique   In contrast to NGT, the **delphi technique** never allows decision participants to meet face to face. Instead, a problem is identified, and members are asked through a series of carefully designed questionnaires to provide potential solutions. These questionnaires are completed independently. Results of the first questionnaire are then circulated to all group members (who are still physically separated). After viewing the feedback, members are again asked their opinions (to see if the opinions of others on the first questionnaire caused them to change their own minds). This process may continue through several iterations until group members' opinions begin to show consensus.

The decision-making process includes a variety of problems. Individuals and groups have various biases and personal goals that may lead to suboptimal decisions. Moreover, groups often censor themselves. Even so, techniques such as those discussed here aim to minimize many of these problems by insulating individual participants from the undue influence of others. This allows individuals greater freedom of expression, and the group receives far less filtered or slanted information with which to make its decision. Thus, although not perfect, these techniques can give managers mechanisms to improve both the quality and the timeliness of decisions made in organizations.

CONCLUDING COMMENTS

The decision-making process typically has two aspects: problem formation and problem solution. Individually, people often select solutions that meet their minimum objectives rather than spending extra time and energy trying to find the solution that maximizes their objectives. However, to appear rational, they often construct objectives and criteria after the fact to justify the decision they have already made. Groups add a social dynamic to the decision-making process that, depending on the dynamics, can result in either better or worse decisions than individuals might make on their own. The decision of how much to involve others is a function of several factors: the potential participants in the decision, the nature of the problem and decision, and the environment in which the problem exists and the decision needs to be made. Understanding these basics provides a foundation for awareness of how cultural values can influence decision making and how managers can make effective decisions in an increasingly global and culturally diverse environment.

KEY TERMS

bounded rationality (administrative man) model 236

brainstorming 256

cross-functional teams 244

decision making 229

delphi technique 256

devil's advocate 249

dialectical inquiry 255

escalating commitment 250

formulation 229

Gresham's law of planning 239

groupthink 247

heuristic 236

multiple advocacy 255

nominal group technique 256

nonprogrammed decision 238

opportunity 231

problem 231

programmed decision 238

rational (classical) model 231

retrospective decision (implicit favorite) model 237

satisficing 236

sequential attention to alternative solutions 236

solution 229

standard operating procedures (SOP) 239

structured debate 255

subjectively expected utility (SEU) model 233

REVIEW QUESTIONS

1. What are the two stages in decision making?
2. What is the basic premise of the rational (classical) model of decision making? How does it differ from the bounded rationality model?
3. What are the primary advantages of the bounded rationality model of decision making?
4. What is satisficing? How does it differ from satisfying?
5. How does the retrospective decision model work?
6. Describe Gresham's law of planning.
7. Describe the normative model of decision making and leadership. What implications for management follow from this model?

8. Discuss the advantages and disadvantages of group decision making compared with individual decision making.
9. When is it appropriate for a manager to be more participative in decision making?
10. Describe the phenomenon of groupthink. What are its symptoms? What are its outcomes?
11. How can we overcome groupthink?
12. Identify examples in your own life of escalating commitment to past decisions.
13. How can managers work to overcome the effects of escalating commitment to past decisions?
14. Compare and contrast the nominal group technique and the delphi technique of decision making.
15. What are some of the more prominent roadblocks to effective managerial decision making?
16. How can cultural values affect decision making?

DISCUSSION QUESTIONS

1. If your subordinates expect you to be consistent in your decision making style, but you believe that different decision making styles are appropriate for specific situations, how can you take this contingency approach and yet not seem inconsistent to your employees?
2. Think of someone you know personally who is an effective decision maker. What key characteristics would you use to describe this manager?
3. What are the strengths and weaknesses of a manager with "good instincts" and who seems to make effective decisions, but whose approach is more like the retrospective than rational model?
4. Japanese and Korean managers tend to spend considerably more time on and involve more people in the problem formulation stage of decision making than American managers do. What are the pros and cons you see with this?

CLOSING CASE

Schwab Trades Security for Uncertainty Online

When a company decides to completely transform the way it does business, the decision is far from automatic. Executives at the venerable investment firm Charles Schwab faced exactly this challenge in a huge, nonprogrammed decision—whether to commit fully to low-cost, Internet trading. The decision not only would shape the future direction of the company but could actually determine the company's life or death.

Several years ago, Schwab had no exposure to the Web. Today, more than $4 billion worth of securities are traded each week on the firm's Web site (www.schwab.com), which is more than half of Schwab's total weekly trading

volume. How did Schwab arrive at this change? During the mid-1990s, several midlevel software researchers at the company presented chief information officer Dawn Lepore and Charles Schwab himself with a demonstration that the two executives recognized as a tremendous potential opportunity for the firm to engage in Web-based stock trading—if Schwab could execute it right. So the executives gathered an independent project team to explore the alternatives. The team, working secretly at first, developed into a separate electronic brokerage unit (called e.Schwab) that reported directly to co-CEO David Pottruck. The unit had to determine how Schwab could compete with the small, deep-discount brokerage firms that had already established themselves on the Internet, or the foray into the Web would not be worth the effort to Schwab. The unit was separate for a reason: "We created e.Schwab because we wanted to learn. But we did not want to risk the whole company," explains Dan Leemon, head of strategy.

One competitive problem was Schwab's traditional reliance on commissions, which were computed on a sliding scale, starting at a minimum of $39.95. The new Web site would charge customers a flat fee of $39 (later dropped to $29.95) for each stock trade up to 1,000 shares. But this price was hardly competitive with those of E*Trade ($15) and Ameritrade ($8). So the company decided against using price as a marketing point. Still, customers hit the Web site in far greater numbers than Schwab managers expected. "We were totally unprepared. Customers began voting with their keyboards, and in two weeks we reached 25,000 Web accounts—our goal for the entire year," recalls Gideon Sasson, the original team's head of technological development (Sasson is now a senior manager). Schwab's online assets ballooned to $81 billion (about 10 times the assets of E*Trade). Yet there were snags.

Possibly because the online brokerage unit had not yet been integrated with the rest of the investment units, regular phone and branch representatives could not help e-mail customers. These customers were allowed only one free phone call a month and were required to direct the rest of their inquiries through e.Schwab e-mail. Those who wanted to speak with a representative more frequently had to keep their regular Schwab accounts active, but then their online discount was reduced. The result was that Schwab customers had to choose between service and price—a situation that many did not find attractive. "So here we were, the No. 1 player, but we had customers who were not happy," says David Pottruck. "That's not a way to build a huge business success." The only way to solve the problem—which could also represent enormous opportunity—it seemed, was to make a total commitment to Internet trading.

The decision was far from easy. It was obvious that customers wanted better, cheaper, more convenient access to Internet trading through Schwab. In fact, Web trading would be faster and cheaper for Schwab as well. But the company's revenues through commissions would be radically reduced—probably $125 million—and neither Wall Street nor the employees who owned 40 percent of the

company's stock were likely to react favorably to the change. So co-chairs Charles Schwab and David Pottruck discussed the situation many times, weighing the alternatives for nearly a year. In the end, Schwab acknowledged, "This isn't that hard a decision, because we really have no choice. It's just a question of when, and it will be harder later."

So the decision was made to go full steam ahead with the Internet. First, however, the independent e.Schwab group had to be integrated with the rest of the organization, and Pottruck and Schwab chose Sasson to facilitate the integration. Within a few months, the revamped trading service was ready—to take a loss. As predicted, both revenues and stock prices dropped dramatically at first. In addition, customers complained about the Web site itself—that it was confusing and difficult to use. But Schwab executives learned an invaluable lesson about what customers want: service. Investors want fast, accurate information that they can understand and use easily. The lowest price is not necessarily the most important factor in an investor's choice of investment firm. So Schwab managers began to address this issue by going to outside sources such as Crédit Suisse, First Boston, and Hambrecht & Quist (who would allow Schwab to distribute their research information) and the Web site design firm Razorfish (who revamped the company's Web site).

How successful the decision to focus on online trading will be is not entirely clear, but the early results seem positive. What is clear is that given the rapidly changing environment of the internet, Schwab's initial decision to venture into online trading will not be its last if it is to remain the leader.

QUESTIONS

1. Do you think that the initial decision to maintain the e.Schwab group as a separate unit was wise? Why or why not?
2. What steps might Schwab managers take to monitor and evaluate the results of its online trading efforts?
3. What steps might Schwab managers take to balance the risk and uncertainty of their decisions as they progress with online trading?

Sources: Erick Schonfeld, "Schwab Puts It All Online," *Fortune,* December 7, 1998, pp. 94–100; Schwab Web site, www.schwab.com, accessed December 4, 1998.

PART 4

Organizing and Staffing

CHAPTER 10

ORGANIZATIONAL STRUCTURE AND DESIGN

LEARNING OBJECTIVES

After studying this chapter, you should be able to:

- Explain the concepts of organizational structure and design.
- Explain the concepts of differentiation and integration and their role in organizational structure and design.
- Describe mechanisms for differentiation and integration.
- Describe the various structures for organizations and their strengths and weaknesses.
- List the environmental factors that influence organizational structure.
- Determine the appropriate organizational structure for a firm given a set of internal and external factors.

Becton Dickinson Restructuring in Europe

The European Union has long promised a pan-European customer and greater ease in the cross-border movement of people, products, and capital within the region. Although reality is still short of the promise, enough progress had been made to force Becton Dickinson, a diversified health care products multinational corporation, to rethink its organizational structure in Europe.

Becton Dickinson, a $2.8 billion firm, had previously focused on the domestic U.S. market but was increasingly turning its attention to international markets. The company organized itself primarily by product and divided its products into two major areas, called sectors. Its Medical Sector consisted of four product groups: hypodermic, diabetic care, intravenous catheter, and operating room products. Its Diagnostic Sector included six product groups: specimen collection, microbiology, immunodiagnostics, primary care diagnostics, cellular analysis, and tissue culture labware. Each of these product divisions was headed up by a division president, who focused mostly on selling products in the United States. In addition, it had an international division that was responsible for all product sales outside the United States.

Becton Dickinson's operations overseas were organized by geography, not product as in the United States. For example, its operations in Europe were organized by country. Becton Dickinson France carried all the firm's products; the country manager of France was then responsible for sales and profits within France. The same was true for Germany, the United Kingdom, and so on. This organizational structure worked quite well because until the early 1990s, countries in Europe had quite different standards and regulations concerning most of the products Becton Dickinson made and sold. However, the formation of the European Union and monetary union in 1999 were expected to reduce the different product standards and make it easier to do business throughout the region.

The European Union held the promise that Becton Dickinson could make a product, such as insulin syringes, to one standard and sell it across all member nations. This would dramatically increase the efficiency of Becton Dickinson's operation in Europe and potentially its profits. However, with this opportunity came an interesting challenge: How should the company structure its operations in Europe?

One obvious solution was to organize in Europe the same way as in the United States, by products. In this case, they would form a European Hypodermic Products Division, a European Diabetic Care Products Division, and so on. However, no one could say how long it would be before hospitals in one country, such as France, would accept the same standards as hospitals in another country, such as Germany.

Another alternative was to organize the entire company by global product. That is, instead of having an international division, each product division would have worldwide responsibility.

Becton Dickinson's U.S.-based competitors were increasingly moving into overseas markets, and foreign competitors were increasingly setting up operations in the United States. The U.S. health care crisis and all the publicity about rising health care costs were exerting downward pressure on prices. Becton Dickinson was thinking carefully about its new organizational structure. Was it ready to go to a global structure? Should it keep its country structure in Europe until the promise of the European Union became reality? Choosing the right organizational structure might make the difference between success and failure in the changing and increasingly competitive environment facing Becton Dickinson.

Sources: "Becton Dickinson and Company Announces Restructuring Plan, One-Time Charges for Third Fiscal Quarter," company press release, May 19, 1998; "Becton Dickinson and Company Announces Executive Vice Presidents," Business Wire, August 4, 1998; "Becton Dickinson Creates Single Bioscience/Diagnostic Business," Business Wire, September 3, 1998.

As the story of Becton Dickinson illustrates, today's complex environment presents a variety of questions of how firms should be structured to survive and prosper. You as a manager must understand the basic building blocks of organizational design to know what options are available. Also, you must understand the basic organizational structures and the general advantages and disadvantages of each. You need to understand the principles linking particular structures, organizational objectives, and the external environment and the key factors that determine a good fit among them. Finally, as a manager, you must be able to apply this knowledge in planning and implementing appropriate organizational structures.

PRINCIPLES OF ORGANIZATIONAL STRUCTURE

organizational structure
the sum of the ways an organization divides its labor into distinct tasks and then coordinates them

organizational design
the process of assessing the organization's strategic objectives and environmental demands and then determining the appropriate organizational structure

organizational charts
graphics illustrating relationships among units and lines of authority through the use of labeled boxes and connecting lines

differentiation
the extent to which tasks are divided into subtasks and performed by individuals with specialized skills

Organizational structure can be defined as the sum of the ways an organization divides its labor into distinct tasks and then coordinates them.[1] **Organizational design** is the process of assessing the organization's strategic objectives and environmental demands and then determining the appropriate organizational structure. Often, organizational structure is talked about in terms of organizational charts. **Organizational charts** illustrate relationships among units and lines of authority through the use of labeled boxes and connecting lines. For example, Exhibit 10.1 shows the organizational chart of Suncor Energy.

While organizational charts represent important aspects of an organization's structure, they do not equal organizational structure. Just as the structure of someone's physical anatomy is more complex than what is visible, so too is an organization's structure more than what can be depicted in a chart. Thus, you must understand the principles behind the differences you see in organizational charts.

Differentiation

To understand organizational structure, the first concept you must understand is differentiation. **Differentiation** is the extent to which tasks are divided into subtasks and performed by individuals with specialized skills. For example, because of the complexity of building a commercial jetliner, Boeing has engineers who specialize in designing airplane doors and others who design seats. The main benefit of differentiation is greater specialization. The key organization structure questions are how much differentiation is appropriate and what activities to divide. To better answer these questions, we first need to look at the four primary types of differentiation: task, cognitive, horizontal, and vertical differentiation.

EXHIBIT 10.1
Suncor Energy Corporate Organization Chart

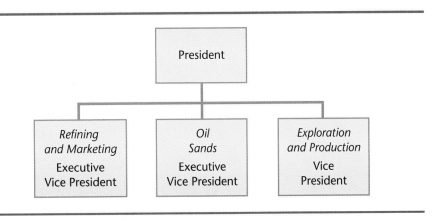

task differentiation
the extent to which tasks are divided

Task Differentiation   The extent to which tasks are divided is referred to as **task differentiation**. As an example, every company needs to keep track of what its competitors are doing. This overall objective can be broken down into many separate tasks, such as reviewing competitors' hiring activities, watching production volume, and tracking their price changes. The more tasks break down, the greater the task differentiation.

cognitive differentiation
the extent to which people in different units within the organization think about different things and think about similar things differently

Cognitive Differentiation   **Cognitive differentiation** exists when people in different units within the organization think about different things and think about similar things differently. For example, accountants typically think about assets and liabilities, while marketing managers think about brand image and market share. However, they might also think about the same thing differently. Accountants might think about organizational performance in terms of financial results, while marketers might think about organizational performance in terms of customer satisfaction. The greater the differences in *what* people think about and in *how* they think about similar things within the organization, the greater the cognitive differentiation. So why is this important? Suppose both design engineers and manufacturing personnel at Boeing need to work together to make a newly designed 777 door operate properly. Greater separation and specialization make this coordination harder because they think about things differently.

horizontal differentiation
the specialization of tasks across the organization

Horizontal Differentiation   **Horizontal differentiation** refers to the specialization of tasks across the organization. The greater the division and specialization of tasks such as marketing, accounting, sales, and production across the organization, the greater the horizontal differentiation. Most medium to large organizations separate financial, accounting, marketing, sales, and production tasks, and therefore have some degree of horizontal differentiation. Horizontal differentiation gives you more specialized knowledge and skills but can make coordination across departments difficult.

vertical differentiation
the extent to which tasks are subdivided and carried out by specialized individuals from the top to the bottom of the organization's hierarchy

Vertical Differentiation   In addition to horizontal differentiation, managers need to determine the appropriate level of vertical differentiation. **Vertical differentiation** occurs when tasks are subdivided and carried out by specialized individuals from the top to the bottom of the organization's hierarchy. A simple way to assess vertical differentiation is to look at how many levels there are in the organization's hierarchy. For example, assuming similar size, the organization that had supervisor, assistant manager, manager, director, vice president, senior vice president, executive vice president, and president levels would have more vertical differentiation than a company with only supervisor, manager, vice president, and president levels.

Integration

integration
the extent to which various parts of the organization cooperate and interact with each other

In contrast to differentiation, **integration** is the extent to which various parts of the organization cooperate and interact with each other. The key benefit of integration is the coordinated movement of different people and activities toward a desired organizational objective. As a consequence, one of the driving forces of integration is interdependence. **Interdependence** is essentially the degree to which one unit, or one person, depends on another to accomplish a required task.

interdependence
the degree to which one unit, or one person, depends on another to accomplish a required task

There are three types of interdependence.[2] *Pooled interdependence* occurs when various groups are largely independent in their functions but collectively contribute to a common output. For example, two product divisions might send products to the same customer to meet the customer's overall needs. *Sequential interdependence* exists when the outputs of one group become the inputs of another group, such as when the raw materials provided by the purchasing department become the inputs of the manufacturing department, whose outputs become the inputs of the sales department. *Reciprocal interdependence* exists when two or more groups depend on one another for inputs, such as when the new product development department relies on the marketing research department for ideas to investigate, and marketing research relies on new product development for new products to test on customers. In principle, the greater the interdependence, the greater the need for cooperation, and thus integration.

Another factor that can influence the need for integration is uncertainty. Uncertainty for a firm refers to the extent to which future input, throughput, and output factors cannot be forecast accurately. The more difficult it is to accurately forecast these factors, the greater uncertainty the firm faces. The greater the uncertainty, the greater the need for integration and coordination.

Integration can be achieved through a variety of mechanisms.[3] The appropriateness of use of each mechanism is related to the level and type of interdependence and the extent of uncertainty.

Rules   Rules essentially establish if–then guidelines for behavior and consequence. For example, the rule may be, if you are going to miss class, then you must notify the professor in advance. In a sense, these rules are the standard operating procedures. In general, the more task independence, the more useful rules are as an integration mechanism. In contrast, the more task interdependence, the less useful rules are as an integration mechanism. If you and a co-worker are interdependent in your jobs, then you have to make adjustments to work effectively together. Rules often work against these required adjustments. In essence, these adjustments are exceptions to the rules.

Goals   As task uncertainty and interdependence increase, the probability that preset rules can effectively coordinate tasks declines (see Exhibit 10.2). Consequently, goals become a more effective coordination mechanism. Instead of

EXHIBIT 10.2	
Shift in the Appropriateness of Rules and Goals	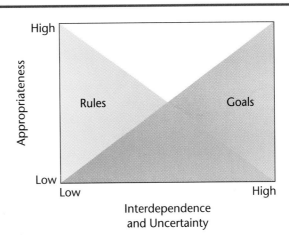

specifying what individuals should do, goals specify what outcomes individuals should achieve. Effective goals define quantitative outcomes and often require high levels of effort to achieve. Specifying the outcomes, but not the process, maximizes individual flexibility in how they get things done, yet facilitates integration by ensuring that people are working toward the same end. For example, university professors encounter students with a wide variety of needs and situations. Rather than provide professors with set rules, the university sets goals in terms of student proficiency. The goals, in terms of learning, ensure that professors are working toward the same end but have the flexibility to respond to specific needs and situations.

Values   In cases of high task uncertainty and interdependence, values become an important coordinating mechanism. Values specify underlying objectives, such as customer satisfaction, but unlike goals, they do not specify quantitative outcomes. High uncertainty combined with high levels of required interdependence means that interdependent employees need something to facilitate interaction and coordination. At the same time, the uncertainty and changing nature of the situation reduce the effectiveness of rules and specific goals as that basis. So shared values can ease coordination under these conditions, because they specify what is important while maintaining flexibility concerning exactly what or how things are accomplished.

Formalization

Organizations vary substantially in how much they use formal or defined structures and systems in decision making, communication, and control. Formal systems specify clear **lines of authority** within an organization, or who reports to whom. Firms with strong formalization rely on the chain of command for decision making, communication, and control. The **chain of command** specifies the sequence of people through whom information and decisions should flow. Formal systems often also stress **unity of command**. This is simply the notion that an employee should have one and only one boss. Additionally, formal systems tend to specify span of control. **Span of control** refers to the number of employees reporting to a given supervisor. Narrow span of control throughout the entire organization will lead to a rather **tall organization structure**, or one that is high in terms of vertical differentiation. In other words, the organization will have multiple reporting layers. Wide span of control throughout the organization will lead to a more **flat organization structure**. In this case, the organization will have fewer layers of supervisors and subordinates. Exhibit 10.3 shows examples of tall and flat organizational structures, as well as span of control.

The decision of whether an organization should be tall or flat or whether a manager should have a narrow or wide span of control is affected by several factors. The more the work is routine, the wider the span of control a given supervisor can effectively manage and the flatter the organization could be. The greater the management capability of the supervisor, the wider the span of control that supervisor can effectively handle. An organization with a large number of capable supervisors could therefore be much flatter than if the reverse were true. Additionally, having capable subordinates who do not require close supervision increases the effective span of control. Thus, an organization that has a large

lines of authority
formal systems specifying who reports to whom

chain of command
the sequence of people through whom information and decisions should flow

unity of command
the notion that an employee should have one and only one boss

span of control
the number of employees reporting to a given supervisor

tall organization structure
multiple reporting layers within the organization brought about by a narrow span of control throughout the entire organization

flat organization structure
fewer layers of supervisors and subordinates within the organization brought about by a wide span of control throughout the organization

EXHIBIT 10.3
Tall and Flat Organization Structures

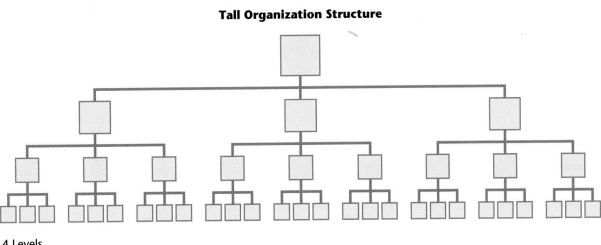

Tall Organization Structure

4 Levels
Span of Control = 3
Total Employees = 40

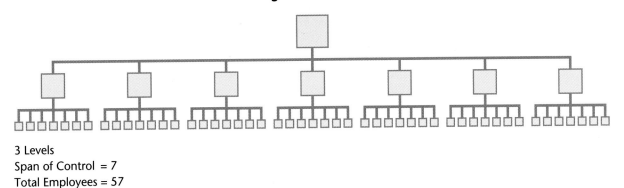

Flat Organization Structure

3 Levels
Span of Control = 7
Total Employees = 57

number of routine tasks performed by capable employees and supervised by capable managers could be quite flat.

Mechanisms such as organizational charts, written job descriptions, policy manuals, operating procedures, financial reports, employee handbooks, and work schedules are all means of creating more formalized organizational structures.

Informalization

An organization's complete structure is not just what is official and formally written down. There are informal dimensions as well. Informal structures for decision making, communication, and control are often not represented in organizational charts, yet they pervade the day-to-day functioning of many organizations. One study that compared U.S. and Japanese firms found that the Japanese relied much more on informalization.[4] Much of the decision making, communication, and control were accomplished through informal, face-to-face meetings between people who did not have formal reporting relationships. As mentioned in the previous chapter, in Japan, this process is referred to as *nemawashi*. In Japanese organizations, *nemawashi* takes the form of informal conversations in which incremental decisions are made so that by the time a meeting is held to make the formal decision, the decision has already been made informally.

Centralization and Decentralization

centralized organizations

organizations in which decision making is restricted to fewer individuals, usually at the top of the organization

decentralized organizations

organizations in which decision making authority is pushed down to the lowest possible level

In addition to the extent to which the organization's structure is formal or informal, the extent to which it is centralized or decentralized is also important. Centralization and decentralization refer to the level at which decisions are made—at the top of the organization or at lower levels. **Centralized organizations** tend to restrict decision making to fewer individuals, usually at the top of the organization. In contrast, **decentralized organizations** tend to push decision-making authority down to the lowest possible level. For instance, European multinational organizations tend to be decentralized and allow units in different countries to make decisions according to local conditions. Often this enables them to adapt to host government demands and different consumer preferences.[5] For many years, Philips, a large multinational electronics firm headquartered in the Netherlands, was viewed as one of the premiere examples of a decentralized international organization. Philips operated in over 60 countries around the world. Many of the larger country units enjoyed considerable freedom and autonomy. For example, even though the V2000 videocassette recorder was developed by the Dutch parent, North American Philips refused to purchase and sell the product in the United States and Canada. Instead, North American Philips purchased a VCR made by a Japanese rival and resold it in the United States and Canada under the brand name of Philips.

Japanese firms, on the other hand, exhibit a stronger degree of centralization and tend not to delegate decisions as frequently as either European or American firms.[6] Most Japanese multinational firms operate like centralized hubs into which information flows, and from which decisions are announced to foreign subsidiaries. In fact, Japanese firms have encountered increasing complaints from host nationals in local subsidiaries about a "bamboo ceiling." This term refers to the exclusion of host nationals from strategic decision making because nearly all key positions in the subsidiary are occupied by Japanese expatriates who are sent by headquarters in Japan to ensure more centralized control.[7]

ORGANIZATIONAL STRUCTURES

Now that we have examined the building blocks of differentiation, integration, formalization, and centralization we can explore different organization structures and the role of these building blocks. Although a variety of structures exist, six structures represent the most common forms. We examine each of these basic structures, although variations can be obtained by combining more than one form. In reality, most organization *do not* have pure forms but have hybrids. Once we have reviewed these basic organizational structures and briefly reviewed their general strengths and

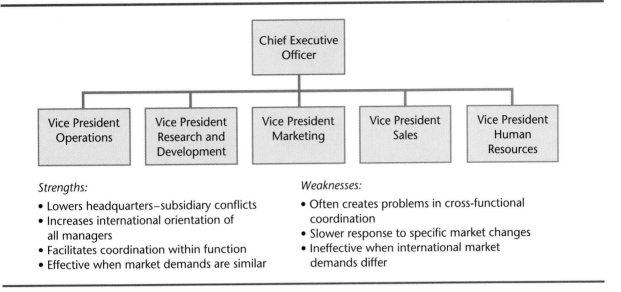

EXHIBIT 10.4
Functional Structure

Strengths:
- Lowers headquarters–subsidiary conflicts
- Increases international orientation of all managers
- Facilitates coordination within function
- Effective when market demands are similar

Weaknesses:
- Often creates problems in cross-functional coordination
- Slower response to specific market changes
- Ineffective when international market demands differ

weaknesses, we can then move to a more detailed examination of the conditions that determine which type of structure you as a manager would want to adopt.

Functional Structure

Perhaps the simplest structure is the functional structure (Exhibit 10.4). The functional structure organizes the firm around traditional functional departments such as accounting, finance, marketing, operations, and so on. This structure is one of the most common organizational structures in part because it separates the specialized knowledge of each functional area through horizontal differentiation and can direct that knowledge toward the firm's key products or services.

Firms with operations outside their domestic borders might also adopt a functional structure. The key difference between a purely domestic organization and a multinational organization with a functional structure is the scope of responsibilities for functional heads in the multinational firm. In a multinational, each department would have worldwide responsibilities. Thus, while each subsidiary would have a local human resource manager, the top human resource manager would be responsible for directing worldwide human resource activities such as hiring, training, appraising, or rewarding employees. This structure is most common when the technology and products of the firm are similar throughout the world.

The major advantage of this structure is that it allows for functional specialization. For example, managers in marketing become experts in that area. The hope is that greater expertise will give the firm an advantage in marketing its products relative to competitors. A functional structure on a global basis reduces headquarters–subsidiary conflicts because operations throughout the world are integrated into their functional areas, and functional department executives are charged with global responsibility. This, in turn, enhances the overall international orientation of managers. For example, the higher a marketing manager rises in the marketing

EXHIBIT 10.5
Geographical/Regional Structure

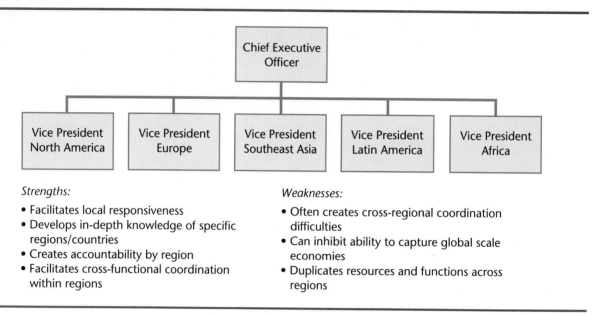

Strengths:
- Facilitates local responsiveness
- Develops in-depth knowledge of specific regions/countries
- Creates accountability by region
- Facilitates cross-functional coordination within regions

Weaknesses:
- Often creates cross-regional coordination difficulties
- Can inhibit ability to capture global scale economies
- Duplicates resources and functions across regions

department, the more that manager needs to think about and understand the firm's global marketing issues.

The weakness of this structure arises when the firm has a wide variety of products and these products have different environmental demands, such as government restrictions or standards, customer preferences, or performance qualities. This weakness is exacerbated when different functional departments experience different demands by geographical area which can create greater cognitive differentiation. For example, if the accounting practices are similar between the United Kingdom and France but the advertising approaches differ, this will tend to exaggerate coordination difficulties between the accounting and marketing departments.

Geographic/Regional Structure

Firms can structure themselves around various geographical areas or regions (Exhibit 10.5). Within this structure, regional executives are generally responsible for all functional activities in their regions. The Western Regional Vice President might be responsible for all key business activities for the states of Washington, Oregon, California, Nevada, Montana, Utah, Idaho, Wyoming, Colorado, Arizona, and New Mexico.

A number of multinational firms also use a geographic/regional structure. This is primarily because customers' demands, government regulations, competitive conditions, availability of suppliers, and other factors vary significantly from one region of the world to another. The size or scope of the region is typically a function of the volume of business. For example, in consumer products companies, the Middle East is often included in the European region because the volume of sales in this area is too small for it to be a separate region. On the other hand, for most oil and gas companies with a geographic structure, the Middle East is a separate region on its own.

One strength of this structure is that it allows a manager to gain in-depth understanding of the market, customers, governments, and competitors within a given geographical area. The fact that regional managers are responsible for all activities within their region also fosters a strong sense of accountability for performance. That is, these managers are expected to meet performance targets and to take corrective action when performance is below expectations. The individual regions are often treated as **profit centers**. In other words, each region's profitability is measured against the revenues it generates and the expenses it incurs.

One of the major weaknesses of this structure is that it can inhibit coordination and communication between regions. Regional managers in the West may not efficiently and effectively share good ideas with managers in the East. Additionally, placing separate production activities in each region can inhibit economies of scale in manufacturing products common to the regions. Placing all functional areas within each region can also lead to duplication of resources. Finally, regional structures can foster competitive behavior among the regions. This can be particularly frustrating for customers who have operations across multiple regions.

profit centers
units in which revenues and expenses are tracked to calculate profits or losses

Product Structure

In a product structure, the firm is organized around specific products (Exhibit 10.6). Each product division is generally treated as a profit center. Typically, each product division contains all the traditional functional departments such as finance, marketing, operations, human resource management, and so on. In multiproduct companies, the product headquarters for different products might not be located in the same place. For example, the headquarters for Honeywell's commercial and residential control systems is in Minnesota, while the headquarters for its commercial flight instruments is in Arizona.

EXHIBIT 10.6
Product Structure

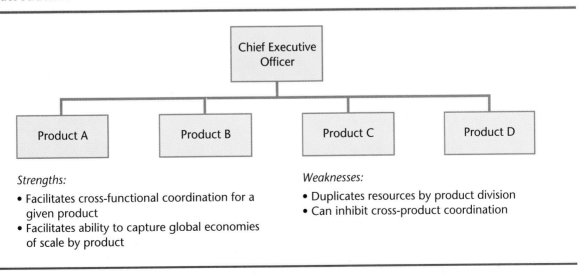

Strengths:
- Facilitates cross-functional coordination for a given product
- Facilitates ability to capture global economies of scale by product

Weaknesses:
- Duplicates resources by product division
- Can inhibit cross-product coordination

Multinational firms also use global product structures. This typically happens when customer needs for a given product are more or less the same the world over. After Becton Dickinson adopted a global product structure, the head of the bioscience/diagnostic business became responsible for global strategy formulation and implementation for those products.

Because all functions are placed within a product division, all departments are focused on the common product. This facilitates coordination among departments. Focus on the product also enhances knowledge about the product and how it should be adapted to maximize its potential in different markets. This, in turn, also identifies elements of the product that are more universal and can be standardized as well as those that are local and must be modified.

The major disadvantage of the product structure is that resources are duplicated. For example, both Product A and Product B have accounting, finance, operations, marketing, human resource, and sales personnel. In addition, structuring by product can inhibit coordination across product divisions, which can create delays or incompatibilities when a single customer purchases products from two or more product divisions.

Division Structure

The division structure can be viewed as an extension of a product structure (Exhibit 10.7). In a division structure, all functional activities are placed within a division, which is typically formed by grouping several related products together.

Like domestic firms, multinational firms can and do use this structure. In this case, each division is charged with worldwide responsibility. Because division structures are generally extensions of product structure, they have many of the same advantages and disadvantages.

One of the strengths of a division structure over a product structure is that duplication of resources can be reduced by having shared functions such as finance, accounting, and human resources for all products within the division. Thus, instead of having human resource managers for each of its drills, saws, and sanders product groups, Black and Decker has a common group of HR managers for its power tools

EXHIBIT 10.7

Division Structure

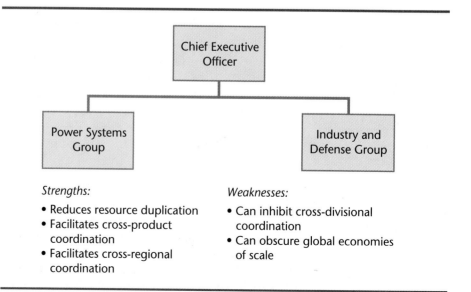

Strengths:
- Reduces resource duplication
- Facilitates cross-product coordination
- Facilitates cross-regional coordination

Weaknesses:
- Can inhibit cross-divisional coordination
- Can obscure global economies of scale

Daimler-Chrysler is organized into seven divisions that include passenger cars and light trucks, commercial vehicles, rail systems, aerospace, automotive electronics, diesel engines, and services. Although manufacturing in the passenger car and light truck division takes place in over 34 countries, operations for Chrysler, Jeep, Dodge, and Plymouth brands are handled under one roof in Auburn, Michigan.

division. Also, for customers who tend to purchase products within a related set, coordination across products is easier in a division versus product structure. This case of coordination can increase customer service and satisfaction. For example, General Electric groups all its medical products within the Medical Systems division. Customers such as hospitals tend to purchase a variety of products from GE, but most of their purchases are within the Medical Systems division.

Customer Structure

As the name implies, customer structures are organized around categories of customers (Exhibit 10.8). Typically, this structure is used when different categories of customers have separate but broad needs. For example, industrial customers might purchase a different set of products than retail customers.

The primary strength of this organizational form is that it facilitates in-depth understanding of specific customer segments. For example, even if wholesale customers in one country are somewhat different from those in another, the focus on wholesale customers can facilitate adaptations in design, manufacturing, advertising, and so on to meet that category of customer needs.

The primary disadvantage is the duplication of resources. Functions such as marketing, sales, and finance tend to be duplicated within each customer division of the company.

Matrix Structure

A matrix structure consists of two organization structures superimposed on each other (Exhibit 10.9). As a consequence, there are dual reporting relationships. That is, one person essentially reports to two bosses. These two structures can be a combination of the general forms already discussed. For example, the matrix structure might consist of product divisions intersecting with functional departments or geographical regions intersecting with product divisions. This is essentially the structure that Procter & Gamble had for many years. The two overlapping structures are based on the two dominant aspects of an organization's environment.

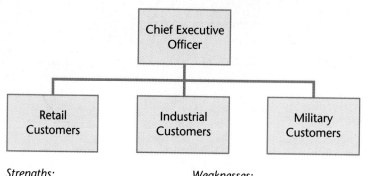

EXHIBIT 10.8
Customer Structure

Strengths:

- Facilitates coordination across functions and regions by customer
- Effective if customer classifications are significantly different

Weaknesses:

- Less effective if differentiation between customers diminishes
- Less effective if differences exist within a customer category across countries

EXHIBIT 10.9
Matrix Structure

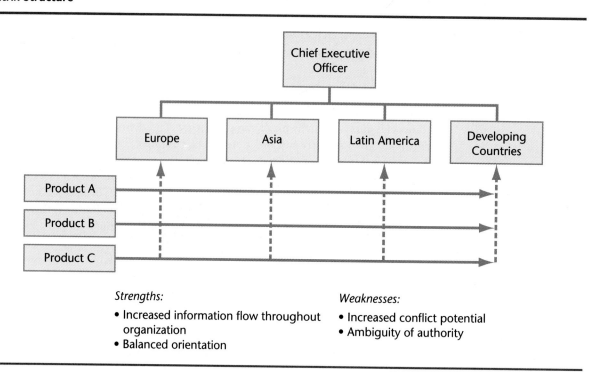

Strengths:

- Increased information flow throughout organization
- Balanced orientation

Weaknesses:

- Increased conflict potential
- Ambiguity of authority

One of the primary advantages of a matrix structure is that it can facilitate information flow throughout the organization. Before key decisions are made, the organization considers the two intersecting perspectives. This helps balance the orientation of the firm so that no single perspective dominates. For example,

MANAGERIAL CHALLENGE

IBM'S RESTRUCTURING

When John F. Akers took over as chairman of IBM in 1985, it appeared the computer giant would experience even more growth than it had in the past. But instead, market share began to slip. The company was relying on sales from its mainframe business, not reacting to the market that was moving toward increasingly powerful minicomputers and personal computers (PCs). Profits took a dive. The company's losses were attributed to heavy competition and IBM's rigid and hierarchical structure, which led to slowness in responding to market changes.

Akers attempted to remedy the problems in 1988 by reorganizing and decentralizing IBM so that decision making would occur closer to the front lines, enabling the company to respond faster. But this seemed to do little to fix the company's problems.

He attempted another reorganization in 1991. In this new structure, Akers divided IBM into 13 units that were to function autonomously for greater task and cognitive differentiation. Nine units were product based, such as personal computers, network systems, and storage devices. Four units covered geographic territories: Asia Pacific, Latin America, Europe/Middle East/Africa, and North America. The units were structured so that some competition between units was likely and interdependence was reduced. Each unit would pursue its own interests, without regard to its effects on other units. The belief was that the individual units would be able to respond to customer needs better and faster because of their smaller size.

Unfortunately, this second restructuring did not stop the downward slide of IBM's profits or stock price. By the end of 1992, IBM reported a loss of nearly $5 billion (one of the largest losses ever reported in the United States) and by January of 1993, its stock had tumbled from highs in the $170s to lows in the $40s. IBM's board of directors then did some internal restructuring, and Akers retired.

With Akers's departure came a new CEO, Louis V. Gerstner Jr. Gerstner quickly scrapped the structure of 13 separate businesses. Instead, he formed a 10-member executive panel of operating chiefs to devise ways that different IBM groups could work together. Gerstner believed that IBM's products had natural interdependence, because a given customer might purchase an entire range of hardware and software products, and he believed that less differentia-

tion was needed, not more. To foster greater integration, he changed the compensation system so that executive pay depended on how the company as a whole performed rather than on how each individual's unit performed.

A major part of the new organization structure was organized around customers. Gerstner established what were termed "industry solution units (ISUs)," or units that would specialize in satisfying the needs for specific industry customers, such as banking, insurance, and chemicals. The belief was that customers in the finance industry were different from those in the chemical industry. Technologies, such as IBM's new Power PC microprocessor chip developed with Apple and Motorola, would then be utilized by the different ISUs in their attempts to find solutions for specific customers.

The new structure required IBM employees to be able to do three specific things better than competitors:

- Understand specific industry and customer needs better than all others.
- Develop technologies and products superior to competitors such as Compaq, Apple, or Hewlett-Packard.
- Understand and leverage those technologies and products across industries and customers.

The new structure simultaneously required some differentiation between the industry customers and integration between product development and ISUs. It also required extensive integration of ISUs on a global basis (e.g., sharing knowledge within the banking industry the world over) and some differentiation by country (e.g., a solution for the Bank of Tokyo may not be 100 percent applicable for Citibank New York). IBM's new structure is a mix of customer, product, and geography. Although IBM's new structure is hard to understand, shareholders like it because they have seen the value of their IBM stock go up more than fourfold over the last few years since the reorganization.

Sources: Stratford Sherman, "Is He Too Cautious to Save IBM?" *Fortune*, October 3, 1994, p. 78; Catherine Arnst, John W. Verity, and Kathy Rebello, "An Exclusive Account of Lou Gerstner's First Six Months," *Business Week*, October 4, 1993, p. 87; "What Went Wrong at IBM," *The Economist*, January 6, 1993, p. 23; Sergio G. Non, "IBM Scrapes by Analyst Estimates for Second Quarter," *TechWeb*, July 20, 1998; Eric Avechard, "IBM's Unix Move Challenges Microsoft," *Wired News*, October 27, 1998.

in Boeing a matrix of functional areas, such as engineering, intersect with project groups, such as the Boeing 777. This matrix brings together the project perspective of the project manager and the technical perspective of the engineering manager.

The major disadvantage of a matrix structure is the conflicts that can arise. If effective conflict resolution is not used, increased conflict can inhibit the organization's ability to respond to changing conditions quickly. Further, this structure also means that many employees have two bosses. They may receive conflicting information or directions. In addition, employees may be forced to choose sides when managers' objectives conflict, and this may hurt the achievement of the organization's goals.

Mixed Organizational Structures

As we mentioned earlier, although there are pure forms, any combination of the basic organizational structures is possible. The typical objective of mixed or hybrid organizational structures is to gain the advantages of one structure and reduce its disadvantages by incorporating the strengths of different structures. IBM's recent restructurings illustrate how it has tried to integrate its strategy, the changing environment, and optimal organizational structure in particular by incorporating a mixed structure design (see the Managerial Challenge box).

DESIGNING ORGANIZATIONS

Now that we have covered the key organizing principles and basic structures, how do we decide how to actually structure an organization? Crucial determinants of appropriate organizational design are the internal and external environments of the organization and the extent to which those environments are simple or complex and static or dynamic. In this section, we explore these considerations and develop a heuristic, or rule of thumb, that can be used in selecting specific organizational structures and design.

As we mentioned earlier, a key factor in determining the match between the environment and organizational structure is environmental uncertainty.[8] Environmental uncertainty is the extent to which the environment is simple or complex and static or dynamic.

Environmental Complexity

Simple environments exist when relatively few internal and external variables need to be incorporated into decision making and these variables are similar. For example, a Bic Pen is made up of approximately seven parts. Each part is produced with relatively low technology, and the assembly of the parts into the final product also involves relatively low technology. At the other end of the continuum, complex environments exist when a great number and dissimilar variables can affect decision making. When Boeing puts together a 747 Jumbo jet, it must assemble over six million parts that range from a simple metal bolt to a panel composed of rare composite materials. Although McDonald's serves hamburgers to millions of customers, the ingredients and technology involved in this service are relatively simple compared with the design and construction of a Boeing 747.

Internal Environment Complexity   In assessing the simplicity or complexity of an organization's internal environment, you can focus on three general factors. The first is the *organization's personnel*. Employees' educational level, technological sophistication, and managerial competence affect complexity. The greater the number of people, the levels of education, and the managerial competencies required, and the greater the dissimilarity among employees, the more complex the organization's internal environment. The second category is the *organization's functional and staff units*, including interdependence among units and technological characteristics. The greater the number of units and the greater their interdependence, technological requirements, and organizational products and services, the greater the complexity. Finally, the *nature of the organization's product or service* and its related goals play a critical role in the internal environment. The greater the number of products and services the firm provides and the greater the number of components within those products or services, the greater the complexity of the organization's internal environment.

External Environment Complexity   A number of factors contribute to the complexity of a firm's external environment. The first category is the *geographic scope of the environment*. The greater the geographic scope, the greater the complexity. This is principally because of the increased probability of differences. For example, the greater the number of countries in which multinational firms operate, the greater the probability of dissimilarities between the countries (their governments, laws, customer preferences, language, etc.). The second category is the *diversity of customers*. The greater the diversity of customers within segments and differences across segments, the greater the complexity. The third category is the *diversity of competitors*. The greater the diversity of competitors in the total number and differences across competitors, the greater the complexity.

Environmental Dynamism

The second element to evaluate the overall uncertainty of the environment is the extent to which the environment is static or dynamic. Static environments may have few or many factors, but these factors tend to remain stable over time. For example, the manufacturing technology for pens has changed little in the last 30 years. In contrast, factors in dynamic environments change rapidly. The fashion industry operates in a relatively dynamic external environment. Benetton faces an environment in which colors, fabric, and styles change not just year to year but season to season. Because the technology in the computer chips industry changes so rapidly, firms such as Intel also face a dynamic environment.

Firms facing dynamic environments often describe them as "white water" environments in reference to the challenges of navigating a raft down the ever-changing rapids of a river. The rapidly changing external environment typically requires quick internal organization changes. However, as we will discuss in Chapter 19, organizational change is not easy. To cope, some organizations essentially contract out part of their organizational structure. For example, Nike has essentially a functional structure, but it contracts out its manufacturing. This enables it to move its manufacturing much more quickly in response to changing environmental conditions than if manufacturing were an internal part of Nike's structure (see the Managerial Challenge box). The popular term for organizations that contract out some or even many of the components of its traditional organization structure is **network organization**.

network organizations
organizations that contract out activities to maintain maximum flexibility in adjusting to the changing environment

MANAGERIAL CHALLENGE

NIKE'S NETWORK STRUCTURE

It is almost impossible to watch TV or read a magazine without being confronted by an ad about the latest, greatest, most snazzy sneakers for basketball, tennis, baseball, aerobics, running, or cross training. Nike has been at the forefront of the athletic shoe industry for many years. However, the industry is characterized by shifts in both technology and style. Black sneakers are in, then they are out, then they are back in again, and then they are "zebra" sneakers (flashy shoes incorporating bold black and white combinations). Nike has over 1,000 models of shoes and introduces over 100 new models each year!

Although Nike has succeeded in turning sneakers into both functional footwear and fashion statement, the fact remains that shoes wear out. As a consequence, even though technology and marketing have pushed the price of Nike's high-end shoes to $200 a pair, there is a limit to what people will pay for shoes that they either grow out of or wear out. Thus, Nike must keep its costs down if it is to remain profitable and competitive.

So how does Nike organize itself to produce 90 million shoes a year and lead the industry in sales and profits in response to these environmental forces?

First, at Nike's headquarters in Beaverton, Oregon, Nike has essentially a functional structure with departments for research and development, product design, and marketing. Although the functional departments are separate, there is a high degree of interdependence. For example, product designers and marketers must work together to come up with next year's new models and to incorporate technical innovations from research and development. Once the blueprints for the new models are ready, they are sent to manufacturing. However, Nike has a very small manufacturing department. How is this possible when it makes 90 million shoes a year? Nike subcontracts nearly all its manufacturing. Nike's emphasis on low-cost manufacturing and speed to

market means it needs to organize itself to minimize its costs and maximize its flexibility.

Over 99 percent of Nike shoes are manufactured in Asia. Nike contracts with approximately 40 factories. As an illustration of the flexibility this provides, consider that over a five-year period, it terminated contracts with 20 factories and initiated contracts with 35 others. When labor costs rose in Korea, it quickly moved production. When factories in the Philippines and Malaysia could not meet required standards, Nike increased the number of shoes coming out of China from a few thousand to nearly 10 percent of its worldwide capacity. Now that there is no longer a U.S. embargo on Vietnam, Nike is analyzing and moving on some of its options there. To ensure this type of flexibility, Nike owns virtually no manufacturing assets.

Instead, Nike uses technology to link its designers and marketers with these far-flung manufacturing operations. Once a blueprint for a new model is complete, it is relayed by satellite to the manufacturer's computer-aided design/computer-aided manufacturing (CAD/CAM) system. Prototypes are produced by the contractors and then shipped via Federal Express back to headquarters. This creates the ability to conceive, design, and prototype new models in two weeks or less.

Once the prototypes are approved and manufacturing can reach Nike's standard of quality, mass production runs begin and the marketing and sales departments get the shoes into the retail distribution channel, such as Footlocker.

Nike's environment and strategy have led to an organizational structure that facilitates low-cost production, quality, and speed by networking manufacturing rather than including it in the formal organization.

Sources: Mark Clifford, "Spring in Their Step," *Far Eastern Economic Review*, November 5, 1992, pp. 56–59; Nike annual report, 1997.

By combining the dimensions of simple–complex and static–dynamic, we can create a four-cell matrix that provides a broad backdrop against which organizational design structures can be placed (see Exhibit 10.10). In general, the more complex and dynamic the environment, the more the organizational structure needs to coordinate different groups' efforts and the greater the speed with which this coordination needs to take place. While Nike's environment may not be as complex as Boeing's, it is perhaps more dynamic. For example, the product cycle times (the time from design to market entry) is measured in weeks for Nike, while it is measured in years for Boeing.

Sheila Silver Library
Self Issue 1
Leeds Beckett University

Customer name: Tannor, William
Asamoah (Mr)
Customer ID: C71901169

Title: Management : meeting new challenges
ID: 1703679290
Due: 25/4/2018,23:59

Total items: 1
18/04/2018 15:16
Checked out: 3
Overdue: 0
Hold requests: 0
Ready for pickup: 0

ITEMS ARE NOW RENEWED AUTOMATICALLY,
EXCEPT SHORT LOANS, HOLDS AND INTER-
LIBRARY LOANS

Need help? Why not Chat with Us 24/7?
See the Need Help? page on the library
website: library.leedsbeckett.ac.uk

EXHIBIT 10.10
Matrix of Organizational
Uncertainty

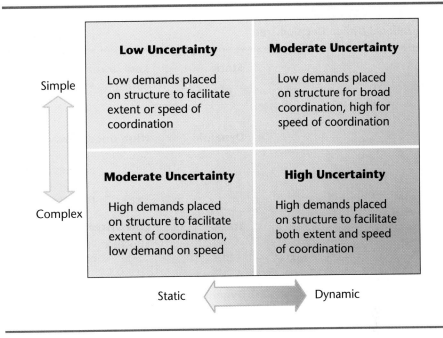

Making Organizational Design Decisions

Now that environmental considerations have been presented, we outline a heuristic that managers can use in making decisions about effective organizational design.[9] This heuristic, like all heuristics, is a simplified set of decision rules (see Exhibit 10.11). Rather than rigidly applying a formula, Exhibit 10.11 shows a general set of principles that help point you as a manager to a general solution. Given all the environmental demands that one firm might face, it is difficult to spell out every level and every department structure. The heuristic instead provides a framework that can guide you through general questions to determine the most appropriate organizational structure.

The first question you must address is the extent to which the environment is simple or complex. A note of caution: Few managers believe their environments are simple. But they need to look outside their industry to the range of possibilities and consider questions such as these:

* How much technology do we use? Often looking at the percentage of research and development expenditures versus sales can provide a guide. Low-technology-intensity firms typically find research and development expenditures to be less than 3 percent of sales. High-technology-intensive firms can spend 10 percent or more.
* How many products do we produce and what are their complexities? A commercial airplane contains 6 million parts; an office chair typically 132. Where does your firm fit?
* How many markets are we in and how different are they? Operations confined to North America and even Europe are less complex than a firm such as Philips, which operates in 60 countries spread throughout the world.

If your organization's environment is relatively simple, then you want to match the level of stability to see what structure would be most appropriate.

EXHIBIT 10.11
Organizational Design Decision Tree

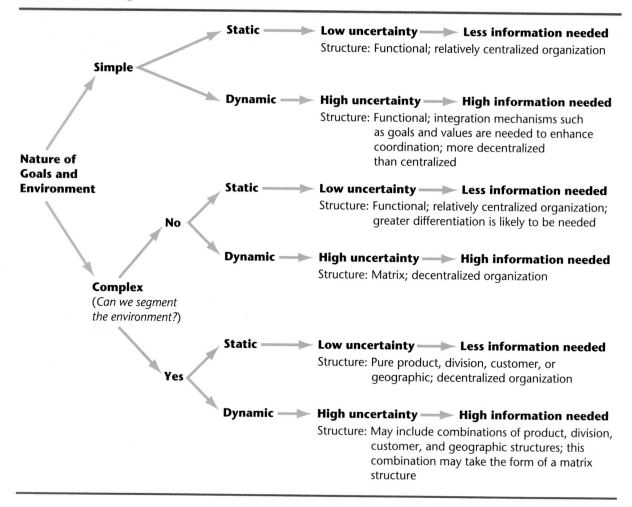

Simple Environments with Varying Stability   Few managers would categorize their environment as static. After all, nothing remains the same forever. The key is to determine the relative level of environmental stability or dynamism. You could examine the length of your product's life cycle or the half-life of technology as means of assessing the dynamism of the environment. For example, the processing capacity of computer chips has doubled nearly every four years for the last several years. That rate of change is dramatic when compared with how long it has taken writing tools to go from dipping a quill in ink to using ballpoint pens.

Simple and Static Environments.   To the extent that the environment is relatively simple and stable, the level of uncertainty is relatively low. Low uncertainty reduces the need for quick and widespread information flows within the firm. This reduces the general need for high levels of integration. Most decisions can be handled through a functional structure without significant decentralization. Integration in this context can largely be accomplished with rules.

Simple and Dynamic Environments.   If the environment is simple and dynamic, then uncertainty and the need for information increase. This context places a greater emphasis on integration. While the functional structure is still appropriate, mechanisms such as goals and values are needed more in this environment.

Complex Environments with Varying Stability   Environments that are judged to be complex require an additional assessment before evaluating their stability or dynamism. Once an environment has been judged complex, it is necessary to determine whether the source of the complexity can be traced to clear categories such as geographic region, market, customer, or product segments. Once a determination about the segmentability of the environment has been made, the next step is to assess the stability or dynamism of the environment.

Complex, Nonsegmentable, Static Environments.   Firms facing complex, nonsegmentable, and relatively stable environments have low uncertainty and low information needs. Consequently, the functional structure is appropriate. Although firms in this environment may have many products in a number of markets, the similarity of markets or products renders the structural separation between functional departments relatively unimportant. Formal rules and goals can effectively coordinate organizational activities. Centralization is somewhat lower in complex and static environments than in simple and static environments.

Complex, Nonsegmentable, Dynamic Environments.   The more complex and dynamic environment emphasizes integration over differentiation. Furthermore, the complexity and dynamism make it unlikely that most decisions can be made centrally or implemented effectively without integration systems. A matrix structure may be appropriate in this context. The areas that are represented in the matrix are determined by the particular demands of the environment. As we mentioned, at Boeing, functions such as engineering intersect in the matrix with projects, such as the new 777.

Complex, Segmentable, Static Environments.   Environments that are complex, segmentable, and static have moderate levels of uncertainty; therefore, firms have moderate information needs. Product or division structures, geographic/regional structures, and customer structures are all appropriate in this context. The choice depends on the dominant variable along which the environment can be segmented. The environment might be segmented primarily by region. For example, Club Med found that its European customers and its American customers differed in terms of how much they were willing to pay for vacations, what type of facilities they wanted, and how they purchased vacation packages (e.g., directly or through independent travel agencies). Furthermore, they found only a small amount (less than 30 percent) were "crossover" customers, i.e., Europeans traveling to American resorts or Americans traveling to European resorts. These differences pushed Club Med in the direction of a regional structure. However, even though the environment can be segmented, its complexity means that it is impossible for senior executives to have all the information necessary to make effective centralized decisions. Consequently, even within a product, divisional, regional, or customer structure, decentralization is more appropriate than centralization. As an example of this type of decentralized decision making, even though the headquarters for N.V. Philips is located in Europe, its first color TV set was built and sold in Canada, its first stereo color TV was developed in Australia, and its programmed word processing typewriter was developed in the United States.

Complex, Segmentable, Dynamic Environments.   Environments that are complex, segmentable, and dynamic generate high levels of uncertainty; therefore, firms have high information needs. Once again, product, division, regional, and customer structures are all appropriate. The choice is a function of the dominant variable along which the environment can be segmented. However, the complexity and dynamism of the environment mean that a variety of managers throughout the organization need to gather and share information. Consequently, centralization is not appropriate. The complexity and dynamism of the environment require a heavy emphasis on integration. Values are the most appropriate integration mechanism in this context.

To the extent that two particular aspects of the environment dominate, a matrix organizational structure may be appropriate. However, as previously discussed, matrix organizations are inherently difficult to manage and require conflict resolution skills, interpersonal competencies, and power and influence abilities significantly greater than those required in alternative organizational structures. Consequently, the matrix structure should be selected after a careful assessment of both the fit between the structure and the environment and the ability of the organization's members to meet these higher demands and skill levels. If organizational members do not have the requisite skills and abilities, specific steps must be taken to train managers before a matrix structure can be implemented successfully.

Moving from Domestic to International Structures

Up to this point, we have mentioned the basic organization structures in terms of both a domestic and international context. Now we want to take a more focused look at organization structure in an international context. Very few firms begin as international organizations. Most start in one country and for a period of time focus on the customers within that country. Although international organizations would be easier to understand if they evolved steadily and systematically, they do not do so.[10] At best, it seems that the development of international organizations can be divided into two basic states: initial international structures and advanced international structures. Although most international organizations do not jump directly into advanced international structure, there is little evidence for a set sequence among the advanced global structures. Rather, the advanced global structures are determined more by the nature of the organization's business and the environment in which it operates.

Domestic Organization with Export Department   As firms venture out from their domestic market to foreign ones, they usually begin with a limited number of products. Typically, the products to be sold in foreign markets are designed and produced in the domestic market. Consequently, the primary international task is exporting the products to foreign markets. At this stage, most firms simply add an export department to their existing structure to handle the specialized tasks, such as international shipping and customs regulations.

Domestic Organization with International Division   Once the volume of exports exceeds the capabilities of a few specialists, firms commonly establish an international division. International divisions typically are responsible for all functional activities relative to international markets. The international division often has its own small department for accounting, finance, marketing, and sales. However, production activities are not usually part of the international division. Products are produced within the normal domestic organizational structure and then modified or simply turned over as is to the international division. Consequently,

U.S. pharmaceutical companies can sell products through their international divisions in Europe and Canada.

the products that tend to be pushed into the international division are those that have broad appeal and for which there are relatively fewer customer differences across countries.

Adding an international division has a number of advantages. First, it is an efficient means of dealing with the international market when a firm has limited experience. The focus on international activities and issues within the division can foster a strong professional identity and career path among its members. It also allows for specialization and training in international activities, which can be valuable later when the firm moves more heavily into the international marketplace and needs individuals with global capabilities. The focus on international markets, competitors, and environments can also facilitate the development of a more effective global strategy. Further, because the top officer of the international division often reports to the CEO (or similar senior executive), international issues often receive high-level corporate consideration and support with this structure.

One major weakness of an international division is its dependence on other divisions for products and support. Because domestic sales of a particular product often make up the largest percentage of the product's overall sales, low priority may be given to international sales. Other parts of the firm that supply products and services to the international division may be unwilling to make modifications that cost them time and money even if the changes would facilitate greater international sales.

Advanced Global Structures   As international sales as a percentage of overall sales increase and as the organization expands into a larger number of countries, it becomes increasingly difficult to maximize the benefits of an international division and minimize the weaknesses. When the organization outgrows its initial international structure, it can choose from among six advanced global structures. As mentioned, there is no particular sequence from one structure to another. These six advanced global structures correspond to the basic functional, geographic/regional, product, division, customer, and matrix structures already discussed, except they have global rather than domestic scope and reach.

Organizing to Think Globally and Act Locally

globalization

the integration of activities on a coordinated, worldwide basis

Given the increasingly international environment in which organizations compete, it is important to examine one other factor that managers must consider when designing organizational structures—globalization or localization demands of the international environment. **Globalization** is the tendency to integrate activities on a coordinated, worldwide basis. Firms are pushed in the direction of globalization when benefits gained from worldwide volume, efficiencies, or economies of scale are significant. These benefits could include economies of scale for production, greater leverage of high-cost distribution networks, and greater leverage of expensive research and development activities. In a variety of industries, the minimally efficient production scale is beyond what could be supported in a single market. If we return to our example of Boeing, the break-even point for a new commercial aircraft is approximately 300 planes, with each plane costing in excess of $100 million. This requires total sales of $30 billion. In order to get an acceptable return on its investment, Boeing has no choice but to try to develop planes that will have global appeal because the U.S. market alone is not big enough. The high level of research and development and scale economies such as these push toward globalization and to centralization of activities such as product development and manufacturing.

localization

the separation of activities on a country-by-country basis due to local differences

By contrast, differences among countries and customer preferences are two key factors that push toward localization. **Localization** is the tendency to differentiate activities country by country. Firms are pushed in the direction of localization when benefits from location-specific differentiation and adaptation are significant and factors such as economies of scale are small. Procter & Gamble recently faced the pressures of localization for a laundry detergent it developed. Although P&G wanted to develop one detergent, Visor, for all of Europe and capture the efficiencies of a single development, manufacturing, and marketing effort, they found significant differences between countries there. These differences pushed P&G from globalization toward localization. For example, it found that Germans prefer front-loading washers, while French prefer top-loading washers. This created a problem. The detergent did not get distributed as well among the clothes when poured into a front-loading washing machine. As P&G discovered, it is not easy to get an entire nation to change from front-loading washing machines to top-loading ones. As this example points out, the greater the differences between countries and the more significant these differences are for a product or service, the greater the need for localization.

Forces can simultaneously push toward both globalization and localization, requiring firms to be globally integrated and locally responsive.[11] In the case of P&G, the manufacturing process pushed for integration because making detergent is basically continuous; that is, like many chemical products, the final product is delivered after a long process of mixing various chemicals in different states and at different temperatures until you get the desired chemical reactions for the final product. This means that the process cannot be stopped at discrete points and finished elsewhere, nor is it economical to alter the process to create different detergents. Both these factors push toward globalization, or the concentration of manufacturing activities without much modification for local market conditions. On the other hand, the significant differences in laundry machines between Germany and France pushed toward localization.

In the case of P&G, it solved the problem by developing a plastic ball into which detergent could be poured and that then could be thrown in with the clothes in a front-loading machine. The plastic ball was designed to dispense the detergent gradually though small holes as the ball bounced around in the clothes while they were being washed.

In general, firms heavily involved in international business face strong pressures for both integration and differentiation. They need specialists for marketing to Germans, dealing with French government officials, and complying with U.S. accounting rules. However, they also face greater needs for integration. These increased information needs can be met in a variety of ways.[12]

Direct Contact   Often, direct contact is an important means of integration by sharing information. One of the largest firms in the world, Matsushita, has an interesting way of accomplishing this. Because research and development is vitally important in the consumer electronics industry, Matsushita has a large central research and development lab. To make sure that managers know what is going on in the lab and to ensure that lab scientists know what the market's emerging needs are, Matsushita holds an annual, internal trade show. Senior managers throughout Matsushita's worldwide operations gather and examine research results and potential new products. Managers also feed back information about market differences, customer preferences, and competitor positioning to research and development scientists. The result is a massive sharing of information that has helped keep Matsushita ahead of competitors.

Liaison   Liaison roles are designed to enhance the link, and therefore information flows, between two or more groups, be they teams, departments, divisions, or subsidiaries. Part of Matsushita's success in the videocassette recorder (VCR) market is due to its purposeful use of liaison. The vice president in charge of Matsushita's U.S. subsidiary was also a member of the senior management committee of the parent company in Japan and spent about a third of his time in Japan. This facilitated the link between headquarters and the United States, which was the most important consumer market for VCRs. In addition, the general manager of the U.S. subsidiary's video department had previously worked for 14 years in the video product division of the production and domestic marketing organization in Japan. This created a strong link between the product division in Japan and the U.S. subsidiary. Also, the assistant product manager in the U.S. subsidiary had spent five years in the central VCR manufacturing plant in Japan. Through these three individuals, Matsushita succeeded in ensuring that vital links at the corporate, product, and factory levels were established between Japan and the United States.

Teams   When integration needs arise across a wide set of functional areas, teams can be an effective integration mechanism. Philips is an example of a firm that utilizes teams as an integrative mechanism. This may stem from the fact that the firm was founded by two brothers, one an engineer and the other a salesman, who worked together in charting Philips's early strategic course. Whatever the origin,

Philips has long had an office of the president, as opposed to a single CEO. The office of the president is composed of a technical, commercial, and financial executive. Furthermore, for each product, there is a team of junior managers from commercial and technical functions. These teams integrate various perspectives and information around a single product to ensure that interfunctional differences are resolved early and that necessary design, manufacturing, and marketing issues are integrated from the outset in an effort to increase the success of the product.

SIGNS OF POOR STRUCTURE–ENVIRONMENT FIT

Even if the organization's structure matches the environment at one point in time, it may not be appropriate forever. Environments change and so should organizational structures. Inappropriate organizational structures block needed information sharing, focus attention away from information that needs to be gathered, and, consequently, hurt decision quality, organizational prosperity, and perhaps even survival. With the wrong structure, managers increasingly make bad decisions, in part because they lack needed information. In the absence of timely, relevant information, effective decisions concerning what products to produce, what quality standards to set, or how to reduce costs, how to advertise, or how to position products against competitors decline.

Since inappropriate organizational design and structures can severely inhibit organizational effectiveness, what are some of the key warning signs that a mismatch exists?[13]

One of the first warning signs is decision makers' inability to anticipate problems. If problems caused by competitors, governments, customers, suppliers, and so on consistently arise without advance notice, this is a warning sign that the organizational structure is inhibiting environmental scanning, data gathering, or information dissemination. If the organization is not designed or structured to correct this problem, decision makers will have to react to rather than anticipate the environment and will be placed at a competitive disadvantage to other organizations.

Another key warning sign is an increase in conflict that prevents effective implementation. This sign, in particular, can indicate that the limits of a functional structure are being stretched and that information exchange mechanisms, such as cross-functional teams, liaisons, or other lateral relations, are needed.

There may also be signs at the individual level. When the number of individuals who do not know what is expected of them or who receive conflicting expectations increases, this is an early warning sign that the organizational structure is not appropriate for the environment.

CONCLUDING COMMENTS

Organizational structures can be thought of as information networks or circuits on a circuit board.[14] The structure influences who talks to whom about what and how often, what information moves through the organization and at what speed. As business and society move from the industrial age to the information age, appropriate organizational structures will be increasingly critical to a firm's success in the marketplace. Likewise, your understanding of and skills at designing effective structures become increasingly critical to your career success. You must be able to quickly and accurately analyze the complexity and dynamism of the internal and external environment.

As cases such as Nike illustrate, the structure has to fit the environment and the organization's objectives. Nike's emphasis on being the innovation leader placed a premium on speed. Its emphasis on low-cost production placed a premium on flexibility. These two combined to suggest that manufacturing should be done outside the formal organization.

In addition, to have a successful managerial career, you need to understand the sometimes-opposing forces of globalization and localization. Successful organizational structures may require you to find solutions that meet both needs simultaneously or to organize various functional activities at different points along the continuum from centralized global activities to decentralized local activities.

In general, designing organizational structure can be one of the more complex activities of management. Its critical role in organizational competitiveness virtually guarantees that managers who understand and are skilled at organizational design will be those who are increasingly given more responsible positions.

KEY TERMS

centralized organizations 270
chain of command 268
cognitive differentiation 266
decentralized organizations 270
differentiation 265
flat organization structure 268
globalization 286
horizontal differentiation 266

integration 266
interdependence 266
lines of authority 268
localization 286
network organizations 279
organizational charts 265
organizational design 265
organizational structure 265

profit centers 273
span of control 268
tall organization structure 268
task differentiation 266
unity of command 268
vertical differentiation 266

REVIEW QUESTIONS

1. Define organizational structure. How does it differ from organizational design?
2. What is the main purpose of organizational charts?
3. What is *task differentiation*, and what is its role in organizational design?
4. Why is cognitive differentiation important in organizational design?
5. What are the key differences between horizontal and vertical differentiation?
6. What are the three major types of interdependence among organizational units?
7. As the level of uncertainty and interdependence increases, how does the usefulness of rules, goals, and values change?
8. How might cultural values influence the degree of formalization in organizational structures?
9. What are the key pros and cons for both centralization and decentralization in organizational structure?
10. Describe the six major organizational structures.
11. How does moving from a purely domestic to an international organization affect organizational structure?
12. What are the critical elements of an organization's internal and external environments that a manager should assess in considering a new organizational structure?

13. What are the four basic elements that influence the uncertainty of an organization's external environment?
14. What role does information play in the context of organizational uncertainty?
15. What is the principal role of direct contact, liaisons, and teams in organizational design?

DISCUSSION QUESTIONS

1. Universities are typically organized by departments or colleges such as business, biology, engineering, political science, and so on. Is this an appropriate structure? What aspects of the environment support this structure? Are there aspects of the internal or external environment that currently or in the near future push in the direction of alternative structures?
2. Organizational design skills are critical to career success, but total organizational design or redesign typically is not put in the hands of newly hired managers. What, then, can you do early in your career to enhance your knowledge and skills besides creating a new structure for an entire organization?
3. What are the organizational structure implications for a firm that is focused primarily on its domestic market but faces foreign competitors in the domestic market and "domestic" competitors who have international operations?

CLOSING CASE

Decentralization at Johnson & Johnson

The structure of Johnson & Johnson, the $16 billion health care giant, is analogous to an octopus. Its giant tentacles, representing 168 separate operating units, spread out over 50 countries around the world. Decentralization has been the hallmark of Johnson & Johnson's organizational structure from the beginning.

Why such decentralization? Some claim that this structure allows the company to deliver more effectively on its "credo"—the code of ethics by which all employees operate. While most companies live by simple mission statements, Johnson & Johnson established a long list of responsibilities to its customers, suppliers, employees, the community, the environment, and its shareholders—in that order. The credo is taken seriously at the company and has been responsible for the steady sales climb over the past several decades.

Johnson & Johnson's decentralization begins with splitting its $16 billion in sales equally among three business segments: consumer products, pharmaceuticals, and professional products. Within each segment are the "group" companies, 33 total, each responsible for a handful of

products worldwide. The 33 group companies are further divided into 168 operating units located around the world.

The mammoth consumer products segment markets some of the industry's most famous brands. First, Johnson & Johnson Consumer Products sells $1.2 billion of Johnson's baby products, Band-Aid Adhesive Bandages, and toothbrushes. McNeil Consumer, another group within the consumer products segment, makes $1.5 billion of Tylenol and other over-the-counter (OTC) drugs. A third group, Personal Products Company, sells $1 billion of Stayfree, Carefree, O.B., and other sanitary protection products.

The pharmaceutical segment includes some 80 prescription drugs, such as Ortho-Novum contraceptive pills and Retin-A acne cream. Because of the company's association with baby products, the Johnson & Johnson brand name is not used on pharmaceutical products.

The professional segment includes companies such as Ethicon, the maker of surgical suture and needles; J&J Orthopaedics, which makes artificial hip and knee joints; Ortho Diagnostic, which makes blood-testing equipment

Johnson & Johnson Simplified Organizational Chart

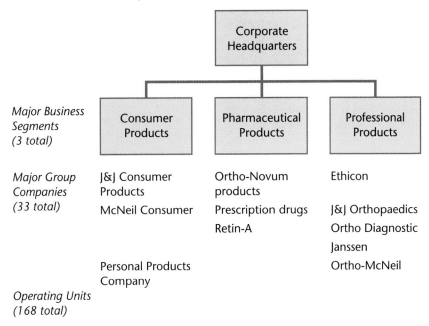

for hospitals; Janssen, which makes antifungal and cancer medicines; and Ortho-McNeil, the professional side of McNeil Consumer, which makes birth-control pills.

The decentralized structure has given the company several competitive advantages. Perhaps the most appealing advantage is the sense of ownership and control that each of the 168 operating units enjoys. Each unit is allowed almost complete autonomy, encouraging an entrepreneurial spirit that is rarely found at large companies. Thus, the units are actually small bureaucracy-busting firms that practice marketing warfare. Decision making and implementation are accomplished at lightning speed.

Another advantage of the decentralized structure is that each operating unit has become a niche player in the business in which it competes. Rather than compete head to head with its giant rivals, such as Merck or Bristol-Myers, Johnson & Johnson companies circumvent the competition and go after specialized markets in many of its businesses. For example, when health care providers began to cut their costs a few years ago, they focused first on the most expensive drugs, such as Merck's hypertension drugs or SmithKline's ulcer medicines, often forcing competitive drugs into a price-bidding war. Since J&J's sales were much smaller in each product segment compared with much of its competition, the company escaped the scrutiny of the health care industry's cost-cutting measures.

For all the success that decentralization brought the company, a downside exists for the future. The fragmentation of businesses has created something just short of chaos, one that even J&J's CEO sometimes finds difficult to organize. Though J&J's family of operating units make efforts

to communicate with each other, each tends to be myopic—that is, focuses on its own business. And while decentralization allows companies to bring products to market quickly, it prevents them from sweeping across international markets. Entering international markets, after all, requires coordination among the different operating units.

Perhaps the most obvious disadvantage is the deliberate duplication of effort and cost among all the companies. Especially costly are the overhead associated with each operating unit and the cost of managing several separate sales forces. Retail accounts, bombarded by scores of salespeople representing different J&J companies, finally forced the company to consolidate its selling efforts. Large customers, such as Wal-Mart, Kmart, and big health care providers, are now served by a team of J&J salespeople. Wal-Mart even has a J&J team devoted entirely to its needs that is stationed in the Bentonville, Arkansas, headquarters.

The cost of duplication becomes more evident when Johnson & Johnson enters international markets. For instance, the separate pharmaceutical and consumer products segments may enter a new market, such as China, at the same time. To avoid making the same mistakes, they must act like a more centralized company and communicate with each other closely to curtail the excessive costs and inefficiency of duplication.

Though the company has tried to consolidate much of its operations, the consolidations may not be enough. As the health care business continues to globalize, more centralized competitors like Merck and Bristol-Myers can storm through many international markets at once with their product launches. A decentralized company such as

Johnson & Johnson must launch independently in each of the markets where it is represented, allowing the operating units full control. Like many companies in other industries, J&J faces the inevitable decision about the amount of centralization it needs for the future. A centralized management structure would allow Johnson & Johnson to better coordinate its global growth. It would also cut costs and help the company become more price competitive in an era of health care reform. However, centralization could destroy the entrepreneurial spirit that has always symbolized J&J's success.

QUESTIONS

1. What are some of the advantages that Johnson & Johnson enjoys as a highly decentralized company? What are the disadvantages?

2. How does this decentralized structure meet the organization's goals?

3. Is Johnson & Johnson's structure based on a globalized or localized approach? What evidence supports your conclusion?

4. If you were the management at Johnson & Johnson, how would you reorganize the company to meet future challenges?

Sources: Brian O'Reilly, "J&J Is on a Roll," *Fortune,* December 26, 1994, pp. 178–85; Allan J. Magrath, "Going to Extremes—Not!" *Sales & Marketing Management,* February 1993, pp. 32–34; "Dusting the Opposition," *The Economist,* April 29, 1995, pp. 71–72; Johnson & Johnson annual report, 1997.

GROUPS AND TEAMS

After studying this chapter you should be able to:

- Describe the similarities and differences between groups and teams.
- Identify and compare different types of groups.
- Name the factors that influence group formation and development.
- Analyze the various structural characteristics of groups.
- Describe the role and effects of norms in groups.
- Distinguish between the two major types of group conflict, and explain why one type can be relatively beneficial for groups.
- Explain how managers can affect the performance of their groups and teams.

Navy SEALS: Elite Team

Sometimes, corporations or other organizations that aspire to high performance look outside their own realm to understand the fundamental nature of teams. For example, they observe how the Chicago Bulls execute a fast break; they read how emergency-trauma teams act collectively to handle an urgent crisis; they listen to the harmonious blending of instruments in world-class quartets. All these and similar groups usually have one thing in common: Though the individuals who make up these teams are outstanding in their own right, they keep their self-interest in check as they perform a single, unifying act.

One of the most elite teams on earth is the U.S. Navy SEALS, the "sea, air, and land" arm of the U.S. Navy. With only 500 officers and 1,800 enlisted personnel, the SEALs weed out recruits early in the program to ensure that they have the best and the toughest commandos in the world. SEAL recruits endure several weeks of one of the most rigorous initial training programs anywhere, climaxing with "Hell Week" at the end of the fifth week. During Hell Week, recruits run miles in heavy boots in the sand, swim miles in the freezing Pacific Ocean, and sprint through obstacle courses again and again. They do calisthenics using heavy logs, as instructors insult them. They paddle for hours in rubber boats while wearing their SEAL uniform—black rubber wet suits, caps, fins, and weapons—on the night ocean. And all of this on only four hours of sleep per night.

At the end of Hell Week, those who remain undergo seven weeks of underwater training, nine weeks of weapons and explosives training, and three weeks of practice parachute jumping. When this basic training period is complete, recruits who have passed must work with an active SEAL unit for six months to prove their worth. Because of the rigors of the training program, only 30 percent of the screened group eventually become SEALs. What is remarkable is that it is not easy to predict who will be successful. The fastest and strongest athletes in the beginning are often not the ones who make it to the end.

One of the primary lessons in the SEAL training program is that an individual will not survive without the help of fellow recruits. As recruits fight eight-foot waves in their tiny rubber boats, they must learn to think together to solve problems, or they will not make it. This philosophy is carried through to the field, where the real work is done. SEALS do not operate alone; their sense of identity is strongly tied to the group. This pride is evidenced in the claim that no dead SEAL has ever been left behind on a battlefield.

Source: K. Labich, "Elite Teams," *Fortune,* February 19, 1996, pp. 90–93.

Increasingly, the practice of management takes place in a context of groups and teams, rather than of individuals.[1] Of course, there will always be a place for the brilliant employee working alone who produces a remarkable innovation or creative achievement. Also, not all individuals or cultures adapt equally well to a group-oriented organizational environment.[2] Yet, more and more around the globe, organizations depend on highly networked and interconnected relationships. Managing such networks requires strong collaborative skills and the ability to work successfully with, and in, groups and teams.

Because so many complex tasks and objectives are beyond the capabilities of a single person, groups and teams, rather than individual employees, will form the fundamental building blocks of 21st-century organizations. Groups develop new products, design automobiles, construct budgets, and formulate strategic plans. Even those who are inclined to be independent entrepreneurs will eventually face this reality test: If an organization is not based on high-performance groups and teams, it cannot compete effectively in tomorrow's world.

In this chapter we begin by examining the nature or essence of groups and teams and identifying the various types of groups that operate in organizational settings. Then we discuss how groups are formed and developed and what some of their most important characteristics are, such as their structure, norms, and degree of cohesiveness. This is followed by an analysis of a critical issue common to many groups, namely, conflict. The chapter concludes with a consideration of the challenges involved in improving group effectiveness.

THE NATURE OF GROUPS AND TEAMS

Groups and teams are so pervasive in modern industrialized societies they are often taken for granted. However, it is important at the outset to be sure that we understand something about their basic nature and about the different types that can exist in organizations.

Are Groups and Teams the Same?

group
a set of people, limited in number (usually from 3 to 20), who have some degree of mutual interaction and shared objectives

team
a type of group that has additional characteristics: a high degree of interdependent, coordinated interaction and a strong sense of members' personal responsibility for achieving specified group outcomes

A **group** is typically defined as a set of people, limited in number (usually from 3 to 20), who have some degree of interaction and shared objectives. A **team**, on the other hand, is a type of group that has additional characteristics: a high degree of interdependent, coordinated interaction and a strong sense of members' personal responsibility for achieving specified group outcomes (see Exhibit 11.1).[3] Also, groups that become teams typically have created a high level of identity about being a member of the unit. These distinguishing features of teams are aptly illustrated, of course, with the Navy SEALs. The SEAL units are groups, but they are also teams. Put simply, all teams are groups, but not all groups are, or become, teams.[4] A major objective in many of today's organizations is to have work groups behave more like teams, although such results cannot be guaranteed. Regardless of whether groups develop into teams, it is useful first to identify the several different types of groups that can exist in any organization.

EXHIBIT 11.1

Changes as Groups
Become Teams

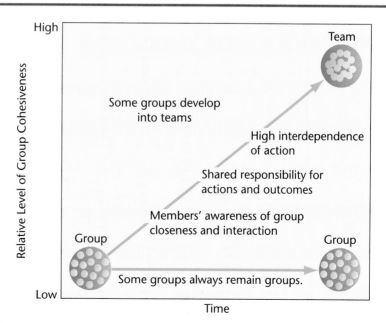

EXHIBIT 11.2

Types of Groups

Type of Group	Features	Examples
Command (Supervisory)	One supervisor with a number of subordinates Relatively enduring Membership changes relatively slowly	Clerical units Manufacturing assembly units Local sales managers reporting to a regional sales manager
Self-Managing (Autonomous)	Leader appointed by the group, not by the organization Expected to foster more "team" feeling	Volvo and Saturn auto manufacturing teams Motorola's Elma, Illinois, plant: more than 50 percent of employees involved in teams* Corning's Erwin plant: half of the employees are involved with teams*
Project/Task Force	Temporary Specific limited purpose Group members are aware of temporary nature of group	Product design teams Management information systems teams to develop upgraded computer systems Term project groups in university classes
Committee	Either permanent or ad hoc Meet only periodically Members have different permanent jobs and/or supervisors Membership typically does not represent an employee's highest commitment	Budget committees Safety committees Promotion review committees
Informal	Group not originated by the organization Voluntary membership Obvious differences and boundaries between members and nonmembers	Group of employees who lunch together on Fridays Van pool group The "water cooler group"

*Examples from S. Jay Liebowitz and Kevin T. Holden, "Are Self-Managing Teams Worthwhile? A Tale of Two Companies," *SAM Advanced Management Journal* 60, no. 2 (1995), pp. 11–17.

Types of Groups

Most people in organizations are part of at least one group, and often of several groups. Examples of the basic types of groups to which an employee could belong are illustrated in Exhibit 11.2 and are described here.

command (supervisory) group
a group whose members consist of a supervisor or manager and all those who report to that person

Command (Supervisory) Groups   A **command (supervisory) group** consists of a supervisor or manager and all those who report to that person; for example, those who report to a particular production supervisor or to a sales manager in a department. Such groups are usually considered to be the basic work units of an organization. Depending on the nature of the tasks assigned to each person, however, the amount of interaction among members may vary considerably from one command group to another. For example, in a clothing manufacturing plant, a group of workers may be assigned to work on a particular style of jeans. They all work to construct the same garment, but because one is sewing the pocket to the leg while another is putting in zippers and yet another is topstitching the waistband, there is very little opportunity for interaction. Contrast this with a marketing team for a toy company, where the members meet frequently to discuss new products, schedule advertising campaigns, and decide on special promotional activities.

Command groups are usually considered relatively enduring, rather than temporary. Also, membership in these groups changes relatively slowly. These factors together affect the nature and quality of the interpersonal interaction among group members. The fact that a person knows he or she will interact repeatedly with the same people for an indefinite length of time can have a powerful effect on relationships with those other members.

Self-Managing (Autonomous) Work Groups (Teams)   A relatively recent, but increasingly important, variant of the command work group is the **self-managed**, or so-called **autonomous**, **work group** that has no formally appointed supervisor. These groups are similar to command groups in that the members coordinate their organizational work as if they all reported to the same formally appointed supervisor. However, the group manages itself on behalf of the organization's objectives, and its members usually appoint their own informal team leader.[5] The group is made up of a number of members with diverse skills that can be applied to the group's task. It generally is responsible for decisions concerning how to accomplish the work—which members will perform which tasks and in which order. They also frequently do jobs traditionally associated with supervision, such as conducting team meetings and solving productivity problems. A major reason that some organizations—Xerox, Procter & Gamble, and General Motors, among others—put together such self-managing units is to develop more teamlike group behavior compared with that of the more traditional command group. When the New York Regional Office of the Department of Veterans Affairs recently reorganized, for example, it abandoned its historically rigid hierarchical structure, opting instead to organize the workforce into 16 12-member, self-directed work groups in which each member has multiple functions. The work groups do not report to a manager as such, but instead they are assigned to a "coach," usually someone who has previously been a supervisor.[6]

The idea of group self-management, however good it appears in principle, may not appeal to all employees who might be affected. Furthermore, it cannot be assumed to fit into all types of cultures.[7] Therefore, managers and organizations who want to establish such groups need to consider potential pitfalls and resistance as well as the possible advantages.

Project/Task Forces   A **project/task force** is a group put together by an organization for a particular purpose; for example, to design a new product or to work on a particular problem (e.g., the Y2K end-of-century computer software problem) that cuts across different organizational units. Such groups differ from supervisory and self-managing work teams in that they are intended to be temporary. Their members know that the group will likely cease to exist once the project or task is completed. This not only changes members' perceptions and their interactions with one another, but it also changes their relationship to the appointed leader of the project or task force group. Because of the nature and importance of the goals and objectives set for them, though, task forces constitute some of the most critical grouplike activities within, and even across, organizations. Illustrations include the following, for example:

---

self-managing (autonomous) work group
a group that has no formally appointed supervisor but is similar to command groups in that the members coordinate their organizational work *as if* they all reported to the same formally appointed supervisor; members usually appoint their own informal team leader

project/task force
a temporary group put together by an organization for a particular purpose

- The *Sacramento Bee*, a highly regarded northern California newspaper, set up a task force to investigate workplace injuries as part of its major review of operations in 1993. The task force developed several recommendations concerning configurations of equipment, training, and work station safety and health. These recommendations resulted in a drop in injury-related costs from $2.2 million in 1990 to $490,000 in 1994.[8]
- In 1995, *People* magazine instituted a task force to investigate the Hispanic market in the United States. The task force made recommendations concerning the possible launch of a new magazine and also whether it should be published in Spanish alone or in a combination of both English and Spanish.[9]
- When quality control numbers stopped improving, Revlon Co. set up a Corporate Quality Control Task Force. The members of the task force were charged with discovering which factors were having a major impact on quality, developing plans to correct the problems, and assigning specific quality-control responsibilities to various departments.[10]
- Duke Power, Bell South, Carolina Power and Light, and 32 independent telephone companies formed a joint task force to develop a $500 million regional personal communication services network.[11]

committee

a group that is either permanent or temporary (ad hoc) whose members meet only occasionally and otherwise report to different permanent supervisors in an organization's structure

Committees   Committees can be either permanent or temporary (ad hoc) in terms of the length of their existence. Typically, the most important feature of committees in organizations is that their members meet only occasionally and otherwise report to different permanent supervisors in the organization's structure (Exhibit 11.3). Thus, interaction is episodic, and for most members this is not the formal organizational group to which they have the highest degree of commitment. For instance, a budget committee may meet several times during a company's fiscal year, with the members likely coming from each of the major departments or divisions. The primary jobs of the budget committee members, however, are in their own organizational work units, not serving together on the budget committee. Nevertheless, such a committee's decisions may have critically important implications not only for its members but also for the larger organization.

formal group

a group that is designated, created, and sanctioned by the organization to carry out its basic work and to fulfill its overall mission

The preceding types of groups are all examples of **formal groups**; that is, groups that are designated, created, and sanctioned by an organization to carry out its basic work and to fulfill its overall mission. Other types of groups also exist in organizations, however.

informal group

a group whose members interact voluntarily

Informal Groups   An **informal group** is one whose members choose to interact voluntarily, not by organizational mandate. A typical example is friendship groups. Although there is no formal joining process, these groups often have fairly obvious boundaries between members and nonmembers. At any given time, people think they know (perhaps incorrectly from the point of view of others in the group) whether they are a member of a certain group or not. Just observing who eats lunch with whom, for instance, is often a clear signal of a friendship group's bound-

EXHIBIT 11.3			
Examples of Committees Present in Many Organizations	• Governance • Executive • Steering • Disaster planning	• Compensation • Finance • Safety • Long-range planning	• Oversight • Audit • Ethics • Public Relations

aries. Such informal groups can be fairly temporary, but more typically they last for considerable periods of time. Most important from the organization's point of view is that friendship and other informal groups can significantly affect the attitudes and performance of their members in relation to organizational tasks and objectives. A set of employees who were originally strangers, for example, might develop into an informal group after carpooling together over a period of time. If the conversations within this group focus on reactions to new organizational policies, then the group may become a significant source of support or opposition to those policies. Research has shown, in fact, that "friendship groups do socialize more; however, they also spend more time discussing the task, are more committed and more cooperative [with each other]."[12]

FORMATION AND DEVELOPMENT OF GROUPS AND TEAMS

Groups in organizations form for many reasons and in many ways. Most often, of course, the company or organization deliberately puts groups together to serve stated organizational purposes. Informal groups, however, are another matter. They form more or less spontaneously on the basis of actions by their members and to serve those members' self-interests, which may or may not coincide with those of the organization.

Factors Influencing the Formation of Groups

The most important factors influencing the formation of groups in organizations are the goals of the organization, the opportunities for routine interaction, and the psychological needs of potential group members.

Organizational Goals The goals and purposes of the larger organization directly affect the nature of its formal groups. The organization creates new groups, whether command, task forces, or committees, based on its judgment that needs are not being met adequately by existing groups. New groups may arise because of organizational growth, changes in the products or services the organization offers, or simply perceptions by key managers that greater efficiency and effectiveness can be gained by adding to, altering, or combining existing groups. General Motors, for example, in 1997 restructured its organization in Europe around a team concept. Each car model (Astra, Corsa, Frontera, Omerga, Tigra, Calebra, and Vectra) was to be represented by its own team consisting of a manager and marketing and advertising representatives.[13]

A key issue for organizations and managers when new groups are formed is whether they will be given adequate resources to accomplish their specific goals.[14] The leader of a team that developed the data storage system for the B2 bomber at Honeywell Defense Avionics stated, "My most important task ... was to help this team feel as if they owned the project by getting them whatever information, financial or otherwise, they needed."[15]

Members who are put together by the organization in a newly created group will likely have questions, such as

- Why are they, rather than someone else, in the group?
- What are the *real* reasons why the group was put together?

- What are their new responsibilities going to be?
- Are the stated objectives for the group realistic and are they the actual goals that will be measured?

Such questions naturally occur to those who will be part of a new group, but they don't always get asked directly or openly. Managers who form groups must therefore anticipate questions such as these, whether or not they are raised explicitly, and must be prepared to provide necessary information and explanations. A manager responsible for putting together a new organizational group also needs to recognize that, as discussed earlier, the formation of a new group does not necessarily mean that a new *team* has been created. There may be the hope that a new group will develop into a team with a strong sense of shared responsibility for the group's performance and output, but cohesiveness and cooperation are not something that the organization or a manager can decree. Organizations cannot simply declare new groups to be "teams" and expect that they will operate that way. Team development depends on managerial skills and follow-up actions to elicit true teamwork in more than name only.[16]

Organizational Proximity   In the formation of groups and their possible development into teams, proximity, or closeness, in working relationships is a key factor. When people have the opportunity to work together, it can facilitate learning about similarities of interests and experiences. These similarities can provide a basis for the development of friendships, which in turn often lead to the formation of informal groups within the formal group. Thus, the firm or company is frequently the indirect, and often inadvertent, initiator of informal groups.

An organization can also interfere with the formation or continuation of groups, purposely or not. This was illustrated recently when a reference specialist on the Democracy and Human Rights team at the reorganized U.S. Information Agency commented after the reorganization: "It's now harder to get together with my fellow librarians and researchers. We all used to be together in library services. Now we are all spread out and assigned to different teams. I miss the contact."[17]

Psychological Factors   Although proximity is a great aid in the formation of informal groups and the development of other types of groups into teams, it is not absolutely essential. Other factors also motivate organizational members to form closer relationships in groups, especially basic human needs for security, social support, self-esteem, and status. By belonging to groups, employees are often able to fulfill needs that may not be well satisfied by the work itself. Thus, the feeling of belonging to a group at work can be highly rewarding for many individuals. It can be, in effect, a significant way for individuals to achieve a distinct social identity that is meaningful both for themselves and for others who interact with them.[18]

Stages of Group Development

Whether groups are formed by the organization or by voluntary actions of individuals, they tend to move through distinct or identifiable developmental stages as they mature.[19] One popular early statement on this issue utilizes an easy-to-remember set of terms for such stages: "forming" (getting acquainted), "storming" (expressing differences of opinion), "norming" (building consensus on basic issues), and "performing" (carrying out cooperative group actions).[20] Although

Stages of Group Development

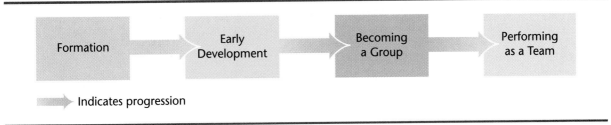

Indicates progression

this model has considerable appeal as a way to think about phases of group development across time, it does not apply universally to all groups. As one set of management scholars has noted, "It seems unlikely that a single sequence can describe the development of all kinds of teams [groups]."[21]

Despite this fact, several identifiable stages do show up with some regularity in organizational contexts (Exhibit 11.4).

Formation   New groups and their leaders face some unique challenges. In particular, in the formation or orientation stage, members need to understand who is in the group, who is leading the group, and where each person is "coming from" in terms of his or her attitude and viewpoint. Nearly all new groups go through this "getting to know you" stage. For example, players recruited from across Great Britain and Ireland for the British Lions rugby team met each other for a team-building workshop prior to their first tour. Initial ice-breaking exercises were used to help develop a feeling of trust and a willingness to use teamwork to reach a goal. As one team member stated, "It meant that we got to know each other as people rather than just rugby players. The tasks forced us out of our cliques."[22]

Early Development   Following a group's formation and initial interactions, an early-development stage settles in that may last for some time, depending on the nature of the group and its tasks. In this stage, members learn what is expected of them, what is acceptable behavior, and how well they relate to each other. Typically, members cautiously exchange, and sometimes jealously guard, information. It is also a time for learning about how opinions within the group overlap or differ on important matters, and, as a consequence, conflicts over group goals or the means to reach them may emerge. An analogy to adolescence in human development might be apt for this stage of group development.

Becoming a Group   In this stage, at least a minimum amount of consensus about group issues begins to appear, as well as a degree of individual identity with the group and its goals. How much consensus and group identity will actually emerge vary widely from group to group at this stage, depending in large part on how well the group is meeting member needs and on how well it is being led. In this stage particularly, organizations and managers can have considerable impact on a group's development and help it to become a true team.

Performing as a Team   In this stage, a group is able to perform like a team and take actions as an entity and not just as individuals. Internally, this means that the group is able to influence members' attitudes and behavior on matters of importance to the group, and externally it means that others in the organization are being affected by its actions. Several years ago, for example, Sterling Winthrop Pharmaceuticals Research Division, a subsidiary of Eastman Kodak Company located in Pennsylvania, constructed a one-million-square-foot complex. Construction was finished early, on budget, and with an exceptional safety record. The company credits that feat to the development of an intense team identity, with members designing their own logo, which was imprinted on almost all items. The team's identity was tied to shared beliefs in cooperation, commitment, and the individual value of each team member.[23]

Each of the preceding four stages can be illustrated by the following story of a project group that was put together in a large consumer products company:

- *Formation:* During a reengineering effort at this company, eight managers from various functions were asked to work together to take on the project of analyzing the company's effectiveness in a number of areas and making performance-enhancing recommendations. In the early group meetings, most people were uncomfortable and unsure. Some were quiet, offering no input and waiting for others to move the meetings along. Some bonded in immediate alliances, and yet others jumped right in and began trying to perform the team's tasks.
- *Early Development:* Soon the group members began to understand the scope of their task. They began to understand who among them really had influence, who the leaders were. Some work was accomplished, and while the members' relationships and confidence improved, overall the group's performance was very low.
- *Becoming a Group:* Next the group began to focus on encouraging group, rather than individual, behavior. They began listening to each other and assessing suggestions in terms of the group's goals rather than as a display of each individual member's goals. They found ways to resolve conflicts and established standards of group conduct.
- *Performing as a Group:* The group now regarded themselves as a team. The next hurdle was learning that they did not always have to agree with each other, that they could disagree and still accomplish their task. They began evaluating all parts of suggestions, coping with divergent opinions and creatively managing their conflict. Their effectiveness and performance steadily continued to improve.
- *Outcome:* Over the 15 weeks of the team's existence (equivalent to one semester), they analyzed the order taking, product scheduling, sales reporting, and pricing processes in their company. They identified and recommended several cost reduction and process improvement plans with their recommendations resulting in savings of $2.5 million to their company.[24]

Returning to the general issue of stages in group development, whether a team's actions across these stages are continuously effective or not is another matter. Events internal or external to the group could still cause it to revert to an earlier stage of development, where it might need to re-form and attempt to become a "performing group" all over again. However, if a group has no specified ending point, that is an "adjourning" phase, there is no inherent reason why the performing stage cannot last indefinitely. To keep a command group or team in this stage continually is a clear managerial and leadership challenge.

CHARACTERISTICS OF GROUPS AND TEAMS

All groups have certain characteristics that affect the degree and types of influence they have on their members and their level of collective performance. Some of these are structural, while others relate to basic features of groups, such as their norms and the degree of cohesion among their members. For all of these characteristics, it is important for leaders and managers to understand their likely effects.

Structural Characteristics

Just as organizations have structure (as discussed in Chapter 10), so do groups, except of course, on a smaller scale. Four of the most essential structural features of groups are size, composition, differentiated roles, and differentiated status (see Exhibit 11.5).

Size As one review of research on groups stated, "Current literature yields a consistent guideline [for determining the best size for a group]: [use] the smallest number of people who can do the task."[25] Similarly, another review of recent studies carried out in the United States found that member satisfaction decreased as groups got larger, and leaders' behavior toward members became more task- and less people-oriented.[26] Likewise, a large-scale study of command group size in 58 offices of a U.S. federal agency found that organizational productivity per employee decreased with increasing size.[27]

What is an optimal group size? Of course, there is no single answer to this question, since it would vary based on the types of tasks facing the group. However, research shows that with increasing group size the sense of personal responsibility for a group's output or performance tends to decrease. The phenomenon of reduced effort per person in larger-size groups has been labeled **social loafing**.[28]

social loafing
the phenomenon of reduced effort per person in large groups

EXHIBIT 11.5

Structural Characteristics of Groups

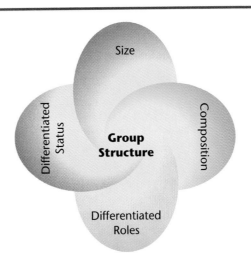

Individuals in larger groups apparently are more likely than those in smaller groups to assume that other members will "carry the load," thus reducing the necessity for their own efforts. In large groups, also, individual members' specific contributions are less easily identified, and this appears to be a major factor in encouraging such "loafing."[29]

There are, however, some approaches that can be used to counter the social-loafing tendency. For example, it is possible to structure group work to encourage full participation by group members. A key lies in the identifiability of an individual's contribution to the final result. One experiment using college swim team members found originally that the athletes swam faster in individual time trials than they did at the same distance and with the same stroke during relays. In the normal situation, only the team time was announced at the end of the race, and the times of individual swimmers were not available. When the relay race was structured so that each individual's time was announced aloud at the end of his or her lap, the individuals actually swam faster during the relay than in the individual heats.

Results such as these suggest that managers may be able to encourage higher individual effort levels on group projects by building in some form of acknowledgment of the contributions made by each member of the group to the final outcome of the project.[30]

Interestingly, additional research seems to indicate that social loafing in groups is less likely to occur in collectivistic cultures (see Chapter 4), such as Asian countries, than in more individualistic cultures such as the United States or Australia because of the much stronger group orientation in collectivistic cultures.[31]

process costs
increasing costs of coordination as group size increases

The other major reason why group performance per person may decrease as group size increases is simply the increasing costs of coordination, or **process costs**. As groups become larger, the number of person-to-person relationships increases significantly, and thus coordination becomes more cumbersome. Also, with larger size come additional opportunities for interpersonal conflicts between individuals and among subgroups within the group.

All of the disadvantages of large group size must be weighed, of course, against the potential advantages of having a more extensive pool of talent, skills, and expertise to boost performance and take on additional problem-solving tasks.[32] Having too few people in a group, especially when tasks are many and complex, defeats the whole purpose of putting together people in the first place. In determining the best size for formal work groups, managers need to consider the probable losses due to process costs in relation to the likely gains due to larger integrated efforts.

Composition   Groups may be composed of individuals who are very similar or very dissimilar. If the former, we describe the group as *homogeneous*. If the latter, the composition would be regarded as *heterogeneous*, or diverse. Most groups these days have some degree of diversity, and many have a great deal. As Exhibit 11.6 shows, there can be different types of diversity within groups, including variations in observable characteristics such as race/ethnicity, gender, and age and variations in underlying attributes such as values, skills, knowledge, and length of time (tenure) in the group and in the organization.[33]

The managerial question, of course, is: Does a greater amount of diversity within groups help or hinder such outcomes as turnover of membership and group performance? Research to date shows that there is no simple answer to this question.

EXHIBIT 11.6

Types of Diversity within Groups and Potential Consequences

Types of Diversity	Potential Consequences
Examples of Observable Attributes • Race/Ethnicity • Gender • Age	**Examples of Affective Consequences** • Satisfaction • Commitment • Identification with the group • Role ambiguity • Role conflict
Examples of Underlying Attributes • Values • Skills and knowledge • Group tenure	**Examples of Cognitive Consequences** • Innovation • Number and quality of ideas **Examples of Communication-Related Consequences** • Communication within the group • Communication outside the group

Source: Adapted from Frances L. Milliken and Luis L. Martins, "Searching for Common Threads: Understanding the Multiple Effects of Diversity in Organizational Groups," *Academy of Management Review* 21, no. 2 (1996), pp. 402–23.

Instead, as shown in Exhibit 11.6, we need to look at the effects of group diversity on more specific and immediate consequences, such as

- Members' reactions (affective consequences), including satisfaction, identification with the group, and conflict within the group;
- The output of members' thinking (cognitive consequences), including the amount of new ideas or innovations emerging from the group; and
- Communication effectiveness, both inside and outside the group.

Research to date is only suggestive and not conclusive, but it tends to show that increased diversity has

- Somewhat negative effects on members' reactions;
- Somewhat positive effects on increasing the quality of the outputs of members' thinking together as a group, presumably because a wider range of opinions and ideas are discussed; and
- Decreased frequency of communication within a group but more communication with those outside a group.[34]

In short, the challenge for managers is to maximize the significant benefits that are possible by having group diversity and to try to minimize potential disadvantages by anticipating what some of those might be and directly addressing them. The Managerial Challenge box on cross-cultural teams at Rhône-Poulenc, Inc. describes how one company met this challenge head-on when putting together and managing groups that have a particular type of diversity: teams with members from different countries.[35] The use of multinational groups is becoming increasingly commonplace, as is the use of increasingly diverse work teams in general.[36] In other words, the diversity challenges for managers are growing, not lessening.

Differentiated Roles In groups of any size, different members perform different roles; that is, they occupy different positions with sets of expected behavior

MANAGERIAL CHALLENGE

CROSS-CULTURAL TEAMS AT RHÔNE-POULENC, INC.

Rhône-Poulenc is one of the largest chemical companies in the world. In an address to the Conference Board in New York City, Peter Neff, CEO of a Rhône-Poulenc subsidiary, discussed some of the challenges he encountered in the mid-1990s while developing it from an $860 million to a $2.3 billion company. In that time period, Rhône-Poulenc employed researchers in a variety of countries including North America, Europe, South America, and Asia. Therefore, one major challenge facing Neff involved training the researchers to work effectively on teams with others from different cultures and training managers to supervise these cross-cultural teams effectively.

Neff learned that "U.S. and French researchers tend to have different perspectives about their work. Americans are generally pragmatic, oriented to creating something that will be used, and expected to develop products that will be sold. The French, on the other hand, tend to be more interested in the pure science, deriving satisfaction through finding solutions to knotty technical problems." He found that the Americans tended to look toward established rules to solve problems while the French were more concerned with the uniqueness of each problem, regardless of what established rules said should be done. Americans focused more on individual rights, the French on how the individual contributed to the organization. Team members had to learn to integrate their attitudes and behaviors to work effectively together.

Neff's view is that "when you bolster one culture, you naturally run the risk of rubbing up against the other." Rhône-Poulenc therefore offers team members specific training and team-building opportunities that teach ways to recognize and manage the problems created when team members come from different cultures. The company actively encourages both self-managing and self-directed work teams. Additionally, Rhône-Poulenc has developed management training programs that attempt to identify managers who can work most effectively in the ambiguous environment of cross-cultural teams. All of these approaches are important because both team members and their managers need to be "secure enough to accept diverse cultures and opinions, and mature enough to manage the creativity and innovation they can ignite."

Source: Peter J. Neff, "Cross-Cultural Research Teams in a Global Enterprise," *Research Technology Management* 38, no. 3 (1995), pp. 15–19.

attached to those positions. This is most vividly illustrated in certain athletic teams, where players have specialized roles when the team is on offense and different roles on defense. Roles in work groups are not always as clear-cut and can range from being fairly general, such as performing analytical duties, to being highly

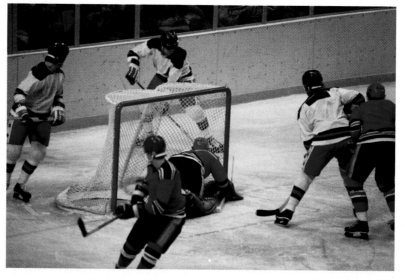

Just like athletic teams, individuals in work groups perform different roles. Each position has a set of expected behaviors.

specialized with specific task assignments, such as monitoring particular pieces of equipment. More and more, however, organizations are attempting to loosen rigid role boundaries in groups and thus generate greater flexibility in meeting unexpected competitive and environmental challenges. The spirit of this change is illustrated in the following quote from the leader of the Electronic Media Team at the U.S. Information Agency: Referring to the new roles of team members, he said, "In the old days, people had very specific job descriptions, and they rarely ventured outside of them. The challenge of teams is to get people and teams moving outside the box" (i.e., to think more creatively about how to fulfill their roles).[37]

One type of role that is assigned or emerges in almost all groups is that of leader. In the past, the leadership role in work groups has tended to be specialized and concentrated in one person, the supervisor. However, the clear trend in today's highly competitive organizations is to attempt to spread the leadership functions of structuring tasks and lending personal support and encouragement as widely as possible among the group's members. This is especially so in so-called self-managing teams discussed earlier, but it also is becoming more common even in typical command groups.[38] For example, at a plant of Texas Instruments in McKinney, Texas, the role of team leader is rotated among group members rather than being assigned permanently to any one individual.[39] The principle involved is that if responsibility for leadership functions is more broadly shared and accepted, the group will be able to respond faster and more effectively to rapidly changing pressures and circumstances.

role ambiguity
a situation in which the expected behaviors for a group member are not clearly defined

Two particular issues that groups face with respect to roles are role ambiguity and role conflict. **Role ambiguity** refers to a situation in which the expected behaviors for a group member are not clearly defined, which can increase the stress level for that person. **Role conflict** emerges when a member faces two or more contrasting sets of expectations, such as taking time to be friendly with customers versus meeting a certain quota of customers to be served during a work period. Effectively managed groups try to reduce role ambiguity and role conflict to minimal levels by sharing information widely and confronting such issues openly and directly.

role conflict
a situation in which a member of a group faces two or more contrasting sets of expectations

status
the standing or prestige that a person has in a group, which can be based on a number of factors such as perceived leadership abilities, seniority, or special skills

Differentiated Status   Not only do members have different roles in groups, they also often have different levels of status or rank. **Status** is the standing or prestige that a person has in a group, and it can be based on a number of factors such as perceived leadership abilities, seniority, or special skills, among others.

Research has shown that status differences can strongly influence interactions within the group.[40] For example, higher-status members tend to receive more communications than do lower-status members, and lower-status members tend to defer to higher-status members when groups are making decisions.[41] Such effects might be especially strong, of course, in high-power-distance cultures, such as those in South America and Asia. However, in cultures with low or medium power distance, effective communication and decision making are likely to be inhibited in groups if status differences and their effects are too extreme. Relevant information would be less likely to be widely shared and thus not be given sufficient attention.

Norms

norms
a group's shared standards that guide the behavior of its individual members

Norms are a group's shared standards that guide the behavior of its individual members. For example, when members of a group behave similarly toward supervisors or outsiders, such as stopping nontask conversations when they enter the room, they are demonstrating the effect of group norms. It would be very difficult, if not impossible, for groups to function if they did not have norms.[42] Each person's behavior would be too unpredictable for coordinated action to take place. Norms also help to reduce ambiguity; thus, they provide members with cues and useful guidelines about how to behave. Such normative information is particularly important for new members of a group who need to learn what is going on in the work situation as rapidly as possible.

Characteristics of Group Norms   An understanding of norms and their significance can be gained by reviewing several of their main features:

- Norms are usually established for the more important issues of concern to the group; for example, rates of minimally acceptable output or performance.
- Norms do not necessarily apply to all members of the group; some apply only to certain members (e.g., the leader), usually based on the status or particular role of those members. For example, it may be acceptable for a senior member of a group, but not for a junior member, to arrive late for meetings.
- Norms vary in the degree of their acceptance by group members; some norms are accepted and endorsed by virtually all members, others by only a majority. For instance, norms regarding how to deal with work problems might be accepted by everyone, but norms regarding desirable attire might be endorsed by only certain members.
- Norms vary in how much deviation members are permitted in following them; in other words, some norms are very loose and permit a great deal of leeway in behavior, while other norms, especially those regarding key group issues, are much more restrictive on members' behavior.[43] For example, a member of a group who talks to outsiders about the group's internal problems might receive severe censure from fellow group members, whereas someone who talks louder than normal during meetings might be tolerated (up to a degree, at least) by group colleagues.

Development of Group Norms   Norms do not suddenly and magically appear in groups. They seldom, if ever, develop in a purely spontaneous way. Rather, they arise out of interaction among group members. An example of a typical norm development process is shown in Exhibit 11.7. Key factors that often have a major influence on the process include the following:[44]

- *Early behaviors:* Typically, initial behaviors, especially in newly formed groups, establish standards for subsequent behavior. In committees, for example, the first few meetings help establish norms about how candid, or how indirect, discussion of sensitive issues is likely to be. Such quickly established norms are often difficult to reshape or change later.
- *Imported behaviors:* Members of a group often bring with them standards of behavior that were prominent in their former groups. The more similar the type and purpose of the previous group were to the present one, the more likely those norms will serve as guideposts in the new situation. "When in doubt, stay with the familiar" seems to be the (sometimes incorrect) watchword of many people in organizations. When a high-status member imports a norm, as in the case of those with acknowledged expertise or high power, the prominence of that norm is likely to be strong. A new chief executive officer

Example of the Development of Group Norms

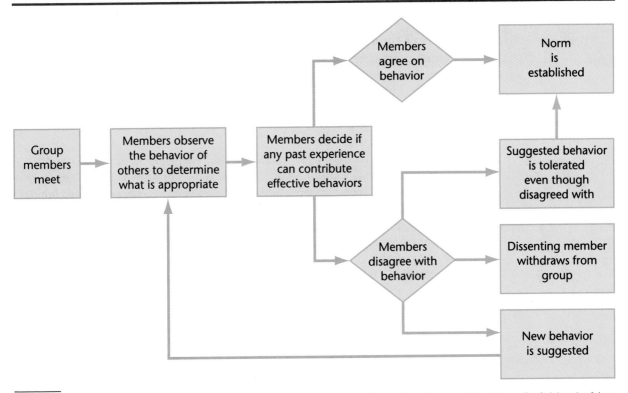

Source: Kenneth Bettenhausen and J. Keith Murnighan, "The Emergence of Norms in Competitive Decision Making Groups," *Administrative Science Quarterly* 30 (1985), pp. 350–72.

(CEO), for example, may believe in a norm of communication "only through channels" regarding suggestions and input from members of the organization, even though this may run counter to the previous norm of openness and the "door is open at any time" fostered by the former CEO. However, because the new CEO has high status, few are likely to challenge this imported norm.

- *Critical events:* A sudden challenge to the group, such as criticism from another group, can create specific and vivid responses that form the basis for how members should be expected to respond in the future. A time of crisis makes people particularly alert to cues in their environment and thus tends to reinforce norms that emerge from that period. In a corporation that has announced layoffs, for example, new norms regarding the overt display of diligent work habits may emerge.

- *Explicitly stated standards:* Not to be overlooked is the fact that leaders or high-status members of a group may simply assert that "this is how we will do it around here!" Newly appointed supervisors and athletic coaches, for example, frequently use this approach with their groups or teams. For example, members of the British Lions rugby team, referred to earlier in this chapter, prior to its first overseas trip mutually developed a set of behavioral norms to guide the team. The explicitly stated (indeed, printed) norms included unity, cohesion, no cliques, discipline concerning the amount of drinking the night before a game, and adherence to the highest standards.[45]

conformity
close adherence to the group's norms by the individual members

Effects of Group Norms   Since norms are, essentially, accepted standards, their primary effect is to shape or influence the behavior of individual members of a group. Thus, norms can be thought of as constraining or reducing the variability of actions and attitudes across a set of group members. That is, the existence of strong norms tends to narrow individual differences in behavior and beliefs. This results in a certain degree of **conformity**, or close adherence to the group's norms by the individual members.

Whether such conformity is "good" or "bad" depends on the perspective of the viewer. If the norms support a manager's goals for a group—say, for example, that everyone should look for opportunities to make creative suggestions to improve the group's effectiveness—then the manager would regard conformity as very helpful. A few years ago, a large, national transit company reorganized around cross-functional groups following a decade of financial and labor problems; about half (42 percent) of the groups were successful and about half (48 percent) were unsuccessful. The groups deemed successful had developed stronger norms of open communication and leadership and behaved more like teams.[46]

If norms conflict with the objectives a manager is trying to achieve, then greater conformity would be regarded as negative. The obvious implication for managers is that they should be as concerned about the content or direction of group norms as about the amount of conformity to them.

From the point of view of the individual member of a group, norms can sometimes be too constraining. In that case, the individual may deviate from the group's expected attitudes and behavior. Such divergent actions or expressed views are potentially troubling to others in the group because they can threaten the group's solidarity and, perhaps in extreme cases, even its existence. Therefore, the group sometimes imposes sanctions on the deviant in an attempt to bring about greater conformity. The classic case in certain Western work situations, particularly at the hourly worker level, is the individual who works faster or slower than the group thinks he or she should. Such persons, sometimes labeled "rate busters" or "slackers," are often subjected to ridicule or ostracism to persuade or force them to work at a rate more in line with the group's norms for production effort.

The degree to which members conform to, or deviate from, a group's norms is a function of several factors, some of which are under managerial control and some of which are not.[47]

* *Ambiguity of the situation:* The more ambiguous the situation, the more likely individuals are to turn to the group for help in interpreting cues and deciding how to behave.
* *Degree of unanimity of the group:* The more the group can agree on a particular norm, the greater the degree of pressure to conform exerted on the individual.
* *Size of the group:* The amount of conformity produced increases with the size of a group up to some maximum, after which greater size has little, if any, effect. The maximum size for producing conformity varies by circumstances, but the effect seems to be strongest up to a size of eight or so members.

- *Past success of the group:* The more successful a group has been in the past, the more likely it is to produce greater conformity to its norms.
- *Identification with the group:* The more individuals identify with a group, that is, the more they see themselves as part of it, the more likely they are to conform to its norms.

The variable over which a manager has the least control is the personality of members. Personality factors that affect group behavior include intelligence (less conforming behavior), a tendency toward authoritarianism (more conforming behavior), and a tendency toward self-blame (more conforming behavior).

Cohesion

cohesion
the degree to which members are motivated to remain in the group

Another major property of groups is their amount of **cohesion**, "the degree to which members are motivated to remain in a group," to *want* to stay in it.[48] Group cohesion is usually considered to have many advantages and to be highly desirable if it can be developed. Indeed, when managers and organizations attempt to turn groups into teams, they are, in effect, trying to generate stronger group cohesion. However, as will be discussed later, high levels of group cohesion may not always result in positive outcomes.[49]

Development of Group Cohesion   There are no surefire ways for managers to build strong cohesion in the groups for which they are responsible. However, the available research suggests three factors that are potentially important for developing greater group cohesion:

- Strong interpersonal attraction among group members;
- High performance and past success of the group; and
- High level of competition with other groups.[50]

The most consistently important of these factors appears to be the first, namely, whether members of the group think they have something in common with other members and tend to like being with them; that is, whether they feel like they belong to a team. The evidence for the other two factors in bringing about cohesion is not as clear-cut, but both past group success and current or anticipated conflict with other groups seem to unite groups and increase their cohesion, especially if strong interpersonal attraction among members is already present. Obviously, a group whose members don't especially like being with each other may disintegrate when faced with competition from external groups, rather than develop greater cohesion. This reinforces the point that few clear guidelines exist that guarantee the development of group cohesion.

Effects of Group Cohesion   Increased cohesiveness of groups can have a number of potential advantages.[51] Chief among these is an increase in the quantity and quality of group interaction.[52]

A second potential advantage of greater group cohesion is that the group has stronger influence on each member to conform to the group's standards or norms. Assuming—and this is a critical assumption—that those norms are positive from the manager's perspective, then this is a significant advantage.

EXHIBIT 11.8	
Effects of High Levels of Group Cohesion	

Positive Effects

- Increased quality and quantity of group interactions
- Strengthened adherence to group norms
- Increased effectiveness in achieving group goals
- Augmented individual satisfaction with group membership

Negative Effects

- Useful or creative ideas may be ignored if they deviate from established norms or values
- Increased probability of developing groupthink
- Potential decrease in intergroup cooperation
- Counterproductive norms may be emphasized

A third possible advantage is that cohesive groups appear to be more effective in achieving goals that group members accept. However, research on this point is not totally consistent. For example, team sports competition would appear to be a setting where high cohesiveness would always bring about better performance. "Unfortunately, ... although some evidence supports [this intuitively appealing assumption], there is also research which fails to provide support."[53]

A final possible advantage of higher group cohesion is that members tend to have greater satisfaction with the group.

As positive as these potential advantages might seem, high group cohesion can be a mixed blessing from a manager's point of view (Exhibit 11.8). First, if the group has norms that do not support the organization's goals, then greater cohesion is definitely a minus. Individuals may be more influenced in the "wrong" direction, as when, for example, a group of workers tolerates sexual harassment, than if there is little cohesion. Another possible disadvantage of strong group cohesion is that deviance from group norms may not be handled effectively. Highly cohesive groups are more likely to reject any deviance, even if it represents creative or discordant ideas that could ultimately be useful to the group. Related to this is the danger that groupthink[54] (previously discussed in Chapter 9) may be accentuated in highly cohesive groups (see the Managerial Challenge box on the Challenger disaster for the dangers of groupthink). Dissenting viewpoints, as expressed in the phrase "devil's advocate," often can be quite useful to a group in causing it to critically test its opinion or decision.

Still another potential disadvantage of high within-group cohesion, but one that is frequently overlooked, is that between-group cooperation may be adversely affected. Most organizations have many work groups; some have hundreds or more. The challenge, from the organization's perspective, is to have these groups and teams work together and interact smoothly and reliably. So it is a concern if higher within-group cohesion hinders intergroup cooperation. For example, in developing and marketing a new product, problems may develop among the production, marketing, and sales departments. If the production group is highly cohesive and has a norm of never allowing outsiders to know they have problems, they may be reluctant to notify other units that a key piece of equipment is not functioning correctly. Without this information, the marketing department might generate unrealistic expectations for the release date, and the sales teams then would promise higher numbers of the product to customers than would actually be available.

MANAGERIAL CHALLENGE

GROUPTHINK AND THE *CHALLENGER* DISASTER

The worst disaster in National Aeronautics and Space Administration (NASA) history occurred on January 18, 1986, when the space shuttle *Challenger* exploded 73 seconds after launch, killing all seven astronauts. Spectators recoiled in horror as the meaning of the flash and fireball sunk in. Then a question arose: How could this have possibly happened? As might be expected, this disaster resulted in immediate in-depth probes of the accident. The investigations revealed that the explosion was caused by a leaky O-ring seal, which failed due to low launch temperatures. However, further analysis suggests that simple mechanical failure may not have been the sole cause of the accident. The phenomenon known as groupthink may have been a contributing factor.

Groupthink symptoms are apparent in the decision to launch the *Challenger*. The night before the launch, a tele-conference took place between managers from the Marshall Space Flight Center, the Kennedy Space Center, and the engineering contractor Morton Thiokol, Inc. (MTI), to discuss the launch conditions. Concerns had been raised because the overnight temperature was expected to be below 20 degrees. No earlier launch had been attempted at such a low temperature. MTI engineers, when queried by their managers, strongly recommended that the launch be scrubbed. They stated that they had documented problems with the O-ring that increased with decreasing tempera-tures. This was not what the flight managers wanted to hear.

NASA and MTI managers had worked together for several years. NASA had a history of 55 successful launches dating back almost 20 years and including the Apollo moon missions, the launch of Skylab, and the previous successful shuttle flights. There had already been one delay in the *Challenger* launch, and NASA managers did not want another. During prior decision-making sessions, engineers had always been asked to prove beyond a shadow of a doubt that the shuttle was completely ready for launch. Now, the engineers were being asked to prove absolutely that the shuttle would fail. This was a decision policy about-face, which allowed the managers to rationalize their deci-sion to launch because the engineers could not provide definitive, quantitative evidence of a failure that had not yet occurred. The engineers could only point to a trend of increasing problems with the O-rings at lower temperatures. The managers decided this was inconclusive and dispensed with any further engineering advice.

At this point, under pressure from NASA management, an executive at MTI expressed the opinion that a managerial decision needed to be made and instructed the vice president of engineering at MTI to take off his engineering hat and put on his management hat. The engineers' recommen-dations were overturned, and the decision was made to recommend a "Go" for the launch. This decision proved catastrophic.

Sources: Gregory Moorhead, Richard Ference, and Chris P. Neck, "Group Decision Fiascoes Continue: Space Shuttle *Challenger* and a Revised Groupthink Framework," *Human Relations* 44, no. 6 (1991), pp. 539–50; Russell P. Boisjoly, Ellen F. Curtis, and Eugene Mellican, "Roger Boisjoly and the *Challenger* Disaster: The Ethical Dimensions," *Journal of Business Ethics* 8, no. 4 (1989), pp. 217–30.

This example illustrates that the active promotion of strong within-group (team) cohesion by managers actually may decrease overall functioning of the larger orga-nization because of increased fragmentation. This situation is sometimes encoun-tered in highly decentralized organizations, where employees show extremely strong loyalty to their own unit, for example, marketing, but considerably less concern for the welfare of other units, say, production, and the need to coordinate with them. Thus, in this case, intraunit cohesion may gain greater autonomy for the unit, but it can hinder the achievement of integrated organizationwide objectives.

GROUP CONFLICT

Just as cohesion is a common feature of groups, so is conflict. Group conflict, that is, disagreement or opposition between or among group members, can occur for a number of reasons and have a variety of consequences. Although the effects of group conflict, such as a marked decrease in cohesion within the group, often can be negative, that is not always so. In fact, some types of conflict, particularly substantive conflict (discussed next), in some circumstances can have positive effects. The important point to remember is that conflict among members within groups is fairly common, and it is not always something to be avoided.

Types of Group Conflict

substantive (cognitive) conflict
differences in ideas and courses of action facing a group

Researchers have generally distinguished two basic types of group conflict: substantive conflict and relationship conflict. **Substantive conflict** is conflict that focuses on differences in ideas and courses of action in addressing the issues facing a group. It is also sometimes called cognitive (thinking)[55] or task conflict.[56] The absence of any conflict can be a sign that the group is not generating a variety of viewpoints and potential approaches for solving problems and making good decisions. Therefore, research indicates that at least some amount of substantive conflict can be beneficial to the group,[57] especially for less routine and more complex tasks.[58]

relationship (affective) conflict
interpersonal differences among group members

The other major type of conflict that can occur in groups, relationship conflict, is usually thought to be almost always dysfunctional. **Relationship conflict** focuses on interpersonal differences and is sometimes called affective or emotional conflict.[59] Research suggests it is a negative type of conflict for groups because it distracts focus from tasks and ideas.[60] It discourages rather than encourages consideration of multiple points of view.

Causes of Group Conflict

There are many potential causes of group conflict, but they can usually be linked to one of the two types of conflict.

The causes of substantive conflict, for example, include

* Ambiguities regarding the task;
* Differences in goals, objectives, and perspectives among group members; and
* Scarcity (actual or perceived) of resources to accomplish group goals.

Two possible causes of relationship conflict are

* Dissimilarities in the composition of the membership of the group, including demographic diversity (in age, ethnic/cultural background, gender, etc.) and status/power differences;[61] and
* Differences in interpersonal styles of individual members.

Several of the potential causes of group conflict can occur together; for example, when a very diverse group that includes several people with distinctive interpersonal styles encounters a highly ambiguous task. When there are such multiple causes, finding ways to deal with the conflict becomes even more difficult, of course.

Managing Group Conflict

Probably the most important managerial objective in dealing with group conflict is to attempt to increase the *ratio* of substantive to relationship conflict.[62] This would particularly include encouraging a culture of openness to express differences of opinion on task methods and objectives, especially novel or creative approaches to the task requirements.[63] In this way, unintended groupthink tendencies can be

Managers are facing increasingly diverse workforces as companies bring teams together. Often, this diversity includes employees from different countries and cultures. These teams may not function well automatically, and companies such as 3M, Colgate-Palmolive, Exxon, and Standard Charter Bank have provided additional training.

intergroup conflict
differences that occur between groups

intragroup conflict
differences that occur within groups

minimized. In addition, managers can clarify and reduce task ambiguities and try to help the group focus on larger goals beyond individual member interests that emphasize the common interests of all the group members.

Most of what we have been talking about so far applies to conflict *within* groups. In organizational settings, of course, conflict *between* or among groups—**intergroup conflict**—can also occur frequently. Strategies for managing **intragroup conflict** apply equally well to intergroup conflict. Therefore, managers should look for opportunities to reduce unnecessary relational conflicts in those intergroup interaction situations and increase the focus on substantive differences. Also, emphasizing larger, common goals can help increase cooperation and thus performance.[64] So, if marketing and production can concentrate on the issue of customer satisfaction—to elevate it to the highest priority—then their differences on how many variations of a product to make and market can be minimized or resolved.

Indeed, senior executives often comment on the creative potential of intergroup conflict. Fred Cunningham, a manager at Keane, an information technology firm in Boston, states, "Put simply, conflict is a potent source of creativity—especially in troubled times. After all, if everything is going smoothly, there's no need to innovate or move to a higher level. When marketing and engineering disagree violently about something, you've got a wonderful opportunity to figure out how to make improvements by meeting both of their objectives." Jerry Hirshberg, president of Nissan Design International in San Diego, goes even a step further by actively encouraging conflict for its "creative abrasion," what he defines as conflict's "ability to transform friction … into opportunities for breakthroughs."[65]

IMPROVING GROUP AND TEAM EFFECTIVENESS

Teams and groups are not static parts of organizations. They come into existence, go out of existence, and change over time. Among the changes that can occur are increases or decreases in effectiveness. Social scientists have focused considerable attention over the years on studying groups, and their findings have resulted in some useful guidelines for managers in attempting to improve the performance of their groups in organizational settings.

Assessing the Effectiveness of Groups

To gain an understanding about how group performance may be improved, we first need to specify what we mean by group effectiveness. That is, what distinguishes highly effective groups from less effective groups? A survey of 61 U.S. companies revealed that about two-thirds used objective quantifiable criteria to measure group effectiveness; these included measures of production output, quality, cost reduction, and turnaround time. A number of the companies also used more subjective criteria including member participation, cooperation, and involvement.[66]

How can we tell when a group is performing especially well? Analyses of research findings by one of the foremost experts on group effectiveness, Richard Hackman, suggest three major indicators (Exhibit 11.9):[67]

1. Whether the group's outputs—products, services, or decisions—are valued by those that receive or use them. Are a committee's recommendations implemented? Does a product development group's creation ever get put into production? Is upper management satisfied with the performance of a customer service unit?

2. Whether the group's capacity for further cooperation among its members is maintained or increased. In early 1994, Walt Disney, Inc., had one of the most talented, experienced, and stable management teams in the movie industry, but its capacity for continued effective interaction was severely tested. The president of Disney, Frank Wells, was killed in a helicopter crash; the production chief, Jeffrey Katzenberg, left in a well-publicized rift when he was passed over for the president's job; and the CEO, Michael Eisner, underwent quadruple bypass surgery.[68] Despite this series of disastrous events, the top group directing the fortunes of Disney was able to maintain the capacity for ongoing cooperation and teamwork in the immediately following years.

3. Whether members gain satisfaction and a sense of growth and well-being from being part of the group. A group or team is unlikely to be regarded by outsiders as effective if its own members do not seem satisfied and are not experiencing feelings of accomplishment by being part of the group.

Most observers would probably say that the first of these criteria of effectiveness—acceptance of the group's outputs by others—is the most important one in organizational settings. However, if neither of the other two indicators can be achieved by a group, it is highly unlikely that it will be able over time to produce

---

EXHIBIT 11.9

Characteristics of Highly Effective Groups

- Any product or service they develop is highly desired and valued by customers.
- Increased cooperation among members is encouraged and achieved.
- Group membership increases individual members' feelings of satisfaction, personal growth, and overall well-being.

Source: J. R. Hackman (ed.), *Groups That Work (and Those That Don't):Creating Conditions for Effective Teamwork* (San Francisco: Jossey-Bass, 1990).

valued output. Thus, all three are important components of group effectiveness and need attention from those who lead groups.

Ingredients Necessary for Group Effectiveness

For a group to perform effectively, it must be able to do three things especially well:

1. Exert enough effort to accomplish its tasks at acceptable levels of quantity and quality;
2. Obtain sufficient knowledge and skills to carry out its work; and
3. Use appropriate strategies to apply its effort, knowledge, and skills effectively.[69]

These three bases for achieving high levels of group effectiveness sound simple, but they are major challenges for organizations and leaders of groups. To assure that these components are actually in place consistently, managers need to address several issues:

Developing Appropriate Group Structures   To be effective, groups need clearly defined tasks and objectives that can motivate their members. They also need a group size appropriate to the tasks and a membership with a sufficient mix of skills and expertise. An illustration of this was provided by the situation faced by Stentor Resource Center Inc. (SRCI). It was charged with developing a solution to the problem of North American telephone companies running out of toll-free 800 numbers. The SRCI team that solved this problem began with 12 people. As it studied the problem and found it needed more expertise, the core group grew to 50. To incorporate all the necessary ideas and concerns, the group expanded. At its largest, the extended "group" of multiple subgroups consisted of 425 members at 17 locations. It included representatives from suppliers, customers, government agencies, and U.S. telephone companies.[70]

Developing Appropriate Support from the Organization   Groups operating within companies and organizations need support from their surrounding environment such as rewards for effective collaboration among members,[71] education and technical training for performing critical group tasks,[72] relief from other duties, and access to necessary information. For example, a few years ago, managers in the U.S. Information Agency (USIA) found that after a reorganization of the agency into self-managing teams, their major problems centered around a lack of administrative support.[73]

Developing Appropriate Coaching and Consultation   Most groups need outside help to reduce potential conflicts, increase coordination in dealing with problems within the group, and provide strategies for approaching the group's tasks.

Exhibit 11.10 provides a summary of the preceding points and shows how the manager's attention to the group's structure, support from the organizational context, and relevant coaching and consultation can help increase each of the three ingredients necessary for group effectiveness: high levels of effort, sufficient knowledge and skills, and appropriate strategies for applying effort and skills. The points

	EXHIBIT 11.10

Enhancing Group Effectiveness

		POINTS OF LEVERAGE	
Necessary Processes	**Group Structure**	**Organizational Context**	**Coaching and Consultation**
Apply ample effort	Motivational structure of group task	Organizational reward system	Remedying coordination problems and building group commitment
Acquire sufficient knowledge and skill	Group composition	Organizational education/ training system	Remedying inappropriate "weighting" of member inputs and fostering cross-training
Develop task-appropriate performance strategies	Group norms that regulate member behavior and foster scanning and planning	Organizational information system	Remedying implementation problems and fostering creativity in strategy development

Source: Adapted from J. R. Hackman (ed.), *Groups That Work (and Those That Don't): Creating Conditions for Effective Teamwork* (San Francisco: Jossey-Bass, 1990), p. 13.

presented and summarized in the exhibit do not provide a cookbook for group or team success. Rather, they are useful guidelines for managers and organizations to consider in approaching *their* task of helping groups to improve performance for themselves and those who rely on the outputs of their work. Likewise, Exhibit 11.11, based on extensive research,[74] provides a helpful checklist for those who assume leadership positions in groups and teams to measure how well they are fulfilling that role in their groups. If team members concur that their leader is in fact doing a good job in these various areas of the role, then it is likely that the group (not just the leader) will perform well.

	EXHIBIT 11.11

A Checklist for Leaders of Groups

How well do you:

- ☑ Encourage members to learn from each other?
- ☑ Recognize and praise members for their contributions?
- ☑ Keep key people outside the [group] informed about its accomplishments?
- ☑ Promptly inform members about major developments that [may] affect them?
- ☑ Give [group] members authority to make [at least some] important decisions?
- ☑ Openly accept and respond to feedback from [group] members?
- ☑ Review the [group's] performance at the end of major tasks?
- ☑ Offer specific and concrete suggestions for how members can improve?
- ☑ Understand what motivates members to work hard?

Source: Adapted from G. L. Hallam, "Seven Common Beliefs about Teams: Are They True?" *Leadership in Action* 17, no. 3 (1997), pp. 1–4.

CONCLUDING COMMENTS

Groups are here to stay. More to the point, they are becoming increasingly vital parts of contemporary organizations operating in a world of accelerated change and competition. Thus, anybody who aspires to become an effective manager or executive in an organization will need to be able to (1) understand different types of groups and how they function and (2) know how to lead them effectively. These are fundamental challenges, but they can be met.

No matter how familiar we are with groups as essential elements of organized activity, they are not as simple as they might seem on the surface. Many people who carry out their own individual work exceedingly well, and who interact very comfortably in one-to-one relationships, often run into difficulties when called on to manage group activity. Groups multiply the number of interpersonal relationships involved, which in turn creates a level of complexity that needs to be assessed and mastered.

To be able to manage groups successfully is a skill that can be learned. It requires deliberate effort to be perceptive and to notice many subtle nuances as well as the more obvious aspects of interpersonal relationships occurring inside groups. Are certain norms forming, and if so, what are the directions of these norms? Is a group developing cohesion, and does it lend support to the organization's larger goals or only to the narrow self-interests of the immediate group? Is there conflict within the group and is it focused on better problem solving or only on potentially destructive personal relationships? Attention to these and similar issues will provide a solid base for leading productive groups.

Successful management of groups also requires constant awareness of how the conditions surrounding groups are changing and how that evolving context will affect what groups do and how they perform. Since groups are parts of larger organizations, keeping track of what is going on elsewhere in the overall organization is essential for managers and leaders. The larger organization can provide a source of support for the group, but it also can provide obstacles if not monitored carefully. Another way of saying this is that just as most individuals in organizations don't work in isolation, neither do groups. The organizational context outside of a group is nearly as important as the interactions that take place inside it in determining how effectively it performs.

Finally, as we noted early in the chapter, there is strong pressure in many of today's organizations for managers to develop their groups to become teams, with all that that term implies. This is not an unrealistic goal, but it can happen only if leaders of groups first learn something about group structure and characteristics and then focus on how to put that knowledge to use day to day. Groups that turn into teams have the potential to vastly magnify the productivity and quality of a set of individuals, as demonstrated in the case of the Navy SEALs, but true teamwork must be created and nurtured by skillful managing rather than simply be asserted as an accomplished fact.

KEY TERMS

cohesion 310
command (supervisory) group 296
committee 298

conformity 310
formal group 298
group 295

informal group 298
intergroup conflict 315
intragroup conflict 315

norms 307

process costs 304

project/task force 297

relationship (affective) conflict 314

role ambiguity 307

role conflict 307

self-managing (autonomous) work group 297

social loafing 303

status 307

substantitive (cognitive) conflict 314

team 295

REVIEW QUESTIONS

1. What are the similarities and differences between a group and a team?
2. What are the major types of groups found in organizations? Give examples of each.
3. What is the fundamental difference between a formal and an informal group?
4. How do organizational goals affect the formation of groups?
5. What are some of the concerns of new group members?
6. How is proximity related to the formation of informal groups?
7. What personal needs may be satisfied by group membership?
8. What are the four stages of group formation? What are the important features of each?
9. What are the structural characteristics of groups? Why is each important?
10. Is there an optimum group size? Why or why not?
11. To what extent is social loafing likely to be equally prevalent in all cultures?
12. How do heterogeneous groups differ from homogeneous ones?
13. What are some of the types of diversity found within groups? What effects can diversity have on group members and on group functioning?
14. Provide examples of role conflict and role ambiguity that illustrate the difference between the two terms.
15. Why are norms important to groups?
16. What are some of the key factors that often have major influences on the development of norms?
17. Is it always good to have a high level of conformity within a group?
18. Can managers affect the level of conformity within a group? Why or why not?
19. What steps can a manager take to deal with groupthink?
20. What are the two basic types of group conflict?
21. Can managers eliminate group conflict? Should they try?
22. What are three major indicators that can be used to identify high-performance groups?
23. What kinds of issues must managers address when attempting to improve group effectiveness?

DISCUSSION QUESTIONS

1. As a manager, would you rather work with highly diversified teams or with more homogeneous teams? Why? Which types would be best for which types of situations?
2. Think about a group in which you have been involved at work, at school, or perhaps while playing a sport. What were the structural characteristics of the group? What were some of its norms? Would you characterize it as a group or as a team? Why?

3. Some students groan and complain when told they must participate in a group project. Why do you think this is? What is it about group work that irritates some students so much? After reading this chapter, can you think of ways to structure and lead a group to gain these individuals' cooperation and motivation?

4. As a manager, if your work group is demonstrating considerable intragroup conflict, what would you do?

CLOSING CASE

*The Team That Wasn't**

The last thing Eric Holt had expected to miss about New York City was its sunrises. Seeing one usually meant he had pulled another all-nighter at the consulting firm where, as a vice president, he had managed three teams of manufacturing specialists. But as he stood on the balcony of his new apartment in the small Indiana city that was now his home, Eric suddenly felt a pang of nostalgia for the way the dawn plays off the skyscrapers of Manhattan. In the next moment, though, he let out a sardonic laugh. The dawn light was *not* what he missed about New York, he realized. What he missed was the feeling of accomplishment that usually accompanied those sunrises.

An all-nighter in New York had meant hours of intense work with a cadre of committed, enthusiastic colleagues. Give and take. Humor. Progress. Here, so far anyway, that was unthinkable. As the director of strategy at FireArt, Inc., a regional glass manufacturer, Eric spent all his time trying to get his new team to make it through a meeting without the tension level becoming unbearable. Six of the top-level managers involved seemed determined to turn the company around, but the seventh seemed equally determined to sabotage the process. Forget camaraderie. There had been three meetings so far, and Eric hadn't even been able to get everyone on the same side of an issue.

Eric stepped inside his apartment and checked the clock: only three more hours before he had to watch as Randy Louderback, FireArt's charismatic director of sales and marketing, either dominated the group's discussion or withdrew entirely, tapping his pen on the table to indicate his boredom. Sometimes he withheld information vital to the group's debate; other times he coolly denigrated people's comments. Still, Eric realized, Randy held the group in such thrall because of his dynamic personality, his almost legendary past, and his close relationship with FireArt's CEO that he could not be ignored. And at least once during each meeting, he offered an insight about the

industry or the company that was so perceptive that Eric knew he *shouldn't* be ignored.

As he prepared to leave for the office, Eric felt the familiar frustration that had started building during the team's first meeting a month earlier. It was then that Randy had first insinuated, with what sounded like a joke, that he wasn't cut out to be a team player. "Leaders lead, followers … please pipe down!" had been his exact words, although he had smiled winningly as he spoke, and the rest of the group had laughed heartily in response. No one in the group was laughing now, though, least of all Eric.

FireArt, Inc., was in trouble—not deep trouble, but enough for its CEO, Jack Derry, to make strategic repositioning Eric's top and only task. The company, a family-owned maker of wine goblets, beer steins, ashtrays, and other glass novelties had succeeded for nearly 80 years as a high-quality, high-price producer, catering to hundreds of Midwestern clients. It traditionally did big business every football season, selling commemorative knickknacks to the fans of teams such as the Fighting Irish, the Wolverines, and the Golden Gophers. In the spring, there was always a rush of demand for senior prom items—champagne goblets emblazoned with a school's name or beer mugs with a school's crest, for example. Fraternities and sororities were steady customers. Year after year, FireArt showed respectable increases at the top and bottom lines, posting $86 million in earnings three years before Eric arrived.

In the last 18 months, though, sales and earnings had flattened. Jack, a grandnephew of the company's founder, thought he knew what was happening. Until recently, large national glass companies had been able to make money only through mass production. Now, however, thanks to new technologies in the glassmaking industry, those companies could execute short runs profitably. They had begun to enter FireArt's niche, Jack had told Eric, and, with their superior resources, it was just a matter of time before they would own it.

---

*HBR's cases are derived from the experiences of real companies and real people. As written, they are hypothetical, and the names used are fictitious.

"You have one responsibility as FireArt's new director of strategy," Jack had said to Eric on his first day. "That's to put together a team of our top people, one person from each division, and have a comprehensive plan for the company's strategic realignment up, running, and winning within six months."

Eric had immediately compiled a list of the senior managers from human resources, manufacturing, finance, distribution, design, and marketing, and had set a date for the first meeting. Then, drawing on his years as a consultant who had worked almost solely in team environments, Eric had carefully prepared a structure and guidelines for the group's discussions, disagreements, and decisions, which he planned to propose to the members for their input before they began working together.

Successful groups are part art, part science, Eric knew, but he also believed that with every member's full commitment, a team proved the adage that the whole is greater than the sum of its parts. Knowing that managers at FireArt were unaccustomed to the team process, however, Eric imagined he might get some resistance from one or two members.

For one, he had been worried about Ray LaPierre of manufacturing. Ray was a giant of a man who had run the furnaces for some 35 years, following in his father's footsteps. Although he was a former high school football star who was known among workers in the factory for his hearty laugh and his love of practical jokes, Ray usually didn't say much around FireArt's executives, citing his lack of higher education as the reason. Eric had thought the team atmosphere might intimidate him.

Eric had also anticipated a bit of a fight from Maureen Turner of the design division, who was known to complain that FireArt didn't appreciate its six artists. Eric had expected that Maureen might have a chip on her shoulder about collaborating with people who didn't understand the design process.

Ironically, both those fears had proved groundless, but another, more difficult problem had arisen. The wild card had turned out to be Randy. Eric had met Randy once before the team started its work and had found him to be enormously intelligent, energetic, and good-humored. What's more, Jack Derry had confirmed his impressions, telling him that Randy "had the best mind" at FireArt. It was also from Jack that Eric had first learned of Randy's hardscrabble yet inspirational personal history.

Poor as a child, he had worked as a security guard and short-order cook to put himself through the state college, from which he graduated with top honors. Soon after, he started his own advertising and market research firm in Indianapolis, and within the decade, he had built it into a company employing 50 people to service some of the region's most prestigious accounts. His success bought with it a measure of fame: articles in the local media, invitations to the statehouse, even an honorary degree from an Indiana business college. But in the late 1980s, Randy's firm suffered the same fate as many other advertising shops, and he was forced to declare bankruptcy. FireArt considered it a coup when it landed him as director of marketing, since he had let it be known that he was offered at least two dozen other jobs. "Randy is the future of this company," Jack Derry had told Eric. "If he can't help you, no one can. I look forward to hearing what a team with his kind of horsepower can come up with to steer us away from the mess we're in."

Those words echoed in Eric's mind as he sat, with increasing anxiety, through the team's first and second meetings. Though Eric had planned an agenda for each meeting and tried to keep the discussions on track, Randy always seemed to find a way to disrupt the process. Time and time again, he shot down other people's ideas, or he simply didn't pay attention. He also answered most questions put to him with maddening vagueness. "I'll have my assistant look into it when he gets a moment," he replied when one team member asked him to list FireArt's five largest customers. "Some days you eat the bear, and other days the bear eats you," he joked another time, when asked why sales to fraternities had recently nose-dived.

Randy's negativism, however, was countered by occasional comments so insightful that they stopped the conversation cold or turned it around entirely—comments that demonstrated extraordinary knowledge about competitors or glass technology or customers' buying patterns. The help wouldn't last, though; Randy would quickly revert to his role as team renegade.

The third meeting, last week, had ended in chaos. Ray LaPierre, Maureen Turner, and the distribution director, Carl Simmons, had each planned to present cost-cutting proposals, and at first it looked as though the group were making good progress.

Ray opened the meeting, proposing a plan for FireArt to cut throughput time by 3 percent and raw-materials costs by 2 percent, thereby positioning the company to compete better on price. It was obvious from his detailed presentation that he had put a lot of thought into his comments, and it was evident that he was fighting a certain amount of nervousness as he made them.

"I know I don't have the book smarts of most of you in this room," he had begun, "but here goes anyway." During his presentation, Ray stopped several times to answer questions from the team, and as he went on, his nervousness transformed into his usual ebullience. "That wasn't so bad!" he laughed to himself as he sat down at the end, flashing a grin at Eric. "Maybe we *can* turn this old ship around."

Maureen Turner had followed Ray. While not disagreeing with him—she praised his comments, in fact—she argued that FireArt also needed to invest in new artists, pitching its competitive advantage in better design and wider variety. Unlike Ray, Maureen had made this case to FireArt's top executives many times, only to be rebuffed, and some of her frustration seeped through as she explained her reasoning yet again. At one point, her voice almost broke as she described how hard she had worked in her first 10 years at FireArt, hoping that someone in management would recognize the creativity of her designs. "But no one did," she recalled with a sad shake of her head. "That's why when I was made director of the department, I made sure all the artists were respected for what they are—*artists,* not worker ants. There's a difference, you know." However, just as with Ray LaPierre, Maureen's comments lost their defensiveness as the group members, with the exception of Randy, who remained impassive, greeted her words with nods of encouragement.

By the time Carl Simmons of distribution started to speak, the mood in the room was approaching buoyant. Carl, a quiet and meticulous man, jumped from his seat and practically paced the room as he described his ideas. FireArt, he said, should play to its strength as a service-oriented company and restructure its trucking system to increase the speed of delivery. He described how a similar strategy had been adopted with excellent results at his last job at a ceramics plant. Carl had joined FireArt just six months earlier. It was when Carl began to describe those results in detail that Randy brought the meeting to an unpleasant halt by letting out a loud groan. "Let's just do *everything,* why don't we, including redesign the kitchen sink!" he cried with mock enthusiasm. That remark sent Carl back quickly to his seat, where he halfheartedly summed up his comments. A few minutes later, he excused himself, saying he had another meeting. Soon the others made excuses to leave, too, and the room became empty.

No wonder Eric was apprehensive about the fourth meeting. He was therefore surprised when he entered the room and found the whole group, save Randy, already assembled.

Ten minutes passed in awkward small talk, and looking, from face to face, Eric could see his own frustration reflected. He also detected an edge of panic—just what he had hoped to avoid. He decided he had to raise the topic of Randy's attitude openly, but just as he started, Randy ambled into the room, smiling. "Sorry, folks," he said lightly, holding up a cup of coffee as if it were explanation enough for his tardiness.

"Randy, I'm glad you're here," Eric began, "because I think today we should begin by talking about the group itself—"

Randy cut Eric off with a small, sarcastic laugh. "Uh-oh, I knew this was going to happen," he said.

Before Eric could answer, Ray LaPierre stood up and walked over to Randy, bending over to look him in the eye.

"You just don't care, do you?" he began, his voice so angry it startled everyone in the room.

Everyone except Randy. "Quite the contrary—I care very much," he answered breezily. "I just don't believe this is how change should be made. A brilliant idea never came out of a *team.* Brilliant ideas come from brilliant individuals, who then inspire others in the organization to implement them."

"That's a lot of bull," Ray shot back. "You just want all the credit for the success, and you don't want to share it with anyone."

"That's absurd," Randy laughed again. "I'm not trying to impress anyone here at FireArt. I don't need to. I want this company to succeed as much as you do, but I believe, and I believe passionately, that groups are useless. Consensus means mediocrity. I'm, sorry, but it does."

"But you haven't even *tried* to reach consensus with us," Maureen interjected. "It's as if you don't care what we all have to say. We can't work alone for a solution—we need to understand each other. Don't you see that?"

The room was silent as Randy shrugged his shoulders noncommittally. He stared at the table, a blank expression on his face.

It was Eric who broke the silence. "Randy, this is a *team.* You are part of it," he said, trying to catch Randy's eye without success. "Perhaps we should start again—"

Randy stopped him by holding up his cup, as if making a toast. "Okay, look, I'll behave from now on," he said. The words held promise, but he was smirking as the spoke them—something no one at the table missed. Eric took a deep breath before he answered; as much as he wanted and needed Randy Louderback's help, he was suddenly struck by the thought that perhaps Randy's personality and his past experiences simply made it impossible for him to participate in the delicate process of ego surrender that any kind of teamwork requires.

"Listen, everyone, I know this is a challenge," Eric began, but he was cut short by Randy's pencil-tapping on the table. A moment later, Ray LaPierre was standing again.

"Forget it. This is never going to work. It's just a waste of time for all of us," he said, more resigned than gruff. "We're all in this together, or there's no point." He headed for the door, and before Eric could stop him, two others were at his heels.

QUESTIONS

1. In what stage of development is FireArt's strategy team? What characteristics of the team point to this stage of development?
2. Do you believe Eric Holt is an effective team leader? Why or why not? What could he do to improve the effectiveness of the team?
3. What is the underlying attitude behind Randy Louderback's behavior? Why may he be trying to undermine the success of the team?
4. Categorize the type of conflict this group is experiencing (i.e., is it related to a task or to personality)? How could the conflict be reduced?

CHAPTER 12

MANAGING HUMAN RESOURCES

LEARNING OBJECTIVES

After studying this chapter, you should be able to:

- Discuss why human resources are key to the success or failure of a firm.
- Explain why the effective management of human resources is a key to the career success or failure for all managers.
- Identify key factors in an organization's external and internal environment that affect human resource management.
- Describe the basic activities of human resource management.
- Discuss key contemporary challenges to effective human resource management.

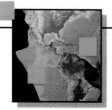

Brunswick's Global Human Resource Challenge

"The world is bigger than a bowling ball." This is the message that senior executives were trying to communicate to Brunswick's 20,000 employees. Brunswick, a U.S.-based $3 billion firm, is a leader in the recreation market. In addition to its traditional and well-known lines of bowling and billiard products, it is also the world's largest manufacturer of recreational boats, including SeaRay, Bayliner, Baja, Procraft, and Astro boats, holds a dominant position in fishing tackle through its Zebco line of products, and is a leader in health and fitness with its LifeCycle products. Brunswick dominates the U.S. market in all its major product lines but only 18 percent of its revenues are from outside the United States. To continue to grow, it must expand into global markets. According to one senior executive, "We are number one in the United States in virtually every product line we have. We need to expand our activities into the global marketplace."

When asked what was the biggest constraint to the implementation of this strategy, an executive replied, "People. At the moment we do not have the human resources necessary to implement our globalization strategy." Brunswick faces many challenges as it tries to expand internationally. For example, Brunswick is expanding into Brazil. Although Brazil has thousands of lakes and rivers waiting for people to enjoy them by boat, it also has laws that restrict the importation of boats costing more than $3,500. The obvious solution is to manufacture boats in Brazil. However, this solution is not as easy to implement as it seems. A variety of human resource challenges first must be met.

One of the first challenges Brunswick faces is determining whether there is a market for recreational boats in Brazil. This seems like a market research challenge, but for many firms like Brunswick, it is more fundamentally a human resource challenge. The critical human resource issue is: Does Brunswick have the people capable of assessing the recreational boat market in Brazil?

Even if Brunswick can assess the Brazilian market and even if that assessment is positive, it still faces several human resource challenges. Can the firm find the skilled people it needs in the Brazilian labor market in sufficient numbers and at a wage that will enable them to manufacture boats cost-effectively? If not, then the potential for Brunswick boats in Brazil is just that—potential.

If Brunswick determines the market is there and skilled labor is not a problem, it faces an additional human resource challenge: Who should it select to run the Brazilian operation? Does Brunswick have anyone with the necessary skills to succeed in the job? The manager must understand how to socialize and train new employees to ensure that they perform their jobs effectively. The manager must be capable of establishing reward systems that will motivate employees to perform well and stay in the company.

Without adequate answers to these human resource management questions, Brunswick's strategy may look great on paper but never translate into real results.

Source: Personal communication with Brunswick senior management.

Brunswick's dilemma illustrates two key issues: (1) firms' ability to survive and prosper in the future is increasingly a function of the human resources they have and (2) as a manager, your career success or failure depends on how well you manage human resources. We can all think of firms whose success seems tied to products, technology, or strategy, not people. Where would Apple be without the Macintosh or iMac? Would Sprint be a player in long distance without fiber optics? Clearly these and other "golden eggs" seem to be at the heart of certain firms' fortunes. True, but the key to any golden egg is a goose. Golden eggs do not just materialize. Without bright, capable, and motivated people, Apple would not have the Macintosh or iMac. Without people who recognized the growing need for data transmission and the superiority of fiber optics for transmitting digital data, Sprint would not have even made it to the starting line. In short, people invent and utilize technology; people gather, analyze, and disseminate information; people formulate and implement strategy. Thus, Brunswick's dependence on people for its future success is not unique or even uncommon. Both the quality of firm's strategy and the success of its implementation depend on getting the right people and maximizing their performance and potential.

You still may wonder why effective human resource management is the key to your career success. Imagine yourself as a manager in Brunswick for a moment. As a manager, you would need to get things done through people. How do you make sure that you have the right people in your unit and that they maximize their performance and potential?

- You need the ability to *recruit* and *select* the right people.
- You need the ability to effectively *socialize* and *train* people in your unit.
- You need the ability to effectively *evaluate* their performance.
- You need the ability to determine *reward* systems that will motivate high performance.
- You need to know what additional experience or education your subordinates need to *develop* and advance in their careers.

As we will explore throughout this chapter, the *right* people, *effective* training, *appropriate* performance appraisal, *successful* reward systems, and *needed* development opportunities are functions of your firm's strategy and the demands, constraints, and opportunities provided by the environment.

Exhibit 12.1 incorporates these various perspectives into a framework of human resource management (HRM). As the figure illustrates, specific human resource activities (planning, job analysis, recruiting, selecting, socialization and training, job design, performance appraisal, compensation, development) exist within the context of the firm's strategy and environment. The fit of these human resource activities with the strategy and environment leads to competitive advantage for the organization and for the individual manager. To fully understand these relationships and terms, we need to examine each aspect of the framework individually. We will then reintegrate them at the end of the chapter.

To understand the framework in Exhibit 12.1, we review briefly the notion of competitive advantage. You recall from Chapter 8 that competitive advantage is created through the achievement of all the following:

- Doing things better than others do them.
- Doing things that are difficult for others to replicate.
- Doing things that customers value.
- Doing things that are difficult to substitute.
- Doing things that have greater than average cost-value margins.[1]

There are two main points to keep in mind concerning competitive advantage and human resource management. First, the five factors that provide firms with competitive advantage also can provide individuals with an edge in the labor market. Second, for both organizations and individual managers, these five factors are accomplished through people. As a consequence, superior ability to manage people can be a key competitive advantage.

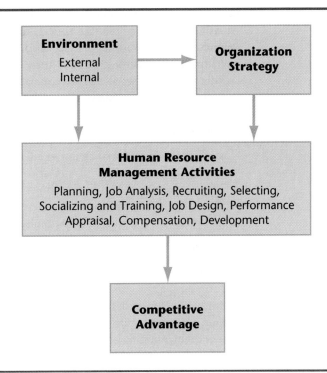

HUMAN RESOURCE MANAGEMENT AND COMPETITIVE ADVANTAGE

Let's now take a closer look at how effective human resource management can create competitive advantage for both the organization and you as an individual manager.

HRM and Organizational Competitive Advantage

People are at the heart of any firm's competitive advantage. This is because *all* activities within an organization can be traced to human involvement and capabilities. But this may seem counterintuitive given the importance of technology in today's marketplace. In the auto industry, direct labor has declined from 30 percent to less than 7 percent for most manufacturers. For example, many French, German, British, American, Korean, and Japanese automobile manufacturers have 10 percent to 20 percent of their painting and welding done by robots. Some firms even advertise automated functions as keys to improved quality. Where is the human element in robots painting or welding cars? People determined whether the quality and consistency of paint and welds were dimensions through which the firm could compete effectively; people assembled and analyzed the information on various robots and made purchasing decisions; people decided how and where to install robots in the factory; effective recruiting, selecting, training and socializing, performance appraising, rewarding, and developing activities put capable people in the position to make all these and other critical decisions. Poor human resource activities could lead to the wrong people being in critical positions, which in turn would lead to poor decisions and weakened ability to compete. General Electric (GE) provides a positive example. By undertaking a variety of changes in hiring, training, appraising, and rewarding people, GE achieved significant productivity increases. In fact, from 1981 through 1992, these productivity increases saved the company $600 million. These savings are equivalent to the profits GE would likely get from acquiring a *$6 billion business!*[2]

HRM and Individual Competitive Advantage

Just as the effective management of human resources can lead to competitive advantage for a company, it can also give you a competitive advantage in your managerial career. Just as firms compete with each other in the marketplace, so too do individuals. The reality is that there are many fewer positions of responsibility than people who would like to occupy them. Because managers must get things done through other people, their promotability is largely dependent on the performance of other people. Consequently, all managers need to effectively plan for their future personnel needs, analyze the jobs over which they have responsibility, identify and attract the right candidates, select the best people, orient and train them, design and redesign subordinates' jobs, evaluate how well or poorly they are doing, encourage and motivate them to perform well, and develop them for greater opportunities and responsibilities in the future.

One of the most enlightening studies on the importance of effective human resource management and career success looked at cases of career derailment. The study found that the number one reason for managerial career derailment, or, in other words, the number one reason why managers who *got on* but then at some point were *bumped off* the upwardly mobile career track, was their inability to successfully carry out the activities associated with effective human resource management.[3] Consequently, managers who gain a competitive advantage at human resource management activities place themselves in a superior position for upward movement and greater opportunities and responsibilities.

ENVIRONMENT AND HRM PRACTICES

Part of what determines whether a particular human resource management activity is effective is the environment that surrounds the activities. As we discussed early in this text, a firm's environment can be segmented into its external and internal components. As we examine both, it should become clear that the environment is one of the most important factors in determining appropriate HR practices and effective HR management—and ultimately the success or failure of a firm or manager.

External Environment

The external environment of a firm has many possible components, as we have explored in previous chapters.[4] Because each one of these components can significantly affect the success or failure of organizations and individual managers, we briefly review key segments of the external environment and discuss their impact on human resource activities.

Laws and Regulations Perhaps the most significant external environmental factor for human resources is the legal and regulatory environment. In countries like the United States, laws and regulations are the source of both challenges and frustrations for organizations and individual managers. Laws and regulations affect virtually every human resource activity, from recruiting to development. For example, a group of flight attendants for Delta Airlines recently filed suit because Delta had weight limits for flight attendants. The suit claimed discrimination because while the weight limits were applied to all flight attendants, both male and female, there were no similar standards applied to pilots. Delta first argued that the weight limits were legal because certain size limitations were necessary for flight attendants to perform their jobs in the limited space on planes. Despite this argument, Delta later dropped the weight requirements for all flight attendants.[5]

Exhibit 12.2 provides a summary of the laws enacted in the United States that have had a significant impact on human resource practices and policies. The basic intent of most of this legislation has been to ensure that equal opportunity is provided for both job applicants and current employees. Because the laws were intended to correct past inequalities, many organizations have implemented **affirmative action programs** to ensure that organizational changes are made. These programs may involve such things as taking extra effort to inform minority candidates about job opportunities, providing special training programs for disadvantaged candidates, or paying special attention to the racial or gender mix of employees who are promoted.

As business globalizes, laws in the United States have begun to have implications outside its formal borders. For example, the Civil Rights Act of 1991 was passed requiring U.S. firms to abide by the same nondiscrimination laws relative to their U.S. personnel overseas as their U.S. employees residing in the United States.[6] One of the specific implications of this law is that unless a particular host country prohibits women from occupying managerial positions, a U.S. firm cannot discriminate against a woman candidate being sent overseas on assignment even if the norms and values of the host country would make it difficult for a women to be effective. Consider that at the time the law was passed only 3 percent of U.S. **expatriate employees**, or employees sent overseas on temporary assignments of three to five years, were women and 41 percent of all U.S. managers were female. This suggests that there may have been some gender bias in the selection of U.S. expatriate managers in the past. Add to this the fact that increasingly, U.S. firms are *requiring* an international assignment as part of a person's development for top management positions. Given that only 3 percent of those receiving this opportunity are women, U.S. firms may find that they face a severe **glass ceiling** problem (i.e., an invisible barrier that prevents women from promotion to the highest executive ranks) and lawsuits because of gender discrimination against women relative to international assignments.

Countries to which managers might be sent for development opportunities only complicate the situation. For example, since Japan is the United States's second largest trading partner, U.S. firms are likely to send employees to operations in Japan. However, in Japan, less than 1 percent of all managers are women. This may suggest that in the traditionally male-dominated society, female expatriate managers from the United States might have difficulty being successful. Yet, the Civil Rights Act of 1991 mandates that the gender of a U.S. candidate cannot be a factor in the selection decision. It is interesting to note that despite initial inclinations to think

affirmative action programs
hiring and training programs intended to correct past inequalities for certain categories of people based on gender, race and ethnicity, age, or religion

expatriate employees
employees sent overseas on temporary assignments of three to five years

glass ceiling
an invisible barrier that prevents women from promotion to the highest executive ranks

EXHIBIT 12.2

Major U.S. Federal Laws and Regulations Related to Human Resource Management

Act	Requirements	Covers	Enforcement Agency
Thirteenth Amendment	Abolished slavery	All individuals	Court system
Fourteenth Amendment	Provides equal protection for all citizens and requires due process in state action	State actions (e.g., decisions of governmental organizations)	Court system
Civil Rights Acts of 1866 and 1871 (as amended)	Grant all citizens the right to make, perform, modify, and terminate contracts and enjoy all benefits, terms, and conditions of the contractual relationship	All individuals	Court system
Equal Pay Act of 1963	Requires that men and women performing equal jobs receive equal pay	Employers engaged in interstate commerce	EEOC
Title VII of CRA	Forbids discrimination based on race, color, religion, sex, or national origin	Employers with 15 or more employees working 20 or more weeks per year; labor unions; and employment agencies	EEOC
Age Discrimination in Employment Act of 1967	Prohibits discrimination in employment against individuals 40 years of age and older	Employers with 15 or more employees working 20 or more weeks per year; labor unions; employment agencies; federal government	EEOC
Rehabilitation Act of 1973	Requires affirmative action in the employment of individuals with disabilities	Government agencies; federal contractors and subcontractors with contracts greater than $2,500	OFCCP
Americans with Disabilities Act of 1990	Prohibits discrimination against individuals with disabilities	Employers with more than 15 employees	EEOC
Executive Order 11246	Requires affirmative action in hiring women and minorities	Federal contractors and subcontractors with contracts greater than $10,000	OFCCP
Civil Rights Act of 1991	Prohibits discrimination (same as Title VII)	Same as Title VII, plus applies Section 1981 to employment discrimination cases	EEOC
Family and Medical Leave Act of 1993	Requires employers to provide 12 weeks of unpaid leave for family and medical emergencies	Employers with more than 50 employees	Department of Labor

Source: Raymond A. Noe, John R. Hollenbeck, Barry Gerhart, and Patrick M. Wright, *Human Resource Management: Gaining a Competitive Advantage* (Burr Ridge, Ill.: Richard D. Irwin, 1997), p. 107. Copyright 1997. Reproduced with permission of The McGraw-Hill Companies.

that women expatriates would have a more difficult time in Japan than male expatriates, research actually suggests that women expatriates do just as well as men in Japan.[7]

It is important to keep in mind that the intent of most of the legislation and regulation in the United States is designed to provide equal opportunity. This, however, does not prevent organizations from using certain criteria that you might think of as discriminatory, if it can be demonstrated that the criteria are **bona fide occupational qualifications (BFOQ)**, or qualifications that have a direct and material impact on job performance and outcomes.[8] For example, you might think that not hiring male employees who have a mustache or beard (or requiring them to shave them before being hired) would constitute discrimination. However, Disney has such a policy for its theme park workers and has prevailed when taken to court. The reason for their success in keeping the policy despite legal challenges is they are able to demonstrate a statistically significant positive customer reaction and satisfaction with male park cast members who are clean shaven versus those who are not. In Disney's case, being clean shaven is a BFOQ.

Customers Who a firm's customers are and what they need may have a significant impact on the type of people the organization needs to hire, the training they will need, how they should be evaluated, and what rewards will motivate them to best serve the customers' needs. Customers are the lifeblood of all businesses. Who are the customers? How many of them exist? How much money do they have, and are they willing to spend? How easy or difficult is it to reach them? How well do the firm's products or services match customers' needs and desires? These questions represent some of the critical ones that firms must address when assessing their customers and determining supportive human resource management practices. GE provides an interesting illustration of how firms might view customers. One unit of GE is organized around key customer accounts, and when it is time to fill a customer account executive position, GE includes the customer in screening the potential candidates for the position.[9]

Competitors Competitors constitute an additional important segment of a firm's external environment. Like customers, the nature of competitors significantly influences the type of people a firm needs and the best way to manage them. How many competitors exist? How extensive are their resources, including human resources? What comparative advantages do they have? How sustainable are those advantages? How much attention do they pay to other competitors? How do they try to create competitive advantage? These are key questions firms must address when evaluating this critical segment of their environment. Many of the U.S. auto firms significantly underestimated the resources and determination of Japanese competitors to succeed in the American marketplace. As a consequence, General Motors, Ford, and Chrysler had to lay off literally thousands of workers as they shrank their production capacity to match their declining market share. Better human resource practices might have enabled U.S. auto firms to compete more successfully with their Japanese competitors.

Suppliers Suppliers can also influence the appropriateness of human resource management practices. Few firms can provide all of the materials and inputs they need for all of their products and services. They must usually purchase them from others. What is the level of supply and demand for needed inputs? Do certain suppliers have extensive control over key inputs? What is the quality level from suppliers? These represent some of the critical questions concerning suppliers. For example, in order to be more cost competitive, GM has focused on scanning the entire globe to find low cost suppliers. This has required hiring purchasing staff

bona fide occupational qualifications (BFOQ) qualifications that have a direct and material impact on job performance and outcomes with stronger global orientation and training them in areas such as international negotiation and cross-cultural communication.

Economy   Economic conditions can also affect appropriate human resource management practices. For example, unemployment rates can have a significant impact on wages and benefits that firms may have to pay to attract qualified candidates. They can also affect the types and number of candidates available.

Culture   Cultural conditions and social values constitute an additional aspect of the environment to which firms must pay attention when formulating human resource management policies and practices. Previously we defined culture as the values that are passed from one generation to the next through symbolic means such as words, stories, and ceremonies.[10] The importance of culture is perhaps most obvious when a firm tries to conduct business outside its home country and discovers that what was successful at home does not work abroad. For example, Seiko, the Japanese watch maker, found that its normal performance appraisal form for supervisors was not effective in China. The form was just too ambiguous for Chinese supervisors, who wanted much more detail regarding expectations. A firm may also need to provide additional training to help employees deal with cultural differences.

Internal Environment

A firm's internal environment has an important impact on human resource management effectiveness.[11] Although there are a variety of aspects of a firm's internal environment, the nature of its products and services and its overall corporate culture are two that have a particular impact on effective human resource management.

Products and Services   The nature of a firm's products and services is a critical aspect of its internal environment. How complex or simple is the product or service? Is it an office chair with 134 separate parts or a commercial jet with 6 million? How static or dynamic is it? Is it a product that has changed little in the last 50 years such as a lead pencil, or is it a product that has changed dramatically just within the last 5 years, such as a computer memory chip? These considerations determine the required skill level of employees or the extent to which employees need to be flexible and adapt to change. These and other characteristics in turn have a significant influence on recruiting, selection, training, compensation, and development activities.

Organizational Culture   The culture of the organization also is a critical internal environmental factor as we discussed in Chapter 4. Just as societies develop values and patterned behaviors, so too do organizations. These values influence not only how members in the organization see and interpret the world but how they react to it as well.[12] For example, consider that at the beginning of the motorcycle industry in Japan, the number one firm was Tohatsu. Have you ever heard of a Tohatsu motorcycle? During the growth stages of the motorcycle industry in Japan, Tohatsu's conservative culture led it to expand quite slowly. In contrast, the current number one motorcycle firm in the world, Honda, took a very aggressive growth strategy. In fact, at one point, Honda was using debt so heavily to finance its growth that it had $7 of debt for every $1 of equity (typically ratios greater than

1:1 are considered risky). Honda's maverick culture and values influenced its aggressive response, and it took advantage of what it perceived as a significant growth opportunity.[13] So the reason you probably never heard of Tohatsu motorcycles is the aggressive culture and people at Honda put Tohatsu out of business. The culture also determined the type of people who were recruited, how they were selected, the type of orientation and socialization they received, the content of the training they received, and the nature of the development experiences they were given.

ORGANIZATIONAL STRATEGY AND EFFECTIVE HRM

The second major context within which we must place human resource practices is the strategy of the firm. You will recall that a firm's strategy is a plan of how to achieve competitive advantage.[14] A strategy typically includes a determination of which activities the firm wants to focus on to gain comparative advantage as well as what it sees as its core competencies. Remember also that the traditional view is that to be successful, there must be a fit between the external environment and a firm's strategy.

Just as strategies must fit the environment, so too must HR practices fit the firm's strategy. We have already argued that ultimately a firm's core competencies reside in its people. To succeed, the firm must have the right people at the right place doing the right things and doing them well. This is primarily accomplished through HR activities. For example, getting the right people is a function of the firm's external and internal recruiting and selection activities. Getting people doing the right things and doing them well is largely a function of the firm's performance appraisal and reward practices. But it is important to point out that the appropriateness of a given recruiting or selection practice is a function of the firm's strategy. Without considering a firm's strategy, it is hard to say that a given HR practice is good or bad per se.

HUMAN RESOURCE MANAGEMENT ACTIVITIES THAT GET THE RIGHT PEOPLE

To this point, we have explored the link between competitive advantage and human resource management and have also briefly examined the importance of the fit between HRM practices and the firm's strategy and environment. We now outline the key HRM activities listed in Exhibit 12.1.

Simplified, there are two main HRM goals: (1) getting the right people and (2) maximizing their performance and potential. Although there are a number of activities related to these two general categories, all managers need to get the right people into the right place at the right time and then help them maximize their performance and future potential. For example, a brilliantly creative person might be right for a firm that competes through product innovation such as 3M but the wrong employee for an organization that competes via cost leadership and low fares such as America West Airlines.

Getting the right people cannot be accomplished without understanding and aligning HRM activities with the corporate strategy. Although it is necessary to discuss each of these activities separately, you should not forget that they are related and that success or failure in one activity can significantly influence the success or failure of another. For example, Disney's ability to select "cast members" (employees) with a happy disposition to work in its theme parks enhances the effectiveness of the "friendly service" training they receive. These two activities combined help keep millions of "guests" pouring through the gates into the parks each year. We now give you a brief overview of the critical human resource activities that all managers must understand and master to be successful.

Planning

Human resource planning activity is concerned with assessing the future human resource needs and creating plans for how to fulfill them. At the organizational level, HR planning is sometimes a shared responsibility among HR specialists and other functional area executives such as accounting, finance, marketing, and operations. The key objective is to determine how many and what type of employees the firm needs at a point in the future, say one or five years hence, considering the firm's strategy and the general business and economic environment. For example, based on demographic trends and economic growth expectations, many Japanese firms determined in the mid-1990s that there would be a labor shortage in Japan of approximately two to three million people by the turn of the century. As a consequence, they started to automate, move operations offshore, examine immigrant labor, and accelerate recruiting efforts to cope with the expected labor shortage. In planning for future human resource needs, a firm's executives might determine that the number of future employees needed will increase, remain the same, or decline and that the type of employees needed will change or remain constant.

Individual managers must also be concerned with and skilled at human resource planning. Managers must determine the number and types of employees they will need in their units and develop a plan of how to get the right people. Just as with the organization, a given manager cannot distinguish between a "right" and "wrong" employee without thoughtful consideration of the firm's strategy. For example, after his departure from Apple, Steven Jobs started a company called NeXT to compete in the high-end computer and work station market. After the first few years, Jobs decided to shift the firm's strategic orientation from hardware to software. For managers in product development, this meant that they needed more programmers than engineers and that they initially needed fewer employees overall. So, before employees are recruited and selected, adequate planning is vital, and failure to do so can result in too few people, too many people, or the wrong kind of people to achieve the firm's strategy and compete in its environment. Finally, although human resource departments often have responsibilities for long-range employment planning for the organization, individual managers must also plan to be sure they get the people they need and want. Indeed, even individual employees must plan for their own development, training, future jobs, and so on to reach their personal career goals.

Job Analysis

job analysis
determination of the scope and depth of jobs and the requisite skills, abilities, and knowledge that people need to perform their jobs successfully

Job analysis is a critical but often overlooked human resource activity. **Job analysis** is concerned primarily with determining the scope and depth of jobs and the requisite skills, abilities, and knowledge that people need to perform their jobs successfully.

For example, Motorola recently decided to shift its strategic orientation away from simply filling customer orders to world-class quality. After making this shift, managers at Motorola analyzed the nature of factory jobs under the new strategy and discovered that factory jobs required employees who could read at the ninth grade level and who had a basic understanding of simple statistics such as means and standard deviations. This analysis provided valuable information that Motorola incorporated into its HR planning process. Unfortunately for Motorola, many of its current employees were underqualified. Managers faced the decision of whether to try to train the existing employees and get them to the level required or to let some of them go and replace them with more capable employees who could handle the new quality control systems and procedures.[15]

At the managerial level, job analysis is critical to effective recruiting and selection activities. Once you have a clear idea of what a given job requires, you can determine for whom to look and where to find them. The specifics of the job analysis might lead you to look within the firm or outside, to search for someone just out of college or currently working, or to emphasize certain skills over others. A thorough job analysis could even help you as a manager determine not just whom to select but how to select them. For example, the job analysis might tell you that the job is so complex that a psychological test that reliably assesses a person's mental complexity might be one method to incorporate in an overall selection plan.

Recruiting

Recruiting is primarily concerned with determining the desired candidate pool and attracting candidates to the organization and the specific open positions. As with the other activities we have already discussed, the desired pool of candidates cannot be determined without considering the firm's strategy. Whom you want is a function of whom you need.

Whether you can get the type of person you want is a different story. Can you offer the people you want what they want? Can your competitor offer more to the people you want?

Let's consider the first question. The key to knowing whether you can offer people what they want is to find out what they do want. Consider the case of UPS in Germany. When UPS expanded into Germany, managers had a difficult time selecting good drivers because they simply were not attracting high-quality applicants. Several factors contributed to this, most notably the fact that the brown UPS uniforms were the same color as the Nazi youth group during World War II. UPS was not offering what high-quality prospective drivers wanted and was, in fact, offering something (brown uniforms) they did not want.

The second question is *not* simply a matter of whether you can offer candidates more money than a competitor. People are not motivated only by money. Rather, it is important to consider work environment, meaningful work, flexible benefits, and opportunity for advancement as factors that could attract candidates to your organization.

Once you have assessed these two questions, you have a variety of approaches to generate job candidates. Each one has its strengths and weaknesses and as a consequence should be used as the situation dictates.

job posting
an internal recruiting method whereby a job, its pay, level, description, and qualifications are posted or announced to all current employees

Job Posting   **Job posting** is a popular internal recruiting method whereby a job, its pay, level, description, and qualifications are posted or announced to all current employees. Increasingly, posting is done electronically through e-mail. Job postings help ensure that all qualified employees have an opportunity to apply for a particular job. Job posting can also help current employees have a better idea of the types of jobs available and the qualifications needed to be successful in those jobs. This

Many companies recruit internally by posting jobs on bulletin boards or on the company intranet. Job postings ensure that all qualified employees have an opportunity to apply for a particular job before the search is extended outside the company.

can allow them to plan their careers. On the negative side, job postings can generate unqualified applicants who need to receive explanations about why they were unqualified and did not get the job. Without adequate explanation, they are likely to wonder whether the job was really "open" when it was posted. If employees begin to doubt the process of posting jobs, it can generate skepticism and limit candidates and therefore also limit the posting's effectiveness.

Advertisements   Advertisements in general or specialized publications can also be an effective means of generating job candidates. National business newspapers such as *The Wall Street Journal* cast a wide net. Professional magazines such as *Personnel Administrator* cast a very specialized net. Regional or local publications, such as your city newspaper, focus on the local labor pool. Increasingly, the Internet is being used as a source of advertising job openings. As use of the Internet matures, it is likely to develop regional and industrial segments that will facilitate a more targeted advertising of jobs.[16] The major downside of advertisements is the time and expense of screening out and rejecting unqualified candidates.

Employment Agencies   Employment agencies can also be effective in generating job candidates in some fields. The agency's effectiveness is largely a function of how well it understands your organization and the requirements of the specific job. Agencies tend to be expensive and usually not cost-effective for low-level and low-paying jobs. In contrast, most openings at the senior management level use executive search firms as part of their recruiting efforts. As their fee for finding an acceptable candidate, these firms typically charge at least one-third of the successful candidate's first-year compensation.

Employee Referrals   Managers may find current employees a great source for job candidates. Current employees with tenure in the organization understand the organization, its culture, and often the particular job that needs to be filled. They usually know something about an applicant as well: work history, educational background, skills and abilities, personal characteristics, and so on. Given that their recommendation puts their own reputation on the line to some degree, current employees tend to recommend individuals whom they believe will do well. Their personal relationship with the recommended candidate allows employees not to just sell the company on the individual but to sell the individual on the company. In general, research suggests that current employee referrals are one of the most effective recruiting methods. Employee referrals are less effective when the firm is looking for a different type of employee than they currently have. Current employees tend to recommend people like themselves. So a company pushing into international activities or new technology may find that employees don't know people in these new areas to then refer.

School Placement Centers   School placement centers are also a popular source of job candidates. These offices can range from high schools, technical schools, and junior colleges, through universities and advanced degree programs. If given adequate time and clear job specifications and requirements, school placement centers can do much of the prescreening work, filtering out unqualified candidates. This can save the firm significant time and money in the recruiting process. Schools are increasingly using video conferencing capabilities to set up "virtual" interviews and online job fairs. Technology helps firms broaden the field, allowing them to reach places to which they may not be able to travel physically. The weakness of school placement centers is that they often deal with so many companies and students that they may not know enough about either to conduct ideal screening.

Selecting

Successful selection is a function of effective planning, analyzing, and recruiting, as well as applying appropriate selection techniques.[17] Even if you get the right set of candidates before you, you need to be able to determine which one is best for the job. For example, international banks such as Bank of America or Citibank have no trouble attracting people to overseas positions, because international experience is important in the increasingly global banking industry. However, managers selected for overseas assignments sometimes fail and have to return home early at a cost of about $150,000 per employee. The early returns not only cost the company but also hurt employees' careers. These failures are partly a function of poor specification of the characteristics that predicted success in an overseas assignment and limited use of selection techniques beyond an unstructured interview.[18] On the domestic front, the Managerial Challenge box illustrates how LaSalle Bank goes about recruiting and selecting new hires.

   One of the key points to keep in mind relative to any selection technique is that if legally challenged, the organization must be able to demonstrate that the selection technique is valid. A **valid selection technique** is one that can differentiate between those who would be more successful in the job and those who would be less successful. For example, educational background is often used in selecting new hires because knowledge typically has a proven relationship with job performance. That is, it is hard to perform well in a job for which you do not have the requisite education and knowledge. There are a variety of selection techniques; each has its own strengths and weaknesses.

valid selection technique

a screening process that differentiates those who would be successful in a job from those who would not

MANAGERIAL CHALLENGE

RIGHT PLACE, RIGHT TIME

As Senior Vice President of Commercial Banking, Lamont Change manages the small business lending division of LaSalle Bank, a major banking institution in Chicago, the fifth largest in the state of Illinois. In this position for five years, Change manages a staff of five professionals and three administrative support persons. His professional staff is composed of three white males, one Hispanic male, and one African American female. The support staff members are all African American females.

In his 22-year history in the banking industry, Change says he has seen a shift in demographics. "There's been a significant growth in white female professionals," he claims. The growth has not been as dramatic, however, for African American males or females.

The professionals working with Change are responsible for analyzing credit, managing existing customer relationships, and generating new business. Sometimes the addition of a staff member is a strategic choice, he admits, and will open up new business possibilities for his division.

The individuals in his division are valuable resources to the bank, and he carefully evaluates any hiring decisions based on several criteria. Change works mostly with head hunters when looking for new personnel. "When I am hiring new people, I ask myself what the growth pattern is in this division. I ask myself the question, 'What do we need?'" Most often, Change has found that he needs more experienced people, and, consequently, he must find professionals who have 5 or 10 years of banking experience under their belt. These seasoned professionals most often come from outside the LaSalle Bank community. At other times, he may make a hiring decision based on communities with which his division hopes to establish new relationships. Hence, hiring a Hispanic male and an African American female made good

business sense. "At times I ask myself what markets are we looking to participate in," he says. But first and foremost, he looks at a candidate's qualifications.

Change has hired less-experienced persons through the bank's training program. LaSalle recruits new college graduates and rotates them through various departments, with recruits working in each department for several months. In this way, they get to understand the workings of the bank and to determine their special interest. At the same time, managers in each area get a chance to look at the recruit and determine whether he or she would fit into their department.

For people starting at lower levels, Change says there is a prescribed career path. "Up to a point there is a map that outlines a pattern for growth," he says, and he as manager can spell that out to the employee and encourage the individual on this path. At some point, though, as people advance in the company, professionals have to be creative and have to create opportunities for themselves. Either way, whether a junior-level employee or a more senior one, the employee has to take charge of his or her own career. "My responsibility," says Change, "is to have opportunities available so that the employee can be successful." Some people he has hired, Change claims, have advanced within his division. For others, however, there has been nowhere to go, and he has seen them promoted out of his department.

Change admits, with both hiring and advancing those he has hired, he's looking mostly at employees' skills and what they bring to the unit. But at the same time, the external environment has encouraged hiring and promotions to individuals outside what used to be the demographic profile of a bank official. This has created opportunities for females of any race and for African American and Hispanic males and has given LaSalle a competitive advantage.

unstructured interview
one in which interviewers have a general idea of the questions they might ask but do not have a standard set

structured interview
one in which interviewers ask a standard set of questions of all candidates about qualifications and capabilities related to job performance

Interviews The most widely used selection technique is the interview. In most cases, the interview is unstructured. An **unstructured interview** is one in which interviewers have a general idea of the types of questions they might ask but do not have a standard set. As a consequence, interviewers might ask different candidates different questions. With different questions and responses, comparing candidates can be like comparing apples and oranges. Not surprisingly, a major weakness of unstructured interviews is that they tend to have low levels of validity.[19] In contrast, **structured interviews**, in which interviewers ask a standard set of questions of all candidates about qualifications and capabilities related to job performance, can be quite valid. Validity can be further enhanced by carefully recording interviewee responses on a standardized form and taking approximately the same time in each interview.

Work Sampling There are a variety of techniques that could be classified as work sampling. Essentially, all these techniques attempt to simulate or exactly duplicate the job the person would be doing if hired. The underlying rationale is straightforward: If you perform poorly or well in the work sample, you would likely perform similarly in the real job. In general, the main strength of work sampling techniques is they make a reasonably accurate prediction of how an individual will do in a job. The main drawback is they tend to be time and cost intensive. Research supports the validity of work sampling techniques.

assessment centers

a work sampling technique in which candidates perform a number of exercises, each one designed to capture one or more key aspects of the job

Assessment centers are one particular work sampling technique. Typically, candidates are required to go through a number of exercises, and each exercise is designed to capture one or more key aspects of the job. For example, a supervisor's job might require good prioritization skills. The assessment center might have an "in-basket" exercise to assess this skill. The exercise consists of an in-basket filled with letters, memos, and reports that the candidate must read and then prioritize. The individual's ability to recognize and respond to high-priority items comes out during the exercise. In general, research supports assessment centers as an effective selection method for new hires as well as for individuals moving up in a firm.[20]

work simulation

situations in which job candidates perform work they would do if hired or work that closely simulates the tasks they would perform

Work simulation techniques typically involve situations in which job candidates perform work that they would do if hired or work that closely simulates the tasks they would perform. For example, when Nissan set up its new assembly plant in Tennessee, it required potential line workers to assemble flashlights to assess manual dexterity, a key requirement for assembly line workers. At Motorola, technical writing job candidates are given a piece of equipment, shown how to use it, given time to practice using it, and then are required to write a technical description of the equipment and operation manual. This gives Motorola a clear idea of those who can write technical material well.

Written Tests Written tests are also widely used. This is in part due to the fact that the tests can be administered cost effectively to a large number of job candidates. Cognitive ability and intelligence tests measure an individual's general cognitive complexity and intellectual ability. Although the validity of these tests has been mixed, they do seem to be acceptable predictors for supervisory and management jobs. Personality tests are much more controversial. While they can be reasonably good predictors of people's ability to work well with other particular personalities, they have not been good overall predictors of job performance.[21] Integrity tests are a more recent development. These tests try to assess the general level of a person's honesty. In general, they seem to be of debatable validity.[22] Written tests have the advantage of generally being inexpensive to administer, but the results are more valid regarding general performance and success than for success in a specific job.

Background and Reference Checks Background checks are essentially efforts to verify factual information that applicants provide. Between 10 and 15 percent of applicants either lie about or exaggerate factual information. As a consequence, checking to make sure people graduated with the degrees they claim, from the schools they cite, held the titles they claim, with the responsibilities they described can be quite valuable. The objective of reference checks is to get candid evaluations from those who have worked with the job candidate. However, recent legal judgments against past employers that made negative statements about previous employees have led employers to provide only factual information, such as title, years employed, and so on. Consequently, reference checks are declining in value.

Physical Examinations   Companies that require physical examinations as part of the selecting process typically do so because the job has high physical demands. In addition to helping them select physically qualified candidates, physical exams also protect firms. First, the physical exam information may help firms reduce insurance claims. Second, it may help protect the firm from lawsuits by identifying high-risk applicants, such as someone who might experience a heart attack from the physical strains of the job. However, given recent legislation in the United States, managers must be careful to ensure that the physical requirements being screened in the examination are in fact related to job performance and are not sources for discrimination.[23] Consequently, physical examinations are good for screening out people who are inappropriate for the physical demands of the job but are not terribly helpful at differentiating who is most suited for the job.

HUMAN RESOURCE MANAGEMENT ACTIVITIES THAT MAXIMIZE PERFORMANCE

Once the right people are in the right positions, the organization needs to ensure they are performing well. What constitutes maximum performance and potential is largely a function of the organization's strategy. For example, 3M chooses to compete on new product innovation and strives to have the majority of its revenue come from products that are less than five years old. It, therefore, needs employees who can think of and test new ideas. For 3M, maximum performance and potential are largely defined in terms of employee innovations. Based on this, 3M undertakes a variety of activities to maximize employees' creativity. We now explore five specific categories of activities that can significantly influence employee performance and potential.

Socialization and Training

Just as early life experiences can shape the general character, personality, and behavior of people, so too can early training and socialization experiences shape important aspects of employees' performance.[24] For example, early training and socialization each affects (1) the probability that new hires will stay with the firm, (2) the extent to which they will perform well, and (3) the degree to which they will develop to their full potential.

Many of the specific training and socialization actions (e.g., new hire orientation sessions) are carried out by individual managers, so as a manager, you need to understand how these early experiences influence new hires. If we return to the example of 3M, recall that the firm places a significant emphasis on competing through innovation. Consequently, it is important that the early training and socialization experiences not only communicate this message to new hires but also begin to encourage innovative behavior.

Managers can use a variety of training methods to enhance the performance and potential of employees. We cover several here. Although early career training is important, in today's changing environment, training and learning are likely to become career-long activities to stay competitive, especially as technology changes continue to mount.

Orientation   One of the first opportunities for an organization to shape the expectations and behavior of new employees is during orientation programs.[25] Typically, these programs provide a broad overview of the industry, the company and its business activities, its key competitors, and general information about working in the company (such as key policies, pay procedures, and fringe benefits). Work unit orientation sessions are typically more narrow and are generally designed to help the new employee get up to speed on the new job, co-workers, work unit policies and procedures, and expectations. In maximizing the effectiveness of orientation programs, managers should consider the following recommendations:

- Keep paperwork to a minimum to avoid information overload. Do include paperwork that must be completed immediately.
- Include an informal meeting with the individual's immediate supervisor.
- Alternate heavy information, such as that related to benefits and insurance, with lighter live or video presentations from corporate officers.
- Provide a glossary of terms unique to the organization.
- Match each new employee with a "buddy" (i.e., an experienced worker) based more on personality compatibility than similarity of jobs.[26]

On-the-Job Training Techniques   On-the-job training (OJT) is the most widely used training technique in organizations. As Exhibit 12.3 illustrates, there are a wide variety of techniques that a manager can use to train employees. Over your career, you will likely be exposed to most, if not all, of these approaches.

Off-the-Job Training Techniques   Off-the-job training can also be used with positive effect. The most common off-the-job training approach is the classroom-based program. The program may be only an hour, or it may be several weeks in length. It may be conducted by in-house experts (i.e., employees of the company) or by outside experts from industry or education, such as a university professor. The program may involve lectures, case studies, discussions, videos, or simulations. Individual-based programs are also increasingly popular. Formal correspondence courses are sometimes used when employees have different learning speeds and motivations but the learning objectives are clear. Computer-assisted programs are also used when employees have different learning speeds and motivations. Current technology now allows for text, graphics, and a variety of visual displays as well as interaction. Many programs now adjust content and difficulty level in real time based on how well the individual is doing.

Training Objectives   Orientation and training programs can have a variety of objectives. However, at a fundamental level, these programs are intended to address employee technical, interpersonal, or conceptual abilities. Technical skills can range from being able to read and perform simple math to being able to program a supercomputer. As mentioned earlier, when Motorola made a strategic commitment to quality, it discovered that over a third of its employees could not read, write, or do math at a level that the new quality control program required. This discovery led to a massive technical training effort.

EXHIBIT 12.3

On-the-Job Training Techniques

1. *Expanded Responsibilities.* This training technique expands the job duties, assignments, and responsibilities of an individual.
2. *Job Rotation.* Also called *cross-training,* this practice moves individuals to various types of jobs within the organization at the same level or next-immediate-higher level for periods of time from an hour or two to as long as a year.
3. *Staff Development Meetings.* Meetings are usually held offsite to discuss facts of each individual's job and to develop ideas for improving job performance.
4. *"Assistant to" Positions.* Promising employees serve as staff assistants to higher-skill-level jobs for a specified period of time (often one to three months) to become more familiar with the higher-skilled positions in the organization.
5. *Problem-Solving Conferences.* Conferences are held to solve a specific problem being experienced by a group or the organization as a whole. It involves brainstorming and other creative means to come up with solutions to basic problems.
6. *Mentoring.* A guide or knowledgeable person higher up in the organization helps a new employee "learn the ropes" of the organization and provides other advice.
7. *Special Assignments.* Special tasks or responsibilities are given to an individual for a specified period of time. The assignment may be writing up a report, investigating the feasibility for a new project, process, service, or product, preparing a newsletter, or evaluating a company policy or procedure.
8. *Company Trainers.* Special programs can cover such topics as safety, new personnel procedures, new product or services, affirmative action, and technical programs.
9. *Outside Consultants.* Recognized experts are brought to the company to conduct training on such topics as goal setting, communications, assessment techniques, safety, and other current topics of importance. They often supplement training done by company trainers.
10. *Consultant Advisory Reviews.* Experts in specialized fields meet with various managers and employee groups to investigate and help solve particular problems. The emphasis is on problem solving rather than training.
11. *Reading Matter.* A formal program is created to circulate books, journals, selected articles, new business material, and so on to selected employees. An effective program also includes periodic scheduled meetings to discuss the material.
12. *Apprenticeship.* Training is provided through working under a journeyman or master in a craft. The apprentice works alongside a person skilled in the craft and is taught by that person. Apprenticeship programs also often include some classroom work.

Source: Adapted from W. P. Anthony, D. L. Perrewé, and K. M. Kacmar, *Strategic Human Resource Management* (Fort Worth, Tex.: Harcourt Brace Jovanovich, 1993).

Because very few employees work in isolation, improved interpersonal abilities are the target of a wide variety of training programs. Programs might address skills such as effective listening, conflict resolution, negotiation, and coaching. In a recent study, executives cited poor interpersonal skills as one of the biggest problems in new college or MBA graduates.[27]

The final category is conceptual abilities. This category includes a variety of skills and abilities, such as problem solving, decision making, planning, and organizing. A given training program might be designed to address just one of these categories, two, or all three.

Regardless of the category the program is designed to target, most successful programs provide participants with several things:

- An understanding of what the correct behavior is and is not.
- A clear knowledge of why certain behaviors are correct or incorrect.

- A clear understanding of the keys for behaving correctly.
- Sufficient opportunities to practice the desired behaviors.
- Feedback on performance with further opportunities to practice and improve.

Job Design

job design

the structuring or restructuring of key job components

Job design is focused on the structuring or restructuring of key job components. Thus, while job analysis focuses on what the components of a job are, job design is the process of determining which components ought to be put together and how they should be arranged. In some texts, this activity would be much earlier in the sequence than we have placed it. In general, for a brand new job that has never been filled before, job design does take place early in the sequence. Also, traditionally jobs were designed and then appropriate people were selected to fit into the jobs. The reality of today's dynamic and global environment has changed that approach. In some cases, it is possible and appropriate to design jobs and then try to match people to them, but in other cases, jobs might need to be designed or redesigned to fit the available people. There are also situations that require a combination of both fitting the person to the job and fitting the job to the person. For example, **job sharing** involves two people working part time in the same job. Effective job sharing requires two individuals who can coordinate well and have similar capabilities. It has become popular with working mothers, who are faced with balancing family and economic/professional demands. Increasingly, technology is allowing managers to design and redesign jobs in ways not possible before.

job sharing

situation in which two people work part time in the same job

reengineering

fundamental rethinking and radical redesign of business processes to achieve dramatic improvements in critical, contemporary measures of performance, such as cost, quality, service, or speed

During the early and mid-1990s, reengineering become a popular concept regarding the design or redesign of work. **Reengineering** is the fundamental rethinking and radical redesign of business processes to achieve dramatic improvements in critical, contemporary measures of performance, such as cost, quality, service, or speed.[28] Computer and information technology today have allowed organizations to design more enriched, satisfying, and productive jobs. Increasingly, organizations are looking at ways to give employees more flexibility in the way their work is accomplished. Technology is one way to provide that flexibility. Maximizing subordinates' performance and your unit's performance is your goal as a manager regarding effective job design.

Performance Appraisal

Before organizations or managers can encourage or correct the actions of employees, they must know how the employees are doing. Performance appraisal is concerned with (1) establishing performance objectives and standards, (2) measuring performance against those standards, and (3) providing feedback to employees concerning that measurement and evaluation.[29] As we stated before, the objectives of the job and the standards against which performance is measured must be driven by the strategy of the firm. When Motorola decided that it would compete on quality, it set "six sigma" as its standard. A six-sigma quality standard allows for only 3.4 defects per one million opportunities. For Motorola, this had wide-ranging implications from the factory floor to the corporate kitchen. On the floor, this meant that only 3.4 products per million could have a defect. For the kitchen, it meant that only 3.4 muffins for every million baked could be burnt. While six sigma was not immediately achievable for Motorola, the strategic intent did have a significant impact on the standard against which employees' performance was evaluated.

Graphic Rating Scale

Employee Name:_____   **Dept.** _____

	Excellent	Good	Average	Fair	Poor
1. Quality of Work	☐	☐	☐	☐	☐
2. Quantity of Work	☐	☐	☐	☐	☐
3. Cooperation	☐	☐	☐	☐	☐
4. Dependability	☐	☐	☐	☐	☐
5. Initiative	☐	☐	☐	☐	☐
6. Job Knowledge	☐	☐	☐	☐	☐
7. Attitude	☐	☐	☐	☐	☐

For most managers, performance appraisal is perhaps the most important, yet most difficult, human resource activity. This difficulty is not only because of the complexity of evaluating past performance and setting future performance targets, but because performance appraisals involve communicating to employees how they are doing relative to established targets. Often employees are not quite measuring up to established standards, requiring feedback for corrective action; however, few people like to give or receive negative feedback. Still, without this feedback, neither individuals nor organizations can maximize performance. As a consequence, all managers need to understand the key factors that drive effective performance appraisal systems and be skilled at implementing them.

Graphic Rating Scales   Perhaps the most popular method of providing performance feedback is through graphic rating scales (see Exhibit 12.4 for an example). A graphic rating scale typically lists a set of qualities on which the employee is evaluated. The level of performance on each of these items is then rated in terms of a graduated scale. The scale typically ranges from 1 to 5. The degree of specificity concerning the definition of each point on the scale can range from one word descriptors (e.g., 1 = poor) to complete sentences (e.g., 1 = Does not meet the minimum standards).

The popularity of graphic ratings is due to two main factors. First, they are relatively quick and easy for managers to complete. Given that most managers have many employees whom they must evaluate and that managers typically do not get a reward for high-quality evaluations, they have a natural incentive to complete the evaluations as quickly as possible. Second, because the evaluation items and the rating scale are common across employees, it is easy to quantify the results and compare employees' performance ratings.

However, there are two key limitations that as a manager you should keep in mind relative to graphic rating scales. First, the characteristics being evaluated may not be clearly defined; thus, they are left to individual interpretation. Consequently, one manager might focus her interpretation of "interpersonal skills" on conflict resolution abilities, while another manager might focus his interpretation on listening skills. Given the two different interpretations, it is difficult to compare the employees evaluated by the two different managers. Furthermore, the two different managers might have different interpretations of the rating scale. One manager might only allow the top 5 percent of employees to receive a high rating of "5 = excellent." Another manager might interpret a "5" as applicable to the top 20 percent of employees. Once again, the different interpretations would make comparing employees rated by different managers difficult. This incomparability is important because over 85 percent of firms use performance appraisals to determine merit increases, bonuses, and promotions.

behaviorally anchored rating scales (BARS)
a performance appraisal system in which the rater places detailed employee characteristics on a rating scale

Behaviorally Anchored Rating Scales   Behaviorally anchored rating scales **(BARS)** are designed to keep many of the advantages of the graphic rating scales and reduce the disadvantages. The general design of BARS is similar to graphic rating scales in that managers rate employee characteristics using a quantitative scale. However, the characteristics are specified in greater detail and described in terms of behaviors rather than abstract qualities. Likewise, the scales are much more tied to descriptions of specific behaviors rather than ambiguous terms (see Exhibit 12.5 for an example). The greater specificity and link to behaviors reduces, but does not eliminate, the potential for noncomparability of ratings across different raters.[30] However, some potential for manager bias remains.[31]

360-degree feedback
performance appraisal system in which information is gathered from supervisors, co-workers, subordinates, and sometimes suppliers and customers

360-Degree Feedback   The primary rationale behind 360-degree feedback appraisal systems is that an individual's performance should be viewed from multiple perspectives.[32] Most **360-degree feedback** systems involve collecting appraisal evaluations from an individual's boss, peers, and subordinates. In some companies, evaluations are also collected from suppliers and customers, depending on the nature of interaction the employee has with these constituencies. The positive aspect of 360-degree feedback is that because data are gathered from multiple sources, employees are encouraged to focus on all key constituencies. This reduces the tendency, for example, to simply cozy up to the boss and work poorly with peers or subordinates. The major drawback is the time and energy it takes to collect, process, and effectively feed the data back to the individual. Estimates are that about 25 percent of U.S. companies now use some form of 360-degree evaluation and that by the year 2005 the percentage will have doubled.[33]

Effective Performance Feedback   Regardless of the system of evaluating employee performance, the results of the evaluation need to be fed back effectively to employees to make a positive difference in their performance. First, if expectations concerning unacceptable, acceptable, or superior performance were not clear to the employee prior to the appraisal, negative assessments will not likely influence future motivation or performance. Consequently, performance expectations must be clear and acceptable to the employee from the beginning. Second, if the employee believes that, as the manager, you are biased in your observations, your assessment will not have the effect you desire. This is why recording both

EXHIBIT 12.5

Behaviorally Anchored Rating Scale Example

Position: _____
Job Dimensions: _____

Plans work and organizes time carefully so as to maximize resources and meet commitments.	9	
	8	Even though this associate has a report due on another project, he or she would be well prepared for the assigned discussion on your project.
	7	This associate would keep a calendar or schedule on which deadlines and activities are carefully noted, and which would be consulted before making new commitments.
	6	As program chief, this associate would manage arrangements for enlisting resources for a special project reasonably well, but would probably omit one or two details that would have to be handled by improvisation.
Plans and organizes time and effort primarily for large segments of a task. Usually meets commitments, but may overlook what are considered secondary details.	5	This associate would meet a deadline in handling in a report, but the report might be below usual standard if other deadlines occur on the same day the report is due.
	4	This associate's evaluations are likely not to reflect abilities because of overcommitments in other activities.
	3	This associate would plan more by enthusiasm than by timetable and frequently have to work late the night before an assignment is due, although it would be completed on time.
	2	This associate would often be late for meetings, although others in similar circumstances do not seem to find it difficult to be on time.
Appears to do little planning. May perform effectively, despite what seems to be a disorganized approach, by concerted effort, although deadlines may be missed.	1	This associate never makes a deadline, even with sufficient notice.

Source: Table from *Strategic Human Resource Management* by William P. Anthony, Pamela L. Perrewé, and K. Michele Kacmar, p. 456, copyright © 1993 by Harcourt Brace & Company, reproduced by permission of the publisher.

critical incidents

recording of specific incidents in which the employee's behavior and performance were above or below expectations

positive and negative **critical incidents** is important. This simply involves the recording of important, specific incidents in which the employee's behavior and performance were above or below expectations. This record then allows you to avoid remembering only the most recent events and also facilitates your ability to talk about specifics in the appraisal interview.[34] This brings us to a brief list of recommendations for an effective performance appraisal interview:

1. Review key work objectives, goals, or standards against which the employee's performance is measured.
2. Summarize employee's overall performance by reviewing specific positive and negative incidents.
3. Discuss causes of weak performance and listen carefully to the employee's explanation.
4. Discuss alternative means of improving future performance and encourage employee input.
5. Establish an agreed approach, timetable, and review process for future improvement.
6. Establish key objectives, timetables, and standards for the upcoming performance period.
7. Leave the meeting on an encouraging and positive note.[35]

These may seem like simple steps, but they can go a long way to improving the effectiveness of one of the most difficult yet important human resource challenges you face as a manager.

Compensation

Although rewards and compensation can be instrumental in getting the right people, their primary function is retaining and maximizing the performance of employees once they have entered the organization. Rewards by their nature are designed to encourage desired behaviors. As already discussed, desired behaviors must be linked to the firm's strategy. Thus, reward systems also must be linked to the firm's strategy.

Unfortunately, employees are often rewarded for doing one thing and yet expected to do another. For example, as Motorola began to shift from simply shipping products to producing world-class quality products, employees continued to be rewarded for timely shipments (with quality levels well below six sigma). Furthermore, employees were punished if shipments were late, even if quality levels of the late shipments approached six sigma. Because rewards were not aligned with the firm's new strategy, results of the six-sigma effort at Motorola were less than what senior executives expected. As another example, most stock brokers at retail brokerage firms are rewarded with bonuses based on the volume of transactions they complete. This leads many brokers to "churn" individual investors' accounts. That is, brokers buy and sell shares in order to generate commissions even though the investment objectives of the investors did not justify such frequent transactions. As a consequence of this churning and the associated fees charged to customers, investors often take their accounts to competing brokerage firms. In the end, the reward structures encourage churning, but churning ultimately hurts firm revenue and broker commissions because customers defect.

pay structure
a range of pay for a particular position or classification of positions

broad band systems
pay structures in which the range of pay is large and covers a wide variety of jobs

Pay Most firms establish a pay structure based on the level in the company and type of position. A **pay structure** establishes a range of pay for a particular position or classification of positions. Traditionally, pay structures were hierarchical and segmented. Most companies are now moving to **broad band systems** in which the range of pay is large and covers a wide variety of jobs.[36] Exhibit 12.6 provides a graphic illustration of a traditional pay structure and a more modern broad band system. The major advantage to a broad band system is the greater flexibility it

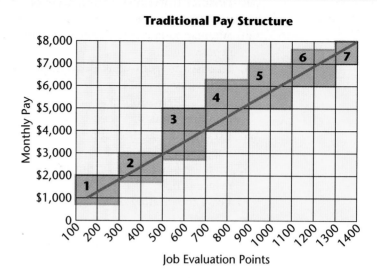

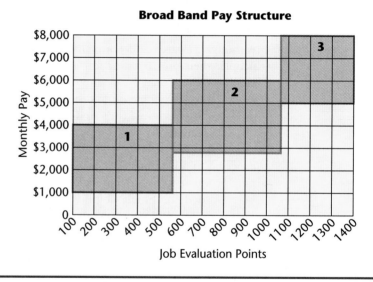

EXHIBIT 12.6

Traditional and Contemporary Pay Structures

gives organizations to match pay to individual value and changing labor market conditions.

Another important pay trend is the movement away from an individual's total compensation package being primarily composed of salary and toward a greater portion of compensation being at risk.[37] **At-risk compensation** is simply pay that varies depending on specified conditions. These conditions might include the general profitability of the company; hitting particular budget, revenue, or cost savings targets for a unit; or meeting specific individual performance targets. Increasingly, companies are placing a higher portion of total compensation "at risk." This is primarily because if total compensation is made up of salary and if salaries are raised at a level comparable to inflation, inflation and subsequent salary increases can add significantly to company costs. On the other hand, if a higher percentage of compensation is tied to performance, higher compensation costs only occur with higher

at-risk compensation

pay that varies depending on specified conditions, including the profitability of the company; hitting particular budget, revenue, or cost savings targets for a unit; or meeting specific individual performance targets

incentive plans
systems that tie some compensation to performance

performance. Consequently, **incentive plans**, or approaches that tie some compensation to performance, are increasingly being spread throughout the organization, whereas traditionally they were reserved for only the most senior managers.

Benefits   Traditional benefit plans include items such as medical, dental, and life insurance. In the past, companies used to compete for employees and retain them in part through offering attractive benefit plans. However, as companies added more and more features to the plans to make them attractive to a broader base of employees with differing needs, companies found themselves paying 20 to 40 percent of salary in benefits. To reduce the soaring benefit costs and yet meet differing employee needs, companies began to offer **cafeteria-style plans** in which employees had a set number of "benefit dollars" that they could use to purchase the specific benefits that fit their particular needs.

cafeteria-style plans
benefit plans in which employees have a set number of "benefit dollars" that they can use to purchase benefits that fit their particular needs

Rewards and Motivation   Although much of the responsibility for reward and compensation systems is placed on the human resource department, effective rewards are more than the dollars paid out in salaries and bonuses or the dollars tied up in health care and other benefits. Although individual managers can influence pay increases and the like, they also have the greatest control over equally powerful rewards such as recognition and praise. Consequently, it is important for you to understand the broad range of rewards and how they influence the performance of your employees. We cover that subject in detail in Chapter 13.

Career Systems and Development

career paths
sets and sequences of positions and experiences

One of the most powerful motivators for people to join organizations and to perform is the opportunity to grow and develop.[38] Career and employee development systems are designed to respond to that particular motivation and to ensure that the human capabilities needed in the organization are being developed. What **career paths** (i.e., a set and sequence of positions and experiences) organizations want employees to have to prepare for certain responsibilities is largely a function of the firm's strategy. For example, Sony is simultaneously trying to capture global efficiencies and respond to local market conditions. Sony tries to capture economic efficiencies by manufacturing nearly all its small, hand-held video cameras for markets throughout the world at a single factory in Japan. Yet, it also tries to sell these cameras in a way that appeals to the different local tastes across the globe. Consequently, Sony places a high premium on international experience for career paths that lead to the top of the organization. Sony also competes on integrated team design. That is, individuals from various functional areas such as market research, engineering, sales, and finance work together at the outset of a new product development. Consequently, Sony places a premium on employees working in several functional areas over the course of their careers, or what is referred to as **cross-functional job rotation**.[39]

cross-functional job rotation
opportunities for employees to work in different functional areas and gain additional expertise

While responsibility for organizational career and development systems is often that of the human resource function, individual managers are those most knowledgeable about the development needs of specific employees and are often those to whom individual employees go in search of career guidance. In addition, managers develop reputations as being effective or ineffective at employee development, and these reputations influence the quality of subordinates managers attract, which in turn affects the performance of their unit. Consequently, while some may view employee career pathing and development as an activity for which the HR department is responsible, it is actually a critical activity at which all managers must be skilled.

CHALLENGES FOR EFFECTIVE HUMAN RESOURCE MANAGEMENT

Both organizations and individual managers face a number of challenges in their efforts to manage human resources effectively. All of the challenges have existed for some time, but their intensity and rate of change have risen dramatically within the last decade or so. Indications are that they will remain challenges in the foreseeable future and, if anything, increase in intensity and importance.

Workforce Diversity

Effective management of workforce diversity is a growing management challenge. Historically, diversity in the United States was defined in terms of differences along traditional racial categories. Today, most organizations think of workforce diversity in terms of a wide range of factors, including age, gender, race, religion, cultural background, education, and mental and physical disabilities. Estimates are that the presence of Hispanic women in the U.S. workforce will increase 71 percent between 1990 and 2000; that Asian women will increase 65 percent; that African American women will increase 29 percent; that African American men will increase 22 percent, and that white males will account for only 15 percent (an increase of only 8 percent) of the incoming labor force by the year 2000 (see Exhibit 12.7). The diversity of backgrounds raises a variety of human resource management questions. For example, with the need to reach out to such a diverse group of potential employees, what types of recruiting efforts will be effective and avoid unintended discrimination? How can the diverse backgrounds, perspectives, and talents of employees be effectively managed?

As a manager, you will increasingly be responsible for subordinates of wide diversity. Within the United States, the growing minority populations and their

EXHIBIT 12.7	
Increasing Diversity of U.S. Workforce	

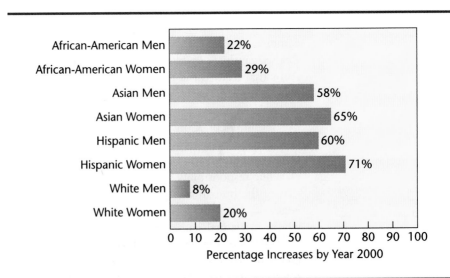

increasing access to education and the jobs that follow, plus steady immigration into the United States from throughout the world, virtually guarantee that you will work with a diverse set of subordinates, peers, superiors, customers, and suppliers. In addition, the increasing globalization of business means that you are likely to work with people from around the world who have cultural, language, political, economic, social, educational, and philosophical backgrounds that are quite different from yours.

Managing Workforce Diversity   While there are ethical arguments for why organizations should embrace diversity, efforts to effectively manage workforce diversity typically are justified in terms of business reasons. These reasons include the following:

- Need to attract enough capable workers to meet turnover and growth demands of the business
- Enhanced creativity and innovation when solving problems
- Knowledge and understanding of the diverse marketplace and customers

The experience of most organizations, however, is that these advantages are hard to obtain. Just as multiple perspectives, values, and ways of thinking can bring new insights and creativity to a problem, they can also create a significant management challenge. Diverse workgroups often encounter the following problems:

- Communication problems and misunderstandings
- Mistrust
- Conflict and incompatible approaches to resolving the conflict
- Lower group cohesiveness and greater subgroup formation based on elements of diversity such as language, race, or gender

Given the potential benefits and the significant challenges of effectively managing workforce diversity, we review some general guidelines for you as a manager to follow:

- *Know yourself.* How much exposure have you had to people with different ethnic, racial, religious, educational, or cultural backgrounds to your own? How tolerant and understanding of the differences have you been? How comfortable were you? How curious were you?
- *Prepare yourself and your employees.* How skilled are you and your employees at listening, conflict resolution, negotiation, and communication?
- *Provide support.* To what extent are there support groups for employees with minority backgrounds to keep them from feeling unappreciated and wanting to leave the organization? To what extent do minority employees have mentors who can help them understand and become an effective part of the organization?
- *Guide behavior.* To what extent do you monitor the behavior of your subordinates and peers? How consistent are you in providing positive reinforcement of behaviors that foster tolerance of and effective use of diversity? To what extent do you privately provide negative feedback to individuals who display intolerance or other problem behaviors?

From both a domestic and international perspective, workforce diversity is only going to increase. One of the ways you can distinguish yourself from others and add value to your organization is through your understanding of the ability to work effectively with subordinates, peers, customers, and suppliers with diverse backgrounds. The Managerial Challenge box, "Marriott Provides a Step Up," profiles one company that has successfully met the diversity challenge.

Competition

Perhaps no single factor has placed a brighter spotlight on human resource management than the increased level of competition. The sources of this increase vary, but their challenge to effective human resource management is constant.

Customer Orientation   Few will debate the rise in customer expectations or the increasing number of firms trying to respond to higher customer demands as a great source of increased competition. Explanations for the dramatic rise in customer demands and the resulting increase in customer orientation within firms abound. They range from advances in information technology that allow customers to become more educated about products and services and their choices to a focus on the higher levels of general education in the population at large. For example, in the United States, just between 1975 and 1990 the percentage of people with four-year college degrees rose from 18 percent to 26 percent. One of the specific manifestations of this rise in customer expectations and customer orientation is the "quality movement." Many firms instituted total quality management (TQM) programs, designed to improve quality in all aspects of their business. For most organizations, a significant improvement in product quality also requires a significant improvement in the quality and skills of their people.

Empowerment   A related but slightly different result of increased competition is the movement toward empowerment. Empowerment, employee involvement, and participative management all involve employees more fully in decision making and problem solving activities within the business.

Empowerment has emerged as a response to competition for at least two fundamental reasons.[40] First, to have a stronger customer orientation, you need to know what customers want. Generally, people closest to the customer have the best sense of this. Pushing decision-making authority down the organization and enabling employees to make decisions that affect the products or services is a way to satisfy customers—and do so more quickly. It also leads to increased employee satisfaction. Second, empowerment has emerged in response to competitive pressures to trim the "fat" out of organizations. Empowering employees can significantly reduce the number of supervisors and managers and their associated costs. As costs come down, customers can be offered better values—more of what they want for less money.

However, the movement toward employee involvement or empowerment presents significant challenges to human resource management. For example, research has demonstrated that efforts to empower and involve employees work best when employees desire more responsibility and opportunities for input.[41] This same research also points out that not all employees want more responsibility. Can enough workers be found and hired that desire greater responsibility, or will too many workers demand their right to a boss who tells them what to do, how to do it, and when it is to be done by? Are there some countries in which the notion of worker involvement is contrary to cultural norms? These questions point out only a few of the many challenges that empowerment places in front of effective human resource management.

MANAGERIAL CHALLENGE

MARRIOTT PROVIDES A STEP UP

For Marriott International, like other large hotel chains, maintaining a core of low-paid workers to do basic services has become an increasing challenge. Although projections point to a rising need for skilled workers, the U.S. marketplace still needs unskilled workers. The problem is that with unemployment figures logging in at less than 5 percent during most of the middle and late 1990s, some companies seeking workers who are willing to work for low wages have found themselves hard pressed. Although little attention had been paid to the needs of this group of workers, Marriott acknowledges how critical they are to its financial success and view this group as strategic to growth. "It's critical that we become more skilled at managing this workforce," admits Donna Klein, who directs work-life programs for Marriott.

Problems are common with low-paid, unskilled workers. Many in this group may be recent immigrants. Some lack education or cannot speak English. Others may lack good work habits or have problems managing life and money well. Domestic problems ranging from violence and abuse to the lack of adequate child care are prevalent. Moreover, cultural differences may affect the success of these workers.

Admittedly, this group of people has long been taken advantage of. It wasn't until recently that Marriott, which now has model programs, started to study a section of its hourly wage workforce. They realized that a three-year-old program offering child care benefits barely scratched the surface of the problems of this group. One finding was that about one-quarter of workers in this group had literacy problems, mostly with English. So Marriott initiated an on-site English as a Second Language (ESL) training program conducted during work hours, to help serve the needs of its employee group that spoke some 65 different languages. The business reason? Workers able to speak English could better serve their guests. Now more than half the Marriott hotels in the United States have active ESL programs.

Classes, however, won't solve all the problems. Managers discovered they were spending a lot of their time doing what they called "baby-sitting." They offered advice about family conflicts, helped employees figure out child care solutions, and on occasion even loaned money to employees to pay urgent bills. "Many managers spend 15 percent of their time doing social work," noted Clifford J. Erlich, Marriott's senior vice president for human resources. And although that may produce a more productive workforce, it represents "time not spent dealing with customer issues."

In response, Marriott instituted programs to deal with problems and conflicts. The approach, which is both formal and informal, includes things such as employee stock

options, a social service referral network, parenting classes, and day care. These programs are relatively inexpensive but produce a loyal and stable group of workers; Marriott's turnover rate is below its competitors'. And they have as their objective three constituencies—the worker, the guests, and, maybe more important, the stockholder, who benefits from Marriott's ability to keep wages stable.

Marriott's Pathways to Independence is a six-week program geared to turning welfare recipients into productive workers. In this model program, welfare recipients are taught basic business skills, like showing up for work on time, as well as important life skills, like money management and self-esteem. For Marriott, this $5,500-per-person investment (half funded by federally funded local agencies) has produced a new labor pool, with a 13 percent turnover rate, which is well below the national industry average. Now workers can dial Associate Resource Line, a national toll-free referral service connecting workers with social services. A new program in Atlanta is experimenting with a 24-hour subsidized child care center, called the Inn for Children.

Critics of Marriott view their programs as paternalistic. But some significant success stories illustrate how Marriott has increased value to the company while improving the quality of life for the individual—people like Thong Lee, who has been with the company 16 years. A bartender in the Seattle Marriott, he learned English through classes at the hotel and has used his stock and pay to buy several rental properties. He also remembers when his boss shut down the hotel laundry for a day so the entire staff could attend Lee's mother's funeral. Sabrina McWhite grins when she shows off the book bag she bought her daughter and says, "I feel so good I could give it to her." McWhite completed Pathways to Independence program, learned money management, and got help finding dependable child care so she could make it to work regularly.

What is clear about the program is this—Marriott is noticing the significance of this pool of workers. And the workers themselves are experiencing an improved quality of life. And by keeping hourly wages from spiraling dramatically upward, Marriott continues to be competitive in a fierce market. In fact, a recent issue of *Fortune* magazine rated Marriott in the top five of the 50 best companies for Asians, blacks, and Hispanics—an impressive accomplishment.

Adapted from Joanne Gordon, "The New Paternalism," *Forbes*, November 2, 1998; "Best Companies for Asians, Blacks, and Hispanics," *Fortune*, August 2, 1998.

Time-Based Competition   An additional result of increased competition is the increased emphasis on time, such as shorter product life cycles, shorter product development cycles, quicker responses to customer complaints, quicker processing and delivery of customer orders, faster rollouts of products across countries, and faster responses to competitors' moves. For example, with the launch of its new premiere sports car, the Viper, Chrysler cut its normal product development time from five years to under three years. All of this increased speed naturally requires increased flexibility. If the content of jobs is changing rapidly, how can you as a manager conduct an effective job analysis? Does this change the nature of the job analysis from static tasks (e.g., processing orders) to dynamic processes (e.g., fulfilling customer needs)? Does this mean that employees should be selected more for their fit with the organization than for their fit with a particular job? With increased emphasis on speed and flexibility, how can organizations or individual managers effectively plan their future human resource needs? As more firms seek time-based competitive advantages, they will discover a variety of new human resource challenges.

Globalization

Globalization also poses a significant challenge to human resource management. Many argue that the world is getting smaller. However, from a human resource perspective, the world is getting larger! If you look at the history of almost any multinational corporation (MNC), at the beginning the firm operated in one or a very limited number of countries. As it grew, it expanded into more and more countries. Telecommunication and transportation technologies in particular have facilitated this expansion. Now companies such as Philips and Citicorp operate in over 70 countries around the world. For them, that translates into employees speaking over 40 different languages, dealing with 70 different governments, interacting with 10 different major religions, and coping with hundreds of different customs, holidays, and traditions. As companies expand into new countries and cultures, the world for them gets larger and more complicated.

Most firms cannot simply avoid expanding overseas. Consider where the workers will be in the future compared with where they are now. Exhibit 12.8 indicates that most of the future workers will be in developing countries. Given that most of the large MNCs are headquartered in developed countries and most of the workers in the future will be in developing countries, continued expansion abroad seems inevitable.

As firms expand outside their home countries, they will confront a variety of HRM challenges. For example, do the selection techniques that work in one country also work in another? Can one performance appraisal form be applied in all operations around the globe? Must reward systems be adapted and changed from one country to the next? If they must be adapted, how can a firm avoid the risk of employees perceiving these differences as inequitable? What must a firm do to ensure that it provides development opportunities for employees in all its operations? For example, recently a Korean multinational firm was seeking to fill its top global marketing position. Is the best possible person for this job only a Korean? How does any global firm ensure that it finds and develops the best possible talent wherever in its worldwide operations that talent might be located? When a firm needs to send employees outside their native countries as a means of developing their international skills and abilities, how does it effectively select these individuals?

EXHIBIT 12.8

Where the Workers Are

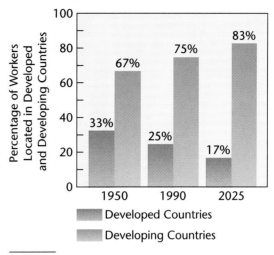

Source: U.S. Department of Labor, 1997.

How should these employees be trained prior to their international assignments? How can these individuals be effectively evaluated when factors such as real changes in exchange rates, government price controls, and other external factors can significantly influence bottom-line results of overseas operations? These are just a sampling of the questions and human resource management challenges raised by today's increasingly global environment.

Dual Careers

Couples in which both partners work full time in professional, managerial, or administrative jobs are typically referred to as dual career couples. The proportion of dual career couples has risen dramatically over the last 20 years.[42] The implications for human resource management are varied. For example, promotions that involve relocation from one part of the country to another can be difficult. In an increasingly global environment, international assignments can also be difficult for dual career couples. Most couples do not want to be separated by thousand of miles for three to five years. However, the spouse may not be able to get a transfer to the same country. Furthermore, work visa restrictions may prevent employment of the spouse in that country even if a transfer or interim job could be located. To cope with this challenge, companies are expanding their spouse relocation assistance programs and also forming informal associations to exchange information about transfers and job opportunities to help each other out.

Sexual Harassment

Over the last 10 years, sexual harassment has become a major workforce issue, especially given the significant financial penalties that can be assessed to organizations that allow it to occur. Sexual harassment takes two basic forms. The first is sometimes termed *quid pro quo* and involves requests or implied suggestions that sexual relations are required in exchange for continued employment or benefits

Sexual harassment often involves actions that create a "hostile environment," such as inappropriate jokes, touching, or comments.

such as promotion. The second form involves actions that create a "hostile environment." A hostile environment can be created through jokes, touching, comments, pictures, and other means of communicating unwanted sexual innuendo. Sexual harassment suits have increased dramatically over the last several years. As a consequence of the judgments (which are often several hundred thousand dollars), companies are increasingly offering training programs to try to help managers understand the law and avoid incidents of sexual harassment.

CONCLUDING COMMENTS

In this chapter, we presented human resource management as a set of activities performed by all managers rather than a set of functions locked within a human resource department. A company's human resources are its most fundamental source of competitive advantage. In addition, individual managers can create competitive advantages for themselves in their careers through superior management of human resources. In particular, managers who can match their management of human resources with the strategy of the organization may find themselves in a superior position relative to their peers.

As a manager, it is unlikely that you will want to leave activities such as recruitment, selection, training, or development of your employees entirely to the human resource department. While human resource departments in most companies play a formal role in all the activities we have covered in this chapter, if you want to get the right people and maximize their performance, you will need to be involved in and skilled at these activities as well.

Relegating HR activities to a specific department is an old school of thought and not reflective of today's environment. As business continues to push toward being knowledge based, the effective management of people in whom critical intelligence and knowledge reside becomes increasingly important. As an executive of an engineering service firm said to us, "I watch the company's assets walk out the door at the close of business each day." From that perspective, effective human resource management becomes a central job of every manager.

KEY TERMS

affirmative action programs 329

assessment centers 339

at-risk compensation 348

behaviorally anchored rating scales (BARS) 345

bona fide occupational qualifications (BFOQ) 331

broad band systems 347

cafeteria-style plans 349

career paths 349

critical incidents 346

cross-functional job rotation 349

expatriate employees 329

glass ceiling 329

incentive plans 349

job analysis 334

job design 343

job posting 335

job sharing 343

pay structure 347

reengineering 343

structured interview 338

360-degree feedback 345

unstructured interview 338

valid selection technique 337

work simulation 339

REVIEW QUESTIONS

1. What are the key components of competitive advantage?
2. Why are people the key to a firm's competitive advantage?
3. Why must you as a manager be skilled at human resource activities?
4. Why must a firm's strategy match its environment?
5. What are six important external environmental factors that have an impact on human resource management?
6. What are the key human resource activities at which you must be skilled?
7. Describe five effective means of recruiting new employees.
8. What does it mean for a selection technique to be valid?
9. What is the primary difference between structured and unstructured interviews and what effect does this difference have?
10. What is the basic rationale for work sampling as a selection method?
11. Identify three written tests used in selection and describe their validity.
12. Why are reference checks of little use in selection?
13. List the five things that can be done to make orientation programs more effective.
14. Define *reengineering* and explain its use in organizations.
15. What are the key differences between graphic rating scales and behaviorally anchored rating scales?
16. List seven steps that can be taken to make performance appraisal sessions more effective.
17. Why are organizations moving away from traditional pay structures to more broad band pay structures?
18. What is a cafeteria-style benefit plan?
19. Describe at least one major challenge for HRM in the future and explain why it is important.

DISCUSSION QUESTIONS

1. Think about the best and worst boss you ever had. To what extent did human resource management skills differentiate the two? In particular, which skills?
2. As you look forward to a future management position, what HRM strengths and weaknesses do you feel you have?
3. If you look at your university, what HR activities does it perform well? What are needed improvements?
4. What do you think will be the most challenging HR activities in the future?

CLOSING CASE

Alliant Diversity Training

In the 21st century, corporate America is encountering a number of trends that affect the composition of its workforce. First, the U.S. population, and thus its workforce, is growing more slowly than it has in the past few decades. Second, the average age of this workforce is rising, and the pool of younger workers is shrinking. Third, women are becoming a more important component of the labor pool, and ethnic minorities are representing a larger share of incoming workers. Fourth, immigration, which accounts for much of the U.S. population growth, has a profound effect on the workforce. As a result of these trends, U.S. firms are facing issues largely ignored in the past: a skilled labor shortage, the restricted physical abilities of older workers, increased demand for family-friendly benefits, and language barriers.

Some companies have reluctantly accepted the trends, while others have embraced them wholeheartedly. One such company is Alliant, formerly Wisconsin Power and Light (WP&L), in Madison, Wisconsin. Alliant is the state's largest electricity and gas distributor. The company has focused on diversity of human resources as a key goal to compete effectively in the future. Erroll B. Davis Jr., the president and CEO, states, "A focus on a diverse workforce is a necessary evolution for our company, both from a cultural and a business perspective.... Because the workforce of the future will be more diverse, [our] efforts now are focused on understanding, respecting, and valuing the differences of our employees. This will allow us to fully utilize our human resources for a competitive advantage in the marketplace."

The company defines diversity as differences in gender, race, age, physical and mental abilities, lifestyles, cultures, education, ideas, and backgrounds. As such, it has expectations about diversity: All levels within the organization will appreciate diversity; employees will seek out different perspectives; and employees at all levels must be intolerant of behaviors that are inconsistent with the company's

mission to build and nurture a diverse workforce. Unlike many companies which pay lip service to the "D" word, the power utility has put its goal into action by involving all parts of the organization.

In 1991, a Diversity Steering Team was created with the goal of training employees about diversity issues. The team consisted of 15 members representing every level of the labor hierarchy and a mix of genders, races, and ages. The team's first step was to conduct an employee survey. Surveys were sent to 1,571 employees, and the team received a response rate of 65 percent, high for any type of research. The survey asked for employee perceptions on a number of diversity issues, such as affirmative action, job satisfaction, interpersonal relationships, and work attitudes. After analyzing the results, the team reached several conclusions. An important one was that employees were generally confused about the company's definition of diversity and its expectations regarding diversity. The team recommended that the company build a formal training program for all employees, called the Diversity of Workforce Awareness Workshop.

The premise of the training program was that once employees understood the range of perspectives that exist in a diverse workforce, they would become more aware of the benefits it carried. The training program consisted of an eight-hour workshop. To communicate the commitment of senior management to diversity, a vice president or department manager opened each workshop. Then a facilitator explained the benefits of diversity, stated the company's expectation of employees, and helped them recognize behaviors that are consistent or inconsistent with diversity. All participants received a workbook designed to guide them through important topics covered during the workshop.

The most important element of the workshops, however, was the involvement of employees. Two exercises were designed to engage employee participation and to help them think through issues. In the first exercise, each employee was asked to name specific actions he or she would take to support diversity. A second exercise had employees create a list of diversity ground rules. For example, one group created the rule that "all offensive jokes and language should be eliminated from the work-place." Another group created a rule that started as "respect the ideas of others" and later changed it to "accept, understand, respect, and celebrate our differ-ences." The active participation of the employees helped them carry the momentum back to their own work stations.

The Diversity Steering Team started its pilot training program and two years later, all 2,500 employees had completed diversity training. Feedback from employees was generally positive, and most seemed to believe that the training helped them to support diversity in their own work groups. The Steering Team then carried its diversity mission to outside suppliers and contractors who represent the company to ensure that all behaviors are consistent with the corporate mission.

This commonsense approach to diversity training is innovative in two ways. First, rather than make the human resource department solely responsible for diversity, the company has the support of top management. Second, the diverse composition of the Steering Team helped it address diversity on a larger scale. At Alliant, every part of the busi-ness now supports diversity, and the company has made a long-term commitment.

QUESTIONS

1. Why is Alliant so committed to diversity of its human resources? How will the company benefit from its mission?
2. Do you believe that the company is forcing the issue of diversity too much? Why or why not? Is it necessary to make training mandatory for all employees?
3. Surveys conducted by independent labor boards indi-cate that it is difficult to quantify the effects of diversity. How might a company measure the effects of a diversi-fied workforce? If a company ignored it own workforce diversity, how might it be affected?

Source: Adapted from Nancy Mueller, "Wisconsin Power & Light's Model Diversity Program," *Training & Development*, March 1996, pp. 57–61.

PART 5

LEADING

CHAPTER 13

MOTIVATION

LEARNING OBJECTIVES

After studying this chapter, you should be able to:

- Analyze the motivational forces present in a specific situation.
- Differentiate between the various content and process theories of motivation and indicate how each can be helpful in analyzing a given motivational situation.
- Explain how job enrichment can influence an employee's motivation.
- Compare and contrast the various approaches to reinforcement and describe their relative advantages and disadvantages for use by managers.
- State how goal setting can affect motivation.
- Name the major types of social influence on employees' motivation and explain how each type can impact motivation.
- Describe how values and attitudes toward work can influence motivation.

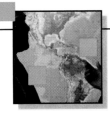

What Will Motivate the Factory Worker of the New Century?

Adlai John Warner had planned to go to college after he returned from the Vietnam War, in which he was an intelligence specialist. But life events intervened—he married and started a family, and instead went to work as a laborer for Acme Metals Inc., near Chicago. He needed to earn enough money to support his family, and his job at Acme Metals provided that. Rachelle Cook, on the other hand, wanted to get ahead in her career as a nurse. But this was difficult to achieve for a mother of two children, who would have had to pursue a four-year degree, raise her children, and work at her job, all at the same time. So when she heard about Medrad, a medical-equipment maker in Pittsburgh that claimed to invest in its workers, she applied for a job—and was hired.

Both of these factory workers were motivated to apply for and achieve in their jobs, each for different reasons. John Warner was motivated by the need to feed and care for his family; Rachelle Cook was motivated by the desire to achieve her career goals. As the new century arrives, workers and companies face both old and new challenges in discovering and satisfying what motivates employees to perform their best on the job. With the rapid development of new manufacturing technologies, companies are able to automate many manufacturing tasks, thus cutting the need for unskilled or semiskilled laborers. But someone has to know how to run the computers that control these operations—and so the very workers who might have decided to skip college or even technical school in favor of good factory wages (John Warner earned up to $60,000 per year) are now faced with the need to be retrained or lose their jobs.

Some of these workers have been able to turn the threat of losing their jobs into an opportunity for advancement. Instead of opting for the early retirement from Acme Steel that many of his coworkers took when faced with job loss or the seemingly daunting task of training, John Warner took a battery of skills tests in reading, math, communications, and technology. He qualified for a job as a maintenance technician and began his new training in the classroom trailers that Acme set up right next to the mill. Acme paid Warner and other trainees to spend nine months, full time, learning everything they needed to know to function in a new, high-tech plant. "We're being exposed to things we've never been exposed to," notes Warner. He was probably motivated to take part in the training program by several factors—the need to continue supporting his family, the incentive provided by the company in the form of paid wages during training, and the desire to advance to a more fulfilling job.

Rachelle Cook was also motivated to turn adversity into opportunity. When she began her employment at Medrad, she found herself stuck on the night shift at $10 per hour, assembling syringes. "Everyone could see I was miserable," she recalls. Cook wasn't content with her circumstances, so she applied for every new opening that came up at Medrad, and when the company decided to institute teams in its factory, Cook became part of a pilot program that offered courses in conflict resolution, problem solving, and customer–supplier relations. She did so well in the program that she was selected for a career development program that put her on the track for a management position either as a trainer or as a customer service supervisor. The program satisfied Cook's need for achievement and highlighted her interest in working with people, both of which were contributing factors to Cook's motivation.

Each of these examples illustrates how both employees and their companies can find ways to address the issue of motivation on the job as technology alters the manufacturing workplace. This chapter explores further the many different motivational issues that managers must consider in their efforts to develop a productive workforce.

Source: Stephen Baker and Larry Armstrong, "The New Factory Worker," *Business Week*, September 30, 1996, pp. 59–58.

Managers who successfully motivate their associates are rewarded with high performance. However, that is not easy to accomplish. Understanding the forces that motivate behavior has been a continuing challenge for managers ever since the beginning of the industrial age. Typical issues might include such questions as: What causes some people to put more effort into their work than others? Why do certain individuals seem to have definite goals and objectives at work but others don't? Why does one individual or one group differ from other individuals or other groups in their persistence in courses of action?

Although these are common questions in work organizations throughout the world, as we saw in the opening story, the answers may vary considerably from one individual or group to another and from one country or culture to another. This, in a way, is the fascination of motivation as a topic. What might work in motivating Employee A might be totally ineffective in motivating Employee B. An approach that is generally successful in Mexico could have absolutely no effect in Germany. An action by a manager in a U.S. company might have a strong positive impact on the motivation of older employees but not younger ones, while the same action by a manager in, say, Korea could have the reverse effect. To repeat: Potentially effective motivational approaches are strongly influenced both by individual differences and by organizational and cultural circumstances.

When we use the term "motivation," regardless of the setting, what does it mean? **Motivation** can be thought of as the set of forces that energize, direct, and sustain behavior. These forces can come from the person, the so-called "push" of internal forces, or they can come from the environment that surrounds the person, the so-called "pull" of external forces. It is therefore essential for managers to recognize the importance of *both* sets of factors when they are analyzing motivational causes of behavior. The Managerial Challenge box explores the role that motivation can play in athletics and in other settings.

An overemphasis on one set of forces to the exclusion of the other can lead to a faulty diagnosis and to actions that do not solve motivational problems. For example, a manager might assume that her subordinate's level of sales calls is low because he is lazy, when in fact appropriate incentives have not been provided that tap his needs or interests. The manager would thus be attributing the cause to lack of an internal, push force, whereas a more accurate diagnosis in this case would focus on deficient pull forces. This kind of misreading of motivation, which is easy to do, could lead to the loss of a potentially valuable employee. Likewise, an assumption that a clerical worker is doing an especially good job in order to please his supervisor would be putting weight on external or pull forces to explain his motivation, while perhaps not giving enough credit to internal push forces. This worker might be a person who is highly motivated no matter what kind of supervision or direction he receives. In both of these examples, a broader view of motivational factors might lead to a more accurate and useful assessment.

Throughout this chapter, different types of motivational forces will be examined, with particular emphasis on what psychologists and other behavioral scientists have

motivation
set of forces that energize, direct, and sustain behavior

HOW IMPORTANT WAS MOTIVATION?

Readers of the sports pages around the United States woke up on Sunday morning, September 14, 1997, to some very surprising stories about the previous day's college football games. They read that: UCLA had defeated the University of Texas 66–3, Washington State University had defeated the University of Southern California 28–21, and Purdue University had defeated Notre Dame 28–17. Why were these scores surprising?

In preseason predictions that year, the UCLA-Texas game was expected to be a close, hard-fought battle between two highly regarded teams. However, UCLA had lost its first two games of the season against teams it was expected to beat. So UCLA was actually the underdog going into its third game, against Texas on Texas's home field. In fact, the Los Angeles newspapers had been very critical of how UCLA had played in those first two games. Thus, not only was UCLA's win over Texas somewhat surprising, but the 63-point margin of victory was a shock to football fans in Los Angeles, Texas, and everywhere else.

The outcome of the Washington State-USC game was not a total surprise, but it was notable because Washington State had not beaten USC at USC in 20 consecutive games—a span of 40 years!

Notre Dame was a clear favorite over Purdue, especially because Purdue had had a disastrous season the year before and was not expected to fare much better, despite the arrival of a new coach. Purdue had even been described in the press before the game as "the Big Ten Conference's doormat of the 1990s." That Purdue even played Notre Dame close, let alone actually defeated their cross-state rival, astonished Notre Dame and Purdue fans alike.

In any highly competitive sports games, differences in athletic talent are probably the major contributor to the eventual outcomes. But in these three games, were the winners *that* much more talented than the losers? It is highly doubtful. Was superior coaching the key? Certainly, coaching played an important role in these games, but it alone was probably not the complete answer to why the three underdogs won. That leaves motivation as a likely factor.

One way we can analyze these three games is from a push–pull motivational perspective. For the UCLA team, the critical LA newspaper accounts clearly provided a strong pull force. That, coupled with the push force of the players' own embarrassment over their previous play and their frustrated need for achievement, provided a high level of overall motivation. For Washington State, the pull force of the knowledge of the year-after-year losses to the more well-publicized USC football teams, combined with the push force of their widely reported confidence in themselves, their quarterback, and their coach, raised their overall motivation to an exceedingly high level. In the case of Purdue, the need to raise their own self-image ("We needed to believe in ourselves and feel better about ourselves" was the way their new coach put it) amounted to a strong push, and a pull was the knowledge that everyone else expected Notre Dame to win.

Motivation wasn't the only variable accounting for these upsets, but it was critical. So, the question is: In activities in organizational situations aside from athletic contests, how much difference does motivation make in the outcome? Or, are sports so uniquely different from ordinary work life in organizations that no comparisons or generalizations are possible?

had to say about the content and process of motivation. First, though, we begin with a framework to analyze the sources of motivational forces in the work situation. Following that, several major behavioral theories of motivation are examined. In later sections of the chapter, attention is focused on how goals, reinforcement systems, and the social environment of work can affect the strength and direction of motivation.

SOURCES OF MOTIVATION

As shown in Exhibit 13.1, there are three basic categories of variables that determine motivation in the work setting:

* Characteristics of the individual
* Characteristics of the job
* Characteristics of the work situation

EXHIBIT 13.1
Key Variables That Influence Motivation

INTERNAL (Push Forces)	EXTERNAL (Pull Forces)	
Characteristics of **The Individual** (examples)	Characteristics of **The Job** (examples)	Characteristics of **The Work Situation** (examples)
Needs • For Security • For Achievement • For Power Attitudes • About Self • About Job • About Supervisor • About Organization Interests • Hobbies, Travel, Reading • Sports	Feedback • Amount • Timing Work Load Tasks • Variety • Scope Discretion • How Job is Performed	Immediate Social Environment • Supervisor(s) • Workgroup Members • Subordinates Organizational Actions • Individual Rewards • Group Rewards • Reward Policies • Training and Development • Pressure to Perform

The first category, the individual's characteristics, is the source of the internal, or push, forces of motivation, what the employee *brings* to the work setting. The individual's contributions to motivational forces consist of three major subsets of variables: needs, such as the need for security, self-esteem, achievement, or power; attitudes toward self, a job, a supervisor, or the organization; and interests, such as hobbies, travel, reading, or sports.

The second and third categories of basic causal variables refer to the external, or pull, forces of motivation. Characteristics of the job focus on what the person *does* in the work setting. These include how much immediate feedback on performance the person receives, the work load, the variety and scope of the tasks that make up the job, and the degree of discretion the person is allowed in meeting the requirements of the job.

The other external category, work situation characteristics, refers to *what happens* to the individual. This category has two sets of variables: the immediate social environment composed of the supervisor(s), members of the work group, and subordinates; and various types of organizational actions, such as, for example, reward and compensation practices, the availability of training and development, and the amount of pressure applied to achieve high levels of output.

Taken together, the three major categories of variables—individual, job, and work situation—can serve as a useful framework for analyzing the sources of motivation, whether in Bangkok, Lima, or New York. Focusing on them also forms a good basis for considering the major behavioral theories of motivation relevant to managing in organizational settings that are presented in the next section.

Accepting and implementing employee suggestions may be a source of motivation for some employees because it gives them a feeling of empowerment.

BEHAVIORAL THEORIES OF MOTIVATION

Several behavioral theories of motivation are particularly relevant for managers. Each of these theories highlights one or more of the variables just discussed and shown in Exhibit 13.1. Each theory also provides managers with useful perspectives for understanding motivational challenges and problems and for ways to deal with them.

Before examining the basic features of these motivational theories, however, it is important to note that almost all were developed by *American* behavioral scientists. Thus, an obvious question is: Do these theories apply only in the context of American culture and society, or are they also useful in analyzing motivation in other societies and cultures?[1] Unfortunately, the answer is not yet clear. Based on the available evidence, the best answer is that some of the theories do have relevance beyond the American context, but others may have fewer universal applications. However, these theories should not be automatically rejected because they originated in a particular cultural context, nor should they be routinely accepted as applying equally well across different cultures.

Psychologists who have studied the topic typically have categorized motivation theories into two types: content theories and process theories, as shown in Exhibit 13.2. The two types together provide us with a deeper understanding of motivation.

Content Theories

content theories
motivation theories that focus on what needs a person is trying to satisfy and on what features of the work environment seem to satisfy those needs

Content theories focus on what needs a person is trying to satisfy and on what features of the work environment seem to satisfy those needs. Such theories try to explain motivation by identifying both internal factors, that is, particular needs, and external factors, particular job and work situation characteristics, that are presumed to cause behavior. Two content theories, need hierarchy and acquired needs, are concerned with identifying internal factors, and one, the two-factor theory, is concerned with identifying external factors.

EXHIBIT 13.2

Types of Motivation Theories

	CONTENT THEORIES	**PROCESS THEORIES**
FOCUS	• Personal needs that workers attempt to satisfy • Features in the work environment that satisfy a worker's needs	• How different variables can combine to influence the amount of effort put forth by employees
THEORIES	• Maslow's Need Hierarchy • McClelland's Acquired Needs Theory • Herzberg's Two-Factor Theory	• Equity Theory • Expectancy Theory

Need Hierarchy Theory   The most prominent need hierarchy theory was developed a half century ago by psychologist Abraham Maslow.[2] Maslow's theory has had a certain appeal to managers, probably because it is easy to remember and contains five types of needs that are arranged in a hierarchy of strength and influence (as shown in Exhibit 13.3).

The five needs in Maslow's hierarchy (starting with the most essential or prepotent) are:

- Physiological: Needs for the most basic essentials of life, such as air, water, food, shelter, and so on.
- Security (safety): The needs to feel safe and secure and not to be threatened by circumstances in the surrounding environment that might jeopardize continued existence.
- Social (belongingness): The needs to be loved, to interact and relate to other people, and to be accepted by them.
- Esteem: The needs for a sense of one's own worth and competence and for recognition of that worth from other people.
- Self-actualization: The needs to be personally fulfilled, to feel a sense of accomplishment, and especially, to develop one's own unique capabilities and talents to the highest possible level.

Maslow's need hierarchy

theory that states people fulfill basic needs, such as physiological and safety needs, before making efforts to satisfy other needs, such as social and belongingness, esteem, and self-actualization

The essence of **Maslow's need hierarchy** is that an individual is motivated to satisfy the most basic or potent needs first (such as physiological needs) and then, if those are satisfied, move to the next level. According to the theory, someone who has fulfilled her basic biological and security needs will then concentrate her effort on the next level of need in the hierarchy, namely, social or belonging needs. However, if that person's security needs should become threatened, she will revert to focusing on these needs and will ignore social or belonging needs until or unless the threat has passed.

A good example of this theory occurred a few years ago at a plant of Ahlstrom Fakop, a Polish subdivision of Finnish paper and power equipment manufacturer A. Ahlstrom. Managers at the plant were having trouble motivating employees in the formerly state-owned enterprise. Offering incentive pay had not worked. Only

EXHIBIT 13.3
Maslow's Hierarchy
of Needs

Maslow's Hierarchy of Needs

EXHIBIT 13.3
Maslow's Hierarchy of Needs

when managers let employees know that no one would be laid off if sales targets were reached did employee morale pick up. Many of the employees were more concerned with keeping their job than with their pay level as their country moved from a state-controlled to a market economy.[3]

An even more extreme example of this principle occurred in 1995 in the Los Angeles area. Young Thai nationals were working in garment workshops under conditions that approached slavery. For example, they were not even allowed to leave the building in which they lived and worked (for up to 18 hours per day) for months and even, in some cases, years. The need hierarchy theory would clearly predict that such workers would not have been concerned with satisfying belonging, esteem, and self-actualization needs. Even the minimum satisfaction of their physiological and safety needs was in jeopardy, let alone that of higher-order needs.[4]

The key to understanding a person's motivation, then, from a need hierarchy perspective, is to identify that person's most basic need that is not yet satisfied. For the Thai garment workers in Los Angeles, this level would be the most basic: physiological needs. Once a need has been satisfied, it ceases to be a motivator unless its fulfillment is threatened again. But, if it is threatened, that more basic need becomes the focus of attention, as in the Polish manufacturing plant example.

Many questions can be raised about the need hierarchy theory. For example, do the needs occur in the same hierarchical order across all cultures and countries? Probably not. The theory was developed in an American context, and there is no convincing evidence that the hierarchy is universal, either from country to country or from one person to the next. As one knowledgeable scholar has argued, based on extensive research findings from a number of countries:

> *Maslow's hierarchy puts self-actualization (achievement) plus esteem above social needs, above security needs. This ... is a description of a value system, the value system of the U.S. middle class to which the author belonged. I suggest that ... for [some] countries [such as Greece and Mexico], security needs should rank at the top; for [other] countries [such as Denmark and Sweden] ... social needs should rank at the top; and [for still other] countries [such as Portugal and Chile], both security and social needs should rank at the top.*[5]

Not only does the hierarchy of needs probably not have the same order across different cultures, it almost assuredly is not ordered the same from one individual to another. Furthermore, different individuals have quite different thresholds for satisfaction of a given need before they try to satisfy the next level. For example, someone who as a child grew up in a family whose financial resources were extremely scarce may go to inordinate lengths to assure current financial security as an adult even though the person is quite well off. Such individual differences in both the order of needs and the threshold for satisfying them clearly adds complexity for managers who attempt to base actions on the theory.

Since Maslow's need hierarchy was not developed specifically for the work situation, it has been difficult for researchers to determine its validity or usefulness in predicting behavior in organizational settings. Probably the greatest value of the theory is that it provides a way of thinking about motivation that highlights the issue of psychological needs, and the differing strength of those needs, that a person could be trying to satisfy at work.

A somewhat more simplified variation of need hierarchy theory was published subsequent to Maslow by behavioral scientist Clay Alderfer. His alternative version, labeled ERG theory for Existence-Relatedness-Growth, collapsed Maslow's five levels into three and provided a more straightforward way of thinking about need hierarchies. Although sharing many similarities with Maslow's original theory, ERG theory differs in some respects.[6] For example, it presumes that different levels of needs can be active at the same time and thus a lower level does *not* have to be completely or even mostly satisfied before higher need levels can emerge. Also, Alderfer's version suggests that even though a lower-level need has already been satisfied, a person may revert to focusing on that level if he or she is frustrated in trying to satisfy a higher level. Thus, an employee blocked in trying to gain opportunities for increased personal growth because she keeps getting assigned routine tasks may concentrate instead on socializing at work and thus gaining even more satisfaction (than before) of relatedness needs. ERG theory presents an interesting alternative to Maslow's earlier, more complicated version, but the key point is that both theories focus on individuals' attempts to satisfy particular types of needs and how that can affect their level and direction of motivation.

From the standpoint of individual managers in an organization, there is probably relatively little they can do personally to affect employees' satisfaction of basic physiological needs. They frequently do, however, have an opportunity to help ensure that employees' safety needs are not threatened and, within the limits of company policy and economic conditions, that security needs are met as much as possible.

With regard to satisfaction of employees' higher-order needs, managers can use their imagination and creativity to play a much more prominent and influential role. Many actions could help employees obtain satisfaction of social, esteem, and even self-actualization needs. For example, at Branch-Smith, Inc., in Fort Worth, Texas, managers encourage their employees to "report" on fellow employees. As part of a program called "Caught in the Act," they ask employees to write a short note of praise when they see another employee performing exceptionally well. These write-ups are then posted on the employee bulletin board and also reproduced in the company newsletter.[7] In this example, satisfaction of the needs of both parties is probably increased: self-actualization needs of the initiator for the "selfless" act of taking the time and trouble to write up the deeds of another employee, and esteem needs of the recipient through public recognition.

One company's managers provided its employees with an innovative opportunity to satisfy self-actualization needs a few years ago in the insurance industry. For its

150th birthday, the New York–based firm of Johnson and Higgins planned a day of community involvement in children's causes for all 8,500 of its employees. The efforts included painting bedrooms at homes of wards of the court, doing home repairs for the families of poor children, repairing and painting classrooms at elementary schools, and even helping children hurt by the Kobe earthquake in Japan. The program was such a success with its employees that executives of Johnson and Higgins plan to make it an annual event. Clearly, for some employees, this program provided an opportunity to obtain satisfaction at the very highest level of the need hierarchy.[8]

acquired needs theory

motivation theory that focuses on learned needs that become enduring predispositions for affiliation, power, and achievement

Acquired Needs   Another content theory that is centered on needs was developed by an American psychologist, David McClelland.[9] This **acquired needs theory** focuses on learned, or acquired, needs that become "enduring predispositions" of individuals, almost like personality traits, that can be stimulated or activated by appropriate cues in the environment. McClelland considered three of these needs to be especially important (and hence his theory is sometimes referred to as the "three-need theory"): affiliation, power, and achievement. However, most of the attention others have given to the theory of acquired needs has concentrated on the need for achievement.

In McClelland's theory, a person who has a high need for achievement is someone who habitually strives for success or attainment of goals *in task situations* (though not necessarily in other types of settings). The research data collected by McClelland and his associates indicate that high need achievement individuals prefer to

- work on tasks of moderate difficulty
- take moderate risks
- take personal responsibility for their actions
- receive specific and concrete feedback on their performance

In other words, high need achievers want challenges, but realistic challenges, not impossible ones. Especially important from a managerial perspective, McClelland's theory suggests that the need for achievement can be increased by "appropriate" training, that is, by showing people how to recognize and respond to relevant achievement cues. As might be guessed, this feature of the theory has proved to be quite controversial, since many experts doubt the extent to which permanent changes in need for achievement can be brought about by such training.

Is a need for achievement a universal motive? Is it, for example, as prevalent in Brazil as in the United States, or in India as much as in Germany? A study that was carried out across 20 countries appeared to show that achievement, along with power, *can* be considered a universal motive.[10] Although countries with quite different cultures—for example, very different attitudes toward individuality and collectivism—were included, the study indicated that a high achieving type of person could be found in each country or culture, but that type was always oriented toward individuality. The findings suggest that the percentage of high-achieving people varies considerably from country to country, but there are definitely people of this type in every culture that has been studied: "It seems that the primary goal of achievers everywhere is to attain recognition for themselves."[11]

Interestingly, research findings show that there was a fairly large change in the level of achievement motivation in both Japan and the United States in the first several decades after World War II.[12] There was a definite overall decrease in achieve-

EXHIBIT 13.4
Herzberg's Two-Factor Theory: Motivators and Hygiene Factors

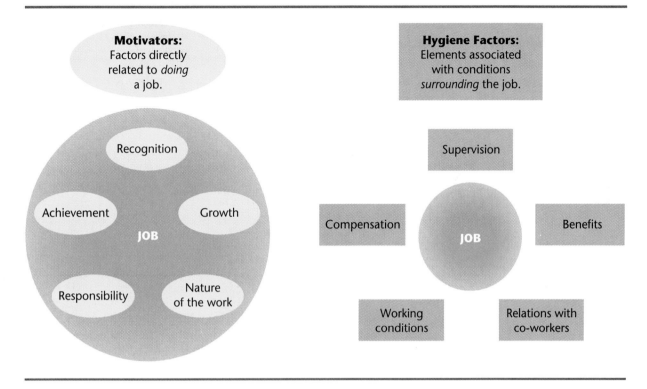

ment motivation in Japan between the 1970s and the beginning of the 1990s, especially in younger generations. This could be due, in part, to the increase in overall prosperity in Japan during that particular time span. On the other hand, younger people in the United States showed higher levels of achievement motivation at the beginning of the 1990s than their counterparts did in the late 1960s and early 1970s, perhaps reflecting the decreasing levels of economic security that occurred in the United States over that time span. Taken together, these findings seem to reinforce the conclusion that achievement motivation can be influenced by strong forces in the larger societal environment, such as changing cultural attitudes toward work and changing economic conditions. Research from the mid-1990s, incidentally, appeared to indicate that achievement motivation remained somewhat lower in Japan than in the United States, but that could change again with future societal changes in the two different countries.[13]

Two-Factor Theory   In the early 1960s, Frederick Herzberg, an American psychologist, proposed a motivation theory that came to be called the "two-factor theory."[14] The **two-factor theory** focused on the distinction between factors that can increase job satisfaction ("motivators") versus those that can prevent dissatisfaction but cannot increase satisfaction ("hygiene factors"). As shown in Exhibit 13.4, motivators are "intrinsic" factors directly related to the *doing* of a job, such as the nature of the work itself, responsibility, personal growth, and the sense of achievement and recognition directly received by performing the work. The other set, "extrinsic" or "hygiene" factors, is associated with conditions *surrounding* the

two-factor theory
motivation theory that focuses on the presumed different effects of intrinsic job factors (motivators) and extrinsic situational factors (hygiene factors)

EXHIBIT 13.5

Herzberg's Two-Factor Theory: Differential Effects of Hygiene Factors and Motivators

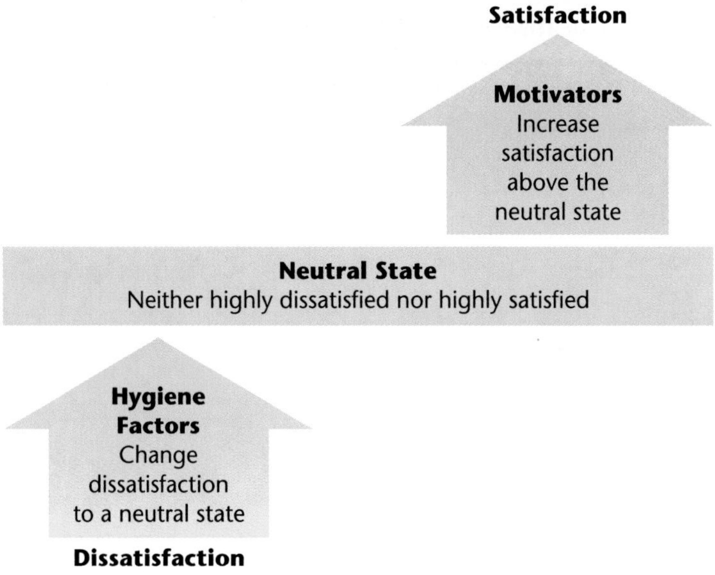

Satisfaction

Motivators
Increase satisfaction above the neutral state

Neutral State
Neither highly dissatisfied nor highly satisfied

Hygiene Factors
Change dissatisfaction to a neutral state

Dissatisfaction

job. Included in this set are supervision, relations with co-workers, working conditions, and company policies and practices related to benefits and compensation. The theory predicts that, as shown in Exhibit 13.5, the intrinsic factors work only in the direction of increasing satisfaction and the extrinsic factors work only in the direction of decreasing dissatisfaction.

The two-factor theory proved an immediate hit with practicing managers because it contains a relatively simple message: If you want to motivate employees, focus on improving how the job is structured—what they *do*—so that they obtain positive job satisfaction. Simply taking care of the hygiene factors can prevent dissatisfaction but will have no effect on positive motivation.

Although intuitively appealing, the two-factor theory has been criticized by many scholars as being overly simplistic. For one thing, research has shown that satisfaction and motivation are not the same thing. Reacting positively to something, such as being pleased with doing a more challenging set of tasks, does not necessarily mean that you will have increased motivation or a stronger desire to perform the job better. Therefore, although changing the nature of the work can often lead to an increase in intrinsic satisfaction, it does not necessarily follow that motivation to perform is increased. Critics contend that the theory blurs the distinction between satisfaction and motivation. Also, subsequent research has shown that it is not possible to distinguish cleanly between variables that only increase satisfaction from those that only decrease dissatisfaction.

Implications for Job Design   Despite these and other criticisms, however, the widespread attention given to the two-factor theory has had one very important consequence in the years after it was proposed: an increased emphasis on the design of jobs; that is, on the combinations of specific tasks put together to form particular jobs.[15] If nothing else, the two-factor theory was responsible for influencing other organizational scholars, as well as employers, to consider the issue of how the content of jobs affects the motivation to perform those jobs, and whether it is possible

job enrichment
increasing the complexity of a job to provide greater responsibility, accomplishment, and achievement

job characteristics model
approach that focuses on the motivational attributes of jobs through emphasizing three sets of variables: core job characteristics, critical psychological states, and outcomes

to provide increased opportunities for employees to experience greater feelings of responsibility, accomplishment, and achievement. The general approach to designing jobs that tries to provide such opportunities is called **job enrichment**.

One of the most comprehensive approaches to the design of enriched jobs with high potential for increased motivation has been labeled the "job characteristics model."[16] Developed by two organizational scientists, J. Richard Hackman and Greg Oldham, the **job characteristics model** emphasizes three components, as shown in Exhibit 13.6:

- Core job characteristics, such as skill variety and task significance
- Critical psychological states, such as experienced meaningfulness of work and experienced responsibility for outcomes of the work
- Expected outcomes, such as high internal work motivation and high work effectiveness.

EXHIBIT 13.6
The Job Characteristics Model

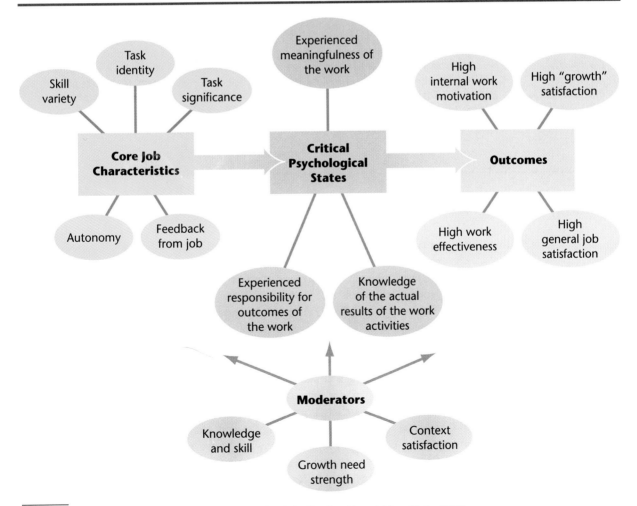

Source: Adapted from J. R. Hackman and G. R. Oldham, *Work Redesign* (Reading, Mass.: Addison-Wesley, 1980).

EXHIBIT 13.7

Core Job Characteristics in Job Characteristics Model

Core Job Characteristics	Definition	Example
Skill variety	The degree to which a job requires a variety of different activities in carrying out the work, involving the use of a number of different skills and talents of the person.	The aerospace engineer must be able to create blueprints, calculate tolerances, provide leadership to the work group, and give presentations to upper management.
Task identity	The degree to which a job requires completion of a "whole" and identifiable piece of work, that is, doing a job from beginning to end with a visible outcome.	The event manager handles all the plans for the annual executive retreat, attends the retreat, and receives information on its success from the participants.
Task significance	The degree to which the job has a substantial impact on the lives of other people, whether those people are in the immediate organization or in the world at large.	The finance manager devises a new benefits plan to improve health coverage for all employees.
Autonomy	The degree to which the job provides substantial freedom, independence, and discretion to the individual in scheduling the work and in determining the procedures to be used in carrying it out.	R&D scientists are linked via the company intranet, allowing them to post their ideas, ask questions, and propose solutions at any hour of the day whether at the office, at home, or on the road.
Feedback from job	The degree to which carrying out the work activities required by the job provides the individual with direct and clear information about the effectiveness of his or her performance.	The lathe operator knows he is cutting his pieces correctly, as very few are rejected by the workers in the next production area.

Source: Adapted from J. Richard Hackman, and Greg R. Oldham, *Work Redesign* (Reading, Mass.: Addison-Wesley, 1980).

The Hackman-Oldham model also includes factors (called "moderators") such as individual differences in growth need strength that affect the likelihood that enriched jobs will lead to the desired outcomes. Clearly, not every employee wants more responsibility, autonomy, and the like, but many do. The message for managers from this model is that if they can create or adjust jobs to include more of the "core characteristics" (see Exhibit 13.7), they may be able to increase the motivation of many of the employees who work in those jobs. Indeed, a useful way for managers, who often have highly enriched jobs themselves, to think about enriching the jobs of their subordinates is to make those jobs more like their own.

The efforts of many companies over the past couple of decades to gain the benefits of job enrichment are nowhere better illustrated than in the changes that have taken place in some production systems formally organized in assembly-line fashion. Many typical assembly-line jobs are dull and repetitive, but significant changes in some companies' production operations have resulted in employees learning more than one task and rotating among a number of tasks that make up the job. At Saturn Corporation, a subsidiary of General Motors, and at Volvo's Uddevalla plant in Sweden, automobiles are constructed by teams of workers, rather than being assembled on a traditional line where one person bolts the chassis while another installs the steering wheel. The workers' individual jobs are designed so that a vehicle is constructed by one team working together to complete the entire job. Employees are thus not doing single, repetitive jobs where they never see the finished product. From a motivational perspective, these redesigned jobs not only enhance opportunities for achievement but also help instill a sense of pride in the finished product.[17]

Process Theories

process theories

motivation theories that deal with the way different variables combine to influence the amount of effort people put forth

Process theories of work motivation deal with the way different variables combine to influence the amount of effort people put forth. In other words, while content theories address the issue of which variables affect motivation, process theories focus on the issue of how variables affect it. The two most prominent process theories are equity theory and expectancy theory.

equity theory

motivation theory that focuses on individuals' comparisons of their circumstances with those of others and how such comparisons may motivate certain kinds of behavior

Equity Theory   Developed in the early 1960s by psychologist Stacy Adams, **equity theory** proposes that individuals will compare their circumstances with those of others and that such comparisons may motivate certain kinds of behavior.[18] As one observer has pointed out, a particularly vivid example involves professional athletes:

[Such] athletes often make the news by demanding that their contracts be torn up before their terms expire. The reason for this apparent lack of respect for contract law usually has to do with feelings on the part of these athletes that the rates of pay agreed to in their contracts are, by some standard [of comparison], not fair.[19]

Equity theory, as shown in Exhibit 13.8, assumes that people know what kind of effort and skills they put into their jobs and what kinds of outcomes (salary, promotions, etc.) they receive from their employer. The theory also assumes that individuals are likely to compare their ratios of inputs to outcomes to the ratios of other relevant people such as colleagues or acquaintances (in or outside their organization). Such comparisons determine whether the person feels equitably treated. The most important assumption, as in the example of the professional athletes just cited, is that if the comparisons result in feelings of inequity, the person will be motivated to try to make changes to reduce such feelings.

Equity theory states that individuals have a number of ways to reduce their feelings that others are "doing better" than they are. One way is to increase their own outcomes, such as getting a salary increase or obtaining a promotion. Another response might be to decrease their inputs; for example, they might try to put less effort in the task and still receive the same level of outcomes, if possible. A third action might be to leave their current situation so that they can obtain a new outcome/input ratio.

If people do not think they are being rewarded equitably, they have other ways of dealing with the situation. They might simply change the object of their comparison—that is, they might decide to compare themselves to different people, for example neighbors instead of work colleagues, whom they think have ratios more similar to their own. This involves no change of behavior but only a change in the way of looking at a situation. Likewise, people might re-evaluate the inputs and outcomes of those with whom they are comparing themselves, as in "she has more skills than I thought she did" or "his job isn't as good as I thought it was."

Except in very limited experimental situations, equity theory has not been very successful in predicting which method of dealing with inequity a person will use in

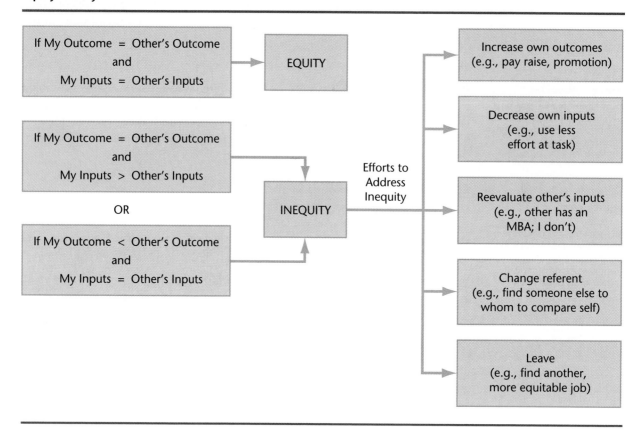

EXHIBIT 13.8

Equity Theory

a given situation. However, the chief value of this theory is that it highlights the importance of perceived equity and the role of comparisons to others' circumstances in affecting motivation. In effect, equity theory emphasizes the *social* nature of motivation.

Expectancy Theory   Psychologist Victor Vroom formulated a motivation theory for application to work settings based on people's expectations.[20] Although details of the theory can get complicated, the basics are easy to understand and are diagrammed in Exhibit 13.9. **Expectancy theory** focuses on the thought processes people use when they face particular choices among alternatives, particularly alternative courses of action. With reference to the work situation, the theory (in simplified form) proposes that individuals have two kinds of expectancies, or beliefs, that can affect the amount of effort they will choose to put forth. One such belief, effort to performance (E→P), is the probability that a certain amount of effort will lead to a certain level of performance: "If I try to do this, will I succeed?" The other expectancy belief, performance to outcome (P→O), is the probability that a particular level of performance will lead to particular "outcomes" or consequences: "If I succeed, will I get praise from the boss?" The third key variable in the theory is the **valence** (V), or anticipated value a person attaches to an outcome: "How much will I like praise from the boss if I get it?"

expectancy theory

motivation theory that focuses on the thought processes people use when they face particular choices among alternatives, particularly alternative courses of action

valence

the anticipated value a person attaches to an outcome

EXHIBIT 13.9

Basic Components of Expectancy Theory

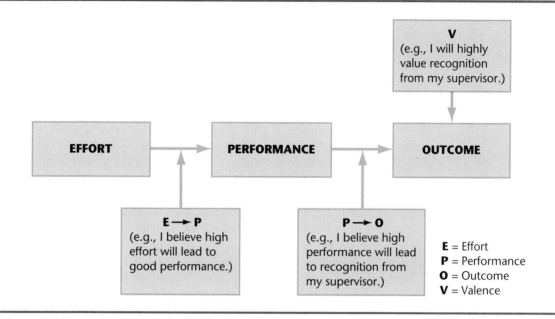

Expectancy theory states that the three key variables interact in a *multiplicative,* not additive, manner to determine the choice of the amount of effort to expend to perform a particular task:

$$\text{Effort} = E{\to}P \times P{\to}O \times V$$

Since, according to the theory, these three variables are multiplied to determine level of effort, a low value in any one of the three would result in the prediction of very low motivation. For example, even if a sales representative strongly believes that a certain level of performance (e.g., meeting a sales quota) will lead to a very desirable reward (e.g., positive recognition from her supervisor), her motivation will be low if she does not also have a strong expectation that effort will lead to that level of performance. To restate: *Both* expectancies and the anticipated value of the outcome must be high for a person to be highly motivated.

A number of implications for managerial practice flow from this theory. For each of the theory's three key variables, managers can take steps to increase employee motivation. The E$\to$P expectancy can be changed by a variety of methods. If a person believes he doesn't have the skills needed to reach a certain level of performance, such self-perceptions can be changed. Through additional training and further practice, and by appropriate guidance and counseling, managers can help employees build their confidence that a particular level of effort will lead to a desired level of performance (thus influencing the E$\to$P expectancy). Employees who believe they are capable of performing well will be more motivated to achieve their goals.

Additionally, by consistently recognizing accomplishments, managers can increase employees' perceptions of the probability of obtaining a desired outcome if they have performed well (thereby influencing the P$\to$O expectancy). How many times, however, do employees perform at a level strongly desired by the organization only to find that, from their perspective, the organization ignores or does not sufficiently recognize the accomplishment? If this happens continually, the level of motivation is certain to decrease.

On the other hand, the reverse is true: If difficult but desired levels of performance are reached and the supervisor or organization recognizes it in an explicit way, future levels of motivation can be increased. Employees are more motivated to perform well when they have a very strong expectation that they will be rewarded. This is the situation for the sales force at AMP, Inc., a manufacturer of equipment interconnectors in Harrisburg, Pennsylvania. Members of the sales force participate in the "Percentage Club." Under this plan, the company sets goals equal to last year's sales plus a targeted percentage increase for the coming year. The salespeople who meet or exceed these goals know with certainty that they will earn one week at a five-star resort.[21]

Finally, providing rewards that employees value highly is another way that managers can also influence motivation. Employees are more likely to strive for a particular outcome or reward if the prospect of receiving that outcome is valuable to them. This puts a premium on managers and organizations to learn what is, and what is not, rewarding for their employees.

Application of expectancy theory in motivation is clearly affected by cultural circumstances. For instance, in certain countries in the Middle East, where there is a strong emphasis on fate, attempts to change effort→performance (E→P) expectancies might not succeed. Likewise, attempts to single out an individual for public praise in a collectivistic culture, such as in many Asian countries, would not likely have as positive an effect on that person's performance as it might in Germany or Australia, where individualism is a stronger characteristic. An approach that considers how individuals calculate potential benefits to themselves in pursuing one course of action over another seems more relevant to most Western cultures than to cultures that place less emphasis on personal gain.

Although the psychological process described in expectancy theory is itself not necessarily culturally bound, since it could occur anywhere, the frequency with which it occurs probably is. For any culture, however, the key point is that expectancy theory is probably most useful in understanding and predicting levels of motivation that involve deliberate choices in the amount of effort to be put forth, rather than routine behavior that is largely determined by habit.

To conclude this section on expectancy theory, a conceptual model based on the theory, the Porter-Lawler model, is presented in Exhibit 13.10.[22] This model provides an overall framework for understanding the motivational process from an expectancy theory perspective. As can be seen in Exhibit 13.10, the model starts with the basic assumptions of expectancy theory about (a) what determines effort (boxes 1 and 2), and then shows (b) what affects the degree to which high levels of effort will result in organizationally desired performance (boxes 3, 4, and 5), which in turn (c) can lead to rewards that then result in a level of satisfaction (boxes 7A, 7B, and 8). Summarized briefly, the key components of the model are the following:

1. Value (valence) of Reward: The desirability of a particular reward.
2. Perceived Effort→Reward Probability: The likelihood that a given level of effort will lead to the desired reward (note that Box 2 combines the E→P and the P→O expectancies).
3. Effort: Mental and physical energy devoted to tasks.

EXHIBIT 13.10

The Porter-Lawler Model

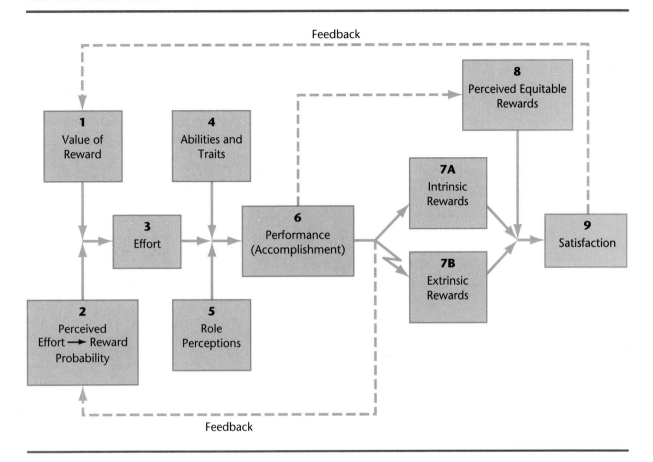

4. **Abilities and Traits:** The basic capabilities of the individual that will determine how well effort can be converted into performance.

5. **Role Perceptions:** The individual's understanding of the direction of the effort to be applied to achieving performance; that is, knowing exactly where, when, and how effort is to be expended; inaccurate role perceptions could be viewed as "misguided efforts."

6. **Performance:** A particular level of accomplishment.

7A. **Intrinsic Rewards:** Rewards that individuals provide to themselves as the direct result of performance, such as a "feeling of accomplishment."

7B. **Extrinsic Rewards:** Rewards (such as pay increases, promotions, praise) that can be provided by the organization for performance *if* the performance is judged to be adequate or better and *if* the organization is willing and able to provide such rewards; the conditional nature of such rewards is represented by the arrow between box 6 and box 7B.

8. **Perceived Equitable Rewards:** The amount or level of rewards that the individual believes should be provided by the organization as the result of particular performance.

9. **Satisfaction:** The individual's reaction to the level of rewards received in relation to the level of rewards anticipated.

Note that the model suggests there are two critical feedback loops in this motivational process that will affect future motivation to perform: one from the strength of the relation of performance to the level of intrinsic and extrinsic rewards received (that is, the strength of the relation of box 6 to boxes 7A and 7B) feeding back to perceived probabilities of effort leading to particular rewards (box 2); and the second from the level of satisfaction obtained (box 9) feeding back to the desirability of a particular reward (box 1). These feedback loops reinforce the notion that motivation is an ongoing, evolving process.

The relevance of the Porter-Lawler model for managers is that it shows exactly at what points they can affect the level of motivation (effort) of those who work for them. Thus, managers potentially can influence employees' motivation by

- identifying what rewards are valued by their subordinates;
- influencing subordinates' beliefs about whether their efforts will lead to desired rewards (box 2);
- increasing subordinates' understanding of exactly where they should direct their efforts (box 5);
- making sure that desired extrinsic rewards are given following particular levels of performance (box 7B); and
- providing a level and amount of extrinsic rewards that are consistent with a reasonable level of expected rewards (box 8).

The Porter-Lawler model provides a useful framework for thinking about motivation as a process. However, like the expectancy framework in general, it does not imply that each step is necessarily a deliberate decision by the employee or manager. As noted earlier, many instances of day-to-day performance and responses to it consist of more or less well-learned and often habitual actions and thus do not involve overtly conscious choices. Therefore, the model is only meant to indicate where managers or employees might make deliberate choices *if* they are trying to influence the process. The model is intended to aid in understanding the process of motivation, not predict the precise level of motivation of a particular individual in a given set of circumstances.

MOTIVATION AND GOALS

Modern approaches to motivation emphasize the concept of goals and the importance of goal setting.[23] The notion of goal, a desired end state, highlights the importance of intention, what people attempt to do in a given situation. "Goal setting theory assumes that human action is directed by conscious goals and intentions."[24] Therefore, if managers can influence goals and intentions, they can directly affect performance. The level at which goals are set is a potentially powerful determinant of motivation, and obtaining a person's commitment to particular goals is crucial.[25]

The findings from goal-setting research point to two basic conclusions:

- More challenging (higher or harder) goals result in higher levels of effort than easier goals.
- Specific goals result in higher levels of effort than vague goals.[26]

Goal setting research shows that goals need to be both challenging and specific in order to obtain a higher level of effort on the part of employees.

It appears that incentives, such as money or positive feedback on performance, only have an effect on effort if they are connected to the setting and acceptance of specific and challenging goals.[27]

Paula Hankins, manager of a Pier 1 Imports store in Nashville, Tennessee, used specific goals to motivate her employees to increase their sales during the holiday season. She decided to post the sales numbers from the previous season and the sales goal for the current season where everyone could see them. In this way, Hankins thought the sales personnel would be motivated to improve. She was gratified when the first day's sales level showed a 40 percent increase over the same day a year before, which was even higher than the 36 percent increase she had set as a goal.[28]

Despite consistent findings in a number of well-controlled experiments, one dimension of goal setting has produced inconsistent and often contradictory results. This is the issue of whether goals that are set through a process of participation (by those who will be asked to meet them) result in higher performance than goals that are arbitrarily assigned by someone else such as a supervisor.

Recent research suggests that cultural factors may be particularly influential in determining whether participation is effective in the goal-setting process.[29] A study jointly conducted on American and Israeli university students showed that *lack* of participation had a much more serious negative effect on the Israeli students than on the American students. The authors of this study interpreted the findings as consistent with cultural differences between the two countries. "The results lead to the conclusion that the difference between Israelis and Americans is not their attitude toward participation but their reaction to assigned goals."[30] This research suggests that participation in goal setting will be more effective in countries and cultures where expectations of collective decision making exist, including decisions about goals. When such cultural expectations (or norms) are weaker, as in the United States, participation in goal setting may have much less effect.

THE ROLE OF REINFORCEMENTS AND CONSEQUENCES

reinforcement theory
motivation theory that examines the effects of consequences on motivation and behavior

Actions that occur *before* behavior takes place, such as setting goals, are considered *antecedents* to performance. Such antecedent actions can influence behavior, especially by clarifying expectations. However, events that happen to the individual *after* behavior, the *consequences* of performance, also can have a powerful effect on determining future motivation by reinforcing tendencies to continue or discontinue that behavior.[31] (Refer back to the three major determinants of motivation in Exhibit 13.1.) **Reinforcement theory** examines the effects that consequences have on motivation and behavior. Consequences can be positive, neutral, or negative and can vary from insignificant to overwhelming.

In the work situation, consequences can come from the work group, the supervisor, the organization, or any combination of the three. Frequently, as in the case of employees who perform far above the average for their group, the consequences from one source (e.g., supervisor) may be positive while those from another source (work group colleagues) may be negative. Regardless, motivation to increase or to decrease particular behavior can be strengthened as a result of these responses to behavior, and thus reinforcing consequences represent a potentially powerful set of tools for managers in influencing performance. That is, they are powerful tools *if* those reinforcements are applied appropriately. As will be clear from the discussion that follows, this is not always easy to do.

Reinforcement Approaches

Analysis of the different reinforcement approaches focuses on whether particular behaviors will likely be repeated or lessened.

The two principal approaches that can be used to *increase* the probability of behavior desired by the manager or organization are positive and negative reinforcements:

positive reinforcements
desirable consequences that, by being given or applied, increase the likelihood of behavior being repeated in the future

Positive Reinforcements   **Positive reinforcements** are desirable consequences, often referred to as "rewards," that, by being given or applied, increase the likelihood of behavior being repeated in the future. (Note the distinction in reinforcement theory between the terms "desirable" and "desired": "desirable" refers to consequences that the person receiving them finds pleasing; "desired" refers to behavior that someone else, such as a supervisor, wants to increase.) In many instances, the use of positive reinforcements, such as a manager praising an employee for good performance, strengthens the likelihood of that desired behavior in the future, especially if such praise is not seen by the subordinate as routine or insincere. However, positive consequences also can inadvertently reinforce undesired behavior.[32] For example, an employee may take a shortcut at considerable risk to the organization to achieve an important performance goal. The employee's manager congratulates the person for reaching the goal so quickly but does not realize that the risky behavior is also being reinforced.

One of the foremost experts on the use of rewards and reinforcements, Steven Kerr, suggests that for positive reinforcements (rewards) to be effective in motivating behavior in organizational settings, they should have the following attributes:

- Equitable: The size of rewards should be roughly related to the quality and/or quantity of past job-related performance.
- Efficient: Rewards must have some capacity for affecting future performance; for example, by making clear that a particular level of future performance will lead to a desired reward.
- Available (i.e., capable of being given): Managers and organizations should not talk about or offer rewards that are not readily available or are available in such small amounts as to be seen (by recipients and others) as not rewarding at all. As Kerr states: "Organizations with minuscule salary increase pools spend hundreds of management hours rating, ranking, and grading employees, only to waste time, raise expectations, and ultimately produce such pitiful increases that everybody is disappointed and embarrassed."
- Not exclusive: The possibility of obtaining rewards should not be limited to only a small percentage of employees. The more that people are "ineligible" or excluded from the possibility of obtaining rewards, the less likely that a given reward could have a widespread effect.
- Visible: To be effective in having more than a very limited impact on the motivation of a number of people, rewards should be visible not only to recipients but also to others who possibly could obtain them in the future.
- Reversible: This attribute of effective rewards does not, of course, refer to a reward that can be taken away once given. Rather, it refers to rewards that can be denied or not given in the future, if circumstances warrant. The classic example in modern business organizations is the bonus. Unlike a pay raise that is, for all intents and purposes, built into a person's compensation forever, a bonus can clearly be a one-time-only reward. It also is a type of reward that can be given again in the future. That feature provides managers with a great deal of flexibility.[33]

negative reinforcements

undesirable consequences that, by being removed or avoided, increase the likelihood of a behavior being repeated in the future

Negative Reinforcements   The *removal* of undesirable (i.e., negative) consequences, that is, consequences that a person performing an act does not want, can *increase* the likelihood of that behavior being repeated in the future. The removal of such undesirable consequences is called a **negative reinforcement**, just as the addition of desirable consequences is called a positive reinforcement. In both cases, they are *reinforcing* if they cause behavior to be maintained or increased. For example, a salesperson, working in a sales territory with very difficult and demanding customers, finds that by putting in extra effort, the unpleasant experiences he has been encountering have been removed when he is transferred to a different territory. If he believes the transfer was a result of his hard work, the removal of the undesirable consequences (the difficult territory with difficult customers) has reinforced the likelihood of high levels of effort in the future. In this instance, both the company and the salesperson benefited from the negative reinforcement.

Negative reinforcements, however, can also work against the best interests of the organization. For example, if a supervisor finds that giving a particular subordinate an "average" rating results in avoiding the very unpleasant interactions with the subordinate that have occurred in the past when the subordinate was given well-deserved "below-average" ratings, the supervisor's current action is negatively reinforced. The results are that the subordinate continues subpar performance and the organization is deprived of accurate information on the subordinate that may be crucial in future promotion decisions.

Both of these reinforcement mechanisms—positive reinforcements and negative reinforcements—maintain or increase particular types of behavior and performance. Thus, they provide managers with potentially potent ways to increase desirable behavior. However, if care is not taken, their use instead can lead to continuation or increases in undesirable behavior.

In contrast to these two reinforcement mechanisms for maintaining or enhancing particular behaviors, two other methods involving consequences, discussed next, are methods to decrease the probability of particular behaviors.

punishments

undesirable consequences that are applied to decrease the likelihood of behavior being repeated in the future

Punishments   Punishments are negative consequences given following behavior to decrease the likelihood it will be repeated. In some organizations, punishments are seen as an effective way to prevent undesired behavior. In many other organizations, however, punishments are discouraged, often because their use is seen as either inappropriate or ineffective. Also, they can have inadvertent undesirable effects. An example of an undesired effect of a deliberately applied punishment is a situation in which a penalty is applied for excessive absenteeism, yet the behavior that is reinforced is not better attendance but more sophisticated excuses for being absent. This example illustrates that it is typically quite difficult in organizations to make sure that punishments have only the effects intended and no other effects.

There are many examples of unintended punishment, with possible undesirable consequences. These include giving added pressure and responsibilities to someone who has shown that she can handle stress, or giving additional committee assignments to the person who has shown that he is exceptionally responsible in meeting commitments. Unless a manager is highly alert, unintended punishments happen more often than might be expected.

extinction

the absence of positive consequences for behavior, lessening the likelihood of that behavior in the future

Extinction   Another approach to decrease behaviors is to avoid providing any positive consequences as the result of that behavior. This process is referred to as **extinction**. It is a well-demonstrated research finding, and a fact of everyday work life, that behaviors that do not lead to positive reinforcements tend not to be repeated, or at least not repeated as much. One of the best examples of this in organizational settings is safety behavior. Often, safe work behavior is simply taken for granted by supervisors and is not explicitly reinforced. As a result, because safe behavior typically requires extra time and effort, employees gradually lose motivation to take these extra steps, and eventually an accident occurs. Other examples of extinction occur when an employee puts in extra effort on a key project but receives little or no recognition or acknowledgment from the boss, and when an employee has repeatedly "gone the extra mile" for the organization yet is one of the first to be laid off in a downsizing. In each case, the motivation to behave similarly the next time would not likely be strengthened.

The effects of each of these approaches to the use of reinforcements are summarized in Exhibit 13.11.

Planned Programs of Positive Reinforcement

Organizations often institute programs to apply systematically the principles of reinforcement theory (often called behavior modification or applied behavior analysis programs). These programs involve four basic steps:

EXHIBIT 13.11

Reinforcement Approaches and Their Effects

Reinforcement Approach	Managerial Action	Effect	Example
Positive reinforcement	Provide desirable consequence	**Increase probability** of behavior being repeated	Highway construction supervisor receives bonus for each day a project is completed ahead of schedule.
Negative reinforcement	Remove undesirable consequence	**Increase probability** of behavior being repeated	Management stops raising output quotas each time workers exceed them.
Punishment	Provide undesirable consequence	**Decrease probability** of behavior being repeated	Habitually tardy crew member is fined the equivalent of one hour's pay each day he is late to work.
Extinction	Remove desirable consequence	**Decrease probability** of behavior being repeated	Group member stops making unsolicited suggestions when team leader no longer mentions them in group meetings.

1. Specify desired performance precisely. (Example: "Lower and keep accident rate below 1 percent.")
2. Measure desired behaviors. (Example: "Monitor safety actions A, B, C, and D.")
3. Provide frequent positive consequences for specified behaviors. (Example: "Give semiannual monetary rewards for performing a procedure safely 100 percent of the time.")
4. Evaluate the effectiveness of the program. (Example: "Were accidents kept below 1 percent over the previous six-month period?") Then make progress public knowledge.[34]

Programs of this type have been effective in a wide variety of work settings and in parts of the world as diverse as the Middle East, Scandinavia, and the United States.[35] It is important to point out, however, that the effectiveness of the basic principles of reinforcement does not depend on formal company programs for their application. Any person in a managerial position can utilize these principles. They will be likely to have their greatest effect on the third of the three elements that make up the definition of motivation—the persistence of behavior.

SOCIAL INFLUENCES ON MOTIVATION

Although the point is sometimes overlooked, understanding motivation involves more than simply analyzing individual behavior. As we saw in Chapter 11, if our concern is about behavior in organizational work settings, it is crucial to recognize the powerful influence of the social context, particularly the individual's immediate work group as well as supervisors and subordinates.

Influence of the Immediate Work Group

The immediate work group affects many aspects of a person's behavior, but one of the strongest effects is on motivation. This is particularly true for organizations operating in cultures and countries that have strong collectivist tendencies and traditions, such as those in Asia and Latin America.[36] In such cultures, the individual is likely to be heavily influenced by the **in-group**, the group to which the person belongs, but less influenced by others who are not members of the in-group. Although stronger and more prevalent in collectivist cultures than in some others, group influences on individuals' motivation can occur in almost any culture or organization, given appropriate circumstances.

What are those circumstances? Primarily, they involve (1) the existence of a group in which an individual is a member, the in-group, *and* especially (2) the strong desire of the person to be part of that group and to receive that group's approval. When this situation exists, the level of effort or motivation a person exerts almost certainly will be affected by the group's influence.

The direction of social influence on motivation will likely depend on the group's norms (as defined in Chapter 11). When those norms support the organization's goals, the influence will be to increase levels of motivation. When the norms oppose the organization's objectives, the influence will be to decrease levels of motivation to perform. And, as originally demonstrated in a study many years ago, the more cohesive a group is, the more it can affect performance motivation in either direction—up or down.[37]

The motivational influence of a person's work group can affect aspects of work behavior other than just levels of performance. For example, a study of teenage workers in fast-food restaurants demonstrated that when an employee decided to leave the organization, it increased (not decreased) the desire of close friends to continue working at the restaurant. Although such a result might seem unexpected, the researchers explained the finding by hypothesizing that the friends who remained working at the restaurant had to re-examine ("justify") their reasons for staying, which resulted in a stronger determination to do so.[38] Thus, the social influence of the work-group friends in this study clearly affected motivation of at least one type of behavior: staying with the organization.

Influence of Supervisors and Subordinates

Supervisors and subordinates, not just work group peers, are also part of the immediate social environment that can influence motivation. The impact of supervisors or leaders on the motivation of their employees is linked to their control of powerful rewards and potential major punishments, as we discussed earlier. However, it is important to emphasize that the motivational impact of someone in a supervisory position is not the same for all subordinates. In other words, although the person next highest in the organization typically has a strong effect on the motivation of those he or she supervises, that effect is often uneven. The same supervisor can be a source of increased motivation for some employees and a source of dampened motivation for others.[39] Much depends on the one-on-one interpersonal relationships that are developed over time in each supervisor–subordinate pair.

Subordinate employees themselves are not without influence on the motivation of their superiors, especially through their ability to punish behavior by subtly

in-group
group to which a person belongs

withholding rewards. Although subordinates typically do not have the same amount of reward leverage over their superiors as is the reverse case, they are not powerless.[40] For example, they could withhold some expertise that only they have (and that the supervisor may not have) when not pleased with an action of the supervisor. A systems analyst, unhappy with the assignment she has been given, could resist pointing out some key technical details to her boss. Although such subordinate behavior is unlikely to be overt, it can affect the supervisor's motivation to act in the future in ways that produce these kind of reactions.

Influence of the Organization's Culture

Not to be overlooked is the impact that the culture of the larger organizational context (beyond the work group) can have on employees' motivation. As one management scholar emphasized, "From a management perspective, [corporate] culture in the form of shared expectations may be thought of as a social control system."[41] This influence on motivation is exercised primarily through norms, in this case the *organization's* expected patterns of appropriate and acceptable behavior. Just as with a peer group, the more that an individual desires to remain part of an organization, the more he or she will be influenced by that organization's culture. The organization can be considered simply a larger type of group, with its culture often having less direct influence on motivation than the immediate work group, but with impact nonetheless. Organizations that have gone through mergers or acquisitions know only too well that the imposition of unfamiliar cultural features and norms can have potentially devastating effects on the motivation of the members of the "new" entity.[42]

INFLUENCE OF VALUES AND ATTITUDES TOWARD WORK

No analysis of motivation in the work setting can be complete without consideration of the influence of an individual's values and fundamental attitudes toward work. Such values and attitudes are especially sensitive to cultural differences within a country or across countries. Managing in a global context requires attention to these differences if one is to understand work motivation beyond the culture(s) of a person's own group or country, as is illustrated by the Managerial Challenge box, "Motivating High Performance in Global Settings."

Values

Chapter 4 has already provided a general discussion of culture and cultural values. With that as a backdrop, we can look at the role of those values as they specifically affect motivation. As a reminder, values are enduring beliefs that a specific mode of conduct or end state of existence is preferable.[43] As this definition implies, values can be "end state," as in the case of "equality" or "liberty," or they can be "instrumental" and influence means to ends, such as the values of being cooperative, supportive, or competitive. Both kinds of values affect motivation levels because they influence what members of a particular culture consider crucially important. That in

MANAGERIAL CHALLENGE

MOTIVATING HIGH PERFORMANCE IN GLOBAL SETTINGS

As companies expand into other countries, expatriate managers may encounter difficulties in determining what motivates host-nation employees. This has happened, for example, to Western managers who have been involved in joint ventures as well as other business arrangements in China, where the culture and economy are so different from those of their home countries. For these managers, figuring out what motivates their Chinese employees is like trying to learn the Chinese language itself—the characters are different, the sounds are different, nuances are different. Many of the usual assumptions on which Western managers rely—such as a predictable level of work ethic, expectation of rewards for individual initiative, even the implied threat of dismissal for poor performance—tend not to exist in a work culture that has been subjected for several decades to a quite different set of governmental and social influences. So what can a manager do in these circumstances?

One manager discovered the cultural importance of developing personal relationships with employees because their perception of time and the importance of deadlines differs greatly from typical Western ideas. "Until you developed personal relationships with the employees they didn't see any [personal] responsibility to get the work done on time," this manager notes. Another manager describes other ways to use relationship-based motivators. "I used ... [small] incentives such as [personal] thank you notes."

An outgrowth of personal relationships as motivators is the mentoring system—between expatriates and locals—which seems to work well in many instances. One manager describes such a system as "designed to ensure that employees are happy with the jobs and satisfied with their scope of work, and the mentor may also help off-the-job with some personal issues." Training is an additional benefit of the mentoring system—employees get personal guidance in how to perform their jobs.

Western managers in China quickly discover an apparent lack of initiative on the part of Chinese employees, largely because Chinese state-run businesses have not in the past emphasized deadlines or results; in other words, there is no endpoint to the work. Furthermore, such employees often show up late to work because they have had no motivation or work history to do otherwise. So clarifying job descriptions and goals is an important task for expatriate managers.

Finally, and most important, American and other Western managers have learned that financial incentives are most effective when they are based on the success of the enterprise as a whole, rather than on individual efforts. "If you try and tie [incentives] to individual performance, then you create an administrative nightmare," because employees do not understand the connection. "It is better to keep things as simple as possible."

Managers experienced in operating only in their home countries face different types of motivational challenges as their organizations continue to expand operations around the world, and they need to be constantly on the lookout for new and creative ways to meet those challenges. What works in one country may not work in another, but a willingness to set aside preconceived opinions and be open to new ideas may be the best resources an expatriate manager has.

Source: Andrew Sergeant and Stephen Frenkel, "Managing People in China: Perceptions of Expatriate Managers," *Journal of World Business* 33 no. 1 (1998), pp. 17–34.

turn can influence goals and intentions. Values also affect what kinds of behaviors individuals will find rewarding and satisfying.[44]

Exhibit 13.12 shows how one set of scholars summarizes core value differences among three cultures from diverse parts of the world: American, Japanese, and Arabic.[45] Obviously, the valence (desirability) of different rewards would be quite different across these three cultures. Thus, from an expectancy theory framework of motivation, for example, managers supervising employees from these three cultures would need to consider the types of rewards to offer in return for high levels of performance. The same conclusion would apply to the results of a study of members of four distinct cultures residing within the same country, in this case, Australia.[46] As Exhibit 13.13 shows, there are some striking differences, as well as some similarities, in desired end states of culturally diverse Australians. For example, "high

Differences in Core Values among Three Cultures

	American	Japanese	Arabic
Core Values	Competition Risk Taking Material Possessions Freedom	Group Harmony Belonging	Reputation Family Security Religious Belief Social Recognition

Source: Reproduced by permission. Adapted table 3.3 from *Multicultural Management 2000* by Farid Elashmawi and Philip R. Harris, Ph.D. Copyright © 1998, Gulf Publishing Company, Houston, Texas, 800–231–6275. All rights reserved.

income level" was ranked second (out of 11) as a goal by Anglo-Saxon Australians, third by Chinese Australians, sixth by those of Lebanese descent, and tenth by aboriginal Australians. On the other hand, "maintaining family status" was ranked first by Lebanese Australians, fifth and sixth by the Chinese and aboriginal respondents, and ninth by those of Anglo-Saxon background. All four cultural groups, it should be noted, ranked "loyalty and devotion to employer" similarly—near the bottom, demonstrating that different cultures can rate some key values more or less the same. An organizational workforce in Australia composed of members of these four different cultural groups would clearly not react in the same way to certain responses from their managers at work.

EXHIBIT 13.13

Different Goals of Australians from Different Cultural Backgrounds

Goals[a]	Anglo-Saxons	Chinese	Lebanese	Aborigines
Financial independence	1	2	5	7
High income level	2	3	6	10
Maintaining family needs	3	4	2	1
Promotional and advancement	4	7	8	9
Self-fulfillment	5	8	7	5
Community respect	6	1	3	3
Family approval	7	6	4	4
Freedom to do what you like	8	10	11	8
Maintaining family status	9	5	1	6
Community helping and sharing	10	9	10	2
Loyalty and devotion to employer	11	11	9	11

[a]Goals are ranked from 1 to 11, with 1 being the most important.

Source: J. Holt and D. M. Keats, "Work Cognitions in Multicultural Interaction," *Journal of Cross-Cultural Psychology* 23, no. 4 (1992), pp. 421–43.

To illustrate the role of cultural values in influencing the motivation of particular behaviors, it is instructive to focus on the dimension of "individualism–collectivism" that was first discussed in Chapter 4. As you recall, individualism is the subordination of a group's goals to a person's own goals, whereas collectivism is the subordination of personal goals to the goals of a collective, (which frequently is an extended family but may also be a work group).[47] An interesting line of research dealing with this dimension of culture as it affects motivation was carried out with Asian and American college students. The research project compared the preferences of the two sets of subjects for allocating rewards to members of work groups: according to "equality" (every member gets an equal share of the rewards) or according to "equity" (members are rewarded in proportion to their individual contributions). The findings showed that although both Asian and American college students generally preferred equity as the basis for rewards, students from Hong Kong and Korean backgrounds tended to put relatively more emphasis on equality than did the Americans. This is in line with the basic hypothesis that those who are raised in a culture that values collectivism will be influenced by this value when put into a work situation. They will be more likely than those raised in an individualistic culture to consider the needs of everyone in their group, even if this means deviating somewhat from the generally preferred equity reward allocation. The research also showed that while Asian student subjects have a greater tendency to use equality as an allocation basis for rewards to in-group members, they did not necessarily extend this tendency to members of out-groups. Thus, Asian students were apparently distinguishing clearly between those two types of groups.[48]

Attitudes toward Work

Understanding how different groups or cultures view the meaning of work, that is, how much the activity of working is valued, helps us to gain additional insight into motivational differences across cultures. The famous sociologist Max Weber was one of the first to call attention to the role that the meaning of work has in influencing motivation in industrial societies. His contention was that in Christian countries of his era (late 19th and early 20th centuries), Protestant religious values emphasized and supported hard work and the accumulation of wealth, and thus he coined the well-known phrase "the Protestant work ethic."[49] According to Weber, many people in the United States and in northern European countries were assumed to be guided by such an ethic, whether or not they were literally "Protestants."

work centrality
the degree of general importance that working has in the life of an individual at a point in time

A body of scholarly research carried out in the last decades of the 20th century on the meaning of work focused especially on **work centrality**, defined as "the degree of general importance that working has in the life of an individual at a point in time."[50] To measure work centrality, researchers asked working adult respondents to rate the importance of work to them and also to compare its importance to other major life roles such as leisure, family, and religion. The resulting overall score for seven countries, on an index from low to high, is shown in Exhibit 13.14. At the time the data were collected in the early 1980s, work was much more important and more central in life experiences in Japan than it was in any of six other countries including Germany, the United Kingdom, and the United States.

Somewhat similar research conducted in the United States on a large, nationwide sample of MBA students compared the relative importance attached to four

EXHIBIT 13.14

The Relative Importance
(Centrality) of Work in
Seven Countries

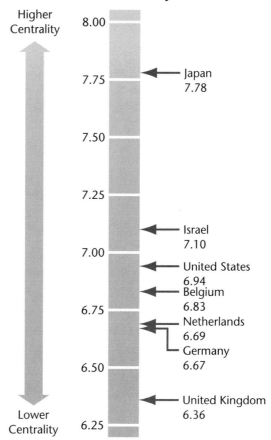

Mean Work Centrality Index

Higher Centrality

8.00

7.75 ← Japan 7.78

7.50

7.25

Israel 7.10

7.00

United States 6.94

Belgium 6.83

6.75

Netherlands 6.69

Germany 6.67

6.50

United Kingdom 6.36

Lower Centrality

6.25

Source: Adapted from MOW International Research Team, *The Meaning of Working: An International Perspective* (London and New York: Academic Press, 1985).

areas of life: family/friends, career/work, freetime/relaxation, and wealth.[51] As can be seen in Exhibit 13.15, the MBA respondents in 1993–1994 ranked those areas as follows: family/friends as most important, followed by career/work and freetime/relaxation, and wealth as least important. However, the interesting story in Exhibit 13.15 is the comparison of rated importance of the four areas by the MBA students to similar ratings of a sample of employed "business professionals" who were surveyed some 12 years earlier, in 1982 ("wealth" was not included in the earlier survey). The relative importance of the three comparable areas is the same for both groups, but the MBA students of the early 1990s attach significantly more importance to "freetime/relaxation" than did the business professionals of the early 1980s. The same survey of MBA students also compared male and female students in their ratings of the four aspects of life. As shown in Exhibit 13.16, the female MBA students rated "freetime/relaxation" as more important than "career/work," while the reverse was true for the male students.

EXHIBIT 13.15

Comparison of Business Professionals 1982 and MBA Students 1993–1994

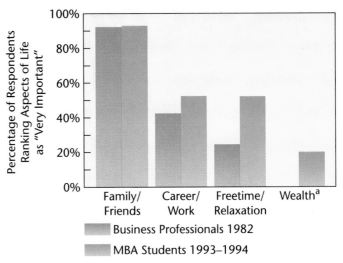

a Importance of wealth was not surveyed in 1982.

aImportance of wealth was not surveyed in 1982.

Source: Adapted from M. K. Dugan et al., *Selections, the Magazine of the Graduate Management Admission Council* 14, no. 2 (1998), pp. 10–18.

EXHIBIT 13.16

Comparison of Male and Female MBA Students 1993–1994

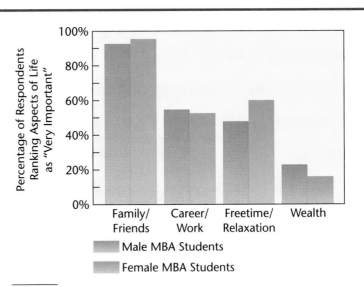

Source: Adapted from M. K. Dugan et al., *Selections, the Magazine of the Graduate Management Admission Council* 14, no. 2 (1998), pp. 10–18.

What are the motivational and managerial implications of such research findings that examine the meaning and importance of work in different cultures and groups? First, it shows that since work does not generate the same relative degree of importance, compared with other significant life areas, from all employees, managers face different motivational challenges relating to different sets of employees or in different cultural contexts. Second, since the nature of the meaning of work appears to vary to some degree among different categories of employees or from country to country, the findings indicate that specific incentives such as pay raises or time off will not have the same motivational effect in all situations. The message is that managers need to realize that there are likely to be differences not only in motivational patterns from person to person but also in patterns across relatively large sets of organizational members. A sensitivity to work values and attitudes, and how they are distributed across groups as well as individuals, can be highly useful for managers in addressing motivational issues and problems.

CONCLUDING COMMENTS

Motivation is a topic that interests both the organizational scholar and the practicing manager. For organizational theorists and researchers, the topic represents a major scientific challenge to gain insight and knowledge, especially knowledge that can be transformed into better-performing organizations. For managers, a good understanding of the topic provides potentially great leverage in positively influencing the work behavior and performance of those who work with and for them.

As we emphasized early in this chapter (Exhibit 13.1), thinking about motivation in terms of the three variables—individual, job, and work context—that together determine levels of motivation provides an essential framework for understanding motivational issues and problems. Knowing what the individual *brings* to the work situation (the internal "push" forces), what the individual *does* in the situation (part of the external "pull" forces), and what *happens to* the individual (the other part of the "pull" forces) provides basic clues for making accurate motivational diagnoses.

Armed with this framework, it is possible to make practical use of the several behavioral theories concerning motivation. For the manager, the theories, both those that relate to *what* motivates people (the content theories) and those that relate to *how* people become motivated (the process theories), are not ends in themselves. Rather, they should be seen as means or aids to gaining a deeper understanding. They provide multiple perspectives that are necessary for gaining insight into the interaction of a fairly complex set of forces.

Being able to analyze and examine the roles of goals, reinforcements, and values and attitudes provides an additional dimension for those who have to put motivation into practice. Knowing how goals can be used effectively, how the use of various types of reinforcements can create quite different effects, and how the values and attitudes that people bring with them to the work situation (and which are also further developed at work) can shape their responses to motivational initiatives, provides additional managerial insights.

Finally, and particularly important, is the necessity for managers of today's multicultural and often multinational workforces not to have a self-centered and ethnic-centered view of how to motivate other people. We are all prisoners, to some extent, of the narrow focus of our own particular cultural, ethnic, and socioeconomic backgrounds. But this will get us into more trouble in managing motivation than anything else. It is crucial, therefore, in attempting to become effective motivators, not to assume that everyone else is like us and will react the same way that we would.

KEY TERMS

acquired needs theory 372
content theories 368
equity theory 377
expectancy theory 378
extinction 386
in-group 388

job characteristics model 375
job enrichment 375
Maslow's need hierarchy 370
motivation 365
negative reinforcements 385
positive reinforcements 384

process theories 377
punishments 386
reinforcement theory 384
two-factor theory 373
valence 378
work centrality 392

REVIEW QUESTIONS

1. What is motivation?
2. What is meant by "push" forces? "pull" forces? Give examples of each.
3. What are three major characteristics that determine motivation in organizations? What are some of the variables within each?
4. What is the difference between a content theory and a process theory of motivation?
5. What are the levels in Maslow's need hierarchy? What determines when a person is likely to move from one level to the next?
6. What are some of the characteristics of an individual with a high need for achievement?
7. Which theory is based on motivator and hygiene factors? What effects are these factors presumed to have on an individual's motivation?
8. How can managers affect motivation by changing job content?
9. According to equity theory, what might happen if a worker thought he or she was putting in more effort than a co-worker, yet the co-worker received a higher salary or larger bonus?
10. What is the basic equation that represents expectancy theory? Explain in words what each variable means.
11. According to expectancy theory, what can a manager do to increase an employee's motivation?
12. What is the difference between intrinsic and extrinsic rewards? Give an example of each. Is one better than the other?
13. What kinds of goals increase motivation? Is it important for managers to help workers set goals?
14. How are antecedents related to consequences and reinforcement?
15. What attributes do positive reinforcements need to have to be effective in motivating behavior?
16. What is the difference between a negative reinforcement and a punishment? Give an example of each.
17. Does the effect of values on motivation differ among cultures?
18. What is work centrality? Why is it important for managers to understand this concept when attempting to improve motivation?

DISCUSSION QUESTIONS

1. You have taken a job as production manager in the electronics plant your company has just bought in Hungary. Your subordinates will be local workers, and your primary goal is to increase their productivity through increasing their motivation. Which motivational theories would you use? Are there any you think would not apply? Why?

2. Is the use of positive reinforcement always the best approach to motivational problems? When might other types of "consequences" be more appropriate?

3. Examine some of your own goals. How did you set them? Were they effective in motivating your performance? If you analyze them in terms of goal-setting theory, how would you change the way you set them in the future?

4. Both equity and expectancy theory suggest that individuals make conscious, reasoned choices concerning their performance. When would a person be most likely to do this? Have you ever seriously analyzed a work situation in the ways suggested by these theories and then changed your behavior as a result?

5. Which motivational forces are stronger: push or pull? Or are they equal? How might their relative strength change with different circumstances? Why?

CLOSING CASE

Motivating Leo Henkelman

Despite his bearlike stature, Leo Henkelman was invisible to his employer. To Sandstrom Products, he was nothing more than a strong-backed laborer, a paint mixer who attended to the mill for over a decade. The plant was full of such employees, who came to work each day, did their job, complained about the college-educated lab technicians, and collected their paychecks. The money was good and the work was steady, but still Henkelman could not help thinking, "This ain't living." Things would have to change, not only at work but in his personal life.

Henkelman's first job out of high school had been in the slaughterhouse where his father was the foreman. Five days a week, on a shift that began at 3:00 AM, his task was to stand in the production line and hammer purple USDA stamps onto the sides of every carcass of beef that passed by. The work was extremely boring, but the pay was decent. He may have stayed at the job longer had he not had a fight with another employee who landed in the hospital. It was his father who fired him.

After a short stint in construction, Henkelman landed a job at Sandstrom Products, a $5.5 million maker of paints, coating, and lubricants. He started as a paint runner, the bottom job at the plant, and spent his days putting paint into cans and putting the cans into boxes. After a year, he

was promoted to a mill operator and began mixing paints in a blender, following the formulas supplied by the labs. Henkelman's work environment was the plant floor—dark, noisy, and reeking of strong fumes. Adjacent to the plant was the lab, filled with college-educated professionals who wore white shirts and carried business cards. In his work, Henkelman was forced to interact with the lab, particularly if a formula did not work. Time after time, he would suggest solutions to the problem, and the lab basically rejected his ideas. Extremely frustrated, Henkelman realized that the company was not interested in his brain but in his brawn.

To solve the problems with paint mixing, Henkelman learned to rely less on the formulas supplied by the labs and more on his own experience. Although the mill operators helped each other, the lab mandated that they were to follow the formulas or else. Henkelman admitted that "we did a lot of things under the cover of 'Don't tell nobody that we did this, but we're gonna check this out to see whether it works, because we don't believe the guys in the lab.'" The ongoing feud between the blue-collar plant and the white-collar lab was not only costly and inefficient to the company, but demeaning to all parties involved. As the product quality suffered, customers began to drop off, and Sandstrom saw its profits eroding.

Finding little at work to challenge him, Henkelman sought solace in spending time with friends at bars after work. On many days, he would show up for work with a hangover, only to turn around and return home sick. On other days, he drove around with friends and lost track of time, forgetting to show up for work at all. Once, he was arrested and lost his driver's license. Realizing that he needed to straighten out his life, Henkelman sought help and slowly began to change his life. Then he underwent back surgery, which caused him to miss three months of work, and his wife threw him out of the house. For a while, he lived on the edge of despair, wondering if his life would ever change.

In the meantime, Sandstrom's future was severely threatened. For the past five years, the company's net income was negative. Jim Sandstrom and Rick Hartsock, the company's top executives, knew that they had to make radical changes. Employees were not solving problems as they should, and morale at work was at a record low. Ironically, Rick Hartsock realized that to save the company from failure, he would have to hand the reins to the employees to solve their own problems. It was then that the company decided to experiment with a motivation technique it called "open book management."

Like many of his colleagues, Leo Henkelman was skeptical. "Just another fad," he thought. What did appeal to him, however, was the focus on results and not on process. Under open book management, the top brass would provide the objectives and allow employees to figure out how to achieve them through creative problem solving, teamwork, and individual initiative. Hungry for the trust and respect that were offered to him, Henkelman signed up for three teams right away: plant equipment, process control, and merit pay.

The first task for the plant equipment team was a proposal to buy a new $18,000 forklift. The old forklift was over 20 years old and, according to its driver, unreliable and unsafe. The team completed a cost and productivity analysis and presented it to the corporate heads. But management argued that, while it was not a bad idea to buy a new forklift, funds were limited and could be used for something more worthwhile. Henkelman could not help but feel let down and began to feel skeptical again. Same old story, he thought. However, a few days later, Henkelman and his team were surprised to learn that the forklift expenditure was approved. Spirits boosted, Henkelman said, "It gave me the idea that we *can* make a difference. It made me feel that we weren't doing all this work for nothing."

As Sandstrom transformed into a company managed by its employees, Henkelman saw the barriers to information begin to fade away. Where the lab had always ruled over the technical manuals, Henkelman and the other plant workers were now allowed to consult them if they wanted

to resolve an issue. He eventually even received a password that gave him access to the formulas on the computer, an event unheard of in prior times. No longer paralyzed in a specific job role, he could update the formulas so the process flowed more smoothly. His attitude began to change in his work.

Henkelman's life began to turn around at the same time. He stopped drinking and got an apartment, where he lived alone. With so much spare time, he went into the office and explored the computer, teaching himself about the business. He filled his empty hours, but more importantly, he filled himself with knowledge, with confidence, and with hope. As a virtual new "owner" in the company, he thought it was his duty to understand every aspect of the business. In the old days, he had only learned what he needed to know to do his narrow job well. Now he wanted to understand the entire process, to help grow the business.

Henkelman and the members of the merit pay team took on the challenge of redesigning an entirely new compensation system. Plant managers had previously used a mixture of seniority and favoritism to compensate their employees, and the subordinates had always been unhappy about this. The workers believed that pay should more closely reflect performance: how useful a worker was on the job, how much a worker knew, and how well tasks were done. These beliefs were not altogether contradictory to that of management; both wanted a highly skilled and effective workforce.

The first proposal drawn by the team offered plant workers incentives to cross-train in their jobs. However, when management and the team fully analyzed the numbers, they both concluded that the proposal was unrealistic. Rather than dismiss the issue, however, management asked for a proposal that made fiscal sense to almost everyone. Deep in the middle of the analysis, Henkelman came to the realization that he was beginning to think like an owner, not like an hourly employee. The new proposal found a way to pay for the added costs of training but at the expense of some paychecks. Some members of the team quit, but Henkelman was determined to stick it out. After months of hard work—meeting formally, debating with coworkers, striking a balance between paying incentives and maintaining equality among workers—the team came up with an innovative compensation system, which was eventually adopted by the company.

This was a critical turnaround in Henkelman's career. Despite the demands that management made on the team's process, Henkelman felt needed and alive for the first time in his working career. He noted, "Because of that I felt and still feel today that I have control of my destiny."

His attitude completely overhauled, Henkelman sought other responsibilities within the company to tap into his strengths. Taking a major promotion, Henkelman was put in charge of scheduling production and even became plant manager for a while. What he found is that neither job suited him. Always a doer, he found it difficult to delegate tasks to others. In a few months, a technician job opened up in the lab. Generally, technicians had college degrees in chemistry, and Henkelman had not even taken chemistry in high school. But Bob Sireno, the lab's technical director, wanted Henkelman for the job. He eventually got it.

Henkelman put away his blue-collar shirt and moved into the lab. He would still do what he had always done—make paint—but instead of following orders, he would guide the process from the beginning to the end. His new job allowed him to work with customers, to develop new formulas, and to use his hands-on experience to solve problems where other less-experienced chemists had failed. Bob Sireno admitted that in a year's time Henkelman had developed skills that had taken college graduates five years to develop. When a complex problem appeared, it was Henkelman who was chosen to solve the problem—shirt sleeves rolled up and mind determined to make it work.

With a new identity and a new attitude about work, Henkelman remains a valuable team member to Sandstrom Products. Instead of dreading the feuding and the tedium of mixing paint, he now looks forward to each new day, wondering what challenges he will overcome.

QUESTIONS

1. Using Maslow's hierarchy of needs, identify the basic needs that Leo Henkelman was attempting to fulfill. How did these needs manifest themselves? How were these needs eventually satisfied?

2. Assess the variables that affected Leo Henkelman's motivation—characteristics of the individual, of the job, and of the work situation.

3. Using the Job Characteristics Model (Exhibit 13.6), analyze Leo Henkelman's motivation: (a) as a worker on the plant floor prior to the introduction of "open book management;" and (b) as a technician in the laboratory.

4. The company's open book management approach was designed to get all employees to focus on helping the business make money. What do you think of "open book management" as a tool for motivating employees? In what kind of organizational circumstances would it work best? In what kind of circumstances might it be ineffective?

Source: Republished with permission of *Inc.* magazine, Goldhirsh Group, Inc., 38 Commercial Wharf, Boston, MA 02110. "Before and After," David Whitford, June 1995. Reproduced by permission of the publisher via Copyright Clearance Center, Inc.

CHAPTER 14

LEADERSHIP, POWER, AND INFLUENCE

LEARNING OBJECTIVES

After studying this chapter, you should be able to:

- Describe the fundamental nature of leadership as part of the managerial role.
- Compare and contrast leading and managing.
- Identify the different types and sources of power available to a leader and analyze some of their potential effects.
- Identify the basic components of the leadership process and state how they interact with each other.
- Discuss the components of the leader–follower relationship.
- Differentiate among charismatic leadership, transactional leadership, and transformational leadership.
- Explain how culture and industrialization may impact leadership practices in different ways.

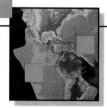

Abraham Lincoln: Leadership Model for Yesterday and Today

Mt. Rushmore doesn't contain any carved figures of CEOs. But it does contain carvings of four leaders: George Washington, Thomas Jefferson, Theodore Roosevelt, and Abraham Lincoln. Many Americans like to perpetuate the image of Abraham Lincoln as a country boy who read his way to a law degree—and, ultimately, the presidency—without formal training. It makes people feel as though anything is possible if they try hard enough. It makes each citizen feel as if he or she has the potential to be a leader.

Abraham Lincoln was, indeed, a country lawyer before becoming a politician. He was successful at his profession, and thus fairly well off financially. He was also a consummate leader. His success—as a lawyer and as a president—largely depended on his ability to use power wisely and to communicate honestly with the people he wanted to influence. As president of the United States, Lincoln held plenty of power; he had the capacity to exert influence on people and policies. But power alone did not make Lincoln a leader; rather, his skill at delegating authority by allowing others to make decisions about details, his quest for knowledge about public opinion, his ability to communicate his thoughts clearly and concisely, his willingness to compromise, and his famous honesty all contributed to his success as a leader. For instance, Lincoln had the power (and the desire) to abolish slavery, but he understood that nearly half the nation depended on the practice socially and economically. So he proceeded with small policy changes, each intended to convince the American public that the abolition of slavery was the only way to end the devastating Civil War and ultimately save the United States.

Lincoln also had charisma—in other words, he was able to inspire people to think and act as he did. Part of his charisma was his ability to speak the language of ordinary people. His speeches and public papers were filled with wit, puns, and colorful but clear arguments and calls for action. His sense of humor saved him from some sticky situations and showed the American public that he was human. And his legendary honesty not only served him well in office during one of the most difficult stages of American history, it is probably the single characteristic most often attributed to Lincoln, nearly 150 years after his presidency.

What might today's CEOs and managers learn from Lincoln's leadership style? First, honesty and integrity may be the strongest and most enduring qualities of any leader. Second, listening carefully to employees, even when they are offering criticism, can provide valuable information. Third, a willingness to compromise may benefit the organization. When analyzed this way, Lincoln's success seems attainable to any person aspiring to become a managerial leader.

Source: David Herbert Donald, "Leadership Lessons from Abraham Lincoln," *Bottom Line*, February 15, 1996, pp. 13–14.

Leadership is an undeniably critical managerial process. Without leadership, organizational performance would be minimal. Indeed, it would be difficult if not impossible to talk about the accomplishments of 20th-century organizations of all types—whether in business, government, education, or other settings—without referring to the role that leadership played in those successes. So it is a given that leadership is important to organizations, and, of course, to society at large. What is not so clear is how to increase its presence and effectiveness. That is the managerial challenge.

Leadership is, above all, a process of influence, as the opening story about Abraham Lincoln illustrates. As such, leadership can occur *potentially anywhere* in an organization. Leadership is not a set of behaviors limited to the chief executive officer, the executive vice president, the director of manufacturing, the regional marketing manager, or, for that matter, a sports team's coach or its captain. It is a process that can be exhibited by almost anyone, at almost any time, and in almost any circumstance.

However, although acts of leadership in an organization can be widespread and commonplace, often they are not. The central issue, then, both for organizations and for individual managers, is to turn the potential for exercising leadership into reality. The very fact that so many articles and books have been, and continue to be, written on the topic of leadership is a good indication that this challenge is not being met well by either the typical organization or the practicing manager.

In this chapter we will first confront an age-old question, "What is leadership?" and then explore how the answers help us understand the relationship between leadership and its close cousins, influence and power. This provides a background for analyzing the nature of the leadership/influence process: the traits and characteristics of people who are most likely to become leaders; the types of behaviors that leaders typically exhibit; the role and influence of followers, including the leader–follower relationship; and the situational circumstances most likely to affect the success of leadership attempts. The chapter concludes by taking a close look at some contemporary issues involved in the practice of leadership in today's rapidly changing organizations, not only in the United States but around the world.

THE BASICS OF LEADERSHIP, POWER, AND INFLUENCE

Throughout this chapter, it is important to keep in mind that although leadership is a familiar everyday term, it nevertheless is far more complex than we might assume. For that reason, it is an especially interesting and intriguing subject. It is also a topic that is easy to oversimplify and therefore one that often leads to conclusions that are incorrect, misleading, or unjustified. In fact, we could say, "It's not what we don't know about leadership that is the problem; it's what we know that isn't so."

What Is Leadership?

Let us take a look at how organizational scientists have defined the term *leadership*. Unfortunately, there is no clear consensus because, as one prominent scholar observed some years ago, "There are almost as many definitions of leadership as there are persons who have attempted to define the concept."[1] Consistent with most definitions, however, we define **organizational leadership** as an interpersonal process involving attempts to influence other people in attaining some goal. This definition, therefore, emphasizes leadership as a social influence process.

organizational leadership
an interpersonal process involving attempts to influence other people in attaining some goal

While there is general agreement that leadership is an influence process, there is less agreement on (a) whether the definition must refer only to influence used by those occupying designated leadership positions ("manager," "coach," etc.), (b) whether the influence must be exercised deliberately and for the specific attainment of the group's or organization's goals, and (c) whether compliance of others must be voluntary. Our view on each of these issues follows.

Acts of leadership behavior *can be exhibited by anyone* in an organization and are not limited only to those holding designated leadership positions. In particular, this means that leadership should not be thought of as occurring only, or even mostly, at the top of the organization. Leadership behavior is not confined only to the Lee Iacoccas, the Estée Lauders, the Jack Welches, the Margaret Thatchers, and the Vince Lombardis of the world. Leadership can also be seen in the actions of the first-line supervisor who inspires her subordinates to increase attention to safety procedures to avoid production downtime. Leadership is demonstrated by the group member who champions his team's new product. Leadership is shown by the human resources manager who makes sure—without being ordered to—that those in the HR division treat all applicants for positions with the company respectfully and equitably. Leadership is exhibited by workers who set an example for their coworkers by continually seeking ways to improve processes and working conditions.

Ordinarily, however, positions that are labeled managerial or supervisory usually have more opportunities to exert leadership. Also, leadership behavior is expected more frequently from supervisors and managers than from other types of roles. Such expectations often profoundly affect the behavior of both those who hold such positions and those around them. Expectations count. For instance, in a company such as pharmaceutical giant Johnson & Johnson, which prides itself on its dedication to ethics in management, subordinates expect their managers to demonstrate such standards—to lead by example. A manager who does not abide by the ethical principles of the company, or who is even perceived as not adhering to them, may lose first the trust of his subordinates and then the ability to be an effective leader.[2]

People act as leaders for many reasons, and their efforts are not necessarily aimed solely at the attainment of a group's or organization's goals. In other words, leaders' motives can be directed at multiple objectives, including their own as well as, or instead of, the organization's. Motives are seldom pure, but we assume explicitly that effective organizational leadership requires organizationally relevant goal-directed behavior, regardless of any other personal objectives.

Use of coercion to gain compliance ("do this or you will be fired" threats) is not typically considered leadership. However, the dividing line between what is, and is not, coercion is often very difficult to determine. Thus, whether others' responses must be purely voluntary is not an easy question to answer. When other people comply with someone's attempts at leadership, the reasons may be many and the degree of willingness can range from grudging to enthusiastic. The safest generalization is this: the greater the degree of purely voluntary actions by followers toward the leader's intended direction, the more effective the leadership.

effective leadership
influence that assists a group or an organization to meet its goals and objectives and perform successfully

The preceding discussion raises a further key issue: What is **effective leadership**? Put most simply, it is influence that assists a group or an organization to meet its goals and objectives and perform successfully. This implies that effective leadership is enabling behavior—that is, it is behavior that *adds* and thus helps other people accomplish more than if there had been no such leadership.[3] Obviously, there are many examples from the past and present—Abraham Lincoln, Cynthia Trudell (Chapter 1), and the highly respected American military and civic leader Colin Powell,[4] just to name a few—who could be mentioned in this regard. By their actions, they have added a leadership ingredient to the sum of the efforts of many people and thereby helped them to achieve together more than they would have otherwise. Again, effective leadership augments and assists by unlocking the potential that resides in a collection of people.

Leading and Managing: The Same or Different?

Leading and managing are two activities that take place in all organizations, and the two terms often are used interchangeably. The processes appear to be similar in many respects. The question is: Do they completely overlap, or are they distinctly different? The answer depends on how the two terms are defined, especially "managing."

The case for viewing leadership as different from management has been made in recent years by several prominent behavioral science scholars.[5] They focus on the role of leaders in creating vision for organizations or units, promoting major changes in goals and procedures, setting and communicating new directions, and inspiring subordinates. This set of activities is then contrasted with such "managerial" functions as dealing with interpersonal conflict, coping with complexities, planning and organizing, and, in general, implementing goals set by others (the leaders).

When leading and managing are defined in these ways, then, of course, they are different. However, if managing is considered from a broader perspective, as it is throughout this book, then the two activities do not differ as much as might appear on the surface. That is, managing *ought* to involve most of the kinds of activities that are included in the leader's role. Removing such "leading" activities from managing makes an artificial distinction between the two and relegates managing to a routine, almost trivial activity—which it is not.

The relation of leading to managing can be illustrated by use of a Venn diagram, similar to those encountered in mathematics classes. Such diagrams consist of circles that are completely independent of each other, circles that overlap one another completely, or circles that partially overlap. Imagine all the leaders from one organization in one circle and all the managers from that same organization in another. The two circles are likely to be partially, but not totally, separate (as shown in Exhibit 14.1). A person can be leader, and a person can be a manager; but many people are *both* leaders and managers. Leadership is a component of management, but management involves more than just leadership. Thus, although not all leaders are managers, and not all managers are leaders, modern organizations need most of their managers to engage in leadership behavior such as fostering innovation and

---

EXHIBIT 14.1

The Overlapping Roles of Leaders and Managers

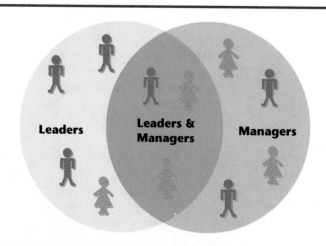

Leaders

Leaders & Managers

Managers

creativity, finding better ways to achieve or exceed goals, and inspiring other people. Consequently, in this chapter and in this book, we view organizational leadership as a process that should be included as a significant part of the managerial role.

LEADERSHIP AND POWER

power
the capacity or ability to influence

It is virtually impossible to consider leadership as a type of social influence without also taking into account the idea of power. **Power** is typically thought of as the capacity or ability to influence, and thus the greater a person's power, the greater the potential for influencing others. Power can be thought of as a basis for exerting influence. It can be used "to change the course of events, to overcome resistance, and to get people to do things that they would not otherwise do."[6] However, the fact that a leader, or anyone else, has power does not guarantee that he or she will use it—or use it well. Possession and use are two different matters.

Whether a leader will use power depends on many factors. One principal reason it is not used, even when it is available, is because of the anticipation of possible undesirable consequences from its use. The use of power is often believed to generate negative reactions. As has been said, "For many people, power is a 'four-letter' word."[7] The famous, but somewhat exaggerated, statement of this view of power was made more than a century ago in Britain, when Lord Acton wrote to Bishop Mandell Creighton that "power tends to corrupt [and] absolute power corrupts absolutely."[8]

It is not too difficult to think of an organization where power has been used inappropriately by a would-be leader. This was illustrated several years ago when a chief executive officer of a consumer products manufacturer was removed from office, even though he had presided over a major turnaround that had brought the company out of bankruptcy. The reason he was dismissed was because of the way he used his power to intimidate subordinates. On occasion, he even threw objects at them when he was angry. His actions so severely damaged morale at the company that the board of directors had no other option but to find a new CEO.[9]

It would be misleading, however, to regard power only from the perspective of the damage it can do. In many circumstances, a leader's skillful use of power can produce positive outcomes. In fact, frequently the problem in organizations is not that leaders use too much power but rather that they fail to use the power available to them.[10] This was noted by two behavioral scientists who have studied leadership extensively when they said: "These days power is conspicuous by its absence. Powerlessness in the face of crisis. Powerlessness in the face of complexity...."[11]

Types and Sources of Power

position power
power based on a person's rank in an organizational structure

personal power
power based on a person's individual characteristics

Power, however it is used, does not arise spontaneously or mysteriously. Rather, it comes from specific and identifiable sources. The two major types of power, based on their sources, are position powers and personal powers.[12] **Position power** is based on a manager's rank in an organizational structure and is given to the manager by superiors. **Personal power** is based on a person's individual characteristics and is in part given by subordinates. The Managerial Challenge box, "Katherine Hudson Turns 'No' into 'Yo,'" describes how one CEO uses both.

Clearly, someone who wants to be a leader could have large amounts of both types of power, which should facilitate the exercise of influence. On the other

MANAGERIAL CHALLENGE

KATHERINE HUDSON TURNS "NO" INTO "YO"

Katherine Hudson is a CEO and president who loves to say "yo." "Yo"—slang for "yes"—is now in the dictionary, Hudson likes to point out. Why is "yo" so important to this midwestern executive? It's now the slogan of W.H. Brady Co., the firm she is proud to head. But W.H. Brady, which manufactures more than 30,000 identification products such as high-tech labels, signs, and portable industrial printing systems, wasn't always a "yes" company. When Hudson took over at Brady after a successful, 24-year career at high-profile Eastman Kodak Co., the company was a conservative, micromanaged, tightly insular organization in which employees rarely shared information or ideas. In fact, keeping secrets was practically part of company policy.

"If I had to put it in one sentence ..." recalls Hudson, "I was convinced that Brady was a company waiting to happen, that it was a company with enormous potential and opportunity, and that my job was to put together a leadership team that would help the folks in the organization unlock all of the opportunities. And the challenge for the management team was to grow the company without losing the family feel to the organization."

So Hudson decided to throw open the doors—literally. When she first arrived in her new office, she discovered that the door wouldn't stay open, so she bought a doorstop. Using both her position power as an upper-level executive and her personal power as an approachable manager, she encouraged employees of all levels to talk with her about the company, its products, their jobs, their ideas. She listened. Then she held a series of strategy meetings, to which she invited employees representing every level of the company, and began to create goals and solutions for the company.

At the first meeting, Hudson and 50 of her senior managers addressed the culture of the corporation itself. "We asked ourselves about the culture of the company—one that had been built on innovation, independence, and the entrepreneurial spirit," says Hudson. Hudson wanted to keep that spirit, but do away with the part of the culture that had evolved to promote secretiveness and a lack of personal initiative. In other words, she wanted to turn Brady into a "yo" culture instead of a "no" culture.

The strategy meetings were key to Hudson's success at influencing and motivating her managers and workers. "We gave the people who attended a ton of tools, presentations, videos, and we even translated the outcome of the meeting into foreign languages," Hudson notes. Employees attended seminars on subjects ranging from financial information to personal development.

Hudson's skillful use of her position power as well as her personal power has helped her energize the company, ultimately meeting some major corporate challenges. "Hudson has stimulated an entire organization," observes Kim A. Stulo, a financial analyst and vice president with Robert W. Baird & Co., an investment banking firm. "Before, it was a sleepy, slow-growth type of company that focused on cost containment. She has brought the various divisions closer together, and there is more cooperation between the divisions. I think her broad vision and strategy have been very successful."

Source: Brian S. Moskal, "From 'No' to 'Yo,'" *Industry Week* 246, no. 16 (September 1, 1997), pp. 50–56.

---

hand, a would-be leader might be low on both, in which case the task of leading obviously would be made more difficult. For instance, a lower-level manager who lacks initiative in developing new products or programs and who is a poor communicator, with little tact, would find it difficult to inspire subordinates to put out extra effort to reach new goals. This manager lacks personal power and would be unlikely to gain a promotion—thus also failing to increase his position power. In many situations, though, a potential leader who is low on one type of power, for example, occupying a relatively junior-level position, can compensate for that by having very strong personal leadership characteristics that are recognized by other people regardless of the person's formal status in the organization.

To help us better understand the nature of power in organizations, it is helpful to think about several subtypes of position power and personal power (Exhibit 14.2).[13]

EXHIBIT 14.2	
Types and Amount of Power	

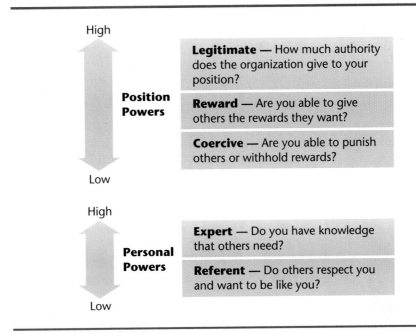

Position Powers   A person's position in an organization provides a base for the exercise of this type of power. Specifically, the major kinds of power that are attached to a position include legitimate power, reward power, and coercive power.

legitimate power (formal authority)

a type of position power granted to a person by the organization

Legitimate Power.   **Legitimate power** is a type of position power granted to a person, say a manager, by the organization. It is sometimes called **formal authority**. In the work setting, such power is intended to give a manager a designated right to expect compliance by his or her employees. Both parties, in effect, agree in advance that requests by the manager are appropriate, within reason, and both parties agree that the subordinates are obligated to respond to those requests.

In today's organizations, with increasing levels of education of the workforce and changing societal norms about what is "legitimate" authority, the effectiveness of this type of power has distinct limits. Often, subordinates will disagree about the scope of a manager's authority; that is, they question the boundaries of what are "appropriate requests." For example, many managers used to expect their secretaries or assistants to make personal appointments for them and perform other non-work-related services. Today, the relationship between a manager and her assistants has changed, and these types of requests are generally not considered legitimate.

The precise scope of legitimate authority in today's complex organizations is frequently ambiguous, and the resulting agreement between manager and subordinate can typically be more implicit than explicit, leaving room for potential conflict. In addition, the extent of a manager's formal authority is bounded by subordinates' perceptions of that person's credentials. If the basis of a person's selection for a managerial position is questioned, the leverage of legitimate power is somewhat reduced. For example, take a medium-size firm where the CEO decides to appoint a close relative who has little knowledge of the business to an executive-level position that in the past has been filled by employees who have worked their way up through the ranks. In this case, subordinates may not acknowledge that the relative has a right to the formal power that would normally be associated with the position, and thus they might not respond to requests rapidly and enthusiastically. This would probably be especially the case in many Western work situations, but perhaps not as much so in Asian cultures, where family connections are viewed as more appropriate for determining who should occupy high-level positions. In essence, though, in most organizational settings, formal authority represents power, but it definitely is not unlimited power.

reward power

a type of position power based on a person's authority to give out rewards

Reward Power. One of the strongest sources of position power for any manager is **reward power**, that is, the authority to give out rewards, especially differing amounts of highly valued rewards to different people. In any hierarchy, this power can have significant effects on others' behavior because it involves dispensing relatively scarce, but desired, resources. Only a few people, at most, can receive plum assignments; only one or two subordinates usually can be given the largest yearly performance bonus; only one person can be awarded the promotion.

Because the use of reward power can have such potentially important consequences, a manager needs to be alert to how his administration of rewards is being perceived. Aside from their direct impact, rewards can have a signaling effect. They let subordinates know, for example, where they stand with the boss. Microsoft Corporation, for example, is known for its lower-than-average starting salaries and grueling work schedules. In the middle of the year, however, CEO Bill Gates puts on an annual extravaganza, at which he recognizes a few of his hardest workers, his most dedicated and creative code writers. He gives them what the salary doesn't, something even more important: his approval.[14]

The power of rewards can extend not only beyond those who directly receive them but also beyond a short period of time. For these reasons, a manager needs to use this power carefully and skillfully. The exercise of reward power obviously can increase the motivation of people who receive the rewards or reinforcements, as we discussed in Chapter 13 and as illustrated in the Microsoft example. However, it also can *decrease* the motivation of others who do not receive them or receive what they regard as insufficient.

coercive power

a type of position power based on a person's authority to administer punishments, either by withholding something that is desired or by giving out something that is not desired

Coercive Power. **Coercive power** is the power to administer punishments, either by withholding something that is desired, such as a raise, or by giving out something that is not desired, such as a letter of reprimand. In typical organizations, such power is used sparingly these days, at least directly and overtly. However, coercive power is sometimes used indirectly in the form of implied threats. A manager, for instance, can let it be known that noncompliance with her requests will result in assignment to the least desired projects or committees. A manager in charge of assigning shift work could subtly influence subordinates by assigning those who do not agree with his policies to a series of split shifts.

As we discussed in Chapter 13, a major problem with the use of coercive power is that it can cause recipients to avoid being detected by disguising their objectionable behavior, rather than motivating them to perform in the desired manner. Furthermore, the use of coercion can generate retaliation. Threatening employees with reduced hours or a pay cut if they don't take on more duties or accept a less than generous incentive plan might result in work slowdowns, increased number of faulty parts, or complaints to government regulators. Any of these actions would obviously be counterproductive.

It should also be noted that although people with higher-level positions have greater ability to apply coercive power, its use is not confined to managers and supervisors. Potentially, anyone has coercive power. A lower-level employee can

Design expertise helps a manager of an architectural or engineering firm be an effective leader.

harm someone higher by, for example, withholding valuable information or making a situation more difficult than it might otherwise be. This use of coercive power by subordinates may be subtle, but in some cases it may actually be quite effective for that reason.

Personal Powers   Personal powers are attached to a person and thus stay with that individual regardless of the position or the organization. For those who want to be leaders, personal powers are especially valuable because they do not depend on the actions of others or of the organization. The two major types are expert power and referent power.

Expert Power.   **Expert power** is based on specialized knowledge not readily available to many people. It is precisely because many people do *not* have a particular knowledge that makes expertise a potential source of power. The potential is translated into actual power when other people depend on, or need advice from, those who have that expertise. The best example of expert power in everyday life is the physician–patient relationship. Most people follow their doctors' directives not because of any formal position power but because of the potential negative consequences of ignoring their expertise. Given the increased percentage of knowledge workers (i.e., those who have some special expertise) and the increased use of sophisticated knowledge in many types of contemporary organizations, it is becoming imperative for most managers to have some type of expertise. Having expertise may not necessarily set a manager apart from her subordinates, but not having it may greatly diminish the effectiveness of various forms of position power.

Expert power is not confined to higher organizational levels. Some of the most specialized, and yet most needed, knowledge in an organization can be possessed by lower-level employees.[15] One only needs to observe a boss trying to find a particular document in a file to appreciate the expert power that an administrative assistant often has in certain situations; or to watch the high-level executive waiting impatiently while the technician makes repairs on the computer or fax machine. These examples illustrate the fact that dependencies create an opportunity for

expert power
a type of personal power based on specialized knowledge not readily available to many people

expertise to become power, whatever the location in an organization or the position of the person having the specialized knowledge.

Referent Power.   When people are attracted to or identify with someone, that person acquires what is called **referent power**. This power is gained because other people "refer" to that person. They want to please that person or in some way receive acceptance. Referent power can be recognized by subtle occurrences. A subordinate, for example, may begin using gestures similar to those of his superior or even imitating certain of his unique speech patterns. More importantly, the subordinate may find his opinions on important work issues becoming similar to those of his boss.

For anyone in a leadership position in a work setting, being able to generate referent power is clearly a great asset. It is a cost-free way to influence other people. Referent power makes it possible to lead by example rather than by orders. A manager can use her referent power to change work habits, for example. If she comes in early, stays late, takes shorter breaks, and finishes her work rather than putting it off until the next day, her subordinates may model themselves on her behavior and change their own work habits as well.

The problem with referent power, however, is that it is not obvious how such power can be developed. There is no formula for how to increase your referent power, and making attempts to get others to like or admire you can frequently cause the opposite reaction. Certain personality attributes may help, but they are not necessarily the same traits from one person to the next. Rather, referent power of a potential leader seems to be built up over time by consistent actions and behavior that cause others to develop admiration.

A particularly strong form of referent power, sometimes labeled *charisma,* is discussed later in this chapter. When a leader possesses the qualities of charisma, less questioning of the leader's actions occurs.

Using Power

There are at least four key issues for managers to think about in relation to the use of power:

- How much power should be used in a given situation?
- Which types of power should be used?
- How can power be put to use?
- Should power be shared?

How Much Power to Use?   The answer to this question seems to be: use enough to achieve objectives but avoid using excessive power. Using too little power in organizational settings can lead to inaction, and this is especially the case when change is needed but strong resistance exists. Often, managers seem reluctant to wield power because of anticipated opposition. Yet, the raw use of power is sometimes the only way to accomplish significant change. "Managing with power means understanding that to get things done, you need power—more power than those whose opposition you must overcome."[16]

Using too much power, though, also can be a problem. When more power is used than is necessary, people's behavior may change, but resentments and reactions often are self-defeating to the power-user in the long run. In many organizational situations, people have a sense of what is an appropriate amount of power. If

referent power

a type of personal power gained when people are attracted to, or identify with, that person; this power is gained because people "refer" to that person that sense is violated, a manager may actually undermine his power for the future. Excessive use of power in work organizations, like excessive use of police force in civil disturbances, can result in potentially severe negative reactions.

Which Types of Power to Use?   Answers to this question depend on characteristics of the situation and circumstances: what has happened before, what type of change is needed, what amount of resistance is expected, where opposition is located, and the like. Each type of power, whether a position power or personal power, has particular impacts. Some types of power, especially referent and expertise, have relatively low costs. That is, their use generates little direct opposition. Thus, they seem to be the powers to use whenever possible. The problem, however, is that they may not be strong enough to have an impact. If a manager has very little referent power, then using that method is not likely to accomplish much. Similarly, if the expertise of the manager is not perceived as high, regardless of the actual degree of expertise, then subordinates are unlikely to be motivated to change. In such cases, the use of a form of position power, such as formal authority or reward power, might be necessary. However, the risks of creating negative reactions are increased, thereby lessening the effects of such power.

How Can Power Be Put to Use?   Power, in its various forms, provides the basis for influence. However, power must be converted into actual manager/leader behaviors. The skillful use of different types of power is a type of expertise that can be developed. This means that the total amount of power available to a manager is not a fixed quantity but rather can be expanded or contracted over time.

influence tactics
specific behaviors used to affect the behavior and attitudes of other people

To put power to use involves **influence tactics**, that is, specific behaviors used to affect the behavior and attitudes of other people. A number of such tactics have been studied,[17] and a representative sample of them is shown in Exhibit 14.3. Obviously, different types of power match up with some tactics more than others. For example, a high degree of expertise would support the use of rational persuasion. Someone possessing a great deal of referent power could more effectively use inspirational appeals than could someone with less referent power. A leader with little position power would have trouble using legitimating tactics.

The other major factor affecting the use of specific influence tactics is the circumstances of the situation, particularly in regard to the targets. Thus, if the target of influence is a person higher up in the organization structure, pressure would likely be an inappropriate and ineffective tactic. Likewise, exchange might work very well with a peer but perhaps be unnecessary with a typical situation involving subordinates. On the other hand, rational persuasion could be a potentially useful tactic in a wide variety of situations, whether with superiors, peers, or subordinates.

empowerment
sharing of power with others

Should Power be Shared?   In recent years, the concept of empowerment has become prominent in management literature.[18] In its broadest sense, **empowerment** simply means the sharing of power with others, where those with high amounts of power increase the power of those with less. In organizational terms, this means that those higher in the formal structure provide more power, especially with regard to decision making, to those lower in the structure. This, of course, can be done organizationwide, but it also can be done by the individual manager/leader.

EXHIBIT 14.3
Types of Influence Tactics

Rational Persuasion
Using arguments and factual evidence to persuade others that a proposal or request is viable and likely to result in the attainment of task objectives

Inspirational Appeals
Making a request or a proposal that arouses enthusiasm by appealing to the other people's values, ideals, and aspirations or by increasing their self-confidence

Consultation
Involving others in planning a strategy, activity, or change for which their support and assistance are desired

Ingratiation
Using praise, flattery, or especially friendly behavior to get others to respond favorably when asking for something

Personal Appeals
Using appeals to the other people's feelings of loyalty and friendship when asking for something

Exchange
Offering an exchange of favors, or indicating a willingness to reciprocate at a later time to gain others' help in accomplishing a task

Coalition Tactics
Asking the aid of others to persuade the target of influence to do something, or using the support of others as a reason for the target to agree

Legitimating Tactics
Establishing the legitimacy of a request by claiming the authority or right to make it, or by verifying that it is consistent with organizational policies, rules, practices, or traditions

Pressure
Using demands, threats, frequent checking, or persistent reminders to influence other people to do what is wanted

Source: Adapted and reprinted from *Leadership and Decision-making* by Victor H. Vroom and Phillip W. Yetton, by permission of the University of Pittsburgh Press. © 1973 by University of Pittsburgh Press.

For empowerment to take place, managers cannot simply declare that those below them have more power. They must provide the necessary means, such as, for example, delegating more formal authority to make specified decisions, offering increased training opportunities to develop expertise and self confidence, providing more resources and access to information to be able to implement effective decisions, and avoiding the sudden withdrawal of shared power at the first sign of trouble. Subordinates must be allowed to learn to use their increased power. Those who advocate empowerment suggest that it is a key leadership practice for helping organizations to achieve high performance and, especially, to cope successfully with major changes and transitions.[19] While these advantages seem obvious, leaders engaging in empowering actions, nevertheless, will need to consider carefully how much power to share and how to enable others to share that power. Empowerment is a potentially effective leadership approach, but it is not by itself the answer to all organizational performance issues.

LEADERS AND THE LEADERSHIP PROCESS

We now turn from how leadership is related to power, and how the hierarchical structure of organizations influences the uses of different kinds of power, to examine leadership as a process. This process has three fundamental elements in organizations: leaders, followers, and situations. Even though the role of leader typically gets most of the attention, all three factors must be considered to gain a comprehensive understanding of how the process unfolds. As shown in Exhibit 14.4, what has been termed the "locus of leadership" is the intersection of these three variables: where and when the leader with a particular set of characteristics and behaviors interacts with a specific set of followers in a situation with certain identifiable characteristics.[20] Each element influences, and is influenced by, the other two variables, and a change in any one will alter how the other two factors interact.

The impact of each of these three variables on the basic leadership process will be discussed in more detail in the sections that follow. We begin in this section with the leader: specifically, leaders' traits, leaders' skills, and leaders' behaviors.

Leaders' Traits

traits
relatively enduring characteristics of a person

One critical component of what leaders in managerial roles bring to the work setting is their **traits**, that is, the relatively enduring characteristics of a person. The scientific study of the role of leaders' traits has had a somewhat rollercoaster history: At the beginning of the 20th century, the "great man"—note that it was not the "great person"—view of leadership was in vogue. That is, leaders, almost always

EXHIBIT 14.4

Locus of Leadership: Intersection of the Basic Components of the Leadership Process

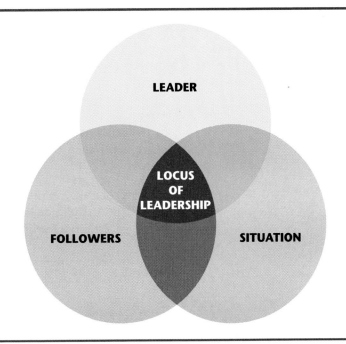

EXHIBIT 14.5

Leaders' Traits

Source: Adapted from S. A. Kirkpatrick and E. A. Locke, "Leadership: Do Traits Matter?" *Academy of Management Executive* 5, no. 2 (1991), pp. 48–60.

thought of as only men in that era, were assumed to have inherited combinations of traits that distinguished them from followers. The notion, then, was that those destined to be leaders were "born" not made. As years passed, however, this theory faded away because of the difficulties of proving that traits were, in fact, inherited. Instead, the focus shifted in the 1920s and 1930s to a search for specific traits or characteristics—such as verbal skills, physical size, dominance, self-esteem—that would unambiguously separate leaders from nonleaders.

The current view is that although specific traits do not invariably determine leadership effectiveness, they can increase its likelihood.[21] As shown in Exhibit 14.5, among the traits that research has indicated are most apt to predict effective leadership are drive, motivation to lead, honesty/integrity, self-confidence, and emotional maturity.[22]

- *Drive:* A high level of energy, effort, and persistence in the pursuit of objectives.
- *Motivation to lead:* A strong desire to influence others, to "be in charge." Such a person is comfortable with the use of power in relating to other people.[23]
- *Honesty/Integrity:* Trustworthiness. Someone with this trait is a person whose word can be relied on consistently and who is highly likely to do what he or she says.[24]
- *Self-Confidence:* A strong belief in one's own capabilities.[25] People with this trait set high expectations for themselves and others,[26] and they tend to be

optimistic rather than pessimistic about overcoming obstacles and achieving objectives. Obviously, in contrast to honesty/integrity, this is a trait that in the extreme can be a negative. It can result in a sense of infallibility and in an attitude of arrogance that can alienate potential followers. In other words, too much self-confidence can lead to what has been called "the shadow side of success."[27] That is, too much success in leadership, paradoxically, can produce the seeds of later leadership problems.

Bill Walsh, the former head coach of the San Francisco 49ers professional football team, touched on the pitfalls of inflated self-confidence when he noted: "It's astonishing how many executives operate on sheer optimism. While emergency drills are standard practice for the military, police, hospital staffs, sport teams and other organizations ..., other businesses—no less vulnerable to crises—proceed with a 'what, me worry?' attitude."[28] No matter how much confidence managers have in themselves, their staffs, and their employees, nothing substitutes for preparation. The manager who relies on self-confidence at the expense of planning is setting the scene for potential disaster.

- *Emotional Maturity:* Remaining even-tempered and calm in the face of stress and pressure. Persons with maturity tend to be accurate in self-awareness about their own strengths and weaknesses; moreover, they are less likely to be self-centered and to be unduly defensive in the face of criticism.[29]

It is important to note that most of the research on traits has involved only, or mostly, men, and the extent to which the findings would generalize to both genders remains a subject for further research. Also, it is important to re-emphasize that traits, such as those listed, do not guarantee that a person will become a leader or will necessarily lead effectively. Very few people possess every critical trait at an exceptionally high level. However, if a person has one or more of these relatively enduring characteristics, the probabilities for successful leadership are increased. Traits provide potential, but other factors such as skills, attitudes, experience, and opportunities determine whether the potential will be realized.

Finally, with respect to traits, it should be stressed that most of the research on the relationship of personal traits to leader effectiveness has not considered the effects of culture. It has focused primarily on Western, mostly American, work environments. Whether traits can universally predict successful leadership is still an open question. It may be that in at least some other cultures other, or different, traits would be equally or more influential. In fact, the very notion that particular personal qualities or leadership traits are critical to successful influence is open to question in many non-Western cultures, such as those in Southeast Asia. In countries such as Korea or Malaysia, for example, a person often is in a leadership position by virtue of ownership or family position, and others show respect for that reason rather than because of certain personality features.[30]

Leaders' Skills

skills
highly developed abilities and competencies

The other major category of personal characteristics that potential leaders bring to organizations consists of **skills**, that is, highly developed abilities and competencies.[31] Skills emerge through a combination of aptitude and education, training, and experience. Three types have been identified as especially critical for managerial leadership tasks: technical, interpersonal, and conceptual (see Exhibit 14.6).

EXHIBIT 14.6

Leaders' Skills

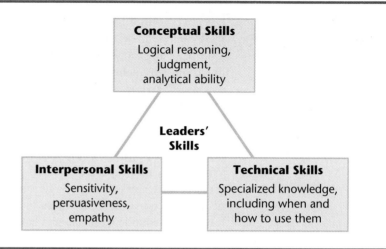

The Managerial Challenge box illustrates how one manager, Don Shula, used all three types of skills as a successful leader.

Technical Skills   Technical skills involve specialized knowledge about procedures, processes, equipment, and the like and include the related abilities of knowing how and when to use that knowledge. Research shows that these skills are especially important early in managerial careers when leadership of lower-level employees is often part of the role, with one of the challenges being to gain the respect of those being led.[32] In addition, technical skills seem to be a particularly critical factor in many successful entrepreneurial start-ups such as those involving Steve Jobs and Steve Wozniak at Apple Computer and Edwin Land at Polaroid.

Technical skills, whether in an entrepreneurial situation or in a larger organizational setting, are frequently necessary for managing effectively, but usually they are not sufficient. In fact, an overreliance on technical skills may actually lower overall leadership effectiveness. The first Apple computer was designed and built by Jobs and Wozniak, and it was their technical skills that started and expanded the fledgling company. However, as Apple grew, due in large part to their technical virtuosity, their skills in this regard became relatively less important as they were able to employ technical specialists. They were not, however, always readily able to exchange those technical skills for other equally impressive leadership skills. As a result, the company had to search for other managerial talent, with mixed success. (After gaining considerable managerial experience in other business endeavors, Jobs did subsequently return to lead Apple—with the assistance of able managers— in the late 1990s).[33]

Interpersonal Skills   Interpersonal skills (e.g., sensitivity, persuasiveness, empathy) have been shown to be important at all levels of management, although particularly so at lower and middle levels.[34] A longitudinal study of career advancement carried out at AT&T found evidence that such skills, measured early in careers by psychological assessment methods, were one factor that predicted advancement in

MANAGERIAL CHALLENGE

DON SHULA AS LEADER: SUCCESS BASED ON SKILLS

"He has incredible knowledge of the game. He can see all twenty-nine people at the same time—twenty-two players and seven officials. He knows what they're all supposed to be doing and when they're supposed to be doing it. It's unbelievable." Jim Tunney, a veteran football official, is describing Don Shula, the legendary former National Football League coach, first of the Baltimore Colts and later of the Miami Dolphins. With 325 wins, Shula holds the record as the most successful coach in NFL history. Now a member of the Football Hall of Fame, Shula may also be one of the most respected football coaches in history.

A coach has the position power to influence players, as Shula did, but that doesn't automatically make the coach a leader. What made Shula a true leader, as so many players, officials, sports journalists, and fans viewed him? Jim Tunney hints at Shula's skills. First, Shula had technical skills. He thoroughly understood the game of football and knew when and how to use his knowledge to motivate his players. Second, he had excellent interpersonal skills, which ultimately earned him the respect of his players, motivating them to give him their best performance. "He was tough when he had to be," recalls John Mackey, former tight end for the Colts. Dan Marino remembers, "I was real excited to be drafted by Miami, because I remember Coach Shula saying he expected me to work hard and compete for the job right away. He put a lot of pressure on me early, and I see now that was good for me. He had me call all my own plays in practice and during exhibitions that first year, which made me study a lot harder and develop more than I would have otherwise." Jimmy Cefalo, former player turned sports-

caster, sums it up this way: "He was a role model for so many of us, and it had nothing to do with football."

Third, Shula had superb conceptual skills. He not only understood every play of every game, he clearly grasped the big picture as well. "We went from being a team that had absolutely no organization to one that was totally organized," says Nick Buoniconti of Shula's early years with the Miami Dolphins. "Don was not going to put up with the mistakes of the past." Strong safety Dick Anderson concurs. "Every minute of every day was planned," he says. Shula was able to analyze his organization and make positive changes.

Shula also possessed the rare quality of knowing when he himself had to change. Part way through his tenure with the Dolphins, Shula recognized that he needed to abandon his basic philosophy that the best football game was a running game and adopt the philosophy that a passing game was best for his team—because the abilities of his players were more suited to passing. "I think what coaching is all about is taking players and analyzing their abilities, then putting them in a position where they can excel within the framework of the team winning," notes Shula, summing up his 33 years of leadership in one sentence.

Sources: Don Shula and Ken Blanchard, *Everyone's a Coach* (New York: HarperBusiness, 1995), p. 124; Greg Cote, "Don Shula's Career: The 1960s," *Miami Herald*, June 29, 1997 (from HeraldLink); Gary Long, "Don Shula's Career: The 1970s," *Miami Herald*, July 6, 1997 (from HeraldLink); Greg Cote: "Don Shula's Career: The 1980s," *Miami Herald*, July 13, 1997 (from HeraldLink); Greg Cote, "A Legend in the Hall," *Miami Herald*, August 3, 1997, (from HeraldLink); Armando Salguero, "This Is the Ultimate Honor," *Miami Herald*, July 27, 1997 (from HeraldLink).

managerial ranks 20 years later.[35] However, though lack of these skills has been shown to prematurely limit managerial advancement even when other skills were present, such skills alone are unlikely to guarantee significant managerial achievement.[36] Exhibit 14.7 summarizes the findings of one study that investigated reasons why some fast-rising executives eventually "derailed" or plateaued in their managerial careers even when they appeared to start out with acceptable levels of interpersonal skills. As put compellingly by a pair of leadership researchers, referring to those with these skills but who lack other capabilities, "The charming but not brilliant find that the job gets too big and the problems too complex to get by on interpersonal skills [alone]."[37]

Conceptual Skills Often called cognitive ability or cognitive complexity, conceptual skills—such as logical reasoning, judgment, and analytical abilities—are a

EXHIBIT 14.7

Who Succeeds? Who Doesn't?

Potential leaders share traits early on:	Those who don't quite make it:	Those who succeed:
Bright, with outstanding track records	Have been successful, but generally only in one area or type of job.	Have diverse track records, demonstrated ability in many different situations, and a breadth of knowledge of the business or industry.
Have survived stressful situations	Frequently described as moody or volatile. May be able to keep their temper with superiors during crises but are hostile toward peers and subordinates.	Maintain composure in stressful situations, are predictable during crises, are regarded as calm and confident.
Have a few flaws	Cover up problems while trying to fix them. If the problem can't be hidden, they tend to go on the defensive and even blame someone else for it.	Make a few mistakes, but when they do, they admit to them and handle them with poise and grace.
Ambitious and oriented toward problem solving	May attempt to micromanage a position, ignoring future prospects, may staff with the incorrect people or neglect the talents they have, may depend too much on a single mentor, calling their own decision-making ability into question.	While focusing on problem solutions, keep their minds focused on the next position, help develop competent successors, seek advice from many sources.
Good people skills	May be viewed as charming but political or direct but tactless, cold, and arrogant. People don't like to work with them.	Can get along well with different types of people, are outspoken without being offensive, are viewed as direct and diplomatic.

Source: Adapted from M. W. McCall, Jr. and M. M. Lombardo, "Off the Track: Why and How Successful Executives Get Derailed," *Technical Report #21* (Greensboro, N.C.: Center for Creative Leadership, 1983), pp. 9–11.

relatively strong predictor of leadership effectiveness.[38] These skills are often the major factor that determines who reaches the highest leadership levels of the organization. A clear example of someone who was selected for a CEO job precisely because of his conceptual skills was Jack Welch at General Electric. He became CEO of GE in 1981 and immediately set out to restructure the organization with the objective of making it more globally competitive. His concept of the company included wiping out its bureaucracy to develop a more flexible organization. At the same time, however, he also championed a new corporate culture, one based on greater empowerment of the employee.[39]

Leaders' Behaviors

For leadership to occur, traits and skills must be transformed into behavior. Thus, considerable research has focused on leaders' behaviors and their impact on subordinates and followers. As far back as the 1950s, researchers zeroed in on two fundamental types of leader behaviors: those involving assistance in the direct

	Task Behaviors (Initiating Structure)	People Behaviors (Consideration)
EXHIBIT 14.8 Leaders' Behaviors	Specifies roles and tasks Plans assignments Schedules work Sets performance standards Develops procedures	Is friendly Is supportive Shows trust and confidence in subordinates Shows concern for subordinates' welfare Gives recognition to subordinates for their accomplishments

performance of the task and those involving the interpersonal relationships necessary to support task performance. These two types have been called by different names over the years, but probably the easiest terms to remember are "task behaviors" and "people behaviors." Examples of these behaviors are shown in Exhibit 14.8.

task behaviors

behaviors that specify and identify the roles and tasks of leaders and their subordinates, such as planning, scheduling, setting standards, and devising procedures

Task Behaviors The key aspects of **task behaviors**, also termed "initiating structure" behaviors, center on specifying and identifying the roles and tasks of the leaders themselves and their subordinates. Such behaviors involve planning assignments, scheduling work, setting standards of performance, and devising the procedures to carry out the tasks.

people behaviors

behaviors that focus on interaction, such as being friendly and supportive, showing trust and confidence, being concerned about others, and supplying recognition

People Behaviors This dimension of leader behaviors has also been termed "consideration" or "relationship oriented." Essentially, the **people behaviors** include being friendly and supportive, showing trust and confidence in subordinates, being concerned about their welfare, and supplying recognition for their accomplishments.

Usefulness of the Leader Behavior Categories Because of the consistency with which these two dimensions of leader behavior have been identified in a wide variety of research studies over the years, you might expect that the most effective leaders would rate high on both dimensions—that is, both strongly task oriented and strongly people oriented.[40] This has not been conclusively demonstrated. Nevertheless, it appears that effective leaders have at least a moderate level of both types of behavior.[41] Also, it has been fairly consistently found that leaders who score highest on people behaviors tend to have the most satisfied subordinates.

Relevant to the issue of the types of leader behaviors is the question of whether female leaders demonstrate different patterns of leader behaviors from those displayed by males. Some research has been said to show that women are more likely than men to exhibit high levels of people skills and that consequently men and women have different leadership styles. However, this issue has been surrounded by considerable controversy. To date, there is insufficient evidence to draw decisive conclusions.[42] What seems clear is that the *individual* differences among women and among men are probably far more important than any relatively small overall average difference between the two gender groups.

Considering all of the research that has been carried out on leader behaviors across nearly five decades, the principal message for those in managerial positions would seem to be this: Effective leaders need to focus on *both* structuring the work (task behaviors) *and* supporting and developing good interpersonal relationships with and among subordinates (people behaviors).

FOLLOWERS AND THE LEADERSHIP PROCESS

We now turn our attention to the second key component of the leadership process: those who receive the leadership and influence, namely, followers or subordinates. The amount of research on followers has been considerably less than that for leaders. This is understandable, given the historical emphasis in Western societies on the role of leaders, but it represents a somewhat distorted and probably misleading picture of the complete process.

Followers provide significant opportunities for, and sometimes constraints on, successful leadership.[43] The U.S. Military Academy at West Point recognizes this point by utilizing cadets' first year to instruct them in the basics of followership. As a former West Point instructor stated: "[New] cadets don't know how to lead soldiers well. They don't know how to motivate or train or reward or discipline effectively." Consequently, the first year is used to teach them to be good followers and in so doing to demonstrate to them what makes an effective leader.[44]

What Followers Bring to the Process

Followers, of course, have characteristics similar to leaders: personality traits, past experiences, beliefs and attitudes, and skills and abilities. What may be different, though, are the amounts and nature of these characteristics in relation to the leader's. In fact, rarely would they be exactly the same. Also, in a work setting, followers frequently have a lower position power than the leader. However, in increasingly flatter and less hierarchical contemporary work organizations, the difference is not likely to be as great as in the past. Such a decrease in the difference between followers' and leaders' formal authority is changing the very nature of the leadership process in today's organizations and presenting new challenges to would-be leaders. Also, in contemporary organizations, leaders cannot assume that they possess more expertise and knowledge than those in a follower position.

Not to be overlooked, moreover, is the fact that almost every leader is also a follower of someone else in the organization. Thus, most people in organizations have to learn how to become good followers as well as good leaders.

A classic example of someone who turned a subordinate or follower's role into a future top executive role was a former president of the United States, Dwight Eisenhower. His Army career progressed slowly following his graduation from West Point and, in fact, it took him some 26 years to be promoted to the rank of colonel just before World War II began in 1939. By 1943, however, he had been advanced over 360 more-senior officers to be made a four-star general and named Supreme Commander of Allied Forces in Europe. The fact that he had served as an outstanding subordinate for his superiors, Generals Douglas MacArthur and George C. Marshall, as well as being a leader of those who reported to him, was more than a minor factor in his ascendancy to a top executive position.[45] Learning how to be effective in a follower role can be a significant ingredient in becoming an effective leader, but this is not the same thing as saying that all followers can or will become good leaders.

Effects of Followers' Behavior

Leaders influence followers, but the reverse is also true: Leaders act, followers respond, and leaders react to those responses. Especially important in these evolving interactions are the followers' perceptions of the leaders; that is, the followers' views of a leader's characteristics and the reasons for the leader's behavior. It appears that followers often check their perceptions against the traits they think leaders *should* possess and the behaviors they *should* display.[46] In effect, followers seem to develop what have been called "implicit leadership theories," and they tend to judge a leader's actions against particular standards or expectations they have in mind.[47] When expectations aren't met, followers may blame leaders for a group's or organization's failures; likewise, when expectations are met, leaders typically get the credit.

Some theorists argue that leaders in organizations, just like certain stars of athletic teams, frequently get excessive—and sometimes undeserved—credit or blame for outcomes they may not have affected decisively.[48] It seems that no story concerning Microsoft, for example, can be written without mentioning Bill Gates. Rightly or wrongly, he has become the icon of the company. Articles commending or criticizing new software, such as the Windows 98 program, seem to place all of the praise or blame squarely on the leader at the top: Bill Gates.

The Leader–Follower Relationship

As we have discussed, in organizational work settings leaders and followers engage in reciprocal relationships: The behavior of each affects the behavior of the other. In cases where a leader has direct contact with a group of followers, such as in a work unit, two-person leader–follower relationships are built between a supervisor and each subordinate. Research shows that these relationships may vary considerably in scope and content from one leader–follower pair to another.[49] That is, how Susan as the leader (supervisor) relates to John as a follower (subordinate) in carrying out the work of the unit may be quite different from how Susan as leader relates to Sam as a follower.

leader–member exchange (LMX) theory
a relationship-based approach to leadership that focuses on the importance of strong, mutually respectful and satisfying relationships between leaders and followers

This line of research has led to the development of a conceptual approach to leadership that focuses on leader–follower relationships: **leader–member exchange (LMX) theory**.[50] Based on this theory, an increasing body of research appears to suggest that the quality of such two-person relationships can strongly influence the effort and behavior of subordinates.[51]

The focus of LMX theory is on the types of relationships that are developed between leader and follower rather than on only the behavior of the leader or of the follower. As described in the theory, the leader's central task is to work with followers on building strong, mutually respectful, and satisfying relationships. However, the degree to which such relationships develop depends as much on the behavior and performance of the follower as on the actions of the leader.[52] Also, developing such deep relationships is not always easy, and one of the major issues for the leader is that this approach can be time-consuming. In fact, as shown in Exhibit 14.9, in later versions of the LMX theory, the leader–member relationship is viewed as taking time to develop across different stages—for example, from that

EXHIBIT 14.9

Development of Leader–Member Relationships over Time

Relationship Characteristic	Relationship Stage		
	Stranger	**Acquaintance**	**Maturity**
Relationship-building phase	Role-finding	Role-making	Role implementation
Quality of leader–member exchange	Low	Medium	High
Amounts of reciprocal influence	None	Limited	Almost unlimited
Focus of interest	Self	→	Team

Time

Source: Adapted from G. B. Graen and M. Uhl-Bien, "Relationship-Based Approach to Leadership: Development of Leader–Member Exchange (LMX) Theory of Leadership over 25 Years: Applying a Multi-level Multi-domain Perspective," *Leadership Quarterly* 6, no. 2, Special Issue: "Leadership," (1995), pp. 219–47.

of a "stranger" interaction, to an "acquaintance" relationship and, ultimately, to a "mature partnership."[53]

LMX theorists stress, of course, that not all leader–follower relationships develop to the partnership phase, and some may not get to even the acquaintance stage. However, if the mature relationship phase can be reached, each party can exercise sizable influence over the other for the benefit of themselves and the organization. Many aspects of this theory are too new to have been validated extensively, but the LMX approach is notable for placing emphasis on how leader–follower relationships develop and on the potentially important consequences that can flow from high-quality relationships.

SITUATIONS AND THE LEADERSHIP PROCESS

The third key element in the analysis of the leadership process is the situation surrounding the process. In addition to followers, the two most important categories of situational variables are tasks and the organizational context.

Tasks

The nature of the work to be performed provides a critical component of the situation facing leaders. Change the task, and the leadership process is highly likely to be changed. Research evidence across many studies indicates that several of the most important dimensions of tasks that affect the leadership process include whether they are relatively structured or unstructured and whether they involve high or low levels of worker discretion.[54] For example, a manager of a group of newly trained but relatively inexperienced tax preparers at a firm such as H&R Block would probably need to use a fairly high degree of task-oriented leadership to

Managing a group of highly educated scientists may require a more person-oriented, less directive form of leadership because of their experience and competence.

be sure that precise guidelines were being followed in analyzing clients' often-complex returns. Alternatively, a project leader in charge of reviewing the work of a group of highly educated scientists doing advanced research in a pharmaceutical company such as Merck would probably be more concerned with ensuring a continuous flow of new scientific information and securing additional funding for the group even when it appears they are not producing immediately useful results. This manager might use a more person-oriented, less directive form of leadership with the research staff.

Organizational Context

The term "organizational context" in this instance means both the immediate work group (those who come in direct face-to-face contact with a leader) and the larger organization (composed of all individuals and groups who do not usually have frequent direct personal contact with a leader). A number of features of the organizational context can affect the leadership process. Of particular importance is the fundamental culture of the organization, that is, its history, traditions, and norms. Someone who has come out of a large and comparatively slow-moving company such as a utilities firm (before deregulation) probably would find that the style of leadership he used effectively there is not equally effective in a fast-changing start-up entrepreneurial firm such as Netscape Communications. The reverse, of course, would be equally true. A leadership style consistent with the funlike informal culture at Ben & Jerry's Ice Cream would not necessarily work at a larger and more traditional firm in, say, the banking industry. These may be extreme cases, but they illustrate that an organization's culture is highly likely to determine what forms of leadership will succeed. In addition to culture, other important parts of the organizational context include its structure (Chapter 10), its human resource policies (Chapter 12), and its pattern of controls (Chapter 16).

CONTINGENCY PERSPECTIVES ON LEADERSHIP

The leader. The followers. The situation. Each is essential for telling the story of leadership. But it is the *interactions* of the three variables that determine the results of the leadership process in particular circumstances. Common sense, as well as theories of leadership, would tell us that no specific approach to leadership, regardless of the characteristics of the leader, the followers, and the situation, will work equally well all the time. Thus, beginning in the 1960s, contingency theories of leadership that focused on describing combinations of key variables necessary for leadership effectiveness were developed. Three of the more prominent of these contingency theories, each identified by the name(s) of its major proponents, are Fiedler's LPC (least preferred coworker) contingency theory, House's path–goal theory, and Vroom and Yetton's normative decision model.

Fiedler's LPC Theory

Fiedler's LPC (least preferred coworker) theory
a contingency theory of leadership that identifies the types of situations in which task-oriented or person-oriented leaders would be most effective

Fiedler's LPC theory grew out of a program of research that centered on leaders' attitudes toward their "least preferred coworker" (LPC).[55] That is, leaders were asked to rate, on a series of scales (e.g., "pleasant–unpleasant," "supportive–hostile," "open–guarded") the person from their present or past work experience with whom they could work *least* well. Thus, leaders who rated this person relatively harshly received low LPC scores, whereas leaders who rated their least preferred coworker relatively favorably received high LPC scores. Basically, a leader's LPC score was interpreted to indicate the degree to which a leader was especially task oriented (low LPC score) or person oriented (high LPC score).

Fiedler's theory was that leadership effectiveness would be contingent on the type of leader (low or high LPC) and the favorability of the situation for the leader. According to the theory, a favorable situation for the leader is when relations with subordinates are good, the task is highly structured, and the leader has considerable position power. An unfavorable situation would be when these conditions are the opposite. For example, a vice president of finance who has been assigned the task of preparing the company's annual report, who will be able to work with the same team that produced last year's report, and who also is regarded as excellent by top management would be in a highly favorable situation. In contrast, the leadership situation would be less favorable for a senior manager asked to develop a new product in conjunction with a subordinate who had hoped to be promoted into the position now held by the new manager. The theory predicts, as shown in Exhibit 14.10, that *low* LPC leaders, that is, those most task-oriented, are most effective in highly favorable or unfavorable situations, such as that encountered by the VP of finance in our example, whereas high LPC leaders will do best in moderately favorable or unfavorable situations. The reasoning, according to the theory, is that task-oriented leaders do not need to be especially sensitive to interpersonal relations in very favorable situations, and in very unfavorable situations a strong task orientation by the leader is the only approach that will work. Conversely, when situations are neither especially favorable nor unfavorable, the theory presumes that leaders more attuned to other people's feelings will do best.

The LPC contingency theory has been the object of considerable research over the years. Reviews of this research indicate some support for it, but various details of the theory have been criticized.[56] Probably its chief value is that when it was originated in the 1960s, it highlighted the importance of the situations leaders face,

EXHIBIT 14.10

LPC Theory

SITUATION	
Favorable (for leader)	**Unfavorable (for leader)**
Good subordinate relationships Highly structured task Leader with high amount of position power	Poor subordinate relationships Unstructured task Leader lacks position power
LEADERS	
Low LPC Perspective	**High LPC Perspective**

Rates least preferred coworker
  harshly
Task oriented
Most effective when situation is
  either highly favorable or
  highly unfavorable
	Rates least preferred coworker
	  favorably
	Person oriented
	Most effective when situation is
	  neither highly favorable nor
	  highly unfavorable

and it suggested how those conditions could make it harder or easier for leaders of particular types to be effective.

House's Path–Goal Theory

path–goal theory of leadership

a contingency theory of leadership that focuses on the leader's role in increasing subordinate satisfaction and effort by increasing personal payoffs for goal attainment and making the path to these payoffs easier

House and his associates in the 1970s proposed what was termed a **path–goal theory of leadership**.[57] Essentially, this perspective emphasized that the leader's job was to increase subordinate satisfaction and effort by "increasing personal payoffs to subordinates for work-goal attainment and making the path to these payoffs easier to travel by clarifying it, reducing roadblocks and pitfalls, and increasing the opportunities for personal satisfaction en route."[58]

The path–goal analysis of the factors involved in leadership effectiveness draws heavily from expectancy theories of motivation (as discussed in Chapter 13). Thus, it assumes that the leader's role is to influence subordinates' expectancies for being able to convert their efforts into performance that leads to desired rewards. Also, much like the LPC contingency theory just discussed, path–goal theory emphasizes two basic types of leader behavior: supportive leadership (people oriented) and directive leadership (task oriented). In addition, as with LPC and other contingency theories, path–goal theory assumes that a particular leadership approach will work better in some task situations than in others. As illustrated in Exhibit 14.11, if tasks are frustrating, boring, or highly stressful, supportive leadership behavior is assumed to help increase subordinate enjoyment and reduce anxiety, thereby raising effort and satisfaction. If tasks are intrinsically enjoyable and interesting, it is assumed that supportive, people-oriented leadership will have little net effect.

Directive, task-oriented leadership behavior, according to the theory, becomes especially important when tasks are varied and unstructured *and* when subordinates are inexperienced. Such directive behavior is assumed to reduce ambiguities in the situation and to clarify the paths to successful task performance. On the other hand (see Exhibit 14.11), if subordinates are highly experienced and competent *and* tasks are relatively structured, directive leadership behavior will be superfluous and possibly even resented.

EXHIBIT 14.11
Path–Goal Theory

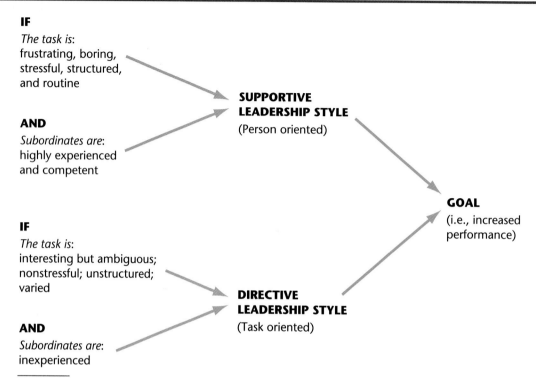

Source: Adapted from R. J. House, "A Path–Goal Theory of Leader Effectiveness," *Administrative Science Quarterly* 16, no. 5 (1971), pp. 321–39.

As with Fiedler's LPC contingency theory, the main contribution of House's path–goal theory has been to provide additional insights into the interactions among leader behavior, task characteristics, and follower competencies, and to identify which interactions are most likely to result in more productive and satisfying outcomes. Its value is in helping potential leaders to think systematically about what types of behavior on their part might work best in what types of situations.

Vroom and Yetton's Normative Decision Model

normative decision model

a contingency model that prescribes standards to determine the extent to which subordinates should be allowed to participate in decision making

Strictly speaking, Vroom and Yetton's **normative decision model** is not a model of leadership.[59] However, it addresses a major issue faced by leaders: the extent to which subordinates should participate in decision making. It is also a contingency model in that it is designed to help leaders determine how much and what type of subordinate participation to use in particular situations. The model is not simply analytical; it also *prescribes* when to use participation as a result of that analysis. Thus, it is called a "normative" model because it provides standards or rules for making such decisions.

The model focuses on two key variables that determine the effectiveness of decisions when measured by group performance: quality and acceptance. Decision

EXHIBIT 14.12 Normative Decision-Making Model: Decision-Making Styles	

Decision Style[a]	Definition
AI	Leader makes the decision alone.
AII	Leader asks for information from team members but makes the decision alone. Team members may or may not be informed what the situation is.
CI	Leader shares situation with each team member and asks for information and evaluation. Team members do not meet as a team, and the leader alone makes the decision.
CII	Leader and team members meet as a team to discuss the situation, but the leader makes the decision.
G	Leader and team members meet as a team to discuss the situation, and the team makes the decision.

[a]A = autocratic   C = consultative   G = group

Sources: V. H. Vroom and P. W. Yetton, *Leadership and Decision-Making* (Pittsburgh, Pa.: University of Pittsburgh Press, 1973); V. H. Vroom and A. G. Jago, *The New Leadership: Managing Participation in Organizations* (Englewood Cliffs, N.J.: Prentice Hall, 1988).

quality refers to the merit or degree of excellence of the course of action that is chosen. The quality of a decision becomes more crucial as the consequences of that decision become more important and when considerable variability exists among alternatives. Examples would be when important goals are being set or when major procedural changes are to be made. Decisions about relatively trivial matters such as where to place a piece of office equipment would not require significant decision quality.

Decision acceptance refers to the amount of subordinate commitment to implementing the chosen alternative. Acceptance is especially important when high levels of subordinate effort and motivation are needed to execute decisions after they are made. If a decision can be implemented directly by the leader without involving followers, then it would not matter a great deal whether decision acceptance was high.

The Vroom–Yetton model proposes that leaders have five basic decision-making procedures available, as shown in Exhibit 14.12. These procedures range from highly autocratic (termed AI in the model), where the manager makes the decision or solves the problem alone, to highly participative (termed G), where the group itself makes the decision. In determining which procedure to use in given situations, a manager could train herself to ask a series of yes-no questions, in a decision-tree style of inquiry, as shown in Exhibit 14.13. As can be seen, the decision tree involves eight components of a situation—the amount of information possessed by the manager and the subordinates, the likelihood that subordinates will accept an autocratic decision, and so forth. By answering this series of questions about the situation, a leader should be able to choose a procedure that will result in effective decisions.

This model (and later versions of it) has been found to have a fairly high level of validity in predicting successful decisions, and it has been used extensively in management development programs.[60] However, as previously noted, although it is a contingency model that is relevant to leadership, it only deals with a portion of total

EXHIBIT 14.13

Normative Decision-Making Model for Leaders' Use of Participation: Decision-Tree Questions

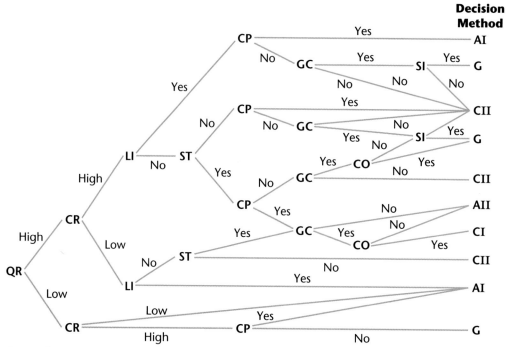

State the Problem

QR How important is the quality of this decision?

CR How important is subordinate commitment to the decision?

LI Do you have sufficient information to make a high-quality decision?

ST Is the problem well structured?

CP If you were to make the decision by yourself, is it reasonably certain that your subordinates would be committed to it?

GC Do subordinates share the organization goals to be attained in solving this problem?

CO Is conflict among subordinates over preferred solutions likely?

SI Do subordinates have sufficient information to make a high-quality decision?

Source: Adapted and reprinted from *Leadership and Decision-making* by Victor H. Vroom and Phillip W. Yetton, by permission of the University of Pittsburgh Press. © 1973 by University of Pittsburgh Press.

leadership behavior: the extent of use of participation in group decision-making behavior.

Substitutes for Leadership

One other important contingency perspective needs to be considered. It is not a leadership theory as such, but it raises significant issues for managers to consider—namely, in some circumstances, there can be substitutes for leadership.[61] That is, a

EXHIBIT 14.14

Examples of Possible
Substitutes for
Leadership

Source: Adapted from S. Kerr and J. M. Jermier, "Substitutes for Leadership: Their Meaning and Measurement," *Organizational Behavior & Human Performance* 22, no. 3 (1978), pp. 375–403.

greater use of leadership behaviors is not always the only, or even the best, solution for some managerial problems. In certain work settings, other approaches can at least partially substitute for increased leadership or even for poor leadership. Examples of some possible substitutes for leadership are shown in Exhibit 14.14.

For example, extensive training and experience can reduce the need for leadership direction in such fast-paced and complex jobs as air traffic controller or police emergency work. The speed required for decisions in these job situations often would not allow time for intervention by a leader, so prior training substitutes for such influence. Furthermore, in many technical and professional jobs in organizations, high levels of earlier formal education reduce the need for close supervision. It is safe to assume that an attorney or scientist or computer programmer working for a company will probably not need the same amount of supervision, and certainly not the same type, as an employee in a more routine job. Too much attempted leadership of such professionals would probably hinder, rather than facilitate, their performance. Similarly, workers in jobs that supply considerable amounts of intrinsic satisfaction, such as those involving an exciting new product or service, would be unlikely to need leaders to increase their motivation. These examples point to the conclusion that the amount and type of leadership required can vary considerably from situation to situation. Too much attempted leadership or too much of a particular leadership approach sometimes can be as dangerous for the organization—and the would-be leader—as not enough.

in addition to substitutes for leadership, there are also "neutralizers," that is, aspects of the organization or work situation that can defeat the best efforts of leaders. Examples would be inflexible organization procedures that do not allow leaders sufficient freedom of choice, or an organizational reward policy that does not allow the leader to have any influence on the amounts of rewards for exceptional performance. Thus, neutralizers, like substitutes, emphasize the importance of situational contingencies and how they can impact the effectiveness of leadership as well as the need for it.

CONTEMPORARY LEADERSHIP ISSUES

In recent years, scholars in the field of leadership have raised several issues that have become increasingly important for management practice. Three of these issues are charismatic leadership, transformational leadership, and leadership across different national cultures, and each of these issues has some interesting implications for managers.

Charismatic Leadership

As mentioned earlier in this chapter, when we were reviewing types of personal power, charisma is an especially strong form of referent power. The term *charisma* has a theological origin and comes from the Greek word for "gift." It literally means "divinely conferred gift." Its relevance for organizational settings was first highlighted in the early decades of the 20th century by the sociologist Max Weber.[62] He described the **charismatic leader** as someone who has influence over others based on inspirational qualities of the individual rather than on that person's formal power or position. Thus, followers or subordinates are assumed to identify with that person because of those exceptional qualities. Many people, of course, would like to think they are endowed with charisma, but only relatively few people have these special powers. If they were common, they wouldn't be exceptional.

The term *charisma* has been used particularly in the political sphere to describe those who are especially influential with large numbers of people. Examples include historical figures such as Mahatma Gandhi, Joan of Arc, Winston Churchill, Martin Luther King Jr., and John F. Kennedy. In the business world, such people as Lee Iacocca, Sam Walton, Richard Branson, and Charlotte Beers (see the Managerial Challenge box, "Passion at the Helm") come to mind.

It is only in the last couple of decades that the concept of charisma has been used explicitly in scholarly examinations of organizational leadership.[63] One of the first such analyses focused on the specific traits and behaviors of charismatic leaders, such as

- Strong needs for power
- High levels of self-confidence
- Strong beliefs in their own ideas.[64]

In terms of their behaviors, charismatic leaders, more than other types of leaders, are especially likely to

- Model desired behavior
- Communicate high expectations for followers' performance

charismatic leadership
leadership by someone who has influence over others based on individual inspirational qualities rather than formal power

- Be concerned with, and try to influence, the impressions of others
- Emphasize ideals, values, and lofty goals

Another analysis of leadership from a charismatic perspective focused on particular types of leaders' behaviors that seem to enhance effects on followers.[65] These include

- Emphasizing a vision for the organization that represents a major, but achievable, change;
- Taking innovative or unorthodox types of actions to achieve goals; and
- Demonstrating self-sacrifices on behalf of the organization.

This perspective highlights the idea that anything a leader can do to create follower dissatisfaction with the status quo, and to offer innovative solutions, as Charlotte Beers did, will increase the probability of attributions of charisma to the leader. (See Exhibit 14.15 for a set of attributes of charismatic leaders, based on the scholarly analyses just discussed.)

Since charisma is a type of "special power" possessed by relatively few people, can a typical manager or leader try to increase his or her charisma? It is clear that no one can create this type of power simply by assuming they have it, or by asking for it or demanding it. It must be generated or conferred in some fashion. Although

EXHIBIT 14.15

Attributes of the Charismatic Leader

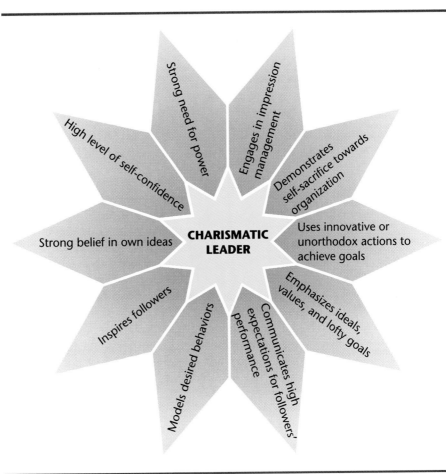

MANAGERIAL CHALLENGE

PASSION AT THE HELM

Charisma is a word that well describes Charlotte Beers, the recently retired CEO and chairwoman of Ogilvy & Mather Worldwide, one of the largest advertising agencies in the world. Beers, described by some as the diva of Madison Avenue, was renowned for making theatrical entrances into client meetings and then greeting clients with a slight drawl and a pointed question: "Now, you're going to give us this business today, aren't you?"

It makes sense that someone with the kind of style that Beers exuded would be running an advertising agency. Some of her exploits are legendary, like tossing her Jaguar keys on the conference table when courting the Jaguar account and launching into an emotional description of the relationship between an owner and her Jag.

Known for calling clients "honey" and pouring on the charm in a southern accent, Beers developed a style uniquely her own. "Yes, I call CEOs 'honey,' but to me, that's wry Texas humor. I'm likely to say the most outrageous thing in the room—to liven things up."

Beers was clear about the importance of the personal touch. "One of the biggest mistakes women make in business is that they aren't friendly enough," she said. But it takes more than style to successfully lead a company, and Beers proved herself quite worthy of the position.

Beers, an advertising veteran who resigned from a mid-sized Chicago agency, landed at Ogilvy & Mather at a time when the agency was floundering. The agency had lost several key accounts and, according to industry sources, staff morale was at an all-time low, with many key veterans jumping ship.

Stepping into her new office at Ogilvy & Mather, Beers had more to deal with than just dwindling billings and falling revenues. What she faced was clearly a leadership challenge. Not only did Beers have to increase revenues, she also had to rouse the troops.

So instead of marching in with spreadsheet in hand and hammering away at the need for profits, she chose to inspire and started preaching "passion." This, she claimed, was the essence of what was needed to bring Ogilvy & Mather back from the dead.

This sense of passion was something she modeled for her staff. Relying on referent power, she worked to inspire and influence those working for her. Beers believed strongly that real leadership doesn't stay anchored in stuffy decorum. "So many CEOs are impeccably logical, but they don't lift your heart. They rely too much on the way things should be done," Beers said. "I believe in provocative disruption."

She didn't stop at this, but pushed her associates to high levels of performance, while trying to revive in Ogilvy & Mather staffers a sense of pride and excitement about their agency.

Following up this work inside the agency, she pushed the idea of "brand stewardship to clients." The response was

few managers have the personality traits to easily or spontaneously produce the levels of charisma that certain renowned business and political leaders have achieved, many leaders can increase the chances that their subordinates will be motivated to follow them and work with and for them. The kinds of behaviors summarized in Exhibit 14.5 are ones that almost anyone can develop.

One final point should be raised about charisma: its potential downside. That is, charisma can be used for harmful ends as well as good. Society and the world at large are only too familiar with how an apparently extreme level of charisma was used by certain "leaders," such as, for example, Adolf Hitler in Nazi Germany before and during World War II and the cult figure Jim Jones of Jonestown mass suicide fame, with disastrous consequences. Charisma represents special power, but that does not guarantee that it will always be used for worthy goals.

Transformational Leadership

In some ways, the concept of **transformational leadership** is similar to charismatic leadership. The two ideas both involve the notion of being able to motivate followers to make major changes or to achieve at very high levels. Thus, the original concept of transformational leadership, authored by a political scientist, James M. Burns, described it as a process in which "leaders and followers raise one another to

transformational leadership

leadership that motivates followers to ignore self-interests and work for the larger good of the organization to achieve significant accomplishments; emphasis is on articulating a vision that will convince subordinates to make major changes disdain by some advertising insiders, who suggested the idea was pretentious. For Beers it represented the responsibility the agency has to the client. Brand stewardship means the agency has to determine the "character" of the brand before it can successfully promote it. Reaching this kind of insight involves knowing how the brand affects the consumer. However, such an investment pays off, according to Beers. "If you have a passionate understanding of what a brand is about, who would ever take that brand from you?"

This idea, which she pushed while calling on clients all over the world, did not receive enthusiastic support within Ogilvy & Mather. But Beers clung to it. "I had to shepherd the idea because our own people were unconvinced." That, of course, didn't daunt her and with characteristic style. Beers claimed, "Consensus is a poor substitute for leadership." In time, "brand stewardship" was on the lips of agency staffers and their clients.

Things started to turn around when the agency landed the Jaguar account. "It's a timely shot of adrenaline for Ogilvy's New York office. We've been working long and hard, and have had a rough spell," said G. Kelly O'Dea, the executive director of world wide client service. Another agency executive claimed that a new breeze of optimism was blowing at the Ogilvy & Mather offices. "There's a sense that things are going somewhere."

But the feather in the cap for Beers was landing the IBM account, a nearly $500 million contract for Ogilvy & Mather.

Under Beer's direction, the agency won back American Express and acquired such clients as Kodak and Swatch, both companies with an international market. In fact, during her stay at Ogilvy & Mather, billings increased from $5.5 billion to $7.6 billion. This improved business resulted in new assignments for various staff members and a renewed vitality for the agency.

Charlotte Beers represents a charismatic leader who inspired and influenced clients and agency staffers alike. The result was what *Fortune* magazine called "a most impressive turnaround" of Ogilvy & Mather.

Sources: Patricia Sellers, "Women, Sex & Power," *Fortune* 134, no. 3 (August 5, 1996), pp. 42–56; Laura Petrecca, "O&M's Beers to Cede CEO Title in the Fall," *Advertising Age* 67, no. 32 (August 5, 1996), p. 2; Amanda Troy Segal, Mark Landler, Eric Schine, Laura Zinn, et al., "Corporate Women," *Business Week* no. 3269, Industrial/Technology Edition (June 8, 1992), pp. 74–83; Gary Levin, "Can Charlotte Beers Revive O&M?: Why Beers Chose O&M," *Advertising Age* 63, no. 15 (April 13, 1992), pp. 1, 58; Melanie Wells, "Charlotte's Agenda: More Top Executives," *Advertising Age* 63, no. 30 (July 27, 1992), pp. 3, 41; Melanie Wells and John P. Cortez, "With Jaguar on Board, What's Next for O&M," *Advertising Age* 63, no. 29 (July 20, 1992), p. 4.

higher levels of morality and motivation."[66] Later refinements of this approach, by social scientists specifically addressing organizational contexts, emphasized that leaders are transformational even if they don't necessarily appeal to "higher levels of morality and motivation," as long as they motivate followers to ignore their own self-interests and instead to work for the larger good of the organization.[67] Put another way, attributions of charisma to leaders are strongly affected by what they are like as people, but attributions of transformational qualities are largely based on what they do.

Transformational leaders, like charismatic leaders, inspire their followers. However, this is not done just through followers' identification with the leader, as in the case of charismatic leadership, but also through empowering and coaching followers. It is in this latter respect that the concept of transformational leadership differs from charismatic leadership. With transformational leadership, followers are not required to be highly dependent on their leaders. Also, whereas instances of charismatic leadership are rare, transformational leadership behavior is assumed to be potentially possible almost anywhere throughout the organization.[68]

Those who advocate greater transformational leadership in organizations contrast it with so-called **transactional leadership**, as shown in Exhibit 14.16. The latter is regarded as leadership that emphasizes the exchange of rewards or other

transactional leadership

leadership that focuses on motivating followers' self-interests by exchanging rewards for their compliance; emphasis is on having subordinates implement procedures correctly and make needed, but relatively routine, changes

EXHIBIT 14.16

Transformational versus
Transactional Leadership

	Transformational Leadership	Transactional Leadership
Leader gains subordinates' compliance by:	Inspiring, empowering, and coaching followers	Exchange of rewards and benefits
Appeals focus on:	Organizational and "common good" interests	Self-interest
Type of planned change:	Major organizational change	Routine changes

benefits for compliance by followers. Transformational leadership is seen as an approach that especially emphasizes organizational or "common good" interests, whereas transactional leadership is seen as focusing more on followers' self-interests. In many respects, however, this distinction is somewhat artificial, since individuals often act for both their own interests *and* organizational interests.

Another distinction drawn between transformational and transactional leadership by some experts is that the former involves motivating subordinates to make major changes, while the latter involves the implementation of routine changes and procedures. Again, this distinction is not always clear-cut in many organizational situations.

In any event, a transformational perspective does focus on motivating people to make relatively significant, or even unusual, achievements and accomplishments. Several studies have recently explored how transformational leaders influence their followers to achieve such exceptional results. One study of 12 CEOs found that transformational leaders (a) recognized the need for major changes, (b) helped subordinates prepare for and accept such changes, and, especially, (c) were particularly skillful in persuading subordinates to accept a new way of doing things—a new vision—in the organization. The study indicated that transformational leaders

- Viewed themselves as agents of change
- Were thoughtful risk-takers
- Were sensitive to people's needs
- Stated a set of core values to rally around
- Were flexible and open to learning
- Had good analytical skills
- Had considerable confidence in their vision for the organization[69]

Another study of 90 leaders in both the corporate world and the public sector came to similar conclusions:

[Transformational leaders] paid attention to what was going on, they determined what parts of events at hand would be important for the future of the organization, they set a new direction, and they concentrated the attention of everyone in the organization on [that new future]. This was ... as true for orchestra conductors, army generals, football coaches, and school superintendents as for corporate leaders.[70]

It is clear from these studies that transformational leadership (a) can occur in widely varying circumstances, (b) emphasizes a particular focus on a vision and how to implement it, and (c) requires considerable perseverance and dedication by the

EXHIBIT 14.17

Guidelines for
Transformational
Leadership

Those Who Want to Be Transformational Leaders Should:

Develop a clear and appealing vision
Develop a strategy for attaining the vision
Articulate and promote the vision
Act confident and optimistic
Express confidence in followers
Use early success in small steps to build confidence
Celebrate successes
Use dramatic, symbolic actions to emphasize key values
Lead by example

Source: Adapted from G. Yukl, *Leadership in Organizations,* 3rd ed. (Englewood Cliffs, N.J.: Prentice Hall, 1994).

leader. Exhibit 14.17 summarizes a set of guidelines for those who aspire to transform their organizations or their parts of organizations.[71]

Leadership across Different National Cultures

A final issue with respect to leadership, power, and influence is this: Does leadership differ fundamentally across national cultures, or do the similarities outweigh the differences? The answer is that nobody knows for sure, although researchers are attempting to find answers.[72]

As some observers point out: "*Leadership* is a fairly modern concept. It did not appear in English-language usage until the first half of the 19th century and has been primarily the concern of Anglo-Saxon influenced countries. Prior to that, and in other countries, the notion of *headship* has been more prominent, as in the head of state, chief, or other *ruling* [italics added] position."[73] Or, as another scholar put it, "The universality of leadership [as a part of the managerial role] does not ... imply a similarity of leadership style throughout the world."[74]

Experts on Southeast Asia, for example, point out two essential cultural features that affect leadership situations and the use of power and influence in that area of the world: requirements for order and compliance and requirements for harmony.[75] The first of these cultural "requirements" involves traditional values that support the acceptance of hierarchies, conformity, and deference to authority. The necessity for the cultural value of harmony involves not only obligations of the subordinate to the superior but also obligations of the superior to respect the subordinate and care for his or her welfare. Clearly, this is a quite different leadership style than is found in most Western societies. In most Asian cultures, for example, this style can be summarized in the word *paternalism,* where a leader is regarded as the provider ("father") who will take care of the subordinate in return for responsible behavior and performance.

Despite such differences related to cultural norms and traditions, some similarities in leadership practices—for example, the greater use of subordinate participation—are appearing with increasing regularity around the world, owing to spreading industrialization. Thus, forces for *divergence* in leadership and influence practices due to culture are combating forces for *convergence* due to industrialization and increasing levels of education associated with it. Results from the most recent large-scale investigation of attributes of effective leadership across more

Examples of leader attributes universally viewed as *positive* **+**	Examples of leader attributes universally viewed as *negative* **−**	Examples of leader attributes viewed as *positive or negative* depending on the culture **+/−**
+ Trustworthy	− Noncooperative	+/− Ambitious
+ Encouraging	− Irritable	+/− Individualistic
+ Honest	− Dictatorial	+/− Cunning
+ Decisive	− Ruthless	+/− Cautious
+ Communicative	− Egocentric	+/− Class Conscious
+ Dependable	− Asocial	+/− Evasive

Source: R. J. House, "Cultural Influences on Leadership and Organizations: Project GLOBE," in W. Mobley (ed.), *Advances in Global Leadership,* vol. 1 (Stamford, Conn.: JAI Press, 1998).

than 60 different national cultures appear consistent with this conclusion.[76] As Exhibit 14.18 shows, according to the data collected for this study, certain leader attributes, such as "trustworthy" and "decisive," are universally (across all cultures) viewed as positive. Likewise, certain other attributes, such as "dictatorial" and "asocial" are universally viewed as negative. The reactions to other leader attributes, however, such as "cautious" and "ambitious," are highly contingent on the particular culture and thus are viewed positively in some cultures but distinctly negatively in other cultures.

Because of expanding industrialization, the need for effective leadership has become a worldwide phenomenon, but exactly how that need is being met in specific organizations and in specific countries still appears to be influenced by cultural circumstances and traditions. Nevertheless, the picture of varying leadership styles and practices around the world at the end of the 20th century may change dramatically by the end of the first decades of the 21st century.

CONCLUDING COMMENTS

Every manager should also want to be a leader, and an effective leader at that. Every manager has the potential to *become* a more effective leader. But, for most people, becoming an effective leader is not an easy or quick task. Most of us, unfortunately, are not endowed with brilliant charismatic qualities. Therefore, we don't necessarily begin a managerial job or career with an extremely high degree of referent power. Rather, a managerial position provides us with a certain amount of position power, and we also probably have acquired at least some degree of expertise. From that point on, it is a matter of gaining additional expertise and building our own referent power based on our actions and the example we set. It's also a matter of learning how to diagnose situations where leadership is called for and how to get the most out of whatever resources we have available. Not easy, but doable.

To make accurate diagnoses of leadership situations requires reasonable insight into, and an accurate assessment of, our own personal strengths, the attitudes and capabilities of those we are trying to lead, the nature of the jobs to be done, and the organizational environment. In other words, leadership is not just action. It involves good planning, good observation, and, especially, good thinking. Knowing what to look for is half the battle of knowing what to do in a leadership context.

Behavioral and organizational science has provided some useful perspectives on the leadership process, and many of those theories and approaches were discussed in this chapter. No single theory itself provides a foolproof formula for guaranteeing success as a leader. (Only some articles and books in the popular media can do that!) However, the conceptual models and ideas in this chapter can be helpful in stimulating your thinking about the process of leadership and what you may want to consider in developing your own distinctive approach to this critical managerial function.

Finally, it is important to keep in mind that effective leadership, despite attempts to oversimplify it, is a fairly complex topic. There are plenty of leadership dilemmas and paradoxes that make decisions difficult, such as: act quickly and decisively, but take time to involve others and gain their commitment; use power, but don't overuse it; be consistent, but be flexible; be task oriented, but don't forget to be people oriented; and, like nuclear disarmament negotiators, "trust, but verify." Those who can master these contradictory pulls and tugs by looking at the big picture will be the ones who are more likely to become effective leaders in the long run. Even in the short run, though, remember that leadership can be exercised almost anytime and anywhere in the organization by almost anyone, regardless of position or depth of experience. In other words, intent counts for a lot in leadership and its effects.

KEY TERMS

charismatic leadership 430
coercive power 408
effective leadership 403
empowerment 411
expert power 409
Fiedler's LPC (least preferred coworker) theory 424
influence tactics 411
leader–member exchange (LMX) theory 421

legitimate power (formal authority) 407
normative decision model 426
organizational leadership 402
path–goal theory of leadership 425
people behaviors 419
personal power 405
position power 405
power 405

referent power 410
reward power 408
skills 415
task behaviors 419
traits 413
transactional leadership 433
transformational leadership 432

REVIEW QUESTIONS

1. Why can leadership be characterized as a social influence process?
2. Who can be expected to exhibit leadership in an organization?
3. What is effective leadership?
4. How do leading and managing differ?

5. What is power?
6. What is position power, and what are its three components?
7. Who can utilize coercive power?
8. What are the two types of personal power discussed in the text?
9. What factors help to determine what type of power will be most effective?
10. Can leadership be taught?
11. What are the three fundamental components of the leadership process in organizations?
12. What is the "locus of leadership"?
13. Summarize the history of thought on the importance of leadership traits.
14. What are three types of skills that are especially critical for managers?
15. Compare task behaviors to people behaviors, in relation to leadership.
16. Why is it important to consider the characteristics of followers?
17. Explain why LMX theory is considered a relationship-based rather than a leader-based approach.
18. How can a company's culture affect a manager's leadership effectiveness?
19. What is meant by a contingency theory of leadership?
20. What issues pertaining to leadership are central to Fiedler's LPC theory?
21. Which contingency theory draws heavily on expectancy theory?
22. From a contingency theory perspective, in what type of situation might a more directive approach to leadership be called for?
23. How do decision quality and decision acceptance affect the effectiveness of decisions?
24. Explain how training or experience can act as a substitute for leadership.
25. What is the difference between charismatic and transformational leadership?
26. Are leadership practices similar across cultures?

DISCUSSION QUESTIONS

1. Think of a specific leader in your work situation, in a friendship group, on a sports team, or in the news. What types of power does he or she appear to use? Is this person an effective leader? Why or why not?
2. Would you prefer to work for a directive or a supportive leader? Why? What would be the potential advantages and disadvantages of working under each type?
3. Look at the decision tree on p. 428. Do you think that a manager can really use this tool? To what extent should managers try to change their leadership style to suit different situations?
4. Think of someone you view as having charisma. How does it manifest itself? Do you think that person was born with a fixed amount of charisma, or did that person learn to increase it? Do you think the positive aspects of that leader's charisma outweigh any potential negative aspects?

CLOSING CASE

The New Supervisor

Grace Reed had been working at the County Medical Society Answering Service for 18 months when she received a promotion to shift supervisor. She was quite excited, as she had worked very hard to develop the technical skills for answering calls and the interpersonal skills used in communicating with patients and their doctors, to master the variety of procedures used by the organization to document each call and its response, and to show her desire for the promotion by volunteering for overtime and holiday work. Finally, she had been promoted. However, now she faced problems she had not anticipated. How was she to convince her friends to take her seriously as their new boss? How was she going to maintain her friendships and still maintain the discipline needed in this workplace?

The San Mateo County Medical Society's physicians were extremely disappointed in the level of dedication and care shown by the former county answering services, which handled not only physicians but business and private accounts as well. They decided to start their own answering service. Their operators would handle only medical calls, would be better trained to recognize urgent and emergency calls, would receive better benefits, and would be paid at a higher rate than the competing answering services. The doctors believed that by structuring the enterprise in this way, they could attract and retain the best possible workers. They would also have the largest available worker pool from which to choose and therefore would not have to worry about being able to find replacement operators if it was necessary. They hired a professional manager to oversee the day-to-day operations, and each shift had a supervisor whose responsibilities included routine scheduling of workers; recognition of and planning for especially heavy days and shifts; handling complaints from doctors, hospitals, pharmacies, or patients concerning the handling of their calls; learning how to operate new equipment and subsequently training their operators in its use; and maintaining the high level of service required by the physicians. These duties were in addition to working her or his own eight-hour shift.

Grace was the fourth operator hired by the organization, and the first operator promoted from the ranks to be supervisor (rather than hiring an outside supervisor). When she was first hired, she was lucky to train with a very experienced, competent operator. She modeled her own skills on those of her trainer and worked diligently to handle the most calls with the fewest mistakes and even fewer complaints. Where the other operators handled only 60 to 70 individual incoming lines, Grace routinely handled 100 to 120 lines, including some of those with the highest volumes of calls. She not only cleared her own calls but

frequently assisted other operators in clearing their backlogged messages. When extremely difficult calls came in, such as suicide calls or nuisance calls from patients to whom even the doctors did not want to talk, it was often Grace who was asked to handle them. She rapidly developed excellent relationships with all of "her" doctors, their staffs, and even their families. During her first year, she was named operator of the month five times. In her second year, she worked with the existing supervisors to learn how to schedule the workers and received advanced training in the other office operations and procedures beyond answering calls.

Although the work was extremely fast paced and required concentration, there was always time for talking with the other operators, joking, and having fun. Strong friendships grew among the operators, who frequently socialized after hours and on their days off. There was a strong feeling of family in the office. The high levels of training and pay led to extremely low turnover rates. There were always waiting lists of applicants for the positions. If an operator wished to leave, he or she had no problem finding work at hospitals or for the phone company. Morale was generally high due to the respect the operators felt they received from "their" doctors for the high-quality work they performed, the higher levels of pay and benefits they received in comparison with operators at other organizations, and the high degree of friendship among operators.

Her friends at the answering service threw Grace a party when she received her promotion. Everyone who wasn't working attended. Everyone was happy for her and sincerely wished her well. They all knew now that you could be promoted from the ranks! Grace was anxious to assume her new responsibilities and even try some new procedures she had been devising.

Within a month, Grace wasn't nearly as happy with her promotion as she had thought she would be. Her friends, who were now her subordinates as well, didn't seem to pay attention to her suggestions concerning their job performance. They ignored her instructions and frequently treated them as a joke. She worked many hours planning schedules only to have the operators switch shifts, leave early, or arrive late, saying they were sure she wouldn't mind because she understood all of their personal complications with their romantic relationships. She was their friend after all; of course, they knew she would cut them some slack. And her best friends seemed to be some of the worst offenders.

Grace soon realized that her new position was missing one thing—authority to go with her new responsibilities. She had no authority to sanction any of her subordinates:

she couldn't dock their pay, make them work overtime, or cut back on their hours. She couldn't shorten their lunch breaks or eliminate their coffee breaks. Any such sanctions could only come from the overall company manager. If she tried to insist that a new procedure be used or that scheduled hours be worked and the operator balked, she had no recourse. If she complained to the manager, she would be viewed as unable to do her job. She couldn't complain to her friends, because they were part of the problem. She tried acting very authoritarian and harshly insisting on the new methods. She was met with hostility, and her friends stopped talking to her. One day she had had enough and berated a group of her friends about how they gave her no respect, they were uncooperative, and they weren't doing their jobs, and she was fed up with it. After all, she didn't ask them to do anything she wasn't willing or able to do herself. Morale was plummeting (hers as well as the other operators') and productivity was falling. Grace felt like a failure at the job she had worked so hard to get, and, even beyond that, she felt she was losing her friends.

Grace knew that something was going to have to change. She needed to try something new, to somehow regain the respect of her subordinates and find a new way to inspire improved performance and efficiency and restore morale. And she had to accomplish all this while maintaining her friendships with the other operators.

QUESTIONS

1. Which traits, skills, and behaviors associated with successful leaders does Grace possess? Are there characteristics she could enhance to improve her leadership ability?

2. Why did Grace have problems making changes and maintaining discipline when she first was promoted to a position that required leadership?

3. Analyze Grace's leadership situation in terms of her sources of power: Are there types of power she couldn't or shouldn't use? What types of power could she draw on, and how could she use those types to greatest effect?

4. Are there substitutes for leadership present in this situation? What neutralizers must Grace overcome to be an effective leader?

CHAPTER 15

COMMUNICATION AND NEGOTIATION

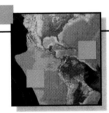

A Communication Collision

It was a car lover's dream. Two brothers, Jack and John Goudy, left their desk jobs to open their own auto repair shop. At first, just the two brothers did brake jobs and replaced exhaust systems. Then, as business grew, they hired a few workers and moved to a larger shop. Within a decade, Two J's Auto Repair was cranking in sales of half a million dollars per year, but then those sales reached a plateau and gradually began to decline. So John, who was in charge of sales and accounting, searched for a new way to improve business. He found it: technology. John began to institute cutting-edge technology in the shop. Now he had to convince his workers, including Jack, who spent more time in the shop than in the office, that his strategy for rebuilding Two J's would be successful.

John convened a staff meeting to communicate his new vision to the employees. Armed with graphs and charts, he talked about profit sharing, employee involvement, and state-of-the-art technology. "From today on, we're a completely different business," he predicted. He did not know how prophetic that statement would prove to be. John's audience did not share his enthusiasm; in fact, they did not understand his message at all because they had received no previous training in the areas of finance, human resources, or technology. They didn't understand the vocabulary he used or the ideas he was presenting. "It was a sea of blank faces with an occasional mutter here and there," John recalls. Thus, the flow of miscommunication at Two J's began.

John purchased a new computer-information system, which reduced the amount of paper communication generated by the office. But employees eventually discovered that the original estimates and the final invoices did not match each other, which caused them to believe that he was withholding work hours—and pay. He installed a closed-circuit TV in the shop so that, when customers phoned to inquire about the status of their repair, he could glance quickly at the monitor and answer them. Unfortunately, shop workers believed that John had installed the TV as a surveillance tool, and they resented his mistrust.

Although John had provided his employees with an elaborate explanation of the profit-sharing plan (which they did not understand), they were skeptical of it because of mixed messages he sent: John often groaned about poor profits but would suddenly arrive at work driving a new sports car. Sensing declining morale, John started to hold daily "release meetings," designed to let employees voice their frustrations and concerns. But even these backfired. "John talked about working together like a football team," says one employee. But the meetings quickly dissolved into lectures. "John talked, we listened." Another employee observes, "It was clear John didn't care much about what we thought. He was too excited about his big ideas."

Jack, meanwhile, tried to serve as a go-between, between John and the workers. "John wasn't working in the shop anymore," he explains. "Unfortunately, he dismissed their ideas when they offered suggestions." Eventually, even Jack and John could be heard fighting in the office. "They routinely got into yelling matches, one threatening to walk out on the other," says one veteran Two J's worker.

Finally, despite John's efforts to attract new customers and provide better, faster repairs through technology, workers began to leave the shop for other jobs. At first, he did not understand what had gone so wrong. And he admitted that he never realized how grueling running his own business could be; he knew that communication was not his strong point. "Every day there were questions," he comments. "After a while, they just ground me down." When the company hit rock bottom, John began to get the message. He began to recognize the importance of communication—not only with customers, but with his own workers—to the success of any business. He began to make small changes. "Now [when I attend staff meetings], I bring a yellow pad, scribble, and listen." This chapter is about the importance of communication—whether it takes place via yellow pad or computer—throughout an organization.

Source: Elizabeth Conlin, "Company Profile: Collision Course," *Inc.* 14, no. 13 (December 1992), pp. 132–42.

It is easy for most people to communicate. We do it all the time. Communicating effectively, however, is a different matter.[1] Accurate and persuasive communication within and between organizations, person to person, person to group, or group to group, is frequently, and sometimes unexpectedly, difficult, as the opening example demonstrates. Receivers often do not have a complete understanding of what the senders mean. But the heart and soul of **communication** is exactly that: the process of transferring information, meaning, and understanding from sender to receiver. And carrying out that process convincingly and proficiently is an absolute essential for a manager to exercise leadership. In fact, it is hard to conceive of successful leadership in the absence of excellent communication skills. The first step for a manager to become an outstanding leader, therefore, is to become an outstanding communicator.

In this chapter, we start with an overview of the basic communication process, followed by an examination of the modes of communication: verbal, nonverbal, and electronic. These topics provide a background for the next section on the organizational context of the communication process as it affects managers. Although the organization can facilitate managerial communication, it also can be one of the key sources of barriers to communication—interpersonal, organizational, and cultural—which are discussed in the following section. This section in turn is followed by one that, appropriately, focuses on some of the steps that managers can take to reduce or overcome these barriers.

The final parts of the chapter focus on one particular area of communication that is especially critical for managers—negotiation. In those sections, we discuss the impact of cultural influences on negotiation strategies and on the negotiation process itself. Throughout this chapter we need to keep in mind a basic perspective: Although communication is a universal human activity, successful communication is not habitual. It requires motivation, skill, and knowledge.

communication

the process of transferring information, meaning, and understanding from sender to receiver

BASIC MODEL OF COMMUNICATION

How do people communicate? How do they send and receive messages? What factors can disrupt communication? Let's look first at the basic model of the communication process (Exhibit 15.1).[2]

All communication involves *four actions* and *five components*. The four actions are encoding, sending, receiving, and decoding. The five components are sender, message, medium, noise, and receiver. The actions and components combine to transfer meaning from the sender to the receiver (see Exhibit 15.1). The sender originates the message by **encoding** it, that is, by constructing the message. The message is the content of the communication. The sender then transmits the message through a medium. A **medium** is the mode or form of transmission, not the message itself. Examples of media are spoken words, gestures and facial expressions,

encoding

the act of constructing a message

medium

the mode or form of transmission of a message

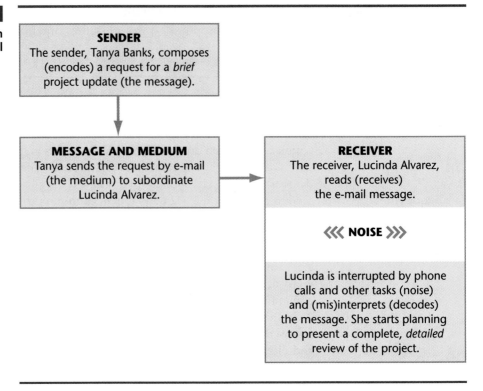

EXHIBIT 15.1

Basic Communication Model

decoding
the act of interpreting a message

noise
potential interference with the transmission or decoding of a message

video, written memos, faxes, and e-mail messages. The receiver acquires, or receives, the message by hearing it, reading it, or having it appear on a fax or computer. The receiver then begins **decoding** the message, that is, interpreting it. Sometimes distractions interfere with the message; these interferences are called **noise**. Noise contributes to misinterpretations of the original message, and it is only through feedback, or verification of the original message, that communication problems may be located and corrected.

The basic model of communication is fundamental and universal. That is, it occurs whenever communication takes place regardless of the culture or organization. However, while the basic acts and components of the communication process are the same everywhere, *how* the acts are carried out and the *nature of the components* are deeply influenced by cultural, organizational, and even personal contexts.[3] Who can send messages to whom, what kinds and what volumes of messages are sent, by what medium are messages transmitted, what sort of interference or noise is likely to occur, and what cues are available for decoding are just some of the many examples of the types of communication issues that can vary from manager to manager, from organization to organization, and from country to country.

MODES OF COMMUNICATION

Communication can occur in either a verbal mode or a nonverbal mode, as shown in Exhibit 15.2. Each mode has particular characteristics and issues that an effective manager must understand.

EXHIBIT 15.2

Modes of Communication

	VERBAL MODE (Language used to convey meaning)		NONVERBAL MODE
	Oral	**Written**	**NONVERBAL MODE**
Examples	Conversation Speeches Telephone calls Videoconferences	Letters Memos Reports E-mail Fax	Dress Speech intonation Gestures Facial expressions
Advantages	Vivid Stimulating Commands attention Difficult to ignore Flexible Adaptive	Decreased misinterpretation Precise	Effectiveness of communication increases with congruence to oral presentation Can emphasize meaning
Disadvantages	Transitory Subject to misinterpretation	Precision loss in translation Inflexible Easier to ignore	Meanings of nonverbal communication not universal

Verbal Communication

Most of us think of spoken words when we think of verbal communication. The key, however, is not that the words are spoken but that words—language—are used to convey meaning. Consequently, when we talk about verbal communication, we mean *both* oral and written communication.

Oral Communication   The spoken word has the potential advantages of being vivid, stimulating, and commanding attention. In most organizational situations, it is difficult for receivers—the listeners—to ignore the words spoken or the person speaking to them. Just think about the last time someone spoke to you directly. Even if you weren't interested in what the person had to say, wouldn't it have been difficult to simply ignore the person, turn, and walk away?

Also, oral communication is exceptionally flexible for both the sender and receiver. While you are speaking, you may try to make a point a certain way but along the way change your words in order for the listener to understand you. Because oral communication is generally interactive, it can be quite responsive and adaptive to circumstances. However, this mode of communication has the major disadvantages of being transitory (unless recorded) and subject to considerable misinterpretation. Even when individuals use the same language, the subtle nuances of the spoken word may be missed or incorrect meaning attached to them. Oral communication between those whose first languages differ, as in many management situations today, simply multiplies the chances of intended meaning going awry.

Written Communication   When messages are put in writing, as in letters, memos, electronic mail, and the like, the opportunity for misunderstanding the

The advantage of oral communication is that it is flexible, interactive, and commands attention.

words of the sender are decreased. The receiver may still misinterpret the intended message, of course, but there is no uncertainty about exactly what words the sender has used. In that sense, written communication has precision. However, not everyone writes well, and so greater precision does not necessarily lead to greater understanding. This is further complicated when the words need translation from one language to another. For example, Americans often write when requesting action "at your earliest convenience," meaning that the request is somewhat urgent, but Europeans frequently interpret it to mean they can respond whenever they want. Or consider how Northwest Airline's slogan "Give Wings to Your Heart" was translated into Chinese: "Tie Feathers to Your Blood Pump." Because the writer/sender does not know immediately how well or poorly the message is getting across, written communication has the disadvantage of not being very flexible. In addition, it is often not as vivid or compelling as oral communication. Although you might find it difficult to ignore someone speaking to you, it would probably be much easier to ignore a letter you received.

Nonverbal Communication

In direct interpersonal communication, nonverbal actions and behaviors often constitute significant messages. A whole range of actions, or lack of them, has the potential for communicating. The way you dress, speak words, use gestures, handle utensils, exhibit facial expressions, and set the physical distance to the receiver are just some of the many forms of nonverbal communication.

As a manager, keep in mind that when verbal and nonverbal messages are contradictory, receivers often may give more weight to the nonverbal signals than to the words used. For example, you may say to employees, "I have an open door policy. Come and talk to me whenever you need to." However, if you never seem to be able to find the time to see them or rarely look up from your work when employees enter, they will soon come to believe the nonverbal message, "I'm busy," rather than the verbal message, "I encourage you to talk with me."

JOHNSON & JOHNSON MAINTAINS LINKS THROUGH VIDEOCONFERENCES

Johnson & Johnson (J&J)—a multinational with 168 operating companies in 53 countries—has nearly 30 videoconference facilities worldwide. John Sheanhan, vice president of communications, believes that used properly, videoconferencing is both productive and economical. The benefits include

- Reduced travel costs
- Face-to-face meetings
- Visual aids
- Increased productivity and efficiency
- Immediate information exchange
- Faster response time
- Fewer meeting delays and cancellations
- Improved management communications
- Speedier decision making

The Raritan, New Jersey, and the Zurich, Switzerland, offices of the RW Johnson Pharmaceutical Research Institute (part of J&J) hold joint monthly reviews. In the past, they had to hold the reviews by phone or fly a few people from one side of the world to the other. In the first videoconference, six European experts made a presentation to 22 American professionals. The total cost of the meeting, not including the cost of the videoconference rooms and equip-

ment, was $3,500, less than the cost of bringing one American expert to Switzerland. Today, the cost of this same meeting is only slightly above $1,000.

In most of the J&J videoconference rooms, there are four cameras. Two cameras cover the standard six-seat table (though the rooms have a seating capacity of 22 situated behind the main six seats). The third camera provides close-ups when needed. The fourth camera is used for visual aids—charts, graphs, and so on. A variety of graphic images—photographs, computer-generated graphics, videos, slides—can be captured and beamed to colleagues halfway around the world.

From J&J's perspective, the positives of videoconferencing are many. For example, managers can now engage in interactive discussions rather than reading static reports. John Sheanhan believes that this has resulted in more creative solutions and ideas. He also claims that discussions that would simply not have happened in the past are occurring today. And although some meetings still require travel, they tend to deal with more complex issues and last for several days.

Source: Anthony DeMarco, "Videoconferencing: J&J's Global Link," *Facilities Design and Management* 12, no. 6 (1993), pp. 56–57.

Of course, when nonverbal messages are consistent with the spoken message, the odds of effective communication taking place are increased. For example, suppose that in addition to saying you had an open door policy you looked up when employees entered, made eye contact with them, smiled, and turned away from your computer and the report on which you were working. In combination, what sort of message do you think you would be sending?

The problem for modern managers working with employees from different cultural backgrounds and working across international borders is that there are no universal meanings to the various nonverbal actions. For example, the traditional "OK" sign in the United States is a gesture for money in Japan and is a rather rude gesture in Brazil. You might think that just toning down your nonverbal gestures would be a good way to avoid inadvertent wrong messages. Such an effort would be fine in Finland, but someone in Italy or Greece might infer from your subdued nonverbal cues that you are uninterested in the discussion. Because there is no simple answer, you should learn about the nonverbal cues and gestures of countries and cultures with which you deal the most.

Electronic Communication

Today, electronic mail, or e-mail, has emerged as one of the fastest-growing forms of communication. Ten years ago, you would have been amazed to see someone's e-mail address on a business card. Now, if it's not there, you wonder why. In a recent nationwide survey, 34 percent of the responding executives indicated that e-mail was their number-one choice for business communication.[4] With e-mail you now can communicate routinely with people in another office just down the hall or in another part of the world. With e-mail and faxes, you can send a message simultaneously to dozens or even hundreds of people. Videoconferences have also emerged as a business communication too (see the Managerial Challenge box). A decade or so ago, sophisticated systems that could allow two groups in different locations to see and talk to each other cost $500,000, plus $2,000 an hour for transmission. Now the same systems cost less than $20,000, with $200 an hour for transmission.

THE ORGANIZATIONAL CONTEXT OF COMMUNICATION

Managers do not deal with communication in the abstract. Rather, they deal with it within an organizational context. The structure and processes of organizations powerfully shape the nature and effectiveness of communication that takes place within and between them.[5] Organizations, whether businesses, hospitals, or government agencies, have a set of defining characteristics, all of which affect communication in one way or another.[6] Thus, organizations

- Are composed of individuals and groups
- Are oriented toward goals
- Have differentiated functions
- Have intended coordination
- Have continuity through time

Organizations of any size, regardless of country, are not simply a random set of individuals who by chance come together for a brief period with no purpose. The fact that they have goal orientations, structures, and coordination greatly influences the nature and amount of communication that takes place. This influence can be analyzed in terms of directions, channels, and patterns of communication.

Directions of Communication within Organizations

Because organizations of any degree of complexity have both differentiated functions and more than one level, the directions of communication within them can be classified according to the level for which they are intended:

downward communication
messages sent from higher organizational levels to lower levels

upward communication
messages sent from lower organizational levels to higher levels

lateral communication
messages sent across essentially equivalent levels of an organization

- **Downward communication** is sent from higher organizational levels to lower levels; for example, from the organization's top executives to its employees, or from supervisors to subordinates.
- **Upward communication** is sent from lower organizational levels to higher levels; for example, from nonmanagement employees to their supervisors, or from a manager to her boss.
- **Lateral communication** is sent across essentially equivalent levels of an organization; for example, from one clerical assistant to another, from the manager of Product A to the manager of Product B, or from the marketing department to the engineering design department.

The topics covered in organizational communication vary according to their direction. As shown in Exhibit 15.3, downward communication typically involves such matters as goals, objectives, directions, decisions, and feedback. Upward com-

EXHIBIT 15.3
Directions of Communication within Organizations

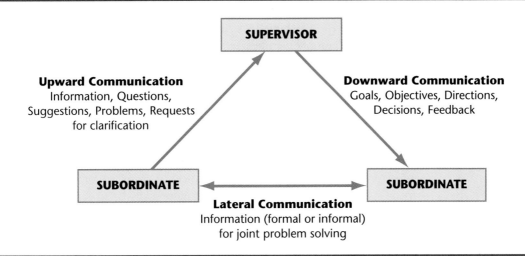

While the subject matter of communication in a particular direction tends to be fairly similar in most medium to large organizations, the culture of the organization (or the culture of the country in which the organization resides) can affect the process. For example, in an organization in which authority and hierarchy are stressed, upward communication might be more formal than in an organization with a more egalitarian culture. As a simple illustration, in the hierarchical organization, a conversation might start with the subordinate addressing a superior several levels above as Mr. or Ms. Jones. In many countries, such as Korea, the conversation might start by addressing the superior by his or her title, such as Director Park. In organizations with less emphasis on hierarchy, the conversation might start by addressing the superior by his or her first name. Likewise, organizational or country culture can influence the frequency and flavor of upward communications. For example, in organizations with strong hierarchical values, upward communication tends to be less frequent.

In summary, organizational communications flow upward, laterally, and downward. The direction of the communication has a significant impact on the type of communication that is likely to take place. However, the culture of the organization and the region or country in which the organization is located can further determine the exact form that communication will have and even the frequency of each direction of communication.

Channels of Communication within Organizations

Organizational channels, or routes of communication, consist of two fundamental types: formal and informal. Both types are essential for organizational functioning, and neither type can easily substitute for the other.

formal communication channels

routes that are authorized, planned, and regulated by the organization and that are directly connected to its official structure

Formal communication channels are those that are authorized, planned, and regulated by the organization and that are directly connected to its official structure. Thus, the organization's designated structure indicates the normal paths for downward, upward, and lateral formal communication. Formal communication channels (shown in Exhibit 15.4) are like highlighted roads on a road map. They specify organizational members who are responsible for tasks and communicating information to levels above and below them and back and forth to adjacent units. Also, formal channels indicate the persons or positions to whom work-related messages should be sent. Formal channels can be modified, and thus they have some flexibility, but they can seldom be disregarded.

informal communication channels

routes that are not prespecified by the organization but that develop through typical and customary activities of people at work

Informal communication channels are communication routes that are not prespecified by the organization but that develop through typical interpersonal activities of people at work. Channels can come into existence and change or disappear rapidly, depending on circumstances. However, they may also endure in many work situations, especially where individuals have been working together over a period of time. If a specific pattern becomes well established, it would ordinarily be called a "network" (to be discussed later).

Several important features of informal communication channels should be noted:

EXHIBIT 15.4

Formal and Informal Channels of Communication in Organizations

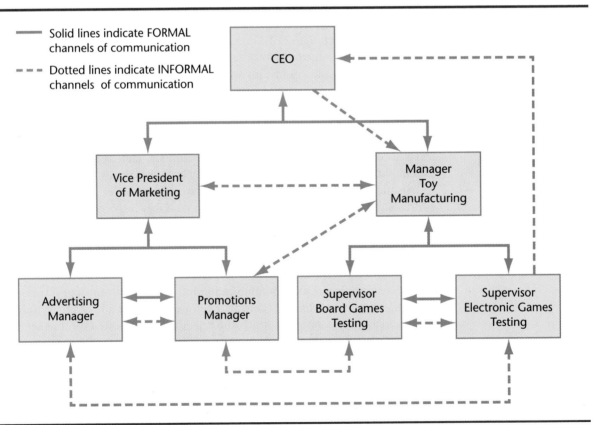

EXHIBIT 15.5	**Formal Communication Channels**	**Informal Communication Channels**
Characteristics of Formal and Informal Communication Channels	• Authorized, planned, and regulated by the organization • Reflect the organization's formal structure • Define who has responsibility for information dissemination and indicate the proper recipients of work-related information • May be modified by the organization • Minor to severe consequences for ignoring them	• Develop through interpersonal activities of organization members • Not specified by the organization • May be short-lived or long-lasting • Are more often lateral than vertical • Information flow can be very fast • Used for both work-related and nonwork information

- They tend to operate more often in the lateral than in the vertical direction compared to formal channels (see Exhibit 15.5) because they are not designated by the organization and its top officials.
- Second, information flowing through informal channels often moves extremely fast, principally because senders are highly motivated to pass information on. The so-called grapevine is a classic example of rapid transmission of messages through informal channels.[7]
- A third feature is that informal channels carry work-related as well as nonwork information. Just because channels are informal does not mean that only gossip and other messages unrelated to jobs and tasks are carried by them. In fact, crucial work-related information is frequently communicated in this way. Of course, some of the messages passed through the informal channels may contain inaccuracies or be negative, and thus seen by some managers as a source of problems. However, few organizations could exist for long if they had to rely only on formal communication channels.

Patterns of Organizational Communication

communication networks

identifiable patterns of communication within and between organizations, whether using formal or informal channels

Identifiable patterns of communication that occur with some regularity within and between organizations, whether using formal or informal channels, are typically called **communication networks**. Put another way, communication networks are stable systems of interconnections. Thus, networks involve consistent linkages between particular sets of senders and receivers. For example, as shown in Exhibit 15.6, a middle-level divisional marketing manager in Los Angeles might have a particular network that involves her boss in New York, three key managers in other departments in the New York headquarters, her seven subordinates located in major Western cities, and two outside vendors of market research data. Another network for the same manager might involve two lower-level managers in other units in the Los Angeles office and their former colleague and old friend who is now a sales supervisor in Chicago and who has access to inside information on how well new marketing approaches are working in that region.

An example of a larger, more organizationwide network would be the Coca-Cola Company's worldwide pattern of communication relationships between its headquarters in Atlanta and its bottlers and distributors. Of course, networks can

EXHIBIT 15.6

Examples of Two Organizational Communication Networks

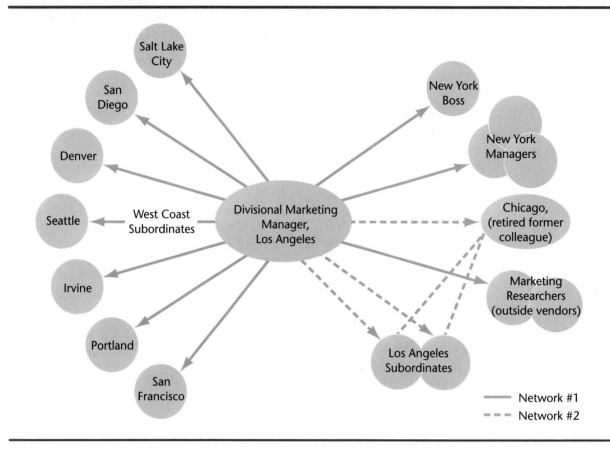

Salt Lake City
San Diego
Denver
Seattle — West Coast Subordinates
Irvine
Portland
San Francisco

Divisional Marketing Manager, Los Angeles

New York Boss
New York Managers
Chicago, (retired former colleague)
Marketing Researchers (outside vendors)
Los Angeles Subordinates

——— Network #1
- - - - Network #2

also be formed across organizations as well as within. This is what often happens when certain sets of managers from two companies—such as Dow Chemical Company and Korea's LG Chemical Company, for example—have to work together on issues that arise in an international joint venture, the LG Dow Polycarbonate Ltd., in this case.[8]

The importance of communication networks to managers is that they can provide significant and regular sources of information, both of the formal and informal type, that might otherwise take a much longer time to obtain if the various links had to be set up from scratch each time some new topic or problem came up. Also, when managers are members of established networks, it can make it easier for them to influence the other people or groups involved in the networks. Consequently, for both of these reasons, managers need to pay particular attention to what networks they can, and want to, be a part of and to the composition of those networks. It is no accident that the term **networking** has come to signify a process that has the potential for gaining advantages for a manager (or anyone for that matter) by having one or more sets of individuals or groups with which one can interact easily and regularly, and with whom one can communicate a sense of confidence and trust.

networking
a process of developing regular patterns of communication with particular individuals or groups to send and receive information

In traditional Western organizations, it has always been relatively easy for males in management positions to establish various networks with other males (thus providing the basis for the phrase "old boys network"). However, at least until very recently, it has been much harder for women and members of underrepresented ethnic groups to establish similar helpful networks in their organizations. Recent research suggests, in fact, that organizational networks involving individuals from these groups are different in terms of both composition and relationships from the traditional networks composed primarily of white males.[9] It does not make such networks any less important or useful to managers from these groups, but does serve to emphasize that network patterns of communication in organizations can vary based on a number of different situational circumstances, including the age, gender, and ethnicity of individuals.

BARRIERS TO COMMUNICATION

Although the organizational context provides numerous opportunities for managers to engage in effective and productive communication to assist in leadership efforts, there are likewise many barriers related to that context that can interfere with the communication process. Such barriers can arise from several different sources, including interpersonal, organizational, and cultural (see Exhibit 15.7).

Interpersonal Barriers

Obstacles to interpersonal communication can occur with either the sender or the receiver. The burden is simultaneously on both the sender and the receiver to ensure accurate communication. It is, however, the sender's obligation to choose

EXHIBIT 15.7
Barriers to Communication

Level	Origin of Barrier	Affects Communication Between:
Interpersonal	Selective perception Frame of reference Emotion Language Nonverbal cues	Individuals or groups
Organizational	Hierarchical (barriers resulting from formal structure) Functional (barriers resulting from differences between functional departments)	Individuals and/or groups within an organization Individuals and/or groups in different organizations Organizations
Cultural	Language High/low context culture Stereotyping Ethnocentrism Cultural distance	Individuals or groups in different organizations with different national cultures Individuals or groups from different organizational cultures Individuals or groups from diverse cultural backgrounds within an organization

the language and words—to encode the message—carefully to carry the greatest precision of meaning. Precision is especially important if the sender is trying to persuade the receiver to do something in a language or communication style different from what the receiver prefers. For example, if you are talking with your boss trying to convince him or her to authorize a new project and you use an informal style and choice of words, your boss may not be receptive if he or she prefers a more formal approach. You will probably need to adjust your style for the communication to be effective.

The receiver, of course, is often the source of communication breakdowns. For example, the receiver might have a **selective perception** problem.[10] That is, the receiver may unintentionally screen out some parts of the intended message because they contradict his beliefs or desires. For example, you might stress the increased productivity from a proposed project, but your boss is focusing on the estimated cost of the project. Although selective perception is a natural human tendency, it hinders accurate communication, especially when sensitive or highly important topics are being discussed. Another way to state this point is that individuals tend to adopt **frames of reference**, or quick ways of interpreting messages that help them make sense of complex communications, but these shortcuts may prevent the intended message from being received.[11]

Emotions can be another barrier.[12] How the receiver feels at the time can influence what gets heard or how it gets interpreted. You certainly have had the experience of feeling that someone was "touchy" or overly sensitive when responding to your message. As a consequence, comments that normally would be taken as mere statements get taken as criticisms.

Language can also be a barrier. Even for people who speak the same language, words mean different things depending on a person's age, education, gender, and so on.[13] For example, saying "That's a bad haircut" to a 50-year-old means something completely different than if it was said to a 15-year-old. The 50-year-old will likely interpret the words to mean that the barber did a poor job. The 15-year-old will likely take the statement to mean he looks cool.

Nonverbal cues can also be barriers to effective communication in two basic ways. First, people can send nonverbal signals without being aware of them, and therefore create unintentional consequences.[14] For example, you might make minimal eye contact with your boss while trying to convince her to approve your proposed project, and yet be unaware that you are doing so. Your boss might think the project has merit but interprets your low level of eye contact as an indication that you are hiding something. Your boss could then reject a project that she might otherwise have authorized. Second, as we have already touched on, nonverbal cues can mean different things to different people.[15] A weak handshake might indicate politeness in Indonesia but communicate lack of confidence in Texas.

Organizational Barriers

Just as interpersonal barriers can limit communication, so can organizational barriers. Such barriers can interfere with communication between individuals or groups within the same organization, between individuals or groups from two different organizations, or between entire organizations. The basis of these barriers lies within the hierarchical structure of organizations. All organizations of any complexity have specialized functions and more than one level of authority. This spe-

selective perception
the process of screening out some parts of an intended message because they contradict our beliefs or desires

frames of reference
existing sets of attitudes that provide quick ways of interpreting complex messages

cialization creates a situation that is ripe for communication difficulties. For example, one person might come from marketing and the other from research and development. The person in marketing might think nothing of exaggerating while the person from research and development always understates her points. Consequently, the marketer might see the R&D scientist as unimaginative and boring, while the scientist might view the marketer as superficial and careless. In addition, the two parties might come from different levels in the organization. The differences between responsibility and level of authority could cause a senior executive to expect an explanation of the broad impacts on the entire organization of a proposed project and a junior technical expert to focus on the detailed schedule of the project.

Cultural Barriers

Communication and culture are tightly intertwined. Culture cannot exist without communication, and human communication only occurs within a cultural context. Since the act of communicating is so closely connected to the surrounding environment, culture can ease or hinder it. Thus, similarity in culture between senders and receivers facilitates successful communication—the intended meaning has a higher probability of getting transferred. Differences in culture hinder the process. The greater the cultural differences between sender and receiver, the greater the expected difficulty in communicating. Therefore, other things being equal, it should be easier, for example, for an American manager to communicate with an Australian subordinate than with a Greek subordinate.

Organizational cultures can also differ. The industry of an organization, for example, can influence its internal culture as we pointed out in Chapter 3. Therefore, it is more likely that an executive at Warner Brothers could communicate successfully with an executive at Disney than with an executive at Exxon. It is not that extreme cultural differences prevent good communication; rather, the possibilities for breakdowns in communication increase in proportion to the degree of differences in the background and customs of the two parties.

The extent to which a sender and receiver differ in a high-context or low-context communication style also significantly influences the effectiveness of the communication. As we discussed in Chapter 4, individuals in high-context cultures tend to pay great attention to the situational factors surrounding the communication process and as a consequence substantially alter what they say and how they say them based on the context.[16] (See Exhibit 15.8.) Individuals in low-context cultures tend to pay less attention to the context and so make fewer and smaller adjustments from situation to situation.[17] Although the greatest difference in high and low context is across countries, there are also such differences across organizations. For example, Japan is a high context culture that has three distinct levels of language that a speaker uses depending on his or her status compared with that of the listener. Thus, there are actually five different words for "you" that are used depending on relative rank and status. However, even within Japan, communication is much more high context in Mitsubishi Heavy Industries than in Nintendo.

What is most problematic when individuals from high- and low-context cultures communicate is that each often forms negative interpretations about the other's communication approach. Individuals from low-context cultures tend to interpret the wide swings in words and style indicative of people from high-context cultures

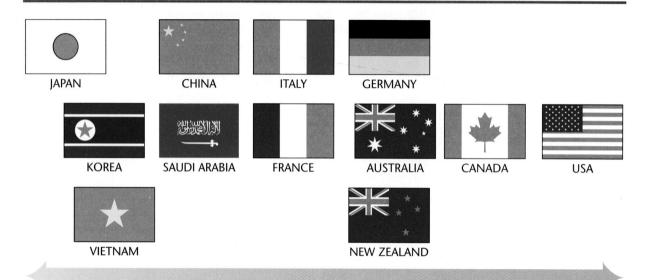

EXHIBIT 15.8

Communication Differences in High- and Low-Context Cultures

JAPAN   CHINA   ITALY   GERMANY

KOREA   SAUDI ARABIA   FRANCE   AUSTRALIA   CANADA   USA

VIETNAM   NEW ZEALAND

HIGH-CONTEXT CULTURES
- More and greater adjustments in messages
- Rank of receiver will probably affect message and medium
- Nonverbal communication cues may be very important
- Medium may be as important as message

LOW-CONTEXT CULTURES
- Fewer and smaller adjustments in messages
- Rank of receiver may or may not affect message or medium
- Nonverbal communication cues not as important
- Message is more important than medium

as evidence of insincerity, hypocrisy, and even instability. These interpretations make trust difficult and at the extreme can make effective communication impossible. On the other hand, individuals from high-context cultures view the lack of change in communication style of individuals from low-context cultures as evidence of immaturity, selfishness, or lack of sophistication.

In cultures such as that of Japan, managers are taught that to communicate effectively, you should "say what you mean, and mean what you say."[18] Vague directives and instructions are seen as a sign of poor communication skills. The assumption, therefore, is that the burden of proof for effective communication is on the speaker. In contrast, in cultures such as those in Arabic countries and in Latin America, the assumption is that both the speaker and the listener share the burden for communicating effectively. In cultures in which speaker and listener share communication responsibilities, chances of unpleasant encounters and direct confrontations and disagreements tend to decrease.

Managers in today's global businesses need to recognize cultural differences and how they can affect communication. In increasingly diverse work settings, culture is of paramount importance because it allows you to anticipate communication problems and make appropriate adjustments in advance.

ethnocentrism
the belief in the superiority and importance of one's own group

Probably the greatest single cultural barrier that can affect communication across different departmental, organizational, regional, or national cultures is ethnocentrism.[19] **Ethnocentrism** is the belief in the superiority of one's own group and the related tendency to view others in terms of the values of one's own group. Ethnocentrism leads individuals to divide their interpersonal worlds into in-groups and out-groups. As we discussed in Chapter 11, in-groups are groups of people with whom you identify and about whom you care.[20] Members of the in-group tend to be trusted, listened to, and have information shared with them. Members of out-groups tend to be viewed with suspicion and are not given full information. This type of behavior exists in organizations as well as in interpersonal interactions. When British European Airways merged with British Overseas Airways Corporation some years ago to form the British Airways that we know today, the ethnocentric orientation of each side almost led to the bankruptcy of the merged unit, which lost nearly $1 billion before the communication barriers were overcome.

Another cross-cultural barrier to communication closely related to ethnocentrism is stereotyping, the tendency to oversimplify and generalize about groups of people. The more firmly held the stereotype by a communicator, the harder it is to overcome preconceived expectations and focus on the specifics of the message that is being sent or received. Stereotyping occurs both within and between cultures and thus it affects communication in virtually all organizational settings. For example, suppose you are a technical service manager in a software company and the president has a strong stereotype of people in your position. Generally, the president sees technical service managers as focused on details and unable to see the big picture. With a strong stereotype of this sort, the president may not recognize that you understand and are considering competitive implications (not just the technical ones) of a new software tool.

cultural distance
the overall difference between two cultures' basic characteristics such as language, level of economic development, and traditions and customs

A third major cultural barrier to communication can be labeled **cultural distance**.[21] This concept refers to the overall difference between two cultures' basic characteristics such as language, level of economic development, and entrenched traditions and customs. Cultural distance was illustrated by a study that gathered 21 senior executives from major corporations in Japan, the United States, Brazil, the United Kingdom, and India for a five-week period of cultural explorations. The executives attended lectures and seminars, built rafts and climbed cliffs together, and even traveled in fact-finding teams to the countries represented. Nevertheless, observers reported that communication remained a problem the entire five weeks.[22] Although much of the difficulty came from obvious language differences, a more subtle difficulty came from cultural differences. Many of the Japanese managers, attempting to fit in, adopted American nicknames, but they actually hated being called by them. The Americans couldn't understand why the Japanese were so quiet, not realizing that they felt that it was unwise to speak first at a meeting. The more senior the Japanese executive, the more he listens, and the executives on this trip were quite senior. Similarly, a development project undertaken by Alcan Aluminum Ltd. of Canada and the Chinese National Nonferrous Corporation brought together managers from both firms to learn more about each other's culture. Even though a set of managers from China spent a whole year in Canada studying North American business methods, effective communication remained an elusive goal throughout the period for both sides.[23] Such examples emphasize that the degree of cultural distance between organizational employees from different nationalities represents a potentially very difficult communication barrier to overcome. The severity of the problem should not be underestimated.

IMPROVING COMMUNICATION

The various barriers that were discussed in the preceding section can interfere with effective communication, but there are ways of dealing with, or overcoming, them. That is the subject of this section: approaches that will help to improve your communication as a manager in organizations. The following paragraphs summarize some of the most important methods for reducing barriers and communicating successfully.

Improving Listening Skills

When the subject is improving communication skills, most people first think of improving their speaking or writing skills. However, contrary to popular belief, probably the single best thing you can do to enhance your communication skills is to focus on improving your receiving rather than sending skills.

Be More Openminded   Stereotyping, enthnocentricity, rigid frames of reference, and selective listening can all become barriers to comprehending the intended message of a sender, so one of the first things to do to enhance listening skills is to spend time developing a greater awareness of personal tendencies in the direction of any of these problems. Once you have a better awareness of these tendencies, you can monitor and control them during conversations. Part of the reason for direct and conscious attention to this area is that most people speak at about 120 words per minute and yet can listen at about a rate of 1,000 words per minute.[24] This creates the opportunity for the mind to wander or make judgments about what we are hearing. These tendencies can distort what is heard and how it is interpreted.

empathy
the ability to put yourself in someone else's place to understand their feelings, situation, and motives

Develop Empathy   Once personal tendencies have been examined, the next step is developing empathy. **Empathy** is identifying with and understanding the other person's feelings, situation, and motives. To some extent, this requires thinking about the situation of other people. What are their feelings relative to the topic at hand? What are their motivations? Why are they talking about what they are? These and other questions can help you enhance your understanding of the personal context of the message being sent.

Listen Actively   The next step to improving communication is to take actions to ensure that the receiver hears and understands what the sender is trying to communicate. In conversations, making eye contact is a good way to help speakers feel comfortable and convinced that you are sincerely interested in understanding what they have to say. It is important to focus more on the content of the message than the style of its delivery. Even if people are not choosing the best words or are making grammatical errors, they may have something quite valuable to communicate. Focusing on style over substance can cause the value of the message to be missed. To make sure you understand what is being said, ask clarifying questions. Also, even when you think you have understood the message, it is a good idea to paraphrase, that is, restate what you think the message is. This can be put in the form of a question or statement. For example, you could ask, "So are you saying that ...?" or you can put it more directly by saying something such as, "What I understand you to be saying is ...."

Observe Nonverbal Cues   As we discussed earlier in this chapter, nonverbal cues are critical to effective communication.[25] Listening more open-mindedly and actively to the words is only part of the task. You also need to concentrate on observing nonverbal cues. In cross-cultural settings, this means that you need to remember that a nonverbal cue or gesture can have different meanings in different cultures. There is little substitute for learning about the nonverbal cues and gestures of the culture of those with whom you will be interacting.

Improving Sending Skills

There are many situations in which you will be the sender of a message. Effective communication can be enhanced by developing better sending skills.

Simplify Language   One of the first things a sender can do to enhance communication is to simplify the language in the message. Clearly, what is simple will vary depending on the audience. Simplifying may involve eliminating jargon that may not be familiar to all members of the audience. It may also involve choosing more succinct and active words and shorter sentences. Perhaps the best clue for spotting complicated and passive language is excessive use of prepositions. The more prepositions in a sentence, the higher the likelihood that the language could be simplified and the message could be stated more directly.

Organize Writing   Executives consistently complain about the poor writing skills of new managers.[26] Their complaints lie not in spelling or grammar mistakes, though clearly these should be eliminated, but in the lack of logical thought processes. As a manager, you are likely to write more reports and memos than you may want, and the effectiveness of those written communications will have an important impact on your career. Consequently, developing good writing skills is vital to being an effective manager. Nothing substitutes for practice.

Understand Audience   Perhaps the single best thing a sender can do to enhance the effectiveness of communications is to understand the audience.[27] For example, consider the following questions, which come from the material we have covered thus far in the chapter:

- What is the direction of the communication (up, lateral, or down), and does the receiver have any expectations concerning this type of communication?
- Is the communication formal or informal, and how should it be structured to have the intended impact on the receiver?
- Are there expectations from the receiver about the explicitness or implicitness of the message you want to send?
- Does the receiver have any biases for or against certain modes of communication (e.g., for or against e-mail, face-to-face conversations, and so on)?

If you do not understand the person or persons to whom you are sending a message, it is almost impossible to answer these questions. Knowing your audience

EXHIBIT 15.9

Tips on Being a More Effective Cross-Cultural Communicator

1. Study general principles that apply to all types of intercultural communication.
2. Learn about the fundamental characteristics of the other cultures with which you will be working.
3. For high-context cultures, learn as many details in advance about the target organization(s) and their specific individual representatives.
4. For high-context cultures, use at least a few words or phrases in the listener's language.
5. For high-context cultures, be especially careful about body language and tone of voice.
6. For low-context cultures, organize written communications so that the major points are immediately and directly stated.
7. Study and respect communicators' preference for greater degrees of formality, especially compared with the typical American approach of casual informality.

(i.e., the receiver or receivers) is critical to improving your sending skills. Knowledge of the audience is particularly important in cross-cultural settings, and Exhibit 15.9 lists some tips to improve cross-cultural communication.

Organization-Level Improvements in Communication

Organizations can take steps to change their policies and methods for how and when managers should communicate. Unfortunately, guidelines for this more structural approach are not as well developed as those for individual managers. A recent study of research and development laboratories within 14 large multinational firms, however, did provide some suggestions.[28] The study produced strong evidence for the importance of **gatekeepers**, or so-called "boundary-spanning" individuals who are at the communication interface between separate organizations or between units within an organization. Large companies especially need to be able to structure the activities of gatekeepers to maximize their usefulness to the communication process and to make sure that the most critical information is both sent and received. Findings from the study indicated that communication could be improved by implementing rules and procedures that increased formal communication, replacing some face-to-face communication with electronic communication, developing particular communication networks, and even creating a centralized office to manage communication activities.

gatekeepers
individuals who are at the communication interface between separate organizations or between different units within an organization

COMMUNICATION AND NEGOTIATION

negotiation
the process of conferring to arrive at an agreement between two different parties, each with their own interests and preferences

In the last sections of this chapter, we focus on one particular type of communication that is especially crucial to management, namely, negotiation. **Negotiation** can be thought of as the process of conferring to arrive at an agreement between two parties, each with their own interests and preferences. The purpose of negotiation is to see whether the two parties can arrive at an agreement that serves their mutual interests. Since reaching an agreement inherently involves communication, negotiation and communication are inseparably linked. Thus, the negotiation process can be considered a special case of the general communication process.

The Importance of Negotiation to Managers

Today's managers often find themselves in the role of negotiator. Previously, managers assumed the role of quality checker after work was completed, but in a dynamic environment where employees increasingly make decisions, often as a member of a team, managers have taken on the role of facilitator—ensuring that all parties can agree on a common course of action.

A certain amount of disagreement is healthy in any organization; otherwise, the organization would stagnate and lose its competitiveness. Negotiations about disagreements can occur between units or departments within an organization as well as between individuals. For example, the manager of the marketing department may negotiate with the head of the engineering department to try to agree on the features for a new product. Consequently, as such an example illustrates, the principles of negotiation can apply to the settlement of any disagreements that a manager might encounter inside or outside an organization.

compromise

part of negotiation in which parties agree to receive only part of what they wanted

Managers have available several potential tactics for use in negotiation. The key to negotiation is for the interested parties to come away with an agreement on what they are willing to give up and what they will receive in exchange, in other words, a **compromise** is often needed. In compromising, neither party gets everything they want, but they mutually agree to receive part of what they originally wanted. Compromise involves dividing up existing resources so that each party gets a portion of those available.

collaboration

part of negotiation in which parties work together to attack and solve a problem

Another useful tactic for managers who are involved in negotiation is to lessen the competition between the two parties (an "I win, you lose" situation) and establish collaboration (a "we all win" situation). **Collaboration** is an attempt to get both parties to attack a problem and solve it together, not have one party defeat the other. Thus, they may use creative approaches to brainstorm solutions, that is, to increase the total amount of resources so that all receive more, pull in other parties to assist with a problem, or look outside the organization for assistance—whatever can help solve a problem and provide parties with better solutions. As previously discussed in Chapter 11, often managers can assist the negotiating parties to concentrate on substance and improving a problem with a *system* in an organization, rather than on the *people* using the system and their interpersonal differences.

Finally, if managers find that negotiations are extremely complex and the parties seem emotionally invested in the outcome, they can often request intervention by a neutral third party. Sometimes managers within an organization but outside the problem may be asked to serve in this role. The third-party negotiator can serve the role of judge, mediator, or devil's advocate. In the role of a judge, the manager handles negotiations and decides on the best course of action, which parties then agree to follow. In mediation, the manager controls the negotiation process, but someone else makes the final decision based on the arguments presented—possibly a senior executive in the organization. As we have discussed in other chapters, a devil's advocate asks questions that may oppose the interests of both parties. The attempt here is for all parties to consider positions that they may not originally have considered.

In today's global organizations, managers may also become involved in negotiations across national borders. With advances in transportation and communication

EXHIBIT 15.10

Important Characteristics Needed by Negotiators in Four Countries

U.S. Managers	Japanese Managers	Chinese Managers (Taiwan)	Brazilian Managers
1. Preparation and planning skill[a]	1. Dedication to job	1. Persistence and determination	1. Preparation and planning skill
2. Thinking under pressure	2. Ability to perceive and exploit power	2. Ability to win respect and confidence	2. Thinking under pressure
3. Judgment and intelligence	3. Ability to win respect and confidence	3. Preparation and planning skill	3. Judgment and intelligence
4. Verbal expressiveness	4. Integrity	4. Product knowledge	4. Verbal expressiveness
5. Product knowledge	5. Listening skill	5. Interesting	5. Product knowledge
6. Ability to perceive and exploit power	6. Broad perspective	6. Judgment and intelligence	6. Ability to perceive and exploit power
7. Integrity	7. Verbal expressiveness		7. Competitiveness

[a]Note: Characteristics are listed in order of importance.

Source: J. L. Graham and Y. Sano, *Smart Bargaining: Doing Business with the Japanese* 2nd ed. (New York: Harper Business, 1988).

technologies, coupled with the general worldwide reduction of controls over cross-national flows of capital, organizations engage in increasing amounts of foreign trade and international business partnerships. All of this activity greatly increases the importance of managers' abilities to negotiate successfully in cross-national circumstances as well as in one's own organization or country.

Key Factors in Negotiation

Analysis has shown that there are three principal variables that determine the outcome of negotiations: the people involved, the situation, and the process itself.[29] Research from an array of internationally-oriented studies also indicates that each of these variables is strongly influenced by cultural differences.[30]

People Although there are some cultural differences in preferred negotiator characteristics, there seem to be some traits and abilities that are fairly universal for the task of negotiation. They include good listening skills, strong orientation toward people, and high self-esteem, among others.[31] In addition, ability to be influential in the home organization appears to be a commonly preferred personal attribute.

Opinions about the qualities of effective negotiators do vary in different countries, however. Exhibit 15.10 lists the qualities U.S. and other managers think are important for effective negotiators. As the exhibit indicates, the opinions about the qualities of effective negotiators vary considerably by culture. For example, U.S., Japanese, Chinese (Taiwan), and Brazilian managers differ in the importance they attach to "ability to win respect and confidence"—it is rated much higher in the two Asian cultures than in the other two cultures. For American and Brazilian managers, planning skills and judgment and intelligence rated as more highly desired negotiator characteristics than they did in the two Asian cultures. But there are also differences even between the two Asian cultures. The Japanese placed highest importance on "dedication to the job," whereas "persistence and determination" ranked number one with the Taiwanese.

Situations of Negotiations   The second major variable affecting negotiation outcomes is the set of situational circumstances. Probably the most important are location of the negotiations, the physical arrangements, the emphasis on speed and time, and the composition of the negotiating teams.

Location.   Typically, there is a strong tendency to want to negotiate on your own turf or at neutral sites, especially for critical negotiation. The so-called "home court advantage" seems to be universal; everyone feels more comfortable and confident, and has greater access to information and resources, when negotiating at home. For international negotiations, negotiations conducted in a manager's own offices or even in his or her home country can be a psychological advantage.

Characteristics of locations, however, can vary by culture. For example, in the United States almost all negotiations occur in a formal setting, such as an office or conference room. In contrast, in Japan and Mexico, where relationship-building is crucial, major parts of the process are likely to occur in an informal or nonwork setting, such as a restaurant or golf course. In Korea, the final contract produced from the negotiations is likely to be signed in a formal and public setting rather than in someone's office.

Physical Arrangements.   The usual American approach to setting up a room for negotiations is to place the two parties on opposite sides of a table, facing each other, which has the obvious effect of emphasizing competing interests. Other arrangements are possible, including seating the two parties at right angles or along the same side "facing the problem" or at a round table where all are part of the total problem-solving effort.[32]

Physical arrangements for negotiations typically place two parties on opposite sides of the table, but alternatives such as seating the parties at right angles can be used to place less emphasis on competing interests.

Emphasis on Speed and Time.   Americans typically avoid wasting time. They want to "get right to the point" or "get down to business." Other cultures differ from that viewpoint. In Mexico or China, for example, the norm is to invest considerable time in relationship building and other activities not directly related to the central negotiation process. Consequently, in such cultures, speed is sacrificed, and the effectiveness and efficiency of subsequent negotiations often hinge on how well relationships have been developed.

Composition of the Negotiating Teams.   The composition and size of teams representing the two parties in negotiations can also influence negotiations. For example, the more people involved at the negotiation table, the more preparation that needs to be done to ensure that the team presents a united front. The composition of the team in terms of decision-making authority is also important. If individuals at the table have authority to make binding decisions, the negotiations are generally more efficient than if they do not.

Team composition can vary significantly by culture. In countries that are sensitive to status differences and ranks (for example, Singapore, India, Venezuela, Japan), having similar status, position, age, and authority between the negotiating teams is much more important than in other countries (e.g., New Zealand, Canada, United States). The size of negotiating teams also can differ markedly by culture. In the United States, where go-it-alone heroes are admired, team size is ordinarily much smaller than in more collectivist-oriented cultures such as those of Taiwan, China, and Japan. The resulting mismatch in size can communicate unintended messages. Taiwanese, for example, might interpret a single negotiator or a small team as a sign that the other party does not consider the negotiations to be important. Similarly, Americans might interpret the presence of a large team from a Taiwanese firm as an attempt to intimidate them with numbers.

The Negotiation Process   The third, and probably most crucial, variable determining the outcome of negotiations is the negotiating process itself. Exhibit 15.11 shows the five common stages in the negotiation process. This process is basically the same across all cultures.[33]

Stage 1: Planning and Preparation.   This stage involves laying the foundations through advance planning and analysis prior to any face-to-face interactions. At this stage, individuals or teams conduct background research, gather relevant information, and plan their strategy and tactics. In addition, preliminary decisions are made about what the objectives will be and what can and cannot be conceded during the course of the negotiations.

Stage 2: Relationship-Building between Negotiating Parties.   This stage is commonly referred to as "nontask time," in which each side attempts to establish comfortable working relationships with the other side. As we pointed out earlier, Americans are inclined to make this stage briefer and believe such activities are relatively unimportant. On the other hand, negotiators from some other cultures such as Latin America, the Middle East, and Asia believe exactly the opposite. Research suggests three types of behaviors during this stage: developing trust, developing personal rapport, and establishing long-term association.[34]

Stage 3: Information Exchange.   In this stage, each party attempts to learn about the needs and demands of their counterparts. Managers from the United States often attempt to hurry through these activities with an attitude of "you tell me what you want and I will tell you what I want."[35] In contrast, managers from

EXHIBIT 15.11

The Five Stages in the
Negotiating Process

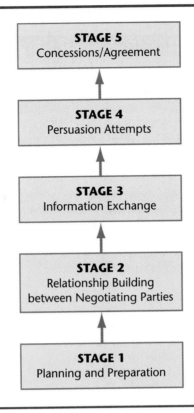

EXHIBIT 15.11

The Five Stages in the
Negotiating Process

Asian cultures take a much more indirect, more drawn out, and more thorough approach to acquiring and exchanging information. Arabic and Latin American managers appear to follow a similar approach, except that the latter are even more leisurely in their use of time at this stage.[36]

Stage 4: Persuasion Attempts. This stage focuses on attempts to modify the position of the other party and to influence that side to accept the negotiator's desired set of exchanges (e.g., an exchange of a certain price for a certain quantity or quality of goods or services). American managers usually treat this as the most important stage, with assertive and straightforward efforts to obtain a desired conclusion. Such persuasion can sometimes involve the use of warnings or threats to try to force the other party to agree.[37] Managers from Arabic countries tend to show similar tactics as those of Americans at the persuasion stage, but they are less inclined to hurry. Negotiators from Asian cultures take a slow, careful approach but do not tend to use direct assertiveness in persuasion until later in the negotiations. As reported in one research study, "when not sure of the offer, they frequently resort to the tactics of 'pretending to lack authority' or 'deliberately delaying [a] counter offer.'"[38] Managers from Latin American cultures tend to use a mixture of approaches during this stage by showing a moderate degree of assertiveness but also a willingness to use the tactic of "calculated delay" when this seems advisable.[39]

Stage 5: Concessions/Agreement. At this final point, if reasonable progress has been made, compromises and concessions are made that permit each party to take away something of value. Since American managers tend to begin the negotiation process with positions fairly close to what they will finally accept, they do not have

MANAGERIAL CHALLENGE

AMERICAN–JAPANESE NEGOTIATIONS

The United States is Japan's largest trading partner. Japan is the United States' second-largest trading partner after Canada. Given the critical economic (as well as political and military) relationship between the two countries, opportunities for negotiations occur frequently. Unfortunately, the two countries differ substantially in their approaches to negotiations.

If you think of negotiations as a dance, then Americans and Japanese are moving to quite different music and, as a consequence, toes get stepped on during the process. Based on the five fundamental processes of negotiations, we can map the importance each culture places on each stage and how much time each tends to spend at each stage. As the diagram illustrates, the differences in patterns make for an awkward dance.

Both Americans and Japanese value and spend time on preparation, but Japanese spend slightly more time. However, they differ dramatically at Stage 2. While Americans place relatively little value on, and do not spend much time on, developing relationships, Japanese are just the opposite. Japanese also spend more time on, and more highly value, the exchange of information than Americans.

Both cultures place significant value on persuasion and on the conclusion of negotiations. However, the two critical timing differences are that by the time Americans want to be well into the persuasion stage (Stage 4), the Japanese are just wanting to end the relationship-building stage (Stage 2). As the diagram also demonstrates, Japanese tend to take more time overall for negotiations.

At the conclusion of negotiations, when negotiating with each other, Americans typically rely on long and extremely detailed contracts that explicitly spell out the obligations of each party and the penalties for noncompliance. In Japan, on the other hand, written agreements are often quite short and only describe the general intentions and obligations of the two parties. The last paragraph of such agreements in Japan may simply state that if disagreements arise, both parties will try to resolve them in good faith.

Unless adjustments are made on one side or the other, or by both parties, even though the two cultures share the same basic sequence of negotiation stages, misunderstandings can easily develop from the difference in importance attached to each stage and how long each stage typically lasts.

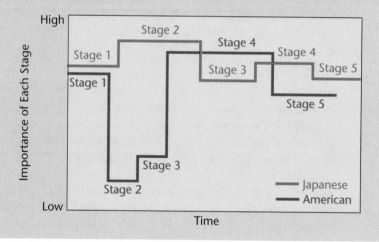

much leeway for concessions.[40] Managers from Arabic and Latin American countries seem to open negotiations from more extreme positions, which permit them to offer concessions late in the process. Managers from Asian countries often employ "normative appeals" (such as "it's your obligation") to try to get the other party to offer concessions.[41]

The Managerial Challenge box explores the five stages of negotiation between two cultures—Japan and the United States.

CONCLUDING COMMENTS

As we emphasized at the beginning of this chapter, being able to become a good communicator, and to know how communication works as a process in an organizational context, is essential for becoming an effective manager and leader. In fact, most experienced managers will tell you that communication skills are vital to career success, and a variety of studies support this claim. The first key to becoming a better communicator as a manager is to understand the basic communication process. But that is only a starting point. Although the process seems simple enough, the major challenge is to be able to implement that process successfully on a regular and consistent basis. That, in turn, requires applying your knowledge about the nature of organizations and some of the other key functions of managing (such as planning, organizing, and leading) that have already been discussed in previous chapters.

If good communication were easy, then everyone would be able to do it, and do it often. However, in any organizational context, there are always barriers and obstacles that interfere with effective communication. It is critically important, therefore, to be very aware of these potential obstructions in order to be able to take steps to overcome and deal with them. Communication, in fact, is an excellent example of a management activity where there is a great cost to naiveté and inexperience and a great benefit to be gained by awareness and analytical insight. Very few people are naturally superb communicators, but there is ample opportunity to become a much better communicator if you focus effort on developing that awareness and insight.

With respect to the importance of communication and negotiation, it is especially helpful in your management career if some understanding of the process of negotiation can be added to your repertoire of communication skills. As we noted in the chapter, negotiation is a particular type or form of communication—because of the up-front recognition and acknowledgment of different interests and preferences as the starting point for the process. Various factors, such as cultural differences, can increase the difficulty and complexity of the process. Again, however, like communication in general, being able to become a better negotiator is a capability that can be improved through developing greater expertise and understanding about the process and through practice that involves thoughtful analysis and careful consideration of the results and how and why they were obtained.

KEY TERMS

collaboration 461
communication 443
communication networks 451
compromise 461
cultural distance 457
decoding 444
downward communication 448
empathy 458

encoding 443
ethnocentrism 457
formal communication
   channels 450
frames of reference 454
gatekeepers 460
informal communication
   channels 450

lateral communication 448
medium 443
negotiation 460
networking 452
noise 444
selective perception 454
upward communication 448

REVIEW QUESTIONS

1. Why is oral communication usually more compelling than written communication?
2. What is it about oral communication that allows it to be flexible?
3. Why must nonverbal cues be consistent with verbal cues for the intended message to be communicated effectively?
4. What are the principal advantages of e-mail?
5. What are the potential benefits of videoconferencing?
6. What are the typical differences in content of upward, downward, and lateral communication within organizations?
7. What are the typical characteristics of formal communication channels?
8. Why do informal communication channels tend to operate more in lateral rather than vertical directions?
9. How are selective perception and frames of reference related?
10. In what way can emotions become a barrier to effective communication?
11. What are the principal differences between high-context and low-context cultures relative to communication?
12. What is ethnocentrism and how does it impair effective communication?
13. What are the key differences between stereotyping and ethnocentrism?
14. How can an organization's culture affect the three basic directional flows of communication?
15. What are the key elements of active listening?
16. Why does simplifying language tend to improve communication effectiveness?
17. What are the three principal variables involved in nearly all negotiations?
18. Describe each of the five stages of negotiations and how they can contribute to the overall outcome.

DISCUSSION QUESTIONS

1. Despite the considerable emphasis that most companies and other types of organizations put on communication, why do you think that many employees feel there is inadequate communication with and from their managers?
2. Assume that you are now working in the first truly management position in your career. What is likely to be the most important communication issue/problem you will face in the first few months in that position?
3. Will the probable continued increase in electronic communication within and between organizations be likely to increase or decrease the communication issues/problems faced by the typical manager? Explain the reasoning behind your answer.
4. How can a knowledge of the basics of negotiation assist managers in doing their day-to-day activities, especially in regard to exercising leadership and influence? Can you provide examples?

CLOSING CASE

Collaboration Software: Revolutionizing Organizational Communication

We used to think of communication as a spoken conversation, a written memo, a combination of gestures. The computer has changed that, and perhaps even changed the way organizations are structured and managed. Only a few years ago, Lotus developed a software package called Lotus Notes, which allowed workers to trade notes on projects, schedule meetings, and share databases. Then a Xerox researcher, Pavel Curtis, came up with an idea for even more flexible communication by computer; he cofounded PlaceWare, Inc., and began to market his new product.

PlaceWare software provides its users with an opportunity to interact with others much the way they might in an Internet chat room. For instance, PlaceWare's first product was a virtual auditorium that contained colorful graphics. A manager can "take the stage," give a presentation complete with slides or other illustrations, and get feedback from an "audience" that might be scattered around a building, the country, even around the world. This way, hospital doctors can attend a virtual seminar; salespeople can attend a virtual training session; regional managers can hold a nationwide virtual meeting. They can listen to a presenter, ask questions, even converse among themselves. What has this meant, in tangible terms, for various companies?

Management consultants at McKinsey & Co. have been able to set up virtual chat rooms to discuss problems and solutions for clients. "There is no single expert who can duplicate the power of a large group of people with different experiences," notes John Hagel III, a McKinsey principal.

Using a similar product—Dassault's Catia, marketed by IBM—Chrysler gathers engineers, designers, and even factory workers to help design a new automobile or improve the design of an existing one. "Any time anyone changes a bolt, we can see how it affects every aspect of the car," says Peter Rosenfield, director for advanced technology planning at Chrysler.

With a third product, created by Netmosphere, a sales manager in San Francisco can send a message to a salesperson in Fresno asking that he or she call on a particular customer. The salesperson must answer the request with a clear yes or no; he or she cannot ignore the message or fudge an answer. Furthermore, the Netmosphere program is capable of sending out automatic reminders and even automatically noting completed tasks on a virtual schedule. This cuts down on the amount of busywork for a sales manager, allowing the manager to focus on training, development of new customers, and other important communication.

With collaboration software, often called groupware, a committee of managers at Xerox can review proposals for new products and inventions, then set priorities to pursue. They can communicate with each other—as well as designers and engineers—by attaching audio comments and even screen drawings to a presentation. "The software allows us to do more complex work much more quickly," says Thomas Moran, a scientist for Xerox. "It also gives us the capability to go back later and analyze the work process itself."

In all of these cases, communication is faster, more precise, and more effective. Everyone who needs to be involved can be involved simultaneously, so problems can be raised, addressed, and solved.

Software like this functions in another way, as well: It can showcase lower-level employees who now have the forum to present their ideas and solutions; it can also highlight workers who contribute less than is expected to their organization. Employees now have greater access to senior managers and greater knowledge about what is happening companywide (including globally). This means that, while an organization may still have a formal hierarchy, greater access to information and ease of communication among employees of different levels may begin to flatten the organizational structure. "There's no doubt that this type of technology can level organizations and empower different people," observes Eric Hahn, senior vice president of Netscape. (Hahn founded a firm called Collabra, which made collaboration software that featured on-line discussion groups. He later sold the company to Netscape.)

The new generation of collaborative software has removed some potential barriers to effective communication (such as overzealous or ineffective gatekeepers), even changed the channels and direction of communication (the lines between formal and informal communication may be blurred, and communication may travel upward, downward, or laterally at once). Thus, future managers will most likely factor this new technology into their communication styles, taking advantage of the flexibility it offers them.

QUESTIONS

1. How can managers maximize the advantages of this type of communication software?

2. What are likely to be the managerial problems that arise with using this software?

3. Could this type of software be used in almost any type of organizational situation? Where might it work best and least well?

Sources: Rita Koselka, "The Hobby That Is Changing the Business World," *Forbes,* October 6, 1997, pp. 104–108; Mike Heck, "Meet Me on the Internet," *InfoWorld,* 20, no. 23 (June 8, 1998), p. 74.

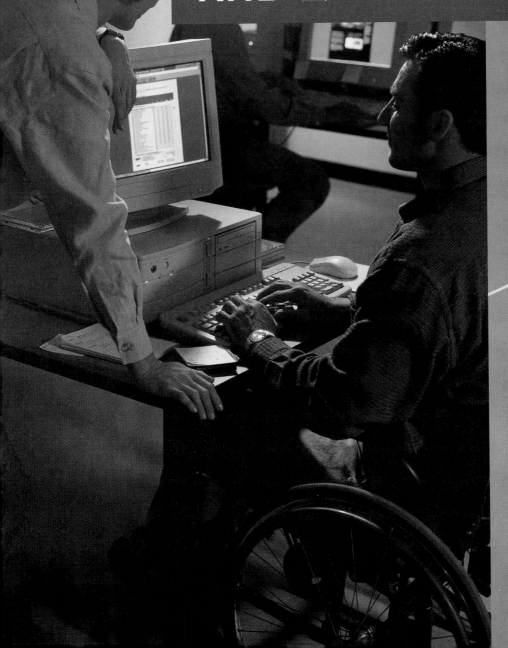

PART 6

MONITORING AND EVALUATING

CHAPTER 16

CONTROL

After studying this chapter, you should be able to:

- Discuss the effects of too much or too little control in an organization.
- Describe the four basic elements of the control process and the issues involved in each.
- Differentiate between the different levels of control and compare their implications for managers.
- Explain the concept of standards and why they are so important in organizations.
- Compare bureaucratic and clan controls.
- Identify the important qualities required for information to be useful in the control process.

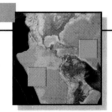

How Much Control Is Enough?

Can a single individual topple an entire multinational corporation? The answer is, surprisingly, yes. The lack of control at Barings' investment bank sank the 233-year-old British bank and rocked the financial world. In early 1995, a 28-year-old trader caused one of the most spectacular collapses in modern financial history. When the dust finally settled, Barings had suffered trading losses in excess of $1 billion. Ironically, just two years earlier, Peter Baring, the company's CEO, had stated in a speech, "[Financial] derivatives need to be well controlled and understood, but we believe we do that well here."

Baring Brothers was one of the oldest and most prestigious banks in Great Britain, a bank to the House of Windsor. In 1803, one of the Baring ancestors had financed the Louisiana Purchase for the United States. Barings' money had also helped to keep British armies in the field during the Napoleonic Wars. The Baring family had run the firm for 233 years, and Peter Baring was carrying on the tradition.

In 1992, Barings sent Nick Leeson to assume a post as the chief trader of Baring Futures in Singapore. Leeson traded futures contracts on the

Nikkei 225, Japan's version of the Dow Jones index. His job was to exploit the small differences in the buying and selling of these contracts, otherwise known as arbitrage. The trading of futures was considered a relatively safe bet, since generally only small profits or losses could be racked up at one time. But Leeson became more sophisticated in his trading knowledge, and he became more bullish.

On January 17, 1995, a massive earthquake devastated Kobe, Japan, and the Nikkei responded with uncertainty. Later that month, the Nikkei plunged more than 1,000 points. For Barings and for Leeson, this natural disaster turned into a financial disaster. The traders in the Far East panicked, and in particular Leeson.

Leeson laid huge bets on the rebound of the Nikkei. While traders at other investment banks cut their losses, Leeson sank Barings' money into billions of dollars' worth of futures contracts that would only make money if the Nikkei rose. Traders in Tokyo and Singapore watched, but they figured that the bets that Barings was making were offset by hedges in other areas. But this turned out not to be the case. For every percentage point that the Nikkei slipped, Barings lost tens of millions of dollars. Eventually, the losses exceeded Barings' net worth.

Whether senior management really knew what was going on in Singapore is not clear. Someone at the London headquarters knew, because Leeson had bought bets with borrowed funds, a common practice. As Leeson's bets lost, Barings in London funneled $900 million to Singapore to offset the losses. By late February, the Nikkei had not bounced back, and Leeson and his wife skipped town.

Barings went bankrupt on February 26. As British regulators took control of the bank, Interpol, the international intelligence agency, sent out an alert to all governments in neighboring countries to find Leeson. A few days after the bank's collapse, the "rogue trader" walked into the arms of police at Germany's Frankfurt airport.

How could such a large, prestigious bank like Barings be so naïve to the public activities of a single trader?

Sources: Pavia Dwyer, "Descent into the Abyss," *Business Week,* July 1, 1996, pp. 28–29; Stephen D. Kaye, "Ripples from a Fallen Bank," *U.S. News & World Report,* March 13, 1995, pp. 68–72; Bill Powell, Daniel Pedersen, and Michael Elliott, "Busted!" *Newsweek,* March 13, 1995, pp. 36–43.

Managerial control problems occur in sophisticated organizations and in all countries. The example in the opening paragraphs makes this abundantly clear. If a major multinational corporation such as Barings can have difficulties with control, so can organizations of smaller size, fewer resources, and less complex systems. Likewise, if these kinds of problems can develop within a firm headquartered in the

United Kingdom and doing business across the globe, they can occur in any location or culture where managerial activity takes place. Exercising effective control is a universal and exceedingly important managerial challenge.

Probably the most critical part of that challenge, for individual managers as well as for organizations, is where to draw the line between too much control and too little control. Most of us can think of examples from our own work or other group experiences where we have encountered the downside of excessive control by individuals or supervisors or the organization itself through its rules and regulations. At the extreme, overcontrol conjures up images of "Big Brother," where you cannot make a move without first obtaining permission from someone higher up in the organizational structure.[1] More typically, too much control can result in resentment and squelched motivation.

At the other extreme, too little control, as illustrated in the opening example, can expose an organization and its managers to very costly risks. In milder forms, undercontrol contributes to sloppy operations and failure to utilize resources efficiently and effectively. Errors or mistakes can increase, and the organization may not know where or when problems are occurring and, particularly, how to fix them. In severe cases, the potential consequences can be catastrophic for the organization, as they were for Barings.

Exercising control, then, presents not only major challenges for managers but also difficult dilemmas. The issue gets further complicated by the fact that, as we will discuss later, there are different types of control. A certain type of control may be quite effective in one situation but very ineffective or even damaging in different circumstances. The bottom line is that managers, no matter where they are in an organization or at what level, will have to deal with fundamental questions of control.

To explore the issue of control, we first look at the role that control plays in organizations and the way it relates to other managerial functions such as strategy and planning. Next, the four basic elements of the control process—establishing standards, measuring performance, comparing performance against standards, and evaluating results (and, if necessary, taking action)—are reviewed. Following this is a discussion of the different levels of control (strategic, tactical, and operational) and the various forms of control. The chapter concludes with an examination of factors that can influence control effectiveness, such as the focus, amount, and cost, and how consideration of these factors leads to crucial managerial choices.

THE CONTROL FUNCTION IN MANAGEMENT

control

regulation of activities and behaviors within organizations; adjustment or conformity to specifications or objectives

On the face of it, the word "control" sounds negative. It can mean restraints, constraints, or checks. This clearly connotes restricted freedom of action—an idea that many people, especially in some cultures, may find troublesome. Certainly, within the context of organizations, **control** involves regulation of activities and behaviors (see Exhibit 16.1). To control, in an organizational setting, means to adjust or bring conformity to specifications or objectives. In this sense, then, the control responsibilities of managers do involve restricting somebody's freedom. A manager cannot control without restricting. However, whether this is good or bad for the individual or group that is the object of the control, for the manager who determines the amount and type of control, and for the organization at large depends on the consequences of the control and whose perspectives are being considered.

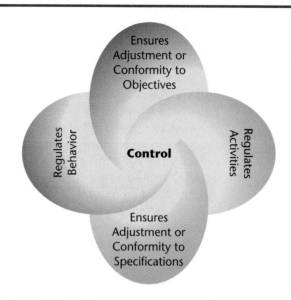

Some amount of control in organizations is unavoidable. The very essence of organizations is that individuals give up total independence so that common goals and objectives may be accomplished. As one organizational scholar put it, "The coordination and order created out of the diverse interests and potentially diffuse behaviors of members is largely a function of control."[2] Thus, control is a fundamental characteristic of organized activity. Managers should always keep in mind, however, that control is a means to a goal and is not the goal itself (see the Managerial Challenge box, "Steak Right").

The managerial function of control comes at the end of a chain of the other major functions of planning, organizing, and leading. (Indeed, that is why a chapter on control is almost always found toward the end of management textbooks.) If those prior functions are carried out well, generating positive responses to controls will be much easier. Conversely, if major problems exist in planning, organizing, and leading, almost no amount of attention to control is likely to work very well. In this sense, effective control is a managerial function that depends heavily on the other functions that precede it. When they work well, control tends to work well. When they don't, control can become a major headache for a manager.

Control can also be thought of as an independent, or causal, variable because the results of control efforts can inform and improve the planning process of the organization. Control is thus part of a feedback loop into planning and organizing (see Exhibit 16.2) that can help managers adapt to changing circumstances and conditions. When either the internal or external organizational environment changes, good control systems let managers know if the current ways of operating are still meeting objectives. For example, during the late 1980s and 1990s, sales agents within Prudential Insurance Company increasingly tried to increase their revenues and their personal bonuses based on increased sales through "churning." The churning involved persuading customers who had long-standing policies with built-up cash value to take out new, bigger policies on the promise that these new policies would not cost them more. Customers were not told that the cash values of their old policies were being used to pay the higher costs of the new policies. So

MANAGERIAL CHALLENGE

STEAK RIGHT

For fine restaurants, cooking is an art, not a science. The reputation of the food at fine restaurants is usually a function of the chef and his or her creativity. So the ideas of standardization and tight control are generally alien to upscale restaurants.

This is not the case with Morton's Restaurant Group, a company that has more than 30 expensive steak houses and runs many aspects of them with McDonald's-type precision. Morton's CEO, Allen J. Bernstein, firmly believes that tight controls are the key to his firm's financial success. Within 10 years, the company quadrupled the number of its restaurants, and net income has risen as well.

The controls start with the "bible." This phone book–thick illustrated binder prescribes, ingredient by ingredient, the preparation of the 500 items coming from the kitchen. The binder exactly specifies everything from the sauces to a medium rare porterhouse steak. The presentation of the food is also not open to individual interpretation. Color photographs line the wall of every Morton kitchen. Evaluation of presentation then becomes a relatively easy matter. Either the dish to be served looks like the photograph, or it doesn't. The push for control is so stringent that each restaurant has a food and beverage controller, a 12-hour-a-day job, focused on tracking the movement of every item. Even the potatoes must meet rigorous standards.

"I weigh every potato," says Andrew Moger, a food and beverage controller in the Manhattan Morton's. "They have to be at least a pound apiece."

The adherence to portion regulation and presentation is coupled with a successful cost control and inventory tracking system. "We have systems in place that can tell us if we've lost a single steak," says President Thomas J. Walters. This is no small matter with such valuable inventory .

The result is a consistent atmosphere and a dependable menu. Customers come to Morton's with complete confidence. "I like knowing what to expect," says one regular customer who uses Morton's for business entertaining. "You never worry about the food or service. When business is involved, you can't trust things to chance."

The consistency produced by the highly developed control system has made Morton's a desirable tenant in the buildings it rents. This is important given the company's plans for further expansion. "Landlords want to use us as an anchor," explains CEO Bernstein. "We're in demand because developers can get other tenants if we're there. Of course, they want their new Morton's to be like the old ones in every way." And they will be.

Source: G. Collins, "A Big Mac Strategy at Porterhouse Prices," *The New York Times*, August 13, 1996, pp. C1 and C4.

EXHIBIT 16.2

Control's Feedback Loop

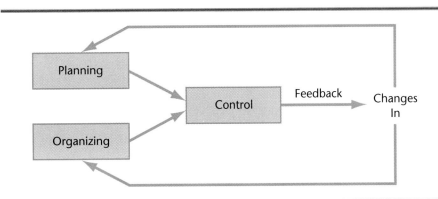

while the customers were not laying out any more cash in monthly premiums than they did before, the new policies were, indeed, costing them. An audit performed by Coopers & Lybrand in 1994 warned senior management of excessively high turnover among "mature policies." Unfortunately for Prudential, while this control provided an early warning signal, managers did not do enough to investigate, and the company was hit by a raft of lawsuits.[3]

THE BASIC CONTROL PROCESS

The basic elements of the control process in an organizational setting are simple and straightforward (see Exhibit 16.3):

1. Establish standards
2. Measure performance
3. Compare performance against standards
4. Evaluate results (of the comparison) and, if necessary, take action

Each of these basic components involves important managerial attention and decisions.

Establish Standards

Specification of what management expects is absolutely critical at each step of the control process. This starts at the top of the organization and, ideally, should eventually involve every level of employee. First and foremost, those at the highest levels should be able to articulate a vision and formulate broad strategic goals for the organization. For example, as we saw in Chapter 8, Microsoft had a vision of having its operating system on every personal computer. From this example, it is easy to see how **standards**, or targets of performance, might be developed. Without a strategic vision and goals for the overall organization, managers in various parts of the organization find it difficult to develop meaningful and agreed-upon performance yardsticks.

The establishment of standards, wherever they exist throughout the organization, requires as much specificity as possible. The reason for this is that measuring performance against standards cannot be readily accomplished if the standards are vague. A standard of "efficiently responds to customer complaints," for example, does not provide usable guidelines for determining whether the standard has been

standards
targets of performance

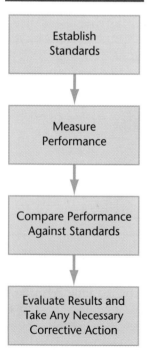

EXHIBIT 16.3

The Basic Elements in the Control Process

Establish Standards

↓

Measure Performance

↓

Compare Performance Against Standards

↓

Evaluate Results and Take Any Necessary Corrective Action

The service standard for Caterpillar dealers is to provide around-the-clock support to customers around the world, enabling customers to obtain service and spare parts delivery anywhere in the world within 24 hours.

EXHIBIT 16.4

The Effect of Specificity of Standards on Performance Measurement

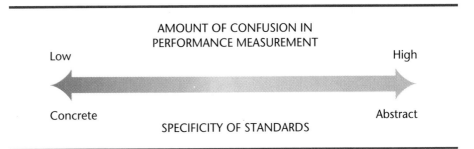

AMOUNT OF CONFUSION IN
PERFORMANCE MEASUREMENT

Low   High

Concrete   Abstract

SPECIFICITY OF STANDARDS

met. A standard of "responds, on average, to three customer complaints per hour" would permit an objective measurement of performance.

However, for some aspects of performance, especially in higher-level and more complex jobs such as those in research laboratories, it is often not possible nor even desirable to set up easily quantified standards. In those positions, the most important elements of performance may be the most difficult to measure. Moreover, in the earlier example, the *quality* of response to customer complaints may be more important than the *rate* of response, but quality is more difficult to measure. As shown in Exhibit 16.4, the more abstract the standard, the greater the possibility of confusion in measuring performance, and the greater the problem of gaining the acceptance of those measurements by members whose performance is being assessed.

Two other issues also arise in the establishment of standards (see Exhibit 16.5). One revolves around the issue of who should set the standards. In general, research has shown that in setting such standards as budgets, participation by those who will be affected is beneficial in two respects.[4] First, because they have had some opportunity to influence the standards being set, those affected are more likely to be committed to meeting them. Second, involving those who have to meet the standards often results in a useful exchange of information and expertise that, in turn, results in more appropriate standards. At Tenneco Gas, a unit of Tenneco Inc., for example, each employee negotiates with his or her supervisor to produce a performance agreement that includes detailed information on how that employee will be responsible for hitting specific performance targets.[5]

EXHIBIT 16.5

Issues in Establishing Standards

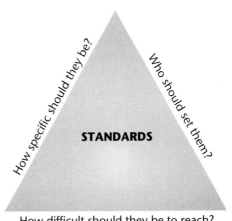

STANDARDS

How specific should they be?

Who should set them?

How difficult should they be to reach?

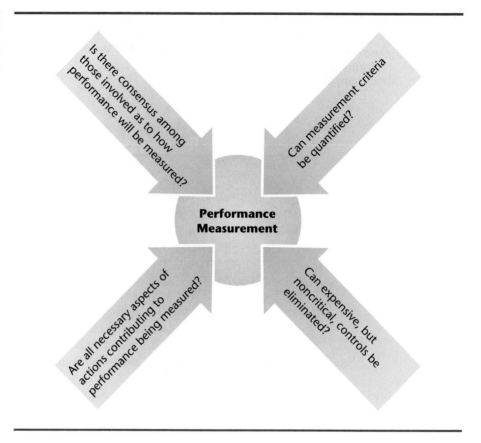

EXHIBIT 16.6

Issues in the Measurement of Performance

Is there consensus among those involved as to how performance will be measured?

Can measurement criteria be quantified?

Performance Measurement

Are all necessary aspects of actions contributing to performance being measured?

Can expensive, but noncritical, controls be eliminated?

A second issue is the degree of difficulty of the standards themselves. As we saw in the chapter on motivation, the research on goal setting points to the conclusion that difficult but achievable goals seem to result in the highest levels of performance.[6] Similar views have been expressed regarding the budgetary process. Thus, "the ideal budget is one that is challenging but attainable" (that is, where there is "at least a 50 percent chance of achieving the budget amount").[7] Achievable budget standards are regarded as desirable because they reduce the motivation to manipulate data and focus only on short-term actions at the expense of long-term objectives. Achievable budgets also have the potential for increasing morale and generating a "winning atmosphere."[8] This assumes, as noted, that the budgetary targets are not only attainable, but also reasonably difficult. Here, again, where to draw the line between goals that are too challenging and those that are not challenging enough is itself a managerial challenge.

Measure Performance

The second step in the basic control process is the measurement of performance, the actions of people and equipment that the organization wants to monitor (see Exhibit 16.6). In the mid-1980s, the Bank of America faced a crisis. Both its stock price and earnings per share had been dropping precipitously for several years, and in 1985 the bank suffered a loss of half a billion dollars. This situation was blamed on, among other factors, "runaway operating expenses, sloppy credit monitoring, [and] loose controls...."[9] The CEO at the time resigned, and a former CEO, Tom

Clausen, was brought back to rescue the company. He immediately impressed upon the employees the importance of measuring and controlling costs. He provided data showing that the bank spent $.70 to obtain $1 of business. He set a goal of reducing those costs, and within a year he managed to lower the figure to $.63 and get the bank on the road to recovery.[10] If specific and concrete standards have been set, as in this example, measurement is facilitated and there is more likely to be agreement on *how* performance is to be measured.

When readily quantifiable criteria do not exist, however, it becomes especially important to obtain as much consensus as possible about the way in which performance is to be assessed. To use an analogy, when true/false or multiple-choice tests are used in a class, the score a student receives is seldom contested (even though the quality of the questions often is). On the other hand, the score given to the answers on a test composed of essay questions is frequently disputed between student and teacher. The more the instructor and the class members can agree in advance about the qualities of good answers and on how the essay questions will be graded, the more likely that the measurement process will be accepted. This occurs even though the measurement process is clearly subjective. Similarly, in work situations, gaining up-front commitment to the performance measurement methods will reduce later complaints about what those measurements showed and what they mean to individuals and to the organization.

Since performance in many jobs involves multiple activities, it is important for measurement to be comprehensive. If only some aspects of performance are measured, results can be misleading; they can skew the data that are used for the next two steps in the control process, especially the taking of action to change performance. Companies such as Kodak, Corning, Polaroid, and Exxon utilize a comprehensive control technology called "Stage-gate" throughout the life of a project. Each project is divided into several stages with "gates" between them. Collectively, the gates act as comprehensive quality control checks that have to be passed before the gate will open, allowing the project to move on to the next stage. This allows management, at each gate, to review the progress of the project and decide whether it merits continued funding.[11]

Finally, even though measurement should be comprehensive, not everything that possibly could be measured should be measured. Measurement has a cost, and the usefulness of the information obtained may not justify the costs. The issue here is one of criticality, that is, what is measured should be highly relevant to the goals of the organization. Activities that are necessary but that do not provide relevant indicators of progress toward goals do not justify the expense to measure them.

Compare Performance against Standards

Comparing performance results against previously set standards is the third step in the control process. Just as performance measurement is strongly influenced by the standards, so are comparisons affected by the kinds of measurements available. If key measurements have *not* already been built into the system, it is usually not possible to go back and reconstruct them for purposes of comparison. Sometimes managers realize too late that appropriate comparisons cannot be made.

When several dimensions of performance have been measured, this step in the process can involve multiple comparisons. If those comparisons all point in the same direction, interpretation is relatively straightforward. However, the picture of performance that emerges from a set of comparisons may be inconsistent or contradictory. That is, some comparisons may show good adherence to standards and targets, and others may reveal problems. So managers need to know how to interpret the patterns of comparisons and to draw appropriate conclusions. A single negative comparison may outweigh a number of positive comparisons, or vice versa.

For example, after a major restructuring, Safeway found that its sales per grocery store had nearly tripled and its sales per employee had also risen by 70 percent. Overall profits were up, but customer satisfaction scores were down. What is a manager to make of this? In Safeway's case, sales per store and per employee as well as overall profits were up because it had sold off or closed its least profitable stores (many of which were operating at a loss). All of this might paint a very positive picture. However, the fact that customer satisfaction was down was potentially a very bad sign. Grocery stores make money through volume. Therefore, if dissatisfied customers were to start spending less at Safeway and more at competitors, the positive results could deteriorate rapidly. Consequently, placing too much emphasis on per-store sales compared with customer satisfaction would be a control mistake.

In this third control step, managers need to compare expected performance with actual performance. These comparisons often involve both subjective estimates as well as objective ones. However, even if the comparison involves only objective, quantitative numbers, judgment is still needed. For example, suppose Safeway's customer satisfaction numbers were down from 5.5 to 5.2. Anyone can compute that customer satisfaction had declined by 0.3 point. However, the key question is, "Is this drop significant?" The answer to this question requires managerial judgment.

Evaluate Results and Take Action

The fourth step, evaluate results and take action, is arguably the most difficult managerial task in the entire control process. The results that emerge from the performance comparisons may or may not require action. Managers need to consider whether any single comparison or a pattern of comparisons require action to be taken. If actual performance deviates from expected performance, how much of a difference is required before something is done about that difference? That question has no single answer. It requires evaluation of the importance and magnitude of the deviation.

An analogy illustrates what is involved in this type of judgment. In industrialized countries, the directors of the national banking system, the Board of Governors of the Federal Reserve System in the case of the United States, periodically receive the most current data about the national economy, for example, the unemployment rate, the consumer price index, the index of consumer confidence, the rate of new starts in home building, and the like. These data are compared against predetermined benchmarks, and then a decision must be made about whether to take action (e.g., increase interest rates). The problem for the board, as for any manager in an organization, is to determine which data are most important and how much of a change is significant. However, the issue is even more complicated. Managers must determine whether a slight change in the same direction for all of the indicators is more or less important than a major change in just one indicator. As any macroeconomist would testify regarding the national economy, this type of judgment is not easy.

The other basic judgment that must be made in this fourth step is *what* action to take if the pattern and size of deviations from expected performance are determined to be significant. Managers need knowledge about the causes of the deviation as

EXHIBIT 16.7

Outcomes of Performance Measurement

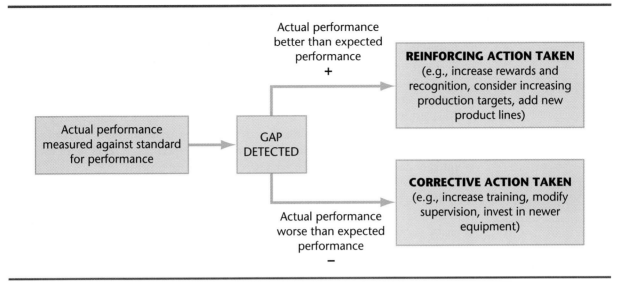

well as about the potential actions that are possible. Recently, McDonald's, one of the largest advertisers on U.S. television, discovered through their quarterly review of advertising that spending at their main advertising agency was $20 million over budget. Consequently, the company took several steps to correct the situation: It requested that TV networks pay the company back in cash rather than free airtime when a sponsored event does not produce sufficient viewership, it reduced the number of 60-second ads and substituted less costly 30-second ads, and it shifted advertising from expensive networks to cheaper cable channels.[12]

Clearly, the evaluation and action step of control requires managers to have strong diagnostic skills as well as a certain level of expertise. Sometimes, the causes of a problem may be easily recognized, but which actions to take may be extremely difficult to decide. Conversely, the most effective actions may be well known, if only the causes could be clearly identified.

If a manager discovers major negative differences between performance and standards, some type of action is clearly needed because failure to act can lead to more severe problems in the future. However, if the deviations are major but positive, the necessity for action is usually much less (see Exhibit 16.7). Nevertheless, positive differences may provide valuable insights about unexpected opportunities that should be pursued. For example, a major maker of baby food discovered stronger-than-expected sales of its new line of toddler foods in Florida. Further investigation revealed that the increased sales were not due to a higher-than-expected number of toddlers, but to older customers with teeth problems who bought the product because it was easier to chew. This led to a whole new line of packaged foods targeted at this particular customer segment.

To help maintain positive performance, employees who are doing better than expected can be given increased recognition and rewards to reinforce their excellent performance. Likewise, sales that exceed their forecast may mean that production should be increased or the product line should be extended. Costs that are below target may suggest an efficient practice that could be duplicated for other employees to follow to reduce the costs even further. In short, it is as important to evaluate surprises on the upside as it is on the downside.

One other issue is involved in determining what action managers should take in the case of significant deviations from standards (whether in the positive or negative direction). This is the judgment about whether the standards are correct and the performance is the problem, or whether the performance is appropriate but the standards are too difficult or too easy. If a great deal of effort and care has been used in setting the standards and participation in setting them was broad, then the issue is probably likely to be one of performance. If, though, the standards have been set hastily or without appropriate input from relevant parties, then performance may not be the problem. This kind of issue points out once again the tight interconnection of the four basic steps of the control process.

SCOPE OF CONTROL IN THE ORGANIZATION

Even though the four steps of the control process are similar wherever they occur in organizations, the scope of what is being controlled can vary widely. This, in turn, affects how the steps are actually put into use. A bank provides a simple illustration. The bank manager may need to assess whether she has an adequate level of deposits relative to outstanding loans. The scope is quite broad because the outcome of this assessment could affect the entire organization. If the ratio is too low, the bank may need to reduce its level of lending or try to get more deposits. On the other hand, the manager may also need to evaluate the ratio of human bank tellers to automatic teller machines at each branch. In this case, the scope is much narrower because the issue only involves a small part of the bank's activities. In the former instance we would label the scope as "strategic," and in the latter it would be regarded as an "operational" control issue. These represent two of the three major categories of control scope. The third, and intermediate between strategic and operational, is a category typically called "tactical."

In the remainder of this section, we look at the issues involved in each of these three types of control classified by the breadth of their scope. However, it is useful to remember that no hard-and-fast boundaries separate the three types (see Exhibit 16.8). The differences between strategic and tactical control issues often are

---

EXHIBIT 16.8

Scope and Overlap of Control Issues

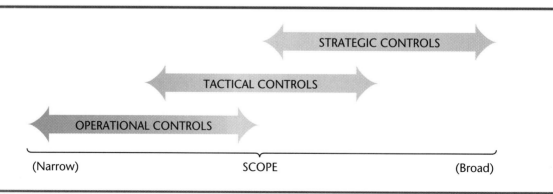

blurred, and likewise, it is not always clear whether a control issue should be considered tactical or operational. Nevertheless, the three categories help remind managers where they should focus their attention.

Strategic Control

strategic control

assessment and regulation of how the organization as a whole fits its external environment and meets its long-range objectives and goals

As discussed in Chapter 8, strategy refers to the direction for the organization as a whole. It is linked to the mission of the organization and to the basic plans for achieving that mission. Thus, **strategic control** is focused on how the organization as a whole fits its external environment and meets its long-range objectives and goals. Strategic control systems, where they exist, are designed to determine how well those objectives and goals are being met.

A particular challenge in formulating strategic controls is the fact that strategic goals are broad and, especially, long term. This means that such goals typically are more abstract than goals for particular units. Consequently, setting strategic standards and measuring strategic performance can be especially challenging. For this reason, research has shown that only a relatively small number of firms in both Europe and the United States have yet set what could be termed strategic control systems.[13] The numbers will undoubtedly increase in the future, but important obstacles interfere with establishing such systems.

A significant factor that affects whether strategic control systems can be set up and whether they will be effective is the unpredictability of the external environments in which many organizations operate and from which they obtain resources. This also makes it difficult to develop standards and measures that are relevant for more than short periods of time. In fact, it is particularly difficult for firms to develop useful criteria for assessing the long-term performance of individual managers.[14]

Environmental conditions for multidivisional companies and those with several different types of strategic business units (SBUs) affect how much leeway each division or SBU is given in determining its own competitive strategies for dealing with its particular markets.[15] Metropolitan Life Insurance Company learned the difficulty of this challenge the hard way. The company, like many others, decentralized in the 1970s. The corporate headquarters gave considerable control over products offered and sales approaches to its individual field offices. However, in 1994, a major problem occurred. It was discovered that sales agents in one of its Florida offices were targeting nurses nationwide to sell life insurance policies described as retirement accounts. Premiums for the insurance were labeled as retirement fund "deposits." This misleading practice eventually resulted in repayments and other compensation to some 31,000 clients, with costs totaling over $100 million. As a result, top corporate management recentralized the control function, and branch offices now have much less autonomy over products offered and agent compensation.[16]

As this example illustrates, the issue is essentially one of how much strategic control systems should be centralized versus decentralized, and how much variation should be allowed by unit. Such a decision involves not only matters of strategy but also of organization structure (Chapter 10).

Research indicates that "the efficiencies of managing through centralized control may be greater ... when the operating environments of divisions in multidivisional organizations are relatively stable and predictable" (see Exhibit 16.9).[17] However, when there is more uncertainty in the environment, centralized control becomes inefficient. In other words, in relatively turbulent environments, it is difficult for

EXHIBIT 16.9

Degree of Centralization of Control in Relation to Environmental Stability

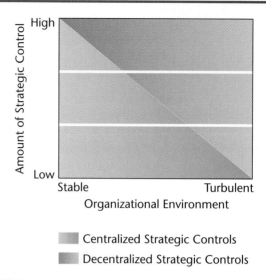

centralized strategic control systems to keep up with events, and, consequently, more responsibility for control must be delegated to the divisions. When the environment is changing rapidly, as it is for many companies these days, too much reliance on organizationwide strategic goals and standards of performance that are set too far in advance can interfere with the needed speed and flexibility of the various operating units to respond effectively to the environment.[18]

As shown in Exhibit 16.10, both the degree to which it is possible to measure precisely how well performance conforms with strategic goals and the degree of turbulence or uncertainty in the environment can affect the value of having strategic control systems.[19] They are most likely to be useful when measurement is easy and operating environments are relatively calm, as in the case of the cement industry. Although this industry basically follows the ups and downs of the construction industry, the factors that significantly affect these movements are relatively well known. For example, changes in interest rates have a significant impact on building booms and busts. As rates go down and money is cheaper to borrow, construction increases. As rates go up and money becomes more expensive to borrow, construction decreases. Thus, for a concrete firm, strategic controls such as being number one in sales in a region can be relatively useful.

Conversely, strategic controls are probably least useful when exact measurement is difficult and the environment is fluctuating rapidly. As recently as five years ago, putting up a Web site for a company involved contracting with a vendor that specialized in the unique and various languages used on the Internet. Companies providing such services have seen their world change dramatically. New languages and tools have emerged so that almost anyone with a little skill and knowledge can create a professional-looking Web site. In such a turbulent environment, strategic goals do not last long. Therefore, strategic controls are of more limited value in these types of organizations.

Strategic control is especially challenging in international organizations. Even with advances in communication and transportation technology, Sydney is still a long way from Paris. Consequently, strategic control across a worldwide organization

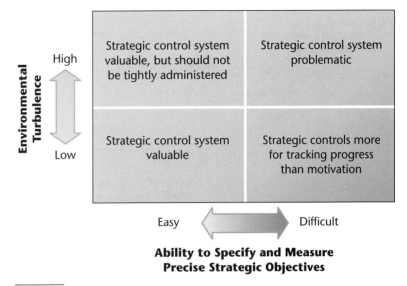

Source: M. Goold and John J. Quinn, "The Paradox of Strategic Controls," *Strategic Management Journal* 11, no. 1 (1990), pp. 43–57 (p. 55).

that crosses cultural, economic, social, political, and religious borders and is 16 time zones away is significantly more difficult than for a purely domestic organization.

Tactical Control

tactical control

assessment and regulation of the day-to-day functions of the organization and its major units in the implementation of its strategy

Tactical control focuses on the implementation of strategy. Thus, this level covers the fundamental control arrangements of the organization, those with which its members have to live day to day. Tactical control forms the heart and, one might say, the soul of an organization's total set of controls. Four of the most important types of tactical control systems are financial controls, budgets, the supervisory structure, and human resource policies and procedures.

The first two types of control, financial and budgetary, contain elements of both strategic and tactical control systems. To the extent they focus on the entire organization, they tend to be more toward the strategic end of the continuum (see Exhibit 16.11), and the more they focus on specific units within an overall organization, they tend to be toward the tactical end. We have chosen to discuss them in this section since they most often focus on organizational units, but keep in mind that they, especially financial controls, can also be used as well for some strategic control considerations.

Financial Controls   Financial controls include several important quantitative ratios involving key financial statistics. Although such financial data are always generated at the organizationwide level as well as at the organizational-unit level, they are especially useful at the unit level as a form of tactical control.

profitability

ratio of cost to benefit

The data used for the most important financial controls involve a basic cost–benefit analysis. For example, ratios relevant to the **profitability** of a given unit are constructed from revenue data (benefit) in relation to given amounts of investment

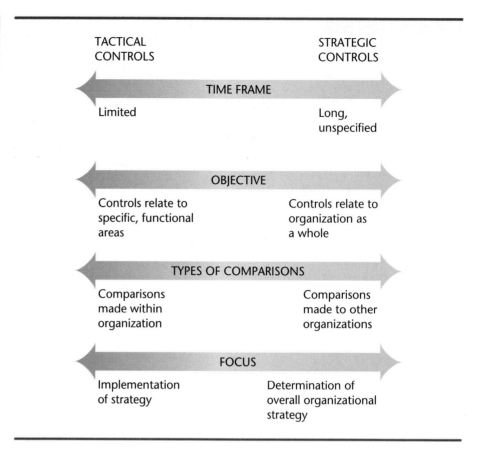

EXHIBIT 16.11

Characteristics of Strategic and Tactical Control

ROI (return on investment)
measure of profitability obtained by dividing net income by the total amount of assets invested

ROE (return on equity)
alternative term for ROI

liquidity
measure of how well a unit can meet its short-term cash requirements

leverage
ratio of total debt to total assets

efficiency (activity)
ratio of amount of sales to total cost of inventory

(cost). The ratio is called **ROI** (return on investment, or alternatively, **ROE**, return on equity) and compares the amount of net profit before taxes (the numerator of the ratio) to the total amount of assets invested (the denominator). Thus, a unit that has a profit of $500,000 for a given year from invested assets of $10 million would have an ROI of 0.05 for that year. If another unit generated that same amount of profit on invested assets of only $5 million, its ROI would be 0.10 and would thus be considered to have had superior financial performance—it generated equal benefit for less cost.

Other financial ratios that are commonly used to assess unit performance include, in addition to profitability ratios, those related to **liquidity** (current assets in relation to current liabilities), which provides an indication of how well the unit can meet its short-term cash requirements; **leverage** (total debt to total assets), which provides an indication of ability to meet long-term financial obligations; and **efficiency** or **activity** (e.g., amount of sales in a given period in relation to cost of inventory used to generate those sales), measuring how efficiently assets are utilized.

Examples of these four types of ratios for two organizations in the retail industry for the year 1997 are shown in Exhibit 16.12. It can be seen from the exhibit that The Limited had a lower ROI than The GAP that year, roughly equivalent liquidity and leverage ratios, and a slightly less efficient use of inventory. Had these been two units within the same larger organization, one would say that for this year The GAP unit was doing better insofar as financial performance was concerned.

EXHIBIT 16.12
Examples of Company Financial Ratios

RATIO	FORMULA	COMPANY			
		THE GAP, INC.		THE LIMITED, INC.	
PROFIT					
Return on Investment	$\dfrac{\text{Net Profit before Taxes}}{\text{Total Assets}}$	$\dfrac{854{,}242}{3{,}337{,}502}$	0.25	$\dfrac{400{,}390}{4{,}300{,}761}$	0.09
LIQUIDITY					
Current Ratio	$\dfrac{\text{Current Assets}}{\text{Current Liabilities}}$	$\dfrac{1{,}830{,}947}{991{,}548}$	1.85	$\dfrac{2{,}031{,}151}{1{,}093{,}412}$	1.86
LEVERAGE					
Debt to Asset	$\dfrac{\text{Total Debt}}{\text{Total Assets}}$	$\dfrac{1{,}753{,}516}{3{,}337{,}502}$	0.52	$\dfrac{2{,}255{,}804}{4{,}300{,}761}$	0.52
ACTIVITY					
Inventory Turnover	$\dfrac{\text{Sales}}{\text{Inventory}}$	$\dfrac{6{,}507{,}825}{733{,}174}$	8.88	$\dfrac{9{,}188{,}804}{1{,}101{,}877}$	8.34

(Ratios for the fiscal year ending January 31,1998. In 1,000 of U.S. dollars.)

The important point here, regarding the various financial ratios, is not the detailed steps that need to be taken to calculate the ratios. Rather, it is that when the ratios are calculated, they can be used to *compare* one organization, or one unit, to another. Thus, it is the comparative nature of the ratios that provides managers with information needed to take action during control. The numbers used to calculate a ratio, such as inventory turnover, for example, will show whether the ratio is relatively unfavorable, and if so, an examination of the two components used in the ratio will also indicate whether the problem seems to be in the amount of sales (too low) or in the amount of inventory (too high) or both. In other words, financial ratios can provide a very useful diagnostic tool for managers to determine where to take control action to improve situations.

Another financial measure is sometimes used for control purposes in business organizations. That measure is called the **break-even point (B-E P)**. Essentially, a B-E P analysis is a quantitative formula used to determine what volume of some product or service must be sold before a firm's fixed and variable costs are covered by the next sale. That is, the break-even point is where the selling price of a unit of a product/service minus its variable costs exceeds the fixed costs for that unit. In equation form:

B-E P = Fixed costs (FC) divided by selling price (SP) minus
variable cost (VC) per unit; thus,

B-E P = FC/(SP − VC)

break-even point (B-E P)
amount of a product or service that must be sold to cover a firm's fixed and variable costs

Once again, the details of calculation are less important than what this analysis can provide to assist managers in control efforts. Clearly, the lower the fixed costs, the fewer the units of goods or services that need to be sold for a break-even point to be reached. Likewise, the lower the variable costs, the higher the profit per unit and therefore the fewer the units that need to be sold to reach that point. Break-even analysis, then, provides a way for managers to determine whether new products or services have a reasonable potential to make a profit, and managers can then exercise control before new ventures are undertaken. Even more important, for ongoing operations, a break-even point analysis focuses managers' attention on reducing or controlling the two categories of costs—fixed and variable—to take the pressure off the need to sell larger volumes.

An example of where a break-even point analysis can illustrate comparisons between two organizations or units within them is provided by the airline industry. Many of the larger airlines have set up separate subsidiary airlines to handle short-haul commuter routes. These units of the larger parents can be operated on relatively small volumes of passenger traffic because lower costs, such as a lower wage-base for pilots, produce a relatively low break-even point. Similarly, certain independent airlines, if they are especially efficient (such as Southwest Airlines, which flies only one type of aircraft and uses smaller and less expensive airports), can charge very low fares on many of their routes and still make a profit.[20]

Although a B-E P analysis can provide extremely useful information for managers for control purposes, such an analysis also has limitations. Looking strictly at the numbers of a B-E P analysis may discourage certain decisions that could ultimately result in very profitable activities that do not initially appear to be profitable. Also, it is not always easy to allocate costs between fixed and variable categories, and it is sometimes difficult to project costs accurately, especially variable costs. Like other financial controls, a break-even point analysis can be an aid to exercising effective control, but it is not by itself a guarantee of wise decisions. What it does do, however, is highlight the potential advantages to be gained by controlling specific types of costs.

Budgetary Controls Budgets are used in almost every organization, and, like financial controls, can sometimes be considered elements of a strategic system. **Budgetary controls**, however, are more usefully viewed as a significant tactical control because they focus on how well strategies are being implemented. In contrast to purely strategic control, budgetary controls

budgetary control

a type of tactical control based on responsibility for meeting financial targets and evaluating how well those targets have been met

- Typically cover a relatively limited time frame (usually 12-month or 3-month periods).
- Focus exclusively on one type of objective (financial).
- Usually cannot be used to compare a total organization's progress relative to its competitors.[21]

Anyone occupying a managerial position both is controlled by budgets and uses budgets to control others. A budget is a commitment to a forecast to make an agreed-upon outcome happen.[22] Thus, it is more than a forecast, which is simply a prediction. A budget is designed to influence behavior so that forecasts or plans for expenditures and (where relevant) revenues can be achieved. It "controls" by assigning responsibility for meeting financial targets and for evaluating how well those targets have been met. It would be difficult indeed to maintain an organization if none of its members were held accountable for limits on expenditures.

	EXHIBIT 16.13
	Issues in Budgetary Control

Issue	Questions
Rolling budgets and revision	Should the budget period be for 12 months followed by another 12-month budget a year later, or should a calendar quarter be added each time a new calendar quarter begins? Should the budget remain fixed for the budget period or should it be revised periodically during the period?
Fixed or flexible budgets	Should performance be evaluated against the original budget or against a budget that incorporates the actual activity level of the business?
Bonuses based on budgets	Should incentive compensation, if any, be based on actual versus budgeted performance, or on actual performance against some other standard?
Evaluation criteria	Should the budget used to evaluate performance include only those items over which the evaluated manager has control, or should it include all unit costs and revenues appropriate to the managerial unit?
Tightness of the budget	What degree of "stretch" should there be in the budget?

Source: Adapted from N. C. Churchill, "Budget Choices: Planning vs. Control," *Harvard Business Review* 62, no. 4 (1984), pp. 150–64, (p. 151).

When using budgets as a form of control, managers face several important issues, as shown in Exhibit 16.13. One is the question of whether to use a fixed budget for a specific period, usually 12 months, and stick with those numbers, or to revise it midway during the period based on changes in operating conditions. AT&T's Universal Card Services division, for example, uses what is termed a "rolling planning process." The term "budget" has been dropped because the organization believes it implies a "calendar-year mentality" that encourages managers to spend their entire budgeted allotment by the end of the year, whether their projects are succeeding or not. In its new 18-month planning process, funding for all projects is reforecast and readjusted each quarter. A rolling budgetary process with relatively frequent revisions, such as the one at the Universal Card Division, has the advantage of being more current and therefore more accurate, but it also can take more managerial time and effort.[23]

Another budget issue is whether compensation bonuses should be based on the achievement of budgetary targets. It sounds good but has the great disadvantage of encouraging budget games, because the person being evaluated has an incentive to provide high cost and low revenue estimates. This way the person has a higher probability of hitting the targets and earning a bonus. Thus, managers who supervise the preparation of budgets need to be alert to how a bonus system of this type can distort estimates and thus undermine control.

A third budgetary control issue involves the question of whether those responsible for meeting specified targets should be evaluated only on expenditures and revenues over which they have direct control or whether they should be evaluated on a final "net" figure based on all costs and revenues for a given unit. The former results in a more direct link between managerial behavior and budgetary responsibility, but the latter is the ultimate "bottom line," especially for publicly-held corporations. For example, as a manager of a sales unit, you might have strong control over the revenues that your unit generates and the money spent on travel expenses. When these travel expenses are subtracted from sales, your unit might look very good. However, if your unit also uses marketing and promotion materials to get these sales, they may need to be factored into the overall assessment. Otherwise, you may overspend on marketing and promotion activities.

The final, and perhaps most important, managerial control issue regarding budgets is how tight or loose to make them. Should a budget require those charged with meeting it to make an extra "stretch"? As we have said before in the chapter on motivation, research indicates that the best performance results from goals that are challenging but achievable. Since budgets represent goals, this conclusion seems highly relevant to the issue of budgetary control.

supervisory structure
a type of tactical control based on reporting levels in an organization

Supervisory Structure The basic **supervisory structure** of an organization is probably the most widespread tactical control system that a typical organizational member encounters. The amount and form of such control varies considerably from organization to organization, but almost always exists in some form. In organizations of any size, there is always someone or some group to which an employee or manager reports. Even in the most collegial and least bureaucratic types of work organizations, such as research laboratories and universities, some sort of reporting structure almost always regulates the activities of each member. However, such supervisory control structures, like other controls, can fail.

Several years ago, it was discovered that the supervisor of the Risk Management Department of a major multicampus university had embezzled $1 million in the preceding four years. This occurred because of a lack of supervisory control above her level, since this employee, herself a supervisor, was authorized to write checks for hundreds of thousands of dollars without having to receive approval from superiors. As a result of the discovery of the embezzlement, the university now requires regular and spot audits, approval of all claim agreements by the university's legal office, and periodic rotation of check-writing authority.[24]

human resource policies and procedures
a type of tactical control based on the organization's overall approach to utilizing its human resources

Human Resource Controls **Human resource policies and procedures** are a fourth major type of tactical control that affects everyone working in an organization. We have discussed these in detail previously in Chapter 12, but what is important to stress about them here is that they provide a number of different opportunities for control (see Exhibit 16.14):

- Selection procedures can specify the range of abilities that will be brought into the organization.
- Training can enhance the consistency with which skills will elevate performance to meet standards.
- Appraisal and evaluation methods reinforce desired behavior and discourage undesirable levels of performance.
- Compensation can motivate efforts in particular directions as opposed to other directions.

An example of human resource procedures that reinforce desired behavior occurred when ABB Vetco Gray, Inc., a large oil field manufacturing and service company headquartered in Houston, Texas, introduced a more comprehensive

EXHIBIT 16.14

Opportunities for Control in the Human Resource Function

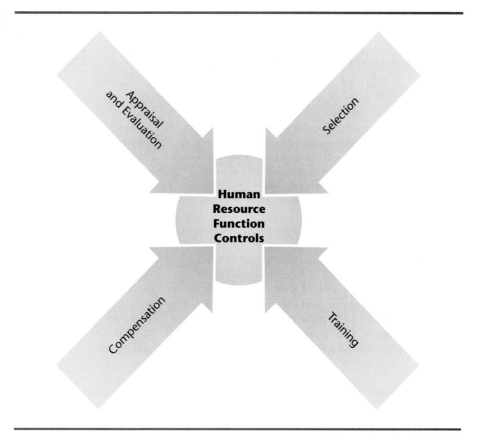

EXHIBIT 16.14

Opportunities for Control in the Human Resource Function

performance measurement system. Among other actions, it decided to link behavior more closely to pay. The company asked each department to establish up to three bottom-line targets. The departments then tracked performance in relation to these targets so that employees could see directly how their actions affected the company's profit.[25]

Because the effects of human resource policies and procedures are so extensive, they are also very powerful means of control, as illustrated in the accompanying Managerial Challenge box. When used with skill and deftness, they are a significant aid to the achievement of organizational objectives, as in the above Vetco Gray example. When used ineptly, and with heavy-handedness, they can hinder organizational progress.

If this were not a big enough challenge, in international organizations perceptions of what is too much oversight can vary considerably from one country and culture to another. For example, tight monitoring of a manager's time and movements is more accepted in countries such as Thailand; however, managers in Australia are likely to react quite strongly and negatively to tight monitoring.

Contrasting Approaches to Using Tactical Controls   As we have said, almost every organization, whether for profit or nonprofit, has the basic tactical control systems of financial controls, budgets, supervisory structures, and human resource policies and procedures. The ways in which tactical control systems are implemented say a great deal about an organization—what it is like to work there and how effective the control is. These control systems characterize an organization and

MANAGERIAL CHALLENGE

HUMAN RESOURCE CONTROL AT ALLEN-BRADLEY

Allen-Bradley is a subsidiary of Rockwell International. It produces electronics and high-level automated industrial control products. When it first joined Rockwell, Allen-Bradley had serious problems with overstaffing, absenteeism, and tardiness. The overstaffing was solved through immediate layoffs. Unfortunately, this hurt overall morale, and absenteeism rose even higher. After investigating the problem, managers determined that there was no official control in place to either monitor or discipline absenteeism.

Implementing a new control policy raised many serious questions: (1) Should the policy reward those who consistently showed up for work or punish those who missed work? (2) Should the policy be focused on punishment at first and then, once most people are complying, focus on rewards? (3) How should acceptable and unacceptable attendance be defined? (4) How should tardiness be defined and what levels would be considered acceptable or unacceptable? (5) Who should be monitored? Should it be hourly workers or all employees?

Rather than use historical comparisons to set standards, managers at Allen-Bradley went outside the firm and benchmarked other manufacturing firms. They found that the U.S. national average for manufacturing firms was about five acceptable absences per year. In terms of tardiness, they obtained benchmark information from the Merchants and Manufacturers Association. Based on this information, they set six occurrences of tardiness in one year as the maximum number allowed. They decided that the policy would punish those who violated the standards. Employees showing up late for work more than six times in a year would face a series of disciplinary measures. If an employee was late 15 times during one year, he or she would be fired.

In terms of who should be monitored, they decided that all employees, hourly as well as salaried, would be monitored. The necessity for the policy and its provisions was explained carefully to all the employees.

To monitor the results, a biweekly report was issued by the human resource department showing the current status of all employees. Within 25 months, absenteeism had dropped 83.5 percent. This saved the company nearly $60,000. Additionally, as problem employees saw that they were in trouble and headed toward increasingly harsh disciplinary measures, they tended to quit rather than wait for the inevitable firing.

Source: Adapted from J. Stinson, "Company Policy Attends to Chronic Absentees," *Personnel Journal,* August 1991, pp. 82–85.

---

are a critical part of its identity. For these reasons, it is important to specify and discuss the two fundamental approaches to tactical control: (a) imposed, or bureaucratic, control and (b) elicited, or commitment or clan, control (see Exhibit 16.15).[26] Most organizations use a combination of these two approaches but also tend to emphasize one over the other.

bureaucratic control

an approach to tactical control that stresses adherence to rules and regulations and is imposed by others

Bureaucratic control stresses adherence to rules and regulations and a formal, impersonal administration of control systems. Thus, for instance, Exxon has a thick operating manual for refinery managers. It specifies everything from what capital budget requests need what type of approval to equipment maintenance schedules. This approach highlights rational planning and orderliness. It heavily emphasizes detecting deviance from standards. But its foremost feature, in a control sense, is that control is *imposed on* the person, group, or activity. From an employee's perspective, "others" do the controlling.

commitment (clan) control

an approach to tactical control that emphasizes consensus and shared responsibility for meeting goals

Commitment, or **clan**, **control** stresses obtaining consensus on what goals should be pursued and then developing a shared sense of responsibility for achieving those goals. It is called a "clan" approach to control because of the emphasis on generating shared values, as in a set of close relatives, and on mutual assistance in meeting performance standards. For example, Meridian is a producer of training films that focuses on a clan approach. There is no real policy manual. Employees are given general goals and basic budgets within which they need to work. The com-

EXHIBIT 16.15

Control in Bureaucracy and Clan Structures

Type of Control	Social Requirements[a]	Control Approach	Informational Requirements
Bureaucracy	Norm of reciprocity Legitimate authority	Adherence to rules and regulations Formal and impersonal Emphasis on detecting deviance Imposed on the individual	Rules
Clan	Norm of reciprocity Legitimate authority Shared values, beliefs	Stresses group consensus on goals and their measurement Mutual assistance in meeting performance standards Uses deviations as guidelines in diagnosing problems Control comes from the individuals or groups	Traditions

[a]Social requirements are the basic agreements between people that, at a minimum, are necessary for a form of control to be employed.

Source: Adapted from William G. Ouchi, "A Conceptual Framework for the Design or Organizational Control Mechanisms," *Management Science* 25, no. 9 (1980) 833–47 (p. 838).

pany relies on employees' understanding of, and commitment to, the organizational objectives as the primary means of control. Unlike the bureaucratic approach, the clan approach tends to treat deviations from standards more as a basis for diagnosis than for taking corrective action. Its foremost feature, in a control sense, is that control is viewed as being *elicited from,* rather than imposed on, the person, group, or activity. From an employee's perspective, the employee or his or her group, rather than others, does the controlling.

On reading these descriptions of the two basic approaches to managerial control, you might wonder why every organization doesn't use a commitment approach. It sounds as if it would function better for both the organization and those who work in it. However, things are not that simple. Creating a genuine clanlike atmosphere among employees, especially in large organizations, is extremely difficult. It takes time and also considerable managerial effort. It may not succeed, or, more likely, exceed only partially. If a true clanlike, high-commitment culture is not created, an organization cannot rely on self-control by individuals or groups to exercise sufficient control. However distasteful it may sound, some amount of bureaucratic managerial control seems necessary for most complex organizations.

Even from the perspective of the organization member or employee, self-imposed clan control may not be as satisfying as it would seem at first glance. A recent study of a small manufacturing company illustrates the point.[27] This company converted its traditional hierarchical structure, which emphasized a high degree of supervisory control, to a structure that was built around self-managing work teams. In the first phase of the transition, the teams spent a good deal of time developing consensus on what constituted, both collectively and individually, good work for the teams and good patterns of behavior that would translate those standards into action. In the second phase, the teams developed strong norms regarding expected behavior. Experienced team members expected new workers to buy into the teams' values and act according to their norms.

Under the old system, supervisors tolerated some slackness among the workers. But in the team system, the members exercised their newfound authority with much less patience. In converting to a clan approach to control, the teams' norms tended to get formalized—that is, to become self-imposed rules. As one team member said: "If we can just get our code of conduct in writing, then everyone will know what to do. We won't have so many problems ... if we can just get it written down." The researcher studying this company stated, "The teams had now created, in effect, a nearly perfect form of control ... an essentially total system of control almost impossible to resist.... The team members had become their own masters and their own slaves." Such clan control had developed into (in the researcher's term) an "iron cage."

The previous example serves to emphasize the point that no single approach to managerial control will work well in all situations. It also shows that whatever approach is chosen will have its own unique problems as well as its advantages.

Operational Control

operational control

assessment and regulation of the specific activities and methods an organization uses to produce goods and services

Operational control, as the name implies, regulates the activities or methods an organization uses to produce the goods and services it supplies to customers and clients. It is control applied to the transformation of inputs into outputs, such as the actions that produce a car, administer therapy to an ill patient, cook and serve a restaurant meal, send a satellite into the sky, or write computer software. In short, operational control "is where the rubber meets the road." Exhibit 16.16 gives further examples of operational controls.

The overall management of operations (as discussed in the next chapter) involves a number of critical and often technical issues. Here, we focus specifically on an overview of the control process relating to operations. Operational control can be analyzed by relating it to the three basic elements involved in any type of service or goods production: inputs, transformation, and outputs (Exhibit 16.17).[28] These three elements can be related to the location of control in the production process: before transformation occurs, or **precontrol**; during transformation, or **concurrent control**; and after transformation takes place, or **postcontrol**.

precontrol

a type of operational control that focuses on the quality, quantity, and characteristics of the inputs into the production process

concurrent control

a type of operational control that evaluates the conversion of inputs to outputs while it is happening

postcontrol

a type of operational control that checks quality *after* production of goods or service outputs

Precontrol of Operations   This form of operational control focuses on the quality, quantity, and characteristics of the inputs into the production process—for example, the purity of steel, the grade of beef, the number of passengers, the age of patients, the test scores of entering students, the aptitudes of job applicants. Such pre-control is illustrated by a specification that the rail transport organization, Conrail, set up for its suppliers of communication products. It began requiring suppliers to guarantee that the parts they provide will continue to work even if struck by lightning. As a result, Conrail cut the number of communication failures resulting in train delays from 300 to 3 per month on its Selkirk–New York–Chicago route.[29]

The more stringent the control over the quality of inputs, the less need for control at the later two stages. The higher the quality of army recruits, for example, the easier it is to train them to be competent soldiers. However, there is a cost involved in exacting precontrol standards. Higher-quality inputs typically cost more, and the effort to ensure that the quality is high also increases costs. Nevertheless, those costs in many cases may be well justified by what is saved in the later control steps

EXHIBIT 16.16 Examples of Operational Controls	

EXHIBIT 16.16

Examples of Operational Controls

Factor Requiring Control	Example
Passenger safety	General Motors has used crash test dummies for a number of years. Now they are developing a virtual safety lab that will use advanced computer systems to model the forces involved in any crash. They will be able to control for type of vehicle and type of accident, as well as gender, size, and position of the passengers. They will not only be able to predict external injuries but the amount and type of injuries to specific internal organs.[1]
Lumber movement	Mill 5 at Avison Lumber Co.'s sawmill in Molalla, Oregon, is able to accurately control the lumber milling process using computerized control of the motion of hydraulic cylinders used to move the lumber.[2]
Access to FBI locations	The Los Angeles office of the Federal Bureau of Investigation has developed a personnel access control system combining optics technology that reads fibers in a photo ID card sometimes backed up by keypads requiring personal identification numbers. Access to the parking structure is also controlled.[3]
World Wide Web access by employees	Sequel Technologies, located in Bellevue, Washington, has developed a software package that allows employers to track the Internet sites visited by their employees similar to how the phone company logs telephone calls. This technology allows supervisors to monitor how productively employees use their on-line time.[4]

Sources: Data from
[1]D. Deitz, "Crash Test Dummies Get Smarter," *Mechanical Engineering* 118, no. 4 (1996), p. 130.
[2]"Edgar System Key Part of Major Mill Upgrade," *Forest Industries* 119, no. 5 (1992), pp. 24–25.
[3]K. Hodgson, "Mission Possible: The FBI's Single-Entry Solution," *Security* 30, no. 7 (1993), pp. 10–11.
[4]J. Martin, "Hunting Down the Porn Freaks," *Fortune* 136, no. 2 (1997), p. 116.

and by the positive evaluation of the eventual goods and services. In other words, customers may be willing to pay more for better products and services.

Concurrent Control of Operations   Concurrent control involves real-time assessment of the quality of the transformation process, that is, evaluation of the conversion of inputs to outputs while it is happening. For example, Distribution Services of America, which operates warehouses and fills orders for large clients such as Nabisco, has installed a real-time inventory tracking system, which utilizes radio frequency communication between warehouse management and workers on the floor. As orders from customers come in, they are relayed to workers on the floor. Since implementing the system, DSA has reduced its order processing time for customers by 40 percent and has achieved 99.5 percent accuracy in filling orders.[30]

Other typical examples of concurrent control are the monitoring of a customer service representative's performance while handling a telephone inquiry or the

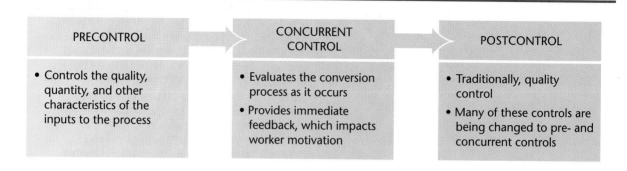

EXHIBIT 16.17
Operational Controls

PRECONTROL	CONCURRENT CONTROL	POSTCONTROL
• Controls the quality, quantity, and other characteristics of the inputs to the process	• Evaluates the conversion process as it occurs • Provides immediate feedback, which impacts worker motivation	• Traditionally, quality control • Many of these controls are being changed to pre- and concurrent controls

inspection of fruit while a batch is proceeding along a conveyer belt to the canning machinery. This type of control is designed to provide immediate feedback so that operations can be changed rapidly to decrease errors or increase quality. To have effective concurrent control procedures, however, managers must give considerable attention in advance to how such systems are designed and implemented. Also, managers need to be aware that this kind of control can have strong impacts on the motivation of those carrying out the operations, since the feedback is so immediate and often very direct.

Postcontrol of Operations Postcontrol was the traditional form of control in manufacturing—checking quality *after* a product (TV sets, shoes, furniture, etc.) was produced. Thus, companies typically have had quality control inspectors or whole departments that checked the rate of defective products and then decided what to do if those rates were too high. For example, Toyota inspects each car coming off the assembly line on a basic list of criteria. It also randomly inspects cars based on a significantly longer and more detailed list of quality criteria. In recent years, the role of quality control has been greatly diminished, with the increasing emphasis on pre- and concurrent control. The adage has been: "*Build* quality into the product, rather than inspect quality into the product."[31] Also, the more contemporary approach to operational control has transferred responsibility to those doing the operations and away from separate evaluators at the end of the process.

total quality management (TQM)

an approach to control that integrates quality objectives into all management functions to continually achieve superior quality

Total Quality Management The two features of operational control just mentioned—comprehensiveness and operator responsibility—form two of the cornerstones of what has come to be called **total quality management (TQM)**.[32] The details of the TQM approach will be covered in the following chapter on "Operations Management." The important point to emphasize here is that TQM is an approach that encompasses all aspects of operational control—pre-, concurrent, and postcontrol—within an integrated management framework. It links issues of control to other management functions including planning, organizing, and, especially, leading. The objective is to make a massive and coordinated attack on achieving superior quality and on unceasing efforts to keep improving that quality even further. Control processes, as such, are involved in the TQM approach, but they are only one part of a much bigger whole.

FACTORS IN CONTROL EFFECTIVENESS

Regardless of good intentions, control systems in organizations may break down completely, as illustrated at the opening of this chapter, or they may not work very well. There can be many reasons for this, but alert managers can take the initiative to reduce these possibilities. The effectiveness of control is very much under the control of managers. Again, there are no automatic prescriptions or rules of thumb for managing the control process well. Instead, managers can use certain potential sources of influence to increase the probabilities of success. In this section, we look at some of the key factors that determine the effectiveness of controls (see Exhibit 16.18).

Focus of Control

The decision of where to focus control in an organization involves critical choices based on what actions and outcomes should receive the greatest attention. The guiding principle for focusing control is that it should be closely linked to the strategic goals and, particularly, the planning process of the organization. For example, in Chapter 4, we talked about Nordstrom's strategic focus on customer service. As a consequence, while the company would probably not be wise to ignore inventory controls, the focus would need to be on how to maintain a high level of customer satisfaction.

To be most effective, planning should be part of the control process, and control should be part of the planning process. Priorities should be set to select what is to be intensely monitored and controlled and what is to be given less attention. As software firms have found out, for example, little is to be gained from requiring star programmers to come to work on a precise schedule, given that the real objective is to produce innovative software. It is worth considerable control effort in that kind of organization, however, to make sure that the software that is written is as absolutely error-free as possible. Conversely, it is extremely important for restau-

EXHIBIT 16.18
Key Factors in Determining the Effectiveness of Controls

Key Factor	Concerns
Focus of control	What will be controlled? Where should controls be located in the organizational structure? Who is responsible for which controls?
Amount of control	Is there a balance between over- and undercontrol?
Quality of information collected by the controls	Is the information useful? Is the information accurate? Is the information timely? Is the information objective?
Flexibility of controls	Are the controls able to respond to varying conditions?
Favorable cost–benefit ratio	Is the information being gathered worth the cost of gathering it?
Source of control	Is control imposed by others? Is control decided by those who are affected?

The critical control process for administering medication was revised at a prestigious Boston hospital after two cancer patients were mistakenly treated with an overdose of a toxic drug.

rants to have their serving personnel be on time so that service is given promptly, whereas an occasional small mistake in taking a customer's order could be tolerated.

The focus of control refers not only to what is to be controlled but also to where control should be located in the organizational structure. This means paying careful attention to which people or positions in the structure have responsibility for different types and areas of control and how broad or narrow is the scope of responsibility. Control responsibility that is too diffuse can lead to omissions, and responsibility that is too concentrated can result in bottlenecks and decision delays. For example, if too many different people are assigned responsibility for quality control of a complex set of equipment, each may assume that one of the others has taken care of a particular problem, and, as a consequence, some aspect of control gets left undone. On the other hand, if only one person is charged with inspecting all the pieces of equipment, that person may get overloaded, with the result that some critical detail gets inadvertently overlooked. Either way, effective control could be compromised.

Amount of Control

As we discussed at the beginning of this chapter, one of the greatest control challenges for any organization or manager is to determine the appropriate amount of control. The consequences of these choices can mean the difference between life and death of an organization, as illustrated by the Managerial Challenge box, "Control: Too Much or Too Little?" Effective control involves finding a balance between overcontrol and undercontrol. Often, less-experienced managers tend to apply more control than is necessary in their eagerness to demonstrate that they are "in charge." This in turn can produce unintended resentment and resistance. Thus, new managers need to be aware of this tendency and moderate it.

When managers have more experience, they have a better basis for gauging the minimum levels of control that will get the job done without incurring unjustified

MANAGERIAL CHALLENGE

CONTROL: TOO MUCH OR TOO LITTLE?

Controls that are too tight can make it difficult for an organization to function at its best. But controls that seem tight to some organizations may be just right for others, just as one size of jeans does not fit everyone. Consider the case of C.R. England, a long-haul refrigerated trucking company based in Salt Lake City. The very nature of the business itself, which requires shipping goods as quickly as possible from one destination to another to maintain freshness, dictates the necessity of tight controls. C.R. England's executives and managers needed to find the most efficient way to transport its customers' products across the country without having their employees feel as though they were prisoners.

"We want to run this place like the cockpit of a jetliner, where you have hundreds of different instruments before you at all times and know exactly where you are," explains Stephen Glines, vice president for technology. Thus, C.R. England relies on strict centralized control that is maintained by a state-of-the-art computerized system that monitors every operation, from arrival times to billing accuracy, to how well the company's repair shop treats its truckers. Every worker receives a weekly letter grade assessing performance, based on computerized data such as the number of minutes it takes to wash a truck or complete a bill. "I don't think anyone likes to be this closely monitored. But most people start using the information as a learning tool." In fact, this may be the key to the success of England's tight controls: Employees actually view them as a positive strategy rather than a negative one. Since the company instituted these controls, turnover—in an industry whose average is 100 percent a year—has dropped 25 percent. And the company has gained a competitive edge, after losing money a decade ago. "I don't see anyone within leagues of where they are," notes William Davidson, head of Mesa Research, a consulting firm in Redondo Beach, California. "C.R. England captures

information on everything and recycles it back through the engine to improve performance."

How about controls that are too loose? Just as a loose pair of shoes can make its wearer stumble, so can loose controls cause an organization to slip and fall. This was the case with Pan Am, the once-venerable airline that suffered from what appeared to be nearly a complete lack of controls. When Pan Am declared itself in trouble financially, businessman Albert Dunlap and a crew of colleagues decided to examine the company to see if it was a worthwhile investment. They found a frustrating—and frightening—lack of controls. At Pan Am offices and ticketing counters, they discovered employees reading books instead of answering phones or issuing tickets. They unearthed $1 million a month in spare parts that were unaccounted for out of a maintenance facility at Kennedy Airport in New York. They were dismayed by shabby offices and wondered at the condition of the planes themselves. They determined that the airline was offering flights to places that customers didn't want to go. They discovered that the company had no assets and that management was spending capital that the company did not have. Finally, they learned that the airline had unfunded medical and pension liabilities of $1.2 billion; in other words, Pan Am had a negative net worth.

Dunlap and his colleagues determined that Pan Am was not a company in which to invest. Six months later, the company went out of business. Although it is impossible to say with certainty whether the company could have been saved, it appears that Pan Am suffered from a companywide lack of basic controls. One can speculate whether stronger controls would have made a difference.

Sources: "Measure It to Manage It," *Fortune,* February 6, 1995, p. 78; Albert J. Dunlap, *Mean Business* (New York: Fireside, 1996), pp. 234–37.

risks. Even seasoned managers often find it difficult to judge correctly the degree of control required, and problems of undercontrol can crop up where least expected. No predetermined "right" amounts of control apply to all work situations. The best guideline for a manager to follow is to view the amount of control as something that, within limits, can be adjusted. Additionally, the undesirable consequences of excessive control and the dangers of too little control need to be made part of careful assessments of performance requirements and not inadvertently or casually overlooked. As we have already mentioned, involving those who will be directly influenced by the control measures in setting the amount of control increases the chances that an appropriate level of control is set from the outset. In addition, if adjustments need to be made, this initial involvement will likely reduce the resistance to needed changes.

Quality of Information

Effective control requires knowledge based on data; that is, it requires good information. Four characteristics that determine the quality of information are usefulness, accuracy, timeliness, and objectivity.

Usefulness   Not all data collected for control purposes are equally useful in managerial operations and decisions. Sometimes data that were once useful continue to be collected, even though the original purposes for obtaining that information have disappeared. Such a situation was discovered several years ago at a division of the Borg-Warner Corporation. Because of major changes in the operating environment at this automotive transmission unit, the company decided to find out which accounting reports, if any, were actually helpful to managers. Did the information contained in the reports actually assist managers to do their jobs better? The answer was a resounding "no." Investigation indicated the accounting department thought they were gathering data that two separate groups could use: corporate managers and plant managers. Yet, it turned out that the information being disseminated was of assistance only to the first group. As a result, the accounting department worked with operations managers in the plants to develop control reports that would help them do their particular jobs more effectively.[33]

Accuracy   Data or numbers that are inaccurate or misleading not only fail to provide a good basis for control steps but also breed cynicism among those whose performance is being measured. Since control actions, especially those designed to change behavior that does not meet agreed-upon standards, can have such powerful effects, it is vital that substantial effort be put into obtaining data that are absolutely valid. Otherwise, no information is better than inaccurate information.

Timeliness   Even accurate data, if they arrive too late, are not useful. This is true for any organizational actions, but especially so for purposes of control. In the fast-paced world of global business, data that are out of date are of virtually no use. For effective control, information must arrive on time to those who can take action and make any required changes. In everyday life, information that arrives to truck drivers 10 minutes after the wrong route has been taken is not very useful. Effective control systems require speed.

Objectivity   Objectivity, especially as it relates to control, is something of a two-edged sword. Almost everyone would agree that objective facts are better than subjective, and possibly biased, opinions. However, for some kinds of performances, objective data may not be possible to obtain or even may be misleading. In diving competition, objective measurement of the exact height that a diver jumps off a springboard may be much less important than the subjective opinion of an experienced judge about the form of the dive. Similarly, in organizations, some of the most easily measured activities, and therefore the most easily controlled, may be relatively insignificant for the achievement of major, strategic goals. All other factors being equal, objective information would be preferred, but in many situations, those other factors may not be equal, and thoughtful judgments rather than unimportant "facts" may provide the best basis for action decisions.

For example, in a customer service call center, it is relatively easy to gather objective data on the length of time a customer service agent spends on the phone with each caller. However, comparing the number of callers served by each agent may not tell you the most important thing—how well each customer was served. In fact, if the number of calls answered becomes the key performance measure, customer service agents may begin to provide poor service in order to get customers off the phone quickly and move on to the next customer, thereby maximizing the number of calls they take in a day. In this case, it is clear that the objective data (i.e., the number of calls taken) may not be the most important data (i.e., how well the customer is served). Measuring customer service may require a supervisor randomly listening in on service calls or going to the cost and effort of trying to measure customer satisfaction by polling customers who have called in to the service center.

Flexibility

For control to be effective, its procedures must respond to changing conditions. Organizations and managers get accustomed to control procedures that are already in place. It is a human tendency to stay the course when things appear to be going well. But that tendency can defeat effective control. Well-designed control systems should be able to account for changing circumstances and adjust accordingly. Rigidity of control systems usually is not a feature to be prized. Flexibility is.

Favorable Cost–Benefit Ratio

The designs of some control systems look good on paper, but they prove to be impractical or costly to use. To be effective, the benefits of controls must outweigh both the direct financial costs and the indirect costs of inconvenience and awkwardness in implementation. Elaborate, complicated control systems immediately raise the issue of whether they will be worth the expense involved. Sometimes, the simplest systems are nearly as effective. Consider again our customer service call center example. While objective customer satisfaction data may be preferable to subjective supervisor evaluations, the cost of obtaining satisfaction ratings directly from customers may be significantly more and not provide much better information than well-trained supervisors.

Of course, some situations may call for intricate controls because of the extremely high costs that would occur from unacceptable performance. Organizations that must carry out certain activities associated with high levels of hazard—such as nuclear power plants, military weapons units, and federal air traffic control agencies—need to invest heavily in control systems that ensure an exceedingly high degree of reliability. Consequently, they must make costly investments in, for example, continual training, redundant staffing, and very expensive equipment to control operations and reduce the possibility of a catastrophic accident to absolute minimum levels.[34] In such cases, high control costs are obviously justified.

Sources

The source of control often affects the willingness of organization members to work cooperatively with the system. In recent years, many organizations have changed from bureaucratic control to control that relies on members' monitoring their own or their team's performance. Thus, the source of control is shifted, and the change may increase positive reactions because employees have more trust in a process over which they have some influence.

Similarly, controls that provide information from equipment or instruments often seem less resented and more fair than controls involving what can be viewed as the sometimes arbitrary actions of supervisors. This principle was illustrated at UNUM Insurance Company, which installed an elaborate information system (involving more than a $30,000 investment in hardware and software per employee) that helps improve the performance of the company's information systems professionals by measuring the amount of work to be done, identifying errors as they occur, and helping to correct those errors. The affected employees "participate in the counting, the defect identification, and the elimination." These employees accept the errors identified by the new system much more readily than from supervisors because the system has no personal "axe to grind."[35] For any type of control, the source has a great deal to do with the acceptability of the system. Acceptability, in turn, affects how well control systems work in practice and not just in theory.

CONCLUDING COMMENTS

Control is a crucial, albeit many times difficult and sometimes even unpleasant, managerial function. As we have emphasized repeatedly throughout this chapter, the challenge for managers is to make wise decisions about how much, and where, control needs to be used, and then how to apply that control. Control is essential, but many a manager and even many an organization have run into severe difficulties because this managerial function has not been well handled.

Knowing the basic elements of the control process is a helpful start in gaining perspective about how to exercise appropriate control. Understanding some of the pitfalls and obstacles that can interfere at each of these steps provides a basis for avoiding unnecessary rookie mistakes. Not many managers would have the aspiration to be a great "controller," but likewise, most would not like to be known as excessively naïve about the need for control. Keeping in mind the factors that influence control effectiveness—such as the focus, amount, and degree of flexibility—is a way to reduce the chances of unintended control blunders and improve the probabilities of success.

Clearly, control is a matter of both science and art. On the one hand, there are a variety of quantitative measures of individual, group, and organizational performance. Particular areas, such as finance and operations, tend to use many quantitative control measures because they deal with things that are easy to count (e.g., money, products, defects). However, just because something can be easily measured doesn't mean it should be. Likewise, just because something is hard to measure doesn't mean it should not be. The key to managerial success relative to control is making good judgments and *then* good measurements. Without good judgment concerning what, how, and when to measure something, the measurements are of little value. Control can add real value to an organization, but that outcome is not guaranteed unless managers with judgment make it happen.

In the following two chapters (Chapters 17 and 18) in this part of the book, we examine two areas that are especially important when it comes to managing the control function in organizations, areas that often present particularly difficult challenges to managers. One is operations, that is, the transformation of resources into goods and services, the other is information technology, the use of hardware and software to convert data into useful information for organizational purposes.

KEY TERMS

break-even point (B-E P) 489
budgetary control 490
bureaucratic control 494
commitment (clan) control 494
concurrent control 496
control 475
efficiency (activity) 488
human resource policies and
    procedures 492

leverage 488
liquidity 488
operational control 496
precontrol 496
postcontrol 496
profitability 487
ROE (return on equity) 488
ROI (return on investment) 488
standards 478

strategic control 485
supervisory structure 492
tactical control 487
total quality management
    (TQM) 498

REVIEW QUESTIONS

1. What is meant by "control" in organizations?
2. Is the control function linked to other managerial functions? Which ones? How?
3. What is meant when control is described as an independent variable?
4. What are the four elements of the control process?
5. Who is responsible for setting standards?
6. What are standards and how are they used in organizations?
7. When measuring performance, is it helpful to collect only quantifiable data?
8. What is the limiting factor in comparing performance against standards?
9. Which is the most difficult managerial task in the control process? Why?
10. What happens when a gap is detected between expected performance and actual performance?
11. Compare strategic, tactical, and operational control. Why are the boundaries between each not always clear?
12. What is the relationship of the external organizational environment to the development of strategic controls?
13. Contrast budgetary control with strategic control.
14. What is the main focus of tactical control?
15. List and discuss four types of tactical controls.
16. Describe four managerial control issues involving budgets.
17. What is the fundamental difference between bureaucratic control and commitment (clan) control?
18. Define operational control.
19. What is the relationship between pre-, concurrent, and postcontrols of operations? Which type is best?
20. What are the seven factors of control effectiveness?
21. What factors determine the usefulness of information to the control process?

DISCUSSION QUESTIONS

1. Do you think it is possible for an international firm to have a common control system even for a single activity, such as manufacturing, when it has plants in countries such as India, Australia, Japan, the United States, and Germany? Explain your answer.

2. If you were the manager of your university's control system for exams, would you tighten or loosen the amount of control? For what signals would you look to determine whether your adjustments were appropriate?

3. In general, do you think that people respond to control systems or that control systems respond to people? In other words, will people generally conform to the tightness or looseness of a control system, or should the tightness or looseness of the control system depend on the nature of the people involved?

4. If you were a worker and management wanted to tighten controls over your job, what would they need to do to get you to go along with tighter controls?

CLOSING CASE

Mercedes Benz: Gaining Control of the American Road

Picture two friends, middle-aged men who love hunting, fishing, and tinkering with race cars together. They sound like brothers, or childhood buddies. But they aren't. One is Billy Minges, an Alabama businessman who owns a small company called Cain Steel. The other is Karl Sauer, a German manager at the Mercedes Benz plant in Vance, Alabama. How did Mercedes Benz find itself in Alabama? How did two men from such different backgrounds become friends? How is the experiment working out?

Germany-based Mercedes has been increasingly faced with two major problems: money and market. German labor costs about 50 percent more than American labor does, particularly labor in the Deep South. Thus, margins on German-manufactured cars are slim. And the American market, particularly for the new model that Mercedes wanted to produce—a luxury sport-utility vehicle priced at about $35,000—is crucial to Mercedes' future success. So the company decided to find a location in the United States where it could build the new cars cheaply and market them to the consumers most likely to buy them. Vance, Alabama, was the final choice.

From the start, issues of control surfaced. The German company's corporate culture, from its rigid management style to its precise way of building cars, clashed with the work habits of its newly employed Alabamans. For instance, German workers wait for instructions and follow them; their American counterparts try to find quicker, easier ways to get the job done. Mercedes has a strict system for building its cars, called SMPs (standard methods and procedures), which has been designed by its engineers. The SMPs defined exactly the way each task is to be completed every step of the way. German Mercedes workers are accustomed to the SMPs and follow them

without question; the SMPs establish certain manufacturing standards that ultimately ensure consistent quality among Mercedes automobiles. To help the Americans along, the SMPs were posted throughout the new factory where they could easily be read. Workers were expected not to deviate from procedure in any way. If a line worker was finished using a wrench, for instance, he or she was to follow the SMP guide to learn where to put the tool down.

Mercedes' American workers needed some time to adjust to this focus on control. In addition, they needed to get used to the personalities and management styles of their German employers. "The Germans are very blunt and don't beat around the bush," observes Charlene Paige, one of the American hires. "You don't get politeness out of them about work…. They are such perfectionists." Many of the American workers viewed the Germans as rigid and humorless.

On the other hand, German managers viewed the Americans as careless and superficial. Not following the SMPs is tantamount to saying that a worker doesn't care about the quality of the cars he or she is building. Responding negatively to criticism—which is intended to improve the product—is as good as saying that customer satisfaction doesn't matter. "[American workers] are not used to really open feedback," comments Andreas Renschler, CEO of the Alabama plant. "The Americans always want to hear that they're doing a good job." Despite these differences, the Mercedes plant appears to be successful, so far.

As the Germans grow more comfortable with the surroundings and their American counterparts, they may want to examine American approaches to setting standards that are just as effective as their own. And as the American workers grow to understand the reason for such strict operational controls, they may be able to see why a Mercedes has the reputation of being one of the best-built cars in the world.

QUESTIONS

1. Do you think that Mercedes could get better performance from its American workers by relaxing some of its operational controls? Why or why not?
2. How might the use of human resource controls, such as training and evaluation methods, help American workers and German managers get along more successfully at the Mercedes plant in Alabama?
3. Since Alabama is geographically—and culturally—a long way from Germany, what types of challenges does Mercedes Benz face in establishing strategic and tactical controls as they are related to the new Alabama plant?

Source: Justin Martin, "Mercedes: Made in Alabama," *Fortune,* July 7, 1997, pp. 150–58.

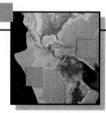

CHAPTER 17

OPERATIONS
MANAGEMENT

LEARNING OBJECTIVES

After studying this chapter, you should be able to:

- Define *operations management* and explain its importance within service and manufacturing firms.
- Explain the factors involved in selecting a facility location.
- Describe the basic types of facility layout designs.
- Explain the importance of capacity and aggregate planning.
- Describe a variety of quality and productivity tools and techniques.
- Describe the components of world-class manufacturing.

1996 Centennial Olympics

The 1996 Summer Centennial Olympics in Atlanta was an event that will go down in history. To successfully pull off such an enormous undertaking, organizers had to consider a number of logistical concerns in planning and managing such a large operation. Just imagine a 17-day event that required or generated the following:

- 48,500 balls for training and competition, including
  - 500 basketballs
  - 750 soccer balls
  - 2,500 baseballs
  - 38,400 tennis balls
- Over 1 million meals served in the Olympic Village that required over
  - 40,000 peaches
  - 3,000 pounds of grits
  - 8,000 pounds of collard greens
  - 31,500 pounds of Vidalia onions
  - 2 million cans of soda

This chapter was written by Helene Caudill of Our Lady of the Lake University and edited by the authors of this book.

- 21 million tons of ice to cool drinks, athletes, and horses (which is enough to make 247 hockey rinks)
- 10,000 tons of trash
- 2,000 portable toilets
- 42,500 volunteers
- 71,000 employees, including
  - 20,000 federal, state, and private security personnel
  - 11,000 transportation personnel
  - 4,050 Olympic committee staff

All of these people and resources were needed to host the 10,500 athletes, the 2 million visitors, and the 30,000 media personnel who visited the games from around the world. The estimated total cost was a whopping $1.7 billion, with over half (57 percent) of these funds required to manage the day-to-day operations of this complex event. Operational control and efficiency are key concerns for any organization's success, and that included the Atlanta Olympic Committee.

Transportation

One particular operational challenge facing the committee was to make sure that athletes and spectators could move about the city easily. One of Atlanta's greatest selling points in winning the right to host the Summer Olympics was its subway system, which was open 24 hours a day during the games. Seating in some vehicles was removed to create standing room for more passengers. But because the system was not originally designed for the Olympics, there was no stop within a mile of the Olympic Stadium. This required using shuttle buses to get spectators to events on time. In total, over 2,000 buses were needed, 1,500 of which had to be borrowed from transit systems across the country. The 11,000-member transportation force hired for the games was the largest ever assembled for a peacetime event. Joel Stone, Director of Transportation for the games, notes that "working out those deals, getting the buses here, and finding a place to keep them has been a big job." In addition, finding qualified people to drive all the buses was a big job, too.

These staffing and scheduling plans were based on the prediction that the majority of 550,000 spectators each day would walk the 1.5 miles or less to reach most of the major events. These plans were also dependent upon a one-third reduction in non-Olympic traffic. To attain this reduction, downtown employers were asked to allow some of their employees to telecommute or take vacation time during the games.

A major reason why transportation flowed smoothly at the games was due to a high-technology traffic management infrastructure called the

Advanced Transportation Management System (ATMS). The ATMS in Atlanta allowed traffic conditions over a wide area, including the major freeways, to be monitored at a central facility. This central facility had the capability of altering signal sequences so that traffic flowed more smoothly through key intersections. The traffic information was also made available to the public through a Web site, as well as through 130 kiosks located around the Olympic venues.

Security

The 20,000 security personnel amassed for the games were braced for everything from credit card scams to outbreaks of violent gangs and terrorist attacks. The security teams were trained by practicing simulated attacks such as a hijacking at Hartsfield International Airport, a kidnapping near Lake Lanier where the rowing events took place, and a chemical attack on the subway similar to the one that had occurred in Tokyo.

Technology also played a big part in the security of athletes and spectators. There were metal detectors at every venue as well as nonlaminated photo ID badges, which incorporated a new kind of high-density bar code and palm-reading device. Individuals passing through high-security checkpoints had their hands scanned to cross-check the badge and its photo with the topographical map of the plan. To enter the highest security area of all, the Olympic Village, athletes were also required to carry a plastic-embedded microchip that emitted a radio signal that was read at a remote site to allow access. Even with all this high technology, no area could be completely safe, as was demonstrated by the bombing at Centennial Olympic Park. But the overall operations of the Olympics were facilitated by numerous technological initiatives. In the end, it was the successful management of people and technology that helped make the games a true success.

Sources: "Atlanta Is Right on Schedule," *Newsweek,* July 17, 1995, p. 64; "The Total Cost of the 1996 Olympics Will Be $17,705,000,000," *Fortune,* July 22, 1996, p. 58; Hoyt Coffee, "High Tech Games," *The Centennial Olympics,* Summer 1996, p. 20; Gary Goettling, "On the Road … Still," *Georgia Tech Alumni Magazine: The Centennial Olympics,* Summer 1996, p. 32; Robin Nelson and Frank Vizarl, "Essential Technology Guide," *Popular Science,* July 1996, p. 63; Mark Starr and Vern E. Smith, "Is Atlanta Ready Yet?" *Newsweek,* July 15, 1996, p. 60; Steve Wuf, Adam Cohen, and Brian Reid, "Ready … or Not?" *Time,* July 15, 1996, p. 48.

As the opening story describing the 1996 Summer Centennial Olympics in Atlanta illustrates, exerting effective control over the coordination of people and technology can be extremely complex. The successful implementation of concepts and techniques involved in operations management was a key to the Olympics' success, just as operations management is a key to the success of all types of organizations. These organizations include large and small, private and not-for-profit, and manufacturing and service firms. Thus, all "operations" require some type of "management" and control in order to provide customers with the products and services they demand, which in turn makes operations management a competitive weapon in today's global economy.

IMPORTANCE OF THE OPERATIONS MANAGEMENT FUNCTION

operations management
a specialized field of management associated with the conversion or transformation of resources into products and services

Operations management is a specialized field of management associated with the conversion or transformation of resources into products and services. In the past, the focus of this field of study had been mainly on manufacturing, and the term *production and operations management (POM)* was commonly used. With the lines between what is strictly a manufacturing firm versus what is strictly a service firm now blurred, the term *operations management (OM)* is a more generic term describing both manufacturing and service-related functions. For example, Microsoft manufactures or produces a number of different software programs, but just as important, it also provides a customer service helpline for its products. Thus, Microsoft would be considered both a manufacturing and a service firm.

Operations management systems obtain inputs and transform them into outputs. Examples of operations management systems are shown in Exhibit 17.1. In terms of a college or university, the inputs would include students, books, and human resources, such as professors, employed by the college or university. The conversion process would be the transformation of these students, books, and professors into the desired output—educated people. These examples further emphasize that manufacturing and service firms are similar in the sense that both require a transformation process that needs to be managed.

EXHIBIT 17.1
Examples of Operations Management

	Primary Inputs	Transformation Process	Outputs
1. Software developer	Ideas, information, knowledge, human resources, computer hardware and software systems, buildings/offices, telephones, customers with questions	Transforms ideas, information, and knowledge into new and revised software programs	Software products and satisfied customers
2. College or university	Students, books, information, supplies, human resources, buildings/offices, utilities	Transforms information and develops skills and knowledge	Educated people
3. Hospital	Medical equipment, supplies, information, human resources, buildings/offices, sick people	Transforms patients who need medical attention	Well patients
4. Automobile factory	Purchased parts, raw materials, supplies, paints, tools, equipment, personnel, buildings, utilities	Transforms raw materials through fabrication and assembly operations	Automobiles
5. Hamburger stand	Meat, bread, vegetables, spices, supplies, human resources, utilities, machines, cartons, napkins, buildings, hungry customers	Transforms raw materials into fast-food products and packages	Fast-food products and satisfied customers

Source: From *Production and Operations Management*, 6th edition, by Norman Gaither. © 1994. Reprinted with permission of South-Western College Publishing, a division of International Thomson Publishing.

MANAGERIAL CHALLENGE

SERVING UP TO 10,000 MEALS A DAY

Throwing a dinner party for friends can certainly pose problems, but just imagine the challenges involved in catering to 1,000 crew members and up to 1,800 passengers on the *QE2,* a prestigious passenger ship that makes transatlantic runs between England and New York. This is the predicament facing Jonathan Wicks, the *QE2's* executive chef and food and beverage manager. With up to 10,000 meals to serve daily, the biggest challenge for him and his 550-person food-and-beverage crew is achieving customer satisfaction by maintaining high-quality, consistent meals.

One way Wicks overcomes this problem is by ordering quality ingredients: "We try to have a partnership with our producers and suppliers." In reference to the *QE2's* top supplier of fruits and vegetables, with whom the ocean liner has been in partnership for 10 years, Wicks notes that "they know the ship and they understand our procedures." With unfamiliar suppliers, Wicks must be much more concerned with quality control. This has been the case in the past for expensive caviar. With demand far exceeding supply, unethical dealers have been caught filling tins with low-grade fish eggs to bring them up to their two-pound weight.

Another way Wicks and his crew maintain quality and customer satisfaction is by carefully planning menus. Their first step in doing this is to analyze the passenger lists; American and British passengers have different tastes in foods. The staff must also keep up with the current trends toward healthy eating.

Wicks also takes the initiative to manage by "walking around." With 13 kitchens, 9 restaurants, 15 bars, and a large buffet operation to manage, he tries to visit the large kitchens at least three times a day. And last, but certainly not least important, Wicks maintains a sense of dedication and enthusiasm that sets an example for the rest of his staff.

Source: Jill James, "*QE2's* Cuisine Operation Is Always Shipshape," *The Dallas Morning News,* August 30, 1996, p. 1M.

Other disciplines are also concerned with the transformation of inputs into outputs. These other "sister" fields of OM include industrial engineering (IE), management science/operations research (MS/OR), and hospitality management. While IE is concerned with many of the same issues as OM, such as facility layout and design, the key distinction between the two stems from IE's roots in the discipline of engineering as opposed to OM's roots in management.[1] Similarly, while OM may apply quantitative decision techniques, such as statistical analysis, these techniques are simply tools for the operations manager to use and are not the focus of the entire discipline as they are in MS/OR. In contrast, hospitality management, which encompasses the management of hotels, restaurants, sports arenas, resort clubs, and cruise lines, may be viewed as a subset of operations management. Both fields use the same management techniques and theories, with hospitality management being focused solely on service issues while OM focuses on both service and manufacturing issues.[2] The Managerial Challenge box, "Serving up to 10,000 Meals a Day," illustrates how the management of the food and beverage services of a cruise ship falls within both OM and hospitality management.

Just as OM integrates with other disciplines and professions, it must also integrate with other areas within the organization itself, as shown in Exhibit 17.2. Although the operations function is often the central focus of a firm, it cannot stand isolated from the other areas of a company. Indeed, decisions made in one area often affect several other areas. For example, the marketing department must work closely with the OM department to ensure that there is enough production capacity to meet sales forecasts.

In particular, operation management's link with the human resource function is of major importance. The people involved lead to the success of any operation.

EXHIBIT 17.2

OM's Link within an Organization

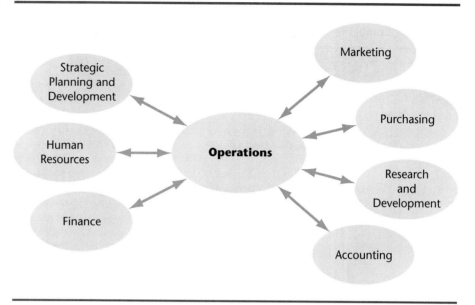

While human resources is normally a specialized function responsible for hiring and recruiting, benefits and compensation, and education and training, operations managers must also effectively manage these functions within their own area. For example, education and training play a key role in the productivity of an organization. A recent survey conducted by the National Center on the Educational Quality of the Workforce (EQW) indicates that a workforce's average level of education has a significant effect on productivity. The results of the survey revealed that in manufacturing firms, a 10 percent increase in education (approximately one year of education) yields an 8.6 percent increase in productivity. Similarly, in nonmanufacturing firms, a 10 percent increase in education yields an 11 percent increase in productivity. The survey also indicates that investments in education increase productivity more than investments in new technology or equipment upgrades.[3]

The operations management function is also very dependent on strategic planning. In reality, the role of the operations function is to support organizationwide strategies. Thus, operations strategy is influenced by the organization's long-term competitive strategies. Specifically, operations strategy translates market needs into operations by developing and implementing plans that support overall corporate objectives. For example, Nike's strategy of being the market leader in innovative athletic-shoe designs means operations must be prepared to start and stop the production of particular shoe models quickly. In turn, this integration of operations with corporate strategy is critical to Nike or any firm in gaining and sustaining competitive advantage. As mentioned in previous chapters, competitive advantage is achieved when the competencies of a firm are utilized in a way that differentiates it from its competitors.

As shown in Exhibit 17.3, the different priorities can be grouped into four categories—(1) cost, (2) quality, (3) time, and (4) flexibility—from which a company must choose to implement an operations management strategy.[4] A company may choose a combination of one or more priorities, but there are always trade-offs in

EXHIBIT 17.3

Examples of Competitive Priorities

Category	Priority	Description	Role of OM	Examples
Cost	1. Low-cost operations	Converting low-cost operations into lower prices can increase demand for products and services.	Managers must address labor, material, scrap, overhead, and other high-cost resources. To lower costs, an additional investment in automated facilities and equipment may be needed.	Generic canned foods Tract homes
Quality	2. High-performance design	A high-performance design may include superior features, greater durability, service helpfulness and availability, safety of products and services, and convenient access to service locations.	Managers must convert marketing demands into products and services desired by their customers. Quality built into the original design is of key importance.	Volvo cars known for safety Pay-at-the-pump gasoline stations
Time	3. On-time delivery	Measures how often delivery-time promises are met.	Managers must use key human resources and automated equipment to meet strict delivery times without allowing quality to suffer.	Pizza delivery Federal Express
Flexibility	4. Customization	The ability to meet the needs of each customer, as well as changing product or service designs.	Managers must ensure that they have a flexible and well-trained workforce. Flexible equipment and facilities are also needed.	Custom-designed swimming pool Cosmetic surgery

Source: Lee J. Krajewski and Larry P. Ritzman, *Operations Management,* (adapted from pages 36–40). © Addison Wesley Longman. Reprinted by permission of Addison Wesley Longman.

choosing one over the other. For example, custom-designed homes take longer and are more expensive to build than modular homes. Also, postal patrons are willing to spend more to have their packages delivered on a priority basis versus parcel post. In each of these cases, an effective operations function is imperative to meet these strategies. As with an organization's overall strategy, once a strategy is chosen, planning begins to bring it to reality.

OPERATIONS PLANNING

To carry out strategic initiatives, an organization must implement them. For the operations manager, the first step is planning. Planning involves decisions regarding the location and interior layout of a facility, the amount the facility should be able to produce or service, and the materials required to produce the firm's products or services. A major planning decision that can have a significant impact on an organization's competitive advantage is the choice of a location.

Facility Location

facility location
the process of selecting a geographic location for a company's operations

Facility location is the process, both objective and subjective, of selecting a geographic location for a company's—or units of a company—operations. The site of a company's (or unit's) facilities can have a profound effect on its operating costs, its ability to compete with its competitors, and, in general, its ability to stay profitable. For example, many companies based in the United States have located some of their assembly divisions in *maquiladoras,* large industrial parks located along the northern border of Mexico. Labor costs in the *maquilas,* or plants located in the *maquiladoras,* are much lower than those in the United States, and these lower wages offset the higher shipping costs. Thus, workers in Mexico assemble parts and then export products back to the home company in the United States. It was predicted that the number of *maquiladoras* would increase significantly by the year 2000. According to WEFA Group Inc., a Mexican forecasting unit, the *maquiladora* sector along the U.S. border planned to add approximately 390 plants by 2000.[5] This would increase the workforce from 579,000 in 1994 to 943,000 by 2000.

There are other factors besides labor costs that effect the decision of where to locate. These other factors include

- *Labor availability.* Does the surrounding population have the right skill mix needed?
- *Proximity to raw materials and suppliers.* Can your suppliers easily access your location?
- *Proximity to markets/customers.* Can your customers easily access your location?
- *Transportation availability.* How far is the nearest airport?
- *Utilities, taxes, real estate costs.* Are there state taxes?
- *Quality of life.* How is the weather where you are considering locating?
- *Quality of government.* Are the attitudes positive concerning new business ventures?

In relation to the attitudes toward business, Austin, Texas, has become a mecca for high-technology firms due to the positive incentives it offers. For example, in 1996, the city of Austin agreed to provide Samsung, a South Korean company, with approximately $40 million in tax relief in exchange for a $1.3 billion semiconductor facility.[6]

Because other factors in addition to tax incentives should be considered when selecting a location, objective decision tools are often used. One such technique is called the factor rating method. An example of how this technique might be used to locate a restaurant is shown in Exhibit 17.4. Despite the availability of objective measures, however, a location decision may be based on something as simple as the wishes of the CEO. In any event, though, the operations manager's role is to illustrate how techniques (such as the factor rating method) can make important strategic decisions (such as choosing the location of a facility) much more objective.

Facility Layout

facility layout
the arrangement of items and people within a facility

Once a company decides where to locate its facility, it must then make another important decision—how the facility will be laid out or designed inside. **Facility layout** refers to the arrangement of items and people within a facility that are needed to help produce an organization's products or services. These items include employee work stations and offices, machines and equipment, and storage areas.

| | EXHIBIT 17.4 |

Facility Location: Factor Rating Method

Scenario
Brian's Cafe wants to add another restaurant site to its existing three restaurants. Listed below are the factors, along with their weights, management considers the most important in a location.

		RAW SCORES (BASED ON 100 POINTS)		WEIGHTED SCORES	
Factor	**Weight**	**Location A**	**Location B**	**Location A**	**Location B**
Labor costs	.15	50	50	7.5	7.5
Labor availability	.20	70	40	14.0	8.0
Customer access	.50	80	85	40.0	42.5
Real estate costs	.10	30	40	3.0	4.0
Tax structure	.05	50	60	2.5	3.0
Total	1.00 (100%)			67.0	65.0

Steps Involved
1. Determine the relevant factors to include.
2. Assign a weight for each factor based on its impact on the organization's objectives. The total weight score should not exceed 1.0, or 100 percent.
3. Develop a scale for each factor (usually 1–10 or 1–100).
4. Score each location for each factor. It is usually best to include a number of key decision makers and average their scores.
5. Multiply the raw scores for each factor by their assigned weight.
6. Total the weighted scores for each location.
7. Make a recommendation based on the scores calculated.

Based on this quantitative approach, location A would be the location chosen. One thing to keep in mind is that although the factor rating method may be an objective technique, assigning the weights and scores for each location often calls for subjective judgment.

The importance of facility layout should not be overlooked because it can affect a number of key areas, including customer satisfaction, human and equipment productivity, material flow, inventory costs, and employee morale and participation. For example, in Korea, office layouts (see Exhibit 17.5) tend to be quite open, with very few walls and private offices. This fosters greater communication and fits with the cultural value of team-oriented versus individual decision making.

The overall objective of facility layout is to provide the means for materials, employees, customers, and information to move efficiently and effectively through an organization. More specific objectives include

- Providing flexibility
- Reducing the costs associated with material handling
- Providing enough capacity to meet demand
- Using human resources productively
- Promoting effective communication within and among departments
- Improving sales and customer convenience

The Managerial Challenge box describes the complexity involved in converting a General Motors assembly plant to meet these objectives.

EXHIBIT 17.5

Typical Office Layout in a Korean Firm

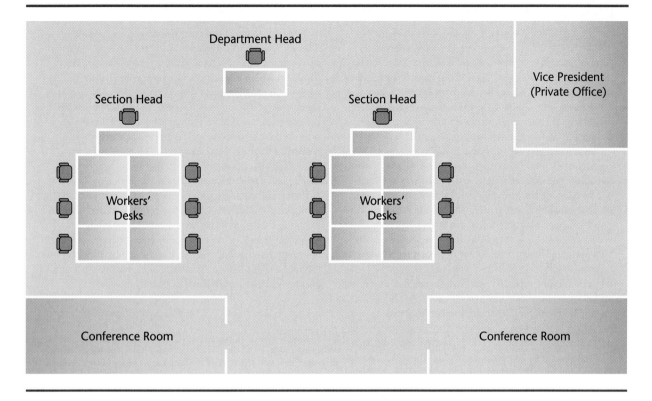

There are three basic types of layout designs: (1) fixed-position layout, (2) product or line layout, and (3) process or functional layout. A fourth design, known as group technology, or cellular layout, is actually a hybrid of the product and process layouts. A brief discussion, with examples, of each of these configurations follows.

fixed-position layout

a facility layout design where the product stays in one location while equipment, supplies, human resources, and other needed materials are brought to the location site

Fixed-Position Layout   In a **fixed-position layout** design, the product stays in one location, that is, it remains fixed while equipment, supplies, human resources, and other needed materials are brought to the location site. This is typical for constructing large items such as airplanes and ships. It is also a typical arrangement for construction sites and movie lots. A common service example is a sit-down restaurant where a food server brings everything to the dining customer, who remains fixed or seated.

product (line) layout

a facility layout design where equipment and work stations are arranged based on the sequence of operations, allowing products to move continuously from one area to another; also known as an assembly line

Product Layout   A sit-down restaurant is in contrast to a cafeteria line, which is an example of a product or line layout. In a **product**, or **line**, **layout**, equipment and work stations are arranged based on the sequence of operations, thereby allowing products to move in a continuous path from one area to another. In the case of a cafeteria line, customers move in the same direction past "food centers" such as salads, meats, deserts, and drinks. Typical product layouts in manufacturing are often termed *assembly lines,* where items such as automobiles are produced. The very funny scene in a classic *I Love Lucy* TV episode is an example of a product line

MANAGERIAL CHALLENGE

GM IS MAKING WAY FOR THE NEW BY BUILDING IN FLEXIBILITY

How do automobile manufacturers keep up with the many changes in consumers' tastes? In the case of the General Motors (GM) plant located in Arlington, Texas, the answer is: by building flexibility into their facility design. A "flex-build" plant, as it is called, is capable of producing more than one car model. This is part of GM's current strategic plan to help it lower production costs and increase its market share.

Since its opening in 1954, the Arlington plant has produced rear-wheel drive cars—most recently, the Chevrolet Impala SS. But with consumers' tastes changing, the last Impala rolled off the assembly line at the end of 1996. In its place, the plant is building more popular trucks and sport utility vehicles such as the Tahoe and Yukon. This product line has helped the U.S. auto industry stay competitive with its Japanese counterparts. Despite the obvious possibility that the current fad for trucks and sport utility vehicles may fade, the conversion of the Arlington plant to a flexible design means added job security for the workers because the plant is able to change from one product line to another fairly easily. According to David Cole, director of the Office for the Study of Automotive Transportation at the University of Michigan, "The local plant is designed for flexibility. The robots, equipment layout, and fixtures are built around the idea of maintaining agility for an ever-changing global market."

The conversion of the plant does not come cheaply though. The estimated $264 million cost is nearly the same as what it would cost GM to build an all-new assembly plant. According to plant manager Herb Stone, "We're taking a Third World body shop into the 21st century." Nearly half of the conversion costs are involved in renovating the plant's automated body shop. The shell of the vehicle is produced in the body shop; the fenders and doors are welded to a vehicle's top and hood. The body must be assembled with great precision so that the other components, such as the seats and dashboard, fit exactly. Because of the precision and consistency required to complete this process, approximately 120 to 150 robots are used. Indeed, the body shop is generally considered the most important area of an assembly plant. Although many modern plants have high levels of automation, it is the ability to reprogram the robots and other equipment to allow for the production of other vehicles that makes a plant truly flexible.

Sources: Terry Box, "Arlington GM Plant Conversion Will Add Flexibility," *Dallas Morning News,* December 16, 1996, pp. D1, D4; Jeanne Graham, "An Epoch Will End in Days at GM Plant," *Fort Worth Star-Telegram,* December 8, 1996, pp. B1, B4; Jeanne Graham, "Historic Transition Is Today at GM Plant," *Fort Worth Star-Telegram,* December 13, 1996, pp. C1, C4.

layout. Lucy and Ethel are employed in a chocolate factory and have trouble keeping up with the production line, so they eat or hide the candy.

process (functional) layout
a facility layout design that groups human resources, equipment, and machines according to functions that do similar type of work

Process Layout   Process, or **functional**, **layout** designs involve the grouping of human resources, equipment, and machines according to activities (functions) that perform similar types of work. It makes sense to utilize a process layout when the products to be produced have different requirements or when customers have unique needs. For example, in a manufacturing facility that has implemented a process layout, all lathes and all stamping machines would be located in their own separate areas. This allows a great deal of variability because materials for a product can be routed to the same processing areas as many times as needed during the product's production. An example of process layout in a service-oriented firm would be a hospital, where similar functions are grouped into departments. Patients may go from the emergency room to x-ray to intensive care and then to a regular medical unit during their stay.

group technology (cellular layout)
a facility layout design that is a hybrid of process and product layout designs

Group Technology   Group technology, or **cellular layout**, consists of machines and human resources that are grouped into work centers or cells containing all the materials, tools, equipment, and operations needed to produce a product or service. This type of layout design has characteristics of both process and product layouts. It

EXHIBIT 17.6 Measures of Capacity	**Type of Organization**	**Output Measures**
	Automobile assembly plant	Automobiles/hour
	Law firm	Billable hours/week
	Oil refinery	Barrels of oil/day
	Electric company	Megawatts of electricity/hour
	Paper producer	Tons of paper/week
		Input Measures
	Jet engine plant	Machine-hours/month
	Airline	Number of seats/flight
	Hotel	Number of rooms, number of beds
	Grocery store	Number of checkout lines
	Warehouse	Cubic feet of space
	Tennis club	Number of courts
	Department store	Number of square feet

Source: James R. Evans, *Applied Production and Operations Management,* 4th ed. (St. Paul, Minn.: West Publishing Co., 1993), p. 194.

is similar to a process layout because the cells are designed to carry out a particular set of processes. It is similar to a product layout because the cells are set up to handle a limited scope of products or services. In general, group technology layouts allow more employee participation than other layout designs because a team of people is responsible for producing a complete product or service and not just a portion of one.

This type of layout is widely used in metal fabricating and computer chip manufacturing. In the service industry, teams of consultants are often grouped together to solve a unique set of problems. In an office layout, offices that have a secretary in each department, as opposed to a centralized secretarial pool, are using a group layout design. The use of a centralized secretarial pool would be an example of a process design.

Capacity Planning

The layout of the facility affects and is affected by the system's capacity. Indeed, a key strategic planning decision in OM is **capacity planning**—determining how much a firm should be able to produce or service. As shown in Exhibit 17.6, measures of capacity include output, as well as input, measures.

Although organizations would like to be able to operate at maximum capacity at all times, no organization could possibly sustain itself at this rate. Rather than run at its **design capacity**, which is the maximum capacity that can be attained under *ideal* conditions, organizations usually run at their effective capacities instead. The **effective capacity** is the percent of design capacity actually expected, and it can be expressed as a simple formula:

Effective Capacity = Expected Capacity/Design Capacity

Organizations may need to add capacity to meet increased demand; however, it is important to consider a number of different options including the timing, amount, and types of capacity to add. For example, if a hospital plans to increase its

capacity planning
the process of determining how much a firm should be able to produce or service

design capacity
the maximum capacity at which a facility can run under ideal conditions

effective capacity
the percent of design capacity a facility is actually expected to maintain

number of beds, it will likely have to increase the number of nurses as well. The wrong type of capacity additions might even lead to financial disaster. For example, airlines that increase their passenger capacity by purchasing large jumbo jets may become less competitive than ones that lease the same capacity, especially if periods of increased demand are temporary. This is partly why outsourcing, or contracting with external vendors to supply products or services to cover capacity shortages, is increasingly being used.

Sometimes fads lead to a capacity dilemma. Consider the cigar craze that swept the nation in the mid-1990s. When annual demand increased over 30 percent from 1994 to 1995, all parts of the supply chain were strained. From tobacco growers, to cigar factories, to cigar box markers and band engravers, demand far outstripped supply.[7] Consolidated Cigar Holdings Inc., the nation's number-one maker, ended 1995 with a backlog of 4.3 million cigars. Even after increasing production capacity in 1996, the company had 18 million cigars on back order. Capacity constraints were further hampered because of the two to five years it can take to grow and age tobacco leaf, as well as the one-year time period required for a new cigar roller to become proficient at the job. Interestingly, by the beginning of 1999, the fad had peaked, and the efforts that manufacturers had made to deal with the capacity shortages worked against them in reverse. The top three premium cigar manufacturers in the United States ended the preceding year with 100 million unsold cigars and did not expect the oversupply to disappear for at least two years.[8]

Frito-Lay faced similar capacity problems in 1995 when it introduced its Baked Lays, low-fat potato chips. All four U.S. production lines capable of producing the snack had to run 24 hours a day, seven days a week, and the company still could not keep up with demand. One of the problems facing Frito-Lay was that the baked chips could only be made on special production lines; existing lines could not be converted easily.[9]

Aggregate Planning

aggregate planning
the process of determining the production or service activities, including the resources, needed to meet forecasted sales demand

While capacity planning looks at long-term, intermediate, and short-term demand, aggregate planning focuses more on the intermediate and short term. **Aggregate planning** is the process of determining the production or service activities, including the resources, needed to meet forecasted sales demand. It provides a broad, or general, operating plan. For example, the aggregate plan for a restaurant would include the total number of customers to be served, but it would not include the specific meals each would consume.[10] These details would be included on the master schedule, which is developed from the aggregate plan. The master schedule includes the forecasted details of the quantity and type or model of each item to be produced or served. In addition, the master schedule includes how, when, and where these items should be produced or served. In the case of a college student, the degree plan is similar to an aggregate plan, while the year's schedule of classes is similar to the master schedule. Once the aggregate plan and master schedule have been completed, materials requirement planning must take place.

Materials Requirement Planning

materials requirement planning (MRP)
a sophisticated computer system, derived from the master production schedule and an inventory database, whose output provides schedules that identify the required raw materials, parts, and assemblies needed during each specified time period

The theme of a **materials requirement planning (MRP)** system is "getting the right materials to the right place at the right time."[11] An MRP system is a sophisticated computer system derived from the master production schedule and an inventory database. Its output provides schedules that identify the required raw materials, parts, and assemblies needed during each specified time period. Firms that implement an MRP system may realize such benefits as reduced inventory, the ability to price more competitively, and better response to customers' demands. Although there are a number of benefits to MRP, implementation of such as system can be quite costly and often requires a higher level of commitment than a company is willing to give.

Operations Scheduling and Control

In addition to MRP systems, which help provide control over production schedules, other tools exist to help control schedules as well. Two such tools are Gantt charts and the program evaluation and review technique and critical path method (PERT/CPM). Inventory management systems also provide additional control over this costly expense.

Gantt Charts   As we discussed in Chapters 2 and 7, Gantt charts are named after Henry Gantt, their inventor, who was a pioneer of the scientific management era. These charts are nonmathematical graphical representations of projects (see Exhibit 7.5). They are useful for determining what specific activities should be included to complete a project on time. They are especially important because they assist in monitoring the progress of a project and are most often used for projects that have a manageable number of activities (approximately 25 or fewer). Projects that are much larger often require a more sophisticated technique known as PERT/CPM.

PERT/CPM

program evaluation and review technique (PERT)/ critical path method (CPM) is a technique for scheduling and controlling large, complex projects

PERT/CPM   The **program evaluation and review technique/critical path method (PERT/CPM)** is useful for scheduling, monitoring, and controlling large, complex projects such as the expansion of a freeway system or the construction of a bridge. Due to the complexity of such projects, a number of PERT/CPM software packages have been developed. Although Gantt charts and PERT/CPM are similar in that both require a complete list of the specific activities involved and time estimates for each, PERT/CPM goes one step farther in helping to maintain control. Specifically, the PERT/CPM technique requires the project manager to determine which activities must precede others and which must follow. These relationships help to determine the critical path through the network of activities. This critical path represents the *longest* time path for the project, and the activities on this path will delay the entire project if any one of them is delayed.[12] For example, laying the foundation for a house would be considered a critical activity because it precedes a number of other activities, such as the electrical and plumbing work. The use of PERT/CPM can also assist managers in rescheduling the noncritical activities of a project—those that can be delayed without causing the entire project to fall behind schedule. Awareness of noncritical activities can help if, for example, there is a staffing shortage and certain activities cannot be completed as originally scheduled.

Inventory Management Systems   Maintaining control over inventory allows organizations to be more profitable. The reason is simple: Companies have to spend money to acquire inventory. The more inventory in the system and the longer it sits idle, the more the money it represents is nonperforming (i.e., non-earning). Excellent inventory control, for example, is a major reason that Dell Computer is so profitable.[13] Because Dell only builds a computer after it has been

economic order quantity (EOQ)

an inventory management model that provides the most economical quantity to order so that total inventory costs are minimized

ordered, it can maintain low levels of inventory. Two of the most basic approaches to inventory management that companies can use to enhance profitability are (1) the economic order quantity (EOQ), and (2) ABC analysis. The **economic order quantity (EOQ)** model was developed in the early 1900s and, thus, has enjoyed a rather long history in the field of OM. The basic premise of the model is to provide the most economical quantity to order so that total inventory costs are minimized. The actual formula is as follows:

$$EOQ = \sqrt{\frac{2 \times U \times S}{C \times I}}$$

where

EOQ = economic order quantity (quantity to be ordered)
U = annual usage
S = restocking or ordering costs
C = cost per unit
I = annual carrying costs

Because the two major costs, ordering costs and annual carrying costs, vary inversely, there are always trade-offs to make. For instance, a company may be able to get a discount for ordering large quantities less often, but there would be an increased cost involved in storing the items.

ABC analysis

an inventory management system that categorizes items to provide information concerning which items require the most control

While the EOQ model assists in making decisions concerning how, when, and how much to order, **ABC analysis** provides information concerning which inventory items require the most attention. In most companies, a small percentage (15–30 percent) of their inventory accounts for the greatest percentage (70–80 percent) of their inventory dollar volume. For this reason, companies are better off putting more effort into controlling and monitoring these high-dollar-volume items compared with the lower-dollar-volume items. For example, many retail stores have placed special security tags on high-priced items, which are likely categorized as A items. These tags help provide the extra control needed to reduce theft.

ABC analysis provides a way to classify inventory items into three value categories (A, B, and C):

1. A items typically account for the top 15 percent of the dollar volume.
2. B items typically account for the next 35 percent of the dollar volume.
3. C items typically account for the remaining 50 percent of the dollar volume.

For a typical office supply company that sells computer equipment, office furniture, and miscellaneous supplies such as paper clips, it is likely that fax machines would be classified as an A item, while desks would be classified as B items, and paper clips would be classified as C items. Based on these categorizations, the firm would want to spend more time keeping better records of the computer equipment compared with the miscellaneous office supplies. The high dollar volume associated with A items is a result of either low cost and high usage or sales, or high cost coupled with low usage or sales. In comparison, items classified as C result from either low demand or sales or low cost that produces low dollar volume.

Critical items that need a great deal of attention are likely to be categorized as A items regardless of their actual dollar volume. This would help ensure that sufficient inventory levels are kept on hand at all times. For example, hospitals would never want to run out of certain life-saving pharmaceuticals; thus, they would likely categorize these medications as A items to help ensure that sufficient levels are always on hand.

Once an organization has dealt with operations planning issues, it needs to consider the productivity and quality of its goods and services. Those two issues determine how competitive an organization will be in the marketplace.

THE PRODUCTIVITY AND QUALITY CHALLENGE

Productivity and quality are two of the most important issues in OM. They are grouped together here because one often leads to the other. To establish effective operations, it is important to know how to define and measure these somewhat abstract concepts. For productivity, two common methods of measurement, time and motion studies and work sampling, are described. For quality, it is important to keep in mind that it is ultimately the customer who determines whether a product or service is of high quality. A number of tools and techniques exist to help improve productivity and quality, including flow charting, benchmarking, outsourcing, designing for manufacturability, statistical process control, just-in-time systems, and supplier partnerships.

Productivity

The renewed interest in productivity is one of the key reasons why there is increased emphasis on OM.[14] The reason for this renewed interest is because productivity is all about the efficient transformation of inputs into desired outputs. Greater productivity typically leads to greater profitability. The simple formula for productivity is

$$\text{Productivity} = \frac{\text{Output}}{\text{Input}}$$

productivity
measurement of how well an organization uses its inputs in producing its outputs

Thus, **productivity** measures how well an organization is using its resources (inputs) in producing its goods and services (outputs). A useful productivity measure for a restaurant would be *number of meals served/waitperson*. For an automobile assembly plant, a useful productivity measure would be *number of cars painted/robot*. Productivity measures such as these can be used for two main comparative purposes. First, a firm can compare itself with similar firms, and second, a firm can track productivity measures over time to identify trends.

Of particular importance to both service and manufacturing firms is labor productivity. To determine the productivity of an employee or a group of employees, work or labor standards are often used. A **work standard** is the amount of time it should take for a trained employee to complete a specific activity or process. The development of work standards involves work measurement techniques. Two popular work measurement techniques are time and motion studies and work sampling.

work standard
the amount of time it takes a trained employee to complete a specific activity or process

The first step in time and motion studies is to review each activity in detail so that unnecessary steps are eliminated. The motto "work smart, not hard" applies here. Only after each process has been carefully reviewed should standard times be developed. Stopwatches are often used to ensure accuracy. In the past, many companies used outside employees to watch and time the employees actually doing the work. More recently, with the philosophy of employee empowerment and teams, co-workers have been used to time their own work groups. This has been the case for New United Motor Manufacturing Inc. (NUMMI), a GM–Toyota joint venture. At NUMMI, team members look for the safest, most efficient and effective way to complete each process at a sustainable pace while timing each other with stopwatches.[15] This involvement has led to greater acceptance of the work standards and increased interest in improving processes.

Work sampling is also a popular way of determining time standards, or, more commonly, the percentage of time spent on each activity during a working day or shift. This method is not as accurate as time and motion studies for setting standards for repetitive, well-defined jobs, but it works well with nonrepetitive work. Work sampling involves sampling the activities performed by an employee or a group of employees at random times throughout a work shift. The assumption is that the percentage of time the specific activities were observed during the observation period is the same as the percentage of time actually spent on the activity.

The key to an effective work sampling study is the development of an observation sheet that lists all the possible activities an employee might perform. A trained observer then marks each activity observed during predetermined random times. To determine the percentage of time spent on a particular activity, the total number of occurrences for each activity is divided by the total number of occurrences for all activities. For example, if a nurse is observed preparing medications 10 times out of 100 observations, then the percentage of time spent on this activity would be 10 percent (10/100). The use of work sampling helps to identify areas of needed improvement. If, for example, patients had complained that they rarely saw their nurse, then work sampling could help determine the percentage of time spent directly with a patient. If this time was below the goal set, then changes in processes and/or staffing levels would likely be needed. These changes, in turn, would improve the quality of patient care. Thus, productivity and quality are directly related.

Quality

Ford Motor Company's advertising slogan, "Quality is job one," points out how important the concept of quality can be to an organization. In today's global economy, companies know that they cannot compete effectively, globally or domestically, without maintaining high-quality products and services. But a company is not the judge of whether it has quality products and services—the customer ultimately decides. Hyundai Motor Co. knows this better than anyone. Although its cars are considered top quality in its home country of South Korea, in consumer markets outside its home country, Hyundai has had trouble with its Rodney Dangerfield image: "They don't get any respect."[16] Because of quality problems with the cars it first introduced into the United States, the company still has the reputation for making cheap products, even though its current cars meet the highest quality standards.

quality
the reliability, durability, serviceability, and dependability of products and services; also defined as fitness for use

Total Quality Management   A popular definition of **quality** is "fitness for use," which is a measure of how well a product or service performs its intended purpose.[17] Other definitions for product quality include reliability (how often a product needs to be repaired), durability (the expected length of time a product should last), and serviceability (the ease, speed, and efficiency of repairing a product). Other definitions of service quality include on-time delivery (the trust that the ser-

total quality management (TQM)

a management approach and philosophy that involves a commitment from all levels of employees to continually strive to make improvements and satisfy customers

vice will be delivered as promised), dependability (the assurance that the service will be provided at the expected quality level), and courtesy (the friendliness and attentiveness of the service staff). All of these definitions are part of a philosophy known as **total quality management (TQM)**.

TQM is considered a management philosophy because it encompasses a commitment from all levels of employees to continually strive to make improvements and satisfy customers. In essence, TQM must be part of the organization's culture in order for a true commitment to quality to be realized. In contrast to traditional quality control efforts where a separate team of experts would normally inspect products or services for defects or errors after completion, TQM emphasizes "quality at the source," i.e., quality inspection at all stages of production or service output. Quality at the source includes quantitative techniques such as statistical process control, as well as nonquantitative techniques such as employee empowerment.

Organizations need to empower their employees so that they will take pride in and a sense of responsibility for their individual output, as well as the output of the entire organization. By involving employees, organizations are obtaining the expertise directly from those who produce the product or provide the service. These individuals are the experts in their areas and should have input on how to improve the quality of the organization's product or service. In addition to employee involvement, a successful TQM philosophy requires a group of committed top managers who can effectively communicate its vision of TQM and provide the strong leadership needed to implement the changes required. And most importantly, a strong focus on the customer's needs and expectations must be paramount.

The goal of exceeding customer expectations was the primary reason why Athens Insurance Center (AIC) implemented a TQM program in the mid-1990s. Part of its TQM effort helped to identify a need to cross-train its agents so that when customers called, they would be assisted immediately instead of having to wait for a particular agent. For AIC, the appeal of TQM was that "it attacks the flaws in the systems and procedures—not people."[18] Indeed, AIC reports that its TQM efforts have helped instill a stronger sense of ownership and pride in their employees, which, in turn, has improved customer satisfaction.

Boeing Co., a maker of commercial and military aircraft, also sees a need for TQM in its operations. The company is focusing on improving quality by eliminating redundant processes, reducing the time to assemble parts, upgrading their information systems, improving supplier relations, increasing its outsourcing, and cutting layers of bureaucracy.[19] These quality efforts are needed for Boeing to survive a sudden downturn, such as sharply reduced orders from particular parts of the world experiencing economic slowdowns (e.g., Asia in the late 1990s). For Boeing, the success of its TQM efforts is imperative for the success of a well-established company.

TQM efforts can also be found in educational settings. "Koalaty Kid," a program sponsored by the American Society for Quality, emphasizes TQM and continuous improvement in elementary schools worldwide. According to Jane Cousins, principal of Johnson Elementary School in Southlake, Texas, "This student-centered approach is aimed at creating a school environment where all students sustain enthusiasm for learning, behave responsibly, feel proud of themselves and their accomplishments, and strive to meet high standards." Part of the Koalaty Kid program includes celebrating student accomplishments. Each six-week grading period, students who have performed above expectations are awarded certificates, stickers, buttons, and stuffed koala bears during a schoolwide assembly. The results have paid off for Johnson Elementary School. Since implementing the Koalaty Kid program in 1992, Johnson Elementary has been recognized as a National Blue Ribbon School of Excellence by the U.S. Department of Education.[20]

The importance that companies—and countries—attach to quality and its management and improvement has resulted in the initiation of several major awards and a significant quality certification procedure. These include the Deming Prize, the Malcolm Baldrige National Quality Award, and ISO 9000 certification, all discussed in the next section.

Recognition of Quality Achievements   The Deming Prize, named after the American statistical control expert, Dr. W. Edwards Deming, was first awarded in 1951. This esteemed prize is sponsored by the Union of Japanese Scientists and Engineers. A Deming Prize is awarded to any company in the world if it meets the standards for statistical quality control instituted by the union. Thus, multiple winners are awarded each year.

In contrast, the Malcolm Baldrige National Quality Award is presented to up to two U.S.-based winners from three categories: (1) manufacturing companies, (2) service companies, and (3) small businesses with fewer than 500 employees. The award was established in 1987 and is named after a former U.S. Secretary of Commerce. The national Institute of Standards and Technology developed the award criteria (see Exhibit 17.7), which includes customer focus and satisfaction, quality and operational results, and human resource development and management. Although the application process is tedious and labor intensive, the status of winning the award has attracted the attention of hundreds of firms that compete for the coveted award each year.

ISO 9000 is a certification procedure rather than an award. Companies that have been deemed compliant have provided documentation to support their quality claims. Thus, ISO 9000 certification does not guarantee the quality of the actual product; it simply relates to the quality processes which the organization prescribes.[21] The quality processes can be documented in a number of places, including employee handbooks, training manuals, and companywide quality manuals. The documentation required for an ISO 9000 audit can be quite time-consuming to complete. LTV Steel, for example, used a broad cross-functional team approach to get itself prepared.[22] A key benefit to going through ISO 9000 certification is that it instills a quality philosophy throughout the organization. For Johnson Controls, obtaining ISO 9000 certification created a better-educated workforce in the company's overall processes.[23] A central focus for all companies vying for the Deming Prize, the Baldrige Award, or ISO 9000 certification is continuous process improvement.

continuous process improvement
incremental and breakthrough improvements in the way an organization does business; also known as business process reengineering and *kaizen*

Continuous Process Improvement   Continuous process improvement, also known as business process reengineering and *kaizen* in Japan, refers to both incremental and breakthrough improvements in the way an organization does business. According to the criteria for the Malcolm Baldrige National Quality Award, several types of improvements are possible, including

1. Enhancing value to customers through new and improved products and services
2. Reducing errors, defects, and waste
3. Improving responsiveness and cycle time performance

An example of *kaizen* can be found at the Toyota Manufacturing plant in Georgetown, Kentucky, where an employee brought in a Bass Boat seat and placed it at his station on the line. A seated position made the installation of parts under the wheel well much easier.

4. Improving productivity and effectiveness in the use of all resources
5. Improving the company's performance and leadership position in fulfilling its public responsibilities and serving as a role model in corporate citizenship

A number of effective quality and productivity tools and techniques are available to make these kinds of continual improvements necessary to remain profitable.

Quality and Productivity Tools and Techniques

There is no substitute for good management and employee relations in making quality and productivity improvements. But in addition to these two basic approaches, operations managers have several other tools and techniques from which to choose. These include flow charting, benchmarking, outsourcing, designing for manufacturing, statistical process control, just-in-time systems, and supplier partnerships.

flowchart
a simple graphical representation of all the steps involved in completing a process

Flowcharting A **flowchart** is a simple graphical representation of all the steps involved in a process. Circles, rectangles, and triangles represent the steps, and arrows show the sequence. Employees actually involved in the process should develop the flowchart. After it is completed, it can be used to identify areas of needed improvement. The U.S. government is in the process of doing just this. After flowcharting the process required to authorize and pay for travel vouchers, a government committee realized that some agencies require as many as 60 steps to complete this process.[24] Some government organizations have already reduced these steps. One did so by reducing the number of signatures required from seven down to one, while another has reduced the time from three weeks to only one day. It costs the U.S. government approximately $37 to $123 to process each trip voucher, but the cost for the best organizations in private industry ranges from $10 to $20 per trip. Such a comparison to best practices is known as benchmarking.

| EXHIBIT 17.7 |

1999 Criteria Used for the Malcolm Baldrige National Quality Award

Category	Items	Examples of Questions to be Answered	Point Value (Maximum Score = 1,000)
Leadership	Organizational leadership	How do senior leaders set directions and seek future opportunities for your organization?	85
	Public responsibility and citizenship	How do you anticipate public concerns with current and future products, services, and operations? How do you prepare for these concerns in a proactive manner?	40
Strategic planning	Strategy development	What is your strategic planning process? Include key steps and key participants in the process.	40
	Strategy deployment	What are your two-to-five year projections for key performance measures and/or indicators? Include key performance targets and/or goals, as appropriate.	45
Customer and market focus	Customer and market knowledge	How do you listen and learn to determine key requirements and drivers of purchase decisions for current, former, and potential customers?	40
	Customer satisfaction and relationships	How do you determine key customer contact requirements and deploy these requirements to all employees involved in the response chain?	45
Information and analysis	Measurement of organizational performance	How do you keep your performance measurement system current with business needs and directions?	40
	Analysis of organizational performance	How do you ensure that the results of organizational level analysis are linked to work group and/or functional-level operations to enable effective support for decision making?	45
Human resource focus	Work systems	How do you design, organize, and manage work and jobs to promote cooperation and collaboration, individual initiative, innovation, and flexibility, and to keep current with business needs?	35
	Employee education, training and satisfaction	How do you enhance your employees' work climate via services, benefits, and policies? How are these enhancements selected and tailored to the needs of different categories and types of employees, and to individuals, as appropriate?	25

Source: Baldrige National Quality Program, Malcolm Baldrige National Quality Award, 1999 Criteria for Performance Excellence.

Benchmarking   Although flowcharting takes an internal look within an organization, benchmarking goes one step further by making comparisons with other, similar companies or companies with similar practices. The basic objective is to select a company with which to make comparisons and then to make internal

EXHIBIT 17.7

Continued

Category	Items	Examples of Questions to be Answered	Point Value (Maximum Score = 1,000)
Process management	Employee well-being and satisfaction	How do you enhance your employees' work climate via services, benefits, and policies? How are these enhancements selected and tailored to the needs of different categories and types of employees, and to individuals, as appropriate?	25
	Product and service processes	What are your design processes for products/services and their related production/delivery processes?	55
	Support processes	How do you determine key support process requirements, incorporating input from internal and/or external customers, as appropriate?	15
	Supplier and partnering processes	How do you minimize overall casts associated with inspections, tests, and process and/or performance audits?	15
Business results	Customer focused results	What are your current levels and trends in key measures and/or indicators of customer satisfaction, dissatisfaction, and satisfaction relative to competitors?	115
	Financial and market results	What are your current levels and trends in key measures and/or indicators of financial performance, including aggregate measures of financial return and/or economic value, as appropriate?	115
	Human resource results	What are your current levels and trends in key measures and/or indicators of employee well-being, satisfaction and dissatisfaction, and development?	80
	Supplier and partner results	What are your current levels and trends in key measures and/or indicators of supplier and partner performance? Include your performance and/or cost improvements resulting from supplier and partner performance and performance management.	25
	Organizational effectiveness results	What are your results for key measures and/or indicators of regulatory/legal compliance and citizenship? What are your results for key measures and/or indicators of accomplishment of organizational strategy?	115

improvements based on those comparisons. Examples of companies that are often used for benchmarking include Xerox and Federal Express, previous recipients of the Baldrige Award. Benchmarking best practices may even lead an organization to decide to outsource certain noncore portions of its business.

outsourcing

contracting out an operation that is considered a noncore portion of the business operation

Outsourcing   Companies that understand and stick to their core competencies have begun to outsource noncore portions of their businesses at an increasing rate. The use of **outsourcing**, or the contracting out of an operation, is widespread. A significant number of health care facilities have outsourced housekeeping and laundry operations for years. More recently, payroll, human resource management, and information processing are also being outsourced by all types of industries. In 1994, Xerox signed a 10-year, $3.2 billion contract with EDS to handle all of its information technology.[25] This deal was part of a large reengineering effort aimed at cutting costs. By allowing EDS to handle all of its information processing, Xerox is able to reduce expenses, particularly hardware expenses and benefits costs associated with fewer employees. Companies that outsource, like Xerox, are able to improve quality and productivity by focusing on their core missions.

designing for manufacturing

designing products for ease of manufacturing so that quality is built into the design process

Designing for Manufacturing   Companies should aim to design products for ease of manufacturing so that quality is built into the design, which, in turn, often leads to increased productivity. **Designing for manufacturing** often means reducing the number of parts required in a product. General Motors succeeded in doing this for its 1997 Corvette, its first new Corvette model in 14 years. The 1997 model had 34 percent fewer parts than its predecessor and a more efficient design, which decreased assembly time from approximately 64 hours to 45, reducing labor costs by about 28 percent.[26]

statistical process control (SPC)

a quantitative tool to aid in making decisions concerning how well a process is performing

Statistical Process Control   **Statistical process control (SPC)** provides an objective tool to make decisions concerning how well a process is performing. Although all companies ideally should have a goal of zero defects, or 100 percent customer satisfaction, in reality, slight deviations cannot be completely eliminated. Thus, organizations try to minimize their occurrence. This is the purpose of SPC, the most common form of which is the process control chart. Control charts should be developed for any quality-related characteristic that may cause defective products or services. Examples include the temperature of fast-food items and the number of complaints from hospital patients. Knowing that a company uses SPC gives consumers greater confidence that the product or service is high quality. Sunbeam-Oster Household Products even advertises that its Accu-read bathroom scale is "precision-manufactured with state-of-the art Statistical Process Control."

The development of a control chart requires taking a sample, computing the average measurement, and establishing the upper and lower control limits. The control limits provide an acceptable range for measurements. Any measurements outside the range are considered unacceptable and cause for investigation. The most important use for control charts is to provide a basis for taking action to determine the causes of good or poor performance. Exhibit 17.8 provides examples of control charts and what actions should be taken based on the measurements plotted.

just-in-time (JIT) systems

inventory management and control systems that have the objective of reducing waste throughout the production and delivery of a product or service; in manufacturing, also known as lean production or value-added manufacturing

Just-in-Time Systems   **Just-in-time (JIT) systems** refer to inventory management and control systems that have the objective of reducing waste throughout the production and delivery of a product or service. In manufacturing, JIT is also known as lean production or value-added manufacturing. The objective is to produce the product or service only as needed with only the necessary materials, equipment, and employee time that will add value to the product or service. JIT is

EXHIBIT 17.8
Quality Control Charts

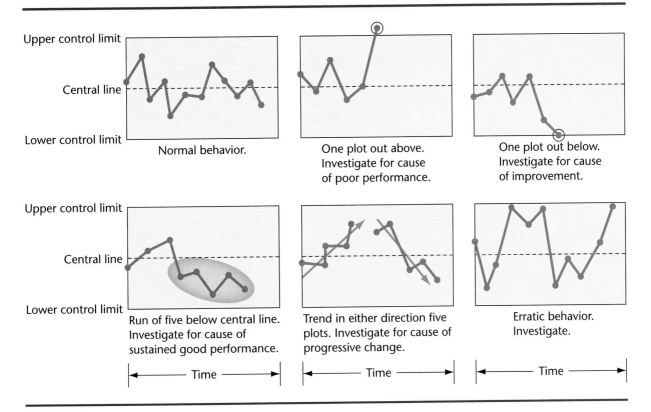

Normal behavior.

One plot out above. Investigate for cause of poor performance.

One plot out below. Investigate for cause of improvement.

Run of five below central line. Investigate for cause of sustained good performance.

Trend in either direction five plots. Investigate for cause of progressive change.

Erratic behavior. Investigate.

known as a pull system, because the demand for the item signals the need to make or provide it. Since pull systems require a high degree of repetitiveness, JIT is not applicable for all organizations, especially those that make customized, one-of-a-kind products or services.

The systematic elimination of waste requires employee involvement at all levels within the organization. Benefits of implementing JIT include

- Reducing inventory levels to only the parts or supplies that are needed at the time
- Improving productivity and quality by reducing labor and equipment time
- Increasing customer satisfaction by decreasing the time required to make and deliver the product or service
- Encouraging employee participation by soliciting ways to make improvements
- Ultimately, increasing profits to the firm

A number of companies that have implemented JIT have found great success. An excellent example is the Converters/Customer Sterile Business Group of Baxter Healthcare Corporation, a producer of single-use supplies, such as disposable drapes and gowns for health care employees and facilities. The division implemented a JIT system and other quality initiatives in 1993.[27] One year later, defects had decreased by 32 percent and the number of days of inventory on hand had decreased by 66 percent. Another very important benefit was that employee

EXHIBIT 17.9

Supplier Relationships

Adversary	Factor	Partnership
Brief	**Tenure**	Long term, stable
Sporadic purchase orders	**Type of agreement**	Exclusive or semiexclusive contracts, usually at least one year
Several sources per item for protection against risk and for price competition	**Number of sources**	One or a few good suppliers for each item or commodity group
Limits on the amount of business with any one supplier	**Volume of business**	High; sometimes supplier dedicates small plant to single customer
High on average; low buy-in bids (below costs) can lead to unstable suppliers	**Price/costs**	Low; scale economies from volume contracts; suppliers can invest in improvements
Uncertain; reliance on receiving inspections	**Quality**	Quality at source; supplier uses SPC and TQM
Customer developed	**Design**	Make use of suppliers' design expertise
Infrequent, large lots	**Delivery frequency/ order size**	Frequent (sometimes more than one per day), small lots, just-in-time
Mail	**Order conveyance**	Long term: contracts. Short term: phone, fax, or electronic data interchange
Packing lists, invoices, count/inspection forms	**Documentation**	Sometimes no count, inspection, or list—just monthly bill
Receiving dock and stockroom	**Delivery location**	Direct to point of use
Very little; black box	**Openness**	On-site audits of supplier, concurrent engineering/design, visits by front-line associates

Source: Adapted from Richard J. Schonberger and Edward M. Knod Jr., *Operations Management*, 5th ed., p. 276, Richard D. Irwin, copyright 1994. Reproduced with permission of The McGraw-Hill Companies.

turnover decreased by 37 percent. A key factor in obtaining benefits such as these from a JIT system is nurturing a positive relationship with suppliers.

Supplier Partnerships Adversarial relationships between buyers and suppliers seem to be a thing of the past. An organization and its suppliers can reap a number of benefits by having a collaborative and trusting relationship with one another. Benefits include increased quality, reduced costs, and better communication. A comparison between an adversarial relationship and a true supplier partnership is shown in Exhibit 17.9. An example of close supplier partnerships was illustrated in the Managerial Challenge box on the *QE2,* where a food and beverage manager must have a trusting relationship with suppliers to ensure the highest quality meals.

Buyers should select companies that they believe will meet their design and manufacturing requirements and that have a record of quality. Chosen suppliers often benefit from the shared information they receive, including production plans of their buyers. In supplier partnerships, buyers frequently visit the manufacturing sites of their suppliers and work with them in producing a better-quality, lower-cost product. For example, in 1993, AlliedSignal, a maker of auto parts and aerospace electronics, narrowed its suppliers for each part to just a few. If offered to double its orders from a particular supplier of aluminum chassis for avionics systems in airplanes and rockets, Mech-Tronics, in exchange for a 10 percent price cut.[28] This agreement has been a win-win situation for both companies.

WORLD-CLASS MANUFACTURING

computer-integrated manufacturing (CIM)
the integration of information systems and equipment in the manufacturing process to produce world-class quality products

The ideal vision of the factory of the future is a fully automated facility that runs without human interaction; however, today's factories rely heavily on humans to devise sophisticated technological systems based on computer information technology. Indeed, computer technology, both software and hardware, has helped make major advances in manufacturing operations worldwide. The term for these sophisticated factories is *world-class manufacturing facilities.* Within these facilities, industrial robots, computer-aided design/computer-aided engineering, computer-aided manufacturing, and flexible manufacturing systems are commonplace. The integration of these automated tools is known as **computer-integrated manufacturing (CIM)**. CIM integrates all these world-class manufacturing technologies, the outcome of which is increased quality, productivity, flexibility, and customer satisfaction.

An example is Allen-Bradley, a division of Rockwell International and a manufacturer of industrial automation controls and systems. In 1985, Allen-Bradley built one of the first CIM facilities, and less than a decade later, it upgraded to an even more state-of-the-art CIM facility. As a result of this investment, Allen-Bradley's products can now be designed, manufactured, and shipped in as few as five months—a vast improvement in a process that once took as long as three years to complete.[29] A closer look at the components of CIM follows.

Industrial Robots

Industrial robots are "steel collar" workers controlled by computers.[30] These machines are versatile enough to manipulate items, move parts and tools, and perform other repetitive tasks, such as spraying paint, on an assembly line. They can also assemble simple mechanical and electrical parts. In addition, they are often sought for tasks that are dangerous for human operators. Approximately one-half of the robots in operation in the United States work in automobile assembly plants. Although many companies are using robots effectively, others have not benefited as

Computer-aided design software is used to generate design drawings and is able to test characteristics such as strength. CAD can communicate the design specifications to software that translates, instructs, and controls the production machinery. This software is known as CAM (computer-aided manufacturing).

greatly. Toyota, for example, discontinued using robots for installing engine blocks. Instead, a worker is able to use a simple power-assist device to position engines in automobile bodies more reliably and with more flexibility than a robot.[31]

Computer-Aided Design/Computer-Aided Engineering

computer-aided design (CAD)/computer-aided engineering (CAE)
computerized systems used to design new products, make modifications to existing ones, and test prototypes

Computer-aided design (CAD)/computer-aided engineering (CAE) is a computerized process for designing new products, making modifications to existing products, and testing prototypes or models of products. CAD/CAE thus replaces the manual and time-consuming process of drafting. The main objectives of these systems are to improve the quality of the designs and to reduce the time required to produce the designs. These two objectives, in turn, reduce the costs involved in manufacturing a product because potential problems can be detected at the design stage. CAD/CAE also allows designs to be stored and transferred for easier revisions. For example, Texas Instruments reduced the time it required to develop a calculator by 20 percent when it was able to send designs electronically.[32]

A more sophisticated form of CAD/CAE is called rapid prototyping, which uses a technique known as stereolithography to build three-dimensional models out of plastic. United Technology was able to use this technology to build a one-sixth model of its Comanche helicopter used for radar testing.[30] The use of CAD/CAE and stereolithography provided the information needed for designers to work quickly to perfect the helicopter's precise design specifications.

computer-aided manufacturing (CAM)
computerized systems used to direct manufacturing processes

Computer-Aided Manufacturing

Once a product is designed via a computer, the next logical step is to allow the computer to manufacture it. **Computer-aided manufacturing (CAM)** refers to the use of computers to direct manufacturing processes. The CAM system can be programmed to guide equipment to perform various manufacturing processes, such as drilling a hole of a specified size, pouring a liquid mixture into a mold, and cutting materials at a certain speed. CAM is most beneficial when the manufacturing process is complex and when frequent design changes are made.[34] The use of a combined CAD/CAE/CAM system can help eliminate duplication between the design group and manufacturing, which not only saves time and money but also improves internal communication among employees within the organization.

Flexible Manufacturing System

flexible manufacturing system (FMS)
automation of a production line by controlling and guiding all machinery by computer

A CAM system normally includes only one machine or process at a time, but a **flexible manufacturing system (FMS)** automates an entire production line by controlling and guiding all machines by computer. Thus, an FMS is a logical extension of a CAM system.[35] It is also the flexibility inherent in an FMS that distinguishes it from a CAM system. This flexibility allows a production line to produce a variety of models with faster setup times. The General Motors assembly plant located in Arlington, Texas, uses FMS to easily switch production back and forth between trucks and sport utility vehicles.

CONCLUDING COMMENTS

Managing operations efficiently is obviously a critical function in organizations—service and manufacturing firms alike. All the best plans and strategies in the world will not amount to a great deal unless operations can be managed and carried out skillfully and effectively. Too many times, companies and other organizations have been headed in the right direction only to run into extreme difficulties because of poor implementation of day-to-day operations. Operations management is clearly a case of where "the devil *is* in the details."

The tools and techniques that have been developed to assist in the management of operations provide a more objective way of making key organizational decisions. As we have seen in this chapter, these techniques assist in such tasks as the selection of facility locations and the interior design of those facilities, scheduling the production of particular goods and services, planning for the optimum amount of capacity, and managing and controlling inventory.

Productivity and quality are the two most well-known and studied facets of OM. Organizations must continually strive to make quality and productivity improvements to compete successfully both domestically and globally. It is important to remember that all employees within an organization, managers and nonmanagers alike, are responsible for productivity and quality initiatives.

In the final analysis, too often the focus on operations management gets placed only on the tools and techniques. However, those tools and techniques are of little value unless people are trained and motivated to use them. Even with that accomplished, their use may not help the organization's ultimate performance unless it is aligned with the organization's strategy. Achieving this alignment and effectively managing the employees using the tools and techniques are the most important of all the challenges related to operations management.

KEY TERMS

ABC analysis 522

aggregate planning 520

capacity planning 519

computer-aided design (CAD)/computer-aided engineering (CAE) 534

computer-aided manufacturing (CAM) 534

computer-integrated manufacturing (CIM) 533

continuous process improvement 526

design capacity 519

designing for manufacturing 530

economic order quantity (EOQ) 522

effective capacity 519

facility layout 515

facility location 515

fixed-position layout 517

flexible manufacturing system (FMS) 535

flowchart 527

group technology (cellular layout) 518

just-in-time (JIT) systems 530

materials requirement planning (MRP) 520

operations management 511

outsourcing 530

PERT/CPM 521

process (functional) layout 518

product (line) layout 517

productivity 523

quality 524

statistical process control (SPC) 530

total quality management (TQM) 525

work standard 523

REVIEW QUESTIONS

1. What is the definition of *operations management*, and how does OM relate to the larger field of management?
2. What factors should be considered when selecting a location for a firm's operations?
3. What type of eating facility has a fixed-position layout? What type has a product layout? Explain.
4. What is the critical path on a PERT/CPM network? What happens when an activity on this path is delayed?
5. How are productivity and quality related?
6. What is the key to an effective work sampling study?
7. Who should define a product's or service's quality?
8. What is the name of the quality and productivity technique that involves presenting a graphical representation of all the steps involved in a process?
9. When companies compare their processes to the best practices of other companies, what is this called?
10. Why might a company consider outsourcing some of its processes?
11. What quality and productivity technique provides an objective way to monitor the performance of a process?
12. What is a JIT system and how would such a system work in a fast-food establishment?
13. How can relationships between a buyer and supplier be improved?
14. Describe what might be included in the factory of the future.
15. For what purposes are industrial robots being used?
16. How can CAD/CAE/CAM help in improving productivity and quality?

DISCUSSION QUESTIONS

1. For many years, consumers seemed to perceive that Japanese-made cars were of higher quality than those made in the United States. Why was this so? What steps, if any, do you think U.S. automakers have taken, or could still take, to improve their image of quality?

2. If you were a cigar manufacturer during the cigar fad, what capacity planning decisions would you have to consider to keep up with continually rising demand rates? What would you do if (as happened) the fad ended and demand dropped?

3. Toward the end of each semester, it often seems as if there is not enough time to get everything done. This is especially true during the fall semester when final exams are approaching and the holiday shopping, wrapping, and mailing need to be done. Devise a Gantt chart listing all possible activities to complete before the end of the fall semester. Also include time estimates for each. How useful do you think a Gantt chart would be for helping you manage your time and projects?

4. A grocery store must tightly control its inventory to remain profitable. How might the ABC inventory management system assist a grocery store manager in doing this? What items might fall into the A, B, and C categories?

5. It is likely that we have all experienced good and bad service at a restaurant. Select a restaurant where you think service was exceptionally good and one where you think service was exceptionally bad. What operations management characteristics did each have? How could the restaurant with poor service improve?

CLOSING CASE

Cranston Nissan

Steve Jackson, general manager of Cranston Nissan, slowly sifted through his usual Monday morning stack of mail. The following letter was one he would not soon forget.

Dear Mr. Jackson:
I am writing this letter so that you will be aware of a nightmare I experienced recently regarding the repair of my 300ZX in your body shop and subsequently in your service department. I will detail the events in chronological order.

August 28
I dropped the car off for repair of rust damage in the following areas:

    Roof—along the top of the windshield area
    Left rocker panel—under driver's door
    Left quarter panel—near end of bumper
    Rear body panel—under license plate

I was told it would take three or four days.

September 1
I called to inquire about the status of the car, since this was the fifth day the car was in the shop. I was told that I could pick up the car anytime after 2 P.M. My wife and I arrived at 5 P.M. The car was still not ready. In the meantime, I

paid the bill for $443.17 and waited. At 6 P.M. the car was driven up dripping wet (presumably from a wash to make it look good). I got into the car and noticed the courtesy light in the driver's door would not turn off when the door was closed. I asked for help, and Jim Boyd, body shop manager, could not figure out what was wrong. His solution was to remove the bulb and have me return after the Labor Day holiday to have the mechanic look at it. I agreed and began to drive off. However, the voice warning, "Left door is open," repeatedly sounded. Without leaving the premises I returned to Mr. Boyd, advising him to retain the car until it was fixed—there was no way I could drive the car with that repeated recording. Mr. Boyd then suggested I call back the next day (Saturday) to see if the mechanic could find the problem. I must emphasize, I brought the car to the body shop on August 28 in perfect mechanical working condition—the repair work was for body rust. This point will become important as the story unfolds.

September 2
I called Jim Boyd at 10:30 A.M. and was told that the car had not been looked at yet. He promised to call back before the shop closed for the holiday, but he never did. I later learned that he did not call because "there was

nothing to report." The car sat in the shop Saturday, Sunday, and Monday.

September 5

I called Jim Boyd to check on the status of the car. It was 4 P.M., and Mr. Boyd told me nothing had been done, but that it should be ready by the next day. At this point it was becoming obvious that my car did not have priority in the service department.

September 6

I called Jim Boyd again (about 4 P.M.) and was told that work had halted on the car because the service department needed authorization and they didn't know how much it would run. At the hint that I would have to pay for this mess I became very upset and demanded that the car be brought immediately to the mechanical condition it was in when it was dropped off on August 28. At this point Ted Simon, service department manager, was summoned, and he assured me that if the problem was caused by some action of the body shop, I would not be financially responsible. I had not driven the car since I dropped it off, and I could not fathom the evidence anyone could produce to prove otherwise.

September 7

Again late in the day, I called Mr. Simon, who said that Larry (in the service department) knew about the problem and switched me over to him. Larry said that they had narrowed it down to a wire that passed several spots where body work was performed. He said the work was very time consuming and that the car should be ready sometime tomorrow.

September 8

I called Mr. Simon to check on the status of the car once more. He told me that the wiring problem was fixed, but now the speedometer didn't work. The short in the wires was caused by the body work. Larry got on the phone and said I could pick up the car, but they would send the car out to a subcontractor on Monday to repair the speedometer. He said that when the mechanic test-drove the car he noticed the speedometer pinned itself at the top end, and Larry thought that someone must have done something while searching for the other problem. I asked him if there would be charges for this, and he said there would not. My wife and I arrived to pick up the car at 5 P.M. I clarified the next steps with Larry and was again assured that the speedometer would be repaired at no charge to me.

The car was brought to me, and as I walked up to it I noticed that the rubber molding beneath the driver's door was hanging down. I asked for some help, and Mr. Simon came out to look at it. He said it must have been left that way after the search process for the bad wire. He took the car back into the shop to screw it on. When it finally came

out again, he said that he would replace the molding because it was actually damaged.

When I arrived home, I discovered that the anti-theft light on the dash would not stop blinking when the doors were closed. Attempting to activate the security system did not help. The only way I could get the light to stop flashing was to remove the fuse. In other words, now my security system was damaged. Needless to say, I was very upset.

September 11

On Sunday evening I dropped off the car and left a note with my keys in the "early bird" slot. The note listed the two items that needed to be done from the agreement of last Friday—the molding and the speedometer. In addition, I mentioned the security system problem and suggested that "somebody must have forgotten to hook something back up while looking for the wire problem." On Monday I received a call from someone in the service department (I think his name was John), who said that the problem in the security system was in two places—the hatchback lock and "some wires in the driver's door." The lock would cost me $76, and the cost of the rest was unknown. The verbal estimate was for a total of $110. I asked him why he did not consider this problem a derivative of the other problems. He said that the body shop and the mechanic who worked on the wire problem said they could see no way that they could have caused this to happen.

I told the fellow on the phone to forget fixing the security system because I was not going to pay for it. At this point I just wanted the car back home, thinking I could address the problem later with someone such as yourself. I told him to have the speedometer fixed and again asked about charges for it. I was assured there would be none.

September 13

The service department called to say I could pick up the car anytime before 8 P.M. He also said that the molding had to be ordered because it was not in stock. The need for the part was known on September 8, and NOW the part must be ordered. This will cause me another trip to the shop.

When I went to the service department to pick up the car, I was presented a bill for $126. I asked what the bill was for, and I was shown an itemized list that included speedometer repair and searching for the security problem. I said my understanding was that there would be no charge. Somebody at the service desk was apprised of the problem and released the car to me with the understanding that the service manager would review the situation the next day.

My car was brought around to me by the same person who brought it to me September 8. As I got into the driver's seat, I noticed there was no rear view mirror—it was lying in the passenger's seat, broken off from its mounting. I was too shocked to even get mad. I got out of the car and asked how something like this could happen without anyone noticing. Jim Boyd said someone probably did not want to own up to it. He requisitioned a part and repaired the mirror mounting.

Mr. Jackson, I realize this is a long letter, but I have been so frustrated and upset over the past three weeks that I had to be sure that you understood the basis for that frustration. I am hoping you can look into this matter and let me know what you think.

Sincerely,
Sam Monahan
555 South Main, Turnerville

QUESTIONS
Answer the following questions from the perspective of TQM.

1. Categorize the quality problems in this case.
2. What are the probable causes of so many mishaps?
3. What specific actions should Jackson take immediately? What should some of his longer-term goals be?

CHAPTER 18

INFORMATION
TECHNOLOGY
MANAGEMENT

LEARNING OBJECTIVES

After studying this chapter, you should be able to:

- Define the concepts and terms managers need for dealing effectively with information technology.
- Discuss ways that effective management of information technologies provides a firm with competitive advantage.
- Describe the role that information systems play in organizations and the importance of managing them responsibly.
- Discuss the impact that changes in information technology have had and continue to have on business.

The Cardinal Rule—Align Information Systems with Strategic Goals

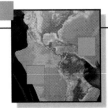

Like many of the other departments at Cardinal Health Company, a pharmaceutical wholesaler based in Columbus, Ohio, the finance department was having difficulty getting the information it needed for critical decisions. A separate information system (IS) department located at the data center in Buffalo, New York, managed Cardinal's information system. The IS department tended to focus on specific tasks rather than how information systems could best support the company's strategic goals and objectives. In addition, poor communication between the two departments meant that often the IS department did not have a clear understanding of the finance department's needs. When staff in finance needed something from the information system, they wrote a description of their needs and sent it to the IS department. The IS department then wrote a program and sent it back to finance. This took considerable

This chapter was written by Eli Cohen and Elizabeth Boyd of the Informing Science Institute and edited by the authors of this book.

time. Even worse, frequently the finance staff discovered that the program wasn't what they really wanted and had to send it back to IS for revisions. Clearly, Cardinal needed a better way to manage its IS function.

One approach some corporations take to dealing with the IS function is to decentralize it and create separate IS areas within each department. However, Cardinal thought this solution could lead to duplication of effort, fragmentation, lack of common standards, and conflict of priorities among departments. Wanting to keep IS centralized, Cardinal embarked on a pilot project within the finance department and hired John DeLeo to fill the specially created position of Corporate Financial Systems Coordinator. His desk was located in the finance department at corporate headquarters in Columbus, but he reported to a director of information systems. DeLeo was charged with aligning information systems functions for finance with Cardinal's business goals. His immediate task was to work on IS projects for finance. His long-term objective was to update the department's financial systems plan in accordance with the department's business needs and the company's overall budget.

One of DeLeo's first steps was to form a Financial Systems Steering Committee comprised of Cardinal's chief information officer (CIO), the vice president of information systems, the chief financial officer (CFO), the treasurer, the controller, the vice president of accounting, and DeLeo. They met every few weeks to review the status of the financial systems, discuss where they wanted them to go, and decide how they were going to get there. DeLeo says these meetings with the top financial managers gave him the perspective he needed to align the business needs of the finance department with the technical capabilities of IS. The committee helped DeLeo change his focus from day-to-day issues, such as general ledger, to higher-level issues, such as how the general ledger application affects the way the department manages company money and how the IS function can be used to provide more value for customers and stockholders.

Another result of this pilot project was that the people in finance are now better educated about what is involved in meeting their information needs. They understand the trade-off between what is possible and what is affordable. DeLeo views the relationship between finance and information systems as a two-way street. Finance describes all the things it wants, and IS describes what it can reasonably do. Together they set priorities and work out a budget for accomplishing agreed-upon tasks. The effect has been to make finance more involved in information functions than ever before.

With this new management structure, Cardinal uses its information system more effectively and ensures that finance managers have access to the information they need for strategic decisions.

Source: Adapted from Andrea Ovans, "Improve IS Department Relations!" *Datamation* 42, no. 16, (October 1996) pp. 66–68; Carl Shapiro and Hal Varian, "Lock 'em up!" *CIO*, October 15, 1998.

information system (IS)

combination of information technologies, people, and procedures organized to provide information for its users

information technology (IT)

computer hardware and software and associated communication equipment that perform data processing tasks

end user

a person, not necessarily technically trained, who uses an information system

To make informed decisions, managers need the right information at the right time and in the right format. In other words, managers need effective information systems. The purpose of an information system is to process data and present the results in meaningful form. Thus, an **information system (IS)** is a combination of **information technologies (IT)** (computer hardware and software and communication equipment), people, and procedures organized to provide information for users of the system. The term **end user** typically refers to a nontechnical person, such as a sales manager who uses a system, as opposed to a technically trained person who designs a system. As Cardinal Health's experience illustrates, one of the main challenges facing managers as end users is how to use information technology and systems to support strategic goals. Cardinal Health adapted a particular solution to its problems, but each organization needs to find the approaches that best fit its strategies, structure, and culture.

INFORMATION IN ORGANIZATIONS

information

that which reduces uncertainty in decision making; usually derived from processing data and presenting the results in a meaningful format

data

raw facts and figures about an entity or event

Managers' questions and problems, as the example of Cardinal Health demonstrates, need to be clearly understood before information technology can provide meaningful answers. **Information** is defined, simply enough, as that which reduces uncertainty in decision making.[1] Thus, information is shaped through both its context and its content. In organizations, the context is the nature of the problems to be solved. Information is derived from **data**, which are facts and figures that have little meaning on their own. However, information is *not* just data that have been processed, but the outcome of processing data and the presentation of results in a context and format that helps decision makers do their jobs by removing some amount of uncertainty from the decision-making process. In other words, information provides meaning. For example, the fact that Pat's sales amounted to $13,570 last month is just data. It becomes information, and therefore meaningful, for a sales manager when given the context that this is a 25 percent increase over the past month or when given the problem "How much did Pat sell last month?"

It should be obvious that information is a valuable resource, and for that reason it must be managed with as much care and thought as the more traditional resources of money, machines, materials, and personnel. Companies, consequently, are asking tough questions about how to use information to stay competitive in the global marketplace. For example, Federal Express and United Parcel Service *add value* to their existing products by giving customers on-line access to information about their service and allowing customers to track shipped parcels. At Caterpillar, information garnered from public records helps marketing staff keep track of com-

By electronically scanning each product sold, grocery stores obtain information about customers' purchases. This information is used for inventory control and marketing.

petitors' market share. Grocery stores track customers' purchases to determine more strategic uses of display space and advertising campaigns.

One of the earliest examples of using an information system strategically to gain competitive advantage is the ASAP system of American Hospital Supply (AHS). AHS placed computer terminals on the desks of its customers (hospital pharmacies) to simplify and speed the ordering process. This use of information technology locked-in customers and provided AHS with increased sales and profit (and also provided customers with better service). Exhibit 18.1 lists examples of how managers use IT to improve competitive advantage.

Because of the importance of information and its management, in recent years most larger companies have placed the top IS manager at the senior level with the title of **chief information officer (CIO)** or vice president of IS. The CIO's mission is to lead the company in using information to create innovative ways of doing business. A CIO must have a technical background in IS, but even more importantly, this person should have "exceptional people skills, political prowess, a broad business view, and change-management skills."[2] To understand the strategic goals of the organization and recommend ways information technology can assist in

chief information officer (CIO)

manager at vice-presidential level responsible for information systems

---

EXHIBIT 18.1

Using Information for Competitive Advantage

Examples of IT Use to Improve Competitive Advantage	Improve Existing Practices	Create New Opportunities
For the individual firm	Automated billing and inventory management systems	Placement of terminals at customers' sites
For the industry as a whole	ATM machines at banks	Internet service providers

achieving them, the CIO should have direct communication with top-level executives and actively participate in senior-level decision making. It is the task of the CIO to work with other senior executives to keep the IS development strategy aligned with the business strategy of the firm. The CIO also, however, should keep corporate expectations for IT realistic, basing decisions on what is most important for the firm, not on what is the latest trend or most state-of-the-art development in IT.

INFORMATION AND MANAGERS

For something to be information, it must be meaningful to the decision maker. Therefore, IS designers must understand what decisions managers actually make. Decisions vary by job within an organization and by the individual within a job.

Amount of Structure in Decisions

As discussed in Chapter 9, the problems or decisions managers face can be classified according to the amount of structure. Since programmed (or structured) problems can be solved by following a predetermined sequence of decision rules or algorithms, a computer can easily solve this type of problem. In contrast, nonprogrammed (unstructured) problems are subjective in nature and depend on experience, intuition, and judgment. Most business problems are considered semistructured, having some aspects for which a computer can provide valuable information as well as other aspects that require the judgment of the manager. For example, the amount of withholding tax to be deducted from an employee's paycheck can be computed and the decision regarding the amount to withhold can be automated. However, a semistructured decision of whether to grant one employee a raise needs human judgment, supplemented by information about past performance that an information system can provide. Information systems vary, as we shall see, by the degree of structure of the problems they address.

In addition to the amount of structure involved in the decision, determining what constitutes information for specific problem solvers varies by level of management and characteristics of the individual.

Organizational Level

As discussed in Chapter 7, managers operate at three major levels—corporate, business, and functional—and the decisions they make can be grouped into three major types (parallel to the three levels of scope of controls discussed in Chapter 16): strategic, tactical, and operational. The information needed at each of the three levels differs in a number of ways. For example, managers at the operational level need information that is current to within days, if not hours, minutes, or seconds. In contrast, managers at the strategic level usually do not require or necessarily benefit from this level of currency; they are usually more concerned with trends or patterns over time. Similarly, a manager at the operational level needs detailed information, such as the number of hours each employee worked last week or the amount of each product sold yesterday, while a manager at the strategic level typically finds summaries more useful. Exhibit 18.2 shows typical information needs of managers at different levels. (Note the similarity of this exhibit to Exhibit 7.1 in Chapter 7.)

EXHIBIT 18.2
Information Needs by Decision Level

	DECISION LEVEL		
	Strategic	**Tactical**	**Operational**
Time Horizon	Long term, 3–5 years	1–2 years	Current year
Information Source	Emphasis on external	Mix of external and internal	Mainly internal
Level of Detail	Summarized	Summarized with some detail	Detailed
Format	Varies from report to report	Fixed format with some special reports	Fixed format
Currency of Information	Relatively old (YTD, patterns)	Mid-range	Up-to-date
Degree of Precision	Accuracy and precision less important than significant changes and estimates	Mid-range	High degree of accuracy and precision
Frequency of Presentation	Irregular and unpredictable, ad hoc	Fairly frequent, fairly regular schedule	Frequent, regularly scheduled
Problem's Degree of Structure	Unstructured and semistructured	Semistructured	Structured

Source: Data derived from G. A. Gorry and M. S. Scott Morton, "A Framework for Management Information Systems," *Sloan Management Review,* Fall 1971.

Individual Differences

Managers differ in their preferred method for receiving and processing information. For example, one executive may want to make a decision after looking at graphs while another likes to study detailed reports with columns of numbers. An information system built to maximize the productivity of one of these executives would be suboptimal for the other. Therefore, information systems need to be designed to take into account both the level of management and individual differences among managers.

TYPES OF INFORMATION SYSTEMS

Over time, as computers became more powerful and sophisticated, and as developers gained better understanding of the information managers need, several types of information systems evolved. These systems can be grouped into two major classifications: (1) those that support the daily operations of the business and (2) those that provide support to managerial decision makers (see Exhibit 18.3).

Information Systems for Daily Operations

Information systems used for daily operations include transaction processing systems and office information systems. These two daily operations systems are used to record routine and repeated business transactions and communications. Also,

| EXHIBIT 18.3 |

Types of Information Systems

they are often the source of raw data that can be used later for managerial decision making.

Transaction Processing Systems   When computers first became available, they were expensive. Therefore, the first computerized information systems performed jobs that provided the best ratio of benefit to cost. These jobs involved high-volume, repetitive daily tasks that addressed clearly defined, structured problems, such as order entry, inventory management, and payroll. Such systems track business transactions for the various functional areas and are called **transaction processing systems (TPS)**. The reports generated by TPSs are generally detailed and of greatest use to managers working at the operational level.

Today, with our ability to connect one computer to another, TPSs have developed from stand-alone systems into systems that communicate with trading partners. Instead of mailing pieces of paper, firms use **electronic data interchange (EDI)** to send data from their computer to another firm's computer using a standardized data format. Firms can request quotations; send purchase orders, acknowledgments, and invoices; inquire about the status of an order; or perform other business transactions. For example, to improve data accuracy and cut costs in the supply chain, Federated Department Stores has notified its suppliers that it wants all bills of lading to be transmitted electronically. Shipping data are transmitted electronically instead of being keyed from paper bills of lading. The reduction in errors

transaction processing systems (TPS)
information systems that perform and track the day-to-day tasks of an organization

electronic data interchange (EDI)
method of sending data from one firm's computer to the computer at another firm

saves drivers the many hours they used to spend reconciling purchase orders with the shipment count.[3]

electronic funds transfer (EFI)
transmission of payments electronically

The real benefit from EDI comes by including in this computer link a shared financial institution, thereby allowing direct payment of bills via **electronic funds transfer (EFT)**. The library at the University of California at Berkeley, for instance, uses this technology. Through its computer systems, the library sends book orders to publishers. When the publisher's computer electronically acknowledges the order, the library's computer generates and transmits a message to its bank that automatically debits the library's and credits the publisher's accounts.[4]

office information systems (OIS)
information systems that focus primarily on communication within the office

Office Information Systems   Office information systems (OIS) aid communication within the office among all levels of workers and managers. This communication includes procedures, reports, or memoranda and may be transmitted in any form (oral, written, image). In the past, the systems designed for office communication were known as *office automation,* but the term *office information systems* (OIS) is now more popular.

Organizations with offices in various parts of the world use e-mail to enable collaboration on projects and thus increase their productivity. E-mail also changes the organizational power structure in that any employee can communicate directly with any other employee, thereby reducing the importance of a hierarchical structure. On the other hand, this ease of communication has dangers as well as benefits. The challenge for managers is to reduce information overload so that it does not interfere with employee productivity.

Documents can get "lost," be they paper (in filing cabinets), microfilm (on reels or sheets), or digital (on computer disk). To find and retrieve a particular document, a document management system is needed. Merely storing documents electronically in a computer system, instead of on paper in filing cabinets, will not make them any easier to find. Document management systems address this problem by filing and retrieving information using key words or full-text indexing. Selleys, a manufacturer of handyman and hardware products near Sydney, Australia, found that a document management system kept it from drowning under a deluge of paper. Bulletins, raw data, catalogues, and reports streamed into the office, filling a continuously expanding bank of filing cabinets. Information was difficult or impossible to find because no one knew how it was filed, and often more than one division would need access to the same document at the same time. Selleys' document management system now scans documents as they are received and stores them on disk in the computer. Documents can later be retrieved by the use of key words or by scanning the full text. Up to 15 people can study the same document at the same time, and the average response time to locate a document is about one second.[5] At Nabisco, payment reconciliation used to take from a couple of days to a couple of months. With a proof-of-delivery document management system, it consolidated 114 scattered paper-based invoice archives into one networked store of document images. Now when a customer needs proof of delivery, Nabisco employees can retrieve an image in less than 15 seconds and fax it while the customer is still on the line.[6]

Managerial Support Systems

Managerial support systems include a large range of systems, many of which fall under the traditional terms of management information system, decision support system, and executive support system. Historically, firms had developed each TPS in isolation from other TPSs. Each one collected data for a particular functional area. However, these data were not related either to past performance or to each other. Thus, TPSs created a huge untapped potential source of information for those working at the tactical and strategic levels. One of the challenges has been to develop ways to integrate these data and provide managers access to the information they represent. As the costs of computing dropped and more complex systems became affordable, several new types of managerial support systems became feasible. Today, many of these types have been combined into a single support system. While the differences among them are no longer distinct, the traditional terms are still helpful for understanding the purposes of these systems.

Management Information Systems   The first type of managerial support system developed was named **management information systems (MIS)**, or information reporting system. Such a system uses data collected from the transaction processing system to provide reports to lower and mid-level managers. Unlike the TPS, these reports can include historical data so that managers can compare one period's activity to prior periods. MIS reports tend to be summaries, produced on regular bases. An example is a report prepared at the end of each month showing the total of each product sold with comparisons to the previous three months and the same month a year ago. Another common MIS report is an exception report, which tracks unusual situations, for example, a list of the 10 fastest- and 10 slowest-moving products during the past three months.

While MIS reports were designed to assist managers, commonly the same reports were provided to a variety of decision makers across many functional areas, and they were not tailored to the specific information needs of an individual manager.

Decision Support Systems   While an MIS is designed to support the information needs of the firm by reporting what has happened, it is not much help to a decision maker who needs insight into what might happen if various alternatives are selected. For example, after a fire destroys a plant, a manager needs to decide whether to rebuild or to expand another plant. This decision, like many others that managers make, is complex and relatively unstructured. What this manager needs is an interactive system that assesses the predicted impact of different courses of actions, that is, "what-if analysis." The class of systems developed to meet these needs is known as **decision support systems (DSS)**. Because semi- and unstructured problems require human judgment, a decision support system is designed to handle the more structured aspects of the problem and provide information from a variety of sources to assist the manager in solving a problem.

Typically, a DSS is not one piece of software but a collection of programs or tools from which the user can pick those best suited for the problem at hand. These programs can range from simple spreadsheet templates to complex modeling programs. In the example of the plant destroyed by fire, the manager could use one or more of these tools to obtain information about the costs and benefits of various plans of actions to recover from the fire. Since this manager may need information about conditions outside the firm, such as tax rates for the plant locations under consideration, the system must be flexible and designed to obtain and use external data. To be effective, it must also be easy to learn and use, with the ability to present information in a wide range of formats. A graphical user interface (GUI, pronounced "gooey") does this by allowing the user to issue commands by selecting icons or pictures.

management information systems (MIS)
management support systems that produce scheduled reports primarily used by operational and mid-level managers

decision support systems (DSS)
programs designed to help a specific manager solve a semi- or unstructured problem

Decision support systems provide information from a variety of sources to assist managers in problem solving. To be effective, the system must be easy to learn and use and have the ability to present information in a wide range of formats.

Executive Support Systems Many top executives found DSS tools more cumbersome and time consuming than useful. They wanted an easy-to-use system with a graphical user interface to provide quick access to information on their business and the ability to present that information in a variety of formats. This demand for instant data-as-you-like-it requires tools that can navigate through the internal data organizations routinely collect as well as provide access to external data. The systems that meet these needs are called **executive support systems (ESS)**, also known as *executive information systems (EIS)* or *employee information systems.*

When presented with one bit of information, often an executive needs to get more specific details about the subject. An ESS enables the executive to drill down through the information to expose underlying trends or problems. For example, a product manager might want to view clothing sales for this year compared with last year, then drill down to see the details on one particular line in one specific sales region. While a DSS is aimed at all managers and is model oriented, an ESS is aimed at top executives and is data retrieval oriented. It lets executives make specific, precise queries and derive specialized reports, projections, and trends.

In Uruguay, an ESS was created to capture and access data needed for presidential decision making. Data about specific areas, such as banking, foreign trade, state income and expenditures, and the economic and employment situations, are gathered by various departments and agencies and made available to the system on a regular basis. The purpose of this system is to provide the president and his ministers with an up-to-date view of the state of the nation on which they can base their decisions.[7]

Groupware Information technology has responded to the growing emphasis on work groups and teams by developing **groupware**, or **group support systems (GSS)** software, designed specifically to help people work collaboratively as well as individually. Some GSSs allow multiple users to create and edit the same document

---

executive support systems (ESS)
information systems designed to provide executives quick access to corporate and external data

groupware, or group support systems (GSS)
software designed to help people work collaboratively as well as individually through information sharing

together. Managers and other users can collaborate on projects by accessing files on their own, as well as co-workers', machines. Employees at Chiat/Day Advertising in New York use a groupware system called Oxygen on a network of computers to simulate a virtual office. Oxygen contains virtual rooms (space set aside in computer storage instead of in a building) where employees can work on group projects. To share project-related information, a staff member places a special icon or image in one of the virtual rooms. From their workstations, other people can enter this room and retrieve the information without knowing exactly where within the computer system the information physically resides. Employees can even dial into the virtual office from a laptop on the road. Project colleagues can set up a conference call by simply clicking on the images that represent the co-workers they want to include.[8]

group decision support systems (GDSS)
software designed to support group decision making

Because strategic decisions are usually made by a group of decision makers, decision support tools have been expanded to create **group decision support systems (GDSS)**. A GDSS electronically joins members of a work team or other group. It facilitates their ability to share data and other computing resources to formulate and solve problems. Other GDSS tools facilitate brainstorming, organizing ideas, and voting. Since input can be made anonymously, users who might otherwise feel intimidated are more willing to express ideas and opinions.

ENABLING TECHNOLOGIES

Up to now, we have focused on the categorization of systems. Let us now turn to information systems from the viewpoint of the technologies that enable managers to use these systems. Although this section portrays these technologies separately, they are, in fact, interrelated and synergistic. The technologies we examine are artificial intelligence, data communications, database management, and client/server architecture.

Artificial Intelligence: Mimicking Human Abilities

artificial intelligence
use of a computer to mimic the behavior of humans and perform tasks that normally require human intelligence

The field of **artificial intelligence (AI)** strives to have a computer mimic the behavior of humans and perform tasks that normally require human intelligence. We examine two types of artificial intelligence designed to help managers make decisions: expert systems and neural networks. They differ in the types of problems they help solve.

expert systems
software designed to solve complex problems that typically could only be solved by highly experienced experts using sets of known rules

Expert Systems   **Expert systems** are designed for problems where sets of rules exist to solve problems. The rules are usually complex and only a small group of highly experienced people (experts) are able do the job well.

Consider the following decision: If an employee worked 1,250 hours in the current year and asks for time off to tend a sick family member, how much time is the company obligated to give? The answer is 12 days under the federal Family Medical Leave Act. However, if the employee lives in Connecticut, by Connecticut statute, he or she is entitled to 16 days over a two-year period. Under the wording of the federal law, if the employee takes 16 days in the first year, he or she is eligible for another 12 in the second year, for a total of 28. A question such as this is only one of the complex problems faced by human resource workers. They need a system that acts as an expert, containing all the rules, applying them against the particular circumstances for each case, and recommending a solution.[9] Among other fields in which expert systems have been applied are finance and medicine.

To create an expert system, a knowledge engineer collects rules by interviewing experts and puts the rules into a computer-understandable format. These rules are stated in the form of "IF <some condition is true>, THEN <take this action>, OTHERWISE, <take this action>."

Neural Networks   Expert systems are useful for situations in which all the rules for making a decision are known. However, many business problems have no *explicit* rules for their solution but do have many case examples that *imply* rules. This type of problem is the focus of a neural network.

Consider the problem of deciding whether to approve or deny a loan application for a given customer. We know that some applicants repay loans promptly and others default, but we do not have rules that accurately predict which is which. However, we do have many historical examples that identify attributes of the applicants, such as their age, income level, and credit rating, and for which we know the outcome. **Neural networks** learn to recognize patterns and relationships between attributes and outcomes in much the same way a human brain does. To create a neural network to assist in deciding whether to extend credit, we would take a piece of software called a neural network shell and "train" it using the historical data with known criteria and known outcomes. After it has processed enough training data, we can enter data about new applicants into the neural network. By comparing the outcomes of past loans with the applicant's characteristics, it is able to guide us in predicting outcomes for future applicants. As we use the system, we add information about the actual outcomes for each of the new cases. Like the human brain, a neural network can continue to learn. As more examples are given to it, it continually refines its ability to predict outcomes.

> **neural networks**
> information systems that, after training on historical data, can learn to recognize patterns and relationships among attributes and outcomes

Because it can handle many more examples than a human can, a neural network is able to find patterns that we cannot. It can perform well even with missing or incomplete data, recognizing and matching complicated, vague, or incomplete patterns. For example, price forecasting, a critical part of commodity trading and price analysis, is viewed as an impossible task by those who believe that market prices are random and that past prices cannot be used as a guide for price behavior in the future. However, when a neural network analyzed monthly figures for wheat and cattle prices over a 20-year span, it discovered the hidden patterns and predicted prices with a reasonable degree of accuracy.[10] Neural networks are also being used by IBM to detect computer viruses. There is usually a lag between the time a virus is unleashed and the typical virus-checking program is updated to detect its presence. However, viruses behave in particular ways. By giving the neural network examples of infected and uninfected code, the neural network learns the patterns that identify a virus, enabling it to detect the presence of a new virus.[11]

Moving Information: Data Communications and Connectivity

A second enabling technology is data communications and connectivity. Today, data and information can be transferred from one location to another almost anywhere in the world at reasonable costs and at near instantaneous speeds. The effect is that business can be conducted and controlled from geographically dispersed locations, connected only by communication links. This requires that managers need to know how to use these advances to their firm's advantage.

Networks: WAN and LAN   When computers were large and expensive, each computer was isolated. All input, processing, and output activities occurred at one site. Later, new communication technology enabled several terminals to be connected to these large computers, creating a **computer network**. Commonly, terminals were connected to the computer over long distances using relatively slow channels, such as telephone wire. This enabled sales data from each region, for example, to be sent electronically to a corporate computer. Such a configuration of connecting computers to other computers over great distances is known as wide area networking (WAN).

With the advent of the personal computer, businesses could afford to provide employees with desktop computers. Since some of the peripheral devices, such as high-speed printers, remained relatively expensive, the personal computers within an office or other small geographic area, such as a campus, were connected to each other and to shared peripheral devices, creating a local area network, or LAN. Typically, data shared among these connected computers were stored on separate, special-purpose computers, called file servers.

Nowadays, business computers large or small are likely to be connected to each other. Commonly, a LAN that processes data for one work group is connected to other LANs at the same site or to a WAN to share results with other locations. Computer networks that are connected to other networks form **internets** (with a lowercase "i"). Often, these internets also connect to the external environment through commercial services such as Mead Data Services.

The Internet   The **Internet** (uppercase "I") refers to a particular internet created in 1969 by the U.S. Defense Department that was designed to be resilient in case of disaster. Computers were placed in a number of secure locations, connected by telecommunication lines in such a way that if one location was disabled, messages would automatically be routed around that location. This system later expanded to bring universities and other research institutions into the network. In the early 1990s, the Internet became available to the general public and commercial businesses.

People often call the Internet an information superhighway, as it consists of three components: (1) the main highway, (2) on-ramps to the highway, and (3) off-ramps to desirable destinations. The highway consists of interconnected communication channels that provide access to geographically dispersed computers. The on-ramps correspond to Internet service providers (ISP) that offer access to the highway (for a fee) and pass along part of that fee to those who maintain the data highway. The off-ramps to destinations are host sites, computers (called servers) on which businesses, universities, and others store content. These host sites are accessible through the Internet. For example, Microsoft has a host site on which it posts information about forthcoming software, fixes to current software, and announcements about job opportunities.

The most common way to use the Internet today is through the **World Wide Web** (www or Web). The Web is a subset of the Internet composed of independently owned systems that present information in the form of pages stored on Web servers. The information on the Web is presented through text, sound, graphics, or other formats that are viewed on the recipient's computer. Pages are linked so that clicking the mouse at a place on one page (a hyperlink) can cause another

computer network
one or more computers connected to other computers, terminals, and/or devices by communication media over which data and messages are transmitted

internets
computer networks that are interconnected to other computer networks

Internet
a worldwide network that is accessible to the public and over which messages may be sent using a common protocol, or format

World Wide Web
part of the Internet composed of independently owned computer systems that work together to provide services in the form of text, graphics, audio, and video and use hypertext to link one page to another

page, located perhaps on a different server in a different country, to be viewed. The Web is built around common standards, such as HTML (hypertext markup language), that enable Web page viewer software (called browsers) from any software publisher to display the page. Most businesses now have Web pages on their host sites. The main site for a business or individual is called its home page. Managers now consider well-designed corporate Web sites a business necessity. One of the challenges facing managers is how to get the most benefit from this new form of corporate identity.

electronic commerce (e-commerce)

electronic business transactions conducted electronically over the Internet

A new and fast-growing business use of the Internet is **electronic commerce (e-commerce)**. Businesses use their Internet connections to conduct transactions electronically, whether those transactions are customer service requests, order processing, or links with suppliers. Federal Express (FedEx) uses the Web to gain competitive advantage through its Virtual Order service. FedEx provides participating companies free user-friendly software to create and maintain an on-line catalog. The company inputs product information and pricing, and FedEx puts the catalog on a FedEx secure server. Customers browse through these on-line catalogs, select products, and charge the purchase to their credit cards. FedEx takes care of credit card number protection and other security measures. It also handles order confirmation and transmission of the order to the firm's site, so the firm does not need special hardware or software. The system prints the shipping label and provides on-line tracking for the packages. Both the customer and the business can track the progress of shipment by entering this number into FedEx's Internet tracking system. As this example illustrates, there are multiple potential advantages to the use of electronic commerce.[12]

intranets

private networks within one organization that use Internet protocols and standards

Intranets   When Amvescap PLC was formed by a merger of Houston-based AIM Management Group and London-based Invesco Funds Group, it needed to be able to communicate and share information among 17 far-flung offices that did not use the same technology. The solution was an intranet. **Intranets** are networks that use the standards and protocols used by the Internet but limit access to employees. The software can run on a variety of computer systems and use the same browsers with which most users are already familiar. This standardization in the presentation of data cuts training costs and enables the use of data from various sources. Already over half of U.S. corporations use intranets and many use their intranets to make up-to-date policies and procedures readily available to employees. Amvescap's intranet includes data about company employees, information about various funds, research notes, and market analysis data.[13]

extranets

private networks that use Internet protocols to share part of a business's information or operations with authorized outsiders

Extranets   Firms' success with intranets has emboldened them to expand access. They have given key outsiders, such as customers and suppliers, access to limited company data via browsers, creating **extranets**. While the general public is given limited access to the firm's Web site, those with the proper passwords can get farther into the system. For example, suppliers can access inventory records and fill out on-line forms to replenish stock. Customers can bring up tailored catalogs or trace the progress of their orders.

American Oncology Resources (AOR) uses an extranet to help fight cancer. Many cancer patients might benefit from participating in one of the cancer-fighting drug trials that pharmaceutical companies conduct, but doctors often don't have information about what trials are available. AOR created a database that stores information about current trials. From PCs in their offices, participating doctors use the familiar browser interface to enter descriptive information about a patient. When the patient data matches the criteria for a trial, the system e-mails the physician, who can immediately enroll the patient in the trial. One participating doctor believes that at least one of his patients is alive today only because of the extranet's timely response.[14]

Storing and Retrieving Information: Database Management

database

an organized collection of data stored in an information system

A third enabling technology is database management. A **database** is an organized collection of data stored in an information system to provide ease of access. When managers say, "I know we have the information, but it is just too difficult to find," a firm knows that it needs to revise how it stores data and retrieves information.

A database management system (DBMS) is a program that organizes and stores data in a way that makes information from the database easily accessible wherever and whenever needed. It also provides a query facility so that managers, without the assistance of a programmer, can create reports. With these tools, managers access the information they need when they need it. As one author put it, "In today's fiercely competitive, fast-paced business world, it is crucial for companies to make better and faster decisions. Many managers are finding that the best way to do this is by deriving greater value from their corporate databases in order to identify trends, gain insight about customers and answer questions like who is buying what, where, and when."[15]

Sharing the Work: Client/Server Architecture

client/server architecture

division of an application into separate components that run on two or more different computers

A fourth technology enabling the advance of information systems is client/server architecture. This chapter has already used the term *server* to denote a computer that provides specialized processing. In the past, applications were processed on just a single computer, the server, and the results were transmitted to users around the firm. With the decrease in cost for computing and data communications, a new way of processing, called **client/server architecture**, has emerged. Using client/server architecture, an application is divided into separate components that run on two or more different computers. Parts of an application, such as how to present information on the screen, may be run on the user's desktop computer, the client. Other parts of the application, such as accessing and processing corporate data, are carried out on a server computer that specializes in that function. These servers can be located anywhere in the world. For example, in Blue Cross and Blue Shield (BCBS) of Ohio's previous system, although terminals were located on the desks of benefits officers, all processing was done on a single large computer. With the growth of customers, BCBS needed a more efficient way to process enrollment data. In place of the terminals, it gave each benefits officer a PC that was set up as a "client" and connected to the main computer, which became the "server." The PC takes care of document imaging and data entry editing as well as presenting the user with an easy-to-use graphical user interface. The server stores all of the necessary customer data and handles all other processing, especially anything requiring a lookup in the database or access to historical data. By assigning to each computer the tasks that it does best, BCBS was able to cut the time to enroll a new group from 30 to 60 days to 2 to 3 days.[16]

MANAGERIAL CHALLENGE

CHUGGING THROUGH THE DATA

Betty Knight, senior manager of Systems Development in the Corporate Support Division of the Union Pacific Railroad, was concerned. Union Pacific had a good track record for collecting data. However, it was stored on hundreds of servers and other computers in multiple formats, making it hard for someone to get the information needed for critical decisions. Knight stated, "If someone requested a report on the maintenance status of our fleet, for example, they got an overwhelming stack of papers." It was difficult and time-consuming to reconcile the information from these reports. To ensure that the highest-quality business decisions could be made throughout the organization, these dozens of disparate systems had to be consolidated into a single timely, consistent, and accurate resource. Marketing could then analyze rates and pricing data in this resource to prepare competitive price quotes for customers. Service Design could use some of the data to design the most cost-effective route for moving customers' goods. Finance could use this resource to analyze profitability. Knight was convinced the solution lay in establishing a data warehouse. Where was she to begin?

Knight decided to start with data generated from accounts payable. This was a comparatively small area, fairly easy to manage; the data were clearly of value to multiple business areas; and the expected benefits were impressive and easily measured. To ensure the success of this project, Knight and her team involved the end users in the early stages, making them aware of the benefits they could receive from active participation. She stated, "The more you communicate with your users, the more they will feel a part of the team, and the more understanding, patient, and proactive they will be in exploiting the technology." Keeping the users in the communications loop helped them understand both the capabilities and the limitations of the system. Getting users to buy into the system is one of the keys to the success of this kind of system.

And a successful project this was, with savings of $500,000 the first year (1992) and projected savings of $2.2 million over the first four years. From this positive beginning, Union Pacific's data warehouse now is a 600-gigabyte repository of corporate information, giving each of over 1,700 users direct access to critical business information.

Source: Adapted from Betty Knight, "The Smart Way to Build a Data-warehouse," *Datamation* 42, no. 16 (October 1996), pp. 91–94; and Craig Stedman, "Users Shoot Holes in Warehouse Tools," *Computerworld*, January 27, 1997, accessed at the *Computerworld* Web site, http://www.computerworld.com/home/print9497.nsf/all/SL4dwi.

Combining Technologies: Data Warehouses

data warehouse

an enterprisewide database that can be accessed, analyzed, and manipulated in multiple ways to reveal patterns

Conventional database management systems are optimized to support operations. To analyze large amounts of data, many firms create a single, enterprisewide database called a **data warehouse**.

The purpose of a data warehouse is to enable managers to gain a deeper understanding of their business, such as customer preferences or geographic trends, by accessing, analyzing, and manipulating a single integrated database in endless, flexible ways. However, the task of creating a data warehouse can be time-consuming and politically sensitive.[17] See the Managerial Challenge box for one company's experience creating a data warehouse.

Traditional methods of data analysis are not well suited for the huge data sets stored in data warehouses. A new approach, *data mining,* uses neural network techniques to detect patterns in the data. These patterns sometimes yield significant, previously unknown patterns useful in making business decisions. In contrast, traditional database query tools require users to know, in advance, the relationships among the data. Query tools are useful if you want to know what percentage of a store's shoppers last month bought pretzels and beer at the same time. But a data mining tool analyzes the buying patterns of beer-buyers and will discover that more of them buy diapers than pretzels, something the user would not have anticipated.[18] Determining which customers are profitable requires a complex analysis of marketing and servicing costs that go into retaining a particular customer and the revenue he or she is likely to bring in. Data mining tools can pinpoint the individual customers who are the most profitable. It can also find those who are the least profitable so that marketing dollars can be released and redirected to the profitable customers.[19] By better understanding customers, organizations and managers can develop more effective sales campaigns and product development strategies that will result in increased revenue and profitability.

HOW INFORMATION TECHNOLOGY IS REDEFINING BUSINESS

Over the past 20 years, computing power per dollar has doubled about every 18 months. One result is that personal computers are now commonplace, both in the office and at home. Likewise, over the same period, ever-more-powerful microprocessors have hit the market with predictable regularity, fueling the exponential growth of the computer industry. As shown in Exhibit 18.4, these changes have had a near revolutionary impact on business.[20] Business leaders embrace these technologies for competitive advantage, the laggards out of competitive necessity.

This section describes three business changes made possible by information technology: telework, outsourcing, and business process reengineering.

Office Work from a Distance: Telework

telework (or telecommuting)
working from remote locations using telecommunication links

The availability of personal computers and telecommunications lines enables office work to be conducted at alternative locations. Field sales representatives have been doing this for some time. Now even hourly employees who would otherwise spend their workday in an office can work at home or at some other site. Because the work travels to the office via telecommunication lines, the term *telecommuting* has been applied to this work arrangement. A better term is **telework**, which literally

EXHIBIT 18.4

Technology Creates New Business Rules

New Technology	Old Rule	New Rule
Shared databases	Information can appear in only one place at one time.	Information can appear simultaneously in as many places as it is needed.
Expert systems	Only experts can perform complex work.	A generalist can do the work of an expert.
Telecommunications networks	Businesses must choose between centralization and decentralization.	Businesses can simultaneously reap the benefits of centralization and decentralization.
Decision support tools	Managers make all decisions.	Decision making is part of everyone's job.
Wireless data communication and portable computers	Field personnel need offices where they can receive, store, and transmit information.	Field personnel can send and receive information wherever they are.
The Internet, Web pages, and interactive video	The best contact with a potential customer is personal contact.	The best contact with a potential customer is effective contact.

means work at a distance. It does not carry with it the limiting connotation of commuting. Home and the field remain common locations for telework. Another option is satellite facilities with smaller central sites. As this practice increases, the "virtual office" sometimes supplants the traditional central office. The virtual office exists not as a single physical location but as a network of workers in multiple locations, with work seen as a process rather than a place. Verifone, based in Redwood City, California, uses this virtual office structure, with most of its employees conducting business from remote sites. Verifone's CEO lives in Redwood City, the CIO operates out of his home in Santa Fe, and the head of human resources conducts business from outside Dallas. All company business is conducted through the company's electronic infrastructure.[21] Studies show that in 1997, 11.1 million workers teleworked at least one day a week, and the Gartner Group predicts 30 million teleworkers by the year 2000.[22]

Telework can make economic sense. Businesses potentially can gain through increased productivity, reduction in real estate costs, and greater employee satisfaction. IBM estimates it saves $75 million annually by having 10,000 salespeople and consultants telecommute. Productivity of those employees has increased 20 percent, and 75 percent of them reported that telecommuting had a positive impact on morale.[23]

The main impediment to telework is learning how to manage teleworkers; the technical issues of such work are relatively straightforward. The American Society for Training and Development (ASTD) found that a successful implementation of telework requires managers to define clearly whether telecommuting in their firm will involve employees working at home or a combination of variable locations and times. Thus, managers need to consider the type of job that would ensure a good fit with telework. For example, salespeople spend much of their time in the field, so telework is ideal for them. However, jobs involving face-to-face contact, needing close supervision, or having many short deadlines may not be well-suited for telework.

Managers also need to pay particular attention to selecting appropriate employees for telework. Some people thrive on the social contact of the office and do not handle well the comparative isolation of telework. Likewise, some workers perceive that being away from the office lessens their visibility and is an obstacle to career advancement. More important than the social aspects or visibility in the organization, however, is an employee's temperament and training. Employees who work at home must be able to manage their time well, be organized, and be able to balance work and family time without undue stress. Most essential of all, telework requires people who are self motivated, who have a high level of self-discipline, and who are able to work independently.[24]

Managers also need to adjust their supervision and evaluation methods and systems for telework to be successful. First, they need to establish clear guidelines and schedules for employees since they will not be in contact with teleworkers daily. Both employees and managers need to understand and agree on what constitutes high-quality work. Second, managers often need to change the way they monitor and evaluate employees in this type of work relationship. Productive telework does not always occur between 9:00 and 5:00, so flexibility is key in communications and the back-and-forth transmittal of work. If managers and their employees can come to terms on control-type issues such as these, then the potential advantages that information systems and technology create for telework can be realized.

Outsourcing Business Functions and Creating Alliances

Telework moves the worker outside the office; outsourcing moves the work itself. Outsourcing refers to contracting the responsibility for part of a firm's operations to a third party. Outsourcing is not new, but it is growing in importance now that data and information can be sent easily through networks to all parts of the world. Commonly, payroll processing, recruiting, and many other day-to-day business processes are outsourced. One reason for outsourcing is that an outside contractor who specializes in the outsourced function—think back to Adam Smith and the "division of labor" principle discussed in Chapter 2—can often do the job faster, better, or less expensively than an in-house, full-time staff or department. At the World Outsourcing Summit in 1998, 35 percent of the managers surveyed said that cutting operating expenses was the primary reason their company outsourced, while 17 percent outsourced to improve quality. However, 31 percent reported that outsourcing some tasks allowed the company staff to focus on its core competencies.[25] When Consolidated Freightways Corp. outsourced almost all of its IS operations to IBM, cost saving was not the primary motive. Staying ahead of the competition was the motivation. Consolidated needed its staff available to concentrate on strategic activities, not managing a data center.[26]

Traditionally, managers have been cautioned not to outsource core activities critical to the strategic mission of the corporation, such as business analysis or product research and development. In identifying activities appropriate for outsourcing, managers need to consider the strategic importance of this activity to the company, as well as whether the task can be performed more efficiently in house or outside. As in any other business arrangement, managers should select a vendor with a proven record of accomplishment and a good reputation. Before outsourcing to another country, other factors need to be considered such as the political stability of that country, restrictions on the flow of data across borders, and the strength of the telecommunication infrastructure.

Today, as vendors gain experience and sophistication with outsourcing, the traditional cautions about which functions to outsource may no longer apply. In many cases, outsourcing is changing into a strategic alliance between a firm and a vendor in which the vendor may handle a strategic application, such as planning and design for new product development. An example of such an alliance is the agreement between Delta Air Lines and AT&T Global Information Solutions. Delta outsourced its IS department to AT&T and created a new company, TransQuest Information Solutions, in which AT&T has a 50 percent stake. TransQuest provides traditional IS outsourcing services to Delta and leverages its assets and its knowledge of airline operations in the marketplace.[27]

Reengineering Business Processes

Businesses continually look for ways to improve—to increase profits by providing better goods and services at less cost—and using computerized information systems is one of those tools. However, computer systems are frequently used just to automate existing business practices, even if those practices are no longer effective. Instead of searching for new, more direct routes for their business processes to follow, some managers have simply "paved over old cow paths," automating what had been done before by hand. This, though, usually does not result in any significant improvements in an organization's functions. Therefore, managers are continually searching for innovative ways to do that.

One such approach to doing things differently that makes major use of information technology is **business process reengineering (BPR)**, which proposes a fundamental rethinking and radical redesign of business processes to achieve dramatic improvements in critical, contemporary measures of performance. BPR differs, therefore, from total quality management, which promotes continually refining and improving existing practices. The four key words in BPR are fundamental, radical, dramatic, and processes. For some businesses, further growth, perhaps even survival, requires a firm to start from scratch, abandoning its outmoded procedures, and drawing completely new maps for its processes. A business must ask itself, "If I were re-creating this company today, given what I know and given current technology, what would it look like?"[28]

Reengineering uses technology, but it also involves people. It can include a redesign of individual jobs and business processes, information systems, organizational structures, and even an organization's culture. The objective of such radical change, of course, is to achieve a breakthrough in business results such as reduced delivery times for products and services, enhanced customer service and satisfaction, or increased profitability. The experience of AFC Enterprises in reengineering its franchise support and other business functions, as described in the Managerial Challenge box, points out that reengineering causes fundamental changes in how businesses operate and thus can affect more than one department's activities, especially in the way they relate to one another. The example illustrates several of the basic elements of reengineering: (1) a process orientation, (2) creativity, and (3) the use of information technology.

One particular type of reengineering effort involving an organization's overall strategy and competitiveness that makes heavy use of information systems is **enterprise resource planning (ERP)**. ERP links all information systems throughout an organization so that managers and employees can have current, instant access to information. The goal of ERP is to spread the knowledge that resides in an organization more broadly and more quickly. It allows managers to monitor quality, product and service availability, customer service, performance, and profitability in *real time*—that is, as they are happening. With such current information at their fingertips, managers can, at least in principle, make better decisions. In effect, ERP systems allow managers to access and process information wherever they are and whenever they need it.

Instituting a reengineering approach as large-scale as ERP systems means an entire redesign of all information systems, and, as such, costs can be prohibitive and therefore can increase the risks. Nevertheless, if an organization's information systems are old and up-to-the-minute information is increasingly difficult to obtain, it may make sense for managers to consider installing ERP and take the risks.

Although information technology is a major enabler of reengineering, it is not enough by itself to ensure success. Clearly, changing the way people work, as reengineering does, is no simple task, and managers need to be intensely involved in, and involve their employees in, such efforts. Otherwise, strong resistance is likely to occur. These and other issues related to using reengineering to make extensive organizational changes are discussed in more detail in Chapter 19. Here, though, it is important to emphasize that reengineering, to have a chance at being

business process reengineering (BPR)
fundamental rethinking and radical redesign of business processes to achieve dramatic improvements in critical, contemporary measures of performance

enterprise resource planning (ERP)
linking of all information systems within an organization to share knowledge

MANAGERIAL CHALLENGE

AFC ENTERPRISES USES IT IN TURNAROUND

When a couple of fast-food chains that specialized in chicken dinners went into bankruptcy, managers and investors formed AFC Enterprises Inc. to take Church's Chicken and Popeye's Chicken & Biscuits under its wing. To turn the franchises around, AFC realized that quick fixes would not do. Instead, it redesigned the franchise businesses using information technology.

At the center of this redesign is AFCOnline, an extranet that promotes communication with and support for AFC's 2,700 restaurants. Through AFCOnline, AFC and franchisees can communicate quickly and easily about the company's latest marketing promotions. "It keeps us updated on what I need to plan for, when I should advertise in a local newspaper, and which coupons to run," notes one Popeye's Chicken franchisee in Wisconsin. The extranet is extremely helpful to new franchisees, giving them step-by-step guidance in how to open and run a new restaurant. This level of support is unusual in the franchise business. "Using state-of-the-art technology to support franchisees puts them ahead of other companies," comments Chris Turner, a VP in Goldman Sachs' leveraged finance group. Even though AFC is smaller than some of its competitors, it leads the pack in the use of information technology to change and grow its business, according to experts.

Before AFCOnline was in place, franchisees had to communicate with the parent company via mail and fax, and AFC field agents had to spend time and money traveling to different restaurant sites to answer questions, solve problems, inform franchisees about new products or marketing strategies, and so forth. Now, franchise partners simply access the AFC support center, which is staffed by consultants who use a Lotus Notes database to help franchisees deal with everything from how much chicken to buy to the price of a deep-fat fryer. AFC still sends out field agents for

quality control and training, but their mission is very specific; they no longer engage in general troubleshooting. Even the field staff, when they make on-site visits, now have access to the extranet through notebook computers. The extranet has helped both AFC agents and franchisees reduce the time it takes to open a new restaurant by as much as one to four months. The sooner a restaurant opens, the sooner the revenues can begin to pour in.

AFCOnline didn't happen overnight; rather, it was part of the process of business process reengineering in which AFC contracted with IT outsourcing expert IBM Global Services to evaluate the company's needs, rethink its processes, and help it use technology to improve and grow. IBM informed AFC that "we would have to overhaul our underlying processes as well as our technology to be competitive," recalls AFC president Dick Holbrook. Another firm, Atlanta-based ILC, developed a sales and inventory forecasting program for AFC, called Franchise Assistant. The new program will help with labor scheduling, restaurant accounting, and sales reporting.

AFC had to find a way to bring its two small subsidiaries back from the brink of disaster; by investing the time, energy, and money in the right information technology, the company was able to redesign many of its business processes. Of course, training its managers—both AFC staff and franchise partners—to use the technology properly has been key to the success of this major change. Communication between managers, as well as quick access to information, has been the real impact of AFC's state-of-the-art technology.

Source: Paula Sinclair, "Extranet Key to Support System," *Informationweek* 699 (September 7, 1998), pp. 41–46.

---

successful in reaching its goals, requires strong upper-level management support and commitment as well as sophisticated applications of information systems.

INFORMATION SYSTEM SECURITY

A major potential problem in managing information systems is guaranteeing their security. A study by the U.S. Government Accounting Office found that while technical measures are helpful, strong policy and personnel measures supported by high-level managers are more important in providing IS security.[29] Managers need to communicate the importance of security throughout the firm by seeing that an IS security plan is adopted and that resources are allocated for its implementation.

EXHIBIT 18.5
Sources of Threats to IS Security

Type of Threat	Source of Threat	Percent of Total	Managerial Response
Accidental	Employees' errors and omissions	65%	Training, software error prevention and detection
Intentional	Unhappy employees	11%	Recognition and rewards
	Dishonest employees	13%	Careful screening of employees; segregation of duties
	Intruders (outsiders)	3%	Virus vaccines, restricted physical and electronic access
Acts of Nature	Floods, fires, earthquakes, etc.	8%	Backups, disaster recovery plan

Source: *MIS Week,* November 27, 1989, pp. 26–32, as cited in James Hicks, *Management Information Systems: A User Perspective* (St. Paul, MN: West Publishing Company, 1993), p. 570; and Jesse Berst, "The Biggest Threat to Your Network's Security," *ZDNet,* April 7, 1998, accessed at http://www.zdnet.com/anchordesk/story/story_1959.html.

Information is a valuable corporate resource that firms must guard and utilize with the same care they give to other resources. Information security can be divided into two major categories: *data integrity* and *confidentiality*, and *accessibility*. Data integrity requires keeping the information accurate and protected against accidental or deliberate unauthorized change, while confidentiality requires that the information is stored so that only those authorized can access it. Accessibility requires that information be available.

Data Integrity and Confidentiality

As Exhibit 18.5 shows, about 90 percent of breeches to IS security come from employees, and the majority of these incidents are accidental, not intentional. Without proper safeguards, employees will unintentionally misenter, access, and even corrupt data. Less than 30 percent of security breaches are intentional, and employees commit the vast majority of these.

The best method to prevent unwanted access to information contained in corporate databases is to establish tight information systems controls. These controls can avoid computer misuse, crime, and fraud. Most IS departments have general operating rules on who can and cannot access what information. Some basic types of controls include the following:

- Input, processing, and output controls—The goal of these controls is to maintain data integrity and security. Policies and procedures can be established to limit who may access and change information. Passwords or sophisticated identification systems (e.g., voice or fingerprint identification) can limit access to input systems and their information output, and backup copies of programs and data can help ensure that data are not lost or corrupted during processing.
- Database controls—The goal of these controls is to identify who within and outside the organization may have access to what data. Identification numbers and passwords can be issued, and, without their use, access to certain data is denied.

Many companies use ID badges to prevent unauthorized access to sensitive areas in information systems facilities.

- Telecommunications controls—These controls are designed to provide accurate data transfer among systems and networks. One example is data encryption, which is a software program that scrambles messages. Only users that have the data "key" may unscramble and read messages.
- Personnel controls—The number and types of employees can be controlled to restrict access to critical information systems. Authorized personnel may be issued passwords or required to carry ID badges or access cards. Limiting access helps prevent computer crime and mistakes.

Managers involved with the IT function have a major role in maintaining information security. They need to focus on the motivation and satisfaction of their employees and to detect dishonest ones if that is necessary. Approaches they can use include such practices (discussed in Chapter 12) as careful initial selection, training, and support of personnel. Investigation and interviews can help weed out those who have exhibited questionable behavior in the past or who may not be suitable for a particular type of job. Once selected, employees need to be trained in how to use and protect the systems, and the training should communicate well-documented policies and procedures for proper computer behavior. In addition, effective reward systems, both actual pay and other forms of recognition, can help motivate employees to be especially vigilant in keeping IS security at a high level in their work.

The accounting principle of segregating duties can be applied to information systems. Just as the person who calculates and prepares a check should not be the one who signs it, the analysts or programmers who create or control the programs should not also be the ones who control or enter the data. This separation of functions reduces error and guards against dishonesty. Technical measures for reducing data entry errors use the computer to check for validity and reasonableness as the data are entered. Similarly, designers should build security measures, such as passwords, into programs to limit access by unauthorized persons.

Accessibility

Floods, earthquakes, and hurricanes can damage or destroy computer installations and all the data stored in them. Even a broken water pipe or a careless smoker can render a system inoperable. Organizations should have disaster recovery plans in place to ensure that information is accessible, even under extreme conditions. Typically, the organization designates certain systems that are so critical they must be continuously available. For example, systems that control cash flow (e.g., invoicing, accounts receivable) and customer service (e.g., inventory and shipping) are designated in a disaster recovery plan. Personnel in the IS unit, in conjunction with managers and employees from the critical business functions, develop emergency alternate procedures and plans based on possible scenarios. Some functions can be performed manually until the system can be accessed; others may need backup systems that can be tapped if the main system goes down. Once a plan is in place, managers and their employees can test the system, similar to the way a fire drill is carried out.

Backup systems involve hardware, software, telecommunications, and personnel. For hardware backup, companies routinely arrange to have compatible computer hardware ready when needed. Such backup systems can be disaster facilities—entire systems offered by a computer vendor—or simply a room in another location where electrical service, telecommunications links, and other backup hardware is available.

Software backup includes not only the programs an organization uses but the databases that store critical information. Duplicate copies are made of all programs and data. At least two copies are made: One is stored on site in the IS unit in case of accidental mishaps; the other is kept off-site in a safe, secure fireproof room. Again, a number of vendors offer software backup and can arrange routine pickup and delivery, but if the organization is small, one or two managers or employees can be designated to run backup software on the system and store the additional copies off-site.

Telecommunications backup can be as complex as arranging entire network recovery or as simple as ensuring one or two critical communication nodes have duplicate components. Often, telecommunications networks already have backup built in. These so-called *fault-tolerant networks* will function when part of the network is disrupted.

Finally, IS personnel must also have backups. Cross-training is the typical method of ensuring that help is available when needed. When more than one individual can perform a needed task, then the organization has assurance that crucial functions can be performed under difficult situations.

ETHICAL ISSUES IN THE USE OF INFORMATION SYSTEMS

Chapter 5 covered ethical issues in general. As information systems give us increasingly sophisticated ways to store and access data, the ethical implications of how to use this information in decision making need to be considered. Decisions that are made ethically, by definition, are made in accordance with principles of right and wrong. To decide whether an action is "right or wrong" requires an ethical analysis that applies such principles to the situation.

EXHIBIT 18.6

Mason's Four Dimensions
of Ethical Issues in IS

Privacy	Just because we now have the ability to collect and store almost any item of data about a person, do we have the right to do this? May we conduct surveillance and monitoring of employees at will?
Access	Who has the right to access what information and for what purpose? How will the tools for access be provided to individuals and to societies?
Property	Who owns information and intellectual property? May a firm sell information, including medical information, about its employees? May it sell demographic information about its customers?
Accuracy	Who is responsible for accuracy of information, and who is accountable for errors?

A senior scholar in the field of information systems (Richard Mason) proposed an oft-quoted framework for analyzing the ethical issues in the use of information. As shown in Exhibit 18.6, this framework classifies IS ethical issues around four main topics: privacy, access, property, and accuracy.[30]

Ethical decision making regarding information is challenging because of the many potential conflicts among different stakeholders. For example, managers' needs to know (to optimize profits for shareholders) may conflict with employees' or customers' rights of privacy. Because of the value of information to organizations and the ease with which information systems can collect it, these conflicts are becoming more apparent, especially with increasing use of the Internet for business. Customers may not know that a company is collecting information on, say, their buying frequencies, types of purchases, and methods of payment. The company's intent for doing so is to help it produce and market products and services to meet their needs. But that information could also be valuable to another firm that sells similar or compatible products. Is it ethical for the company to sell that information to another? Regarding employee privacy, companies can monitor work done on networks by recording the number of keystrokes an employee makes or the amount of time spent at the keyboard. Should companies do so? Similarly, e-mail and phone systems can be monitored. Is e-mail private? Not according to federal law and court decisions. Some firms have even been sued after e-mail that had been deleted was recovered and used to prove employee discrimination lawsuits. The key point is that organizations must set up policies and procedures about what type of information it will collect, who will have access to it, and for what it will be used. Managers and employees all need to know and follow the policies to the letter.

CONCLUDING COMMENTS

Information, as we have emphasized in this chapter, is an extremely valuable resource, and advances in information technology provide organizations with tremendously powerful tools for executing their strategies and attaining their objectives. But ... information technology must be managed, and managed well, if its great potential is to be achieved. That is the core management challenge: to make the costly investments in information technology actually pay off in better organizational performance.

In today's organizations, managers themselves not only need to know how to use information technologies but also, especially, to know and understand the managerial issues that such technology imposes. The advances in information technology bring with them their own new complexities, such as maintaining information systems security and dealing with some very real ethical issues that confront managerial decision making in this area. It is also clear that information technologies provide exceptional opportunities for putting into action creative initiatives, but managers, not technologists, need to be the strategists directing their use. Otherwise, the advantages that information technology and information systems offer are not likely to be fully realized.

Over the years, information systems have evolved in response to the changing needs of organizations and the changing capabilities of information technologies. The evolution of these technologies has given managers significant freedom to rethink how their organizations or their particular units go about doing their most basic activities. Some have not grasped these potentials for fundamental change and hence are still mired in outmoded ways of doing business and in great danger of missing out on what could be accomplished through skillful management of those technologies. Many others, however, have had the vision to see what is possible, and for them the challenge is to implement major changes effectively. That is the subject of the next, and final, chapter.

KEY TERMS

artificial intelligence (AI) 550

business process reengineering (BPR) 559

chief information officer (CIO) 543

client/server architecture 554

computer network 552

data 542

database 554

data warehouse 555

decision support systems (DSS) 548

electronic commerce (e-commerce) 553

electronic data interchange (EDI) 546

electronic funds transfer (EFT) 547

end user 542

enterprise resource planning (ERP) 559

executive support systems (ESS) 549

expert systems 550

extranets 553

group decision support systems (GDSS) 550

groupware, or group support systems (GSS) 549

information 542

information systems (IS) 542

information technology (IT) 542

Internet 552

internets 552

intranets 553

management information system (MIS) 548

neural networks 551

office information systems (OIS) 547

telework (telecommuting) 556

transaction processing systems (TPS) 546

World Wide Web 552

REVIEW QUESTIONS

1. Explain the difference between data and information, and give an example of each.
2. What are the duties and desired characteristics of a CIO?
3. Describe how information needs vary by the level of the decision. Give examples of information or reports that each level would use.
4. What is a transaction processing system? Give three examples from businesses with which you frequently interact.
5. Describe the similarities and differences between the different types of managerial support systems.
6. What is the difference between expert systems and neural networks? Give an example, other than those used in the text, of how each might be used in a business.

7. Describe the Internet and the Wide World Web. What challenges do they pose for managers?

8. Describe a data warehouse and how it might be used by a business. What are some of the problems in constructing one?

9. Explain the terms *telework* and *outsourcing*. How can businesses benefit from these options?

10. What are the major threats to information system security, and what can managers do to reduce these threats?

11. Describe Mason's four areas of information system ethical issues. Give an example, not used in the text, of an issue in each area.

DISCUSSION QUESTIONS

1. In the Managerial Challenge box, "Chugging through the Data," what techniques did Betty Knight use as a change agent to reduce resistance and help ensure the success of her project?

2. How has information technology affected management decision making?

3. Discuss the following statement: "The role of the manager has expanded due to information technology."

4. Some say that to stay competitive, a business must adopt the latest information technologies. Explain why you agree or disagree with this statement.

5. Select an organization or industry with which you are familiar. How is it currently using information technology? How has information technology changed the way it operates? Are there potential uses of IT that have not yet been tapped in that industry?

CLOSING CASE

Using Information Technology to Support Corporate Strategy

Roberts Transportation Services, a division of Roadway Services, recognized a window of opportunity created by the liberalized trade environment within the newly formed European Union (EU). Roberts, based in Akron, Ohio, is the world's largest surface expedited carrier specializing in the transportation of critical and emergency shipments of items that are fragile or valuable or require security provisions, special handling, customized equipment, or full-range temperature control. In 1992, Roberts created Roberts Express Europe (REE), the first company to enter the critical and emergency shipment market in the European Union (EU).

In the early 1990s, the physical distribution of goods within Europe was supply driven. Goods were stored in large distribution centers located in each country in which

a manufacturer did business, and sales within each country were filled from the distribution center located in that country. The advantages of this system included low per-unit shipping costs, since shipments took place in large batches, and the ability to absorb fluctuations in demand. Disadvantages included high inventory levels with their associated costs, difficulty in controlling and coordinating widely dispersed distribution centers, and lack of responsiveness to customer needs. REE estimated that it took 3 to 14 days to move goods through these systems, too long a period for REE's specialized customers.

In view of the number of freight companies existing in Europe, REE managers determined that to succeed in this market, its primary mission must be to place the customer first and reduce delivery time to hours instead of days or weeks. REE would guarantee pickup within 90 minutes in Germany, France, Holland, Belgium, and Luxembourg. It would give a guaranteed delivery time for each shipment and deduct one-fourth of the bill if it was two hours late and one-half of the bill if it was more than four hours late. To respond to the unique needs of its customers, instead of a hub-and-spoke configuration used by companies such as Federal Express, REE would build its physical distribution network country by country using independent subcontractors. Dedicated vans, trucks, or aircraft would pick up a job and deliver it using the same vehicle.

REE was fortunate that its managing director recognized the importance of information technology to the success of the project. The director stated, "Those organizations that will win in the EU need to use computers and telecommunications as a strategic tool and set quality of service as number one." REE developed its information technology strategy and structures at the same time it developed its business strategy and structure. It became clear to REE managers that they would need an innovative information system that could accommodate differences between countries yet provide centralized control of operations. Some of the challenges it faced were

- How to meet the varied restrictions on the flow of data and goods between countries.
- How to transmit information between dispatchers and drivers who might be anywhere on the continent.
- How to handle the differences between countries, such as language, currency, and accounting practices.

Although there has been some progress to reduce restrictions on the flow of data between European countries, significant differences in laws and regulations still exist. It was essential for REE to transfer data about customers and shipments across borders, so REE had to make sure that its IT system complied with all relevant regulations and laws. In addition to restrictions on data, there are many others on the flow of goods. For example, it is unlawful to drive during some weekend hours in Germany, and in France no truck traffic is allowed on weekends in August. Because dispatchers could not make accurate schedules without this information, data on permits, road restrictions, and customs processing all had to be accessible within the system.

The next question was to decide what media to use for transmitting data. Factors to be considered were cost, reliability, and availability. Although it would be less expensive to use the existing public communications service, many countries could not provide the necessary capacity or service reliability. Since customer service was its primary mission, REE decided reliability and efficiency were more important than cost and, therefore, selected a proprietary system that uses two-way satellite communication. The system collects data about shipments and stores those data in a central database. It displays graphic images of shipment

locations on a map of Western Europe at the central facility in Maastricht, the Netherlands. From this map, dispatchers can see the whereabouts of drivers and assign the closest available vehicle to a new order. Now, within 10 minutes a dispatcher can match a shipment to the appropriate vehicle, assign a driver, and schedule an immediate pickup. In addition, the satellite link can be used for direct communication between dispatcher and drivers.

Now that the communication link was selected, what could be done about the differences in language? Although English is often considered the common international language for business, many individuals involved in REE's business do not speak English. REE had to find a way to communicate accurately with both customers and drivers who spoke a single, non-English language. REE built the system so it recognizes the country from which a customer is calling and automatically routes that call to someone at headquarters who speaks that language. Since drivers crossed borders, REE needed a different solution to ensure messages from drivers speaking a variety of languages were interpreted correctly. REE was able to identify 25 frequently used messages, such as, "I am delayed in traffic and will be 15 to 30 minutes late." To send a message, the driver identifies his or her native language and the list of messages appears in that language. After the driver selects the correct message, it is sent to headquarters, where it is displayed in the native language of the dispatcher.

Accounting differences posed an especially complicated problem. Not only do all expenses and revenues have to be accurately allocated to the country in which they occurred, each country has different reporting rules. REE considered two accounting system alternatives. The first option would develop at least a dozen different accounting systems, each tailored to a specific country. The second would have a single, comprehensive accounting system administered from the central office that collected all revenue and expense data and allocated them to the appropriate country. In each country, REE would subcontract with public accounting firms who would use these data to prepare the accounting forms, tax statements, and payroll for that country. REE selected the second option.

The experience of REE reaffirms the importance of integrating business and information technology strategies to achieve competitive advantage. By doing so, REE was able to use IT to help it coordinate the differences across international borders and integrate operations within a multinational corporation.

QUESTIONS

1. Discuss some of the ways REE used information technology to support its mission of prompt customer service.
2. In what ways did REE's mission of customer service influence the structure of its information system?

3. In what ways does REE have a centralized system and in what ways is it decentralized?

4. Federal Express and REE are both shipping companies. Federal Express transports all goods to a central site where they are sorted and sent on to their destination. REE transports each job separately. What do you think are the main reasons each selected its method of delivery, and how does the selected method impact IT requirements for information use by managers?

5. REE would like to get more of its customers to use electronic data interchange. What could REE do to make this option more attractive to customers?

Source: This case was developed from an article by Barry Shore, a professor at the University of New Hampshire, and used with his permission. Further details can be found in Dr. Shore's article "Using Information Technology to Coordinate Transnational Service Operations: A Case Study in the European Union," *Journal of Global Information Management,* Spring 1996, pp. 5–14.

PART 7

TRANSFORMING

CHAPTER 19

ORGANIZATIONAL CHANGE AND RENEWAL

LEARNING OBJECTIVES

After studying this chapter, you should be able to:

- Identify the internal and external forces for change in an organization.
- Discuss the technological, cultural, strategic, structural, procedural, and people focuses for change.
- Analyze the process managers should use in evaluating the need for change.
- Describe the process of organizational change.
- Diagnose the causes of resistance to change and discuss possible approaches to dealing with such resistance.
- Describe three approaches to planned comprehensive organizational change and compare their similarities and differences.

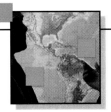

Change at the U.S. Postal Service

As a former branch of the U.S. government, the U.S. Postal Service has always been infamous for its authoritarian, command-and-control management culture. However, in the early 1990s, the Postal Service wanted to change this culture and appointed a new postmaster general. Marvin Runyon was the former chairman of the Tennessee Valley Authority, where he had gained the reputation of a tough but enlightened leader who could effect revolutionary change in an organization that badly needed to compete with private enterprise, such as Federal Express and United Parcel Service.

When Runyon became postmaster general, he promised to transform the Postal Service into a model of modern leadership in which employee involvement and empowerment would rule. What he soon found out, however, is that his good-faith efforts would not change the Postal Service overnight. The Postal Service is one of the nation's largest organizations with a workforce of 700,000, roughly the size of the entire city of Baltimore. Significantly changing direction of an organization that size was like trying to turn a supertanker without running aground in hidden shoals. Among Runyon's biggest challenges was to improve relations between management and the largest unions, the National Association of Letter Carriers (NALC) and the American Postal Workers Union (APWU).

Just after Runyon took control, he announced several strategies he though would put the Postal Service back onto a more competitive course: streamlining management, empowering employees, holding employees more accountable for performance, and introducing work teams to encourage departments to work more closely together. Management began to implement a number of new programs, but not all the changes were popular. Runyon started a long-term automation project that would cut the Postal Service's huge labor costs—by far the largest expense the organization incurs. The $5 billion automation project called for investment in letter-sorting equipment and bar-code readers. Not long after his appointment, Runyon downsized the giant workforce by offering as many as 30,000 early retirement packages. Bill Henderson, then the head of Human Resources, further cut the Postal Service's training force by 40 percent and moved the training headquarters from Washington, D.C., to Chicago.

Although long-time critics of the Postal Service applauded Runyon's much-needed cuts, its management had to deal with the aftermath. Management had not anticipated, for instance, that it would lose more employees than it wanted. Nearly 48,000 workers left, and the Postal Service was forced to pay huge sums as overtime hours nearly doubled for the remaining workers. Many inexperienced workers were suddenly pushed into supervisory jobs, where they had to manage former peers who were overworked and frustrated.

The downsizing of the training department proved to be a costly error. As a leaner workforce was under pressure to move even more mail, supervisors could not take the time to be trained. The fortunate few who could take the time for training found that the severely downsized training staff was incapable of providing it. New supervisors relied on on-the-job coaching from managers until they could enroll in management classes at local universities. Finally, three years after cutting the training staff, the Postal Service acknowledged that the move had not been a great idea and increased the training budget to further support the group.

The greatest disaster of all occurred in the already-unstable relationship between the Postal Service's management and its unions. Though the unions had been encouraged by the announcement of employee empowerment, they had quickly grown skeptical about management's willingness to let go of control. Employee empowerment would allow employees—

including union members—to have a say in the management of the organization and to make their own decisions. Four years into Runyon's tenure, Vince Sombrotto, national president of the NALC, commented that "absolutely nothing has changed. Employee empowerment seemed like a good idea for about 60 days, until management figured out that it meant actually giving up some of their power and letting workers have a say. Now they have returned to their old confrontational style of management by stick."

Despite the improvements in Postal Service finances—it posted three years of gains of more that $1 billion each and halved the outstanding debt that had accumulated over two decades—labor relations are the worst they have been in the last 40 years, according to union officials. The workplace continues to be marked by controversy, a relatively autocratic management style, and labor disputes.

The major organizational changes initiated at the U.S. Postal Service obviously left many unresolved questions. In well-intended efforts to change a huge, bureaucratic organization, did reformers work too quickly? Must change in an organization be *revolutionary* to be effective? Or should it be *evolutionary*?

Source: Adapted from David Stamps, "Going Nowhere: Culture Change at the Postal Service Fizzles," *Training*, July 1996, pp. 26–34; Eric Yoder, "First Class Feud," *Government Executive* 30, no. 2 (February 1998), pp. 23–26; William J. Henderson, "Delivering the Future," *Government Executive* 30, no. 10 (October 1998), p. 61.

Organizations never stay the same, because the world around them never stays the same. From ancient times forward, every organization has had to build the capacity to change into its structure.[1] Thus, making changes and managing that process are essential to the vitality of any organization or company, whether in the 1800s, the 1900s, or the 2000s. However, as the opening story of the U.S. Postal Service's efforts to make significant changes demonstrates, managing the change process is no easy task. The need to change is often obvious, but *how* to make successful changes represents formidable managerial challenges. As Marvin Runyon found out at the Postal Service, and as any manager anywhere discovers sooner or later, there are fundamental issues of change, such as the following, that need to be confronted:

- How much change is enough?
- How fast should change take place?
- How should the need for continual changes be balanced against the need for a minimum level of stability and continuity?
- Who should be the major players in change processes, and what should their roles be?
- Who, exactly, is likely to benefit and who could be harmed by particular changes?

Answers to these and other similar questions will determine the fate of attempted changes in any organization. Certainly, this has been the case so far in the evolving story of the U.S. Postal Service.

This chapter focuses on change in *organizational* settings; that is, in complex contexts where many kinds of changes can take place. Some are very *un*planned and reactive, often involving unpleasant consequences for those who work in organizations. A sudden layoff of a large number of employees to reduce expenses quickly is one familiar example, such as Kodak's 1998 announcement that it would lay off 200 executives and 16,600 employees, or approximately 17 percent of its work-force.[2] Other changes, like that at the Postal Service, are much more planned and often have the intent of transforming the entire organization or at least major parts of it so that sudden, drastic cuts of personnel will not be necessary. The more a change is planned, comprehensive, and apt to bring about basic modifications in the very nature of the organization, the more the terms "organizational development" or "organizational renewal" are applicable. (We also discuss a special use of the term "organizational development" later in the chapter.)

In this chapter we first review why organizations change—focusing on the forces that can cause changes. Particular attention is given to analyzing internal and external forces of change, and on recognizing and diagnosing those forces as they affect the need for change. Particular areas of change are considered next: technology, organizational culture, strategy, structure, processes and systems, and people. These sections provide a background for an examination of managerial choices regarding the preparation, implementation, and evaluation of the change process. The chapter concludes with an analysis of several specific approaches to planned, comprehensive change that are frequently used by managers in contemporary organizations.

FORCES FOR CHANGE

The causes of organizational change originate from both external and internal forces, and a manager must be alert to all of them (see Exhibit 19.1). Sometimes those causes arise almost totally from factors outside the organization such as economic or business conditions, technological developments, demographic shifts, and the like. At other times, the forces are mostly from inside the organization. Internal forces include such factors as managerial decisions to make changes and employee pressures for urgent changes. Often, of course, the total set of causes of change represent a combination of both external and internal reasons.

Forces Outside the Organization

A whole host of forces outside the organization, as discussed earlier in the chapter on external environments, can bring about changes inside it. Here we mention several of the most important.

Economic Conditions   Obvious forces for change affecting business organizations are developments in the economic environment. If the economy is weak, then many companies are likely to reduce their workforces or at least limit hiring, prune low-profit product lines, and the like. For example, from January 1994 to July 1995, DuPont, in anticipation of an economic turndown, shut or sold 58 plants and businesses and reduced capital investment 40 percent below 1990 levels.[3]

EXHIBIT 19.1

Forces for Change

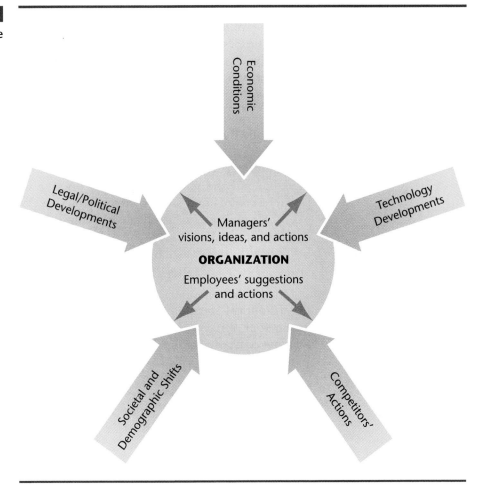

Conversely, if the economy is vibrant and expanding, many firms consider adding new services or products, creating new units or divisions, increasing their geographic areas of operations, and undertaking similar growth changes. Thus, in response to a healthy economy and increasing demand for its motorcycles, Harley-Davidson spent some $800 million between 1995 and 1999 to open two new manufacturing plants.[4]

Analogous to these business-world examples, many nonbusiness organizations, especially governmental agencies, contract or expand in relation to economic conditions because their budgets are directly impacted by those forces. In recent years, for example, the various projects planned by the National Aeronautics and Space Administration (NASA) have been put on slower timetables because of severe budget cuts.[5]

Competitors' Actions Regardless of the state of the economy, most business and many other organizations are likely to be extremely sensitive to moves made by their direct competitors, especially those in response to changes in the market or customers' preferences. The actions of other significant players in the immediate environment often can trigger changes inside a given organization, even when that organization would prefer not to make any changes at that time. For example, in anticipation of competitors' moves in a deregulated utility environment, companies such as Duke Power of North Carolina and Utilicorp of Kansas City searched for new customers outside their traditional geographic markets.[6] Likewise, an international merger between British Petroleum and Amoco caused Exxon to merge with Mobil and form the largest industrial company at that point in time.

Technology Developments   Changes in technology developed outside an organization frequently require it to respond, whether it wants to or not. Technological advances offer both opportunity and threat to organizations, but if they are major breakthroughs and relate directly to an organization's core activities, managers have little choice but to make corresponding changes. Several years ago, for example, the technological achievements of a competitor, Oracle, spurred the managers at Informix to adopt and market a new graphics and video-oriented database. Unfortunately, this change resulted in major losses, a significant drop in Informix's market value, and the departure of key technical personnel.[7]

Legal/Political Developments   When governments make new laws or courts issue new interpretations of those laws, managers need to respond, even when the solutions or types of changes that should be made are not obvious. In the United States, the passage of Title IX of the 1964 Civil Rights Law required universities to provide equal resources and opportunities to male and female students (in relation to their proportions in the student body). Directors of intercollegiate athletics at U.S. universities eventually realized that this would have major implications for their area of activities. Because of tight budgets, however, these particular managers, the athletic directors, found it difficult to add enough women's sports to equalize the proportion of men to women athletes. Nevertheless, some managers handled this situation much better than others and made the changes more quickly and with less conflict within their organizations. Clearly, however, the external force of law in this instance caused changes that would unlikely have come about for any other reason. Also, in this example, the political climate added a force to the legal enactment that hastened attention to the need to make these changes.

Societal and Demographic Shifts   Other types of external forces for change can take longer to develop and be more subtle and difficult to detect, such as changing societal attitudes toward various products, services and practices. Airlines, for example, had to change their practices regarding passengers who smoked. In response to changing levels of customer tolerance to smoking in confined areas, and long before there was any mandatory legislation that required complete abolition of smoking, airlines took steps to create separate sections for smokers and nonsmokers, where formerly they paid no attention at all to whether passengers smoked or not.

Shifting demographic patterns, such as the aging of populations in the United States and Japan in recent years, are another type of slow-moving external force. For example, within the last few years, the U.S. Bureau of Labor Statistics reported that by the year 2005, 29 percent of the U.S. population will be over age 55, and the largest growing segment (40 percent) will be between 45 and 64.[8] Such alterations in the age makeup of society have, for example, challenged retailing firms to change product mixes and take new approaches to sales and marketing.

Before there was mandatory legislation banning smoking on flights, airlines created separate sections for smokers in response to the changing attitudes toward smoking. And before the creation of separate sections, airlines permitted smoking anywhere on the plane.

These kinds of demographic shifts do not take place overnight, of course, but they can exert a powerful force nevertheless.

Forces Inside the Organization

As with external factors, many potential forces inside the organization can cause change to take place. Two of the most important are (1) managerial decisions and (2) employee preferences and pressures.

Managerial Decisions   Managers at any level of an organization operate under certain constraints that limit their freedom of action. However, in many instances they have considerable authority to make changes in their particular parts of the enterprise. Generally, of course, even in this age of flatter organizational structures, the higher up that managers are in an organization, the more leeway and the more power they have to institute change. Managers are often reluctant, though, to use their power for this purpose. Indeed, as pointed out in Chapter 14 ("Leadership, Power, and Influence"), some authorities would argue that managers tend to *under*utilize their power to make changes, rather use too much power.[9] The risk, obviously, is that an attempted change will be unsuccessful, and the manager may end up with less power than before. Therefore, as will be discussed in the next section, one of the most critical leadership issues facing managers is accurately evaluating the need for change. When managers do make decisions to change, though, those decisions can affect the status quo in major ways.

Employee Preferences and Suggestions   Managerial decisions are not the only source of change inside organizations. Lower-level employees often are an excellent source of innovative suggestions for change. The Dana Corporation, for instance, considers employee suggestions to be its best method for discovering new ways to cut costs and improve procedures. In fact, each of the auto-parts manufacturer's

45,000 employees averages an impressive 1.22 suggestions per month. One such suggestion by two plant employees at Dana's Elizabethtown, Kentucky, facility concerned an easier method to stack steel sheets for fabrication. That one suggestion resulted in $250,000 in annual savings.[10] The challenge for managers, of course, is to sort out the creative proposals and hunches that have potential for increased performance and improved work climate from those that would be ineffective if implemented.

In extreme instances, employees may exert overt pressure for changes. In May 1996, for example, truckers in Los Angeles staged a work stoppage, which reduced traffic at the Port of Los Angeles by 80 percent. They took this strong measure to call attention to the financial losses they suffered as a result of the hours-long delays being caused by traffic congestion in and around the terminal.[11]

Managers need to distinguish employee pressures that address legitimate needs for change from pressures that attempt to obstruct or intimidate. Making such judgments wisely and responding appropriately are essential managerial skills, as discussed in the next section. Regardless of the extent to which managers have that skill, however, employees can be a stimulus for change that frequently cannot, and should not, be ignored.

FOCUS OF ORGANIZATIONAL CHANGES

When managers decide that change is needed, or when they realize that they have no choice but to make changes, one of the first issues they face is: What to change? In organizational settings, at least a half dozen components could be altered. Any change involves at least one of these elements of the organization, and most changes involve several. Especially complex and comprehensive changes will involve all six.

Technology

For many organizations, the most obvious and most frequent object of changes is technology (see Exhibit 19.2). This has always been the case in manufacturing and capital-intensive companies, where replacing and upgrading equipment and technology have been the keys to organizational survival and an ability to keep ahead of the competition. In recent years, though, virtually all types of firms, government agencies, and nonbusiness organizations have been giving increasing attention to improving and expanding their information technology.[12] For example, in the late 1980s, the Australian architectural firm of Flower & Samios of Sydney was still doing all its drafting and designing with paper and pencil. Within the space of a few years, the firm converted entirely to computer-aided drafting and design and grew from $20 million a year in projects to over $100 million.[13]

Thus, for almost any organization at the beginning of the 21st century, from the corner dry cleaner to the largest multinational, making changes in technology becomes a prime and nearly continual focal point. The critical issues for managers, however, involve the significant and often unexpected spillover effects of changes in technology on other areas such as structure, processes, and people. New equipment, for example, can result in entirely different patterns of work relationships among employees, and that, in turn, can create considerable confusion. Such effects, if they are major or last a long time, can dilute or even cancel the positive effects of the improvements. A focus on technology is, therefore, a frequent

EXHIBIT 19.2

Examples of
Technological Changes

Technology Focus	Example of Change
Information Technology	Charles Schwab Brokerage spends 11–14 percent of its annual revenues to continually change and update its computer systems.[a]
	Goldman Sachs, Bear Stearns, and the Chicago Mercantile Exchange have all instituted the use of speech recognition computer technology for stock trades registered on the floor of the exchange.[b]
Holography	Kirby Co. now uses NASA holographic technology to design vacuum cleaners.[c]
	Ford Motor Co. now uses laser holography in new car designs.[d]
Computer-Aided Design	Claremont Garments of England switched to computer-aided design to minimize fabric waste in pattern cutting.[e]
Machinery	Widmar Brothers, a large regional brewery in Portland, Oregon, introduced new types of conveyor and inspection systems as part of a new advanced quality assurance program.[f]

[a]Jeffrey Young and Julie Pilta, "Wal-Mart or Western Union? Charles Schwab Corporation," *Forbes* 160, no. 1 (1997), pp. 246–48.
[b]Tatiana Helenius, "Voice Systems No Longer Sci-Fi," *Wall Street and Technology* 15, no. 6 (1997), pp. 52–54.
[c]Stephen J. Mraz, "Sweeping up with New Technology," *Machine Design* 68, no. 19 (1996), pp. 59–60.
[d]Bill Visnic, "Team Taurus—Revisited for 1996," *Ward's Auto World* 31, no. 6 (1995), pp. 26–27.
[e]Brian L. Carr, "Modern Garment Manufacturer and the Role of Work Study," *Management Services* 39, no. 12, (1995), pp. 16–18.
[f]Sandra McBride, "Craft Quality," *Beverage World* 116, no. 1633 (1997), pp. 700–72.

starting point of changes, but it is not necessarily a good indicator of where major problems may occur.

Culture

The culture of the organization, as discussed in Chapter 4, is a second potential focus for change in organizations (see Exhibit 19.3). In its way, changing an organization's culture can be as potent in its consequences as making major changes in technology. In fact, if it were easy to make changes in the culture of an organization, managers likely would try to do so more often. Despite such powerful potential, however, the embedded traditions and accepted ways of doing things that constitute an organization's culture can be extremely difficult to change successfully. Thus, in the mid-1990s, the founder and chairman of apparel distributor Lands' End asked for the resignation of the CEO and also the director of human resources and proceeded to scrap three years of efforts that had tried to change Lands' End's culture. Those efforts had included new personnel evaluation methods, new project teams, increases in meetings, and various devices (e.g., posters, banners) to proclaim the organization's rewritten mission statement. Veteran Lands' End employees resented all these changes, believing that they were counter to the company's long-standing family-like culture, and their reaction doomed the culture-change attempt.[14]

EXHIBIT 19.3

Examples of Cultural Changes

Cultural Focus	Example of Change
Cooperation and Encouragement	Kentucky Fried Chicken's new culture is now based on four points: *Create, Courage, Encourage, Give.* Managers were sent into the field. There are new methods for recognition of employees. Management is encouraging cooperation between headquarters and franchisers.[a]
Friendliness, Customer Orientation	Toys 'R' Us changed to a responsive culture, friendlier to both associates and customers. Management encourages associates to make decisions to enhance customer satisfaction.[b]
Cooperation and Team Focus	Arizona Public Service Company increased interdepartmental cooperation through its Strategic Cultural Change Initiative. It instituted cross-functional teams focused on innovation and operational improvement.[c]
Emphasis on Diversity	The City of San Diego has focused on the value of diversity in its workforce, implementing an extensive equal opportunity training program.[d]
Collaboration and Participation	Vanderbilt University Medical Center's new culture reflects an emphasis on shared governance throughout the organization. Management encourages staff involvement in decision making and strongly emphasizes collaboration and participation at all levels.[e]
Family Feeling	At Chrysler Corporation's assembly plant in Windsor, Ontario, all employees are encouraged to strive for the same goals, to increase their own and others' self-esteem, to listen and respond empathetically, and to request assistance when needed while retaining responsibility.[f]

[a]Steve Brooks, "The Man Who Could Be King," *Restaurant Business* 96, no. 9 (1997), pp. 56–64.
[b]Tony Lisanti, "Concept 2000: A New Era in Design, a New Culture for TRU," *Discount Store News* 35, no. 15 (1996), p. 13.
[c]Samuel M. DeMarie and Barbara W. Keats, "Deregulation, Reengineering and Cultural Transformations at Arizona Public Service Company," *Organization Dynamics* 23, no. 3 (1995), pp. 70–76.
[d]Matti G. Dobbs, "San Diego's Diversity Commitment," *Public Manager* 23, no. 1 (1994), pp. 59–62.
[e]Jill L. Sheer, "Retooling Leaders," *Hospital and Health Networks* 68, no. 1 (1994), pp. 42–44.
[f]Adrian Vido, "Chrysler and Mini-Vans: Are We There Yet?" *CMA Magazine* 67, no. 9 (1993), pp. 11–16.

A key to changing an organization's culture is to start by trying to change its values, since what is valued is the underlying essence of the culture. One company that did make a successful change in its basic culture and values was the Barnes and Noble bookstore chain. Its owner, Leonard Riggio, decided to redefine the individual bookstores as social meeting places rather than just places to buy books. Thus, the cultural milieu of the stores was changed at the beginning of the 1990s by changing the physical layout and appearance of the stores. Small nooks for sitting, reading, talking, and browsing were created, and in some locations coffee bars were installed. The core value of selling books was converted to one of selling entertainment and social interaction. A New York newspaper, in fact, reported that the Barnes and Noble store at 82nd and Broadway had become a favorite meeting place for singles.[15]

Substituting new values for old values is hardly a simple process, though. The assertion of new values in a mission statement is easy. Getting them accepted and, as social scientists would say, "institutionalized," so that they become part of the basic fabric of the organization, is exceedingly difficult.

Barnes and Noble bookstores changed its basic culture and values by adding in-store cafes. The result was a transformation from just a place to buy books to a social meeting place.

Changing a culture, by whatever means, may take a long time and not achieve necessary changes quickly enough. More likely than not, it is easier and less costly for managers to attempt to change other factors, such as strategy or structure. Nevertheless, culture does represent a significant, if difficult, target for fundamental changes.

Strategy

Since an organization's overall strategy, along with its basic mission statement and espoused values, provides major directions for its activities, it can serve as another potent focus of managerial change efforts (see Exhibit 19.4).[16] In contrast to its culture, an organization's strategy or set of strategies may be less difficult for managers to change. Top management typically is more in control in setting strategy than are other parts of the organization and, in fact, is expected to do so. Thus, by announcing strategic changes, which may occur after extensive consultation with all parts of the organization, managers at the highest levels can strongly influence change.[17] Of course, whether strategic changes are then implemented effectively is another matter entirely.

Asserting changes in strategy is vastly different from actually bringing about such changes. This lesson was learned by the appliances business unit of General Electric Company when it embarked on a major expansion into Asian markets in the early 1990s. Initially, the unit's executives formulated a strategy that involved entering into a joint venture with one large manufacturer that would handle production and distribution for all of Asia and India. However, this proved unworkable and the strategy was changed to meticulous research of each market, then tailoring

![EXHIBIT 19.4]

EXHIBIT 19.4

Examples of Strategy Changes

Strategy Focus	Example of Change
Production	Siemens SG's new strategy emphasizes the production of telecommunication equipment rather than consumer electronics.[a]
	Philips Electronics (Europe) is now concentrating on individual rather than corporate consumer electronics production.[b]
Customers	Arizona Public Services Company's strategy now focuses on customer service rather than utility rates.[c]
	Compaq Computer changed its traditional high-quality, low-customer-service strategy to a strong customer-service focus, including hiring 2,000 new sales and support employees.[d]
Price/Quality	Herman Miller, a well-known Michigan firm, changed its strategy from manufacturing strictly high-price, high-quality office furniture to a dual approach that promotes new and reconditioned, less expensive office furniture.[e]
	Thoraldson Enterprises, a $230 million, North Dakota hotel firm, divested itself of its small-town, limited-service hotels in order to concentrate on building more expensive hotels in larger cities.[f]

[a]Lewis H. Young, "European Style Restructuring," *Electronic Business Today* 23, no. 2 (1997), pp. 36–42.
[b]Ibid.
[c]Samuel M. DeMarie and Barbara W. Keats, "Deregulation, Reengineering and Cultural Transformations at Arizona Public Service Company," *Organization Dynamics* 23, no. 3 (1995), pp. 70–76.
[d]David Kirkpatric, "Houston, We Have a Problem," *Fortune* 135, no. 12 (1997), pp. 102–103.
[e]Bruce Upbin, "A Touch of Schizophrenia," *Forbes* 160, no. 1 (1997), pp. 57–59.
[f]Michele Conlin, "Keep It Simple, Keep It Cheap," *Forbes* 159, no. 12 (1997), pp. 81–82.

a mix of products, marketing, and retailing for that market. This new, so-called "smart bomb" strategy permitted the company to achieve an extremely high degree of flexibility in its Asian ventures.[18]

Structure

Changing the structural makeup of organizations is sometimes one of the most valuable tools managers have to create other desired changes, such as improved productivity or more creative problem solving (see Exhibit 19.5). Many structural changes, such as reorganizing on a product basis rather than a geographic one or consolidating major divisions, can be made at the macro, or total organization, level. The top management of AT&T Capital Leasing Services at the end of the 1980s, for example, decided to redesign major elements of the company. The new structure included greater centralization of operations, a flattened hierarchy, and related changes in personnel evaluation criteria. Before implementing the structural changes throughout the organization, however, a pilot program was tested in one of the company's main offices. This pilot program revealed several potentially disastrous flaws that, if the reorganization had been put in place as originally planned, would have resulted in failure of the entire change program.[19]

Other structural changes can be made at the intermediate level, involving such actions as combining or dividing departments or changing locations and reporting relationships within or among units. Still other structural changes can be made at

EXHIBIT 19.5

Examples of Structure Changes

Structural Focus	Example of Change
Combination of Functions/Units	Tenneco, to improve performance and reduce redundancy, combined employee benefits, administration, human resources, supplier development, finance, information technology, and environmental health and safety functions into one new unit to serve all other units of the company.[a]
	Halliburton Company melded nine autonomous energy service units into one organization—Halliburton Energy Services.[b]
Centralization of Information Services	Mobil Corporation centralized all of its information service functions under one global manager.[c]
Reduction of Managerial Levels	National Semiconductor flattened organizational layers and introduced self-directed work teams.[d]
Divestiture	Coca-Cola sold all nonbeverage-related businesses, eliminated managerial layers, and replaced regional offices with country managers who report directly to headquarters in Atlanta.[e]

[a]"Tough Times at Tenneco," *CIO* 10, no. 15 (1997), p. 51.
[b]Dale Jones, "Getting the Job Done," *Baylor Business Review* 13, no. 1 (1995), pp. 2–5.
[c]Daniel Gross, "Getting the Lead Out," *CIO* 10, no. 13 (1997), pp. 62–70.
[d]Rochelle Garner, "Too Much, Too Fast," *Computerworld* 31, no. 9 (1997), pp. 75–76.
[e]"2000 Bound," *Beverage World* 112, no. 1551 (1993), pp. 8–12.

very micro levels, such as forming new project groups or altering the composition of particular jobs or positions. The Mayo Clinic, for example, a few years ago formed a group of 13 examining physicians and 17 staff members into a new unit called its Executive Health Program to specialize in conducting annual physical examinations on over 2,500 executives.[20]

As with changes in strategy, changes in structure are not especially difficult to pull off initially, but making them work to generate the desired effects can be particularly challenging for managers. Research shows that almost no other events in organizations can create as much political maneuvering as potential, or rumored, reorganization changes.[21] The ambiguity of the effects of such changes, coupled with their potential importance for the jobs of those who may be directly affected, causes high levels of anxiety and frequent political activity.

Processes/Procedures

Another major object of change can be the processes or procedures used in, and by, an organization (see Exhibit 19.6). Such changes involve attention to the sequence and manner in which work activities and operations are carried out. For example, Toyota Motor Co. plans to have its hand-finishing process for die manufacturing automated by the year 2000.[22]

Changes in processes and procedures often come about because of prior changes in technology or structure. In this sense, modifications of the way which work is performed, whether by individuals or groups, can be considered residual changes. The purchase of new equipment, for instance, would be a primary change, as in the

EXHIBIT 19.6

Examples of Process/
Procedure Changes

Process/Procedure Focus	Example of Change
Manufacturing	Batch to continuous flow manufacturing. Assembly line to team manufacturing. Elimination of redundant steps.
Quality Control	Process controls placed at each step rather than at the end of the procedure. Defective items returned immediately to originator for correction rather than to a different department.
Accounting/Taxation	Inventory valuation changed from last in, first out to first in, first out. Reporting procedures for capital gains revised.
Education	Class registration changed from in-person to telephone process. New student ID cards changed from annual issue to multiple-year issue.
Banking	Canceled checks kept on microfilm rather than mailing back to originator.

case of the automated finishing operations at Toyota, and the adoption of new procedures because of this equipment would be the secondary change. It is important to note, however, that changes in processes can themselves be primary. For example, Pneumofil, a manufacturing company in North Carolina, made a decision to streamline its customer order processes at one of its new factories. Managers eliminated the customer service department, which did nothing but take the initial order and then pass it on to the factory. Now, instead, the customer deals directly with the Material Department, where one person takes the order, arranges for the necessary materials, cuts the work orders for the appropriate production team, and follows the manufacture of the ordered items through to invoicing and delivery.[23] In this example, no changes in technology have taken place, but the procedures themselves have been changed directly. Such primary changes in process and procedures in total organizational systems are central to the concept of reengineering (discussed in the previous chapter and again later in this chapter).

People

Finally, people—both individuals and groups—can be the focus of major changes (see Exhibit 19.7). Essentially, changes that focus on people involve one or more of four elements:

* Who the people are.
* What their attitudes and expectations are.
* How they interact interpersonally.
* How they are trained or developed.

In the first instance, change can be brought about by adding, subtracting, or interchanging people. Bringing in a new supervisor or transferring a difficult employee from one unit to another are examples of change focusing on the selection and placement of people.

EXHIBIT 19.7	

Examples of People-Oriented Change

People-Oriented Focus	Example Of Change
Selection	Hiring an increased number of minorities, women, physically challenged individuals, rehabilitated individuals, and older workers.
Placement	Bringing in a manager known for the ability to succeed in difficult situations. Moving a successfully functioning team to a new plant to act as role models.
Attitudes	Managers emphasizing ethical, environmental, and safety issues in order to change employee attitudes in these areas. Following through on employee suggestions to improve employee attitudes toward participative decision making.
Expectations	Demonstrating austerity in pay and bonuses for executives in order to reduce employee expectations.
Employee inter-relationships	Encouraging group solidarity through sponsored intergroup sports competitions. Encouraging cooperation through cross-training team members. Reworking reward systems to recognize team efforts.
Enhancement of knowledge, skills, and abilities	Increasing the number of training workshops. Disseminating information of individual, group, and organizational productivity. Paying all or part of tuition for employees seeking higher educational degrees.

The second element, attitudes and expectations, often can be an important focus because people act on the basis of them and they sometimes can be modified without excessive effort or cost by the manager. Providing people with new information or a new way to look at problems, issues, or events has the potential—but no certainty—of creating significant change in their behavior.[24]

Attempts to alter how people relate to each other—such as by being more cooperative with, and more supportive of, each other—represent a third people-oriented change focus.

The fourth and often most lasting people-change approach involves direct enhancement of their knowledge, skills, and abilities, typically through education, training, and personal development activities. Such change can improve the performance of individuals, groups, and even larger units, regardless of any other changes a manager might initiate.

As with other types of changes, however, efforts to change people can be costly. Managers need to weigh the costs of managerial time and effort, and frequently significant budgetary expenditures, against potential benefits such as a more capable workforce, increased creativity and innovation, better morale, and, perhaps, decreased turnover.

EVALUATING THE NEED FOR CHANGE

Is change always necessary? To answer that question, managers should undertake two critical steps. One is to recognize the possible need for change and to correctly assess the strength of that need. The other is to accurately diagnose the problems and issues that the change or changes should address. Misjudgments at either step

EXHIBIT 19.8

EXHIBIT 19.8

Relative Cost of Change

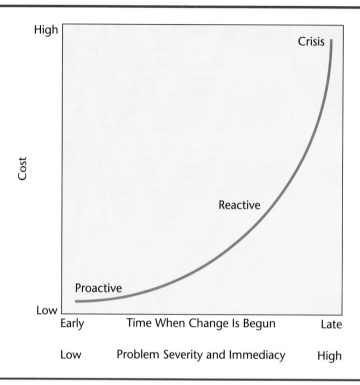

can lead to severe problems, if not outright disaster.[25] Jumping in to make changes before taking *both* these steps is a recipe for almost certain failure.

Recognition and Assessment of the Strength of Need for Change

As we have stressed earlier, making changes is definitely not a cost-free activity (see Exhibit 19.8). Thus, this puts a premium on *not* making changes where the costs will outweigh the potential benefits. It also means that it is crucial to make an accurate assessment of the strength of forces behind the need for change.

Proactive Recognition   Effective managers, no matter where they are in the organization's structure, are those who can recognize needs for change at the earliest possible time. This is because they should have systems and methods in place to monitor the environment in which they and their units operate, and these systems should be capable of detecting clues that may not yet have become obvious warning signs.[26] At the end of the 1980s, Craig Weatherup, a divisional president at PepsiCo responsible for $7 billion in sales and 30,000 employees, demonstrated this principle. He restructured his division to avoid future losses from the potential flattening out of sales that were starting to result from increased competition. Specifically, he and his top management team broke up the division into 107 units to focus on specific customer segments. At the end of three years, the division was poised to meet its 15 percent target in growth in earnings and, as a consequence, saved Pepsi-Cola tens of millions of dollars.[27]

This kind of planned, proactive assessment of the need for change is intended to provide advance notice so that changes can be made sooner, with better planning and potentially with less cost. Methods can range, for example, from elaborate and sophisticated information systems (as discussed in Chapter 18), to more mundane trend-spotting of anomalies in sales reports, to very low tech and informal—but active—seeking out the views of clients, customers, and employees. Central and SouthWest Corporation, a Texas-based electric utility company, for example, decided to use a process of deliberative polling to obtain deeper and better information than one gets from normal attitude survey methods. Thus, the Texas utility began by polling a random sample of customers concerning their feelings about four proposed changes to meet future energy needs in the geographical area. Following this initial polling, the participants were formed into several groups and provided detailed information about the four options. At the end of this extensive educational phase, the participants were polled again, and from this highly informed input, CSW developed its plans.[28]

Reactive Recognition   Not all needs for change can be identified in advance, regardless of how much proactive recognition is attempted. Invariably, some developments in the internal or external environment will take place so quickly or will get to a critical size so unexpectedly that managers must *react to* them rather than *plan for* them in advance. In such instances, the forces for change become too large to ignore, and the issue becomes one of how and when to react rather than whether or not to react.[29] This kind of situation faced the managing director of Ganz-Hunslet, a Hungarian railcar manufacturer, at the end of the 1980s. After the government changed from a socialist to a more capitalist system, his enterprise was suddenly confronted with the need to operate at a profit. With no time to plan for this change, he cut the workforce in half, raised the salaries of the remaining workers, and improved quality in order to sell to the West.[30]

Diagnosing Problems

The recognition that change needs to take place is only a starting point. Much like a physician identifying the source of a symptom in a patient, the next step is to make an accurate diagnosis of what is causing the problem or issue so that changes can deal with it effectively. Initiating changes that do not improve the underlying causes is sometimes worse than making no changes at all. Thus, managers need to avoid premature conclusions about causes. Instead, they should obtain information from a variety of sources, if possible; compare those sets of information to uncover consistent patterns or trends; and, especially, attempt to determine what are the most likely causes.

This type of diagnosis was carried out by the First National Bank of Chicago a few years ago when the bank decided that its process costs were too high and turnaround times too slow in its small business loans department. Before instituting a change, officials attended a roundtable discussion on small business lending sponsored by a local consulting firm, conducted surveys with its customers about proposed process changes, and obtained information on practices at competitors. What was learned by this diagnosis process was that the bank needed to work with small businesses more in the manner that it worked with consumers, rather than in the way it interacted with large businesses.[31] The end result of a comprehensive analysis of this type should be an accurate, valid diagnosis of what, and who, needs to change.

THE CHANGE PROCESS

So far in this chapter, we have focused on the background and context of change in organizations: the forces for change, the types of change possible, and, especially, managers' roles in understanding, assessing, and evaluating the need for change. Now we turn to the change process itself: planning and preparing for it, implementing it, dealing with resistance to it, and evaluating its outcomes (see Exhibit 19.9).

Planning and Preparation for Change

Once a manager or a group of managers has been convinced that change is necessary and that an accurate diagnosis has been made of the causes requiring change, preparation for the changes can begin. As shown in Exhibit 19.10, such planning calls for attention to several important issues.

Timing   Managers are often tempted to initiate something quickly, especially if the need for change seems exceptionally strong. Whether rapid implementation is a good idea or not represents a difficult judgment call. Acting too quickly can lead to changes that are not well planned and that fail because they lack sufficient support. On the other hand, waiting too long to make necessary changes can also be a recipe for failure. In the summer of 1997, Gilbert Amelio, then CEO of Apple Computer, was ousted by the company's board of directors precisely because, according to knowledgeable observers in the industry and "many of Apple's own employees," he did not move "quickly enough to help return the company to profitability" and failed to "act with a sense of urgency."[32] It is clear that the timing of changes can be critical to their success.

Building Support   One of the best guarantees for successful implementation is to build support for change in advance. Developing this foundation requires especially careful consideration of who will be affected by the changes and how they will likely react. This means that managers need to have a clear understanding of the sit-

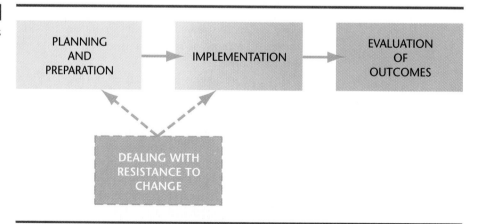

EXHIBIT 19.9
The Change Process

EXHIBIT 19.10

Planning Choices for Change

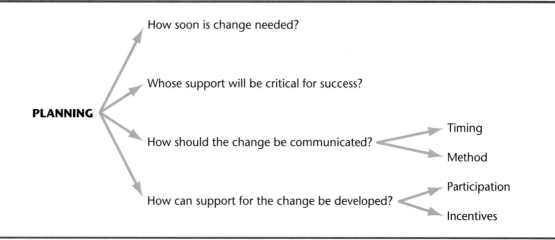

---

uation and circumstances in which the changes will take place if they are to increase the probability of success. It also means that this kind of analysis, in turn, must be followed with support-building activities by the manager. Several of these are discussed here.

Communication   A key step in building support for major changes is to communicate about them in advance to those who will be affected. Cooperation is likely to be enhanced the more that people understand (a) the reasons for the changes and, especially, (b) the ways those changes are likely to impact them. In the early 1990s, General Electric's Fanuc Automation North America plant in Charlottesville, Virginia, changed from a directive "do as I say, no questions asked" form of management to a team-based structure. The success of such a major change was credited to management's commitment to open communication. Top management explained the proposed change to all employees; required hours of training in problem solving, goal setting, and conflict management; and set up scheduled meetings both with individual groups and with the entire workforce.[33] If, in contrast to this example, the reasons for the changes and their anticipated effects cannot be clearly communicated, that may signal that the changes have not been sufficiently planned and they may not have a high enough probability of success. Seldom do changes fail because of too much communication, but they are likely to encounter difficulty when too little information is provided.

Particularly important in using communication to build support for proposed changes is to provide a compelling rationale for those changes. Those to be affected need to know the specific objectives of the changes and how those relate to the larger goals and values of the unit or total organization. For example, Oldsmobile several years ago instituted its "Commitment to the family of Oldsmobile" program. This training program encouraged the company's auto dealers to be cooperative rather than competitive in their relations both with their salespeople and with other local Oldsmobile dealers. The program trained the dealers to understand how cooperation will help them achieve their own personal goal of financial reward as well as the corporation's goal of increased customer satisfaction and sales.[34] In short, as this example illustrates, managers initiating major changes need to communicate a "vision" for where the changes are headed and why.[35]

Also important in communication is to focus special attention on those who are likely to be influential in shaping the attitudes of their colleagues. In other words, extra effort spent on communication with opinion leaders can be a good investment. During the reorganization of Cookson Group, the multibillion-dollar parent corporation of a group of international manufacturing companies, the headquarters treasury unit was given the job of reviewing and revising funding and capital investment policies and practices at each company. The unit found that the key to success was to meet with senior management in each company before starting the review to convince them of the benefits to be gained by the centralization of capital investment procedures.[36]

Participation   During the planning stage, obtaining the participation of those to be affected by changes can help build later support for those changes. Plans can often be improved and commitment gained through such participation. In addition, participation can build trust because those initiating the changes, in effect, are allowing themselves to be influenced about how and when to make the changes. An example of effective use of participation is Xerox Corporation's Chicago-based Customer Business Unit (CBU). The CBU drew 50 people from different functions and levels within the organization, 50 percent management and 50 percent nonmanagement, to meet and determine "a shared future direction for the achievement of a market-driven CBU in the next 24 to 36 months." Over three days, this diverse group hammered out the basic business policy the CBU would follow for the next three years, a policy that all levels of the company were dedicated to implementing.[37]

Of course, the use of participation is not cost free. It takes time and effort on the manager's part and may not be feasible if speed is essential or if it is not easy to arrange for effective participation. Also, participation may backfire if participants' suggestions and requests diverge widely from managers' goals. Furthermore, if those asked to participate sense that their input is not really wanted and that a manager is only "going through the motions," this can quickly lead to a feeling of being "manipulated." In such cases, participation has eroded rather than built support for change. Nevertheless, participation should at least be considered as a viable approach. The real issue is whether the failure to use participation creates more problems for the changes than will the use of participation. The answer is often "yes."

Incentives   One other factor that can help build support for change is to emphasize incentives for those who will be affected. Simply communicating how the change itself will directly affect them in a positive way can often increase support. Examples are the installation of new equipment to make work easier, or reorganization to provide clearer direction, or additional training to add to an employee's repertoire of skills. At other times, providing incentives may involve conferring benefits directly to those affected. This could include, for example, either nonmonetary incentives such as more desirable working conditions, or the use of some form of monetary incentives such as increased compensation for increased responsibilities.

At chemical giant DuPont, those contributing the most to the success of innovations and changes are allowed to work with management to determine the level and type of their reward. These rewards can be as large as sizable monetary awards or as small as dinner for two. At General Electric, the revised bonus system has been tied to a team orientation. No longer do only executives receive bonuses; now all team members involved in solving problems also receive bonuses.[38] Of course, in some circumstances, providing explicit incentives is often not practical. However, in certain instances, offering something tangible in return for support of changes that may cause extensive adaptation and even stress on the part of those affected may be appropriate and may directly encourage stronger support.

Managers should consider some important cautions, however, when weighing the possibility of using incentives to generate support for change. One is that providing incentives to those likely to be most affected may make them feel they are being "bought off." Thus, the use of incentives for change, especially monetary incentives, can potentially boomerang by increasing skepticism and cynicism of managers' motives and thus increase, rather than decrease, resistance to the changes. Furthermore, offering explicit incentives one time for a change may increase the probability that those affected will expect incentives any time a new change is made in the future. Therefore, introducing incentives as a way of building support for change is not something that should be done lightly and without consideration of possible serious, though unintended, side effects.

Implementation Choices

Where planning for change leaves off and implementation of change begins is often difficult to specify because the process is, or should be, more or less continuous. Regardless of where that boundary is, however, implementing change involves several critical choices for managers (see Exhibit 19.11). Three of the most important are discussed here.

Choice of Approach   Earlier in this chapter, we identified six types, or focuses, of change: technology, culture, strategy, structure, process/procedures, and people.

EXHIBIT 19.11

Implementation Choices

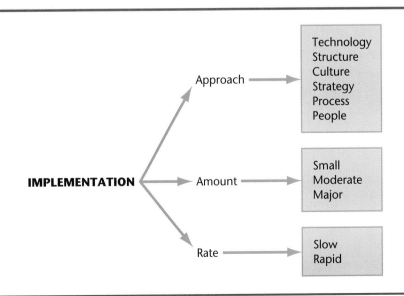

To initiate the change process, one or more of these focuses need to be selected. The choice depends in large part on the objectives to be accomplished, which in turn are linked to the problems identified in the assessment of the need to change. If the major problem is outdated equipment, then, obviously, changing the technology will be the approach of choice. However, if the problem is one of sluggish growth in sales compared with competitors, then the choice of approach is not so self-evident. It could be that the organization is not sufficiently market oriented, which could indicate a need for change in the culture of the organization. That is exactly what took place in the 1980s with the breakup of AT&T. The seven newly created "Baby Bells" were suddenly thrust into an unregulated environment, and employees had to get used to marketing their companies' services rather than relying on their former monopolistic advantage to gain customer business. The managers of these new organizations needed to make substantial changes in their traditional ways of doing business, that is, the culture that had been entrenched for years and years.[39]

Changing organizational cultures also was exactly the approach that was required in a quite different setting when enterprises in former Eastern European countries such as Poland and Hungary were required to shift from operating in socialist-run economies to being effective in market-based economies. During the early 1990s in Budapest, Hungary, the U.S. telephone company Ameritech found two major cultural problems in attempting to oversee the privatization of MATAV, Hungary's telephone company: (1) convincing workers and managers that customer satisfaction is important to organizational effectiveness and (2) encouraging initiative in employees.[40] No simple changes such as replacing managers or buying new equipment would suffice to bring about the magnitude of change that was required in this case.

Often, the problems uncovered in the assessments of the need to change require several simultaneous approaches, such as a new strategic direction for the organization *and* a major modification of its culture and structure that more closely fits this new strategy. This combined set of approaches to change is well illustrated by the change at Eastman Kodak (see the Managerial Challenge box).

Choice of Amount   Even after managers have decided what approaches to take and have started to implement those choices, they must also confront another, but related, set of issues: How *much* change should take place? That is, how comprehensive should the change be, and what parts of the unit or the whole organization should be affected? These questions have no easy answers.

When change is too little, the benefits are not likely to outweigh the costs involved. For example, 3M Corporation tried for several years to fix its magnetic storage business problems through minor cost-cutting changes. After 10 years of escalating losses, it finally divested itself of this part of the company.[41] Even modest changes can take a great amount of effort and cause disruptions that are almost as great as if the change were much more sizable. Thus, managers must decide whether implementing minimal changes are worth these costs or simply wait until the problems are large enough to justify the substantial investments that will be required. The argument in favor of making minimal changes, however, is that even though the immediate cost–benefit ratio may not be favorable, changes postponed until later will be much more expensive; therefore, the longer-term benefits can easily prove the worth of making small changes early.

MANAGERIAL CHALLENGE

TURNAROUND AT KODAK

George Fisher was hired in 1993 as the new CEO of Kodak, following more than a decade of disasters under previous CEOs that included five separate restructurings, the loss of 30 percent of market share, cutbacks of 40,000 jobs, and a huge increase in debt coupled with a large loss in market value.

Several forces pushed such dramatic changes. The first was an attack by its leading competitor, Fuji Photo Film of Japan. Fuji had been moving aggressively into the U.S. market for years, but in 1997 it launched a price war that lowered retail prices by nearly 40 percent on some products.

Fuji was helped in this effort by currency exchange rates. As the dollar appreciated against the yen, Fuji prices were essentially lowered without the company's doing anything. Kodak found it would have to lower its costs by about 15 percent just to keep its profit margins the same and keep its prices competitive with Fuji's as a result of the strong dollar.

Other competitors also hurt Kodak. In a new CD plant in Ireland, Kodak was producing CDs at the cost of about $4 to $5. A Taiwanese competitor entered the business and dropped its price to $1.50. Kodak matched these prices to hang on to market share, but the operation went from making $100 million to losing $100 million.

General economic problems in Asia in 1997 and 1998 also hurt Kodak. Overall, Kodak went from growing at a rate of 20 percent to about 7 percent. The results were serious. Kodak earned only $5 million on sales of $14.7 *billion.*

With all these troubles, Fisher had little choice but to make major changes and make them quickly. He attacked the problem on four major fronts: structure, technology, culture, and people. Structurally, he did several things. First, he sold all businesses unrelated to photography. For example, he sold Sterling Pharmaceutical as well as an optical disk storage business. Next, he divided the company into two divisions—one for traditional photography, the other for digital electronic imaging—and focused the company on the development and marketing of the new digital imaging technology.

While changing the structure and emphasizing this new technology, Fisher also worked to change the culture from a complacent, passive, static one to a high-performance work-force dedicated to continual, rather than incremental, change. He essentially let employees know that if they performed well, they would be rewarded. Otherwise, they could either settle for stagnant pay or leave. He also rescinded the tradition of guaranteed annual raises, replacing them with merit raises. He also announced a special grant of 100 stock options to 90,000 employees.

On the people side, he brought in a cadre of new managers, firing the heads of three of the most critical businesses—consumer imaging, Kodak professional, and digital and applied imaging. One of the new managers he brought in was Daniel Palumbo, as new marketing chief. Analyzing data, Palumbo found that more than 80 percent of all Kodak sales came from less than 20 percent of its products. He quickly eliminated 27 percent of all sales items.

The results of these and other changes will likely not be known for years. But some progress was made. For example, professional photographers at the 1996 Summer Olympics refused to use the free film that Kodak gave them because of its poor quality. By 1998, however, Heinz Kluetmeier, senior photographer for *Sports Illustrated,* reflected a changing sentiment among professionals due to quality improvements at Kodak and the release of a new film, E200. "At one point on my light table, we would not have had any Kodak film. Today [1998] I'm hard pressed to find a few roles of Fuji."

Source: Linda Grant, "Why Kodak Still Isn't Fixed," *Fortune,* May 11, 1998, pp. 179–81.

Changes can be too massive as well as too small. Although managers may be tempted to make big changes once they decide to make changes, they often overlook the potential costs. Of course, very large changes are sometimes what is called for, especially when major changes are occurring in the unit's or organization's environment. Evidence from a longitudinal study of 25 U.S. minicomputer companies founded in the late 1960s, for example, showed that companies that engaged in bursts of very large changes rather than a series of small, incremental changes were better able to cope with an extremely volatile environment.[42]

Major magnitude changes also can have the positive side effect of "galvanizing the troops" so that organization members support the changes as not only necessary but also as inspiring their best efforts. However, as we will discuss later, any

MANAGERIAL CHALLENGE

CHANGE AT MCDONNELL DOUGLAS

In early 1989, John McDonnell, chairman of McDonnell Douglas, held a series of meetings in St. Louis to map out a strategy for a reorganization of Douglas Aircraft (MDA), the airplane manufacturing division of McDonnell Douglas (now owned by Boeing). When the corporate plans were initially formulated, none of the senior executives at MDA were even aware that plans for a reorganization of their area of the company were being considered. The first major part of the reorganization was aimed at the structure of the company. Managers and executives at MDA found out that a major change was occurring when all 5,200 of them were called to a meeting in a hangar and told their jobs no longer existed. The matrix structure of the company was being scrapped and a project structure, with separate and complete functional systems for each project, was to be instituted. The ex-managers were informed that they could apply for the 1,000 newly constituted management positions that would now be open. Many of them did apply and were subsequently put through a battery of personality and leadership tests. Those who did not pass the tests were offered nonmanagerial positions. Prior to the reorganization, the best engineers and scientists had been the managers of the various projects. Now, those who scored best on team leadership potential were the project leaders, without consideration for their technical skills. This structural reorganization left the management of MDA in turmoil.

The second major part of the reorganization involved the rank and file, when McDonnell Douglas announced 17,000 jobs (almost one-third of the workforce) would be cut. Those who remained would be working in a new group structure with much more decision responsibility. This led to problems with the labor unions, whose members were confused about who actually held decision responsibility and accountability. In addition to all these changes, the reorganization called for an increase in the number of projects undertaken at the plant. Some critics suggested that the plant already had too many projects at a time when both the management and rank and file were suffering from confusion and extremely low morale. Overall, the reorganization was characterized as "traumatic and poorly executed," and the results clearly pointed to a change that was too large in scope.

Sources: Rick Wartzman, "McDonnell Douglas Struggles to Revamp," *The Wall Street Journal,* September 6, 1990, p. A4; Ralph Vartabedian, "The Remaking of Douglas by McDonnell," *Los Angeles Times,* October 15, 1989, p. D1.

change can cause resistance, and big changes can cause immense resistance. Thus, too great a change, in effect, can create more chaos and more problems than were there initially. When this happens, no change at all would have been better than the change that was made. This is perhaps particularly well illustrated by changes made at McDonnell Douglas at the end of the 1980s (see the Managerial Challenge box).

Another aspect of the amount of change that needs to be considered is the frequency of changes. In these times of competitive pressures and relative turbulence in many organizational environments, change must be implemented much more often than in the past. In some sense, change is a more or less constant condition. However, if specific changes, especially those of at least moderate size, are made continually, organization members can get mentally and physically exhausted. Imagine, for example, that you are a member of a sales department in a large, geographically dispersed company. First, management decides that sales data should be centralized and installs a new data information system linking all the regions. Next management reorganizes the structure of the department by geographic region rather than by type of product. Next management institutes a team structure linking sales with marketing and research and development personnel for new projects. Each of these changes, by itself, may improve customer satisfaction and employee performance. However, if they all occur within a short space of time, you might not have time to adjust to any one change before finding yourself in the midst of a new change. Therefore, the frequency of changes must be considered along with their size to gauge the effects on those who will have to respond.

The lesson for managers is that great care must be taken in deciding how much change should be implemented. Potential problems exist in making too small or not enough change. Similarly, there can be potential dangers in making too large or too many changes. In particular instances, however, one of these extremes may in fact be the best alternative. The general guideline, therefore, is that the amount of change should fit the severity of the problems, and this should be determined by sound analysis of the strength of the need for change.

Choice of Rate   Just as the amount and frequency of change represent important choices in making changes, so does the rate of change. If the pace of change is too slow, conditions that created the need for it in the first place may again shift significantly so that the wrong problems are being dealt with by the end of the entire change process. Also, change that is too slow can frustrate many people, who want to see at least some early and tangible results in return for their efforts. For instance, suppose a company spent several months putting together new work teams and training employees in decision-making techniques, group processes, conflict resolution techniques, and use of computerized performance tracking. Then, however, suppose it delayed installing the new equipment and software. Employees would likely be frustrated by not being able to put their new knowledge and skills to immediate use.

Change that is too rapid can also cause major problems. Whether the change is primarily technological, structural, procedural, or some other focus, people need to adapt to the rate. Rates that are excessively fast can exceed the typical person's ability to cope and thus increase resentment and resistance. It has even been suggested that in situations of rapid change, the work experience may be so stressful and so damaging to a person's self-identity as to trigger violent behavior.[43]

Of course, managers sometimes deliberately and appropriately make rapid changes. One obvious case is when the forces for change are so overwhelming that swift change is essential, as was the case with minicomputer companies in the late 1960s and 1970s. Survival for even a decade seemed to depend on not only big but also rapid changes.[44] Furthermore, managers sometimes institute a fast rate of change precisely to determine who can keep up and who cannot. In such circumstances, a rapid rate may be a viable change tactic—if the manager has carefully considered what is to be accomplished and what the potential negative consequences or costs might be. In many other cases, however, managers have not adequately assessed the possible costs and benefits and may have simply implemented an abrupt change because of their eagerness to see results quickly.

As with choices about the amount of change, managers often face clear options about the rate of change. However, there is one major difference. When dealing with the rate of change, managers can make mid-course corrections easier than they can with regard to the amount of change. (It is very difficult, for example, to suddenly convert a large change into a small change.) If the initial pace has started slowly, managers can increase it if this appears desirable. Likewise, a change that has started out rapidly can be slowed, allowing for adaptation to catch up with events. Thus, just as the rate of speed of a car can be increased or decreased depending on road conditions, so can the rate of change in organizational settings. Of course, just as in a car, if the rate is changed too often or too drastically, it can be very uncomfortable for those required to adapt. This in turn can reduce confidence in the person responsible for the changes.

Resistance to Change

Those who lead organizations tend to be favorably disposed toward change. They see, from their perspective, the necessity for it and believe it is best for the organization. Consequently, although almost any change carries with it the seeds of resistance, managers are often surprised, and frequently disappointed, by it. Some degree of resistance may be inevitable in organizational changes, but overcoming that resistance is not easy. In this section we examine some of the reasons for resistance and some general approaches for dealing with it.

Reasons for Resistance   The basic reason people resist change can be summed up in an old adage (slightly restated) that is applicable to many organizational circumstances: "The devil people know is preferred to the devil they don't know." Change embodies potential risks and threats for those affected. They think they know how to size up those risks and threats in their present situation, but they are uncertain what they will be in the changed situation. Thus, if all other things are assumed to be equal, the known present will be preferred to the unknown and changed future, and thus change is likely to be resisted. Within this overall context, some more specific reasons for resisting change can be identified.

Inertia.   People in organizations get comfortable with their present ways of doing things. Even if they perceive no increase in risks, people simply find it easier to do things the way they always have rather than to operate or behave differently. Ingrained and overlearned habits die hard.

Mistrust.   Even if those proposing change emphasize positive future consequences, people often doubt that they will actually occur. Such skepticism is especially magnified if change occurs in an existing climate of mistrust or if previous change efforts have failed.

An example is clearly illustrated in a recent change effort by the World Bank. In 1997, the top management of the World Bank attempted to make a major change in the organization's structure and procedures, to model it more as a consulting firm and to reduce perceived overstaffing. To accomplish this, existing managers had to apply for the newly reduced number of management jobs, then selection committees made up short lists of those qualified for each job. Top managers made the final decisions. This change effort resulted in near panic among the bank's managers because of memories of a similar change effort undertaken by the World Bank in 1987. At that time, top management similarly required all employees to resign and then had managers choose whomever they wanted to work for them. This resulted in perceived cronyism, loss of morale, and continued inefficiency. The 1997 change, consequently, revived memories of the debacle 10 years earlier.[45] In such a situation, any supposed positive advantages of a change are likely to be highly discounted by those affected.

Lack of Information.   A third contributing factor to resistance to change can be a lack of adequate information about both the need for the change and what its effects are likely to be. Even a seemingly small change such as a minor reorganization of a specific unit can produce opposition, often of a subtle nature, simply because basic information was not provided.

Anticipated Consequences.   Another reason for resistance can be straightforward assessments of expected gains and losses by those affected; in other words, employees determine what is best for protection of their self-interests. Those affected by the change may consider possible loss of status or influence, which may be ignored or underestimated by the managers who are instigating the change. Calculations of whether a change is "good" and should be supported or is "bad" and should be resisted can be quite different from the viewpoint of those initiating the change and those who receive it. The two sides' self-interests, often defined by each party as also "better for the organization," may be diametrically opposed.

Dealing with Resistance to Change   Resistance to change typically involves more than one of the preceding factors; thus, from a manager's perspective, there is probably no "quick fix" to reduce or eliminate resistance. However, that does not mean that nothing can be done and, therefore, having a framework for analyzing the resistance can be helpful.

Force Field Analysis.   One very useful way of looking at the problem of resistance is what is called a "force field analysis," as first proposed some years ago by psychologist Kurt Lewin.[46] This analysis, as depicted in Exhibit 19.12, uses the concept of *equilibrium,* a condition that occurs when the forces for change, the "driving forces," are roughly balanced by forces opposing change, the "restraining forces." Such a condition results in a relatively steady state that is disrupted only when the driving forces become stronger than the restraining forces. If we apply this analysis to typical organizational changes, we see that managers basically have two choices: add more force for change, such as putting more pressure on subordinates to conform to new procedures; or reduce the resistance forces, such as convincing informal leaders that they will benefit from the change. The basic problem with increasing the driving forces is that this often results in increasing the opposing forces. Therefore, the Lewin analysis suggests that weakening restraints may be the more effective way to bring about change. (This is similar to the old Aesop fable about the contrasting strategies of the wind and the sun who vie to get persons to take off their coats. The sun won.)

What are some ways to reduce resistance to change? Several approaches are the same as those discussed in the section on "Planning and Preparation for Change," since it is in the planning stages that potential resistance can first be anticipated and steps taken to address it. However, not all forms of resistance can be foreseen or dealt with in advance, so various other approaches are also needed in this stage. A set of such approaches, with their associated advantages and disadvantages, are shown in Exhibit 19.13. Particularly important in this exhibit is the column showing the circumstances in which a particular approach is most likely to be effective. The message here is that not all approaches will work in all situations, and a manager must be selective in choosing when and where to use a particular method. Several factors are especially critical in making these choices, such as

- Timing of use of approach
- Cost in managers' and employees' time
- Cost in financial and other resources
- Degree of risk involved
- Importance of the issues involved

Negotiations.   Negotiating too early with those who may resist could be wasted effort because the issues to be negotiated or the degree of resistance may not yet be clear. If resistance is primarily due to lack of information, entering into negotiations too early may only increase resistance, thus strengthening a restraining force.

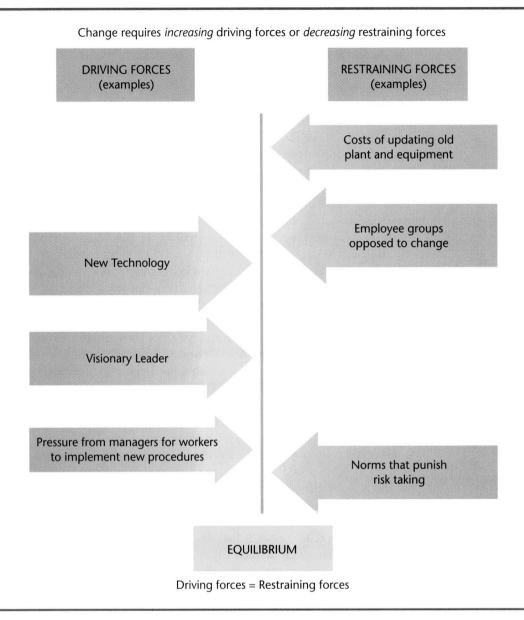

Change requires *increasing* driving forces or *decreasing* restraining forces

DRIVING FORCES (examples)

RESTRAINING FORCES (examples)

Costs of updating old plant and equipment

New Technology

Employee groups opposed to change

Visionary Leader

Pressure from managers for workers to implement new procedures

Norms that punish risk taking

EQUILIBRIUM

Driving forces = Restraining forces

People may resist managers' negotiation efforts since they feel they cannot make intelligent decisions about offers or counteroffers because they lack sufficient information. In this situation, as in the Aesop fable, the other party may feel as though the wind is blowing harder and so it only makes sense to hold on even tighter to the coat.

Participation.   Participation may be very effective in defusing some resistance, or even identifying valid reasons why the change might not work, but it can be a costly use of everyone's time and can be risky for managers because the outcomes

EXHIBIT 19.13
Possible Methods for Dealing with Resistance to Change

Approach	Commonly Used In Situations—	Advantages	Disadvantages
Negotiation and Agreement (e.g., use formal or informal processes to gain advanced agreement to change before implementation)	In which someone or some group will clearly lose out in a change, and in which that group has considerable power to resist	Sometimes major resistance can be reduced or avoided	Can be expensive in many cases if it alerts other groups to want to negotiate too
Participation and Involvement (e.g., involve affected employees in planning the change)	In which the initiators do not have all the information they need to design the change, and in which others have considerable power to resist	People who participate are more likely to be committed to implementing change, and any relevant information they have will be integrated into the change plan	Can be both time-consuming and awkward if participants design an inappropriate change
Communication and Education (e.g., provide increased information to employees concerning the short- and long-term effects of the change)	In which there is a lack of information or inaccurate information and analysis	Once persuaded, people will often help with the implementation of the change	Can be very time-consuming if many people are involved
Facilitation and Support (e.g., offer seminars in stress management, personal development, anger resolution, etc.)	In which people are resisting because of problems in adjusting to the changes	No other approach works as well with problems of adapting to changes	Can be expensive, and still fail
Explicit and Implicit Coercion (e.g., use position power to order change)	In which speed is essential, and the change initiators possess considerable power	It is speedy and can overcome many kinds of resistance	Can be risky if it leaves people angry at the initiators and lowers trust in them

Source: Adapted and reprinted by permission of *Harvard Business Review.* An exhibit from "Methods for Dealing with Resistance to Change" by John P. Kotter and Leonard A. Schlesinger (March/April 1979), p. 111. Copyright 1979 by the President and Fellows of Harvard College; all rights reserved.

are hard to predict. For example, in a setting in which past change efforts have failed or have hurt employees (for example, through layoffs), asking for people's participation may not seem legitimate.

Communication. Communication can be relatively inexpensive, but if it comes too late, it may not have much effect. For example, communicating and emphasizing to employees that a firm's profits have dropped sharply, after layoffs have already been announced, may seem like an after-the-fact attempt to justify the layoff action and may only result in increased levels of mistrust and resistance in the future.

Facilitation. Facilitation and support would probably be welcomed by those who might not want to go along with the changes, but the costs can be substantial. For example, GE hires consultants to help with its "workout" program, a series of "town meetings" in which managers and employees meet for frank discussions of the business situation and to find solutions to key problems. These consultants cost about $5,000 to $10,000 per day in fees plus expenses. At that rate, it doesn't take many days to rack up a sizable bill.

Coercion. Coercion, such as threatening transfers or denying future promotions, is risky and not designed to lessen resistance, but it may overcome resistance in the short term. For this to work, management must have the power to follow through with threats, and the threats must be of sufficient magnitude to motivate compliance on the part of employees. In extreme situations managers may have no other choice, but if this option is chosen, managers need to recognize that it will be highly likely to increase mistrust and resistance to change efforts in the future.

A final point to be made about dealing with resistance to change is that managers should recognize that the amount and nature of resistance may be very useful diagnostic tools to gauge whether the change is appropriate and will actually bring about desired results if implemented. To put this another way, managers need to *listen* to resistance and determine whether they have accurately assessed the need for change and the process of implementation. Just because resistance arises certainly does not mean that the proposed change must be abandoned or postponed. On the other hand, it may be a very important signal that managers ignore at their peril, as illustrated in the following example of an actual situation.

The owner of a small tire store bought three major new power tools for his tire-replacement mechanics. The owner believed that the power tools would improve the performance and satisfaction of his employees—less time and less muscle power would be required. However, within one month, all three tools were out of commission: one had been left in the trunk of a customer's car, one had been run over by a truck, and one had been dropped from a hoist. When the owner probed the reasons for the losses, he found that they were not purely accidental. The employees, who had worked together for over 12 years, could not talk to each other over the noise of the power tools, and they had always enjoyed the camaraderie on the job. Without the opportunity to explain their opposition to the change, they became dissatisfied with their new working conditions and, in effect, sabotaged the new tools.[47] Had the owner appreciated why the employees might resist, he could have considered other, perhaps superior, alternatives.

Evaluation of Change Outcomes

Once change has been carried out, whether throughout the entire organization or within one unit, managers need to evaluate the outcomes. If the effects of changes are not appraised in some manner, managers have no way of knowing whether additional changes are needed and also whether the particular approaches implemented should be used again in similar circumstances. To carry out the evaluation process, three basic steps are required: data collection, comparison of results against goals, and feedback of results to those affected by the changes.

Data Collection The data that can be collected to evaluate the outcomes of change essentially come in two forms: objective, or quantitative, data and subjective, or attitude, data. Both types can be useful to the manager who has implemented change, and often it will be necessary to tap several sources of each type. For example, after introducing major new information technology, a manager could evaluate by measuring changes in output per employee, speed of response to customers, accuracy in reports, attitudes of employee users within the organization, and attitudes of clients who deal with employees using the new technology.

It is important to keep in mind that the collection of different sets of data, such as these, to measure change outcomes may well require significant costs. Therefore, not every type of data that could be collected should be collected. As with other organizational actions, the benefits should be weighed against the costs. The point, though, is that significant sources of data should not be overlooked, and the more types of data that can be collected, the more likely the analysis of the effects will be informative. Also, in most cases, data should be collected at periodic intervals to measure the lasting power of the change. A recent survey showed that two-thirds of companies are using some form of scorecard software to measure everything from financial progress to customer satisfaction. These scorecards can be customized to reflect only the measures the company wishes to track. Then, by targeting the distribution of this kind of data, a company can ensure, for example, that managers from marketing, finance, and research and development are all discussing the same measures in meetings.[48]

Comparison of Outcomes against Goals   Collection of data is only a first step in evaluating outcomes. The crucial next step is the comparison of those outcomes against the goals and various benchmarks or standards set in advance of the change. Without those goals and standards, interpretation of the data will be almost meaningless. To know that sales increased by 3 percent is interesting but lacks meaning unless it can be compared with some explicit objective, such as a 5 percent increase. Likewise, to know that employees' job satisfaction after the change averages 3.5 on a 5-point scale doesn't tell a manager much unless that can be measured against a goal of "at least 3.0." In other words, absolute results are not as informative as relative results. Goals and benchmarks that have been specified in advance of change efforts provide the basis for making meaningful relative comparisons.

Feedback of Results   A final step in evaluating change outcomes is communication of the findings to those who are involved with or affected by the change. Managers seldom, if ever, neglect to provide this information to interested superiors. However, when it comes to subordinates, this step is frequently overlooked or seen as desirable but not mandatory. This may be short-sighted. Failure to provide feedback can leave subordinates and other employees with a sense of frustration, and they may even question a manager's motives for not supplying it. It also can produce an element of distrust, making it even harder to carry out successful changes in the future.

Managers can provide feedback to both superiors and subordinates in a variety of ways, including written reports, direct oral reports and briefings, discussions with small groups, and the like. No one method is more effective than others. The key point is that in nearly all cases, some feedback about the effects of changes is better than no communication at all.

COMPREHENSIVE ORGANIZATIONAL CHANGE APPROACHES

Throughout the earlier parts of this chapter, we have presented general principles and issues relating to organizational change and renewal. Here, in this final section, we look at three specific, but comprehensive, approaches to organizational change. The first is organizational development, which is an approach with a strong behavioral and people orientation. The second is the more engineering-based approach called *reengineering*, which was discussed in Chapter 18. The final part of this section describes what is almost more a particular framework or perspective than a change approach as such, namely, *organizational learning*.

The Organizational Development (OD) Approach to Change

organizational development (OD)

approach to organizational change that has a strong behavioral and people orientation, emphasizing planned, strategic, long-range efforts focusing on people and their interrelationships in organizations

The essence of an **organizational development (OD)** approach to change is its emphasis on planned, strategic, long-range efforts focusing on people and their interrelationships in organizations.[49] While "organizational development" may seem like a general term that could be applied to almost any aspect of the topic of organizational change, as we noted at the beginning of this chapter, it in fact refers to a specific approach to bringing change to organizations. It grew out of behavioral science research as far back as the 1930s and 1940s aimed at improving the communication and quality of interactions among individuals in groups. Researchers put together groups of individuals in sessions away from the workplace in what were termed basic skill training groups, or, as they came to be called for short, **T-groups**.[50] The T-group orientation over time broadened into a focus on interpersonal relationships throughout the larger organization, and hence the attention to *organizational*, not just group, development.

T-groups

groups of individuals participating in organizational development sessions away from the workplace; also called basic skill training groups

Values and Assumptions   The early formulation of what eventually evolved into the OD approach placed particular importance on certain values and assumptions, and they have remained at the heart of this approach to change to this day.[51] One set of these values related to the people in organizations: First and foremost is the assumption that "people are the cornerstone of success in any organizational endeavor."[52] A second value or assumption is that most people desire opportunities for personal growth and enhancement of their capabilities. Another basic value belief about people that underlies this approach to change is that their emotions are as important as their rational thoughts and that, therefore, the open expression of these emotions can be critical in facilitating real change.

The fundamental assumption about organizations in the OD approach is that they are systems composed of interdependent parts, and, thus, a change in any one part can have major effects on other parts.[53] Another assumption is that the way organizations are designed and structured will influence the interpersonal relationships among people in them. In other words, the behavior of people in organizational settings flows not just from their intrinsic nature but also from the conditions they encounter in these contexts—and these conditions can be changed.

Basic Approach to the Process of Change   Lewin's basic OD approach to organizational change involves three seemingly simple steps:

1. Unfreezing
2. Changing
3. Refreezing[54]

These steps are easy to state and remember, but they are not especially easy to put into practice. Unfreezing, essentially, emphasizes the need to get people to examine critically and openly their current attitudes or behavior patterns. In effect, and using a force field analysis, the unfreezing process is designed to decrease the restraining force of existing viewpoints and customary ways of doing things. If change is attempted while the old habits and perspectives are still in place, resistance can virtually be guaranteed. In one sense, you can think of the unfreezing stage as an effort to lower overall resistance to change rather than focusing on specific sources of resistance. Therefore, in an OD approach to change, the initial challenge is to unfreeze existing behavioral patterns by getting people not to take them for granted but to question them and look at their effects. For example, when a certain mine decided to use OD techniques to reduce its accident rate, the first necessary step was to change existing attitudes about safety. This was accomplished by changing the organizational climate concerning safety. Managers began to emphasize safety as a goal, and they allocated funds to improve specific hazardous conditions. They also made it a point to emphasize that every member of the company was responsible for safety. Employees were encouraged to meet and discuss safety issues and come up with ways of doing tasks that would help them by making their work safer. All of these steps helped to convince the miners that management was serious about improving safety conditions, and it primed them to accept and implement required procedural changes. Results of the OD intervention demonstrated a 50 percent reduction in on-the-job injuries.[55]

In the traditional OD approach, both the first and second steps, unfreezing and changing, involve the use of **change agents**, individuals responsible for implementing change efforts.[56] They can be either internal change agents, that is, from inside the organization, often from the human resource area, or they can be external change agents, from outside the organization. In either case, the OD change agent is someone who is not a member of the particular groups or units directly involved. Frequently, this person is a consultant, someone with presumed expertise in helping groups see the need for change and in making changes.

The changes themselves are achieved by the use of one or more **interventions**, that is, "sets of structured activities," or action steps, designed to improve the organization.[57] Some of these interventions, such as fact finding, begin in the unfreezing stage, and others, such as team building and coaching/counseling, take place in the changing stage. Several of the more common types of interventions are shown in Exhibit 19.14.

The priority in the second change stage is on exploring new forms of behavior and relationships. Particularly important at this point is an emphasis on behavioral processes, such as leader–group relations, decision making, intergroup cooperation, and the like. This **behavioral process orientation** is a key distinguishing feature of the OD approach to organizational change.

Merely engaging in new and different ways of behaving, relating, and interacting is not enough for changes to have lasting effects. This is why Lewin included the third stage, refreezing. The intent of this third stage was to make sure that the changes "stick" and that behavior and relationships don't easily return to their former—less effective—states. This means that the new patterns must become, in effect, new habits that are not easily dislodged by a tendency to return to old routines. However, since the time of Lewin's formulation of this three-stage change process many years ago, the goal of refreezing has been converted into the objective of **organizational renewal**. This new focus takes into account the fact that in the contemporary, fast-changing, competitive world, new habits and patterns rapidly become old and outdated themselves and may need to be replaced after relatively short periods of time. Therefore, the emphasis has shifted from refreezing to developing a capacity for renewal, a goal that incorporates flexibility and the ability to change more or less continually.

change agents
individuals who are responsible for implementing change efforts; they can be either internal or external to the organization

interventions
sets of structured activities or action steps designed to improve organizations

behavioral process orientation
key distinguishing feature of the OD approach to organizational change that focuses on new forms of behavior and new relationships

organizational renewal
a concept of organizational change that proposes a goal of flexibility and capability for continual change

EXHIBIT 19.14

Types of OD Interventions

Intervention	Objective	Examples
Diagnostic Activities	To determine the current state of the organization or the parameters of a problem	Interviews Questionnaires Surveys Meetings
Individual Enhancement Activities	To improve understanding of and relationships with others in the organization	Sensitivity training (T-groups) Behavior modeling Life and career planning
Team Building	To improve team operation, abilities, cohesiveness	Diagnostic meetings Role analysis Responsibility charting
Intergroup Activities	To improve cooperation between groups	Intergroup team building
Technostructural or Structural Activities	To find solutions to problems through the application of technological and structural changes	Job enrichment Management by objective New technology introduction
Process Consultation	To disseminate information concerning the future diagnosis and management of human processes in organizations including communication, leadership, problem solving and decision making, and intra- and intergroup relationships	Agenda setting Feedback and observation Coaching and counseling Structural change suggestions

Source: Adapted from Wendell L. French and Cecil H. Bell Jr., *Organization Development: Behavioral Science Interventions for Organizational Improvement* 5th ed. (N.J.: Prentice Hall, 1995), p. 165.

In recent years, the OD approach to change, which formerly was almost a rigid set of procedures that required specific behavioral science expertise in the form of an experienced change agent, has evolved into a more general approach that places more emphasis on the direct use of line managers as potential change agents. Also, many of its intervention methods, such as team-building, have become day-to-day mainstream organizational activities. The OD legacy survives in various forms in many organizations today, but other, newer comprehensive approaches to change have attracted increasing attention from many managers in the last decade or so. Two of these are reengineering and organizational learning.

Reengineering

As discussed in Chapter 18, business process reengineering is a radical redesign of business processes to achieve (intended) dramatic improvements.[58] Information technology, of course, often plays a central role in such reengineering efforts. But the human and managerial issues related to reengineering are also extremely crucial to its success in organizations.

Those reengineering efforts that appear to achieve the most success have both breadth and depth (see Exhibits 19.15 and 19.16).[59] Breadth of reengineering means change in terms of the redesign of a set of processes across a complete business unit rather than a change in a single, limited process, and depth of reengineering means change in a related set of core organizational elements such as roles

EXHIBIT 19.15
Breadth of Reengineering Efforts

Focus	Narrow	Medium	Broad
Examples	Single activity or function e.g., redesign of Accounts Payable process	Multiple activities e.g., redesign of new product development processes	Strategic business activities involved in maintaining an organization's competitive advantage e.g., reorganizing into team structure to improve manufacturing speed and quality
Overall Business-Unit Cost Savings	<1%	3–5%	17%

Source: Adapted from Gene Hall, Jim Rosenthal, and Judy Wade, "How to Make Reengineering Really Work," *Harvard Business Review* 71, no. 6 (1993), pp. 119–31.

EXHIBIT 19.16
Depth of Reengineering Efforts

	Unidimensional Change		Multidimensional Change	
Percentage of Levers Changed	25%	50%	75%	100%
Levers can include: • *Structure* • *Skills* • *IT Systems* • *Roles* • *Measurements* • *Incentives* • *Shared Values*	e.g., Change • Structure • Incentives	e.g., Change • Structure • IT Systems • Incentives	e.g., Change • Structure • Skills • IT Systems • Incentives	e.g., Change •All Levers
Realized Process Cost Savings *(based on 20 detailed case analyses)*	19%	25%	24%	35%

Source: Adapted from Gene Hall, Jim Rosenthal, and Judy Wade, "How to Make Reengineering Really Work," *Harvard Business Review* 71, no. 6 (1993), pp. 119–31.

and responsibilities, structure, incentives, shared values, and the like, rather than any one or two of these elements.

Adequate breadth and depth by themselves, however, are not enough for reengineering to succeed. A major commitment must come from the top of the organization, that is, from key executives (of the total organization or of its major units) who can supply the necessary resources to implement these activities and who can take the time to demonstrate personal involvement in the entire redesign process. Like any comprehensive change approach, for reengineering to be successful requires enormous energy, planning, coordinated effort, persistence, and attention to detail. Without substantial backing, it is likely to fail.

Even under the best of circumstances, however, reengineering does not always produce effective change, and this has caused some disillusionment after the early enthusiasm for it.[60] For one thing, the amount of effort required has not always seemed commensurate with the results obtained. One European commercial bank, for example, saw its reengineering effort yield only a 5 percent cost reduction rather than the anticipated 23 percent reduction.[61] Because of less-than-expected effects, some managers and organizations simply decide not to continue with reengineering projects.

A second reason that some managers have become disenchanted with reengineering, regardless of any positive benefits such as increased efficiency, is that it can cause more or less constant disorder and considerable resistance. For example, although Levi Strauss, the jeans manufacturer, had had some success with its reengineering program started in the mid-1990s, including a reduction in order turnaround time from three weeks to 36 hours, the company decided to slow down the program. It added two years to the projected completion of the project because of turmoil among employees following an attempt to have 4,000 white-collar staff reapply for their jobs in newly structured process groups.[62]

As this example, and others that could be cited, illustrates, reengineering is not exactly embraced by many of those who have to take part in it. In fact, one of the co-authors (Hammer) of the book that popularized this approach, which has its roots in process engineering, has stated that the people aspects of reengineering were not always given enough attention. "I was insufficiently appreciative of the human dimension. I've learned that's critical."[63] Nevertheless, despite its problems, some CEOs and other corporate leaders appear to remain quite positive about the potential positive effects of this comprehensive approach to change.

Organizational Learning

organizational learning

exhibited by an organization that is skilled at creating, acquiring, and transferring knowledge, and at modifying its behavior to reflect new knowledge and insights

Although the concept has been around for some time, it was not until relatively recently that **organizational learning** has become a major focus in approaches to organizational change and renewal.[64] By way of definition, an organization that is good at this process is said to be "skilled at creating, acquiring, and transferring knowledge, and at modifying its behavior to reflect new knowledge and insights."[65] Such an organization, in fact, would be called a *learning organization*. The central idea is that organizations that emphasize this perspective are (1) attempting to change and improve continuously, not just periodically, and (2) basing these improvements on a foundation of new knowledge they have learned.

Several factors have been shown to facilitate learning by organizations:

- Existing and well-developed central, core competencies of current personnel.
- An organizational culture that supports continuous improvement.
- The availability of organizational capabilities (e.g., managerial expertise) to be able to implement the necessary changes.[66]

Clearly, managers and organizations cannot simply decide, or declare, that learning should take place. The elements listed above need to be in place as a starting point if organizational learning is going to lead to any real benefits. Then, a number of activities need to take place to implement fully an ongoing learning process in organizations. Five of the more important are explained here.[67]

Systematic, Organized and Consistent Approach to Problem Solving Similar to the emphasis on scientific method in the TQM approach, a learning process in organizations requires the continual collection of factual data, rather than reliance on assumptions or guesswork, to aid problem solving and decision making. As far back as 1983, for example, all employees at Xerox were trained in problem-solving techniques including how to collect information, generate ideas, and perform data analyses.

Experimentation to Obtain New Knowledge   Learning organizations do not simply solve current problems. They experiment with new methods and procedures to expand their knowledge and gain fresh insights. They engage in a steady series of small experiments to keep acquiring new knowledge consistently and to help employees become accustomed to change. For example, such major manufacturing companies as Corning, Allegheny Ludlum, and Chaparral Steel constantly try new methods and processes to see whether they can improve their productivity. As they become experienced with learning and experimenting, they become less resistant to change in general. Also, however, learning organizations invest in bolder, one-of-a-kind experiments such as substantial demonstration or pilot projects. When General Foods first wanted to test self-managing work teams, it started with such a project on a major scale at its Topeka, Kansas, plant.

Drawing Lessons from Past Experiences   Enterprises with strong learning cultures pay particular attention to lessons from both past failures as well as past successes. They exemplify the old maxim: "It is not having had the experience that is important; it's what you learn from the experience that's important." To do this requires managers and the organization to draw conclusions and not leave such learning to hit-or-miss chance. Because of problems with the development of its 737 and 747 planes, Boeing initiated a three-year project to compare the development of these planes to the earlier, more reliable 707 and 727 planes. This project resulted in a booklet of "lessons learned," which was then used in the development and manufacture of the 757 and 767 aircraft. Likewise, British Petroleum has an ongoing review process that analyzes every major project to derive lessons to be applied to future projects.

Learning from the Best Practices and Ideas of Others   Organizations and their managers that are strongly committed to learning are also humble in a certain respect. They do not assume that they already know how to do everything better than other organizations, whether they are competitors, enterprises outside their own industry or sphere of operations, or customers. They consistently spend resources to scan their environments to gain information and knowledge from a variety of external sources. One common form of this is **benchmarking**, where the best practices of competitors are identified, analyzed, and compared against one's own practices. Thus, for example, the world's leading petroleum producers use reports from Environmental Information Services to benchmark against their competitors in terms of compliance with, and involvement in, environmental issues.[68] In a different kind of competitive industry, Shea Homes of San Diego, California, benchmarks its customer satisfaction not only against other home builders but against other industries, using the Malcolm Baldrige National Quality Award guidelines as criteria. As a result, Shea won the 1996 National Housing Quality award.[69]

Other ways of generating this kind of learning include putting together **focus groups** of customers that spend time in small groups for intense discussions of the

benchmarking
identification, analysis, and comparison of the best practices of competitors against an organization's own practices

focus groups
small groups involved in intense discussions of the positive and negative features of products or services

positive and negative features of products or services. The objective in using these and similar methods is to gain knowledge that would be difficult, if not impossible, to get only from people and available data inside the organization. In other words, learning organizations work hard at not being parochial and insular.

Transferring and Sharing Knowledge   Another core activity of an organizational learning approach is to make sure that the new knowledge that is gained is actually disseminated widely throughout relevant units of the organization. This requires that managers be alert to both the need for information sharing as well as ways to do it. The latter would include such activities as distributing reports, developing demonstration projects, initiating training and education programs, and rotating or transferring those with the knowledge. General Motors, for example, developed a series of specialized tours of its NUMMI plant to introduce new workers to the distinctive procedures being used there. Tours were developed not only for hourly employees but also for upper and middle managers, with each tour concentrating on issues most relevant to the targeted group.

As an approach to change, an organizational learning perspective has much to offer. It places the emphasis on constant attention to the possible need for changes, and it embodies the goal of renewal, of pushing organizations or units within them to continue to reinvent themselves in one way or another through the purposeful and persistent acquisition of new knowledge. The implementation of active organizational learning directly confronts the fundamental issue stated at the beginning of this chapter: Since environments never stay the same, successful organizations can never stay the same. One of the best ways both to keep up with changing environments and to keep ahead of them is for managers to focus intently on instilling a learning culture in their areas of responsibility.

CONCLUDING COMMENTS

Clearly, change in organizations is often necessary—but hardly ever easy. What may seem like an obvious need for change from the point of view of the person in charge, the manager, may not seem that way at all to those who have to adapt and carry out the change. People resist change for a variety of reasons, many of them valid. In general, if people do not *feel* or *believe* in the need for change, at best they are likely to be only apathetic supporters and at worst active resisters of the change initiative. Consequently, creating a felt need for change and a belief in the necessity of change is one of the first and most critical steps in achieving successful change.

As we have discussed in this chapter, producing effective change requires both an analysis of likely sources and reasons for resistance and skillful consideration of the most effective approaches for overcoming that resistance. Once people are "unfrozen," they need a new "state" to move toward. In other words, as a manager, you will need to persuade people that not only is the place where they are currently untenable, but the place where you want them to go is better. This means that before they will become motivated to move ahead with much energy, they need from you a clear sense of how they are going to get from where they are now to the new place you want them to go.

Simplified, change is about helping people you manage answer three basic questions: (1) What's wrong with just staying put? (2) Where do we want to go instead?

(3) How are we going to get there? Without convincing answers to these essential questions, most people are unlikely to change. The stimulating thing about managing change, however, is that no two situations are identical, nor are the people who are involved or affected by the change.

In the final analysis, organizations and managers need to view the condition of "things as they are" with extreme skepticism. Similar to the principle in physics that says "nature abhors a vacuum," the status quo in organizations should be regarded almost as anathema. It is fraught with dangers, many of which are subtle and hard to recognize. Consequently, managers need to be ever alert against becoming prisoners of their own success and just sticking with what has worked in the past. For this reason, to be able to make meaningful changes that lead to organizational renewal in a way that adds substantial value should be regarded as one of the premier managerial challenges of our times.

KEY TERMS

behavioral process orientation 603
benchmarking 607
change agents 603
focus groups 607

interventions 603
organizational development (OD) 602
organizational learning 606

organizational renewal 603
T-groups 602

REVIEW QUESTIONS

1. List the forces that act from outside an organization to bring about change within it.
2. What are an organization's internal forces for change?
3. What components within an organization can be changed? (Hint: the chapter discusses six of them.)
4. What is the key to changing an organization's culture?
5. Is it more difficult to change an organization's strategy or its culture? Why?
6. What elements are involved in attempting people-focused change in an organization?
7. What is meant by proactive and reactive change?
8. What are the three major steps in the change process?
9. What are some of the considerations managers face when planning change?
10. Why is it important to involve in the planning process those who will ultimately be affected by a change?
11. List the drawbacks to using incentives to gain cooperation during a change.
12. Why is it important to be careful in choosing the amount and rate of change? What are the benefits and drawbacks involved in large- and small-scale change? In rapid or slow change?
13. Why do employees resist change?
14. What are some of the ways managers can overcome employees' resistance to change?
15. What is meant by force field analysis?
16. In evaluating the outcome of planned change, what types of data are used?
17. What are the three steps in evaluating the outcome of a planned change?
18. What is the emphasis of the OD approach to change?
19. What are the key steps in the OD approach to change?

20. What is a change agent? Where do they come from?
21. What is the importance of refreezing?
22. How is reengineering different from TQM?
23. What is the difference between the breadth and the depth of reengineering?
24. Describe a "learning organization."
25. How could you tell when you are encountering a learning organization?

DISCUSSION QUESTIONS

1. Going back to the story ("Change at the U.S. Postal Service") that opened this chapter, do you think that Cynthia Trudell (discussed in Chapter 1) would have handled the need for change at the Postal Service any differently than Marvin Runyon? If so, how? Would the consequences have been any different?

2. Think of the last organizational change that affected you. Maybe your university, for example, recently changed some policy on major curriculum requirements or something similar. Were you a supporter or resister of the change? What mistakes did the organization make? What could it have done differently to facilitate the change?

3. The exact outcomes of change programs are often *not* evaluated. Why do you think this is the case?

4. Changes in strategy are generally not effective without changes in other aspects of the organization. Why do you think this is the case?

5. Crisis change is more common but more costly than anticipatory change. What do you think the keys are to effective anticipatory change?

6. How easy, or difficult, is it to convert a traditional organization to a learning organization?

CLOSING CASE

Ford 2000: Change to Begin the Millennium

As we have seen in this chapter, change is perhaps the one constant in today's business climate. Thus, it stands to reason that even the venerable automaker whose founder, Henry Ford, uttered the now-anachronistic motto, "customers can have any color as long as it's black," must bend to the forces of change. Ford *has* changed in the past few years, more rapidly and radically than its competitors, under former CEO Alex Trotman's Ford 2000 plan.

External and internal forces have brought about this massive organizational change. One is a healthy economic climate, which has allowed Ford to embark on profitable projects and stockpile cash against a potential recession (the auto industry, which is capital-intensive, is very vulnerable during a recession). Another is the explosion of new technology allowing rapid communications and the streamlining of processes. A third external force is societal and

demographic shifts—aging baby boomers want different cars from the ones they wanted a decade or two ago. The most important internal force is that of managerial decisions, at all levels. Trotman shook up the status quo at the top level, with reverberations all down the line.

Ford 2000, introduced in the last half of the 1990s, is essentially a global engineering strategy in which one vehicle center is completely responsible for designing and building a particular car category for the entire global market. As part of the overall plan, Trotman intended to close and restructure plants, move production to different sites, drop unprofitable car models (such as the nostalgia-inducing Thunderbird), design and launch new models (such as the wildly successful Navigator), and institute a category management strategy. Under the Ford 2000 plan, a single team now works on each type of car instead of different departments working on functions such as advertising, product specifications, and the like, across all models. Although there was some initial resistance to the change because workers had to be retrained and learn new processes, there was a significant improvement in communication—and streamlining of the overall car manufacturing cycle.

Technology has played a major role in the implementation of Ford 2000. The company's intranet is now a global central repository for data. More importantly, managers have committed themselves to making sure that the intranet provides quality information to the right people at the right time to bolster their decision-making capabilities. Now, all Ford operations use the same quality measurements to make comparisons among product lines, divisions, and even countries. With 120,000 computer workstations located throughout the company, engineers, designers, marketers, and other managers can communicate with each other instantaneously from anywhere in the world. Ultimately, Ford wants to be able to integrate its engineering, manufacturing, and testing into one computer system. If it is successful, the initiative could save the company millions of dollars as well as reduce the time it takes to bring a new car to market. Paul Blumberg, director of product development systems, is optimistic: "With this new software, we could be able to compress our cycle time for new models from 26 months to 15 months in three to five years."

In addition, Ford has restructured its manufacturing process so that it is now based on platform engineering. That is, instead of creating a different "platform" on which to build each car model (at about $400 million per platform), Ford workers can new create several similar models on one platform. For instance, Ford's full-size pickup platform also generates the Ford Expedition and Lincoln Navigator.

All of these changes mean a seismic shift in Ford's organizational culture. Traditionally, Ford has had a reactive culture—one that responded to environmental forces—instead of a proactive culture. Ford 2000 expects managers to change their entire outlook. To help, Ford has instituted financial incentives for its managers. Managers used to receive bonuses based on the company's annual profits. Now their bonuses are tied to such criteria as customer satisfaction and warranty performance. Instead of being surprised at the end of the year by the amount of their bonus, managers now receive quarterly reports telling them how close they are to their targets.

Current CEO Jacques Nasser, who has spent his entire career at Ford, plans to extend the Ford 2000 strategy, looking for more ways to loosen up the company's traditional culture, making it a more agile organization—one that will be better prepared to meet the challenges of the 21st century. He wants to cut another $1 billion in costs, hire more outsiders (who will bring in fresh ideas), expand the retail distribution unit, and, ultimately, transform the organization into a consumer product company. Nasser comments that he wants being different to be part of Ford's new image. "We like to be different because that adds value to everything we do," he comments.

QUESTIONS

1. Do you think Ford 2000 is trying to change too much, too quickly? Why or why not?
2. Considering some of the issues discussed in this chapter, what types of problems might Ford encounter as it presses forward with its companywide change initiative?
3. In what ways does the Ford 2000 plan exemplify the principles of organizational learning and in what ways (if any) does it not?
4. Assuming that the Ford 2000 change initiative instituted in the last half of the 1990s proves to be successful, what are likely to be Ford's organizational renewal issues by the year 2010?

Sources: Todd Nissen, "New CEO's First Strategic Move Has a European Flair," *The Boston Globe,* January 29, 1999, p. E12; Sallie L. Gaines and Jim Mateja, "Ford Makes Move," *The Boston Globe,* January 29, 1999, pp. E1, E12; Alex Taylor III, "The Gentlemen at Ford Are Kicking Butt," *Fortune,* June 22, 1998; David Smith and Greg Gardner, "Can Ford Go It Alone? Nasser: Absolutely," *Ward's Auto World* 34, no. 12 (December 1998), pp. 42–43; Melissa Larson, "Ford Puts Quality Data in Human Hands," *Quality* 36, no. 12 (December 1998), pp. 34–36; Marc Ferranti, "Ford Motor Co.: Automaker Aims for Companywide Collaborative Standards," *Computerworld* 31, no. 49 (December 8, 1997), pp. C14–C15; Ida Picker, "Alex Trotman of Ford Motor Co.: The $10 Billion Man," *Institutional Investor* 31, no. 10 (October 1997), pp. 23–27; Stephanie Bentley and Sean Brierly, "Shifting Gear," *Marketing Week* 20, no. 12 (June 19, 1997), pp. 44–45; Tanya Gazdik and Angela Dawson, "Ford's Shops Await Consolidation," *Adweek* (Eastern ed.) 39, no. 41 (October 12, 1998), p. 5; Greg Gardner, "Well Focused," *Ward's Auto World* 34, no. 11 (November 1998), pp. 40–41.

REFERENCES

CHAPTER 1

1. P. Carlin, "Pure Profit," *Los Angeles Times Magazine,* February 15, 1995, pp. 12–15+.

2. A. E. Serwer, "McDonald's Conquers the World," *Fortune* 130, no. 8 (1994), pp. 103–116.

3. R. Stewart, "A Model for Understanding Managerial Jobs and Behavior," *Academy of Management Review* 7 (1982), pp. 7–13.

4. S. J. Carroll and D. J. Gillen, "Are the Classical Management Functions Useful in Describing Managerial Work?" *Academy of Management Review* 12 (1987), pp. 38–51.

5. H. Mintzberg, "The Manager's Job: Folklore and Fact," *Harvard Business Review* 53, no. 4 (1975), pp. 49–61.

6. L. W. Porter and L. E. McKibbin, *Management Education and Development: Drift or Thrust into the 21st Century?* (New York: McGraw-Hill, 1988).

CHAPTER 2

1. C. A. Rarick, "Ancient Chinese Advice for Modern Business Strategists," *SAM Advanced Management Journal* 61 (1996), pp. 38–43; H. W. Vroman, "Sun Tzu and the Art of Business," *Academy of Management Executive* 11 (1997), pp. 129–30; C. H. Wee, "Fighting Talk," *People Management* 3, no. 21 (1997), pp. 40–44; Y. Y. Wong, T. E. Haher, and G. Lee, "The Strategy of an Ancient Warrior: An Inspiration for International Managers," *Multinational Business Review* 6 (1998), pp. 83–93.

2. C. S. George, *The History of Management Thought* (Englewood Cliffs, N.J.: Prentice Hall, 1972).

3. Ibid.

4. D. Wren, *The Evolution of Management Thought,* 4th ed. (New York: Wiley, 1994), pp. 36–38.

5. Ibid., pp. 31–32. From Adam Smith, *An Inquiry Into the Nature and Causes of the Wealth of Nations,* Great Books of the Western World, vol. 39 (Chicago: Encyclopedia Britannica, 1952; originally published in 1776).

6. Wren, *The Evolution of Management Thought,* p. 32. From Smith, *An Inquiry Into the Nature and Causes of the Wealth of Nations.*

7. Wren, *The Evolution of Management Thought,* p. 45.

8. Ibid., pp. 45–46.

9. George, *The History of Management Thought.*

10. Wren, *The Evolution of Management Thought* (see especially chapter 5).

11. Ibid., p. 73.

12. George, *The History of Management Thought,* p. 83; Wren, *The Evolution of Management Thought,* pp. 76–78.

13. D. A. Wren, ed. and J. A. Pearce II, assoc. ed., *Papers Dedicated to the Development of Modern Management: Celebrating 100 Years of Modern Management: 50th Anniversary of the Academy of Management* ([S.I.]: Academy of Management, 1986).

14. From *Transactions* 7 (1886), pp. 428–32, published by the American Society of Mechanical Engineers. Reprinted in Wren, "Papers Dedicated to the Development of Modern Management," pp. 3–4.

15. P. F. Drucker, "The Coming Rediscovery of Scientific Management," *Conference Board Record* 13, no. 6 (1976), p. 26.

16. Edwin A. Locke, "The Ideas of Frederick W. Taylor: An Evaluation," *Academy of Management Review* 7, no. 1 (1982), p. 15.

17. Charles D. Wrege and Amede Perroni, "Taylor's Pig Tale— A Historical Analysis of Frederick W. Taylor's Pig-Iron Experiment," *Academy of Management Journal* 17, no. 1 (1974), pp. 6–27; Locke, "The Ideas of Frederick W. Taylor," pp. 18–19.

18. U.S. House of Representatives, Labor Committee, "Hearings on House Resolution 8662, A Bill to Prevent the Use of Stop Watch or Other Time-Measuring Devices on Government Work and the Payment of Premiums or Bonuses to Government Employees," (Washington, D.C.: Government Printing Office, 1994), p. 1387. Quoted in Wren, *The Evolution of Management Thought,* p. 127.

19. Ronald G. Greenwood, Regina A. Greenwood, and Jay A. Severance, "Lillian M. Gilbreth, First Lady of Management," in Jeffrey C. Susbauer, ed., *Academy of Management Proceedings,* San Francicso, 1978, p. 2. Cited in Wren, *The Evolution of Management Thought,* p. 143.

20. D. S. Pugh, D. J. Hickson, and C. R. Hinings, *Writers on Organizations* (Beverly Hills: Sage, 1985), p. 64.

21. Ibid., p. 15.

22. A. M. Henderson and T. Parsons, eds. and trans. *Max Weber: The Theory of Social and Economic Organization* (New York: Free Press, 1947), p. 328.

23. R. G. Greenwood and C. D. Wregge, "The Hawthorne Studies," in Wren, "Papers Dedicated to the Development of Modern Management."

24. Ibid.

25. A. Carey, "The Hawthorne Studies: A Radical Criticism," *American Sociological Review* 32 (1967), pp. 403–16.

26. Greenwood and Wregge, "The Hawthorne Studies."

27. Ludwig von Bertalanffy, "General Systems Theory: A New Approach to the Unity of Science," *Human Biology* 23 (1951), pp. 302–61.

28. Tom Burns and G. M. Stalker, *The Management of Innovation* (London: Travistock Publishers, 1961); Joan Woodward, *Industrial Organization: Theory and Practice* (London: Oxford University Press, 1965); Paul R. Lawrence and Jay W. Lorsch, *Organization and Environment: Managing Differentiation and Integration* (Homewood, Ill.: Richard D. Irwin, 1967).

CHAPTER 3

1. M. Porter, *Competitive Strategy: Techniques for Analyzing Industries and Competitors* (New York: Free Press, 1980).

2. "Retail Entrepreneurs of the Year: Harold Ruttenberg," *Chain Store Age* 72 , no. 12 (1996), pp. 68–69.

3. D. Greising, "How High Can the Airlines Fly?" *Business Week* 3436 (1995), pp. 25–26.

4. "Glass with Attitude," *Economist* 345, no. 8048 (1997), pp. 113–115.

5. M. Mecham "Cathay Anticipates 747-500/600 Order," *Aviation Week & Space Technology* 114, no. 13 (1996), pp. 36–37.

6. M. Moynihan, *Global Consumer Demographics* (New York: Business International, 1991).

7. S. P. Seithi and P. Steidlmeier, "The Evolution of Business' Role in Society," *Business and Society Review* 94 (Summer 1995), pp. 9–12.

8. S. Gelsi, "Class for the Masses," *Brandweek* 38, no. 13 (1997), pp. 23–33.

9. "Glass Fibers Make Smokestacks Cleaner," *Machine Design* 67, no. 18 (1995), p. 123.

10. T. Mason and J. R. Norman, "Is It the Last Roundup for Texas Real Estate Tycoons?" *Business Week* 2977 (Industrial/Technology Edition, 1986), pp. 86–88; J. R. Norman, J. E. Davis, M. Ivey, and T. Thompson, "Casualties Start to Pile Up in the Oil Patch," *Business Week* 2932 (Industrial/Technology Edition, 1986), pp. 83–88.

11. C. Miller, "Contractors Fight for Share of Smaller Defense Market," *Marketing News* 24, no. 13 (1990), pp. 2, 17; S. N. Chakravarty, "36th Annual Report on American Industry: Aerospace and Defense," *Forbes* 113, no. 1 (1984), pp. 144–46.

12. B. Johnstone, "Rainbow Warriors," *Far Eastern Economic Review* 147, no. 7, p. 90.

13. B. Caldwell, "Wal-Mart Ups the Pace," *Informationweek* 609 (1996), pp. 37–51.

14. A. D. Neale and M. L. Stephens, *International Business and National Jurisdiction* (Oxford: Claredon Press 1998); A. K. Sundaram and J. S. Black, *The International Business Environment* (Englewood Cliffs: Prentice Hall; 1995).

15. S. J. Kobrin, "When Does Political Instability Result in Increased Investment Risk?" *Columbia Journal of World Business,* Spring 1978, pp. 113–22.; S. J. Kobrin, "Political Assessment by International Firms: Models or Methodologies?" *Journal of Policy Modeling* 3, no. 2 (1980), pp. 251–70; J. D. Simon, "A Theoretical Perspective on Political Risk," *Journal of International Business Studies* 15, no. 3 (1984), pp. 123–43; A. K. Sundaram and J. S. Black, *The International Business Environment* (Englewood Cliffs: Prentice Hall, 1995).

16. J. J. Boddewyn and T. Brewer, "International Business Political Behavior: New Theoretical Dimensions," *Academy of Management Review,* (1994), pp. 119–43; M. Fitzpatrick, "The Definition and Assessment of Political Risk in International Business: A Review of the Literature," *Academy of Management Review* 8 (1983), pp. 249–54; F. T. Haner, "Rating Investment Risks Abroad," *Business Horizons* 22 (1979), pp. 18–23; S. Robock," Political Risk: Identification and Assessment," *Columbia Journal of World Business* 6 (1971), pp. 6–20; R. J. Rummel and D. A. Heenan, "How Multinationals Analyze Political Risk," *Harvard Business Review* 56 (January/February 1978), pp. 67–76; A. K. Sundaram and J. S. Black, *The International Business Environment* (Englewood Cliffs: Prentice Hall, 1995); D. W. Bunn and W. Mustafaoglu, "Forecasting Political Risk," *Management Science* 24 (1978), pp. 1557–67; J. D. Simon, "Political Risk Assessment: Past Trends and Future Prospects," *Columbia Journal of World Business,* Fall 1982, pp. 62–71; R. Friedmann and J. Kim, "Political Risk and International Marketing," *Columbia Journal of World Business,* Winter 1988, pp. 63–74.

17. W. S. Hersch, "EDS Faces Simmering Challenges Despite Posting Strong 4Q Results," *Computer Reseller News* 776, no. 7 (1998), p. 16; "Face to Face: With Jack Smith, President of General Motors," *International Motor Business,* First Quarter 1995, pp. 6–20; L. Colby, "The Fortune Global 5 Hundred: The World's Largest Corporations," *Fortune* 136, no. 3 (1977), pp. F1–F11.

18. J. Lawrence, "P&G Losing Ground in Product Innovation," *Advertising Age* 64, no. 48 (1993), p. 44; J. Lawrence, "It's Diaper D-Day with P&G Rollout," *Advertising Age* 64, no. 39 (1993), pp. 1, 60; J. Lawrence, "Kimberly, P&G Rev Up to Market Latest Twist in Disposable Diapers," *Advertising Age* 63, no. 26 (1992), pp. 3, 51.

CHAPTER 4

1. A. L. Wilkins and W. Ouchi, "Efficient Cultures: Exploring the Relationship between Culture and Organizational Performance," *Administrative Science Quarterly* 28 (1983), pp. 468–81.

2. J. E. Dutton and S. Jackson, "Categorizing Strategic Issues: Links to Organizational Actions," *Academy of Management Review* 12 (1987), pp. 76–90.

3. R. G. Lord and R. J. Foti, "Schema Theories, Information Processing, and Organizational Behavior," pp. 20–48, in *The Thinking Organization.* ed. H. P. Simes and D. A. Gioia (San Francisco: Jossey-Bass, 1986); Wilkins and Ouchi, "Efficient Cultures."

4. D. Druckman, "Nationalism, Patriotism, and Group Loyalty: A Social-Psychological Perspective," *Merson International Studies Review* 38 (1994), pp. 43–68.

5. Personal communication with U.S. Bureau of Labor Statistics, 1997; U.S. Department of Commerce, 1998; and U.S. State Department, 1998.

6. E. Schein, "Coming to a New Awareness of Organizational Culture," *Sloan Management Review,* Winter 1984, pp. 3–16.

7. A. L. Kroeber and C. Kluckhohn, *Culture: A Critical Review of Concepts and Definitions* (Cambridge, Mass.: Harvard University Press, 1952).

8. Schein, "Coming to a New Awareness of Organizational Culture."

9. Ibid.

10. D. McGregor, *The Human Side of Enterprise* (New York: McGraw-Hill, 1960).

11. G. Hofstede, *Culture's Consequences* (Beverly Hills, Calif.: Sage, 1980).

12. J. Rokeach, *The Nature of Human Values* (New York: Free Press, 1973).

13. C. Hawkins and P. Oster, "After a U-turn, UPS Really Delivers," *Business Week,* May 31, 1993, pp. 43–45.

14. Personal communication, 1996.

15. M. Loden and J. Rosener, *Workforce America! Managing Employee Diversity as a Vital Resource* (New York: Irwin, 1991).

16. N. Adler, *International Dimensions of Organizational Behavior* (Boston: Kent Publishing, 1994).

17. Personal communication, 1998.

18. V. D. Miller and F. M. Jablin, "Information Seeking During Organizational Entry: Influences, Tactics, and a Model of the Process," *Academy of Management Review* 16 (1991), pp. 92–120.

19. E. Hall, *Beyond Culture* (Garden City, NY: Doubleday, 1976).

20. I. Ratui, "Thinking Internationally: A Comparison of How International Executives Learn," *International Studies of Management and Organization* 13, nos. 1–2 (1983), pp. 139–50.

CHAPTER 5

1. A. J. Dubinsky, M. A. Jolson, M. Kotabe, and C. U. Lim, "A Cross-National Investigation of Industrial Salespeople's Ethical Perceptions," *Journal of International Business Studies,* Fourth Quarter 1991, pp. 651–69.

2. J. S. Black, H. B. Gregersen, and M. E. Mendenhall, *Global Assignments* (San Francisco, Calif.: Jossey-Bass, 1992).

3. J. Rawls, *A Theory of Justice* (Cambridge, Mass.: Harvard University Press, 1971); J. Greenberg, "A Taxonomy of Organizational Justice Theories," *Academy of Management Review* 12 (1987), pp. 9–22.

4. T. Donaldson and T. W. Dunfee, "Toward a Unified Conception of Business Ethics," *Academy of Management Review* 19 (1994), pp. 252–84.

5. J. M. Jones, "Ethical Decision Making by Individuals in Organizations: An Issue-Contingent Model," *Academy of Management Review* 16 (1991), pp. 366–95.

6. Ibid.

7. P. S. Ring and A. Van De Ven, "Developmental Process of Cooperative Interorganizational Relationships," *Academy of Management Review* 19 (1994), pp. 90–118.

8. D. Robin, M. Giallourakis, F. R. David, and T. Moritz, "A Different Look at Codes of Ethics," *Business Horizons,* January–February 1989, pp. 66–73.

9. C. C. Langlois and B. B. Schlegelmilch, "Do Corporate Codes of Ethics Reflect National Character? Evidence from Europe and the United States," *Journal of International Business Studies,* Fourth Quarter 1991, pp. 519–39.

10. Robin, et al., "A Different Look at Codes of Ethics."

11. Ibid.

12. B. Ettorre, "Ethics Inc.: The Buck Stops Here," *HR Focus,* June 1992, p. 11.

13. M. P. Miceli and J. P. Near, *Blowing the Whistle* (Lexington, Mass.: Lexington Books, 1992).

14. Ibid.

15. M. P. Miceli and J. P. Near, "The Relationships among Beliefs, Organizational Position, and Whistle Blowing Status: A Discriminant Analysis," *Academy of Management Journal* 27 (1984), pp. 687–705.

16. D. Shingler, "Battelle Program Attracts NASA Whistle Blowers," *Business First of Greater Columbus* 4, no. 3 (October 5, 1987), p. 9.

17. M. P. Miceli and J. P. Near, "Whistle Blowing: Reaping the Benefits," *Academy of Management Executive* 8 (1994), pp. 65–71.

18. Miceli and Near, *Blowing the Whistle.*

19. M. Friedman, "The Social Responsibility of Business Is to Increase Its Profits," *New York Magazine,* September 13, 1970, pp. 32–33, 122, 126.

20. A. Smith, *An Inquiry into the Nature and Causes of the Wealth of Nations,* ed. R. H. Campbell and A. S. Skinner (Oxford, UK: Clarendon Press, 1976).

21. Friedman, "The Social Responsibility of Business Is to Increase Its Profits," p. 32.

22. M. Rothman, "Nightmare at Kaufman's," *Business Ethics,* November–December 1994, pp. 15–16.

23. J. Joha, L. Serbet, and A. Sundaram, "Cross-Border Liability of Multinational Enterprises: Border Taxes and Capital Structure," *Financial Management,* Winter 1991, pp. 54–67.

24. Business Roundtable, *Statement on Corporate Responsibility* (New York I: Business Roundtable, October 1981).

25. C. Watson, "Managing with Integrity: Social Responsibilities of Business as Seen by America's CEOs," *Business Horizons,* July/August 1991, pp. 99–109.

CHAPTER 6

1. J. A. Schumpeter, *The Theory of Economic Development: An Inquiry into Profits, Capital, Credit Interest, and the Business Cycle,* trans. Redevers Opie (New York: Oxford, 1961 [1934]).

2. R. Waldinger, H. Aldrich, R. Ward, and associates, *Ethnic Entrepreneurs: Immigrant Business in Industrial Societies* (Newbury Park, Calif.: Sage; 1990); S. J. Birley, "Succession in the Family Firm," *Journal of Small Business Management* 24, no. 3 (1986), pp. 36–43; J. A. Katz, "A Psychosocial Cognitive Model of Employment Status Choice," *Entrepreneurship: Theory and Practice* 17, no. 1 (1992), pp. 29–37.

3. B. J. Bird, *Entrepreneurial Behavior* (Glenview, Ill.: Scott Foresman, 1989); R. E. Boyatzis, *The Competent Manager* (New York: Wiley-Interscience, 1982); D. C. McClelland, *The Achieving Society* (Princeton: Van Nostrand, 1961); D. C. McClelland and D. G. Winter, *Motivating Economic Achievement* (New York: Free Press, 1969).

4. D. F. Jennings, *Multiple Perspectives on Entrepreneurship: Text, Readings, and Cases* (Cincinnati: SouthWestern, 1994); C. Hampden-Turner and A. Trompenaars, *The Seven Cultures of Capitalism* (New York: Currency Doubleday, 1993).

5. N. C. Churchill and V. L. Lewis, "The Five Stages of Small Business Growth, *Harvard Business Review* 83 (1983), pp. 3–12.

6. P. D. Reynolds, "The Great American Incubator," *Inc.,* April 1994, p. 12.

7. J. A. Katz and W. B. Gartner, "Properties of Emerging Organizations," *Academy of Management Review* 13, no. 3 (1988), pp. 429–41.

8. V. H. Trimble, *The Wild Rise and Hard Fall of Chris Whittle* (New York: Birch Lane Press, 1995); D. Greising, "Live by the Hype, Die by the Hype," *Business Week,* October 16, 1995, Books Section, p. 19.

9. U.S. Government Printing Office, *Small Business Scorecard,* 1996.

10. M. A. Maidique and B. J. Zirger, "The New Product Learning Cycle," *Research Policy,* December 1985, reprinted in R. A. Burgelman and M. A. Maidique, *Strategic Management of Technology and Innovation* (Homewood, Ill.: Richard D. Irwin, 1988), pp. 320–37.

11. P. Ghemawat and N. Donohue, "U.S. Airline Industry—1978–88 (A)," Case 9-390-025 [Teaching Note (5-390-169)] (Boston: Harvard Business School, 1989).

12. M. Beer and P. Holland, "People Express Decline: Interview with Don Burr," Video 9-890-508 ("People Express Airlines: Rise and Decline," Case 9-490-012) (Boston: Harvard Business School, 1994).

13. W. G. Lee, "Southwest Airlines' Herb Kelleher: Unorthodoxy at Work," *Management Review* 84, no. 1 (January 1995), pp. 9–12; J. L. Heskett and R. Hallowell, "Southwest Airlines—1993 (A)", Case 9-694-023 (Boston: Harvard Business School, 1994).

14. K. G. Palepu, "Home Depot, Inc.," Case 9-188-148 [Teaching Note (5-190-171)] (Boston: Harvard Business School, 1996).

15. T. A. Luehrman, "Home Shopping Network (Abridged)," Case 9-295-135 (Boston: Harvard Business School, 1995).

16. A. E. Serwer, "McDonald's Captures the World," *Fortune,* October 17, 1994, p. 103ff; see also D. Upton and J. D. Margolis, "McDonald's Corp.—1992: Operations, Flexibility and the Environment," Case 9-693-028 [Teaching Note (5-693-106)] (Boston: Harvard Business School, 1996); J. M. Hertzfeld, "Joint Ventures: Saving the Soviets from Perestroika," *Harvard Business Review* 69, no. 1 (January/February 1991), pp. 80–91.

17. E. M. Rogers and F. F. Shoemaker, *Communication of Innovations: A Cross-Cultural Approach,* 2nd ed. (New York: Free Press, 1971).

18. J. J. Fucini and S. Fucini, *Entrepreneurs: The Men and Women Behind Famous Brand Names and How They Made It* (Boston: G.K. Hall, 1985), pp. 96–99; J. P. Kotter and J. M. Stengrevics, "Mary Kay Cosmetics, Inc.," Case 9-481-126 (Boston: Harvard Business School, 1981).

19. Fucini and Fucini, *Entrepreneurs,* pp. 99–101.

20. J. V. Singh, D. J Tucker, and R. J. House, "Organizational Legitimacy and the Liability of Newness," *Administrative Science Quarterly* 31 (1986), pp. 171–93.

21. P. R. Nayak and J. M. Ketteringham, *Breakthroughs!* (New York: Rawson Associates, 1986).

22. T. Peters, "The Mythology of Innovation or a Skunkworks Tale, Part II, *The Stanford Magazine,* 1983, reprinted in M. L. Tushman and W. L. Moore, eds, *Readings in the Management of Innovation,* 2nd ed. (Cambridge, Mass.: Ballinger, 1988), pp. 138–47.

23. Maidique and Zirger, "The New Product Learning Cycle."

24. Van Doren, *Webster's American Biographies* (Springfield, Mass.: G.C. Merriam Co., (1974), "Richard Warren Sears, 1863–1914," p. 930.

CHAPTER 7

1. J. A. Pearce, K. Robbins, and R. Robinson, "The Impact of Grand Planning Formality on Financial Performance," *Strategic Management Journal,* March–April 1987, pp. 125–34.

2. J. Camillus, "Reinventing Strategic Planning," *Strategy and Leadership,* May–June 1996, pp. 6–12; L. Olson, "Strategic Lessons," *Association Management* 44, no. 6 (1992), pp. 35–39; J. J. Murphy, "Identifying Strategic Issues," *Long Range Planning* 22, no. 2 (1989), pp. 101–105.

3. G. Vastag, S. Kerekes, and D. Rondinelli, "Evolution of Corporate Environmental Management Approaches: A Framework and Application," *International Journal of Production Economics* 43, nos. 2/3 (1996), pp. 193–211; B. Boyd and J. Faulk, "Executive Scanning and Perceived Uncertainty: A Multidimensional Model," *Journal of Management* 22, no. 1 (1996), pp. 1–21; D. Lane and R. Maxfield, "Strategy Under Complexity: Fostering Generative Relationships," *Long Range Planning* 29, no. 2 (1996), pp. 215–31.

4. L. Rouleau and F. Seguin, "Strategy and Organization Theories: Common Forms of Discourse," *Journal of Management Studies* 32, no. 1 (1995), pp. 101–17.

5. R. Bergstrom, "Benchmarking," *Automotive Production* 108, no. 9 (1996), pp. 63–65; J. Vezmar, "Competitive Intelligence at Xerox," *Competitive Intelligence Review* 7, no. 3 (1996), pp. 15–19.

6. A. Bhid, "The Questions Every Entrepreneur Must Ask," *Harvard Business Review* 74, no. 6 (1996), pp. 120–30.

7. E. A. Locke and G. P. Latham, *A Theory of Goal Setting and Task Performance* (Englewood Cliffs, N.J.: Prentice Hall, 1990); A. Lederer and A. Mendelow, "Information Systems Planning and the Challenge of Shifting Priorities," *Information and Management* 24, no. 6 (1993), pp. 319–28.

8. D. Federa and T. Miller, "Capital Allocation Techniques," *Topics in Health Care Financing* 19, no. 1 (1992), pp. 68–78.

9. F. Sunderland and M. Kane, "Measuring Productivity on a Value Basis," *National Productivity Review* 15, no. 4 (1996), pp. 57–76.

10. K. Lehn and A. Makhiji, "EVA and MVA: As Performance Measures and Signals for Strategic Change," *Strategy and Leadership* 24, no. 3 (1996), pp. 34–38; R. Kaplan and D. Norton, "Strategic Learning and the Balanced Score Card," *Strategy and Leadership* 24, no. 5 (1996), pp. 18–24.

11. Bhid, "The Questions Every Entrepreneur Must Ask."

12. L. Kempfer, "Planning for Success," *Computer-Aided Engineering* 13, no. 4 (1994), pp. 18–22; P. Sweet, "A Planner's Best Friend?" *Accountancy* 113, no. 1206 (1994), pp. 56–58; J. Rakos, "The Virtues of the Time-Bar Chart," *Computing Canada* 18, no. 17 (1992), p. 32.

13. F. Harrison, "Strategic Control at the CEO Level," *Long Range Planning* 24, no. 6 (1991), pp. 78–87; A. Di Primo, "When Turnaround Management Works," *Journal of Business Strategy* 9, no. 1 (1988), pp. 61–64.

14. M. Ishman, "Commitment-Compliance: Counterforces in Implementing Production and Inventory Control Systems," *Production and Inventory Management Journal* 36, no. 1 (1995), pp. 33–37.

15. J. White, "Almost Nothing New under the Sun: Why the Work of Budgeting Remains Incremental," *Public Budgeting and Finance* 14, no. 1 (1994), pp. 113–34.

16. W. Llewellyn, "A Review of the Budgeting System," *Assessment* 1, no. 5 (1994), pp. 47–50.

17. E. A. Locke and G. P. Latham, *A Theory of Goal Setting and Task Performance* (Englewood Cliffs, N.J.: Prentice Hall, 1990).

18. M. Erez, P. C. Earley, and C. L. Hulin, "The Impact of Participation on Goal Acceptance and Performance: A Two Step Model," *Academy of Management Journal,* March 1985, pp. 50–66.

19. G. P. Latham and L. M. Saari, "The Effects of Holding Goal Difficulty Constant on Assigned and Participatively Set Goals," *Academy of Management Journal,* March 1979, pp. 163–68.

20. H. Weihrich, *Management Excellence: Productivity through MBO* (New York: McGraw-Hill, 1985).

21. P. Mali, *MBO Update* (New York: Wiley, 1986).

22. R. Rodgers and J. E. Hunter, "Impact of Management by Objectives on Organizational Productivity," *Journal of Applied Psychology,* April 1991, pp. 322–36.

CHAPTER 8

1. G. Hamel and C. K. Prahalad, *Competing for the Future,* (Boston, Mass.: Harvard Business Press, 1994).

2. O. Harari, "Three Vital Little Words," *Management Review* 84, no. 11 (1995), pp. 25–27; G. Hamel and C. K. Prahalad, "Strategy as Stretch and Leverage," *Harvard Business Review* 71, no. 2 (1993), pp. 75–84.

3. D. Calfee, "Get Your Mission Statement Working," *Management Review* 82, no. 1 (1993), pp. 54–57; J. Collins and J. Porras, "Building Your Company's Vision," *Harvard Business Review* 74, no. 5 (1996), pp. 65–77; C. Rarick and J. Vitton, "Mission Statements Make Sense," *Journal of Business Strategy* 16, no. 1 (1995), pp. 11–12.

4. M. E. Porter, *Competitive Advantage* (New York: Free Press, 1985).

5. C. Unruh, "Passage to India," *Journal of Business Strategy* 15, no. 4 (1994), pp. 6–7.

6. J. Younker, "Organization Direction-Setting," *Tapping the Network Journal* 2, no. 2 (1991), pp. 20–23; W. Schiemann, "Strategy, Culture, Communication: Three Keys to Success," *Executive Excellence* 6, no. 8 (1989), pp. 11–12.

7. M. E. Porter, *Competitive Advantage.*

8. C. K. Prahalad and G. Hamel, "The Core Competence of the Corporation," *Harvard Business Review* 68, no. 3 (1990), pp. 79–91.

9. J. Barney, "Looking Inside for Competitive Advantage," *Academy of Management Executive* 9, no. 4 (1995), pp. 49–61; W. Dyer and V. Sighn, "The Relational View: Cooperative Strategy and Sources of Interorganizational Competitive Advantage," *Academy of Management Review* 23, no. 4 (October 1998), pp. 660–79.

10. S. Ghoshal and N. Nohria, "Horses for Courses: Organizational Forms for Multinational Corporations," *Sloan Management Review* 34, no. 2 (1993), pp. 23–35.

11. M. Gort and R. Wall, "The Evolution of Technologies and Investment in Innovation," *Economic Journal* 96, no. 383 (1986), pp. 741–57.

12. C. Anderson and C. Zeithaml, "Stage of the Product Life Cycle, Business Strategy, and Business Performance," *Academy of Management Journal* 27, no. 1 (1984), pp. 5–24.

13. E. Comiskey and C. Mulford, "Anticipating Trends in Operating Profits and Cash Flow," *Commercial Lending Review* 8, no. 2 (1993), pp. 38–48.

14. J. Cantwell, "The Globalization of Technology: What Remains of the Product Life Cycle Model?" *Cambridge Journal of Economics* 19, no. 1 (1995), pp. 155–74; T. Tyebjee, "Globalization Challenges Facing Fast Growing Companies," *Journal of Business and Industrial Marketing* 8, no. 3 (1993), pp. 58–64.

15. J. Barney, "Looking Inside for Competitive Advantage," *Academy of Management Executive* 9, no. 4 (1995), pp. 49–61.

16. M. E. Porter, "Towards a Dynamic Theory of Strategy," *Strategic Management Journal* 12 (1991), pp. 95–117.

17. J. Barney, "Firm Resources and Sustained Competitive Advantage," *Journal of Management* 17, no. 1 (1991), pp. 99–120; Porter, *Competitive Advantage.*

18. D. Bunch and R. Smiley, "Who Deters Entry?" *Review of Economics and Statistics* 74, no. 3 (1992), pp. 509–21.

19. Porter, *Competitive Advantage;* M. Partridge and L. Perren, "Developing Strategic Direction: Can Generic Strategies Help?" *Management Accounting–London* 72, no. 5 (1994), pp. 28–29.

20. D. A. Heenan and H. V. Perlmutter, *Multinational Organizational Development* (Reading, Mass.: Addison-Wesley, 1979).

21. B. Quinn, *Intelligent Enterprise* (New York: Free Press, 1992).

22. H. Mintzberg, "The Strategy Concept I: Five Ps for Strategy," *California Management Review,* Fall 1987, pp. 11–24.

23. F. A. Maljers, "Inside Unilever: The Evolving Transnational Company," *Harvard Business Review,* September–October 1992, p. 2.

CHAPTER 9

1. G. R. Ungson and D. N. Braunstein, *Decision Making* (Boston: Kent, 1982).

2. D. Miller and M. Star, *The Structure of Human Decisions* (Englewood Cliffs, N.J.: Prentice Hall, 1967).

3. H. A. Simon, *The New Science of Management Decisions* (Englewood Cliffs, N.J.: Prentice Hall, 1977); J. Parking, "Organizational Decision Making and the Project Manager," *International Journal of Project Management* 14, no. 5 (1996), pp. 257–63.

4. H. A. Simon, *Administrative Behavior* (New York: The Free Press, 1957).

5. J. G. March and H. A. Simon, *Organizations* (New York: Wiley, 1958), pp. 140–41.

6. P. Soelberg, "Unprogrammed Decision Making," *Industrial Management* (1967), pp. 19–29; D. Cray, G. H. Haines, and G. R. Mallory, "Programmed Strategic Decision Making," *British Journal of Management* 5, no. 3 (1994), pp. 191–204.

7. Simon, *The New Science of Management Decisions.*

8. T. R. Mitchell and J. R. Larson, *People in Organizations* (New York: McGraw-Hill, 1987).

9. E. Harrison, *The Managerial Decision Making Process* (Boston: Houghton-Mifflin, 1975).

10. R. Ebert and T. Mitchell, *Organizational Decision Processes: Concepts and Analysis* (New York: Crane, Russak, 1975).

11. N. Margulies and J. Stewart Black, "Perspectives on the Implementation of Participative Approaches," *Human Resource Management* 26, no. 3 (1987), pp. 385–412.

12. J. Stewart Black and Hal B. Gregersen, "Participative Decision Making: An Integration of Multiple Perspectives," *Human Relations* 50 (1997), pp. 859–78.

13. V. Vroom and P. Yetton, *Leadership and Decision Making* (Pittsburgh: University of Pittsburgh Press, 1973); V. Vroom and A. Jago, *The New Leadership: Managing Participation in Organizations* (Englewood Cliffs, N.J.: Prentice Hall, 1988).

14. R. Hof, "Why Once-Ambitious Computer Firm Quit," *Peninsula Times Tribune,* September 29, 1984, p. B1.

15. K. Eisenhardt and L. J. Bourgeois, "Making Fast Strategic Decisions in High-Velocity Environments," *Academy of Management Journal* 32 (1989), pp. 543–76.

16. I. Janis, *Victims of Groupthink* (Boston: Houghton Mifflin, 1972); M. E. Turner and A. R. Pratkamis, "Twenty-Five Years of Groupthink Theory and Research: Lessons from the

Evaluation of a Theory," *Organizational Behavior and Human Decision Processes* 73, nos. 2, 3 (1998), pp. 105–15; J. K. Esser; "Alive and Well after 25 Years: A Review of Groupthink Research," *Organizational Behavior and Human Decision Processes* 73, nos. 2, 3 (1998), pp. 116–41.

17. B. M. Staw, "The Escalation of Commitment to a Course of Action," *Academy of Management Review* 6 (1981), pp. 577–87; G. Whyte, A. M. Saks, and S. Hook, "When Success Breeds Failure," *Journal of Organizational Behavior* 18, no. 5 (1997), pp. 415–32; D. R. Bobocel and J. P. Meyer, "Escalating Commitment to a Failing Course of Action," *Journal of Applied Psychology* 79, no. 3 (1994), pp. 360–63; J. Ross and M. Staw, "Organizational Escalation and Exit: Lessons from the Shoreham Nuclear Power Plant," *Academy of Management Journal* 36, no. 4 (1993), pp. 701–32.

18. Staw, "The Escalation of Commitment to a Course of Action," p. 578.

19. J. S. Black, H. B. Gregersen, and M. E. Mendenhall, *Global Assignments* (San Francisco: Jossey-Bass, 1992).

20. C. Schwenk and H. Thomas, "Formulating the Mess: The Role of Decision Aids in Problem Formulation," *Omega* 11 (1983), pp. 239–52.

21. A. VanDeVen and A. Delbecq, "The Effectiveness of Nominal, Delphi, and Interacting Group Decision-Making Processes," *Academy of Management Journal* 17 (1974), pp. 607–26; Schwenk and Thomas, "Formulating the Mess."

CHAPTER 10

1. H. Mintzberg, *The Structuring of Organizations* (Englewood Cliffs, N.J.: Prentice Hall, 1979).

2. R. Steers and J. S. Black, *Organizational Behavior* (New York: Harper-Collins, 1993); R. H. Hall, *Organizations: Structures , Process, and Outcomes,* 5th ed. (Englewood Cliffs, N.J.: Prentice Hall, 1991).

3. R. Cyert and J. March, *The Behavioral Theory of the Firm,* (Englewood Cliffs, N.J.: Prentice Hall, 1963); J. R. Galbraith, "Organization Design: An Information Processing View," *Interfaces* 4, no. 3 (1974), pp. 28–36; Hall, *Organizations.*

4. Y. Rhy-song and T. Sagafi-nejad, "Organizational Characteristics of American and Japanese Firms in Taiwan," *National Academy of Management Proceedings,* 1987, pp. 111–15.

5. C. A. Bartlett and S. Ghoshal, "Organizing for Worldwide Effectiveness: The Transnational Solution," *California Management Review,* Fall 1988, pp. 54–74; D. H. Doty, W. H. Glick, and G. P. Huber, "Fit, Effectiveness, and Equifinality: A Test of Two Configurational Theories," *Academy of Management Journal* 36 (1993), pp. 1196–250.

6. J. R. Lincoln, M. Hanada, and K. McBride, "Organizational Structures in Japanese and U.S. Manufacturing," *Administrative Science Quarterly* 31 (1986), pp. 338–64.

7. J. Schachter, "When Hope Turns to Frustration: The Americanization of Mitsubishi Has Had Little Success," *Los Angeles Times,* July 10, 1988, p. 1.

8. R. Duncan, "What Is the Right Organizational Structure?" *Organizational Dynamics,* Winter 1979, pp. 59–79; Hall, *Organizations.*

9. Duncan, "What Is the Right Organizational Structure?"

10. S. Ghoshal and N. Nohria, "Internal Differentiation within Multinational Corporations," *Strategic Management Journal* 10 (1989), pp. 323–37.

11. Bartlett and Ghoshal, "Organizing for Worldwide Effectiveness"; A. Sundaram and J. S. Black, "Environment and Internal Organization of Multinational Enterprises," *Academy of Management Review* 17 (1992), pp. 729–57.

12. Galbraith, "Organization Design"; Bartlett and Ghoshal, "Organizing for Worldwide Effectiveness"; Hall, *Organizations.*

13. Galbraith "Organization Design"; Hall, *Organizations.*

14. I. Nonaka, "Managing the Firm as an Information Creation Process," in J. Meindl (ed.), *Advances in Information Processing in Organizations,* vol. 4 (Greenwich, Conn.: JAI Press, 1991), pp. 239–75.

CHAPTER 11

1. H. J. Leavitt, "The Old Days, Hot Groups, and Managers' Lib," *Administrative Science Quarterly* 41, no. 2 (1996), pp. 288–300.

2. B. I. Kirkman and D. L. Shapiro, "The Impact of Cultural Values on Employee Resistance to Teams: Toward a Model of Globalized Self-Managing Work Team Effectiveness," *Academy of Management Review* 22, no. 3 (1997), pp. 730–57.

3. E. Sundstrom, K. P. de Meuse, and D. Futrell, "Work Teams: Applications and Effectiveness," *American Psychologist* 45, no. 2 (1990), pp. 120–33.

4. M. Cottrill, "Give Your Work Teams Time and Training," *Academy of Management Executive* 11, no. 3 (1997), pp. 87–89; R. D. Banker, J. M. Field, R. G. Schroeder, and K. K. Sinha, "Impact of Work Teams on Manufacturing Performance: A Longitudinal Field Study," *Academy of Management Journal* 39, no. 4 (1996), pp. 867–90.

5. M. H. Safizadeh, "The Case of Workgroups in Manufacturing Operations," *California Management Review* 33, no. 4 (1991), pp. 61–82.

6. J. Thompson, "Joe versus the Bureaucracy," *Government Executive* 27, no. 10 (1995), pp. 50–55.

7. Kirkman and Shapiro, "The Impact of Cultural Values on Employee Resistance to Teams."

8. R. Peterson, "Ergonomics and an Office Renovation," *Editor & Publisher* 128, no. 44 (1995), pp. 14P–15P.

9. J. D. Zbar, "Hispanics Attract Publishers' Notice," *Advertising Age* 66, no. 40 (1995), p. 12.

10. "Employee Empowerment Works for Revlon," *Quality* 34, no. 12 (1995), pp. 59–60.

11. E. Krapf, "Utility Player," *America's Network* 99, no. 11 (1995), p. 40.

12. K. A. Jehn and P. P. Shah, "Interpersonal Relationships and Task Performance: An Examination of Mediation Processes in Friendship and Acquaintance Groups," *Journal of Personality and Social Psychology* 72, (1997), pp. 775–90; "Friends Make Good Teammates," *Quality* 36, no. 1 (1997), p. 12.

13. T. O'Sullivan, "Re-engineering," *Marketing Week* 19, no. 46/2 (1997), pp. 41–44.

14. J. R. Hackman, "The Design of Work Teams," in J. W. Lorsch (ed.), *Handbook of Organizational Behavior* (Englewood Cliffs, N.J.: Prentice Hall, 1987), pp. 315–42.

15. S. Caminiti, "What Team Leaders Need to Know," *Fortune* 131, no. 3 (1995), pp.93–100.

16. Banker et al., "Impact of the Work Teams on Manufacturing Performance."

17. M. A. Abramson, "First Teams," *Government Executive* 28, no. 5 (1996), pp. 53–58.

18. B. E. Ashforth and F. Mael, "Social Identity Theory and the Organization," *Academy of Management Review* 14, no. 1

(1989), pp. 20–39; K. L. Bettenhausen, "Five Years of Group Research: What We Have Learned and What Needs to be Addressed," *Journal of Management* 17, no. 2 (1991), pp. 345–81.

19. J. S. Heinen and E. Jacobson, "A Model of Task Group Development in Complex Organizations and a Strategy of Implementation," *Academy of Management Review* 1, no. 4 (1976), pp. 98–111; B. W. Tuckman and M. A. Jensen, "Stages of Small-Group Development Revisited," *Group & Organization Studies* 2, no. 4 (1977), pp. 419–27; R. L. Moreland and J. M. Levine, "Group Dynamics over Time: Development and Socialization in Small Groups," in J. M. McGrath (ed.), *The Social Psychology of Time: New Perspectives,* Sage focus editions, Vol. 91 (Newbury Park, Calif.: Sage Publications, Inc., 1988), pp. 151–81; Sundstrom et al., "Work Teams;" Bettenhausen, "Five Years of Group Research."

20. B. W. Tuckman, "Developmental Sequence in Small Groups," *Psychological Bulletin* 63, no. 6 (1965), pp. 384–99; Tuckman and Jensen, "Stages of Small-Group Development Revisited."

21. Sundstrom et al., "Work Teams," p. 127.

22. N. Merrick, "The Lions Share," *People Management* 3, no. 12 (1997), pp. 34–37.

23. A. DeMarco, "Teamwork Pays off for Ross and Sterling Winthrop," *Facilities Design and Management* 12, no. 12 (1993), pp. 38–41.

24. S. Convey, "Performance Measurement in Cross-Functional Teams," *CMA Magazine* 68, no. 8 (1994), pp. 13–15.

25. Sundstrom et al., "Work Teams," p. 126.

26. B. Mullen, C. Symons, L. Hu, and E. Salas, "Group Size, Leadership Behavior, and Subordinate Satisfaction," *Journal of General Psychology* 116, no. 2 (1989), pp. 155–70.

27. B. Mullen, D. A. Johnson, and S. D. Drake, "Organizational Productivity as a Function of Group Composition: A Self-Attention Perspective," *Journal of Social Psychology* 127 (1987), pp. 143–50.

28. B. Latane, K. Williams, and S. Harkins, "Social Loafing," *Psychology Today* 13, no. 5 (1979), pp. 104–10; P. C. Early, "Social Loafing and Collectivism: A Comparison of the United States and the People's Republic of China," *Administrative Science Quarterly* 34 (1989), pp. 565–81.

29. Bettenhausen, "Five Years of Group Research."

30. K. D. Williams, S. A. Nida, L. D. Baca, and B. Latane, "Social Loafing and Swimming: Effects of Identifiabilty on Individual and Relay Performance of Intercollegiate Swimmers," *Basic and Applied Social Psychology* 10 (1989), pp. 73–81.

31. W. K. Gabrenya, Y. Wang, and B. Latane, "Social Loafing on an Optimizing Task: Cross-Cultural Differences among Chinese and Americans," *Journal of Cross-Cultural Psychology* 16, no. 2 (1985), pp. 223–42.

32. M. E. Shaw, *Group Dynamics: The Psychology of Small Group Behavior,* 3rd ed. (New York: McGraw-Hill, 1981).

33. F. J. Milliken and L. L. Martins, "Searching for Common Threads: Understanding the Multiple Effects of Diversity in Organizational Groups," *Academy of Management Review* 21, no. 2 (1996), pp. 402–33.

34. Ibid.

35. P. J. Neff, "Cross-Cultural Research Teams in a Global Enterprise," *Research-Technology Management* 38, no. 3 (1995), pp. 15–19.

36. J. Gordon, M. Hequet, C. Lee, M. Picard, et al., "Workplace Blues," *Training* 33, no. 2 (1996), p. 16.

37. M. A. Abramson, "First Teams," *Government Executive* 28, no. 5 (1996), pp. 53–58.

38. C. C. Manz and H. P. Sims Jr., "Leading Workers to Lead Themselves: The External Leadership of Self-Managing Work Teams," *Administrative Science Quarterly* 32, no. 1 (1987), pp. 106–29.

39. Camininti, "What Team Leaders Need to Know."

40. Shaw, *Group Dynamics.*

41. J. E. Driskell and E. Salas, "Group Decision Making under Stress," *Journal of Applied Psychology* 76, no. 3 (1991), pp. 473–78.

42. Shaw, *Group Dynamics.*

43. Ibid.

44. D. C. Feldman, "The Development and Enforcement of Group Norms," *Academy of Management Review* 9, no. 1 (1984), pp. 47–53.

45. N. Merrick, "The Lions Share."

46. R. A. Proehl, "A Panacea or Just Another Headache?" *Supervision* 57, no. 7 (1996), pp. 6–8.

47. Shaw, *Group Dynamics.*

48. Ibid., p. 213; see also N. Nicholson, (ed.), *Encyclopedic Dictionary of Organizational Behavior* (Oxford, U.K.: Blackwell, 1995), p. 199.

49. D. Druckman and J. A. Swets, (eds.), *Enhancing Human Performance: Issues, Theories and Techniques,* National Research Council (Washington, D.C.: National Academy Press, 1988).

50. Ibid.

51. Shaw, *Group Dynamics.*

52. Ibid., p. 218.

53. D. M. Landers, M. O. Wilkinson, B. D. Hatfield, and H. Barber, "Causality and the Cohesion-Performance Relationship," *Journal of Sport Psychology* 4, no. 2 (1982), pp. 170–83.

54. I. L. Janis, *Victims of Groupthink: A Psychological Study of Foreign-Policy Decisions and Fiascoes* (Boston: Houghton, Mifflin, 1972).

55. A. C. Amason, W. A. Hochwarter, K. R. Thompson, and A. W. Harrison, "Conflict: An Important Dimension in Successful Management Teams," *Organizational Dynamics* 24, no. 2 (1995), pp. 20–35.

56. K. A. Jehn, "A Multimethod Examination of the Benefits and Detriments of Intragroup Conflict," *Administrative Science Quarterly* 40, no. 2 (1995), pp. 256–82.

57. Amason et al., "Conflict;" K. M. Eisenhardt, J. L. Kahwajy, and L. J. Bourgeois III, "Conflict and Strategic Choice: How Top Management Teams Disagree," *California Management Review* 39, no. 2 (1997), pp. 42–62.

58. Jehn, "A Multimethod Examination of the Benefits and Detriments of Intragroup Conflict."

59. Amason, et al., "Conflict."

60. Ibid.; Jehn, "A Multimethod Examination of the Benefits and Detriments of Intragroup Conflict."

61. L. H. Pelled, "Demographic Diversity, Conflict, and Work Group Outcomes: An Intervening Process Theory," *Organization Science* 7, no. 6 (1996), pp. 615–31.

62. Amason et al., "Conflict."

63. Eisenhardt et al., "Conflict and Strategic Choice."

64. D. R. Forsyth, *An Introduction to Group Dynamics* (Monterey, Calif.: Brooks/Cole Pub. Co., 1983).

65. S. Caudron, "Keeping Team Conflict Alive," *Training and Development* 52, no. 9 (1998), pp. 48–52.

66. J. Fitz-Enz, "Measuring Team Effectiveness," *HR Focus* 74, no. 8 (1997), p. 3.

67. J. R. Hackman (ed.), *Groups That Work (and Those That Don't): Creating Conditions for Effective Teamwork* (San Francisco: Jossey-Bass, 1990).

68. J. Huey, "Eisner Explains Everything," *Fortune* 131, no. 7 (1995), pp. 44–68.

69. Hackman, *Groups That Work.*

70. C. Stephenson, "How Carriers Can Become More Organizationally Nimble," *Telecommunications* 31, no. 8 (1997), pp. 50–53.

71. R. Wageman and G. Baker, "Incentives and Cooperation: The Joint Effects of Task and Reward Interdependence on Group Performance," *Journal of Organizational Behavior* 18, no. 2 (1997), pp. 139–58.

72. Banker et al., "Impact of Work Teams on Manufacturing Performance;" Cottrill, "Give Your Work Teams Time and Training."

73. Abramson, "First Teams."

74. G. L. Hallam, "Seven Common Beliefs about Teams: Are They True?" *Leadership in Action* 17, no. 3 (1997), pp. 1–4.

CHAPTER 12

1. M. E. Porter, "Towards a Dynamic Theory of Strategy," *Strategic Management Journal* 12 (1991), pp. 95–117; M. E. Porter, *Competitive Advantage: Creating and Sustaining Superior Performance* (New York: Free Press, 1985); J. Barney, "Firm Resources and Sustained Competitive Advantage," *Journal of Management* 17, no. 1 (1991), pp. 99–120.

2. D. Ulrich, "HR Partnerships: From Rhetoric to Results," working paper, University of Michigan, 1994.

3. M. W. McCall and M. M. Lombardo, *Off the Track: Why and How Successful Executives Get Derailed* (Greensboro, N.C.: Center for Creative Leadership, 1983).

4. M. E. Porter, *The Competitive Advantage of Nations* (New York: Free Press, 1990).

5. Personal communication with human resource executive at Delta Airlines.

6. P. Feltes, R. K. Robinson and R. L. Fink, "American Female Expatriate and the Civil Rights Act of 1991: Balancing Legal and Business Interests," *Business Horizons,* March–April 1993, pp. 82–86.

7. N. Adler, "Expecting International Success: Female Managers Overseas," *Columbia Journal of World Business* 19 (1987), pp. 79–85.

8. E. P. Gray, "The National Origin of BFOQ Under Title VII," *Employee Relations Law Journal* 11, no. 2 (1985), pp. 311–21.

9. D. Ulrich, W. Brockbank, A. Yeung, and D. Lake, "Human Resources as a Competitive Advantage," unpublished manuscript, University of Michigan, 1993.

10. E. Schein, "Coming to a New Awareness of Organizational Culture," *Sloan Management Review* 10 (1984), pp. 3–16.

11. J. Barney, "Firm Resources and Sustained Competitive Advantage."

12. J. E. Dutton and S. E. Jackson, "Categorizing Strategic Issues: Links to Organizational Action," *Academy of Management Review* 12 (1987), pp. 76–90.

13. J. C. Abegglen and G. Stalk, *Kaisha: The Japanese Corporation* (New York: Basic Books, 1985).

14. Porter, *Competitive Advantage.*

15. W. Wiggenhorn, "Motorola U: When Training Becomes an Education," *Harvard Business Review,* July–August 1990, pp. 71–83.

16. L. Goff, "Job Surfing," *ComputerWorld* 30, no. 36 (1996), p. 81; M. K. McGee, "Job Hunting on the Internet," *Informationweek* 576 (1996), p. 98.

17. D. Terpstra, "The Search for Effective Methods," *HR Focus* 73, no. 5 (1996), pp. 16–17.

18. J. S. Black, H. B. Gregersen, and M. E. Mendenhall, *Global Assignments* (San Francisco, Calif.: Jossey-Bass, 1992).

19. J. Conway, R. Jako, and D. Goodman, "A Meta-Analysis of Interrater and Internal Consistency Reliability of Selection Interviews," *Journal of Applied Psychology* 80, no. 5 (1995), pp. 565–79; M. McDaniel, D. Whetzel, F. Schmidt, and S. Maurer, "The Validity of Employment Interviews: A Comprehensive Review and Meta-Analysis," *Journal of Applied Psychology* 79, no. 4 (1994), pp. 599–616.

20. L. Rudner, "Pre-Employment Testing and Employee Productivity," *Public Management* 21, no. 2 (1992), pp.133–50; P. Lowry, "The Assessment Center: Effects of Varying Consensus Procedures," *Public Personnel Management* 21, no. 2 (1992), pp. 171–83; T. Payne, N. Anderson, and T. Smith, "Assessment Centres: Selection Systems and Cost-Effectiveness," *Personnel Review* 21, no. 4 (1992), pp. 48–56.

21. S. Adler, "Personality Tests for Salesforce Selection," *Review of Business* 16, no. 1 (1994), pp. 27–31.

22. M. McCullough, "Can Integrity Testing Improve Market Conduct?" *LIMRA's Marketfacts* 15, no. 2 (1996), pp. 15–16; H. J. Bernardin and D. Cooke, "Validity of an Honesty Test in Predicting Theft among Convenience Store Employees," *Academy of Management Journal* 36, no. 50 (1993), pp. 1097–108.

23. B. Murphy, W. Barlow, and D. Hatch, "Employer-Mandated Physicals for Over-70 Employees Violate the ADEA," *Personnel Journal* 72, no. 6 (1993), p. 24; R. Ledman and D. Brown, "The Americans with Disabilities Act," *SAM Advanced Management Journal* 58, no. 2 (1993), pp. 17–20.

24. C. Fisher, "Organizational Socialization: An Integrative Review," in K. Rowland and J. Ferris (eds.), *Research in Personnel and Human Resource Management* 4 (1986), pp. 101–45.

25. B. Jacobson and B. Kaye, "Service Means Success," *Training and Development* 45, no. 5 (1991), pp. 53–58; J. Brechlin and A. Rossett, "Orienting New Employees," *Training* 28, no. 4 (1991), pp. 45–51.

26. W. P. Anthony, P. L. Perrewé, and K. M. Kacmar, *Strategic Human Resource Management* (Fort Worth, Tex.: Harcourt Brace Jovanovich, 1993).

27. L. W. Porter and L. E. McKibbin, *Management Education and Development* (New York: McGraw-Hill, 1988).

28. M. Hammer and J. Champy, *Reengineering the Corporation,* (New York: Harper-Collins, 1993).

29. T. Redman, E. Snape, and G. McElwee, "Appraising Employee Performance: A Vital Organizational Activity?" *Education and Training* 35, no. 2 (1993), pp. 3–10; R. Bretz, G. Milkovitch, and W. Read, "The Current State of Performance Appraisal Research and Practice," *Journal of Management* 18, no. 2 (1992), pp. 321–52.

30. L. Gomez-Mejia, "Evaluating Employee Performance: Does the Appraisal Instrument Make a Difference?" *Journal of Organizational Behavior Management* 9, no. 2 (1988), pp. 155–72.

31. C. Rarick and G. Baxter, "Behaviorally Anchored Rating Scales: An Effective Performance Appraisal Approach," *Advanced Management Journal* 51, no. 1 (1986), pp. 36–39; D. Naffziger, "BARS, RJPs, and Recruiting," *Personnel Administrator* 30, no. 8 (1985), pp. 85–96.

32. D. Bohl, "Minisurvey: 360 Degree Appraisals Yield Superior Results," *Compensation and Benefits Review* 28, no. 5 (1996), pp. 16–19.

33. M. Vinson, "The Pros and Cons of 360 Degree Feedback," *Training and Development* 50, no. 4 (1996), pp. 11–12.

34. J. Lawrie, "Steps Toward an Objective Appraisal," *Supervisory Management* 34, no. 5 (1989), pp. 17–24.

35. C. Roebuck, "Constructive Feedback," *Long Range Planning* 29, no. 3 (1996), pp. 328–36.

36. J. Kanin-Lovers and M. Cameron, "Broadbanding—A Step Forward or a Step Backward?" *Journal of Compensation and Benefits* 9, no. 5 (1994), pp. 39–42.

37. L. Stroh, J. Brett, J. Baumann, and A. Reilly, "Agency Theory and Variable Pay Compensation Strategies," *Academy of Management Journal* 39, no. 3 (1996), pp. 751–67.

38. J. Fierman, "Beating the Midlife Career Crisis," *Fortune* 128, no. 5 (1993), pp. 52–62.

39. Personal communication with vice president of human resources at Sony.

40. N. Margulies and J. S. Black, "Perspectives on the Implementation of Participative Programs," *Human Resource Management Journal* 16 (1987), pp. 385–412.

41. J. Kling, "High Performance Work Systems and Firm Performance," *Monthly Labor Review* 118, no. 5 (1995), pp. 29–36.

42. A. Leibowitz and J. Klerman, "Explaining Changes in Married Mothers' Employment Over Time," *Demography* 32, no. 3 (1995), pp. 365–78.

CHAPTER 13

1. G. Hofstede, "Culture and Organizations," *International Studies of Management & Organization* 10, no. 4 (1980), pp. 15–41.

2. A. H. Maslow, *Motivation and Personality*, 2d ed. (New York: Harper & Row, 1970).

3. R. Jacob, "Secure Jobs Trump Higher Pay, *Fortune* 131, no. 5 (1995), p. 24.

4. K. Schoenberger, P. J. McDonnell, and S. Hubler, "21 Thais Found in Sweatshop Are Released," *Los Angeles Times*, August 21, 1995, p. A1+.

5. Hofstede, "Culture and Organizations," pp. 55–56 and Figure 7.

6. C. P. Alderfer, "An Empirical Test of a New Theory of Human Needs," *Organizational Behavior and Human Performance* 4 (1969), pp. 142–75; C. P. Alderfer, *Existence, Relatedness and Growth: Human Need in Organizational Settings* (New York: The Free Press, 1972).

7. F. Ferris, "Unlocking Employee Productivity," *American Printer* 215, no. 5 (1995), pp. 30–34.

8. M. H. Peak, "Happy Birthday to Us," *Management Review* 84, no. 9 (1995), p. 6.

9. D. C. McClelland, *Human Motivation* (Glenview, Ill.: Scott, Foresman, 1985); D. C. McClelland and R. E. Boyatzis, "Leadership Motive Pattern and Long-Term Success in Management," *Journal of Applied Psychology* 67 (1982), pp. 737–43; D. C. McClelland and D. G. Winter, *Motivating Economic Achievement* (New York: The Free Press, 1969).

10. S. H. Schwartz and W. Bilsky, "Toward a Universal Psychological Structure of Human Values," *Journal of Personality & Social Psychology* 53, no. 3 (1987), pp. 550–62; S. H. Schwartz and W. Bilsky, "Toward a Theory of the Universal Content and Structure of Values: Extensions and Cross-Cultural Replications," *Journal of Personality & Social Psychology* 58, no. 5 (1990), pp. 878–91.

11. M. Erez and P. C. Earley, *Culture, Self-Identity, and Work* (New York: Oxford University Press, 1993), p. 102.

12. J. W. Connor and G. A. DeVos, "Cultural Influences on Achievement Motivation and Orientation: Towards Work in Japanese and American Youth," in D. Stern and D. Eichorn (eds.), *Influences of Social Structure, Labor Markets, and Culture* (Hillsdale, N.J.: Lawrence Erlbaum Associates, 1989), pp. 291–326.

13. A. Sagie, D. Elizur, and H. Yamauchi, "The Structure and Strength of Achievement Motivation: A Cross-Cultural Comparison," *Journal of Organizational Behavior* 17 (1996), pp. 431–44.

14. F. Herzberg, *Work and the Nature of Man* (Cleveland: Worth Publishing, 1966); F. Herzberg, "One More Time: How Do You Motivate Employees?" *Harvard Business Review* 46, (1968), pp. 54–62; F. Herzberg, B. Mausner, B. B. Snyderman, *The Motivation to Work* (New York: Wiley, 1959).

15. R. W. Griffin, *Task Design: An Integrative Approach* (Glenview, Ill.: Scott, Foresman, 1982); J. L. Pierce and R. B. Dunham, "Task Design: A Literature Review," *Academy of Management Review* 1 (1976), pp. 83–97.

16. J. R. Hackman and G. R. Oldham, *Work Redesign* (Reading, Mass.: Addison-Wesley, 1980).

17. "Enriching and Empowering Employees—the Saturn Way," *Personnel Journal* 74, no. 9 (1995), p. 32.

18. J. S. Adams, "Towards an Understanding of Inequity," *Journal of Abnormal & Social Psychology* 67, no. 5 (1963), pp. 422–36; J. S. Adams, "Inequity in Social Exchange," in L. Berkowitz (ed.), *Advances in Experimental Social Psychology*, Vol. 2 (New York: Academic Press, 1965), pp. 267–99; R. T. Mowday, "Equity Theory Predictions of Behavior in Organizations," in R. M. Steers, L. W. Porter, and G. A. Bigley (eds.), *Motivation and Leadership at Work*, 6th ed. (New York: McGraw-Hill, 1996).

19. C. C. Pinder, *Work Motivation: Theory, Issues, and Applications* (Glenview, Ill.: Scott, Foresman, 1984), p. 114.

20. V. H. Vroom, *Work and Motivation* (New York: Wiley, 1964).

21. J. Williams, "Team-Building for Techies," *Incentive* 169, no. 9 (1995), pp. 69–72.

22. L. W. Porter and E. E. Lawler, *Managerial Attitudes and Performance* (Homewood, Ill.: Richard D. Irwin, 1968).

23. M. Erez, "Goal Setting," in N. Nicholson (ed.), *Blackwell Encyclopedic Dictionary of Organizational Behavior* (Cambridge, Mass.: Blackwell Business Publishing, 1995), pp. 193–94; E. A. Locke, "The Motivation Sequence, the Motivation Hub, and the Motivation Core," *Organizational Behavior & Human Decision Processes* 50, no. 2 (1991), pp. 288–99; E. A. Locke and G. P. Latham, *A Theory of Goal Setting and Task Performance* (Englewood Cliffs, N.J.: Prentice Hall, 1990); W. Q. Judge, G. E. Fryxell, and R. S. Dooley, "The New Task of R&D Management: Creating Goal-Directed Communities for Innovation," *California Management Review* 39, no. 3 (1997), pp. 72–85.

24. E. A. Locke and G. P. Latham, "Goal Setting Theory: An Introduction," in R. M. Steers, L. W. Porter, and G. A. Bigley (eds.), *Motivation and Leadership at Work*, 6th ed. (New York: McGraw-Hill, 1996).

25. Erez, "Goal Setting."

26. Ibid.

27. Pinder, *Work Motivation*.

28. K. Helliker, "Pressure at Pier 1: Beating Sales Numbers of Year Earlier Is a Storewide Obsession," *The Wall Street Journal*, December 7, 1995, p. B1.

29. M. Erez and P. C. Earley, "Comparative Analysis of Goal-Setting Strategies Across Cultures," *Journal of Applied Psychology* 72, no. 4 (1987), pp. 658–65.

30. Erez and Earley, *Culture, Self-Identity, and Work,* 1993, p. 107.

31. J. L. Komaki, T. Coombs, and S. Schepman, "Motivational Implications of Reinforcement Theory," in R. M. Steers, L. W. Porter, and G. A. Bigley (eds.), *Motivation and Leadership at Work,* 6th ed. (New York: McGraw-Hill, 1996), pp. 34–52.

32. S. Kerr, "On the Folly of Rewarding A, While Hoping for B," *Academy of Management Journal* 18, no. 4 (1975), pp. 769–83.

33. S. Kerr, *Ultimate Rewards* (Boston Mass.: Harvard Business School Press, 1997), pp. viii–xxi.

34. Komaki, Coombs, and Schepman, "Motivational Implications of Reinforcement Theory."

35. Ibid.

36. H. C. Triandis, "Collectivism vs. Individualism: A Reconceptualization of a Basic Concept in Cross-Cultural Social Psychology," in G. K. Verma and C. Bagley (eds.), *Cross-Cultural Studies of Personality, Attitudes, and Cognition* (London: Macmillan, 1988), pp. 60–95; Erez and Earley, *Culture, Self-Identify, and Work.*

37. S. E. Seashore, *Group Cohesiveness in the Industrial Work Group* (Ann Arbor, Mich.: Survey Research Center, Institute for Social Research, University of Michigan, 1954).

38. D. Krackhardt and L. W. Porter, "When Friends Leave: A Structural Analysis of the Relationship Between Turnover and Stayers' Attitudes," *Administrative Science Quarterly* 30, no. 2 (1985), pp. 242–61.

39. F. Danssereau, Jr., G. Graen, and W. J. Haga, "A Vertical Dyad Linkage Approach to Leadership within Formal Organizations: A Longitudinal Investigation of the Role Making Process," *Organizational Behavior and Human Performance* 13 (1975), pp. 46–78; G. B. Graen and J. F. Cashman, "A Role Making Model of Leadership in Formal Organizations: A Developmental Approach," in J. G. Hunt and L. L. Larson (eds.), *Leadership Frontiers* (Kent, Ohio: Kent State University Press, 1975), pp. 143–65.

40. D. Mechanic, *Students Under Stress; a Study in the Social Psychology of Adaptation* (New York: Free Press of Glencoe, 1962).

41. C. O'Reilly, "Corporations, Culture, and Commitment: Motivation and Social Control in Organizations," *California Management Review* 31, no. 4 (1989), p. 12.

42. E. Schonfeld, "Have the Urge to Merge? You'd Better Think Twice," *Fortune* 135, no. 6 (1997), pp. 114–16.

43. M. Rokeach, *The Nature of Human Values* (New York: Free Press, 1973).

44. Erez and Earley, *Culture, Self-Identity, and Work;* Locke, "The Motivation Sequence, the Motivation Hub, and the Motivation Core."

45. F. Elashmawi and P. R. Harris, *Mulicultural Management: New Skills for Global Success* (Houston, Tex.: Gulf Publishing, 1993), Table 6.2, p. 144.

46. J. Holt and D. M. Keats, "Work Cognitions in Multicultural Interaction," *Journal of Cross-Cultural Psychology* 23, no. 4 (1992), pp. 421–43.

47. H. C. Triandis, R. Brislin, and C. H. Hui, "Cross-Cultural Training across the Individualism–Collectivism Divide," *International Journal of Intercultural Relations* 12, no. 3 (1988), pp. 269–89.

48. K. Leung and M. H. Bond, "How Chinese and Americans Reward Task-Related Contributions: A Preliminary Study,"

Psychologia: An International Journal of Psychology in the Orient 25, no. 1 (1982), pp. 32–39; M. H. Bond, K. Leung, and K. C. Wan, "How Does Cultural Collectivism Operate? The Impact of Task and Maintenance Contributions on Reward Distribution," *Journal of Cross-Cultural Psychology* 13, no. 2 (1982), pp. 186–200; K. Leung and M. H. Bond, "The Impact of Cultural Collectivism on Reward Allocation," *Journal of Personality & Social Psychology* 47, no. 4 (1984), pp. 793–804; K. Leung and H. Park, "Effects of Interactional Goal on Choice of Allocation Rule: A Cross-National Study," *Organizational Behavior & Human Decision Processes* 37, no. 1 (1986), pp. 111–20; K. I. Kim, H. Park, and N. Suzuki, "Reward Allocations in the United States, Japan, and Korea: A Comparison of Individualistic and Collectivistic Cultures," *Academy of Management Journal* 33, no. 1 (1990), pp. 188–98.

49. M. Weber, *The Protestant Ethic and the Spirit of Capitalism,* translated by Talcott Parsons (New York: Scribners, 1958); R. Wuthnow, "Religion and Economic Life," in N. J. Smelser and R. Swedbert (eds.), *The Handbook of Economic Sociology* (Princeton: Princeton University Press, 1994), pp. 620–46.

50. G. W. England and I. Harpaz, "Some Methodological and Analytic Considerations in Cross-National Comparative Research," *Journal of International Business Studies* 14, no. 2 (1983), pp. 49–59.

51. M. K. Dugan, B. Pyne, W. R. Grady, T. R. Johnson, et al., "The New Values of MBAs: Myth or Reality?" *Selections* 14, no. 2 (1998), pp. 10–18.

CHAPTER 14

1. R. M. Stogdill, "Historical Trends in Leadership Theory and Research," *Journal of Contemporary Business* 3, no. 4 (1974), pp. 1–17 (p. 2).

2. R. Levering and M. Moskowitz, *The 100 Best Companies to Work for in America,* rev. ed. (New York: Plume, 1993).

3. D. Katz and R. L. Kahn, *The Social Psychology of Organizations,* 2d ed. (New York: Wiley, 1978).

4. G. Romano, "Never Walk Past a Mistake," *Association Management* 50, no. 10 (1998), pp. 42–48.

5. W. G. Bennis and B. Nanus, *Leaders: Strategies for Taking Charge,* 2d ed. (New York: HarperBusiness, 1997); J. P. Kotter, "What Leaders Really Do," *Harvard Business Review* 68, no. 3 (1990), pp. 103–11; A. Zaleznik, "Managers and Leaders: Are They Different?" *Harvard Business Review* 70, no. 2 (1992), pp. 126–35.

6. J. Pfeffer, *Managing with Power: Politics and Influence in Organizations,* (Boston, Mass.: Harvard Business School Press, 1992), p. 45.

7. D. A. Whetten and K. S. Cameron, *Developing Management Skills,* 4th ed. (Reading, Mass.: Addison-Wesley, 1998), p. 229.

8. G. E. G. Catlin, *Systematic Politics,* (Toronto: University of Toronto Press, 1962), p. 71.

9. M. Davids, "Where Style Meets Substance," *Journal of Business Strategy* 16, no. 1 (1995), pp. 48–52+.

10. Pfeffer, *Managing with Power.*

11. W. G. Bennis and B. Nanus, *Leaders: The Strategies for Taking Charge,* 1st ed. (New York: Harper & Row, 1985), p. 6.

12. B. M. Bass, *Leadership, Psychology, and Organizational Behavior,* (New York: Harper, 1960); A. Etzioni, *A Comparative Analysis of Complex Organizations: On Power, Involvement, and Their Correlates,* (New York: Free Press of Glencoe, 1961); G. A. Yukl, *Leadership in Organizations,* 3rd ed. (Englewood Cliffs, N.J.: Prentice Hall, 1994).

13. J. R. P. French and B. Raven, "The Bases of Social Power," in D. Cartwright (ed.), *Studies in Social Power* (Ann Arbor, Mich.: Institute for Social Research, 1959), pp. 150–67.

14. G. P. Zachary, "The Once and Future Microsoft," *Upside* 7, no. 4 (1995), pp. 16–32.

15. D. Mechanic, "Sources of Power of Lower Participants in Complex Organizations," *Administrative Science Quarterly* 7 (1962), pp. 349–64.

16. Pfeffer, *Managing with Power*, p. 46.

17. D. Kipnis, S. M. Schmidt, and I. Wilkinson, "Intra-organizational Influence Tactics: Explorations in Getting One's Way," *Journal of Applied Psychology* 65, no. 4 (1980), pp. 440–52; L. W. Porter, R. W. Allen, and H. L. Angle, "The Politics of Upward Influence in Organizations," in L. L. Cummings and B. M. Staw (eds.), *Research in Organizational Behavior*, vol. 3 (Greenwich, Conn.: JAI Press, 1981), pp. 109–49; G. Yukl and C. M. Falbe, "Influence Tactics and Objectives in Upward, Downward and Lateral Influence Attempts," *Journal of Applied Psychology* 75, no. 2 (1990), pp. 132–40; G. Yukl, R. Lepsinger, and T. Lucia, "Preliminary Report on the Development and Validation of the Influence Behavior Questionnaire," in K. Clark and M. Clark (eds.), *The Impact of Leadership* (Greensboro, N.C.: Center for Creative Leadership, 1992); G. Yukl and J. B. Tracey, "Consequences of Influence Tactics Used with Subordinates, Peers, and the Boss," *Journal of Applied Psychology* 77, no. 4 (1992), pp. 525–35.

18. Bennis and Nanus, *Leaders*; R. M. Kanter, "Frontiers for Strategic Human Resource Planning and Management," *Human Resource Management* 22, (nos. 1/2) (1983), pp. 9–21; J. A. Conger, "Leadership: The Art of Empowering Others," *Academy of Management Executive* 3, no. 1 (1989), pp. 17–24; J. A. Conger and R. N. Kanungo, "The Empowerment Process: Integrating Theory and Practice," *Academy of Management Review* 13, no. 3 (1988), pp. 471–82; P. G. Foster-Fishman and C. B. Keys, "The Inverted Pyramid: How a Well Meaning Attempt to Initiate Employee Empowerment Ran Afoul of the Culture of a Public Bureaucracy," *Academy of Management Journal* Best Papers Proceedings 1995, pp. 364–68; G. M. Spreitzer, "Psychological Empowerment in the Workplace: Dimensions, Measurement, and Validation," *Academy of Management Journal* 38, no. 5 (1995), pp. 1442–65; G. M. Spreitzer, "Social Structural Characteristics of Psychological Empowerment," *Academy of Management Journal* 39, no. 2 (1996), pp. 483–504; N. M. Tichy and M. A. Devanna, "The Transformational Leader," *Training & Development Journal* 40, no. 7 (1986), pp. 27–32.

19. Bennis and Nanus, *Leaders*; R. M. Kanter, "Frontiers for Strategic Human Resource Planning and Management;" Conger and Kanungo, "The Empowerment Process;" Tichy and Devanna, "The Transformational Leader."

20. R. M. Stogdill, "Personal Factors Associated with Leadership: A Survey of the Literature," *Journal of Psychology* 25 (1948), pp. 35–71.

21. R. G. Lord, C. L. De Vader, and G. M. Alliger, "A Meta-Analysis of the Relation between Personality Traits and Leadership Perceptions: An Application of Validity Generalization Procedures," *Journal of Applied Psychology* 71, no. 3 (1986), pp. 402–41; S. A. Kirkpatrick and E. A. Locke, "Leadership: Do Traits Matter?" *Academy of Management Executive* 5, no. 2 (1991), pp. 48–60; Yukl, *Leadership in Organizations*.

22. Kirkpatrick and Locke, "Leadership;" Yukl, *Leadership in Organizations*.

23. J. B. Miner, "Twenty Years of Research on Role-Motivation Theory of Managerial Effectiveness," *Personnel Psychology* 31, no. 4 (1978), pp. 739–60; F. E. Berman and J. B. Miner, "Motivation to Manage at the Top Executive Level: A Test of the Hierarchic Role-Motivation Theory," *Personnel Psychology* 38, no. 2 (1985), pp. 377–91.

24. Bennis and Nanus, *Leaders*; J. M. Kouzes and B. Z. Posner, *The Leadership Challenge: How to Get Extraordinary Things Done in Organizations* (San Francisco: Jossey-Bass, 1987).

25. A. Bandura, *Social Foundations of Thought and Action: A Social Cognitive Theory* (Englewood Cliffs, N.J.: Prentice Hall, 1986); B. M. Bass, *Handbook of Leadership: A Survey of Theory and Research* (New York: Free Press, 1990); D. C. McClelland and R. E. Boyatzis, "Leadership Motive Pattern and Long-Term Success in Management," *Journal of Applied Psychology* 67, no. 6 (1982), pp. 737–43; A. Howard and D. W. Bray, *Managerial Lives in Transition: Advancing Age and Changing Times* (New York: Guilford Press, 1988).

26. Kouzes and Posner, *The Leadership Challenge*.

27. J. R. O'Neil, *The Paradox of Success: When Winning at Work Means Losing at Life. A Book of Renewal for Leaders* (New York: G. P. Putnam's Sons, 1994).

28. B. Walsh, "Beware the Crisis Lovers," *Forbes, ASAP Supplement*, 1995, p. 17.

29. Bass, *Handbook of Leadership*; Bennis and Nanus, *Leaders*; Howard and Bray, *Managerial Lives in Transition*; C. D. McCauley and M. M. Lombardo, "Benchmarks: An Instrument for Diagnosing Managerial Strengths and Weaknesses," in K. E. Clark and M. B. Clark (eds.), *Measures of Leadership* (West Orange, N.J.: Leadership Library of America, Inc., 1990) pp. 535–45.

30. R. I. Westwood and A. Chan, "Headship and Leadership," in R. I. Westwood (ed.), *Organizational Behavior: Southeast Asian Perspectives* (Hong Kong: Longman, 1992), pp. 118–43.

31. Bass, *Handbook of Leadership*; R. E. Boyatzis, *The Competent Manager* (New York: Wiley, 1982); Howard and Bray, *Managerial Lives in Transition*; M. W. McCall Jr. and M. M. Lombardo, "Off the Track: Why and How Successful Executives Get Derailed," *Technical Report #21* (Greensboro, N.C.: Center for Creative Leadership, 1983), pp. 9–11.

32. Bass, *Handbook of Leadership*; McCall and Lombardo, "Off the Track."

33. J. Cardiff, "The Year in Review," *Computing Canada* 12, no. 1 (1985), Microreport 10; A. Pang, "Apple's Enigma," *Computer Reseller News* 611 (1995), pp. 120–21.

34. Bass, *Handbook of Leadership*.

35. Howard and Bray, *Managerial Lives in Transition*.

36. McCall and Lombardo, "Off the Track."

37. Ibid., p. 26.

38. Boyatzis, *The Competent Manager*; Bass, *Handbook of Leadership*.

39. J. L. Noel and R. Charan, "GE Brings Global Thinking to Light," *Training & Development* 46, no. 7 (1992), p. 28.

40. J. Misumi and M. F. Peterson, "The Performance-Maintenance (PM) Theory of Leadership: Review of a Japanese Research Program," *Administrative Science Quarterly* 30, no. 2 (1985), pp. 198–223.

41. Yukl, *Leadership in Organizations*, p. 75.

42. A. H. Eagly and B. T. Johnson, "Gender and Leadership Style: A Meta-Analysis," *Psychological Bulletin* 108, no. 2 (1990), pp. 233–56; J. B. Rosener, "Ways Women Lead," *Harvard Business Review* 68, no. 6 (1990), pp. 119–25; G. N. Powell, "One More Time: Do Female and Male Managers Differ?" *Academy of Management Executive* 4, no. 3 (1990), pp. 68–75; D. J. Campbell, W. Bommer, and

E. Yeo, "Perceptions of Appropriate Leadership Style: Participation versus Consultation across Two Cultures," *Asia Pacific Journal of Management* 10, no. 1 (1993), pp. 1–19.

43. E. P. Hollander, "The Essential Interdependence of Leadership and Followership," *Current Directions in Psychological Science* 1, no. 2 (1992), pp. 71–75; R. Stewart, *Choices for the Manager* (Englewood Cliffs, N.J.: Prentice-Hall, 1982), cited in E. P. Hollander, "Leadership, Followership, Self and Others," *Leadership Quarterly* 3, no. 1 (1992), pp. 43–54.

44. S. Motsch, "Think Gray," *Incentive* 169, no. 4 (1995), pp. 59–60.

45. Hollander, "The Essential Interdependence of Leadership and Followership," p. 44.

46. R. G. Lord and K. J. Maher, "Alternative Information-Processing Models and Their Implications for Theory, Research, and Practice," *Academy of Management Review* 15, no. 1 (1990), pp. 9–28.

47. B. J. Calder, "An Attribution Theory of Leadership," in B. M. Staw and G. R. Salancik (eds.), *New Directions in Organizational Behavior* (Chicago: St. Clair, 1997); Lord, De Vader, and Alliger, "A Meta-Analysis of the Relation Between Personality Traits and Leadership Perceptions."

48. Calder, "An Attribution Theory of Leadership;" J. Pfeffer, "The Ambiguity of Leadership," *Academy of Management Review* 2, no. 1 (1977), pp. 104–12.

49. G. B. Graen, R. C. Liden, and W. Hoel, "Role of Leadership in the Employee Withdrawal Process," *Journal of Applied Psychology* 67, no. 6 (1982), pp. 868–72; G. B. Graen, T. A. Scandura, and M. R. Graen, "A Field Experimental Test of the Moderating Effects of Growth Need Strength on Productivity," *Journal of Applied Psychology* 71, no. 3 (1986), pp. 484–91.

50. F. Dansereau, G. Graen, et al., "A Vertical Dyad Lineage Approach to Leadership within Formal Organizations," *Organizational Behavior & Human Performance* 13, no. 1 (1975), pp. 46–78; G. Graen and J. F. Cashman, "A Role-Making Model of Leadership in Formal Organizations—A Developmental Approach," *Organization & Administrative Sciences* 6, nos. 2–3 (1975), pp. 143–65; J. F. Cashman, F. Dansereau, G. Graen, and W. J. Haga, "Organizational Understructure and Leadership: A Longitudinal Investigation of the Managerial Role-Making Process," *Organizational Behavior & Human Performance* 15, no. 2 (1976), pp. 278–96; G. B. Graen and M. Uhl-Bien, "Relationship-Based Approach to Leadership: Development of Leader-Member Exchange (LMX) Theory of Leadership over 25 Years: Applying a Multi-Level Multi-Domain Perspective," *The Leadership Quarterly*, Special Issue: "Leadership" 6, no. 2 (1995),pp. 219–47; M. Uhl-Bien and G. B. Graen, "Leadership Making in Self-Managing Professional Work Teams: an Empirical Investigation," in K. E. Clark, M. B. Clark, and D. P. Campbell (eds.), *The Impact of Leadership* (West Orange, N.J.: Leadership Library of America, 1993), pp. 379–87.

51. T. N. Bauer and S. G. Green, "Development of Leader-Member Exchange: A Longitudinal Test," *Academy of Management Journal* 39, no. 6 (1996), pp. 1538–67; C. R. Gerstner and D. V. Day, "Meta-Analytic Review of Leader-Member Exchange Theory: Correlates and Construct Issues," *Journal of Applied Psychology* 82, no.6 (1997), pp. 827–44; Graen et al., "Role of Leadership in the Employee Withdrawal Process;" Graen, Scandura, and Graen, "A Field Experimental Test of the Moderating Effects of Growth Need Strength on Productivity;" T. A. Scandura and G. B. Graen, "Moderating Effects of Initial Leader-Member Exchange Status on the Effects of a Leadership Intervention," *Journal of Applied Psychology* 69, no. 3 (1984), pp. 428–36.

52. Bauer and Green, "Development of Leader-Member Exchange."

53. Graen and Uhl-Bien, "Relationship-Based Approach to Leadership;" Uhl-Bien & Graen, "Leadership Making in Self-Managing Professional Work Teams;" R. T. Sparrowe and R. C. Liden, "Process and Structure in Leader-Member Exchange," *Academy of Management Review* 22, no. 2 (1997), pp. 522–52.

54. A. N. Turner and P. R. Lawrence, *Industrial Jobs and the Worker: An Investigation of Response to Task Attributes* (Boston: Harvard University, Division of Research, Graduate School of Business Administration, 1965); R. W. Griffin, *Task Design: An Integrative Approach* (Glenview, Ill.: Scott, Foresman, 1982); J. R. Hackman and G. R. Oldham, *Work Redesign* (Reading, Mass.: Addison-Wesley, 1980).

55. L. R. Anderson and F. E. Fiedler, "The Effect of Participatory and Supervisory Leadership on Group Creativity," *Journal of Applied Psychology* 48, no. 4 (1964), pp. 227–36; F. E. Fiedler, *A Theory of Leadership Effectiveness* (New York: McGraw-Hill, 1967); M. M. Chemers and F. E. Fiedler, "The Effectiveness of Leadership Training: A Reply to Argyris," *American Psychologist* 33, no. 4 (1978), pp. 391–94.

56. M. J. Strube and J. E. Garcia, "A Meta-Analytic Investigation of Fiedler's Contingency Model of Leadership Effectiveness, *Psychological Bulletin* 90, no. 2 (1981), pp. 307–21; L. H. Peters, D. D. Hartke, and J. T. Pohlmann, "Fiedler's Contingency Theory of Leadership: An Application of the Meta-Analysis Procedures of Schmidt and Hunter," *Psychological Bulletin* 97, no. 2 (1985), pp. 274–85.

57. M. G. Evans, "The Effects of Supervisory Behavior on the Path–Goal Relationship," *Organizational Behavior & Human Performance* 5, no. 3 (1970), pp. 277–98; R. J. House, "A Path-Goal Theory of Leader Effectiveness," *Administrative Science Quarterly* 16, no. 3 (1971), pp. 321–39; R. J. House and G. Dessler, "The Path–Goal Theory of Leadership: Some Post Hoc and A Priori Tests," in J. Hunt and L. Larson (eds.), *Contingency Approaches to Leadership* (Carbondale, Ill.: Southern Illinois Press, 1974); R. J. House and T. R. Mitchell, "Path–Goal Theory of Leadership," *Journal of Contemporary Business* 3, no. 4 (1974), pp. 81–97.

58. House, "A Path–Goal Theory of Leader Effectiveness," p. 324.

59. V. H. Vroom and P. W. Yetton, *Leadership and Decision-Making* (Pittsburgh, Pa.: University of Pittsburgh Press, 1973); V. H. Vroom and A. G. Jago, *The New Leadership: Managing Participation in Organizations* (Englewood Cliffs, N.J.: Prentice Hall, 1973).

60. Vroom and Jago, *The New Leadership*.

61. S. Kerr and J. M. Jermier, "Substitutes for Leadership: Their Meaning and Measurement," *Organizational Behavior & Human Performance* 22, no. 3 (1978), pp. 375–403; J. P. Howell, D. E. Bowen, P. W. Dorfman, S. Kerr, et. al., "Substitutes for Leadership: Effective Alternatives to Ineffective Leadership," *Organizational Dynamics* 19, no. 1 (1990), pp. 20–38; J. P. Howell and P. W. Dorfman, "Substitutes for Leadership: Test of a Construct, *Academy of Management Journal* 24, no. 4 (1981), pp. 714–28; P. M. Podsakoff, S. B. MacKenzie, and W. H. Bommer, "Transformational Leader Behaviors and Substitutes for Leadership as Determinants of Employee Satisfaction, Commitment, Trust, and Organizational Citizenship Behaviors," *Journal of Management* 22, no. 2 (1996), pp. 259–98; S. B. MacKenzie, P. M. Podsakoff, and R. Fetter, "The Impact of Organizational Citizenship Behavior on

Evaluations of Salesperson Performance," *Journal of Marketing* 57, no. 1 (1993), pp. 70–80; P. M. Podsakoff, B. P. Niehoff, S. B. MacKenzie, and M. L. Williams, "Do Substitutes for Leadership Really Substitute for Leadership? An Empirical Examination of Kerr and Jermier's Situational Leadership Model," *Organizational Behavior & Human Decision Processes* 54, no. 1 (1993), pp. 1–44.

62. M. Weber, *Max Weber: The Theory of Social and Economic Organization*, translated by A. M. Henderson and T. Parsons; edited with an introduction by T. Parsons (New York: Free Press, 1948).

63. O. Behling and J. M. McFillen, "A Syncretical Model of Charismatic/Transformational Leadership," *Group and Organization Management* 21 (1996), pp. 163–91; J. A. Conger, *The Charismatic Leader: Beyond the Mystique of Exceptional Leadership* (San Francisco: Jossey-Bass, 1989); J. A. Conger and R. N. Kanungo, "Toward a Behavioral Theory of Charismatic Leadership in Organizational Settings," *Academy of Management Review* 12, no. 4 (1987), pp. 637–47; J. A. Conger, R. N. Kanungo, S. T. Menon, and P. Mathur, "Measuring Charisma: Dimensionality and Validity of the Conger–Kanungo Scale of Charismatic Leadership," *Canadian Journal of Administrative Sciences* 14, no. 3 (1997), pp. 290–302; R. J. House, "A 1976 Theory of Charismatic Leadership," in J. G. Hunt, *Leadership: The Cutting Edge* (Carbondale, Ill.: Southern Illinois Press, 1977); R. J. House, W. D. Spangler, and J. Woycke, "Personality and Charisma in the U.S. Presidency: A Psychological Theory of Leader Effectiveness," *Administrative Science Quarterly* 36, no. 3 (1991), pp. 364–96.

64. House, "A 1976 Theory of Charismatic Leadership."

65. Conger, "Leadership;" Conger and Kanungo, "Toward a Behavioral Theory of Charismatic Leadership in Organizational Settings."

66. J. M. Burns, *Leadership* (New York: Harper & Row, 1978).

67. B. M. Bass, "Leadership: Good, Better, Best," *Organizational Dynamics* 13, no. 3 (1985), pp. 26–40; B. M. Bass and B. J. Avolio, "Developing Transformational Leadership: 1992 and Beyond," *Journal of European Industrial Training* 14, no. 5 (1992), pp. 21–27.

68. Bass, "Leadership."

69. Tichy and Devanna, "The Transformational Leader;" Yukl, *Leadership in Organizations*, pp. 360–63.

70. Bennis and Nanus, *Leaders*, pp. 88–89.

71. Yukl, *Leadership in Organizations*, pp. 368–74.

72. R. J. House, et al., "Cultural Influences on Leadership and Organizations: Project GLOBE," in W. Mobley (ed.), *Advances in Global Leadership*, vol. 1, (Stanford, Conn: JAI Press, 1998).

73. Westwood and Chan, "Headship and Leadership," p. 121.

74. S. Ronen, *Comparative and Multinational Management* (New York: Wiley, 1986), p. 191.

75. Westwood and Chan, "Headship and Leadership," p. 141.

76. House, "Cultural Influences on Leadership and Organizations."

CHAPTER 15

1. S. Bing, "Business as a Second Language," *Fortune* 137, no. 3 (1998), pp. 57–58.

2. K. Krone, F. M. Jablin, and L. L. Putnam, "Communication Theory and Organizational Communication: Multiple Perspectives," in F. M. Japlin, L. L. Putnam, K. H. Roberts, and L. W. Porter, (eds.), *Handbook of Organizational Communication: An Interdisciplinary Perspective* (Newbury Park, Calif.: Sage Publications, 1987).

3. H. C. Triandis, *Culture and Social Behavior* (New York: McGraw-Hill, 1994).

4. "The Business Meeting is Alive and Well … for Now," *Risk Management* 44, no. 9 (1997), p. 6.

5. J. Yates and W. J. Orlikowski, "Genres of Organizational Communication: A Structurational Approach to Studying Communication and Media," *Academy of Management Review* 17, no. 2 (1992), pp. 299–326.

6. L. W. Porter, E. E. Lawler III, and J. R. Hackman, *Behavior in Organizations* (New York: McGraw-Hill, 1975).

7. K. Davis, "The Care and Cultivation of the Corporate Grapevine," *Dun's Review* 102, no. 1 (1973), pp. 44–47.

8. S. Carroll, "Dow, LG in $320 Million Joint Venture," *Chemical Market Reporter* 254, no. 16 (1998), p. 3.

9. H. Ibarra, "Homophily and Differential Returns: Sex Differences in Network Structure and Access in an Advertising Firm," *Administrative Science Quarterly* 37 (1992), pp. 422–47; H. Ibarra, "Personal Networks of Women and Minorities in Management: A Conceptual Framework," *Academy of Management Review* 18 (1993), pp. 56–87; H. Ibarra, "Race, Opportunity, and Diversity of Social Circles in Managerial Networks," *Academy of Management Journal* 38 (1995), pp. 673–703.

10. J. M. Beyer, P. Chattopadhyay, E. George, W. H. Glick, et al., "The Selective Perception of Managers Revisited," *Academy of Management Journal* 40, no. 3 (1997), pp. 716–37.

11. A. Tversky and D. Kahneman, "Rational Choice and the Framing of Decisions," *Journal of Business* 59, no. 4 (1986), pp. S251–78.

12. C. R. Rogers and F. J. Roethlisberger, "Barriers and Gateways to Communication," *Harvard Business Review* 69, no. 6 (1991), pp. 105–11.

13. R. Wilkinson, "Do You Speak Obscuranta?" *Supervision* 49, no. 9 (1988), pp. 3–5.

14. R. Harrison, *Beyond Words: An Introduction to Nonverbal Communication* (Englewood Cliffs, N.J.: Prentice-Hall, 1974).

15. J. A. Mausehund, S. A. Timm, and A. S. King, "Diversity Training: Effects of an Intervention Treatment on Nonverbal Awareness," *Business Communication Quarterly* 58, no. 1 (1995), pp. 27–30.

16. J. H. Robinson, "Professional Communication in Korea: Playing Things by Eye," *IEEE Transactions on Professional Communication* 39, no. 3 (1996), pp. 129–34.

17. T. E. McNamara and K. Hayashi, "Culture and Management: Japan and the West Towards a Transnational Corporate Culture," *Management Japan* 27, no. 2 (1994), pp. 3–13.

18. M. Rosch and K. G. Segler, "Communication with Japanese," *Management International Review* 27, no. 4 (1987), pp. 56–67.

19. C. Gouttefarde, "Host National Culture Shock: What Management Can Do," *European Business Review* 92, no. 4 (1992), pp. 1–3.

20. H. Triandis, "Cross-Cultural Contributions to Theory in Social Psychology," in W. B. Gudykunst and Y. Y. Kim (eds.), *Reading on Communication with Strangers* (New York: McGraw-Hill, 1992), p. 75.

21. S. Carlson, "International Transmission of Information and the Business Firm," *Annals of the American Academy of Political and Social Science* 412 (1974), pp. 55–63.

22. J. Main, "How 21 Men Got Global in 35 Days," *Fortune* 120, no. 11 (1989), pp. 71–79.

23. R. S. Burnett, "Ni Zao: Good Morning, China," *Business Horizons* 33, no. 6 (1990), pp. 65–71.

24. T. D. Lewis and G. H. Graham, "Six Ways to Improve Your Communication Skills," *Internal Auditor*, 1988, p. 25.

25. G. M. Barton, "Manage Words Effectively," *Personnel Journal* 69, no. 1 (1990), pp. 32–40.

26. L. H. Porter and L. E. McKibbin, *Management Education and Development: Drift or Thrust into the 21st Century* (New York: McGraw-Hill, 1988).

27. S. L. Silk, "Making Your Speech Memorable," *Association Management* 46, no. 1 (1994), pp. L59–L62

28. A. DeMeyer, "Tech Talk: How Managers are Stimulating Global R&D Communication," *Sloan Management Review* 32, no. 3 (1991), pp. 49–58.

29. N. J. Adler, *International Dimensions of Organizational Behavior*, 2nd ed. (Boston: PWS–Kent, 1991), p. 185.

30. G. Fisher, *International Negotiations* (Chicago: Intercultural Press, 1980); J. L. Graham, "Brazilian, Japanese and American Business Negotiations," *Journal of International Business Studies* 14, no. 1 (1983), pp. 47–61.

31. J. L. Graham and R. A. Herberger, Jr. "Negotiators Abroad Don't Shoot from the Hip," *Harvard Business Review* 83, no. 4 (1983), pp. 160–68.

32. R. Fisher and W. Ury, *Getting to Yes* (London: Simon & Schuster, 1987).

33. K. Kumar, S. Noneth, and C. Yauger, "Cultural Approaches to the Process of Business Negotiation: Understanding Cross-Cultural Differences in Negotiating Behaviors," in C. L. Swanson, (ed.), *International Research in the Business Disciplines* (Greenwich,Conn.: JAI Press, 1993), pp. 79–90; J. L. Graham and Y. Sano, *Smart Bargaining: Doing Business with the Japanese*, 2d ed. (New York: Harper Business, 1988); B. M. Hawrysh and J. L. Zaichkowsky, "Cultural Approaches to Negotiations: Understanding the Japanese," *International Marketing Review* 7, no. 2 (1990), pp. 28–42.

34. Kumar et al., "Cultural Approaches to the Process of Business Negotiations."

35. Graham and Herberger, "Negotiators Abroad Don't Shoot from the Hip."

36. Kumar et al., "Cultural Approaches to the Process of Business Negotiations."

37. N. Woliansky, "We Do (Do Not) Accept Your Offer," *Management Review* 78, no. 12 (1989), pp. 54–55; Kumar et al., "Cultural Approaches to the Process of Business Negotiations."

38. Kumar et al., "Cultural Approaches to the Process of Business Negotiations," p. 86.

39. Graham and Herberger, "Negotiators Abroad Don't Shoot from the Hip."

40. J. L. Graham and N. J. Adler, "Cross-Cultural Interaction: The International Comparison Fallacy?" *Journal of International Business Studies* 20, no. 3 (1989), pp. 515–37; C. Barnum and N. Wolniasky, "Why Americans Fail at Overseas Negotiations," *Management Review* 78, no. 10 (1989), pp. 55–57.

41. Kumar et al., "Cultural Approaches to the Process of Business Negotiations."

CHAPTER 16

1. G. Orwell, *1984 : A Novel* (New York: New American Library, 1950).

2. A. S. Tannenbaum (ed.), *Control in Organizations* (New York: McGraw-Hill, 1968).

3. L. Scism, "Prudential's Auditor Gave Early Warning Signals about Sales Abuses," *The Wall Street Journal*, August 7, 1997, pp. A1, A4.

4. V. Govindarajan, "Impact of Participation in the Budgetary Process on Managerial Attitudes and Performance: Universalistic and Contingency Perspectives," *Decision Sciences* 17, no. 4 (1986), pp. 496–516.

5. B. Birchard, "Making it Count," *CFO: The Magazine for Senior Financial Executives* 11, no.10 (1995), pp. 42–51.

6. E. A. Locke, "The Ubiquity of the Technique of Goal Setting in Theories of and Approaches to Employee Motivation," *Academy of Management Review* 3, no. 3 (1978), pp. 594–601.

7. R. N. Anthony and J. S. Reece, *Accounting Principles* 7th ed. (Chicago: Richard D. Irwin, 1995), p. 382.

8. Ibid.

9. G. Palmer, "Back on Top," *Banker* 144, no. 824 (1994), pp. 31–34.

10. Ibid., pp. 31–34; A. W.Clausen, "Strategic Issues in Managing Change: The Turnaround at BankAmerica Corporation," *California Management Review* 32, no. 2 (1990), pp. 98–105.

11. R. G. Cooper, "How to Launch a New Product Successfully," *CMA Magazine* 69, no. 8 (1995), pp. 20–23.

12. R. B. Gibson and S. Goll, "Burnett Budgeting Bungle Leaves McDonald's in a Pickle," *The Wall Street Journal*, July 8, 1996, p. B5.

13. M. Goold and J. J. Quinn, "The Paradox of Strategic Controls," *Strategic Management Journal* 11, no. 1 (1990), pp. 43–57.

14. P. Lorange and D. C. Murphy, "Strategy and Human Resources: Concepts and Practice," *Human Resource Management* 22, no. 1/2 (1983), pp. 111–35.

15. J. A. Alexander, "Adaptive Change in Corporate Control Practices," *Academy of Management Journal* 34, no. 1 (1991), pp. 162–93; V. Govindarajan and J. Fisher, "Strategy, Control Systems, and Resource Sharing: Effects on Business-Unit Performance," *Academy of Management Journal* 33, no. 2 (1990), pp. 259–85.

16. M. Quint, "Met Life Shakes up its Ranks," *New York Times*, October 29, 1994, p. 17.

17. Alexander, "Adaptive Change in Corporate Control Practices," p. 181.

18. Goold and Quinn, "The Paradox of Strategic Controls."

19. Ibid., Figure 2, p. 55.

20. L. Fisher, "Success in a Nutshell," *Accountancy* 122, no. 1259 (July 1998), pp. 28–29.

21. Goold and Quinn, "The Paradox of Strategic Controls."

22. N. C. Churchill, "Budget Choice: Planning vs. Control," *Harvard Business Review* 62, no. 4 (1984), pp. 150–64.

23. B. Birchard, "Making It Count," *CFO: The Magazine for Senior Financial Executives* 11, no. 10 (1995), pp. 42–51.

24. A. Wallace, "UC Sues Official over Alleged Embezzlement; University Contends Woman Approved Phony Claims Exceeding $900,000; No Criminal Charges Have Been Filed," *Los Angeles Times*, August 25, 1995, p. A3.

25. J. L. Wilkerson, "Merit Pay–Performance Review: They Just Don't Work!" *Management Accounting* 76, no. 12 (1995), pp. 40–45.

26. J. R. Barker, "Tightening the Iron Cage: Concertive Control in Self-Managing Teams," *Administrative Science Quarterly* 38, no. 3 (1993), pp. 408–37; Goold and Quinn, "The Paradox of Strategic Controls"; W. G. Ouchi, "A Conceptual Framework for the Design of Organizational Control

Mechanisms," *Management Science* 25, no. 9 (1979), pp. 833–48; W. G. Ouchi, "Markets, Bureaucracies, and Clans," *Administrative Science Quarterly* 25, no. 1 (1980), pp. 129–41; R. E. Walton, "From Control to Commitment in the Workplace," *Harvard Business Review* 63, no. 2 (1985), pp. 76–84.

27. Barker, "Tightening the Iron Cage."

28. W. H. Newman, *Constructive Control; Design and Use of Control Systems* (Englewood Cliffs, N.J.: Prentice Hall, 1975).

29. "How Conrail is Building a 'Transparent' Physical Plant," *Railway Age* 195, no. 12 (1994), pp. 41–42.

30. G. Forger, "RFDC and Warehouse Software Cut Order Turnaround Time 40%," *Modern Materials Handling* 50, no. 3 (1995), pp. S8–S9.

31. R. N. Anthony, J. Dearden, and V. Govindarajan, *Management Control Systems*, 8th ed. (Burr Ridge, Ill.: Richard D. Irwin, 1995), p. 437.

32. Ibid.; R. J. Schonberger, "Total Quality Management Cuts a Broad Swath—Through Manufacturing and Beyond," *Organizational Dynamics* 20, no. 4 (1992), pp. 16–28.

33. G. F. Hanks, M. A. Freid, and J. Huber, "Shifting Gears at Borg-Warner Automotive," *Management Accounting* 75, no. 8 (1994), pp. 25–29.

34. K. H. Roberts, "Managing High Reliability Organizations," *California Management Review* 32, no. 4 (1990), pp. 101–13.

35. D. M. Iadipaolo, "Monster or Monitor? Have Tracking Systems Gone Mad?" *Insurance & Technology* 17, no. 6 (1992), pp. 47–54.

CHAPTER 17

1. R. B. Chase and N. J. Aquilano, *Production and Operations Management*, 7th ed. (Burr Ridge, Ill.: Richard D. Irwin, 1995).

2. S. M. Ladki, "Hospitality Education: The Identity Struggle," *International Journal of Hospitality Management* 12 (1993), pp. 243–51.

3. "More Education Increases Productivity," *IIE Solutions*, October 1995, p. 7.

4. L. J. Krajewski and L. P. Ritzman, *Operations Management*, 4th ed. (Reading, Mass.: Addison-Wesley, 1996), pp. 36–40.

5. D. Koretz, "Baxter Created World Class Manufacturing Environment," *IIE Solutions*, December 1995, pp. 18–22.

6. S. A. Forest, "Foreign Plant, Yes. Foreign Wages, No," *Business Week*, December 9, 1996, p. 8.

7. G. DeGeorge, "I'm Rolling as Fast as I Can," *Business Week*, September 2, 1996, p. 46.

8. J. Carrier, "Smoke without the Mirrors: For Cigar Makers Big and Small, the '90s Were Good Years," *New York Times* [on-line edition], December 26, 1998.

9. M. Zimmerman, "Baked Lay's Feeding Frenzy," *Dallas Morning News*, March 13, 1996, pp. 1D, 10D.

10. W. Plunkett and R. Atner, *Introduction to Management*, 5th ed. (Belmont, Calif.: Wadsworth, 1994).

11. Chase and Aquilano, *Production and Operations Management*.

12. B. Render and J. Heizer, *Principles of Operations Management* (Boston: Allyn and Bacon, 1994).

13. G. McWilliams, "Double Barrels Aimed at Dell," *Business Week*, December 9, 1996, p. 6.

14. J. R. Evans, *Applied Production and Operations Management*, 4th ed. (St Paul, Minn.: West Publishing Company, 1993).

15. P. S. Adler, "Time-and-Motion Regained," *Harvard Business Review*, January–February 1993, pp. 97–108.

16. A. Glodstein, "S. Korean Companies Seek Respect in U.S. Markets," *Dallas Morning News*, January 5, 1997, pp. 1A, 21A.

17. J. Juran, *Quality Control Handbook*, 3rd ed. (New York: McGraw-Hill, 1979).

18. L. H. VanHorn, "Improving Results through Total Quality Management," *American Agent and Broker*, June 1997, pp. 47–49, 69–72.

19. S. Browder, "Boeing's Revised Flight Plan," *Business Week*, December 21, 1998, p. 39; A. Dworkin, "Jettisoning the Fat," *The Dallas Morning News*, November 8, 1998, pp. 1H, 6H; A. Reinhardt and S. Browder, "Fly, Damn It, Fly," *Business Week*, November 9, 1998, pp. 150–56.

20. S. Yorks, "Koalaty Kid Program Gains National Attention," *Colleyville News and Times: Southlake Edition* 14, no. 25 (1998), pp. 1, 3.

21. R. Kirshnan, A. B. Shani, R. M. Grant, and R. Baer, "In Search of Quality Improvement: Problems of Design and Implementation," *Academy of Management Executive*, November 1993, pp. 7–20.

22. Q. R. Skrabec, "Maximizing the Benefits of Your ISO 9000 Campaign," *Industrial Engineering Solutions*, April 1995, pp. 34–37.

23. K. Farahmand, R. Becerra, and J. Greene, "ISO 9000 Certification: Johnson Controls' Inside Story," *Industrial Engineering*, September 1994, pp. 22–23.

24. Associated Press, "U.S. Wastes $1 Billion on Travel, Senator Says," *Dallas Morning News*, March 9, 1996, p. 6A.

25. S. S. Rao, "When in Doubt, Outsource," *Financial World*, December 5, 1995, pp. 77–78.

26. K. Kerwin, "Not Your Father's Corvette," *Business Week*, December 23, 1996, p. 44.

27. D. Davis, "Baxter Creates World Class Manufacturing Environment," *Industrial Engineering Solutions*, December 1995, pp. 18–22.

28. S. Tully, "Purchasing's New Muscle," *Fortune*, February 20, 1995, pp. 75–80.

29. K. Blass, "World-Class Strategies Help Create a World-Class CIM Facility," *Industrial Engineering*, November 1992, pp. 26–29.

30. Krajewski and Ritzman, *Operations Management*.

31. D. Brittan, "When Bad Things Happen to Good Factories," *Technology Review*, July, 1996, pp. 14–15.

32. M. Magnut and R. Sookdeo, "Who's Winning the Information Revolution," *Fortune*, November 30, 1992, pp. 110–115.

33. Ibid.

34. Evans, *Applied Production and Operations Management*.

35. Ibid.

CHAPTER 18

1. C. E. Shannon and W. Weaver, *The Mathematical Theory of Communication* (Urbana, Ill.: University of Illinois Press, 1949).

2. C. Koch, "Sitting in the Hot Seat," *CIO*, February 1996, pp. 40–47.

3. C. Sliwa, "Snipper Helps Bills of Lading Go Digital," *Computerworld*, July 13, 1998, pp. 41–42.

4. S. E. Verney and V. McCarthy, "Wired for Profits," *Datamation* 42, no. 16 (October 1996), pp. 43–50.

5. "Imaging Works for Selleys," *LAN Magazine* (Australia/New Zealand) 4, no. 9 (March 1996), p. 34.

6. N. Dillon, "Nabisco Cooks up Storage Savings," *Computerworld*, May 18, 1998, pp. 59, 61.

7. D. Hernandez, R. Gibson, and E. McGuire, "Informatics in Uruguay: Evolution and Implications," *Journal of Global Information Management* 4, no.1 (Winter 1996), pp. 23–31.

8. T. R. Halfhill, "Agents and Avatars," *Byte* 21, no. 2 (February 1996), pp. 69–72.

9. C. Babcock, "Software Turns Middle Manager," *Computerworld*, June 12, 1995, p. 142.

10. N. Kohzadi, M. S. Boyd, B. Kermanshahi, and I. Kaastra, "A Comparison of Artificial Neural Networks and Time Series Models for Forecasting Commodity Prices," *Neurocomputing* 10, no. 2 (March 1996), pp. 169–81.

11. S. Machlis, "IBM Patent Covers Artificial Intelligence Antivirus Effort," *Computerworld*, October 18, 1997, accessed at the *Computerworld* Web site, http://www.computerworld.com/home/online9697.nsf/all/971027ibm199CA.

12. D. Frank, "FedEx Delivers Web's Worth with Business-to-Business Catalog Service," *InfoWorld Electric*, October 9, 1996, accessed at http://www.infoworld.com; and the FedEx Web site, accessed at http://www.fedex.com/us/services/vitalorder/features.html.

13. C. Sliwa, "Intranet Eases Mutual Fund Merger Pain," *Computerworld*, November 17, 1997, pp. 57–59.

14. S. Machlis, "Web Database Helps Doctors Fight Cancer," *Computerworld*, October 12, 1998, pp. 41–42.

15. F. W. Rook, "More Than Just Executive Tool," *Computing Canada* 22, no. 4 (February 15, 1996), p. 38(1).

16. C. Corcoran, "Client/Server Move Gives Insurance Company a Jump on Managed-Care Business," *Infoworld*, September 23, 1996, p. 80.

17. R. L. Scheier, "Timing Is Everything," *Computerworld*, August 5, 1996, accessed at the *Computerworld* Web site, http://www.computerworld.com/home/print9597.nsf/all/SLO8D5rs.

18. D. Richman, "Start-up Brings Data Mining out of the Cave," *Computerworld*, February 5, 1996, p. 45.

19. P. Judge, "What've You Done for Us Lately?" *Business Week*, September 14, l998, pp. 140–48.

20. M. Hammer and J. Champy, *Reengineering the Corporation—A Manifesto for Business Revolution* (New York: Harper Collins, 1993), pp. 92–99.

21. W. Taylor, "At Verifone It's a Dog's Life (and They Love It!)" *Fast Company*, November 1995, retrieved from http://www.fastcompany.com/online/01/vfone.html; and the Verifone Web site, accessed at http://www.verifone.com.

22. J. Langhoff, "The Experts Panel," *Fast Company*, June 3, 1998, retrieved from http://www.fastcompany.com/fc/ask/q980603.html.

23. J. Bresnahan, "Why Telework?" *CIO*, January 15, 1998, accessed at the *CIO* Web site, http://www.cio.com/archive/enterprise/011598_work.html.

24. "Making Telecommuting Work," *Information Management* 9, no. 1/2 (Spring 1996), p. 12.

25. "Why Companies Outsource," *Computerworld*, October 26, 1998, p. 39.

26. J. King, "Shipper Signs IT Outsource Deal with IBM," *Computerworld*, November 16, 1998, p. 24.

27. V. Gurbaxani, "The New World of Technology Outsourcing," *Communications of the ACM* 39, no. 7 (July 1996), pp. 45–46.

28. Hammer and Champy, *Reengineering the Corporation,* pp. 31–32.

29. U.S. Government Accounting Office, "Information Security: Computer Attacks at Department of Defense Pose Increasing Risks," *GAO/AIMD-96-84*, May 22, 1996.

30. R. O. Mason, F. M. Mason, and M. J. Culnan, *Ethics of Information Management* (Thousand Oaks, Calif.: Sage Publications, 1995); R. O. Mason, "Four Ethical Issues of the Information Age," *Management Information Systems Quarterly,* March 1986, pp. 4–12.

CHAPTER 19

1. P. F. Drucker, "The New Society of Organizations," *Harvard Business Review* 70, no. 5 (1992), pp. 95–104; C. K. Wagner, "Managing Change in Business: Views from the Ancient Past," *Business Horizons* 38, no. 6 (1995), p. 812.

2. L. Grant, "Why Kodak Still Isn't Fixed," *Fortune,* May 11, 1998, pp. 179–81.

3. L. S. Richman, "The Economy: Managing through a Downturn," *Fortune* 132, no. 3 (1995), pp. 59–64.

4. D. Machan, "Is the Hog Going Soft?" *Forbes* 159, no. 5 (1997), pp. 114–19.

5. C. Covault, "Kennedy Cutbacks Could Risk Capability," *Aviation Week and Space Technology* 145, no. 10 (1996), pp. 53–54.

6. J. Spiers, "Upheaval in the Electricity Business," *Fortune* 133, no. 12 (1996), pp. 26–30.

7. E. Schonfeld, "Is Informix Toast?" *Fortune* 136, no. 2 (1997), pp. 25–26.

8. J. V. Owen and E. E. Sprow, "The Challenge of Change (Part 1)," *Manufacturing Engineering* 112, no. 3 (1994), pp. 33–46.

9. J. Pfeffer, "Understanding Power in Organizations," *California Management Review* 34, no. 2 (1992), pp. 29–50.

10. R. Teitelbaum, "How to Harness Gray Matter," *Fortune* 135, no. 11 (1997), p. 168.

11. J. Shaw, "Truck and Rail Update: LA Truckers Find a New Home; U.S. Rail Carriers Find New Mates," *World Trade* 9, no. 6 (1996), pp. 60–61.

12. N. Venkatraman, "IT-Enabled Business Transformation: From Automation to Business Scope Redefinition," *Sloan Management Review* 35, no. 2 (1994), pp. 73–87.

13. P. W. Yetton, K. D. Johnston, and J. F. Craig, "Computer-Aided Architects: A Case Study of IT and Strategic Change," *Sloan Management Review* 35, no. 4 (1994), pp. 57–67.

14. G. A. Patterson, "Bad Fit: Lands' End Kicks Out Modern New Managers, Rejecting a Makeover; Employees, Founder Prefer the Old-Fashioned Way, but Is 'Cozy' Outdated?" *The Wall Street Journal*, April 3, 1995, p. A1.

15. J. Champy, *Reengineering Management: The Mandate for New Leadership,* (New York: Harper Business, 1996).

16. A. D. Chandler, *Strategy and Structure: Chapters in the History of the Industrial Enterprise,* (Cambridge, Mass.: M.I.T. Press, 1962); T. L. Amburgey and T. Dacin, "As the Left Foot Follows the Right? The Dynamics of Strategic and Structural Change," *Academy of Management Journal* 37, no. 6 (1994), pp. 1427–52.

17. D. A. Nadler and M. L. Tushman, "Beyond the Charismatic Leader: Leadership and Organizational Change," *California Management Review* 32, no. 2 (1990), pp. 77–97.

18. L. Grant, "GE's 'Smart Bomb' Strategy," *Fortune* 136, no. 2 (1997), pp. 109–10.

19. R. L. Manganelli and S. P. Raspa, "Why Reengineering Has Failed," *Management Review* 84, no. 7 (1995), pp. 39–43.

20. L. A. Armour, "Me and the Mayo," *Fortune* 136, no. 2 (1997), pp. 86–89.

21. D. L. Madison, R. W. Allen, L. W. Porter, P. A. Renwick, et al., "Organizational Politics: An Exploration of Managers' Perceptions," *Human Relations* 33, no. 2 (1980), pp. 79–100.

22. "Technology Trends: Developments in Electric Vehicles, Die-Making, VICS and Advanced Safety Vehicles," *Motor Business Japan,* First Quarter 1996, pp. 62–73.

23. C. F. Sly, "Conquering Internal Process Problems with the Use of Cross-Functional Self-Directed Work Teams," *Hospital Material Management Quarterly* 18, no. 4 (1997), pp. 51–60.

24. S. Ghoshal and C. A. Bartlett, "Rebuilding Behavioral Context: A Blueprint for Corporate Renewal," *Sloan Management Review* 37, no. 2 (1996), pp. 23–36.

25. W. Weitzel and E. Johnson, "Decline in Organizations: A Literature Integration and Extension," *Administrative Science Quarterly* 34 (1989), pp. 91–109.

26. B. Dumaine, "Times Are Good? Create a Crisis," *Fortune* 127, no. 13 (1993), pp. 123–30.

27. Ibid.

28. L. Jones, "Educated Opinions," *Electric Perspectives* 22, no. 1 (1997), pp. 10–17.

29. M. L. Tushman, W. H. Newman, and E. Romanelli, "Convergence and Upheaval: Managing the Unsteady Pace of Organizational Evolution," *California Management Review* 29, no. 1 (1986), pp. 29–44.

30. P. Neuburg, "Shock Treatment in Hungary," *Business London,* July 1990, pp. 58–63.

31. C. Ponicki, "Case Study: Improving the Efficiency of Small-Business Lending at First National Bank of Chicago," *Commercial Lending Review* 11, no. 2 (1996), pp. 51–60.

32. C. Piller, "So What if Amelio's File is Closed? Apple Can Reboot," *Los Angeles Times,* July 10, 1997, p. D1+; J. Carlton and L. Gomes, "Apple Computer Chief Amelio is Ousted; Co-founder Jobs to Assume Broader Role as Search for a Successor Begins," *The Wall Street Journal,* July 10, 1997, p. A3.

33. "Winning Team Plays: The Dream Team," *Supervisory Management* 40, no. 5 (1995), p. 10.

34. V. Alonzo, "Shifting Gears," *Incentive* 168, no. 8 (1994), pp. 76–82.

35. J. L. Porras and P. J. Robertson, "Organizational Development: Theory, Practice and Research," in M. D. Dunnette and L. M. Hough (eds.), *Handbook of Industrial and Organizational Psychology* (Palo Alto, Calif.: Consulting Psychologists Press, 1992).

36. M. MacCallan, "Re-Engineering Treasury at Cookson Group," *TMA Journal* 16, no. 4 (1996), pp. 45–51.

37. R. E. Purser and S. Cabana, "Involve Employees at Every Level of Strategic Planning," *Quality Progress* 30, no. 5 (1997), pp. 66–71.

38. B. K. Spiker and E. Lesser, "We Have Met the Enemy," *Journal of Business Strategy* 16, no. 2 (1995), pp. 17–21.

39. K. Ballen, "Report Card on the Baby Bells," *Fortune* 117, no. 13 (1988), pp. 87–96; P. Coy and M. Lewyn," The Baby Bells Learn a Nasty New Word: Competition," *Business Week,* no. 3205 (1991), pp. 96–101.

40. L. Nameth, "A Hoosier in Budapest," *CFO: The Magazine for Senior Financial Executives* 11, no. 1 (1995), pp. 34–46.

41. T. A. Stewart, "3M Fights Back," *Fortune* 133, no. 2 (1996), pp. 94–99.

42. E. Romanelli and M. L. Tushman, "Organizational Transformation as Punctuated Equilibrium: An Empirical Test," *Academy of Management Journal* 37 (1994), pp. 1141–66.

43. V. Baxter and A. Margavio, "Assaultive Violence in the U.S. Post Office," *Work and Occupations* 23, no. 3 (1996), pp. 277–96.

44. Romanelli and Tushman, "Organizational Transformation as Punctuated Equilibrium."

45. "Shake-Up or Cock-Up?" *Economist* 343, no. 8019 (1997), p. 67.

46. K. Lewin, *Field Theory in Social Science: Selected Theoretical Papers* (New York: Harper, 1951).

47. Spiker and Lesser, "We Have Met the Enemy."

48. J. Kurtzman, "Is Your Company Off Course? Now You Can Find Out Why," *Fortune* 135, no. 3 (1997), pp. 58–60.

49. W. L. French, C. H. Bell Jr., and R. A. Zawacki, *Organization Development and Transformation: Managing Effective Change,* 4th ed. (Burr Ridge, Ill.: Richard D. Irwin, 1994).

50. Ibid.

51. R. Beckhard, *Organization Development: Strategies and Models* (Reading, Mass.: Addison-Wesley, 1969); R. D. Smither, J. M. Houston, and S. D. McIntire, *Organization Development: Strategies for Changing Environments* (New York: HarperCollins, 1996).

52. Smither et al., *Organization Development,* p. 20.

53. Ibid.

54. K. Lewin, "Frontiers in Group Dynamics: Concepts, Method, and Reality in Social Science," *Human Relations* 1 (1947), pp. 5–41.

55. W. L. French and C. H. Bell Jr., *Organization Development: Behavioral Science Interventions for Organizational Improvement,* 4th ed. (Englewood Cliffs, N.J.: Prentice Hall, 1990), pp. 6–7.

56. Smither et al., *Organization Development.*

57. W. L. French and C. H. Bell Jr., *Organization Development: Behavioral Science Interventions for Organizational Improvement,* 5th ed. (Englewood Cliffs, N.J.: Prentice Hall, 1995), p. 156.

58. D. A. Garvin, "Leveraging Processes for Strategic Advantage," *Harvard Business Review* 73, no. 5 (1995), pp. 76–79.

59. G. Hall, J. Rosenthal, and J. Wade, "How to Make Reengineering Really Work," *Harvard Business Review* 71, no. 6 (1993), pp. 119–31.

60. J. B. White, "'Next Big Thing': Reengineering Gurus Take Steps to Remodel Their Stalling Vehicles," *The Wall Street Journal,* November 26, 1996, pp. A1, A10.

61. Hall et al., "How to Make Reengineering Really Work."

62. White, "'Next Big Thing'."

63. Ibid.

64. D. M. Rousseau, "Organizational Behavior in the New Organizational Era," *Annual Review of Psychology* 48 (1997), pp. 515–46; C. Argyris and D. A. Schoen, *Organizational Learning II: Theory, Method and Practice* (Reading, Mass.: Addison-Wesley, 1996); D. A. Garvin, "Building a Learning Organization," *Harvard Business Review* 71, no. 4 (1993), pp. 78–91; E. C. Nevis, A. J. DiBella, and J. A. Gould, "Understanding Organizations as Learning Systems," *Sloan*

Management Review 36, no. 2 (1995), pp. 73–85; E. A. Schein, "How Can Organizations Learn Faster? The Challenge of Entering the Green Room," *Sloan Management Review* 34, no. 2 (1993), pp. 85–92; P. M. Senge, "The Leader's New Work: Building Learning Organizations," *Sloan Management Review* 32, no. 1 (1990), pp. 7–23. ; P. M. Senge, *The Fifth Discipline* (New York: Doubleday, 1990); S. F. Slater, "Learning to Change" *Business Horizons* 38, no. 6 (November/December 1995), pp. 13–20.

65. Garvin, "Building a Learning Organization," p. 80.

66. Nevis et al., "Understanding Organizations as Learning Systems."

67. Garvin, "Building a Learning Organization."

68. J. Levinson, "Benchmarking Compliance Performance," *Environmental Quality Management* 6, no. 4 (1997), pp. 49–60.

69. S. Bady, "Shea Benchmarks Against Other Industries' Best Practices," *Professional Builder*, National Housing Quality Awards Supplement, 1996, pp. 8–12.

CREDITS

Continued from copyright page

NAME INDEX*

Abegglen, J. C., 333n13
Abramson, M. A., 300n17, 307n37, 317n73
Acton, Lord, 405
Adams, J. S., 377n18
Adler, N. J., 104n16, 330n7, 462n29, 466n40
Adler, P. S., 524n15
Adler, S., 339n21
Akers, John F., 278
Alderfer, Clay, 371
Aldrich, H., 148n2
Alexander, J. A., 485n15, 485n17
Alison, Sebastian, 69
Allen, Paul, 194
Allen, R. W., 411n17, 583n21
Allen, Robert, 230
Alliger, G. M., 414n21, 421n47
Allport, G. W., 101n
Alonzo, V., 590n34
Amason, A. C., 314n55, 314n57, 314n59, 314n60, 314n62
Amburgey, T. L., 581n16
Amelio, Gilbert, 588
Anderson, C., 208n12
Anderson, Dick, 417
Anderson, L. R., 424n55
Anderson, N., 339n20
Andreessen, Mark, 144–146
Angle, H. L., 411n17
Angus, Jeff, 228n
Anthony, R. N., 480n7, 498n31
Anthony, W. P., 341n26, 342n
Aquilano, N. J., 512n1, 520n11
Argyris, Chris, 54, 606n64
Armour, L. A., 583n20
Armstrong, C. Michael, 230
Armstrong, Larry, 365n
Arnst, Catherine, 279n
Arpino, Gerald, 240, 241
Ash, Mary Kay, 159, 164
Ashforth, B. E., 300n18
Atner, R., 520n10
Avolio, B. J., 433n67

Babbage, Charles, 36
Babcock, C., 551n9
Baca, L. D., 304n30
Bady, S., 607n68
Baer, R., 526n21

Bagley, C., 388n36
Bailey, Dorothy, 114
Baker, G., 317n71
Baker, George W., 224
Baker, Stephen, 365n
Ball, C. H., Jr., 602n49, 603n55, 603n57
Ball, George, 250
Ballen, K., 592n39
Bandura, A., 414n25
Banker, R. D., 295n4, 300n16, 317n72
Barber, H., 312n53
Barker, J. R., 494n26, 495n27
Barlow, W., 340n23
Barnard, Chester, 51–53
Barney, J., 206n9, 212n15, 213n17, 326n1, 331n11
Barnum, C., 466n40
Bartlett, C. A., 270n5, 286n11, 287n12, 585n24
Barton, G. M., 459n25
Bass, B. M., 405n12, 414n25, 415n29, 415n31, 416n32, 416n34, 433n67, 433n68
Bauer, T. N., 421n51
Baumann, J., 348n37
Baxter, G., 345n31
Baxter, V., 595n43
Beatty, Sally Goll, 225n
Becerra, R., 526n23
Beckhard, R., 602n51
Beer, M., 156n12
Beers, Charlotte, 430, 431, 432
Behling, O., 430n63
Bell, Cecil H., Jr., 604n
Bennis, W. G., 404n5, 405n11, 411n18, 412n19, 414n24, 434n70
Bentley, Stephanie, 611n
Bergstrom, R., 181n5
Berkowitz, L., 377n18
Berman, F. E., 414n23
Bernardin, H. J., 339n22
Bernstein, Allen J., 477
Bertalanffy, Ludwig von, 57n27
Bettenhausen, K. L., 300n18, 304n29, 309n
Beyer, J. M., 454n10
Bhid, A., 182n6, 183n11
Bigley, G. A., 377n18, 382n24, 384n31

Bilsky, W., 372n10
Bina, Eric, 145
Bing, S., 443n1
Birchard, B., 479n5, 491n23
Bird, B. J., 148n3
Birley, S. J., 148n2
Black, J. Stewart, 80n14, 81n15, 81n16, 90n, 92n, 116n, 120n2, 244n11, 244n12, 246n, 253n19, 266n2, 286n11, 337n18, 352n40
Blake, S., 104n
Blanchard, Ken, 417n
Blass, K., 533n29
Bobocel, D. R., 251n17
Boddewyn, J. J., 81n16
Bohl, D., 345n32
Boisjoly, Russell P., 313n
Boje, David M., 167n
Bommer, W., 419n42, 428n61
Bond, M. H., 392n48
Booke, James, 84n
Borgfeldt, George, 167
Bourgeois, L. J., 246, 246n15, 314n57
Bowen, D. E., 428n61
Box, Terry, 518n
Boyatzis, R. E., 148n3, 372n9, 414n25, 415n31, 418n38
Boyd, B., 180n3
Boyd, Elizabeth, 540
Boyd, Jim, 537, 538
Boyd, M. S., 551n10
Bradsher, Keith, 4
Branson, Richard, 430
Braunstein, D. N., 231n1
Bray, D. W., 414n25, 415n31, 417n35
Bray, John Randolph, 167
Brechlin, J., 341n25
Breman, Arnold, 240, 241
Bresnahan, J., 557n23
Breta, R., 343n29
Brett, J., 348n37
Brewer, T., 81n16
Brierly, Sean, 611n
Brislin, R., 392n47
Brittan, D., 534n31
Brooks, Steve, 580n
Browder, S., 525n19
Brown, D., 340n23
Bumaine, B., 586n26, 586n27
Bunch, D., 213n18

*For readers' convenience, note numbers are provided in index. Complete references are found on pages 612–629.

ORGANIZATION/ COMPANY INDEX

SUBJECT INDEX*

*Boldface terms in the index refer to key terms in the text, and the boldface number refers to the page on which the
key term is defined.

640